KT-529-420

China after Deng Xiaoping

THE POWER STRUGGLE IN BEIJING SINCE TIANANMEN

China after Deng Xiaoping

THE POWER STRUGGLE IN BEIJING SINCE TIANANMEN

Willy Wo-Lap Lam

JOHN WILEY & SONS

Singapore   New York   Chichester   Brisbane   Toronto

Copyright ©1995 by   John Wiley & Sons (SEA) Pte Ltd
37 Jalan Pemimpin #05-04
Block B Union Industrial Building
Singapore 2057

All rights reserved

No part of this book may be reproduced by any means,
or transmitted, or translated into a machine language
without the written permission of the publisher

Other Wiley Editorial Offices

John Wiley & Sons, Inc. 605 Third Avenue,
New York, NY 10158-0012, USA

Jacaranda Wiley Ltd, G.P.O.Box 859, Brisbane,
Queensland 401, Australia

John Wiley & Sons (Canada) Ltd, 22 Worcester Road
Rexdale, Ontario M9W 1L1, Canada

John Wiley & Sons Ltd, Baffins Lane, Chichester,
West Sussex PO19 1UD, England

Cataloging-in-Publication Data:

Lam, Willy Wo-Lap
    China After Deng Xiaoping: The Power
Struggle in Beijing since Tiananmen
      p. cm.
      Includes Index
      ISBN: 0-471-13114-8

Printed in the Republic of Singapore

10 9 8 7 6 5 4 3 2 1

For Michelle and Julian

About the Author

A Hong Kong native, Willy Wo-Lap Lam has been writing about China since the mid-1970s. An accredited foreign correspondent in Beijing from 1986 to 1988, Mr Lam is China Editor of the *South China Morning Post*. He is the author of *The Era of Zhao Ziyang* (1989); *Toward A Chinese-Style Socialism* (1987); and several chapters in the *China Review* annual series published by the Chinese University of Hong Kong. Mr Lam is a graduate of the University of Hong Kong and the University of Minnesota.

Mr Lam is a world-renowned sinologist with particular expertise on the Chinese Communist Party; party ideology; the People's Liberation Army; the theory and practice of economic and political reform; political sociology; Chinese culture; and Deng Xiaoping Thought.

Articles by Mr Lam have been picked up by international news agencies (AP, Reuters, AFP, UPI, Kyodo, Central News Agency) as well as by newspapers and magazines in Hong Kong, Taiwan, China, Singapore, Japan, Britain, the United States, Australia and Canada.

His expertise on China has been sought by the global media. He has been regularly interviewed by BBC (TV and radio), the Voice of America, CNN, ABC (US), ABC (Australia), NHK (Japan), SBC (Singapore), CBC (Canada), French International Radio, Swedish Television, Radio Television Hong Kong, TVB and ATV (Hong Kong).

Comments on Willy Lam's previous books

"Lam comes successfully to grips with such difficult topics as price reform, the decentralisation of enterprise management . . . and the prospects of political liberalisation. He is admirably wide-ranging; his interesting chapter on literature and the wealth of his footnotes suggest that he has read everything." — *Far Eastern Economic Review* (1987)

"Among them [books on Zhao Ziyang], Willy Wo-Lap Lam's exhaustive account of Zhao's rise to party General Secretary between 1986 and 1988 is the best . . . Lam's book is a startling inside view of the key players in the turbulent power struggle that led to the [June 4] crackdown. Drawing on scores of interviews, internal party documents and hundreds of official speeches and press statements, Lam, a former Asiaweek correspondent, describes the opposing factions that make up China's government." — *Time* (1989)

Contents

Acknowledgements ix

Preface xi

1. Deng Xiaoping's Controversial Legacy......................... 1

2. Economic Reform:
How Far Down the Capitalist Road?........................... 51

3. The Maoist Restoration:
Class Struggle and the Negation of Reform 135

4. The People's Liberation Army:
Deng's Great Wall of Steel 193

5. Political Reform on Hold:
How the Party Consolidated its Dictatorship.................. 239

6. Succession Politics and the Post-Deng Leadership 323

7. Conclusion:
China after Deng Xiaoping................................. 383

Abbreviations and Glossary 431

Notes 433

Index 479

Acknowledgements

MOST of the best China-watchers are missionaries. It is impossible to know and report on China, and not be struck by the immense suffering, the wasted lives and the unrealised potential. Few sinologists and China journalists can resist the temptation to proselytise, to pray for divine intervention, and to hope against hope that either poetic or heavenly justice will prevail. The corollary is also that quite a few China-watchers are pessimists: the country is too big and chaotic for even a divinely-inspired Helmsman to make it right. And, most Helmsmen that China has had — including the protagonist of this tome — have proved disappointing in one way or another.

My goal in writing this book is simple: to state the facts, to "seek truth from facts", and to throw out some theories, hypotheses and educated speculations. I have been studying and writing about China since the mid-1970s. And I shall be more than rewarded if my readers — particularly officials, businessmen, journalists, educators and students who are in a position to influence China — could get from this humble undertaking some inspiration for tackling the chronic "China problem".

The following friends (not all are in the China field) have over the years offered tea and sympathy; timely tips and warnings; various forms of advice and patronage; and much more. They are: Sir David Akers-Jones, Forrest Anderson, Robbie Barnett, Jasper Becker, Scott Bellard, Dr Maurice Brosseau, Dr John Burns, Dr Thomas Chan Man-Hung, Timothy Chan Tak-yue, Ying Chan, Kent Chen, Chen

x

Chi-pang, Prof Chen Ke-kun, Prof Chen Ku-ying, Windson Chen, Tai Ming Cheung, Chow Yung-ping, Prof Jerome Cohen, Gary Coull, Prof Joseph Cheng Yu-shek, Ching Cheong, Frank Ching, Crys Darewicz, Dr Andrei Denissov, Dr L.K. Ding, Jed Donohoe, Prof Edward Friedman, Bernard Fong, Andy Ho, Ho Pin, Hanson Huang, Citi Hung Ching-tin, Kalina Ip, Andrew Jean, Yanshi Jin, John Kamm, Willem von Kemenade, Prof Kuan Hsin-chi, Carol Lai Pui-yee, Lam Chui-fun, Prof Diana Lary, Johnny Lau Yui-siu, Kevin Lau, Dr Lee Cho-Kay, Eric Lee, Frankie Leung, Dr W. H. Leung, Debra Levine, Diana Lin, Damin Liu, Dr Lo Chi-kin, Paul Loong, Pauline Loong, Lu Keng, Dr Jonathan Mirsky, Mou Chi-wang, Paul Mooney, Robin Munro, Yoshihisa Murayama, Douglas Ng, Tony Paul, Norio Sato, Orville Schell, Prof Ian Scott, Peter Seidlitz, Dr Michael D. Swaine, Anne Thurston, Prof Daniel & Lois Tretiak, William Triplett, Dr Tsang Shu-ki, T.L. Tsim, Dr Jim Walker, Wang Chen-pang, Andrew Wark, Wong Wai-man, Nury Vittachi, Fanny Wong, Xu Simin, Prof Yan Jiaqi, L.J. Yang, Phil Yang, Joseph Yau Sai-man, Russell Young and Zhang Weiguo.

Special thanks are due to the Chinese University Press, Hong Kong, for permission to use material from the four articles that I contributed to *China Review*, *China Review* 1992, *China Review* 1993 and *China Review* 1994: "The Media: The Party's Throat and Tongue Defend the Faith"; "Governing an Intransigent Society"; "Leadership Changes at the Fourteenth Party Congress"; and "Locking up the Floodgates; Striking a Balance between Reform and Repression".

The *South China Morning Post* has been unstinting in its support of my work in general, and this project in particular. Individual segments of this book have made use of material from articles that I wrote for the *Post*; such material has all been rewritten or updated. Editor-in-Chief David Armstrong has my gratitude for much-needed encouragement. I owe much to the former chief editor of the *Post*, Phillip Crawley, for enlightenment and guidance. Present and former colleagues at the *Post*'s China operation — particularly Chris Yeung and Daniel Kwan — have been generous with their advice and forbearance. Andrew Lynch copy-edited the manuscript and gave invaluable help and advice. I must record my heartfelt gratitude to David Chen, my predecessor as China Editor of the *Post* and *raconteur extraordinaire*, for many years of tutelage.

My dear and sweet wife Grace has been an unfailing spiritual support and a fount of wisdom. This book is dedicated to our daughter Michelle Ching-wen and son Julian Wen-chung, in the hope that they will take more interest in China.

Willy Wo-Lap Lam
January 1995
Hong Kong

Preface

I. Whither Chinese Socialism?

"THE revolution has not yet succeeded; comrades, we need to work harder!" The words of Dr Sun Yat-sen, the founder of modern China, had a strange resonance as China stepped more firmly into the post-Deng Xiaoping era in 1995.

The question of the direction of the "Chinese revolution" was posed with poignancy by Chinese Communist Party (CCP) elder Bo Yibo at a conference on Deng Xiaoping Thought and Socialism with Chinese Characteristics in December 1994. Bo, a former vice-premier, cast his eyes over the party's 74-year-old effort to graft socialism on to Chinese soil to fulfil the country's perennial dream of *fuqiang* — "prosperity and strength".

Bo quoted the patriarch's words of wisdom. "We will never make it if we just copy the experience and models of other countries," Deng indicated in the 1930s, arguing that China should not be a clone of the Soviet Union. Deng added in the 1950s: "From the point of view of the entire party, our knowledge [about Chinese socialism] is very insufficient. On socialist construction, we still have a large measure of blindness."

The putative Chief Architect of Reform did not seem to have solved the riddle through the 1980s. Speaking to aides and foreign dignitaries alike, the patriarch admitted that the contours of "Chinese-style socialism" had become less clear. "We were not sure as to what socialism was about," Deng told an African leader in the mid-1980s, referring to the "leftist" mistakes made by

Chairman Mao and Co in the 1960s and 1970s. The only concrete thing that the New Helmsman had to offer was that "socialism is not poverty".

Other reformist lieutenants who had worked for Deng were hardly more innovative. The late party General Secretary Hu Yaobang's attempts at "thought liberation" did not go much beyond his now-famous remark at the grave of Karl Marx in late 1985: "Marxism cannot solve all the problems of today." Hu's successor, former party chief Zhao Ziyang, who was less of an ideologue, tackled the problem largely by skirting it. "For me, socialism is nothing more than [overall] state ownership of the means of production and rewards [to citizens] being distributed in accordance with [the quality of] labour [contributed by each individual]," Zhao said in private, hinting that he would rather steer clear of the theoretical constraints of socialism.

The explorations of Deng, Hu and Zhao were crystallised in the Political Report endorsed by the 13th Party Congress of 1987, perhaps the zenith of the CCP's decades-old soul-searching. The congress conceded that China was still at a "preliminary stage of socialism". It then argued, *á la* Dr Sun, that the comrades should persevere in both the theory and practice of reform, the "revolution" of the day.

In spite of the belief of many that by early 1995, the Middle Kingdom was poised to acquire membership of the developed world, the questions posed by Bo, Deng, Hu and Zhao have remained daunting. Alas, they also risk becoming obsolete: the CCP is being overtaken by events and their "revolution" stolen from them.

The *fuqiang* that China has amassed since the Tiananmen Square crackdown has come about despite — not because of — "Chinese-style socialism". This wealth and vigour is predicated upon the Chinese going one better than Zhao in exercising a collective amnesia: forget about socialism — be it Soviet or Chinese — and just get rich. The questions confronting the post-Deng republic are those of the primitive phase of capitalism: how to lay down rules whereby each individual and enterprise can compete on a level playing field.

The problem for the CCP has become not so much showing the country the way to *fuqiang* but not being left behind by the people: how to stay — and to be seen as — relevant in the wake of the widespread perception even among the 54 million CCP members that socialism and party interference have become a millstone around the neck of progress.

The Beijing leadership is aware of the twin crises of ideology and legitimacy. While panic-stricken, however, the post-Deng leadership with President Jiang Zemin at its core has refused to perform radical surgery on Chinese-style socialism as well as the party's mind-set. The crisis mentality has manifested itself in the hundreds of conferences on Deng Thought that have been held across the land since late 1993. The dominant theme of the conclaves was how to use Deng Thought to save the day. But can Deng — and the leadership that is the beneficiary of his "death-bed blessing" — deliver?

II. The "China Problem" for the Post-Deng Leadership

This book looks at developments in politics, the economy, the army and society since the tragedy of June 4, 1989, and forecasts their progress into the post-Deng era. The common theme is: is the party under Deng and his designated successors able to tackle the problems? Apart from the CCP, what other socio-economic factors and sectors will play pivotal roles? What might China be like five or ten years down the road?

At least on the surface, the country was doing very well by early 1995. With a gross domestic product of more than US$515 billion, China became the world's seventh largest economy in 1994. Foreign reserves hit an enviable US$50 billion. In the same year, the mainland economy enjoyed the world's highest growth rate. In spite of jarring instances such as the Beijing municipal government refusing to honour a lease contract with the fast-food chain McDonald's, overseas investors were rushing in. Equally significant, Beijing, which was feverishly lobbying the West to join the World Trade Organisation, seemed to have made great strides in adopting market economics.

Chapter 2 describes in detail the valiant efforts Deng made to resuscitate economic reform after the gunshots of Tiananmen Square. Particularly after his *nanxun* or "imperial tour of the south" in early 1992, a leap forward was taken in reforms including finance, attracting foreign investment, and the development of the private sector. Deng was practising a "Zhao Ziyang policy without Zhao Ziyang". By late 1994, however, economic liberalisation had reached a bottleneck. It was clear that from that point onwards, the social and economic costs of reform were becoming prohibitive unless commensurate steps were taken to liberalise the political structure.

The impending demise of Deng has exposed more chinks in the regime's armour. The CCP political structure and culture have remained more in tune with the caves of Yan'an, Shaanxi Province (the party's rural base in the 1930s), than with the 21st century. Up until the end of 1994, the leadership was preoccupied with Maoist "ideological political work" as well as "party construction" — euphemisms for indoctrination and promoting absolute loyalty to the party centre. Rule of personality towers over rule of law. The leadership has given up on even the lily-livered attempts at political liberalisation, such as "separation of party and government" advocated by Hu and Zhao in the mid-1980s (see Chapter 5).

Internally, the party lacked institutional mechanisms to ensure that different factions can air their views openly and compete on an equal footing. The Mainstream Clique led by President Jiang faced repeated challenges from both the right (forces represented by the remnant supporters of Hu and Zhao) and the left (the quasi-Maoists). Yan'an-style purges and back-stabbing continued to poison the body politic. Droves of the best cadres left the party to avoid being embroiled in Machiavellian schemes.

Externally, the party had to rely on an army and police-state apparatus to shore up "the dictatorship of the proletariat". Billions of yuan were splashed out on the People's Liberation Army (PLA) and the police even as budgets fell short and most government departments were going through administrative streamlining. Special privileges for men in uniform were boosted. Generals not only had *carte blanche* to do business but were given a big say in policy-making in civilian areas (see Chapter 4).

Another consequence of the failure to retool the political set-up is the growing tension within the regions. In 1994 and early 1995 the Jiang leadership took back powers from local administrations to shore up its position. The political initiatives of localities were blunted as Jiang let more and more Shanghai Faction politicians jump the queue to Beijing. Provincial and municipal chieftains were also hit in their pockets through heavier taxes. Autonomous powers hitherto enjoyed by the regions to "do their own thing" were rescinded in the interest of cutting inflationary investments, boosting grain production, and stopping speculative activities such as real estate. While no single province or city had openly rebelled, most were pursuing their own agendas while going through the motions of supporting the centre.

Worse still, the party's failure to modernise itself has undermined its ability to wage economic reform, now the CCP's only *raison d'être*. In the mid-1990s, Beijing has to tackle those reforms that demand hefty sacrifices on the part of holders of vested interests including industries, factories and individuals. Such minefields include the reform of state enterprises, which inevitably requires massive lay-off of workers. An administration that scores high on legitimacy and popularity could afford bolder moves; it might be in a position to convince the people that it is worthwhile to make short-term sacrifices for long-term gains. The risks in implementing difficult and unpopular measures can also be lessened if there are effective communication channels and, even better, if different sectors of society are allowed a role in policy-making.

Since the CCP is bent on preserving its monopoly on power — and a closed and unwieldy ruling mechanism — it can ill afford risky policies, particularly given the need to contain mass dissatisfaction in the run-up to the patriarch's demise. What the party did was water down the reforms. As we shall see, the Jiang leadership presided over a partial return of central planning in the interest of upholding stability. Measures such as restructuring state enterprises and forming joint-stock companies slowed down in late 1994 because of fear that unemployed workers would take to the streets. Price control and grain coupons were re-introduced to fight inflation.

Another area where stagnation in political change has hurt business and the economy in general is corruption. Companies run by the offspring of senior cadres and army officers have obstructed the economy's march to the market place because of their refusal to part with special privileges, thus making equal competition impossible. And the lack of transparency in the political system and the party's refusal to share power means that its perennial anti-corruption campaign has come to nought.

III. Deng Xiaoping and the Future of the Chinese Communist Party

In the interview given by Deng Rong to the *New York Times* in January 1995, the third daughter of the patriarch seemed to hold out an olive branch to the victims of Tiananmen Square. While defending Deng's decision to let the tanks roll, Deng Rong hinted at the possibility of a reconciliation: "That's something which will be up to those [leaders] who come afterwards." Ms Deng also offered a *mea culpa* for Deng's involvement in the Anti-Rightist Campaign of 1957. "A large number of people who were made targets were actually good people," she said.

It would be unrealistic to expect something as conciliatory from Deng's will, if there is one. The New Helmsman largely halted his own "thought liberation" after the student demonstrations of December 1986, a precursor to the 1989 democracy movement. From 1987 onwards, Deng stopped exploring conundrums such as the role of the party in an increasingly pluralistic society: he began lecturing Chinese and foreigners alike on the "absolute necessity" of stale Marxist concepts including the dictatorship of the proletariat. As Deng told former United States Secretary of State George Shultz in 1987: "Only the socialist system can fundamentally solve the problem of poverty. That's why we cannot tolerate people who oppose socialism . . . Socialist construction is impossible without CCP leadership."

Despite Deng's attempts to mend heaven in the wake of the June 4 disaster, his statecraft remained the same: to maintain a balance among different factions in the party. To prevent the country from imploding, Deng juxtaposed yin against yang, left against right, pro-market economic reforms against the crypto-Stalinist police-state apparatus. At the height of the *nanxun*, Deng boasted about his "one great theoretical invention" — "not engaging in controversy", meaning not taking sides or being infatuated with any ideological viewpoint. Fearful of upsetting the equilibrium, Deng always pulled back at the threshold of a revolution. The New Helmsman proved incapable of following his own instruction about "changing one's brain" — and taking the leap of faith into the 21st century (see Chapter 1).

It would be equally unrealistic to expect bold initiatives from the Jiang faction, which has no other avocation than preserving the vested interests of clique affiliates. The President revived Leninist orthodoxy by building a top-heavy party structure with a rigid chain of command under the Jiang Zemin Office. In Mao's formulation of the Leninist doctrine, "democratic centralism" was nothing more than "the minority [of party members] obeying the majority; individuals obeying the organisation; inferior departments obeying superior departments; and the entire party obeying the *zhongyang* [Central Committee]." Just as in Mao's days, the *zhongyang* stands for the Politburo Standing Committee or, in most instances, just the helmsman.

Jiang masterminded the restitution of many elements of Maoist statecraft, particularly ways to counter "peaceful evolution", the codeword for alleged efforts by the "neo-imperialist West" to turn China into a vassal of capitalism. Desperate attempts were made to resuscitate the country's 800,000-odd CPP cells. The party also lavished inordinate resources on the propagation of a corps of young cadres — those in their 30s and 40s — who would carry the flame of Chinese socialism into the next century.

Chapter 5 and 6 will give a detailed account of the potentials, strengths and weaknesses of leaders including Jiang, Premier Li Peng, Vice-Premier Zhu Rongji, National People's Congress Chairman Qiao Shi and Chinese People's Political Consultative Conference Chairman Li Ruihuan — as well as their younger followers. The political fortunes of cabals such as the Shanghai Faction, the Qinghua Faction, the Communist Youth League Faction, and the Faction of the Alumni of Soviet Colleges are assessed.

Whichever leadership collective takes over from Deng, however, will have to contend with two forces that are ghosts from the Maoist past. One is the still-potent bloc of leftist ideologues who want to stop market reforms and return to Mao's "kingdom of the spirit" (see Chapter 3). While they seem hopelessly obsolete, the Maoists could gain points by appealing to those losers in the reform enterprise who hanker after the egalitarian, non-inflationary days of the early 1950s.

The other force in the polity that might block progress is the army, Deng Xiaoping's "iron wall of steel" against the infiltration of bourgeois-liberal thoughts from the West. To bolster his position as well as that of the party, since becoming Chairman of the Central Military Commission in late 1989 Jiang has curried favour with the generals by granting the PLA unprecedented powers.

One cannot, of course, rule out the possibility of the "healthy forces" within the party coming to the fore after the Jiang Zemin-dominated interregnum.

Apart from the remnant followers of Hu Yaobang and Zhao Ziyang, they include the hordes of cadres who have switched over to business. Some among these non-mainstream elements could initiate internal reform so that the hardline CCP might gradually be transformed into a "soft" socialist party in the East European mode. By early 1995, however, the prospects for this outcome were uncertain.

IV. The Rise of People Power with Chinese Characteristics

Revolution is neither a dinner party nor an armed insurrection: it is a state of mind. Five years shy of the 21st century, do the Chinese have the requisite mentality to propel themselves towards modernisation? This could be the single most important question for China after Deng Xiaoping.

The key to *fuqiang* may lie less and less with the CCP. Much of the energy for ringing in the new might come from what sociologists call the "civil society" — in the Chinese context, whatever is outside the party's domain. It is generally recognised that two forces are indispensable for the leap from monolithic feudalism to modernity, which is characterised by pluralism in politics and culture. The catalysts are economics and education.

Quite independently of the CCP or the government, Chinese have accumulated much wealth. By 1994, private companies and collectively-owned units such as village and township enterprises had displayed wholly-state-owned concerns as the mainstay of industry. The same year, the number of workers employed by non-state units — 120 million — surpassed that of the state sector. In late 1994, household savings hit 2 trillion yuan, in addition to US$20 billion in foreign currencies. In spite of depressed stock prices, more than 10 million *gumin* ("stocks-crazed people") played the markets everyday. Heaps of money and money-making skills have meant that in the cities, the contours of a "Western-style" middle-class have become evident.

And what about education? Theoretically, the proportion of the GNP that China earmarked for education in 1994 — 2.66 per cent — remained abysmal. Opportunities, however, abound for the more resourceful urbanites. Private schools, some with investment from Hong Kong and Taiwan, are sprouting like bamboo shoots in the spring. Even more important is the development of education in the broad sense of the word: exposure to the outside world thanks to the information revolution. Through satellite television, IDD, faxes, modems and the Internet, Chinese are hooked up to the global village. Beijing is spending upwards of US$10 billion to assemble an information highway with the help of Microsoft and other software giants.

The marriage of money and knowledge has resulted in the centre of gravity shifting gradually but irrevocably away from Zhongnanhai, the party headquarters in Beijing, to the civil society. The consolidation of the influence of businessmen and professionals, and intellectuals with independent sources of information has also confirmed the party's irrelevance and impending obsolescence.

There are many ways in which the civil society is challenging the 46-year-old orthodoxy. Firstly, it is going after goals that are not compatible with the Four Cardinal Principles of communism. A late 1994 poll on the objectives of Beijing citizens found that "becoming a millionaire" was the most popular choice. In lifestyle, preference for Hong Kong and Taiwan singers and movie stars had become so overwhelming that the party's Propaganda Department had to restrict the broadcast and circulation of "decadent" music and films. A poll among Beijing primary school pupils revealed that Hong Kong heart-throb Andy Lau was more popular than Chairman Mao.

Secondly, and much more worrying for the CCP, activist members of the civil society are forming groupings to protect and boost their economic and political interests. This will inevitably develop into clashes with a party that jealously guards its prerogatives. Reluctantly, units such as the police, the Ministry of Civil Affairs and the State Industry and Commerce Bureau have permitted some categories of unofficial or "mass" organisations to be set up. They include clubs and associations on environmental issues; the protection of the rights of non-smokers; consumer rights; and even the rights of homosexuals. Not to mention the scores of quasi-private chambers of commerce and trade associations whose hidden agenda is to ensure that non-state-sector businesses have the legal status and clout to compete with state concerns.

The CCP, of course, will not surrender its last line of defence by allowing non-party elements to join the ruling apparatus, let alone mechanisms for maintaining "proletarian dictatorship" such as the army and the police. The siege of Zhongnanhai, however, is hotting up. It also promises to be a major focus of post-Deng Xiaoping politics. Non-party elements will be helped by the growing influence of Hong Kong and Taiwan — as well as the integration of the Chinese economy with the international order.

Chapter 7, the conclusion of this book, forecasts developments in the party and the country into the new century. The fate of China hinges on the outcome of the slugfest within the CCP that will inevitably break out after the demise of the holder of the heavenly mandate. It also depends on the speed with which droves of once-straitlaced party members fall for the many-splendoured world beyond Mao's infamous One-Voice Chamber. Infinite possibilities — most of them non-Marxist and non-socialist — are beckoning for those among the Old Hundred Surnames who are finally taking their fate into their own hands. The 1989 pro-democracy movement could be the first flowering of "people power" in a quasi-feudal system. A new chapter for the world's longest-continuous civilisation opens as its last patriarch gives up the ghost.

1

Deng Xiaoping's
Controversial Legacy

I. Introduction

REBEL political scientist Yan Jiaqi once said: "In China, only one man does the thinking." The exiled dissident was referring to a long line of monarchs stretching from Qin the First Emperor to Deng Xiaoping. It would, of course, be an overstatement to say that the patriarch was, from mid-1989 to late 1994, the sole arbiter of Chinese politics. To do so would be to over-exaggerate the monolithic nature of Chinese communism — and to fail to do justice to the dynamics of factional contention and "people power" with Chinese characteristics.

However, Deng remained very much a first among equals in the octogenarian leadership that ruled China. Perhaps most of the major initiatives of the Chinese Communist Party (CCP) from 1989 to 1994 came from the New Helmsman. While the prestige and credibility of the senior leader had noticeably decreased after the Beijing massacre, it could be argued that Deng had by and large achieved what he had set out to do: to stop the rebellion against the CCP; to re-ignite economic growth and reform; and to break through the diplomatic isolation that had beset China.

A key reason behind Deng's decision to "sacrifice" handpicked successors Hu Yaobang and Zhao Ziyang in January 1987 and June 1989 respectively was that the two had failed to achieve a balance between the two goals — political repression and economic liberalisation. The June 4 crackdown was an instance of the CCP re-assuming an iron-fisted approach to snuffing out challenges from the right. After mid-1989, Deng spearheaded an apparently successful crusade to strike a new balance.

On the one hand, the mechanism of state control, or the dictatorship of the proletariat was reinforced. The campaign against "peaceful evolution" went into high gear. And the police-state apparatus was beefed up even beyond the scale of Mao Zedong and his cohorts. On the other hand, Deng, the progenitor of change, went ahead with economic reform. By late 1991, in Guangdong, Fujian and Hainan provinces and along the coastal belt, the pace of reform had picked up speed. Much of Zhao Ziyang's economic programme was revived. And the country made a great leap rightward after Deng's *nanxun* ("imperial tour of the south") in early 1992. From this stage onwards, the country was irrevocably committed to a quasi-capitalistic path.

Internationally, by early 1992, China had largely been re-accepted into the community of nations. This was illustrated by the success with which the Middle Kingdom had forged new ties with countries as diverse as Indonesia, Singapore, Brunei, Israel and South Africa. Beijing weathered the collapse of the Soviet Union and the Eastern bloc well. By mid-1994, China had emerged as a major player on the international stage. So many Western powers were jostling to get into the China market that even the administration of US President Bill Clinton had to take seriously Beijing's threat of retaliation should Washington decide not to renew its Most Favoured Nation trading status.

By sheer bravado and will-power, then, the Houdini of Chinese politics seemed to have succeeded in imposing a collective amnesia about June 4. By mid-1994, Deng Thought had displaced Mao Thought as the state creed. With China basking in the warmth of double-digit growth, the prestige of the New Helmsman seemed to be nearing another peak.

Yet, as the following sections will make clear, China was never the same after the Tiananmen Square bloodbath. Deng's reputation was inexorably dented. To steady the ship of state after the June 4 fiasco, the New Helmsman had to sacrifice the other half of his reforms: political change. Political reform remained frozen as of mid-1994. It could be argued that things had retrogressed. CCP politics was as dynastic as ever: rule of personality still towered over the rule of law. The system was more monolithic in mid-1994 than it was before the June 4 crackdown. Participation by non-Communist elements in decision-making was less pronounced than it was in the heyday of "liberalisation" under Hu Yaobang or Zhao Ziyang.

The prestige and legitimacy of the CCP continued to decline. Without political reform, corruption got worse, unravelling the moral fabric of the party and society in general. By early 1994, there were unmistakable signals that failure to implement political reform had hurt the ability of the country to absorb the shock of economic reforms. Worse still, with Deng's health becoming more frail by the day, the party had failed to come up with a formula for orderly and democratic succession.

To some extent, these questions will be addressed in the rest of the book. This chapter will concentrate on Deng's psychology and statecraft after the June 4 crackdown: the thinking behind the many initiatives he undertook from 1989 and mid-1994. Sections will be devoted to the patriarch's creative expansion of the open-door policy in the wake of the *nanxun* and his call for "perennial thought liberation". Deng's failure to entertain political reform — and his acquiescence in the Deng Cult — will also be examined. The conclusion will sum up Deng's contributions, his failings, and his dubious legacy.

II. Economics as the Core of National Work

When the then Politburo member Hu Qili met the press in October 1987, he said the 1986 student demonstrations and the ensuing campaign against bourgeois liberalisation were merely a *caju* ("interlude") which would not affect the overall course and outcome of the reform effort.[1] Deng did the same thing after the Tiananmen Square massacre. In both internal meetings and talks to foreign dignitaries, the patriarch tried to reassure the world that reform would stay on course despite the "June 4 contretemps".

In a speech to Premier Li Peng and Vice-Premier Yao Yilin on May 31, 1989 — when the decision to use force against the students had been taken — Deng said that the "counter-revolutionary rebellion" and its aftermath would not affect reform. "The policy of reform and the open door will not change," the patriarch asserted. "It will not change in the coming few decades, and must be upheld from beginning to end." Deng added that the line, goals and policies of the Third Plenum of the 11th Central Committee — which marked the beginning of the "era of reform" — would be preserved. The same goes for the decisions of the 13th Party Congress of late 1987, which hammered out a series of market reforms including a multi-sector economy. Deng pointed out that "even the wording" of the Congress decisions must be kept intact. "The Political Report of the 13th Party Congress has been passed by the entire congress," he said. "Not one word of it can be changed."[2]

Deng also indicated the extent of the reform and open-door policy would be widened, not constricted. "In the past, I talked about creating a few more Hong Kongs," he told Li and Yao. "This means we must open up to the outside world and cannot roll back the reforms. The extent of the open door will be wider than before. We must be bolder in the reform and open-door policy."

Until Deng stopped meeting foreign visitors in mid-1990, he had numerous occasions to hammer home that reform would not only be continued but expanded. For example, Deng told Chinese-American physicist Li Tsung-dao a few months after the massacre that "various policies associated with reform and the open door will not change". "China will do a better job at the construction of the Four Modernisations, and reform and the open-door policy," he added. "China's advancement speed will be even more stable, solid and speedy."[3] The same message was repeated to former president Richard Nixon and then American National Security Adviser Brent Scowcroft in the latter half of 1989.

A. Reviving the Economics-First Imperative

(i) "Talk More About Economics"

When Deng conceived his reform gameplan in the late 1970s, he laid down this golden rule, which became known as the line of the Third Plenum of the 13th Central Committee (1978), or "one centre, two basic points": "Economic construction is the core of national work; on the one hand, we pursue reform and the open-door policy; on the other, we uphold the Four Cardinal Principles." While this credo still carried with it the yoke of Marxism-Leninism, it was an improvement over classic Maoism, which posited class struggle as the centre of the universe.

As we shall see in Chapters 3 and 5, the part about "upholding the Four Cardinal Principles" largely consisted of endless campaigns against "bourgeois liberalisation" and strengthening the tools of the dictatorship of the proletariat. However, Deng wanted to get across the message both to the party and especially to the outside world that the police-state apparatus notwithstanding, China would concentrate on economic construction and reform.

After all, a key component of the Deng Xiaoping Revolution was his emphasis that the nation must slough off its preoccupation with Maoist class struggle and take economic work as the core. "We talked too much about politics and too little about economics," he said soon after taking power in 1978. If the June 4 crackdown was a case of Maoist politics wreaking havoc on economic construction, Deng wanted to repair the damage and, at least until he saw Marx, shift the focus back to economics.[4]

Resorting to a time-honoured ploy in the CCP cosmology, Deng used the ghosts of the past to justify his visions for the future. Soon after the Tiananmen Square bloodbath, the patriarch's handlers recycled a speech delivered by Deng in 1957 entitled "Our Major Task in the Future is Construction". It was in this seminal talk that the New Helmsman first spelled out his credo that

China should concentrate on economics, not politics. "What is our task for the future?" he asked. "There is still some revolutionary work, but it won't amount to much; our major job is [economic] construction." Deng thumbed his nose at leftist commissars whose speciality was "class struggle". "Our party, our cadres have thoroughly learnt the science called class struggle," he said. "However, they are either ignorant of or they know too little about the science of transforming nature."[5]

At about the same time, Deng revived another of his speeches in the late 1950s. In an address to Communist Youth League officials, Deng, then general secretary of the party, appeared to cast aspersions on Maoist-style mass movements. "How easy it is to call a mass meeting, or to issue a summons to action," Deng said. "Beating on the drums, pounding on the cymbals. Make everything loud and noisy. Yet what kind of result will this kind of work accomplish?"[6]

The patriarch's resolve to re-orientate national work to economic development steeled in the wake of the crumbling of communism in Eastern Europe and the Soviet Union. While he agreed with the hardliners that Beijing had to raise further its guard against infiltration and sabotage from foreign and domestic enemies, Deng also made it clear that only through economic growth and improvement in the standard of living could the CCP guarantee its monopoly on power.

In his celebrated briefing to participants in the Seventh Plenum of the 13th Central Committee in December 1990, Deng elaborated on his theory that only economic progress could save Chinese-style socialism. "If the economy improves, other policies could succeed and the Chinese people's faith in socialism will be enhanced," he said. "If not, socialism not only in China but in the rest of the world will be endangered."[7]

One of Deng's key lieutenants, member of the Politburo Standing Committee Li Ruihuan, also felt emboldened to revive the "economics first" argument. On a trip to Hubei Province in late 1990, Li reinstated the old Dengist slogan about "politics subserving economics". While talking to cadres there, Li said ideological and political work must take as its goal the boosting of productivity. "Ideological and political work must serve the goal of economic construction and be subordinate to it," he said. "We must fully arouse the enthusiasm of the people and the masses so that they can diligently promote economic construction."[8]

Chinese analysts said in reviving the "economics first" imperative, Deng was only restating the position for which he was lambasted by the Red Guards during the Cultural Revolution: "Taking productivity as the key criterion." In the Ten Years of Chaos, Deng was criticised for neglecting politics and ideology and concentrating merely on economic development. [9]

(ii) The Big Debate after the Soviet Coup

As we shall see in Chapter 3, the leftists tried their level best to revive Maoist class struggle. This reached an apogee immediately after the failed Soviet coup in August 1991. At an emergency meeting of party elders and Politburo members, leading ideologue Deng Liqun put forward the argument that, faced with the end of communism in the USSR, China must put "combating peaceful evolution as the core [of national work]". This was reportedly seconded by other party elders as well as third-generation hardliners including Li Peng. The premier reportedly said: "If we cannot ensure the socialist orientation of the country, we [the CCP] will lose power no matter how well the economy is developed." Nonplussed, Deng reportedly sat in silence.[10]

The patriarch soon fought back. With the backing of the more moderate elders, principally Yang Shangkun and Bo Yibo, he was able to re-establish a consensus among the leadership: that the CCP must stick to economic construction as the "core". Deng's instructions on the subject was appropriately related by Yang at the national meeting to commemorate the 80th anniversary of the 1911 Revolution, which was held in the Great Hall of the People on October 9, 1991.

"We must rely on economic development to convince those who do not believe in socialism," Yang quoted Deng as saying. "If we achieve small-scale prosperity by the end of the century, the minds [of the disbelievers] will become clearer. And when we have attained the level of medium-scale economic development during the next century, we shall have taken a leap forward in convincing them. The great majority among them [the disbelievers] will realise they made a mistake." This message was so important that national media repeated it several times in late 1991.[11]

Befitting his role at the time as the main executor of Deng's wishes, Yang himself issued a clarion call for the economics-first strategy. "All our work must serve the core of economic construction," he said on the same occasion. "We must not disrupt or interfere with this centrepoint." The former general then added: "Unless there is a massive invasion by foreign enemies, we must unremittingly uphold the goal [of economic progress]."

From the autumn of 1991 to early 1992, members of the Deng camp made the rounds of the provinces reaffirming the "Third-Plenum line". For example, member of the Politburo Standing Committee Qiao Shi, a leading moderate, toured Hainan Island in October 1991. "The line, goals and policies instituted by the party since the Third Plenum of the 11th Central Committee have greatly aroused the enthusiasm of the people and pushed forward economic development," Qiao said. "They are entirely correct."[12]

B. Focus on Science and Technology

A variant of the "economics first" persuasion was the slogan, reinstated after the Gulf War, that the nation should concentrate its resources on science and technology. The paramount leader's directive about "science and technology being the premier production force" was another attempt to ask the nation to concentrate its energy on the economy, this time, technological modernisation.

Deng first launched the "technology first" slogan in a talk to intimates in the spring of 1991. "We must put the highest emphasis on science and technology," the patriarch said. "We must fully depend on and assiduously develop science and technology." Deng's ideas were relayed by his daughter Deng Nan, a Vice-Minister of Science and Technology, first to the General Office of the Central Committee and then to the Politburo.[13]

The edict was given national prominence by Jiang Zemin when he toured Sichuan province in April 1991. "To give a push to Chinese socialist modernisation and the reform and open-door policy, we must give priority to, and fully rely on, science and technology," Jiang told cadres in the southwestern province. "To develop science and technology in a big way is the key to realising the Eighth Five-Year Plan and the Ten-Year Economic Blueprint [for the 1990s]."[14]

At the same time, the Beijing media revealed that it was Deng who had laid the foundation for the country's high-technology programme. In a front-page article on April 23, 1991, the *People's Daily* disclosed that Deng had in March 1986 issued personal instructions for a series of scientific research projects. The scheme, which involved more than 10,000 technical personnel, had since become known as the "March 1986 plan".[15]

The national press also disclosed that in October 1988, Deng had laid down specific instructions for preserving China's *qiaozhi* or global ranking. "Different countries of the world have mapped out strategies for scientific and technological development because the next century will be a century of high technology," the patriarch said. "China must develop its own hi-tech base so that it can belong among the front ranks." [16]

That Deng's message had political as well as economic significance was made clear by Politburo liberal Li Ruihuan. In May 1991, Li asked the entire nation to study the implications of Deng's instruction on technology. "Pushing forward the development of science and technology is both an economic as well as political question," Li said. "Assiduously developing science and technology is the key to realising the strategic goal of the nation." [17] The former Tianjan mayor was warning the ideologues not to push class struggle instead of technological innovation.

C. Reining in the Leftists

During the first year after the June 4 tragedy, a chastised and dispirited Deng lent his authority to a frenetic shift to the left in Chinese politics. Firstly, Deng himself wanted to ensure that there would be no repeat performance of the 1989 democracy movement: hence the very willing blessings he gave to the post-Tiananmen Square repression. Secondly, as we shall see in Chapter 3, Deng himself was subjected to attack by the likes of Deng Liqun over the failure to stamp out bourgeois liberalisation in the mid-1980s.[18]

All along, however, Deng also felt a need to put a damper on attempts by leftists to roll back economic reform under the pretext of fighting "peaceful evolution". Consistent with dynastic political culture, Deng resorted to allegories, subtle hints, and the revival of his own old speeches to drive home his point.

Among the first "reformist" ideals that Deng tried to re-establish after June 4 was his old slogan of "seeking truth from facts" — or doing things according to actual conditions, not "bookism". For example, on August 16, 1989, national newspapers carried a 1956 speech that Deng made to a gathering of international Communist Youth League representatives in Beijing. Entitled "The Integration of Marxism and China's Actual Conditions", the address contained one of the earliest statements by Deng on the need to be pragmatic and to temper the rigid requirements of Marxism with the day-to-day exigencies of Chinese life. He argued that the way ahead for China was "to integrate the general truth of Marxism-Leninism with the actual and practical [conditions] of China".[19]

The patriarch, who coined the slogan "seek truth from facts" in the early 1980s, said the goals of socialism and communism must be achieved bearing in mind the actual conditions of China. He cited the example of the "socialist transformation of the capitalist industry and commerce" in the mid-1950s. "We have adopted the measure of the peaceful transformation of capitalist commerce and industry," Deng said. "In this way, our production has not only avoided damage but has progressed. And while capitalism has been wiped out, we have educated the bourgeois class."

Most important, Deng warned that China must guard against "subjectivism". A major manifestation of "subjectivism", the architect of reform said, was "dogmaticism" or "knowing only certain sentences and words of Marxism and not going by actual conditions". Chinese sources said by releasing the 33-year-old speech, Deng was serving notice on the leftists not to go too far in their revival of Maoism. Specifically, Deng urged them not to jettison market-oriented economic reforms.

In March 1991, Deng upped the ante in his allegorical offensive by releasing yet another old speech: this time, his 1957 address to the All-China Federation of Women. Entitled "What is Important is Constant Work", Deng argued that cadres must do practical work for the masses, and not be contented with futile sloganeering.[20]

It was not until the second half of 1991 that Deng's moderate faction felt strong enough to tackle the leftists head on. Reminiscent of the fire-fighting efforts undertaken by Zhao Ziyang to contain the scope of the Campaign Against Bourgeois Liberalisation in early 1987, Deng and Yang Shangkun masterminded attempts to prevent the fight against "peaceful evolution" from spilling over into the economic arena. For example, the patriarch ruled that the "anti-peaceful evolution" campaign be waged only among cadres, not among the people. Further, the crusade against "US-instigated infiltration" should be carried out outside the nation's economic activities.[21]

With the backing of Deng, Jiang Zemin was emboldened to put the leftists in their place. In the autumn of 1991, the party chief upbraided commissars in the ideological and propaganda establishment for paying "excessive" attention to combating bourgeois liberalisation. "We must be on guard against the peaceful evolution conspiracy," he said in late 1991. "Yet there is no need to talk about it everyday. It will not do to see an enemy behind every tree. The focus of our work must be to build up the country [economically]."[22]

Deng won a sizeable victory at the national meeting of the heads of propaganda departments held in Beijing in January 1992. Then department chief Wang Renzhi, a protégé of Deng Liqun's, said that media units should concentrate on "positive propaganda", especially "achievements in the area of reform, the open door, and modernisation construction". The conclave did not make any reference to fighting "peaceful evolution". The commissars also committed themselves to "encouraging and guiding the people to liberate their thoughts and to open up new avenues".[23] As we shall see in Chapter 3, the reference to "peaceful evolution" largely died out from late 1992.

III. A New "Thought-Liberation" Movement

A. The Theory of the New Cats

"Deng Xiaoping has rediscovered the wheel." This was the reaction of diplomats in Beijing to Deng's efforts to recycle his time-honoured slogan that the criterion for a policy is whether it works. It was during his Christmas Eve 1990 address to the Seventh Plenum that the patriarch officially revived his "theory of the white and black cats" — be it white or black it is a good cat that catches mice. The "new" version of the Dengist wisdom: do not enquire about the nature or "ideological orientation" of a certain economic policy; it should be pursued if it enhances productivity.

Deng attempted to reinstate this credo of economic pragmatism in reaction to efforts by remnant Maoists to revive the "debate of the surnames". A major controversy that hit theoretical and press circles in 1987 and 1988 was whether the country should differentiate between the "surnames" or orientation of a particular policy. Leftists insisted that a "capitalist" reform policy should be jettisoned no matter how promising it may be for economic progress.

For Deng Xiaoping, however, Beijing should adopt any economic policy and measure that promoted productivity or generated wealth. He indicated in late 1990 that it was simplistic to equate market mechanisms with capitalism — and thus bar them from the socialist economy. "Some comrades have equated a planned economy with socialism and market economics with capitalism," Deng said, adding that both the socialist and the capitalist systems had elements of planning and the marketplace. He further argued that planning and market mechanisms were only means to control and distribute resources, not a yardstick for telling socialism from capitalism.[24]

Deng was desperately seeking a theoretical justification for boosting the proportions of market mechanisms at a time when conservatives were turning their back on economic reform under the pretext of maintaining the "purity" of Chinese socialism. Actually, Deng had tried to make propaganda for market forces two months earlier. In an internal speech in October 1991, he underscored the importance of "the organic synthesis of central planning and market mechanisms". Deng, who had begun reform experiments 11 years ago, said the two were "mutually interdependent and one cannot uphold central planning at the expense of market forces or vice-versa".[25]

The patriarch also co-opted others among the Eight Major Elders to speak out in favour of his eclecticism. Then vice-chairman of the Central Advisory Commission Bo Yibo, one of the elders closest to Deng, made a defence of quasi-capitalist mechanisms in late 1990. "Do not regard the commodity economy and the market economy as the monopoly of capitalism," Bo said. "We must make use of the reform and open-door policy to further develop links with the world economy."[26]

Echoing the patriarch, Bo said the Chinese economy must "follow a path of socialism with Chinese characteristics: the synthesis of the socialist planned economy and market regulations". Bo added that market forces were important because "it is an era of business warfare in the international arena". "In the past, the Chinese economy was cut off from the world [economy]," the elder said. "We must make use of the policy of reform and the open door to further promote links with the world economy and to fight for international markets."

From late 1990 to early 1992, Deng's "new cat theory" had become a dominant theoretical weapon for the moderate wing of the party. For example, in a speech in November 1990, Jiang Zemin also spoke of the need for an "organic mix" of planning and market forces. Quoting his mentor, Jiang said: "We must explore a concrete path which is a synthesis between a planned economy and market regulations."[27]

In a July 1991 dispatch, the semi-official China News Service went so far as to say that Deng had been pushing the New Cat Theory — "whether our policies and actual work are correct depends on whether they are beneficial to the development of production forces" — to combat the rising trend of leftism. CNS reported that the patriarch was disturbed by resistance to reform from "unliberated minds" in the party and government. It also said the fact that moderate leaders favoured by Deng such as Jiang Zemin had consolidated their positions augured well for a felicitous outcome for "the long-brewing handover of power to the third generation"[28]

By the time Deng visited Guangdong in January 1992, it seemed he had wangled a promise from the bulk of his colleagues to pay lip service at least to the New Cats Theory. That month, the pro-Beijing newspaper in Hong Kong, *Ta Kung Pao*, quoted another Deng speech which had been "recently" carried by an unspecified mainland media. That address basically recapitulated the old man's Christmas Eve 1990 speech. "We must avoid being mired in a new ideological imbroglio," *Ta Kung Pao* quoted Deng as saying. "We must not equate market economics with capitalism. We must not juxtapose the use of foreign capital against [the Maoist ideal of] autarky."[29]

B. The "Northern Expedition" and Call for New Ideas

The bugle call for "thought liberation" and "new ideas" which was made by the moderate faction a year or so after the 1989 massacre was a case of *deja vu*. The CCP had made the same rallying cry after each cycle of repression. The latest example was in mid-1987, when Zhao Ziyang issued an appeal for new ideas after the Campaign Against Bourgeois Liberalisation. The underlying reason: every time that the party restored Maoist orthodoxy, morale among the cadres and intellectuals nosedived, and the CCP had to foster another round of "tolerance and openness" to mollify this key sector of the polity. After all, without "new ideas", how can economic reform go on?

The first sign that Deng wanted to revive the goal of "thought modernisation" came in a speech made by Jiang Zemin to the heads of the party schools in mid-June 1990. Echoing well-known statements made by the likes of Hu Yaobang and former Politburo liberal Hu Qili, Jiang said Marxism was a "developing creed" and the party must interpret Marxist theory according to

LIBRARY
BISHOP BURTON COLLEGE
BEVERLEY HU17 8QG

the needs of today. "Chinese communists regard Marxism as a science that is steadily developing, never as a rigid dogma," he said. Jiang further noted that under this concept, the party must synthesise Marxism with "China's socialist modernisation drive, the practice of the reform and open-door policy, and new developments in the world situation so as to develop Marxism while adhering to it".[30]

However, it was not until early 1991 that the patriarch rolled up his sleeves and personally took charge of a "thought liberation" campaign to sweep aside the outdated concepts of Marxism. In terms of both content and scale, it was comparable to the intellectual enlightenment that Deng and Hu Yaobang launched soon after the Third Plenum of the 11th Central Committee, when the liberal leaders urged "new thinking" based on the slogan "practice is the sole criterion of truth".[31]

This latest round of "thought liberation" was characterised by Deng himself as the "Northern Expedition". Citing the late Generalissimo Chiang Kai-shek's efforts in the late 1920s to crush the northern warlords with Guangzhou-based troops, Deng indicated that the reformist faction must make use of "new ideas" and political forces in the south, including Shanghai, to smash "ossified thinking" in the capital.

"I made a mistake ten years ago by not turning Shanghai into a special economic zone," Deng reportedly said on a visit to the eastern metropolis in the spring of 1991. "If I had done so, Shanghai would be a lot more different than what it is now; and the entire country would also not be the same." Another version of Deng's remarks: "I want to launch a Northern Expedition and recover territory [lost to conservative thinking]."[32]

The bulk of the "new ideas" was presented in four commentaries in the Shanghai-based *Liberation Daily* from February to April 1991. The writing group of the commentaries — three liberal editors and propaganda officials — was aptly known as Huangpu Ping, which translates as Deng Xiaoping at Huangpu River, Shanghai. "To boost the consciousness of the open door, we must further liberate our thoughts and jettison concepts that are conservative and ossified," Huangpu Ping said. "It won't do without new ideas and new strategies," he added. "It will also not do to simplistically follow [outdated] open door practices of the 1980s."[33]

One commentary cited the Deng dictum: "To wage revolution and pursue construction, we need a batch of trail-blazers who are brave in thinking, brave in exploration and brave in innovations." This recalled the old slogan of Hu Yaobang and Hu Qili that for reform to succeed, the party needed a generation of "new thinking men". Huangpu Ping cited the following examples of "ossified thinking": equating market mechanisms with capitalism; "juxtaposing the open-door policy with the principle of self-reliance, in the process being over-cautious in the use of foreign capital"; failure to uphold reform policies which had been proven by the past decade to be effective.[34]

The commentator went so far as to point out that, in the name of "developing the economy in a sustained and stable manner and not being over-impetuous", some cadres were sloppy in their work, in the process failing to do things that could be done. There seemed little question that Huangpu Ping — and Deng Xiaoping — was zeroing in on central planners in the State Council, in particular Li Peng and Yao Yilin, who were holding up reform under the pretext of being cautious. And it was no accident that soon after the appearance of the commentaries, Li Peng dispatched a high-level team of "investigators" to check out the "background" of the anti-conservative fusillades.[35]

Again in a throwback to the 1979 "thought liberation" movement, Deng and his lieutenants went about testing the loyalty of central and regional leaders by asking them to *biaotai* or voice publicly their views on reform. In the spring of 1991, various leaders, including those with conservative reputations, at least went through the motions of toeing Deng's new line.

For example, in early April, Mayor of Beijing Chen Xitong, a prime advocate of the armed suppression of the student movement, surprised observers when he told local reporters that "thought liberation would be the priority task of 1991". "We cannot make advancements without the liberation of thought," he said. "Practice has shown that whenever the thoughts of the staff of a unit are liberated, its performance would be particularly energetic." Chen was quoted as telling the more "ossified" of his colleagues: "Do not fear market forces. Liberate your thoughts."[36]

In a similar vein, then party boss of Shanxi Wang Maolin, admonished his colleagues to "liberate our thinking in order to steady our faith in reform and the open-door policy". Others who had apparently jumped on the thought-liberation bandwagon included the new Shanghai mayor Huang Ju and the then Governor of Gansu, Jia Zhijie. For example, in an internal talk in April 1991, Huang urged "further liberation of thought" in the solution of the nation's problems. "We must be more broad-minded in our thoughts, more flexible and multi-faceted in our measures," he said.[37]

C. The "New Ideas" in Practice

(i) Deng's Role in the Eighth Five-Year Plan

In spite of his inexorably declining health, Deng was generally more active after June 4, 1989, than in the mid-1980s. The reason is obvious: earlier, the patriarch could count on Hu Yaobang and Zhao Ziyang to formulate and execute his reform programmes. Now, he had to take up the cudgel himself.

Throughout 1990, a major concern for Deng was to ensure the reformist content of the Eighth Five-Year Plan (1991-95) and the Ten-Year Economic Blueprint (1991-2000). In theory, the State Planning Commission, under then vice-premier Yao Yilin, was in charge of the drafting process. However, Deng had, either personally or through emissaries, made known his views to Yao and his drafters. On at least one occasion, Deng upbraided Yao for failing to boost the scale of reform in the plans. This was one reason for Yao's somewhat surprising decision to give up his SPC portfolio in late 1990.

First of all, it was Deng who laid down the idea of the simultaneous drafting of the Five-Year Plan and the Ten-Year Blueprint. Since the 1940s, the CCP had followed the Soviet example of putting together five-year plans on economic development. In a speech in late 1990 however, the patriarch explained the need for a decade-long plan: "On the basis of the previous ten years, we must take a look at the coming decade." "We must uphold whatever was correct in the past ten years, spend more effort on whatever fell short, and rectify whatever is not correct," he added. Chinese sources said Deng was anxious to uphold his record of reform. He also hoped that by fixing a ten-year plan, the reform process would survive his own death.[38]

Specifically, Deng disputed the central planners' argument that the economy must develop in a "sustained, stable and harmonious" fashion, by which the latter meant that speed of growth must be slowed, and the pace of reform contained. Through various emissaries, Deng made clear that the growth rate must be maintained and reform be rendered "faster and quicker" during the 1990s.

Speaking for Deng, Jiang Zemin said in a speech in November 1990 that the speed of economic development must not be dampened if China were to fulfil the pledge made by Deng in the early 1980s that the economy would be quadrupled by the year 2000 and that the country would be "relatively well off" by the middle of the 21st century. "In a developing socialist country like China, it will not do if the economy does not develop at a considerable speed," Jiang said. "If not, the original target cannot be reached." The party leader also said that Beijing welcomed "the free contention of views" among theoreticians on how the Five-Year Plan and the Ten-Year Blueprint should be drafted.[39]

On the question of the speed of development, Deng was able to get the support of individual party elders. For example, in a speech delivered in Shanghai in early 1991, the late president Li Xiannian apparently criticised the foot-dragging by central planners. "It would not do just to steady the pace [of economic development]," said the former state president. "We must go forward. We've been stabilised for too long. It won't do not to make a move."[40]

Aside from the speed of development, Deng also threw his weight around on the equally critical question of the speed of reform. The argument went back to the skirmishes fought throughout the 1980s between Zhao Ziyang and Deng on the one hand, and Li Peng and Yao Yilin on the other. While Zhao talked incessantly about "quickening reform", Li would subtly indicate his caveats by dwelling on the imperative of "deepening reform." This was Li's euphemism for proceeding only with those reforms that would not adulterate the "socialist" nature of the country.[41]

Deng's call for speeding up reform was relayed through then Minister of the State Commission for the Reform of the Economic Structure (SCREC) Chen Jinhua. Chen was an affiliate of the Shanghai Faction that Deng had groomed to carry forward the flame of reform (see Chapter 6). In an interview with the NCNA in October 1990, Chen played up Deng's message that "upholding reform and the open-door policy is one of China's basic state policies". "Not only will we uphold the policy of reform and the open door, but as comrade Xiaoping has demanded, we will render reform better, more rapid and more effective," said Chen, a former vice-mayor of Shanghai.[42]

However, it was not until late 1991 that a consensus was reached within the leadership about rendering "speed up the reforms" as a national rallying cry. Then NPC chairman Wan Li made waves when he boldly talked about "quickening and expanding reform" during a tour to the Shantou and Xiamen special economic zones (SEZs) in October that year. As columnist Da Xia of Guangzhou's *Guangdong-Hong Kong Intelligence* newspaper put it: "People all know what it means when people have used words like 'deepening reform' in the past few years," Da wrote. Until Wan's statement, he said, "not even lip service had been paid to 'expanding' or 'quickening' reform".[43]

Most significantly, Li Peng had by late 1991 and early 1992 totally changed his tone. During his much-publicised visit to Western Europe and the United Nations in January and February 1992, the premier peppered his talks with frequent references to "speeding up the pace of reform".[44] As many commentators pointed out, the hardline leader had at least on the rhetorical level become the most vociferous sponsor of fast-paced reform. For the near term, Deng seemed to have scored a sizeable victory.

(ii) Shanghai and the Coastal Belt

As we shall see in Chapter 2, Deng had by 1991 laid down specific instructions for a "second wave" of his open-door policy. His personal involvement, and in many instances, interference, was instrumental in generating the requisite momentum for market reforms that culminated in the *nanxun* (see next section).

By 1990 and 1991, it was apparent that Deng had designated Shanghai — especially its new zone of Pudong — as the "dragon head" of a new wave of reform for the 21st century. At the same time, the southeast Gold Coast — Guangdong, Hainan, and the SEZs — clawed back much of the prominence and clout they had lost in the first year after the Tiananmen Square shootings. By the time Deng paid his visit to Shenzhen and Zhuhai in January 1992, the zones and open cities in Guangdong had regained their status as "before-the-times" pilot areas for trying out quasi-capitalist methods.

The Pudong Project, which involved the development of the part of Shanghai east of the Huangpu River into a zone slightly larger than Shenzhen, was first talked about by local officials in the early 1980s. It was not until Deng made a detailed inspection of Shanghai in the Lunar New Year of 1990 that the Pudong question was resolved. The patriarch personally gave approval for the use of central government funds for Pudong, since it was unlikely that foreign corporations would underwrite the massive infrastructure projects. From the start, Deng had great expectations for Shanghai and Pudong. "It is not too late to get the Shanghai economy off the ground," Deng told Shanghai cadres in early 1990. "Compared to Guangdong, the speed of economic development in Shanghai could be even faster."[45]

When Deng visited Shanghai during the Lunar New Year of 1991, his enthusiasm for conducting novel experiments there seemed to know no bounds. The patriarch, who toured joint ventures and other plants in Shanghai, including the McDonnell Douglas factory, spelled out the city's role well into the 21st century. "If the policy is right and there is no major problem, I think in 20 to 30 years' time, Shanghai will become a comprehensive international centre for industry, finance and high technology," he said. "It will leave Hong Kong and Singapore in its wake." The patriarch also instructed that Shanghai try out financial reforms, specifically stock exchanges. "The financial market in Shanghai is still at its infancy," he said. "We must learn from the good experience of Hong Kong, Singapore and the international scene, integrate it with the requirements of Shanghai, and proceed steadily."

Apparently trying to lay to rest the qualms of Chen Yun, Deng added: "I heard some comrades are afraid that if the door of the financial market is opened wide, there will be chaos and it will be hard to slam the brake on. Why is there a need to slam on the brake? Marxism has not specified that an open financial market cannot be permitted during socialist construction."[46]

While in Shanghai, Deng apparently also gave instructions on expanding the experiment with stock companies. This was reflected in speeches by the new Shanghai mayor Huang Ju. In an early May address to local cadres, Huang urged "further liberation of thought" in the solution of the economy's major problem of low productivity. "We must be more broad-minded in our thoughts, more flexible and multi-faceted in our measures," he said. To lend authority to his statement, Huang quoted the Deng dictum: "We must rack our brains to make use of the opportunities at this moment to expand the scope of using foreign capital to transform existing large and medium-sized state enterprises."[47]

Huang said that according to the spirit of Deng's recent instructions, it was permissible to set up "pilot points" for the shareholding system. For example, a state company can be turned into a stock concern with the government and collectives owning the bulk of shares, and the rest held by individual residents and foreign companies. Huang even put forward the controversial theory of "one factory, two systems" or "one factory, three systems". Under this schema, while parts of a state factory could be run along traditional lines, others could be contracted out to local entrepreneurs or foreign businessmen and administered along "capitalist lines". The mayor also indicated that chronically unproductive factories should switch to other product lines or to services.

Aside from Shanghai and Pudong, Deng blazed new trails for the introduction of foreign capital to Fujian Province, especially the Xiamen SEZ. In 1990, Deng granted secret audiences to Taiwan tycoon Y. C. Wang, who got assurances from the patriarch that the consortium led by his Formosa Plastics would get "super-special" preferential status. The investment, reported to be worth US$7 billion, would be in Haicang, a new district within Xiamen.

It is a tribute to the residual authority of Deng that when Wang first raised the project with bureaucrats from Fujian and central government departments, the latter dared not make up their minds. However, specially with "united front politics" in mind, Deng was anxious to lure Taiwanese corporate giants. "Give him [Wang] as many preferential conditions and as much of a free hand as he wants," the patriarch instructed. Deng also committed central government funds to beefing up the infrastructure of Fujian, particularly that of the Taiwan investment zones in the province.[48]

And while Deng's policy towards Hong Kong was all along conservative and hardline, he tried his best to entice such moguls as Li Ka-shing and the late Sir Y. K. Pao to invest in the mainland. Deng also played a role in insisting that top Hong Kong businessmen be given a say in the preparation of the transfer of Hong Kong's sovereignty in 1997. Prior to the *nanxun*, many Hong Kong capitalist barons merely demonstrated their "patriotism" by making donations to schools and hospitals. That picture changed dramatically in 1993 and 1994.[49]

IV. The *Nanxun* and the Rekindling of Reform, 1992

Much of history is about hubris. The chronicles of yore would have been half as thick if empires had not over-extended themselves, and if emperors had not tarried beyond their threescore years and ten. For less than two months in 1992, Deng Xiaoping, then 87, played God — and apparently got away with it.

The *nanxun*, or imperial tour of the south, which Deng embarked upon in January and February 1992 would go down in history as a gigantic triumph of the will. Almost singlehandedly, the patriarch succeeded in giving the appearance of blotting out the disgrace of June 4 — and re-anchoring the nation on to a path of reform. Most of the ideas talked about during the *nanxun* had been raised in 1990 and 1991. However, Deng managed to delineate, both during his southern tour and in the ensuing months, a number of concrete policies for expanding and expediting the market reforms.

The results of the *nanxun* were apparent to all by the end of 1994. The pivotal 14th Party Congress of October 1992 endorsed practically all the changes called for by Deng earlier that year and outlined in the sections below, including a comprehensive open-door policy and the unprecedented raising of the role of market forces (see also Chapter 2). After the *nanxun*, Hong Kong tycoons such as Li Ka-shing — who in the past had only made donations to hospitals and colleges in the motherland — became so encouraged that they began committing multi-billion yuan investments for the first time. In 1993, the country absorbed US$30 billion yuan in contracted capital, making China the most investor friendly country in the world.

Above all, the *nanxun* exhortations made it possible for cadres and the people alike to forget about politics for the time being. The party and society became depoliticised: ideology took a back seat and Marxism became wellnigh irrelevant as a tidal wave of *quanmin jieshang* ("everybody going into business") swept the nation.

A. Giving the Market a Big Go

With a bold stroke, Deng predicated the legitimacy of the party not on a heavenly mandate or prophecy from Marx but on solid, measurable economic performance. Basing his judgment on events in the former Soviet Union — and their lessons for China — Deng hinted that the Communist Party might be driven from power if it failed to improve the standard of living of the people. The patriarch's instructions, given to party leaders in cities including Shenzhen, Zhuhai, Wuchang and Nanchang, were collected as party document No. 2 of 1992, which was disseminated among the hierarchy in late spring.[49]

"If we do not implement reform and the open door and do not develop the economy and improve the people's livelihood, we'll be left with only one road, the road to death," the patriarch said. "Had it not been for the fruits of reform and the open door, we would not have been able to pass the test of June 4." Throughout the talks, Deng made his usual reference to the need to uphold socialism and develop spiritual civilisation. His overriding concern, however, was economic development. "Developing the economy is the key to seizing opportunities and self-development," he said.

The *nanxun* talks crystallised the arguments made by Huang Puping about "thought liberation" and the "theory of the new cats". "It does not square with practical conditions to equate a planned economy with socialist economics, or to equate a market economy with capitalism," Deng said in Shenzhen, leaving it beyond doubt that quasi-capitalist policies would no longer be taboo. "Reform requires new methods and new measures that are different from those of a decade ago," the senior leader indicated. "The key to exploring new ideas is further thought liberation."

As we shall see in a later section, Deng insisted that the nation take a new leap forward. "We must be bolder in reform and the open door, and be brave enough to experiment," Deng said. "We cannot be like women with bound feet. Once we have made the calculations, we must bravely forge ahead." He repeated his statement, first made in the mid-1980s, that it was permissible for cadres to make mistakes in the course of reform.

Again, Deng returned to the high-speed model that he had recommended for the nation in the mid-1980s. In general, the patriarch wanted a growth rate of "ten per cent or above", which was substantially higher than the 6 per cent or so prescribed by Premier Li and his fellow planners in 1991.

Analysts were right when they said that by 1992, Beijing was implementing a "Zhao Ziyang policy without Zhao Ziyang". Many of the ideas mooted by Zhao's radical think-tank members became policy in the wake of the *nanxun*. On the heels of the epoch-making Document No. 2 came Documents No. 4 and 5. They extended the open-door policy to different sectors and localities — and expanded the scope of the private sector. Deng, who reiterated he regretted not having made Shanghai a SEZ at the same time as Shenzhen, turned practically all the open cities in China into SEZs. These included the cities along the Yangtze River and the provincial capitals (see Chapter 2).

Party and government units — as well as the cadres working in them — were for the first time allowed to run businesses on the side. Government departments that had economic functions were asked to transform themselves from traditional *yamen* into either service-oriented agencies or outright commercial units. Document No. 5 called for the no-holds-barred development of the services sector, which only accounted for 27 per cent of the GNP. New areas including information, accountancy, consultancy, financial and technological services would receive priority. Foreign funds would be lured into new sectors including commerce, insurance, real estate, tourism, food, culture and health.[50]

As a sequel to his *nanxun*, Deng visited the Capital Iron and Steel Works (Shougang) in May, 1992. During a long briefing to Shougang staff, Deng extended his radical reform programmes to state-run companies. The gist of the patriarch's instructions was that unprecedented autonomy would be given public-sector firms. "More water must be made available so that the fish can thrive," he said of enterprise reform. "The problem is the superstructure. The structure and mechanism [for governing and running enterprises] must be changed. Individual units must have money and autonomy." On the spot, Deng gave Shougang autonomy to set up a bank and to open branches in Hong Kong and overseas cities.[51]

B.The Battle Against Leftism

Judging by the ferocity of the attack mounted by Deng Xiaoping against the leftists, many analysts thought the patriarch might have decided to deal a knockout blow to the remnant Maoists. As we shall see in the later sections, this did not come to pass. Even so, enough salvoes were fired during the *nanxun* to ensure that, at least in the economic sphere, the wings of the leftists were clipped.

Deng coined the slogan that, at least for some time, endeared himself to the nation's demoralised intellectuals: the CCP's priority is to fight leftism. "The party must raise its guard against rightism, but its major task is to prevent 'leftism'," Deng repeatedly said during his tour. The patriarch indicated it was leftist thinking rather than rightist deviation which had the most "deep-seated" influence on the party. "'Leftism' carries with it a revolutionary flavour," he said. "It is as though the more leftist one is, the more revolutionary one appears." The patriarch pointed out that leftism had wreaked havoc on the country, particularly on the economy.

Probably with veteran commissars such as Deng Liqun in mind, Deng accused leftists of putting obstacles in the path of reform. "Leftism manifests itself in regarding reform and the open door as introducing and developing capitalism, and thinking that the danger of 'peaceful evolution' comes from the economic arena," he said, sounding a bit like Zhao Ziyang scolding the Maoists in 1987.

Deng zeroed in on one of the pet theories of the leftists, that of the "surnames": before one tries out a new policy, one must find out whether it is surnamed socialist or capitalist. Deng's argument was unambiguous: a policy is right so long as it promotes productivity. "The criterion for judgment should be whether a policy is beneficial to the development of socialist productivity, to increasing the comprehensive strength of the socialist nation, and raising the people's standard of living," he said.

With uncharacteristic ferocity, Deng called upon those who resisted reform "to go to sleep". In particular, the senior leader was targeting "three types of people" who, he said, must depart the stage. They included people who favoured reform on the surface but who sabotaged it in reality; people who did not understand and failed to implement the policy of taking economics as the core task; and people who failed to promote the economy.[52]

Deng's criticism of individual cadres was not recorded in Document No. 2. But those names very soon leaked out to intellectual circles in the capital. The leading *bêtes noires* were sometimes identified as the New Gang of Four. They were: Politburo member in charge of organisation Song Ping; Propaganda Chief Wang Renzhi; *People's Daily* Director Gao Di; and Acting Culture Minister He Jingzhi. Other leftists lambasted by the patriarch included the party secretary of Beijing, Li Ximing. Li, who played a key role in persuading Deng to use force against the student protesters, openly opposed foreign investment in the capital on the grounds that joint ventures amounted to being "a tail of capitalism".[53]

Encouraged by Deng's initiative, cadres who had long chafed under the yoke of leftism took the opportunity to fire mighty salvoes against Deng Liqun and his ilk. The boldest anti-leftist crusaders were Qiao Shi and Tian Jiyun. For many intellectuals in Beijing, the high point of 1992 came with Tian's *ne plus ultra* speech to the Central Party School on April 25, 1992. Tian, the right-hand man of Zhao Ziyang, cut mercilessly into Maoists by saying they were obsessed with such cruel games as "taking class struggle as the key link". "You struggle against me, I struggle against you," he said. "The end result is that nobody is at peace and the relation between cadres and the masses becomes very strained."[54]

Only half-jokingly, Tian proposed setting up a "leftist special zone" where the followers of Mao would be banished. In such a haven for pariahs, the then vice-premier said, strict planning would be carried out. Food would be rationed and its denizens would not be allowed to go abroad. As we shall see in Chapter 3, the *nanxun* emboldened a large group of liberal intellectuals to organise private gatherings and put together books to denounce leftism.[55]

C. Playing the People and the Regions Card

Taking a leaf from the book of Chairman Mao, Deng was gamely bombarding the headquarters of the central planners and the bureaucrats by appealing for support from the people and the regions. It must be borne in mind that the *nanxun* took place because Deng found it difficult to get his views across in the capital. A year earlier, when Deng was trying to spread the same messages in Shanghai, he met with stiff resistance.

The people's card was evident in Deng's pledge to raise the standard of living. Speaking like a populist politician, Deng said: "Now, the countries and regions around us are developing faster than we do. If we do not develop ourselves or are slow in development, the masses will see where the problem lies after a simple comparison."

At the time of the NPC of 1992, the popular-opinion card assumed elements of a media war when Deng took his case directly to the people. Frustrated that the bureaucrats and central planners in the State Council were watering down his reform initiatives, Deng ordered the national media to broadcast his *nanxun* instructions directly to the 1.14 billion people. As a lead item of the CCTV evening newscast for March 30, 1992, a newsreader read out excerpts of the 10,000-character account of Deng's trip to Shenzhen in January, which first appeared in the *Shenzhen Special Zone Daily*. Excited TV audiences across the country realised that Deng was once again in control.

While the pro-Chinese press in Hong Kong and local papers in Shenzhen, Zhuhai and Shanghai had by late February given accounts of the *nanxun* instructions, the national media had until the end of March failed to follow suit. This is despite the fact that the gist of Deng's talks had already been relayed to mid-echelon and senior party members in the form of Document No. 2. Hardliners in the ideological and propaganda departments had restricted the circulation of the document and in many instances excised the politically sensitive portions.[56]

Again taking a cue from Chairman Mao, the New Helmsman encouraged the regions to demand more autonomous powers from the recalcitrant centre. He gave *carte blanche* to various localities, particularly those along the coast, to go full steam ahead. "Do not put up obstacles if a place has the wherewithal to develop," he said. "Those areas with the qualifications can go faster. There is nothing to fear if [these places] put the stress on efficiency and quality and if their economy is export-oriented." Areas with the requisite qualifications such as Guangdong, Jiangsu and Shanghai were encouraged to move at least one step ahead of the nation.

The patron saint of reform gave a big pat on the back to the much-maligned Gold Coast. He asked Guangdong "to cross a few thresholds" and to catch up with the Four Dragons in 20 years. The patriarch endorsed the status of the province as an "ahead-of-the-times" experimental zone, the "dragon head" for the reform enterprise. Then vice-mayor of Guangzhou Lei Yu quoted Deng as saying; "Guangdong and Guangzhou must expand the reforms. Without reform, the pace of growth will slow down; without reform, things will stop and retrogress."[57]

Before leaving Shenzhen in late January, Deng reaffirmed that the "path of the Shenzhen SEZ" was correct. "We were right in establishing the Shenzhen

SEZ," he said. He reiterated his determination to create a series of "new Hong Kongs" along the coast. In other words, there would be many more Shenzhens and Zhuhais.

D. High-Speed Reforms

Deng subscribed to the general theory of "leaps forward", or, as he put it in the *nanxun*, seizing the opportunity to leapfrog from one threshold after another. "From our experience in recent years, it is possible for economic development to reach a new threshold every few years." Deng, of course, never admitted to succumbing to Mao Zedong's Great Leap Forward mentality. Yet both privately and openly, that was the judgment of conservative economists as well as Western analysts.

One of the most important salvoes of the *nanxun* was his defence of the high-speed model as advocated by himself and Zhao Ziyang — and his subtle critique of Li Peng and Yao Yilin, who launched the three-year retrenchment programme in late 1988.

Deng gave a very positive assessment of the eight years of reform from 1980 onwards, especially the five years from 1984-88, which witnessed a gargantuan annual growth rate of 21.7 per cent. "During this period, the country's wealth saw a tremendous increase and the whole national economy crossed a new threshold," Deng said. For the first time after June 4, 1989, Deng gave indirect praise to his former lieutenants Hu Yaobang and Zhao Ziyang, saying they had made undeniable achievements in the economic field.

Somewhat tongue in cheek, Deng said he was not opposed to the three-year retrenchment programme, saying the economy was indeed overheated and the money supply was excessive. However, he went on to say that whatever achievements the campaign to cure and restructure the economy had notched up were "merely an achievement in stabilising the economy". Further, Deng claimed that the five-year period of high growth was different from the Great Leap Forward because "it had not hurt the organic substance and the mechanism of development". He reiterated that those five years "scored not a few contributions towards expediting development", adding somewhat illogically that had it not been for that speedy development, the three-year retrenchment programme would not have been successful.

In yet another example of politics interfering with economics, in mid-1992 Deng half-persuaded and half-obliged cadres including Zhu Rongji and Chen Jinhua to revise the Eighth Five-Year Plan and the Ten-Year Economic Blueprint to reflect the new imperative of market reforms and fast-paced growth. As we shall see in Chapter 2, those requirements would be reflected in the economic programme contained in the 14th Party Congress. As the semi-official China News Service said in a dispatch in August 1992: "The main theme for the economy in the 1990s is to seek development through speed."[58]

E. Deficiencies of the Nanxun Instructions

With hindsight, it could be said that the *nanxun* was Deng's last hurrah. In early 1992, the 88-year-old still felt confident about visiting Hong Kong in 1997. He still felt fit enough to volunteer to go to Taiwan as head of the Chinese team to "reunification talks" with the Kuomintang.[59] From 1993 onwards, however, it became apparent that his primary interest was nothing more than safeguarding his place in history.

It is, however, equally evident that imperfections in the Deng worldview became apparent in the *nanxun* talks. While the patriarch is widely described by the Chinese media as the Great Architect of Reform, he is no systems engineer. The patriarch scored very low in what the American media like to call "the vision thing". He had no blueprint for such basic issues as how the Chinese economy would integrate with the international marketplace in the 21st century.

On a more concrete level, Deng consistently failed to spell out ways to retool the economy by, for example, privatising state-owned enterprises and drastically expanding the private sector. When commenting on why there was no need to be afraid of the introduction of foreign and private capital in the SEZs, Deng said: "We have a superior [situation]. We have large- and medium-scale state-run enterprises and village and township enterprises. The most important thing is that the administration is in our hands." He added that joint ventures and foreign-owned enterprises were a "beneficial supplement to the socialist economy". In other words, the patriarch was still hesitant about changing the basic nature or structure of the state sector.

Similarly, Deng's attitude towards new-fangled or "Western-style" business practices, for example, stock companies, was less enthusiastic than that of former associates such as Zhao Ziyang. "If we have made the right judgment and the results are good after one to two years of experiments, we should open up [stocks and other businesses]," he said during the *nanxun*. "If they [the experiments] turn out to be mistaken, they should be rectified and [the businesses involved] closed down." This less than overwhelming endorsement was a factor behind the relatively unambitious steps taken by Beijing to open up new markets in 1993 and 1994.[60]

One recalls Deng's similarly ambivalent attitude in the mid-1980s towards the experiment with the SEZs. Faced with pressure from the conservatives, the patriarch shocked Chinese reformers as well as Western businessmen when he said in the summer of 1985 that Shenzhen was only an experiment, — and should it be proven misguided, the experiment could be scrapped.[61]

V. Deng's Last Efforts at Reform, 1993-1994

By late 1993, Deng was a lion in winter. His continuously vigorous push for an aggressive open-door policy and high-speed reform sustained the momentum for market reforms. But the down side of his "interference" in the economy was also getting obvious. Inflation was getting out of control. In 1993, Deng was partially responsible for the near-disastrous delay in tackling the price spirals. Moreover, in the last quarter of the year, the patriarch played a role in the premature end of the austerity programme, which was designed to put the economy back on an even keel.

A. Deng's Instructions in 1993

Deng repeated his roadshow for high growth during a visit to Shanghai one year after the *nanxun*. In a much-publicised talk in the eastern metropolis in January 1993, the patriarch played up his "theory of opportunity": that China must aggressively seize the opportunities still available to it in the last decade of the old century. "Without high-speed development, growth and reform run the risk of retrogressing. We must cross a new threshold every few years."

"I hope you will not lose this opportunity," the patriarch told his compatriots, particularly those along the go-go coast. "For China, there aren't that many opportunities for major development." Deng went on to point out that one notable "opportunity" consisted in the tens of millions of *huaqiao*, or ethnic Chinese, residing abroad. He particularly admonished denizens of Shanghai, "who had already worked hard for one year", to "brave the wind and ride the waves" for another year. "Shanghai should have a facelift once every year, a major transformation once every three years," he said.

Alluding to voices of opposition against his Great Leap Forward gambit, Deng made some token gestures about the need to "look back after going one step forward in order to make a reassessment". "We must pay attention to being stable and steadfast," he said. "We must avoid losses, especially big losses." Yet the emphasis was still on going full steam ahead. "Small losses do not matter. What is needed is to generalise the experience and to rectify the mistakes."[62]

The only substantially new thing that Deng said concerned the bigger role for Shanghai as a financial centre. In the latter half of the year, the patriarch heaped praise on the potentials of Shanghai, known in the 1930s as the "Paris of the East", for being the financial centre of the Far East. "Developing

Shanghai is a major thing," he said. "Shanghai is our strong suit, a short cut [for building up the entire economy]. Shanghai used to be a financial centre in the past, where currencies could be circulated freely. We must go along the same lines in the future. We must rely on Shanghai to ensure that China gains an international position in the world." 63

The Architect of Reform further pointed out the pivotal place of finance. "Finance is very important in a modern economy," he said. "If this sector is well run, the entire economy will be rendered alive." The patriarch also indicated Shanghai must catch up with Hong Kong and Singapore in policies on banking and stock exchanges.

Repeating the tactics he had used in 1992, Deng seized upon every opportunity to egg on local leaders in spite of reservations made by central bureaucrats about a feverish development clip. While on his way from Shanghai to Beijing in February 1993, Deng asked the leaders of Jiangsu Province to go full speed ahead. "Comrade Xiaoping demanded that the growth rate of Jiangsu exceed that of the national average," Governor Chen Huanyou said.64

The message was repeated during Deng's tour of the superhighways of Beijing in October 1993. Accompanied only by a small group of officials and aides, including Vice-Mayor Zhang Baifa, Deng repeated the old edict: "We must ensure high-speed reform and development so that the economy can cross a new threshold once every few years," he said. As Zhang later recalled: "Deng wanted the [economic] speed to go faster. His mind is always filled with this idea."65

As we shall see in Chapter 2, Deng's ideas were generally enshrined in the historic Third Plenum of the 14th Central Committee in November 1993. In spite of his declining health, Deng laid down the overall guidelines for the document on the socialist market economy that was endorsed by the plenum.

B. Deng's Interference in Economic Policy, 1993

When is an overheated economy not overheated? When Deng Xiaoping says so. Running a country as big and difficult as China has its privileges, including, to use a proverb made famous by an ancient monarch, the right to call a deer a horse. During his long career, Deng was caught more than once passing a bear off for a bull. In 1993, the patriarch again got into the act.

One of Deng's most important actions in 1993 was to delay the State Council's action against inflation — and to force Vice Premier Zhu Rongji to call off the austerity campaign earlier than expected. Beginning in late 1992, as signs of the economy overheating were becoming obvious and such planners as Yao Yilin were proposing radical measures to rein in growth, Deng had a sense of *deja vu*. He suspected that, just as in the summer and autumn of

1988, the conservatives were seizing upon "dislocations" in the economy to roll back reform.

In a series of internal speeches in December 1992 and January 1993, the patriarch attacked the planners and practically banished the word "overheating" from the economic lexicon. For example, Deng had this to say on Yao's criticism of the overheating phenomenon: "This is getting ridiculous. What is one to fear about a little heat [in the economy]. It is normal for some problems to emerge in the course of our work; only people who do nothing will incur no mistakes."[66]

In January 1993, Shanghai's *Liberation Daily*, sometimes identified as a mouthpiece of the Deng family, pointed out that "speeding up economic development" must be differentiated from inflation and other ailments. "Speeding up development cannot be taken as overheating the economy," the paper contended. Other media, including the *Economic Daily*, began enumerating on their front pages scores of reasons why the economy was not overheated.

Liberal economists echoed Deng's point that the conservatives were exaggerating the dislocations in order to mothball reform. "The question now is not whether the economy is overheated, it is whether we want to persevere with reform," Professor Wu Jinglin said, apparently paraphrasing internal instructions given by the patriarch.[67]

Deng's hold on the country was such that, unlike 1988, he was able to force cadres from the other camp to recant their views. The most dramatic turnaround was registered by then People's Bank of China Governor Li Guixian. In an interview in December 1992, Governor Li lambasted the signs of overheating and vowed that the country would "severely restrict the scale of credit and the currency in circulation". Later the same day, Li got wind of Deng's objections to "premature retrenchment". He immediately called up the NCNA and asked that those parts of his speech dealing with overheating and retrenchment be taken back. It was too late. The next day Li made it up by issuing a speech saying that the banking system would continue to provide credit for the orderly progress of the economy.[68]

As soon as the drafting team of Li Peng's Government Work Report to the 1993 NPC got under way in January, it was under heavy pressure from the Deng camp to tone down references to hyperinflation and allied ills. Nonetheless, analysts were surprised when, at the opening of the Congress, Li bent over backwards to accommodate Deng's edicts: there was not a single reference in the report to the problem of the overheated economy. The premier merely mentioned that "there are still weak links [in the economy] that need to be corrected". Helping himself liberally to euphemisms, the premier said "the pressure of potential inflation is increasing".[69]

At a press conference soon after the NPC, Li said that "the Chinese economy is not overheated; we need only prevent it from becoming so." Other commentators used similar circumlocutions such as "the inflationary pressure is in danger of being released". At the 1992, when the position of the planners was somewhat stronger, Premier Li had bucked Deng's demands and stuck to the growth rate of 6 per cent a year. At the 1993 Congress, however, the chastised premier opted for an 8 to 9 per cent growth rate. However, by saying that "it is expected that the rate will be exceeded in the course of implementation [of the plans]", Li had in effect given the green light for a repeat of 1992's 12.8 per cent clip in GNP growth.

By June that year, Deng was forced by circumstances to acquiesce in yet another round of the austerity programme (see Chapter 2). However, in early September, Deng called in a group of senior advisers in which he expressed concern that the retrenchment had "hurt the enthusiasm for reform." From that point towards the end of the year, the patriarch raised two new slogans: "Only [fast-paced] development passes the rigorous test of reason"; and the national economy must develop in a "sustained, healthy, and high-speed" fashion. Zhu's campaign to boost macro-economic controls and adjustments ground to a halt.[70]

C. Deng's Reluctant Adieu, 1994

In 1994, the increasingly frail helmsman succumbed to one of the worst sins in politics: selfplagiarism. His appearance on Shanghai TV on the eve of Lunar New Year was a public relations disaster. In addition to problems like shaking hands, near deafness and failure to walk unaided or focus his gaze, the octogenarian mumbled so badly he had to depend on "imperial lip reader" Deng Rong to make himself understood.

The quotes attributed to Deng were hackneyed slogans. He praised the civilian and military leadership of Shanghai for "doing a good job" in 1993. The patron of the East China metropolis said because of its "special qualities and traits, Shanghai has the wherewithal to go faster [in economic development]". Again, Deng regurgitated his "theory of opportunity". According to one version leaked to a Hong Kong paper, the patriarch stressed the fact that "the last few years of the 20th century were advantageous to China". "That's why I think we cannot afford a slow pace in the coming few years," he said. "We must solve economic problems [such as inflation] in the course of [fast-paced] development."[71]

While in Shanghai, Deng also held forth on his vision of the metropolis livening up the economy of the entire Yangtze River zone. "Once the Shanghai economy is developed, the Yangtze River Estuary, the entire Yangtze belt, and the national economy will not be the same." The patriarch also waxed elo-

quent on "perpetual thought liberation". "There is no end to thought liberation," he said. "It won't do to be afraid of this or that. The development of
Shanghai depends on concrete work."[72]

However, during the earlier portion of his tour of Shanghai and environs —
which began in early December 1993 and lasted until mid-February 1994 —
Deng also gave vent to more conservative ideas. He issued a tough warning
against growing centrifugalism. "Nothing can be accomplished if central
authority is weakened," the patriarch reportedly said. "Local governments and
cadres must toe the central line." In spite of his reservations about the severity of the austerity campaign in late 1993, Deng professed support for Zhu
Rongji's efforts to whip the "warlords" into line.[73]

Deng's energy seemed to have petered out by mid-1993. He had nothing
more original to say about reform and the economy. There are grave doubts as
to the authenticity of the remarks attributed to the patriarch. In foreign affairs,
Deng was also quoted in 1993 and 1994 as laying down a hard line towards
Hong Kong Governor Chris Patten as well as the peaceful-evolution tactics of
the neo-imperialist West.[74] There is a high possibility, however, that many of
the quotes were put together if not manufactured by the Deng household as
well as politicians who had to gain from those "imperial instructions".

VI. Deng's Ideology and Statecraft, 1989-1994

Having taken a look at Deng's efforts at mending heaven in the economic
arena, we shall examine the patriarch's ideology and policies in the political
field. While the ramifications of Deng's decisions will become evident in the
following chapters, it is instructive to analyse the background and psychology behind the New Helmsman's statecraft.

A. How to Save the Party

Deng will probably go down in history as the Communist-Chinese politician
who delayed the decay and disintegration of the CCP against formidable odds.
In a way, it can be said that Deng was more successful than Soviet leader
Mikhail Gorbachev, whose mission until the coup of August 1991 was also to
save the Soviet Communist party through reform. Up to the end of 1994, at
least, fans of Deng could say that he had succeeded where Gorbachev had
failed. However, in the longer run, Deng could be held accountable for running up huge costs in putting off the inevitable — and just by a few years.

By the early 1990s, most Chinese were no longer interested in preserving
the party. Deng and other holders of vested interests, of course, saw as their

chief mission the maintenance of the CCP's monopoly on power. The price that the party — and the country — had to pay for this, however, was shared by each and every one of 1.15 billion Chinese.

For almost two years after the Tiananmen Square bloodbath, the propaganda machinery pumped out the same slogan: "stability is the overriding task". This was repeated *ad nauseam* by leaders from Deng and Jiang down to the provincial chiefs. The slogan was somewhat downplayed after the *nanxun*, but was picked up again as signs of instability surfaced in early 1994.

Deng tried to guard the party's near-omnipotence in multifarious ways. The first was boosting the police-state apparatus, including the army, the police and the judicial organs (see Chapters 4 and 5). Secondly, maintenance of stability involved developing the economy, the *leitmotif* of the *nanxun*. Here, it is evident Deng did not exactly follow his own edict about "thought liberation".

In the political field, he was sticking to the time-honoured dictum of "both hands being tough", which was part of the *nanxun* talks. As he put it in early 1992, the campaign against bourgeois liberalisation would last for at least 20 more years. "It is righteous to use the force of the people's democratic dictatorship to consolidate the people's regime," the patriarch said. "We must enforce dictatorship over our enemies." The "enemies" included dissidents and other opponents to the CCP.[75]

The new element in Deng's post-June 4 thinking was his idea of "party construction": the CCP's power must be augmented through institutional means. The CCP would have ultimate control over the government, the army, the legislature, and business. "Deng thinks that one reason for the collapse of the Soviet party was that Moscow's apparatchiks were cut off from day-to-day administration and economic policy-making," said a source close to the Deng family. "The patriarch is convinced that for the party to thrive, it must take an active if not predominant part in government and in the market economy."[76]

This explains the decision by Deng at the end of 1992 to rescind totally earlier ideals about separation of party and government or separation between party and business. This was the reason behind the phenomenon of "cross-leadership" that was achieved at the 14th party congress and the NPC of March 1993 (see Chapter 6). Equally significant was Deng's decision to acquiesce in if not encourage senior cadres and their offspring to go into business in a big way. By late 1993, cadres and their children had monopolised key businesses (see Chapter 5).

The lunge into the business world also had the bonus effect of promoting inner-party unity. Internecine bickering, which had bedevilled party unity since the 1920s, was set aside as members of various cliques devoted their all to making fast bucks. This is particularly true of the sons and daughters of party elders from different shades of the political spectrum. And seeing how well their offspring have done in the business world, even elders who have ideological difficulties with the market economy would tend to connive at Deng's risque reforms.

B. Maintaining Unity within the Party: The Politics of Not Taking Sides

Politics is the art of the possible. Much of the political agenda of Deng after June 4, 1989, however, consisted in the ostrich-like avoidance of conflict and controversies. One of the reasons why Deng appeared a weaker leader than Mao was his obsession with balance: striking a Golden Mean among disparate theories, policies and factions. While this made for at least temporary stability, it also showed that Deng was not a man of convictions — nor was he willing to or capable of pushing an unpopular idea.

Deng's politics of hedging manifested itself in what his lackeys proclaimed to be one of his major theoretical breakthroughs: the "both hands being equally tough" approach to politics. Peppered through Deng's speeches throughout 1989-1994 was this constant theme: develop both material and spiritual civilisation; on the one hand grasp economic reform and development, on the other fight crime and bourgeois liberalisation. In other words, play to either the left or the right according to the needs of the times.

An equally significant aspect of this statecraft of flip-flops, however, was given in the *nanxun* speeches: his claim to be the man behind a "great [theoretical] invention — not engaging in controversy".[77] The patriarch was mainly talking about economic issues. For example, the nation should not worry about whether the economic policies it was pursuing were "surnamed" socialist or capitalist. However, this nihilistic approach to governance had plenty of applications in the political arena. The party, especially its squabbling factions, should steer clear of controversial questions like the verdict on June 4, the issue of succession, and whether the country should proceed with "Western-style" political reform.

In an internal speech in early 1993, Deng made clear that the CCP's future leaders must not be those who were squeamish about ideology. "Whichever [senior cadre] in the party stirs up controversy about ideology or [political] lines must leave their positions," he said. "Whoever in the army stirs up contentions and makes unprincipled accusations will have their positions relieved by the party Central Committee and the Central Military Commission."[78]

As is well known, Deng steadfastly stayed away from contentious issues especially in personnel matters. And to the extent of hurting the quality of the leadership and the welfare of the country. The most glaring example was his tolerance of Jiang Zemin's leftism and the latter's lukewarm commitment to reform. A nominee of the late president Li Xiannian, Jiang was less than enthusiastic about propagating the spirit of the *nanxun*, particularly Deng's anti-leftist crusade. For the sake of overall stability, however, Deng seldom wavered in propping him up as the "core" of the new leadership (see Chapter 6).

Deng's obsession with the theory of balance — and the imperative of not taking sides — also accounted for his failure to build up a solid cadre of followers. The positive element is that, compared with such of his rivals as Chen Yun, Li Xiannian or Deng Liqun, the patriarch did not bend over backwards to put together a Deng clique. In fact, the patriarch was remarkably poor in personnel matters such as taking control of the crucial Organisation Department, which remained a stronghold of leftists from the mid-1980s onwards. As Hong Kong commentators pointed out, after the ousting of Hu Yaobang and Zhao Ziyang, the two arms of the New Helmsman had been chopped off. Until his "discovery" of Zhu Rongji, Deng could not count on a faithful coterie of officials to implement his market reforms. The only exception was the army, where Deng's roots ran deep.

C. The People's Liberation Army as Deng's Private Army

One of the major contributions that Deng is said to have made towards socialism with Chinese characteristics was his theory on army construction. In a mid-1993 article, the *People's Liberation Army Daily* succinctly summarised his ten-point contributions. They included: "In our army, the party directs the gun, not the gun the party"; "Streamline the forces and raise their combativeness"; "Put education and training on to a strategic position"; "Strengthen and improve ideological and political work"; "Render the cadre corps more revolutionary, younger, more intellectual and more professional".[79]

More important than these so-called theoretical inventions, however, was the fact that after mid-1989, Deng rescinded his earlier concept about "defence modernisation" by turning the PLA into the Communist party's private army. During his celebrated talk to the top brass soon after the suppression of the 1989 "turmoil", the then chairman of the Central Military Commission praised the Martial Law Command for saving the CCP by acting as a "Steel Great Wall". Since the crackdown, ideologues in the PLA went about a mega-decibel campaign to promote the party's "absolute leadership" over the army.

The fusion of party and army amounted to a betrayal of the modernisation goal that Deng contemplated in the early 1980s when he created the State Central Military Commission and boosted the powers of the Defence Ministry: the separation of the army and the party, and subsuming the army under civilian, governmental control.

After 1992, things went from bad to worse as the PLA seemed to have gone from being the party's army to the private garrison of a certain clique, namely, the Deng clique. This, at least, seemed to meet the subjective wishes of Deng. Before the falling out between Deng and the Yang Clan, the latter, led by former chief political commissar Yang Baibing, acquitted itself well of the task of "providing an imperial escort" for Deng's new wave of reform. From the *nanxun* to the 14th Party Congress, Deng skillfully used army backing to beat back the challenge of the conservatives and central planners in Beijing.

By 1993 and 1994, the army became a principal guarantee for Deng's succession strategy: propping up the authority of the Mainstream Faction led by Jiang and helping it to maintain supremacy in the post-Deng era. The Beijing-affiliated journal *The Mirror* reported in April 1994 that Deng personally asked senior generals and experienced officers to help Jiang maintain his grip over the PLA. This first became evident at the 14th Party Congress, when Deng appointed Liu Huaqing and Zhang Zhen to be CMC Vice-Chairmen. The patriarch also ensured that the Director of the Deng Xiaoping Office, General Wang Ruilin, play a key role in personnel and disciplinary matters. *The Mirror* reported that since Liu and Zhang were in their late 70s, Deng indicated in early 1994 that he wanted Generals Chi Haotian and Wang Ruilin to continue shoring up Jiang throughout the mid-1990s.[80]

As we shall see in Chapter 4, Deng's reliance on the army to carry out his personal political agenda required that he gave something in return. Thus, the PLA's status as "a state within a state" continued. Political representation of the PLA in the highest councils of the party and government increased to the extent that the army had an inordinately big say even in civilian affairs.

D. Suing for Peace with the Leftists

Deng did not live up to his promises during the *nanxun* to cut the leftist establishment down to size. Heeding the imperatives of the politics of not taking sides, by 1993 he seemed convinced that he had to retain the commissars in order to rein in the bourgeois-liberal modernisers. In late 1992, the following story made the rounds of Beijing about the "three noes" policy of the patriarch: that the verdict on June 4 would not be overturned; the campaign against bourgeois liberalisation must not be forsaken; and that the leftists would not be driven from the political stage.[81]

Up to mid-1994, a number of the leftists decried by Deng during the *nanxun* still managed to hang on to office, or were just given a slap on the wrists. Deng had connived at if not actively approved measures by Jiang and the new Propaganda Department chief Ding Guan'gen to continue to impose a straitjacket in the ideological and propaganda sphere (see Chapter 3).

Deng's love-hate relationship with his nemesis Deng Liqun (Little Deng) is especially remarkable. Commissar Deng, 78, sometimes known as an "underground general secretary", had made no secret of his desire to become head of the party. He had openly poured scorn on Deng's reform, saying it was a negation of orthodox socialism. However, while the patriarch took the initiative at the 13th Party Congress of 1987 to strip Little Deng of all his major positions, he had not removed him from the picture.

The most that Deng did was to make verbal criticisms of his foe. For example, in early 1993 Deng indirectly reprimanded Little Deng, who was trying to regroup his ideologues under the newly-formed China National History Research Society, of which he was president. "It is not desirable for comrade Liqun to engage in factionalism after the 14th Party Congress," Deng said. "Activities by Deng Liqun, including those associated with the History Research Society, are a cause for concern."[82]

E. Reining in the Rightists

(i) Packing the Bourgeois-Liberals off to Exile

While it is probably true that Deng Xiaoping was instrumental in preventing the leftists from mowing down the Zhao Ziyang faction of radical reformers after June 4, 1989, it is quite certain that the patriarch did not want the "rightist" wing of the party to be back in power.

Aside from the fact that he thought Hu Yaobang, Zhao Ziyang and their followers had terminally succumbed to bourgeois liberalisation, there was the consideration of June 4. A full-scale rehabilitation of the rightists would almost amount to a *mea culpa*, an acknowledgement of at least mishandling the student movement. Moreover, there was no knowing whether the rightists, if given power, might one day pin the blame of the massacre on Deng himself.

Deng was thus half-hearted in his treatment of the radical modernisers. Firstly, especially in the first year or so after the Tiananmen Square shootings, he wanted the followers of Zhao to counterbalance the preponderance of the left. Secondly, the nation needed the radical reformists to pick up the pieces of reform. Deng was, for example, instrumental in the partial rehabilitation of three Zhao associates in 1990: Hu Qili, Rui Xingwen and Yan Mingfu.

However, as we shall see in Chapter 6, Deng was adamantly against the rehabilitation of Zhao. At the Ninth Plenum of the 13th Central Committee on October 9, 1992, the party decided to uphold the Fourth Plenum verdict of late June 1989: that the former party chief had supported the 1989 "turmoil" and had split the party. A few months earlier, Bao Tong, a key aide to Zhao, was sentenced to seven years in jail. Chinese sources said the relatively harsh sentence given to Bao and the shabby treatment accorded Zhao bore Deng's imprimatur.

Then there was Deng's falling out with the Yang brothers in late 1992. While there was a strong military dimension to the sidelining of the Yang Clan, the major reason for the fall from grace of former president Yang was again the June 4 syndrome. In the summer of 1992, Beijing was suffused with rumours that Yang was amenable to a revision of the June 4 verdict that might compromise Deng. It turned out that at the time, some senior cadres were asking themselves who gave the orders for the troops to open fire on the students. To which Yang reportedly said: "I have proof of who sanctioned it. I even have a tape recording of it." Needless to say, Yang's statement was a hint that the veteran intelligence chief had the wherewithal to nail Deng if he wanted to. After all, one of the "crimes" Mao cited against Yang during the Cultural Revolution was that he had installed a bug under the chairman's bed![83]

The former president also aroused Deng's suspicion by urging before the October 1992 plenum for a "partial exoneration" of Zhao's mistakes. The elder pleaded that Zhao had made contributions to the party through his economic reforms. Earlier, he had suggested that it might be better not to press charges against Bao Tong.

By late 1992 it had become apparent that there would be no reconciliation between Deng and the party's liberal wing. A key example was Tian Jiyun, then mentioned in some quarters as a potential premier. Apparently because of his ferocious attack against the leftists, the former right-hand man of Zhao Ziyang lost his last chance of being inducted into the Politburo Standing Committee. He was instead given the No. 2 slot in the NPC. Analysts suspected that aside from opposition from the conservative elders, Deng felt that Tian had gone too far in his anti-leftist fusillades.[84]

(ii) Freezing out the Dissidents

Deng Xiaoping's attitude towards dissidents became more uncompromising after the June 4 crisis. Just as the patriarch had the final say over the 15-year jail sentence that was slapped on Wei Jingsheng in 1979, he ensured that such Black Hands behind the 1989 "turmoil" as Chen Ziming and Wang Juntao received hefty terms. This was in spite of the fact that a number of third- and fourth-tier leaders, including Qiao Shi and Li Ruihuan, had in private urged a more conciliatory stance towards bourgeois-liberal intellectuals.

From 1989 to 1994, there were several occasions when Deng appeared to yield by agreeing to the release or parole of dissidents ranging from Fang Lizhi, Wei Jingsheng and Wang Juntao. These gestures of largesse, however, had more to do with the patriarch's anxiety to patch up relations with the United States and to win Most Favoured Nation status. Moreover, the Communist party had by 1991 decided that packing dissidents off into exile was the best way to get rid of the "trouble-makers".[85]

In an essay in May 1993, former Nanjing University professor Guo Luoji wrote perceptively on Deng's visceral hatred of dissident intellectuals. Guo, a former Beijing University philosopher who was exiled to Nanjing by Deng in 1982, recounted the patriarch's judgment on Wei. "Haven't we arrested Wei Jingsheng?" Deng said in 1986. "Has China's reputation suffered because of this? Since we have already gotten hold of him, let's not let him go. China's image has not become worse. Our reputation has actually gone from strength to strength."[86]

Deng's intransigence stemmed from a personal peculiarity. Throughout his long career, there were a few occasions when he conceded about making mistakes in the economy. Yet not once had he owned up to ill-treating the party's rightists. In the first volume of his Selected Works, the patriarch defended his role in persecuting nay-saying intellectuals during the infamous Anti-Rightist Campaign of 1957 and 1958 by claiming they were "brimming with the desire to kill the party".[87]

Most disturbingly, it seems that the patriarch did not learn the lesson of June 4. In a major *People's Daily* article in April 1992, theorist Leng Rong quoted Deng as saying he would not hesitate to use force again to quell a challenge comparable to the 1989 student crusade. "Once the factors of turmoil reappear in the future, we will, if required, not hesitate to use any means to eliminate them as soon as possible," Deng said. "We can use martial law or measures harsher and stricter than martial law, so that we will not be subjected to interference from outside [countries]."[88]

China analysts said Deng probably issued the above warning in the first year after the massacre. That the *People's Daily* disclosed the message at the height of the euphoria after the *nanxun* was obvious: Beijing wanted to disabuse those intellectuals who might have deluded themselves into thinking that a Deng Xiaoping who had re-committed himself to reform would forget about the dictatorship of the proletariat.[89]

VII. The Deng Xiaoping Cult

Whether he wanted to or not, Deng had by mid-1992 to acquiesce at least in the construction of a personality cult around him. As with Mao, the image of an all-knowing, almost supernatural leader was perceived by the CCP's inner circle as the most potent weapon to forge inner-party unity. Moreover, one thing leads to another. Central- and local-level cadres began currying favour with the patriarch by putting out Deng books and holding Deng seminars. Claimants to the throne were also anxious to cast themselves as the "true heirs to and followers of the patriarch".

That the CCP should invest such resources in the apotheosis of Deng reflected the desperation with which the party needed a "new" creed to hold the nation together. On a *de facto* basis, Deng Thought had by 1994 replaced Mao Thought as one of the Four Cardinal Principles. It also helped to justify the future reign of Deng's anointed successors such as Jiang Zemin.

A. The Genesis of Deng Xiaoping Thought, 1992-1993

(i) How Deng Thought Became the State Creed

For almost 14 years after he seized power, Deng, normally an unpretentious, laconic person, studiously avoided all semblance of a personality cult. He resisted attempts by colleagues and underlings to erect "a system of Deng Xiaoping Thought", indicating that only Mao could be accorded the honour of philosopher-king. Deng's theoretical musings were referred to as innovations or ideas, but never collectively — and honorifically — as Deng Thought.

Things began to change, however, in the run-up to the 14th Party Congress, which, among other things, enshrined Deng Thought as the state philosophy. In early 1992, the Chinese-run Hong Kong daily *Wen Wei Po* quoted an internal document as saying that Deng Thought would not only provide guidance to reform and the 14th Party Congress but "had an important and far-reaching significance for the entire enterprise of socialist modernisation and construction." The paper quoted a Politburo member as saying Deng's thinking must be given its due. "It is time to raise the twin concepts of Deng Thought and the Deng Line," the leader reportedly said. "We use Deng Thought to summarise the historical experience of our socialist period; it will also lead us down the road of socialism with Chinese characteristics."[90]

At a national meeting of propaganda officials in January 1993, Head of the Propaganda Department Ding Guan'gen gave the formal call to "use Deng theories to arm the entire party". During a talk to cadres attending the Central Party School four months later, Qiao Shi repeated the message about "arming" the entire CCP with Deng Thought. Somewhat long-windedly, Qiao said the reform and open-door theories "constituted Marxism that has been carried forward and developed by comrade Xiaoping with a new approach after he summed up the positive and negative experiences of a long period of Chinese history and integrated the fundamental tenets of Marxism with contemporary China's reality." The former police chief added that the leadership quality of a cadre would depend on "how far he has studied, mastered and applied Deng's theories".[91]

Cynics would say that what the likes of Ding and Qiao were preaching was, in essence, no different from what the late defence minister Lin Biao or former party chairman Hua Guofeng had to say about the "perpetual correct-ness" of Mao Zedong Thought. Throughout 1993, multifarious conferences and study sessions were devoted to various facets of the thinking of Deng Xiaoping. They ranged from military and foreign affairs to his contributions to building the SEZs and the formula of "one country, two systems."[92]

The most important of the Deng seminars was held in Shanghai in mid-1993 under the auspices of the Propaganda Department and the Shanghai party com-mittee. Politburo member and Shanghai party boss Wu Bangguo pointed out that "to study, propagate and do research on Deng's theories is an urgent and long-term strategic task for the theorists and the party as a whole". "Deng is an outstanding representative and brilliant model of safeguarding, adhering to and developing Marxism, Leninism and Mao Thought," he said. Propaganda chief Ding Guan'gen called on the nation's theoreticians to "be more united, prag-matic, active and creative" in their study and interpretation of Deng Thought. [93]

Then came scores of books on the patriarch. By late 1992, more than 100 million copies of works by or about Deng were in print, meaning Deng-related publications now rivalled Mao's Little Red Book. In terms of variety, books about the New Helmsman had outstripped those about the Great Helmsman. The most stupendous of the tomes was perhaps the *Research Collection on Deng Xiaoping's Life and Thoughts*, put out by the Liaoning People's Press in April 1993. It weighed in at 6 million words and included volumes on 20 aspects of Deng Thought ranging from reform theories to military and foreign affairs.[94]

(ii) Deng Rong's Book on Deng Xiaoping

The personality cult reached new heights with the publication in September 1993 of *My Father, Deng Xiaoping*, by his youngest daughter Deng Rong (aka Xiao Rong). The 460,000-character tome was intended to bolster Deng's posi-tion as a giant in Chinese history. Deng Rong, also the patriarch's private sec-retary, toed the time-honoured — and non-Marxist — line of court scribes and apologists that history is the handiwork of a coterie of demi-gods.[95]

While most of *My Father* only covered Deng's exploits up to 1949, the author eloquently claimed that the Sichuan-born titan was the only Communist-Chinese leader whose protean contributions had edified three revolutionary generations. Deng was not only present at the creation of the party in the 20s and 30s but the prophet-reformer who rectified its mistakes to usher it into the 21st century.

The First Daughter revealed that from the early 30s, when he was hardly 20 years old, Deng began attending Politburo meetings in a secret hideout in Shanghai. Much of the volume was devoted to Deng's larger-than-life dimen-sions as he took part in the Long March, fought the party's early manifestations of leftism, and made mincemeat of the troops of Chiang Kai-shek. As the Chinese-run Hong Kong magazine *Bauhinia* summed it up in a review: "Deng Xiaoping is, in an important aspect, a representative of his age. That great era can be seen through [the life of] Deng."[96]

The Deng Rong school of history seemed oblivious to the fact that, according to Marx, history is the result of shifts in "production relations" and technology, the summation of the sweat and tears of the toiling masses rather than the feats of supermen. A jarring corollary of this *l'etat, c'est moi* approach to historiography is that it is both natural and legitimate to pass the sceptre from one monarch-like figure to the next.

The tome quoted Deng as claiming to be the heir of the late premier Zhou Enlai. In like manner, the crown would be passed on to Jiang Zemin. The highlight of Deng Rong's account of November 8, 1989, the day that Deng quit his last remaining job as CMC Chairman, was his giving his blessing to his successor Jiang — and Jiang's words of gratitude to Deng: "I will not spare the last bit of my energy; I will persevere unto death." The reader is reminded of that other famous episode in Communist-Chinese history: Chairman Mao on his death bed bestowing the crown on Hua Guofeng upon saying, "With you in charge, my heart is at rest."

My Father violated an unspoken party regulation, which has been unfailingly observed since the 20s, against senior cadres writing autobiographies or allowing their offspring to pen hagiographic pieces while they are still alive. In spite of its commercial success, *My Father* was widely criticised by Beijing intellectuals as an effort by the Deng household to revive personality worship of the most vulgar kind.

B. The Apogee of the Deng Cult, 1993-1994

(i) The Third Volume of Deng's *Selected Works*

It takes guts of an otherworldly dimension for a mortal to aspire to the ranks of the gods. Deng, perhaps the last of the Eight Immortals who still called the shots in 1993, made a bold bid for the pantheon. The publication of the Third Volume of his *Selected Works* in November that year represented a feverish, though very non-Marxist, attempt at self-deification.

The 288,000-character book covered 119 pieces of writings and speeches dating from September 1982 to the *nanxun*.[97] The tome was an elaborate effort by the patriarch to ensure his place in history. This is despite the fact that it does not exactly square with dialectical materialism for anyone, let alone a Communist who had studied Marxism for at least seven decades, to lay down rules by which posterity should judge him.

The *Selected Works* was a grand way of saying "I told you so". As befitting the holder of the heavenly mandate, the New Helmsman wanted to dispel all doubts that he had always steered the ship of state in the right direction. On the suppression of the June 4 "turmoil", Deng told a Chinese-American scientist five months later: "It is lucky that I was still around. The matter was handled without difficulty."

The patriarch offered neither excuses nor apologies for his equally tough "handling" of the student movement of December 1986, including the expulsion from the party of dissidents whom he called "mad and reckless to the extreme". Deng also defended his very harsh treatment of Hu Yaobang and Zhao Ziyang, who were accused of "succumbing to the tide of bourgeois liberalisation". *Selected Works* also contained elaborate arguments why he was convinced Washington was spearheading a Western conspiracy to subvert China through "peaceful evolution".

On economic issues, Deng refused to take responsibility for the hyperinflation and panic-buying of late 1988 to early 1989. He also made subtle defences of his high growth model. The only mistake he owned up to was not having designated Shanghai a SEZ early enough. He admitted in a speech in 1992 that "my major mistake was not to have included Shanghai when I started the four SEZs [in the early 1980s]."

The patriarch's lapses on political reform were glaring. In a letter to the Politburo in September 1991, the then CMC chairman said he had retired from his last remaining post in order to "abolish the system of life tenure for cadres". Right to the end, although Deng would part with the crown, he would hold on to the sceptre. Twelve days after the June 4 killings, Deng vowed to "deal severely with corruption and to crack at least 10 to 20 major cases". In talks with foreign dignitaries in 1986, the patriarch promised to make political change keep pace with economic liberalisation, citing the need to "separate the party from the government". None of these pledges materialised.[98]

(ii) The Personality Cult Runneth Over

The national Learn-from-Deng campaign unleashed upon the publication of the Third Volume of his *Selected Works* could be compared to the frenetic waving of the Little Red Book by Red Guards in the early phase of the Cultural Revolution. In a throwback to the worse excesses of the Mao personality cult, Deng Thought was said by propagandists to pack the punch of a "spiritual atomic bomb".

Ministerial-level cadres spent up to a few weeks at the Central Party School plumbing the depths of Deng Thought. Party and government units of all levels organised special sessions to study the edicts. Senior ministers were liberal with encomiums. Vice-chief of Propaganda Zheng Bijian said: "Deng's works were a powerful weapon for educating the people." Director of the Special Economic Zone Office in the State Council, Hu Ping, waxed lyrical on how Deng's ideas had "enriched Marxism-Leninism". Li Peng said Deng Thought had "carried forward, enriched and developed socialism with Chinese characteristics". He added that the diplomatic thinking of Deng was "a complete scientific system". Jiang Zemin called Deng's teachings "a scientific theory that has integrated socialism with patriotism", "a great ideological force" that bound the nation together.[99]

In a commentary in December 1993, the *People's Daily* called upon cadres nationwide to "take the lead in studying and applying well the *Third Volume of the Selected Works of Deng Xiaoping*". In a throwback to the "whateverism" of Mao's chosen heir Hua Guofeng — "whatever the Chairman said was correct" — the commentator asked officials to "self-consciously uphold those [parts] of our knowledge and actions that dovetail with the theories of comrade Deng Xiaoping". "We must self-consciously rectify those [kinds of] knowledge that do not tally with the theories of comrade Deng," the party mouthpiece added.[100]

Also reminiscent of the personality cult of Mao was the way members of the Deng household stole the limelight. Deng Rong became a media star with her best-selling biography, which was also published in Hong Kong, Taiwan, Japan and other countries. Activities on behalf of the handicapped by eldest son Deng Pufang, and the real-estate exploits of second son Deng Zhifang, a thriving businessman, became regular features in magazines. Trips abroad by the two sons and painter Deng Nan — to places including Hong Kong, South Korea, Germany and the US — were big press events. Deng's hometown, Guang'an county in Sichuan, was in November 1993 upgraded into a district that had jurisdiction over four counties and one city. The China News Service reported that provincial authorities had specially transferred a "corps of young and able officials to run the district".[101]

A Research Centre on Deng Xiaoping Theory was set up within the Shanghai Branch of the Chinese Academy of Social Sciences. It is not surprising that one of the heads of the centre was the CASS's ranking expert on Mao Thought, Li Junru.[102] Analysts were quick to point out that immediately after the Cultural Revolution, Deng and his contemporaries had vowed not to engage in Maoist-style self-adulation.

C. Deng's Last Days: A Pathetic Hostage to History

Perhaps nothing better illustrated Deng's "dynastic politics as usual" than the striking similarity between the last days of the New and the Old Helmsman.

With his physical conditions no longer allowing him to pay attention to affairs of state — or to make himself understood — Deng had no choice but to let his palace guards manipulate his last words.

A sizeable amount of the fairly elaborate remarks attributed to Deng from late 1993 onwards must have been assembled by Deng Rong together with a host of spin doctors. One is reminded of palace guards like Jiang Qing and Mao Yuanxin (the late chairman's nephew) putting words into the uncontrolled salivating mouth of the dying Mao.

Not unlike taxi drivers who hung mini-portraits of Mao on the windscreen to ward off the evil spirit, the CCP desperately needed the face of Deng on national television and newspapers — even images that were a pathetic mockery of the New Helmsman who had thrice risen from disgrace — as what the Chinese call "steady-the-heart pills".

Various factions and politicians were doing their level best to twist Deng's words and manipulate the Deng legacy to their own advantage. As in the case of Mao, the followers of Deng — especially those who had ambition for the peacock throne — were jockeying to position themselves as his favoured disciples and heirs apparent. Deng Rong, who is believed to have formed a power pact with Jiang Zemin, repeatedly indicated her father favoured "economic and political stability" and that he had faith in Jiang as the "core" of the third-generation leadership.[103]

Leftists, however, also had a field day interpreting Deng's words to their own advantage. This started in the late 1980s, when the commissars focused on the patriarch's teachings about countering bourgeois liberalisation to bring about a Maoist restoration. After the *nanxun*, the Maoists put their stress on the campaign to "positively, comprehensively and correctly understand and apply Deng Thought". Translation: do not just emphasise Deng's words about market reforms, but pay at least equal attention to his teachings about fighting peaceful evolution.[104]

Indeed, the obverse of any personality cult is the quintessentially Communist-Chinese phenomenon called "hoisting the red flag to counter the red flag". By early 1994, there were signs that the commissars were also playing the game of using Deng's supposed "instructions" to counter Dengism. For example, in the spring of that year, Beijing was abuzz with rumours that Deng had warned against the birth of a "new bourgeois class". "If a new bourgeois class is formed, we will have gone down an evil path," he reportedly said. Also attributed to Deng was this injunction: "In reform we must insist upon two basic principles: the predominance of the public sector, and [all the people] getting rich at the same time." For many analysts, however, this seems more like Little Deng than Deng talking.[105]

In May 1994, Deng Rong disclosed that the sequel to her *My Father, Deng*

Xiaoping would be published in two years. This second volume would presumably take the readers from 1949 to the very end of the patriarch's career. "The most resplendent chapters in my father's life will appear in the second volume," Deng Rong said. And so the myth-making goes on.[106]

VIII. Conclusion: The Deng Xiaoping Legacy

Deng Xiaoping started out on June 4, 1989, to mend heaven. As we shall argue, he partially succeeded. The gaping holes left in the firmaments, however, were due to the fact that Deng failed to transcend his own background and world-view: he failed to "change his [own] brain", to mend his mentality, and to give the near-obsolete party a make-over. His vocation was to touch up a tattered heavenly mandate — not to create a new heaven and a new earth.

In a talk to an African leader in late 1989 entitled "Uphold socialism; prevent peaceful evolution", Deng laid out his ultimate goal: to safeguard the party and socialism. "If China goes about pursuing bourgeois liberalisation, there will certainly be turmoil," he said. "China upholds socialism. There will not be any change." During his *nanxun* talks, he boasted: "There is no doubt in my mind that more and more people in the world will give the thumbs up to Marxism, because Marxism is science."[107]

Like Hu Yaobang, whose most famous saying was "Marxism cannot solve all the problems of today", Deng was aware of the need of radical revisionism. As he told Mikhail Gorbachev less than a month before the June 4 killings: "We can absolutely not expect Marx to provide ready-made answers to problems that come about a hundred or a few hundred years after his death. It is not a true Marxist who fails to use new ideas and viewpoints to succeed and develop Marxism," he said.[108] The problem is that Deng failed to go far enough. He refused to recognise that the days of socialism and Marxism were numbered — and that they might be wiped off the face of the earth before the end of the decade.

Judging by appearances alone, Deng had by mid-1994 pretty much achieved what he had set out to do after the June 4 fiasco: to restore political order and to rekindle economic reform. Amid the heady atmosphere of *quanmin jieshang* ("every citizen going into business"), the wounds of Tiananmen Square seemed to have been healed. The beefed-up security apparatus seemed more than adequate to put down the isolated attempts at challenging authority that had surfaced since mid-1989. Foreign capital was coming back to the country in leaps and bounds. While inflationary, the growth rate of the country was the envy of the world. Above all, Deng could also very well have boasted to Chinese and foreigners alike that the CCP had under his guidance successfully withstood the shock of the fall of the Eastern bloc.

However, a malaise overshadowed the prosperity. Much as Deng had called on the party and nation to "seize the day", precious time was lost in that most vital of modernisation: what Wei Jingsheng called the Fifth Modernisation, that of the spirit. The CCP remained a feudalistic party and Chinese politics did not seem to have emerged from the caves of Yan'an. By 1994, China was still under the rule of personality and the party had become terribly corrupt. The same problems that almost wrecked the party in June 1989 remained un-solved: political stagnation; the fusion between the party, government and the army; no supervision of corruption and other malpractices by the powers-that-be; no rule of law or independence of the judiciary.

It was clear by mid-1994, however, that the 89-year-old was too frail to attempt yet another *nanxun*-like miracle. The candle was flickering in the wind. While economic reform and prosperity seemed assured, the future of the party and socialism was in doubt. So was Deng's chequered legacy.

A. The Limits of Thought Liberation

Deng's foremost contribution to Communist-Chinese statecraft was probably "thought liberation", what he called in the last years of his life "changing one's brain". It is clear, however, that Deng failed, to a considerable extent, to live up to his own standards.

In an early 1994 speech ascribed to Deng, the New Helmsman said: "Society is developing and times are changing. There is no limit to thought liberation. Points of view that are static and metaphysical are against the basic tenets of Marxism."[109] While Deng succeeded in blazing some new trails in economics, he failed miserably in overhauling the party's fundamental approach to governance.

In essence, the political *lunli* or ethos in China remained as feudalistic in mid-1994 as it was in the late 1970s. There are many who would argue that Deng had retrogressed and given up on ideals he himself had espoused when he assumed power in late 1978. The CCP was by 1994 still the Stalinist hotch-potch it had always been. In an internal discussion with fellow party elders in 1993, Deng made this frank admission: "The fate of the party and country cannot be tied to just one person. This easily leads to mistakes, and may bring disaster upon the party and country." On that occasion, Deng was underscor-ing the importance of replacing the "rule by personality" with modern, sys-temic statecraft. Nothing came out of it.[110]

Much of the problem came from the fact that Deng never admitted to his errant ways. Underlying this is the mentality of the heavenly mandate: the ruler automatically loses his mandate and his legitimacy when he admits to having made a blunder. Like Mao, he refused to shoulder the blame for the party's various anti-rightist campaigns. In an internal speech in late 1992, the patriarch admitted that at the enlarged Politburo meeting in January 1987 that dumped Hu Yaobang, the criticism against Hu was "excessive and unbalanced". Yet the patriarch never conceded that the removal of Hu was unconstitutional. The same goes for Zhao Ziyang. Privately, the patriarch expressed regrets over his removal. Yet his handling of the Zhao question remained harsh.[111]

One reason for the retrogression of political reform after mid-1989 was Deng's anxiety to ensure that none of his colleagues or successors would overturn the verdict on June 4. And it is for this reason that he shunted aside relatively moderate and liberal cadres such as Yang Shangkun, Qiao Shi and Tian Jiyun. By the same token, officials with lukewarm commitment to market reforms, such as Jiang Zemin and Li Peng, were tolerated because they could be trusted not to "expose" Deng's guilt.

B. The Party's "Crisis of Morality"

Deng might be held accountable for the unravelling of the CCP's moral fabric — and its unprecedented corruption — in the early and mid-1990s. Since the onset of the business craze after the *nanxun*, Deng as well as other party elders had repeatedly warned against the creeping scourge of corruption. The patriarch reportedly said that if the CCP were to disintegrate in the 1990s, it would not be because of foreign invasion or internal de-stabilisation by anti-socialist elements: the root of death would be corruption.

The *People's Daily* editorial of July 1, 1993, quoted Deng as saying: "We have scored considerable achievements in economic construction and the situation is pleasing. Yet if the [party] style continues to deteriorate, what will be the meaning of economic success?" The patriarch reportedly warned that both the party and the economy would be poisoned, and it would become "a world where corruption and theft hold sway". "Party members and cadres who are corrupt and who seek private gain by using their positions should be sent to the law courts," he said in late 1993. "There should be no ambiguity about it."[112]

A central focus of "party construction" in 1993 and 1994 was to stem out corruption. Yet, Western diplomats and Chinese intellectuals agreed that the point of no return had been reached: corruption, which Jiang Zemin called the "commercialisation of power" or the "exchange of power for money", had already been built into the system.

While nobody has accused Deng of lack of probity in financial matters, rumours concerning the business activities of his immediate family were widespread in the last years of his life. Such of his offspring as Deng Zhifang,

Deng Nan and Deng Rong — as well as sons-in-law He Ping and Wu Jianchang — were by 1993 reported to have become premier red capitalists. For example, Deng Zhifang, the second son, had that year teamed up with such Hong Kong magnates as Li Ka-shing in property and other ventures. Hong Kong's *Next* magazine reported that by late 1993, the Deng family had interests in some 14 publicly listed companies in Hong Kong, which had a book value of more than HK$16 billion.[113]

Worse still, the Deng offspring were also reported to have used their influence to help relatives and cronies get ahead of the pack. The daughters, for example, are believed to have close ties with the Capital Iron and Steel Works (Shougang) in Beijing as well as the Daqiuzhuang conglomerate outside Tianjin. Shougang's connection with the Deng family was a factor behind the patriarch's visit to the company in May 1992 — and the autonomous powers that Deng granted it on the spot. The "king" of Daqiuzhuang, Yu Zuomin, was reported to be a Deng crony. Yu, who treated Daqiuzhuang as his personal fiefdom, was arrested in the spring of 1993 for harbouring criminals. His relatively light sentence, however, was widely perceived to have been due to the influence of the Deng family.[114]

In the vital matter of keeping the party clean, Deng seemed to have retreated from his position in 1988, when he ordered that "no son or daughter of senior cadres could engage in business, starting with my son". Thereupon, the Kanghua business empire run by Deng Pufang was closed. By mid-1994, no one thought Deng would use his influence to clamp down on the business activities of *gaoganzidi*, no matter how corrupt they might be.[115]

C. The Economy: Deng as a Faulty Architect

Deng's title as the Chief Architect of Reform notwithstanding, he was never an imaginative thinker or strategist in economic matters. The "two cats theory" pretty much spanned his entire universe of discourse. During his visit to Shougang in 1992, the New Helmsman was candid about his lack of economic expertise. While praising Zhu Rongji as one of the few senior cadres who knew how the modern economy worked, Deng admitted he was a near-ignoramus in the dismal science. The patriarch's other famous dictum for economic policy was "crossing the river while feeling for the boulders". This trial-and-error approach to management was responsible for a series of well-documented flaws in economic policy.

Deng's status of Chief Architect was marred by a series of leftist, Great Leap Forward-style campaigns. One recalls the heady days of the summer of 1988, when Deng and Zhao Ziyang put the economy into overdrive to speed up growth and to "breach the fortress of the prices" — meaning to consummate price reform at one go. At the time, Deng and Zhao told intimates that China could cushion the shock of "South American-style inflation". The disaster that came out of that experience led to the sidelining of Zhao several months before the Tiananmen Square shootings.[116]

There was almost a repeat performance of 1988 in late 1992 and early 1993. While the economy had begun to boil in the winter of 1992, Deng virtually imposed a ban on the discussion of the overheating phenomenon until the end of March 1993. When the austerity programme started in late June, Zhu Rongji had been put in a passive position. The patriarch's mid-1993 comment on the situation, however, was the following unhelpful understatement: "It is necessary to look back once in a while."[117]

By the summer of 1993, Deng tried to salvage his reputation by reportedly giving his blessings to the series of "investigation work teams" to be sent out to the provinces to re-impose fiscal discipline. "We should make an early decision [on sending down the teams] and make an early announcement," Deng said. "We should be bold and resolute. We should let elements inside and outside the party to inspect and endorse our work."[118] Precious time, however, had been lost because of Deng's interference.

The patriarch was, of course, aware of the dangers of economic leftism. It is just that the "little man in a big hurry" was too impatient for results — and too dictatorial to accept a second opinion. In a talk with a visiting African head of state in 1982, Deng cautioned against the Great Leap Forward mentality. "According to our experience, the pace [of economic development] cannot be too fast and too expeditious," Deng said. "In the past, we were too anxious for results and mistakes occurred. We call them leftist errors. Because of them, the growth rate actually went down."[119]

D. The Propensity to Compromise and the Tunnel Vision

According to Sun Changjiang, a former chief editor of *Technology Daily* and a close adviser to Hu Yaobang, Deng scholars have misquoted a key assessment of the patriarch by Mao: "Deng is a needle in a ball of cotton." Conventional wisdom has it that the Chairman was expressing amazement at the pint-sized politician's guts, his steely resolve in going against the current. Sun said, however, that what Mao actually told Deng was: "You should be a needle in a ball of wool." Mao was upbraiding Deng's lack of resolve and his propensity to climb down from difficult positions.[120]

One of Deng's endearing strengths was his ability to play the Great Balancer and Arbitrator among disparate political factions, Marxist theories, and approaches to the economy. That is why after the demise of the Gang of Four, the entire party turned to him to steady the ship of state. But there is a down side to this readiness to compromise: his Great Leap Forward mentality notwithstanding, Deng was not psychologically well placed to put reform on the fast track. Foreign and domestic intellectuals have long decried his "one step forward; half-a-step backwards" approach to modernisation.

As we shall see in Chapter 3, the most clear-cut example of this yo-yo effect is Deng's ambivalent attitude towards leftism. In spite of the obvious harm that the Maoist ideologues had done to reform — and to his own power base — Deng was unable to sever his own links with leftism and to consign the ideologues to the dustbin of history.

What one might call Deng's character flaw has been reinforced by a lack of a world-class vision. For all his commitment to reform, Deng did not pursue it for its own sake, but as a means to preserve the party — and to protect a clique of holders of special privileges. For all the high marks he earned in the West as a Master Reformer, Deng's Maoist roots were obvious.

This remnant feudalism showed through during the June 4 crisis. It also manifested itself during a meeting with former German chancellor Helmut Schmidt in May 1990, when the patriarch boasted about China not being afraid of June 4-related sanctions. Deng betrayed an element of Maoist autarky when he said: "China was the victim of sanctions for a few decades, from 1949 to 1972. We grew up in the environment of isolationism."[121] If modernisation meant the CCP had to leave the Yan'an caves, Deng would rather stay inside and "eat bitterness" on the Dragon Throne.

E. Deng Xiaoping as Tragic Hero

"After Deng's death, there will be a campaign to criticise the Deng tradition," said exiled political scientist Yan Jiaqi. "This will be as inevitable as torrents after the rainstorm."[122] In spite of the good he had done his country, Deng is considered the last of China's feudal monarchs, an enlightened tyrant but a despot nonetheless. Yan thought that in spite of Deng's liberal leanings, historians would still put him in the same category as Chen Yun or Mao Zedong.

Deng's tragedy, however, is that despite the gunshots on the night of June 3, this need not have been the case. Chinese — the long-suffering, easily-forgiving Chinese — would have been willing to look the other way had the patriarch dwelled less on his feudalist past and listened more to the voices of the new century.

It is, of course, true that even before June 4, 1989, his reputation had taken a beating. During the army parade that celebrated the 35th anniversary of the founding of the People's Republic in 1984, the masses in Tiananmen Square spontaneously cried out: "Xiaoping *ninhao* [you have done well]." At the height of the Tiananmen Square protests in 1989, however, the refrain from the students was: "Xiaoping *ninhao hutu* [you are very dumb]."

Yet even without subjecting himself to criminal proceedings, Deng could have won back the support of most Chinese by making a clean break with the past. The *nanxun* was a heroic effort to save his place in history — and put the nation on to the path to prosperity and strength. And to some extent he succeeded. The radical market reforms that followed probably went further than those conceived by the young advisers of Zhao Ziyang. Also in the *nanxun*, Deng scored points by cracking the whip on the leftists.

If Deng had gone the whole hog and picked up the threads of political reform begun by Hu Yaobang, Hu Qili, Zhu Houze and Zhao Ziyang, the day would have been saved. However, he chose to stay with the ideals of the Yan'an caves. The supremacy of the party, the inviolability of the June 4 verdict, and his status as the Son of Heaven, became an all-consuming obsession. He turned a blind eye and a deaf ear to all that was happening around him: the disintegration of the Eastern bloc, the fall from power of Japan's Liberal Democratic Party, and the formation of the New Party in Taiwan. Deng lost touch. And he would have to pay for it in the history books.

Moreover, there is this ironic twist to the Deng tragedy. In spite of the tremendous price Deng paid in terms of his standing in history, his heaven-mending feats would at most have put off the death of the CCP by a few years. Peaceful evolution was a foregone conclusion. The process through which the colour of the party was being changed had actually been helped along by Deng's reforms. By 1994, such shibboleths as communism, socialism, and "plain living and hard struggle" had become totally irrelevant to the lives of Chinese. Ten years from now, when the dust had settled on the Communist-Chinese empire of the spirit, Deng would be remembered as the fool on the hill who tried to force the earth to spin the other way.

2

Economic Reform: How Far Down the Capitalist Road?

I. Introduction

BILL Clinton's slogan for his victorious campaign for the American presidency in 1992 — "The economy, stupid!" — aptly illustrated the psychology behind Beijing's drive for economic reform in the early 1990s. The Chinese Communist Party (CCP) administration knew full well that economic liberalisation would unleash socio-political forces that would chip away at its monopoly on power. While not being particularly populist, Deng Xiaoping realised the party had to continue with its reforms if it was to avoid the fate that had befallen the Soviet and other East European parties in 1990 and 1991. Deng and the leadership, however, were convinced that they could pursue the so-called East-Asiatic or Singapore model by walking the high wire of economic reform and political suppression.

This chapter will examine the convoluted trajectory of economic reform from 1989 to late 1994. Sections will be devoted to the following points: the restoration of central planning in the two years following the Tiananmen Square massacre; Deng's valiant efforts to reactivate reform, which culminated in the now-famous talks he gave during the *nanxun*, or "imperial tour of the south" in 1992; and the watershed Third Plenum of the 14th Central Committee in late 1993. There will be detailed discussion of two central issues of the political economy: the growth of the private sector and the worsening rivalry between the centre and the regions. The conclusion will look at whether the Singapore model could last through to the late 1990s.

The relatively short-lived restoration of central planning showed up the irrational but tell-tale face of the regime: if the party had a choice, it would stick to the Stalinist diktat economy, which works best towards centralising powers in the party apparatus. As a sharp reaction against the "turmoil" of early 1989, the State Council rolled back liberalisation measures introduced by ousted party chief Zhao Ziyang. It also took steps to cramp the private sector, deemed an ally of the pro-democracy demonstrators.

The conservative reaction to the June 4 crisis lasted until 1991, when Deng tried to pick up the threads of reform. As we saw in Chapter 1, there were the talks delivered by the patriarch in Shanghai in early 1991, some of which appeared in the guise of the Huang Puping ("comrade Xiaoping speaking at Huangpu River in Shanghai") commentaries in *Liberation Daily* in the spring of that year. Then came the *nanxun* talks. By early 1992, even Premier Li Peng, who had always insisted that reform was no more than an effort to "perfect socialism", was talking about "quickening the pace" of economic liberalisation.[1]

By late 1991, the Chinese media had become suffused with calls for "bolder, faster reform". Living up to his reputation as Communist China's philosopher king, Deng drew the right conclusion from the dissolution of the Soviet Union: the party must reaffirm "economic construction" as the "core" of national work. The party would stay in power if, because of the reforms, the living standards of the people were raised.

Many of the market-oriented measures introduced by Zhao Ziyang were resurrected. The shareholding system was rehabilitated. Selected state-owned companies in "pilot-point" cities were granted extra autonomous powers. In Hainan province and other experimental zones, "concessions" were granted to foreign corporations to be developed along international lines.

Deng, however, had to wage a fierce battle against ideologues and central planners who insisted that the lesson to be drawn from the crumbling of the Eastern bloc was that the public sector, or the socialist road, must be shored up. Hence the celebrated "debate over the surnames" — "only reforms surnamed socialist should be carried out". Under orders from Deng, the "surnames controversy" was put to an end.[2]

Yet up to early 1993, the pace for integration with the international market place proceeded gingerly. As Li Peng put it in early 1992, China would need ten years to integrate planning and market adjustments.[3] In other words, at least up to the early 21st century, state fiats would play a heavy role. Only a limited number of state companies would be converted into stock concerns, and even then, the government would retain more than 50 per cent of the shares. While the private sector would be encouraged to grow, it could not challenge the public sector for supremacy.

Then came the watershed Third Plenum of the 14th Central Committee. Many reservations about the private sector or about the public domain being the mainstay of the economy were swept aside as Beijing took bold and irrevocable steps towards the market place.

However, China would not go all out for the Western model. The prevailing thinking as of late 1994 was still that China would not proceed down the road followed by Hungary, Yugoslavia, Poland — or Boris Yeltsin's Russia — by trying to convert the Chinese economy into a total market economy. Rather, the East-Asiatic or Singapore model of a "collectivist" approach to the market place prevailed. By 1994, sufficient bottlenecks had appeared to show that this approach would soon become untenable.

II. Economic Reform, 1989-1991: "Synthesis between planning and the market"

A. The Post-Tiananmen Crackdown: Part-Centralisation, Part-Liberalisation

The post-Tiananmen Square leadership was faced with a dilemma: whether to continue the old policies of reform or to *shou* (recentralise and retrench) unremittingly. The continuation of policies initiated by Zhao Ziyang with the sanction of Deng Xiaoping would spawn problems galore. The expansion of powers wielded by coastal provinces and cities would lead to the diminution of central authority. The growth of a semi-independent class of "red capitalists", managers and professionals would threaten the "dictatorship of the proletariat". And "excessive" reliance on the overseas market and on economic co-operation with the West might abet the "peaceful evolution" plot of the "neo-imperialists". As conservatives such as then vice-premier Yao Yilin put it in late 1989: "The open-door policy must be accompanied by the strengthening of [the spirit of] self-reliance."[4]

However, it is also obvious that even the central planners realised they could not bring back the economic policies of Mao Zedong — or conservative patriarch Chen Yun. Central planning and the "theory of the four balances" put forward by Chen would seem to guarantee a superficial kind of stability: there is no apparent inflation, no disparity of income among citizens, no budget deficit and no foreign debt. However, it is also a tried-and-failed formula for national development: growth is stymied and productivity cannot be spurred.[5]

The result of efforts to meet these competing demands was a half-hearted, wishy-washy compromise: part central planning, part market forces; or central planning in Beijing and market forces in the coastal belt. The so-called "organic synthesis of a planned economy and market adjustment", a phrase coined by Deng Xiaoping in late 1990, became the only economic doctrine at least up to Deng's *nanxun*.[6]

Economists inside and outside China have difficulty seeing how this synthesis can be accomplished. The "organic combination" of state fiats and market forces seems a contradiction in terms. Central planners such as Li Peng and Yao Yilin saw the market place as no more than a necessary evil — a lubricant that, they hoped, would oil the antiquated mechanism called central planning. However, Adam Smith's Invisible Hand only works when it is allowed free play. The market will wilt unless the government takes a back seat.

For about three months in mid-1990, the country's premier business paper, the *Economic Daily*, asked readers to offer suggestions on precisely how the two strange bedfellows can hit it off. After receiving hundreds of letters, the newspaper ended its debate in late July 1990 by publishing a one-sentence comment from a reader from Guizhou that neatly epitomised the imbroglio: "There is no answer on how it can be done."[7]

At a national meeting called in May 1991 to discuss the economic structure, Premier Li confessed that, with reference to economic reform: "It looks as though it has taken us too long a time in materialising this goal." Li went on, however, to defend Deng Xiaoping's masterplan: "It is not an easy task for a socialist country to really combine the superiority of a planned economy with that of market adjustments. This is an unprecedented experiment."[8]

B. Restricting Reform for Political Ends

A basic precept of Marxism is that economics (including matters such as production relations, productivity, the level of technology and so forth) is the "inner structure" of society. This infrastructure in turn determines the "superstructure", which embodies arenas such as politics and culture. To a certain extent, reformists including Zhao Ziyang and his liberal advisers were going by this principle: First liberalise the economy, and then bring about political change. The post-Tiananmen Square leadership, on the other hand, was circumscribing economic reform in order to minimise socio-political liberalisation.

In a few key areas politics impinged on economic reform. The restructuring of state enterprises — billed the premier reform measure for the early 1990s — proceeded half-heartedly because of political considerations. From the point of view of the custodians of the socialist road, this reform should be restricted to injecting "new life" into government business units, not to change their "ownership nature" through privatisation.

In a dispatch in late 1991, the Chinese-run *Wen Wei Po* in Hong Kong quoted a "top-level State Council official" as saying that Beijing was worried about the decreased role of the state sector. The report said that by 1991, the share of state-owned enterprises in the total value of industrial production had slipped to 59 per cent, the lowest since 1949. "State-owned enterprises, especially large- and medium-sized units, represent the public-ownership system," the official was quoted as saying. "This phenomenon is not only an economic but a major political problem." *Wen Wei Po* went on to quote another cadre on the political fall-out of the demise of the public sector: "If the skin is dead, on what will the hair anchor itself?"[9]

Political considerations also underlined the CCP's emphasis on agriculture and the partial revival of the Maoist slogan that "grain is the key link" of the economy. Agriculture had pride of place both in the Five-Year Plan and the Ten-Year Economic Blueprint. Given the widespread signs of disaffection in the cities both among intellectuals and workers, the party was eager to reaffirm its hold on its traditional power base. As General Secretary Jiang Zemin put it at an agrarian conference in June 1990: "More than 800 million of our 1.1 billion people live in the countryside. When the villages are stabilised, and the farmers live a contented life, this will fundamentally guarantee the stability of the nation and society."[10]

The most pervasive influence of politics, however, might have manifested itself in the dearth of new reform ideas. Out of fear of the "bourgeois-liberal" label — and also because of a desire not to co-operate with the "Tiananmen Square butchers" — the most active thinkers of the Zhao Ziyang era stayed silent for two years. Things came to such a pass that the Vice-President of Chinese Academy of Social Sciences, Professor Liu Guoguang, a conservative economist, said new thinking and experiments should not be branded "symptoms of bourgeois liberalisation". Six months after the massacre, Liu told the semi-official Hong Kong China News Agency: "Explorations in theory and practice in the course of reform, including mistakes in policies, should not be simplistically equated with bourgeois liberalisation." "We should encourage bold explorations under the Four Cardinal Principles," he said, as though the two did not contradict each other.[11]

C. Re-hoisting the Flag of Central Planning

A major accusation levelled against Zhao Ziyang was his apparent effort to steer China down the capitalist road. There might be some truth to this. For example, the Political Report of the 13th Party Congress, which marked the high point of Zhao's career, was unabashedly critical of state fiats. "Direct management based on mandatory plans cannot suit the demands of the socialist commodity economy," it said. The Congress called for the gradual retreat of the state, the establishment of a "mechanism where the state regulates the market, and the market guides enterprises".[12]

It is characteristic of the patriarch's famed "balancing act" that when he first enunciated the "organic synthesis" theory in October 1990, Deng never spelled out which was the more important, planning or the market. However, it seemed obvious at the time that since the State Council was controlled by central planners, planning would have pride of place at least in day-to-day economic policy-making.

Speaking about the Eighth Five-Year Plan and the Ten-Year Economic Blueprint, then minister of the State Planning Commission Zou Jiahua said: "The synthesis of central planning and market regulation is a basic principle" of economic policy-making. However, he made it explicit that "the two do not have equal status. Central planning is of primary importance. Market regulations are supplementary." "The national economy must be built on the basis of plans and a well-proportioned development," said Zou, a former Ordnance Minister who is considered an ally of Li Peng. He said state plans would be formulated according to the needs of "socialist economic development", adding that "major strategic resources and important strategic [economic] means" must be put under the control of the central government.[13]

Zou's ideas were representative of his colleagues in the State Council. They were seconded by the Vice-Governor of the People's Bank of China, Chen Yuan. Chen is the eldest son of Chen Yun, author of the infamous "bird cage" theory of state fiats. In a controversial article in the media early 1991, the younger Chen argued that planning was the "basis" of the market. "Planning is the *sine qua non* for the development of the market," he wrote. "Without the support of planning, the market will speedily shrink and disintegrate."

Chen contended that given China's large population and limited resources, planning would be a fact of life for a long time to come. He said that economic policy should consist in the "co-existence of and interplay among" state fiats, indirect macro-economic control and adjustment, and market forces. "At this stage, direct planning is the basis for the development and functioning of the market," Chen said. In the foreseeable future, the state would go on interfering in the market through direct control over the exploitation and distribution of major commodities and through indirect levers in the areas of finance, investment and prices. "It requires a very long historical period for a market to mature under the support of direct planning," he wrote.[14]

Opponents of the "market first" persuasion cited China's "unique characteristics" as excuses for centralisation. In late July 1990, the official China Survey Service (CSS) published a three-year study which concluded that the decade-old modernisation model of market-oriented, fast-track development ill suited the nation's economic realities. Pinpointing China's huge population and chronic shortages in areas including minerals, arable land and technology, CSS recommended a "broad co-ordination of the increasingly scarce resources" in order to ensure their "economical utilisation and proper consumption".[15]

The views of the central planners were by and large enshrined in the Proposals for China's Ten-Year Economic Programme and Eighth Five-Year Plan, which were passed in late 1990. This was in spite of frantic lobbying by Deng Xiaoping to inject more market elements into the plan and the blueprint. In partial deference to the 13th Party Congress Report, the Proposals did say that the general drift of policy-making would be to curtail direct state fiats, and to replace them with non-mandatory "guidance" as well as market adjustments.

However, the Proposals stressed that it was necessary for both short-term and long-term development to "adequately concentrate necessary funds and other resources [in central government] to accomplish well certain major projects which affect the national interest and which can only be done well by the centre".[16] Other aspects of the recentralisation strategy will be taken up later.

D. The Recentralisation Imperative

A major reason behind the centripetal urge was money: the national budget deficit kept yawning wider year after year. If Western accounting practices were followed — meaning that domestic and foreign loans were not counted as "income" — the deficits from 1986 to 1990 would be: 20.8 billion yuan, 24.9 billion yuan, 34.8 billion yuan, 37.5 billion yuan and 50.9 billion yuan.[17] From the late 1980s to 1991, the central government's share of national income slipped from an estimated 60 per cent to 40 per cent. In August 1990, then finance minister Wang Bingqian pointed out that in spite of recentralisation efforts introduced since 1988, "the proportion of the share of the central government in total national income continues to slide." [18]

Free-marketeers have argued that a sure-fire way to generate income is to open up the economy — so that as business mushrooms, state coffers will benefit from more taxes and other contributions. For central planners inured to the traditional autarkist economy, however, the natural impulse was to boost state fiats on how much localities and businesses can spend — and how much they must surrender to the central treasury.

On relations between Beijing and enterprises, a big controversy erupted over whether the responsibility system should be dropped. A major achievement of the decade of reform, the system ensured that enterprises kept the bulk of their profits after giving up an agreed percentage to central authorities. Professor Wang Zhaofei, a researcher at the Institute of Finance and Trade at CASS, however, criticised the responsibility system for contributing to Beijing's financial crisis. "The responsibility system has broken up the normal order of the distribution of finances and taxes," he said. "As a result, the distribution of national income has been weighted in favour of enterprises and localities." In a commentary in late 1989, the China News Service pointed out the system encouraged "short-term behaviour" in many entrepreneurs, who would not make optimum use of his resources — or go in for long-term planning — in their urge to make a fast buck.[19]

There was a half-hearted attempt to introduce another tax system, which was called "the demarcation of tax and profits". Roughly put, it meant that enterprises had to pay multifarious levels of taxes first before they could have access to their profits. The tax rate would be higher than the "contracted percentage" to be rendered to the state under the responsibility system. By early 1992, however, it seemed likely the system would stay. And Capital Iron and Steel Works in Beijing, a pioneer of the system, was again cited in the media as a model enterprise. Efforts were instead concentrated on cutting subventions to perennially loss-making state enterprises (see section on state enterprises).

Fiercer dogfights were waged between the central government and localities. The tug-of-war came to a head at the now-celebrated National Economic Work Meeting held in Beijing in September 1990. The conference was devoted to how the economic pie should be split. Beijing wanted to impress upon the provinces the size of the deficit in 1990, which was close to 12 billion yuan even using the Chinese accounting method. Moreover, central coffers were owed 20 billion yuan in taxes.[20]

In particular, Beijing wanted to abolish the contract financial responsibility system (CFRS), which had since the early 1980s governed revenue sharing between the centre and the regions, especially the coastal provinces and centrally administered cities. Under this schema, a province or city could keep its revenue after surrendering an agreed amount of tax and other contributions to the centre. The system proposed for the early 1990s was called the "segregation of taxes" or the "dual tax system": separate tax bases would be carved out for Beijing and the localities.

Under the CFRS, the percentage of tax and other contributions to the given to Beijing varied from place to place. Guangdong and Shenzhen were the big winners because they were able to retain up to 90 per cent of their revenues. At the September 1990 showdown between central and local authorities, the latter refused to part with their hard-won privileges.

While the minutes of the meeting had not been publicised, Chinese sources said local leaders, led by then Guangdong governor Ye Xuanping and Shandong governor Zhao Zhihao, staged a virtual rebellion. The altercation broke out over the evaluation of the 10 years of reform begun by Deng Xiaoping.

While Li Peng expressed reservations about the reforms, saying they had led to "dislocations", the provincial chieftains said they must be affirmed and written into the Eighth Five-Year Plan. The regional cadres refused to give up the CFRS. An impasse followed. It took the intervention of elder statesman Yang Shangkun before Li Peng could leave the room with some composure. The "compromise" reached was that things would remain the same. As we shall see later, the "dual tax system" would not be introduced until 1994.[21]

E. Taking Back Powers From The Regions

(i) Arresting Centrifugal Tendencies

A central plank of the Deng Xiaoping revolution was *yindizhiyi* ("to each [locality] according to its characteristics"). Powers were devolved to an extent unimaginable in the days of Mao Zedong, one of whose concerns was to prevent the growth of "mountain strongholds" in political and economic matters.

The rational for "creative centrifugalism" was written into the 13th Party Congress Report. "One of the manifestations of the over-concentration of authority is that the powers of grassroots units are excessively concentrated in superior [party and government] departments," the document said. "On the one hand, the leading departments have been minding over things which they should not mind, which they cannot manage well, and which they cannot control. On the other hand, the grassroots lack autonomy, and the enthusiasm of the masses cannot be fully motivated."[22]

It is well known that Zhao Ziyang granted a sizeable amount of autonomy to areas along the southeast coast. However, under Hu Yaobang and Zhao, areas with concentrations of potentially anti-Beijing ethnic minorities — Tibet and Xinjiang — also got a comparatively larger measure of economic freedom. In spite of qualms about potentially destabilising consequences, Xinjiang was permitted to upgrade economic links with Muslim-speaking countries and peoples to its west.

Things went the other way for up to two years after the massacre. As master planner Zou Jiahua put it in mid-1990, Beijing would put as its priority "preventing and countering the centrifugal tendencies and behaviour" of local-level administrations and enterprises.[23] The Proposal for the Eighth Five-Year Plan and the Ten-Year Blueprint said Beijing must "correctly handle the relationship between centripetal and centrifugal tendencies and between the centre and localities." It made no secret of the fact that in the future, the accent would be on "earnestly boosting the macro-level regulations and control powers of central authorities, and raising their effectiveness and authority".[24]

That the centre was ready to act toughly was made clear by Premier Li while on a trip to Guizhou in early 1991. Li called upon cadres in the province to carry out the spirit of the Seventh Plenum of the 13th Central Committee, which had endorsed the plan and the blueprint. The premier said individual provinces were free to devise their own corresponding plan and blueprint, but the latter must be "appropriate to the practical situation in local districts and [government] departments". Referring to the runaway capital-construction projects in some provinces, Li issued mighty caveats against "over-ambitiousness". He said that local plans must be practical: "It will not do without the spirit of striving for better results. However, impetuosity will also be inappropriate."[25]

Specifically, the economic powers that the centre tried to take back from the regions included: the size of capital construction in the locality and its growth rate; its freedom to form economic linkages with neighbouring areas and foreign countries; and its production orientation. As we shall see, the centripetal imperative encountered stiff opposition from the regions, especially coastal provinces and cities.

(ii) A Product Sliding Policy

Zhao Ziyang tended to favour certain regions in the country, mostly the southeastern coast. This became known as the geographical sliding policy: certain districts in the country had priority access to state investment and a larger share of the favourable policies in tax and other areas. The post-Tiananmen leadership tried instead to promote a product sliding policy: vouchsafing the advantages to areas and factories that manufactured the desired types of goods and services. While Zhao had favoured "export-oriented", particularly light industrial products, the central planners went in for areas including agriculture, energy, transportation, and heavy industry. This new sliding policy endured right through to late 1993.

As senior economist Wang Zuo, a staffer with the Policy Research Office of the Guangdong government, put it in late 1989: "With the deepening of the programme to cure and rectify the economy, the country will gradually phase out its policy of favouring the regions and substitute it with the policy of favouring certain industrial sectors." Wang warned that the Pearl River region, for so many years the beneficiary of special privileges, would face a "tough test".[26]

Most indicative of the conservative trend was the emphasis on agriculture, which was a direct result of the ascendancy of the ideas of Chen Yun (see Chapter 3). At a national meeting on agrarian issues in June 1990, agriculture, especially grain production, was reaffirmed as the primary pursuit of the economy. "Feeding 1.1 billion people is the No. 1 concern of this country,"

Jiang Zemin said. "We must further unify our thoughts, and truly put agriculture as the first place of national economic work."[27]

Guangdong Province, a leader in reform since the early 1980s, acknowledged its incompetence in the agrarian area. The semi-official China News Service reported in December 1990 that the province was busy "learning and taking lessons in agrarian reform from Shandong Province". Lin Ruo, then Guangdong party boss and a Zhao Ziyang protégé, went on a special "learning trip" to Shandong in October 1990. "The Shandong experience consists first of all in attaching a high degree of importance to agriculture," Lin said. "Shandong has also put emphasis on agriculture infrastructure and on developing technology." He also praised the eastern China province for promoting "unity" between towns and villages, and between the sectors of agriculture, industry and trade.[28]

The emphasis on heavy industry and related projects reflected the bias of the Soviet-trained central planners, who had a stranglehold on major positions in the State Council. The crowning touch of their industrial strategy was the decision taken in late 1991 and early 1992 to go ahead with the Three Gorges hydro-electric project, which had a price-tag of more than 100 billion yuan. The year 1991 also saw the decision by the central government to form huge conglomerates to develop heavy industrial sectors including petrochemicals, automobiles, minerals and metallurgy. [29]

As we shall see in Chapter 4, the bias in favour of heavy industry was given an added push by the expanding clout of the military. Soon after the Gulf War, Jiang Zemin and Zou Jiahua both talked about the "inter-changeability" of heavy industry and the military sector. Jiang, a former Minister of Electronics, lobbied for more funds for the electronics industries, particularly those with military applications.

F. Debate over the Speed of Growth and Reform

A perennial bone of contention between Zhao Ziyang and Li Peng in the mid-1980s was the speed of growth and reform. Following the ideas of Deng Xiaoping, Zhao favoured break-neck speeds for both growth and reform. After all, a Deng Xiaoping aphorism commonly cited when price reform was waged in 1988 was "short-term pain is better than long-term pain". Li, on the other hand, had always been for stability: that the economy must develop and reform implemented in a "stable, sustained, harmonious" fashion.[30]

Premier Li partially won the battle with the Eighth Five-Year Plan and the Ten-Year Blueprint, which fixed the growth rate for the 1990s at 6 per cent. This by and large reflected the instructions of Chen Yun. In a message to the Politburo written by Chen in late 1990, the conservative patriarch bitterly attacked the "high-speed growth model" of the past few years. Chen said that in economic construction, the party had succumbed to leftist hysteria. "In one-sidedly emphasising and going after high speed, [the party and government] departed from national conditions and the normal law of social development," Chen said. "The result is a bogus type of efficiency, low speed and negative growth."[31]

Li stuck to this theme while touring the major open city of Tianjin in mid-1991. The premier said that while the economy should have an adequate growth rate and that output should expand steadily, "growth should be based on high economic efficiency". "If we seek a high growth rate to the neglect of efficiency, enterprises would make no progress," he pointed out.[32]

This was, of course, almost diametrically opposed to Deng's argument. About one year after Tiananmen Square, the patriarch had again lobbied for his old "high-growth model". In an internal speech in December 1990, Deng made propaganda for a "reasonably high level of growth", arguing that economic efficiency could only be achieved on the basis of a "considerable scale and speed of development." The patriarch further said the scale and speed of growth which he and fellow reformers had determined in the past decade of reform were not based on "subjective conjecture" but on scientific analysis of the nation's resources.[33]

In a dispatch in November 1990, the Hong Kong China News Agency, which often reflects the views of the moderate faction, quoted a group of "relevant economic experts" as saying that "the best speed for Chinese economic development is 11.9 per cent". HKCNA quoted the economists, who had reportedly studied "millions of data", as saying that "economic development should have an adequate speed. If it is too slow, development will be sluggish. Too high a speed will engender constraints." The experts said a growth rate in the range of 8 to 12 per cent was suitable for China.[34]

An equally vehement debate was staged over the pace of reform. Premier Li, again representing the so-called *wending pai* or Faction of Stability, would only endorse progress that did not upset the existing economic structure and socio-political order. Li's comparison between China and the former Soviet Union in late 1990 is instructive. Referring to the radical programme hatched by former president Mikhail Gorbachev to privatise the economy, Li told a foreign delegation in 1990: "China is different from the Soviet Union. We'll have 10 years, and not just 500 days to wage reforms."[35]

G. Controversy Over The "Curing and Rectification" Campaign

Economic historians of the years 1979 to 1991 would easily spot periods of heady reform followed by periods of retrenchment, usually called "curing and restructuring". Partisans of reform liked to interpret the "curing" period as an uncomfortable interregnum, the growing pains of liberalisation. Conservatives, however, regarded the very need for retrenchment as unmistakable signs that the reform strategy had gone awry. For the latter, the austerity drive should be extended until all the basic "errors" of the radical reformists had been rectified.

Allied to the controversy over the speed of growth was the argument over whether and when to call an end to the curing and rectification programme, which started in late 1988. Not surprisingly, central planners wanted to prolong it, fearing that a loosening up of credit and other forms of central control would open the way for inflation, excessive decentralisation and market mechanisms.

The central planners were trying to turn the tables on the reformers. Whereas the latter used to argue that retrenchment was basically a "service" to reform, the former contended that reform should be waged only in accordance with the requirements of rectification. At a conference called in early 1990 by the State Commission for the Reform of the Economic Structure, Vice-Minister He Guanghui said: "The contents, measures and speed of reform must observe the overall situation of curing and restructuring the economy."[36] A dispatch by the semi-official China News Service quoted an "authoritative person" as saying that "in the course of curing and rectifying the economy, reform must not be geared towards the pursuit of speed and newfangled objectives. We must not be impetuous."[37]

Up until early 1991, Li Peng's chief economics adviser, Yuan Mu, insisted that the curing and rectification process should go into the first half of the Eighth Five-Year Plan, meaning 1993 at the earliest. Speaking in January 1991, Professor Liu Guoguang, another Li adviser, said the austerity gameplan should not be prematurely curtailed. Pointing out that retrenchment had achieved results, Liu warned: "The task of rectification remains an arduous one and more efforts are required to persevere with it."[38] Even relatively moderate leaders like Jiang Zemin seemed to be going along with Liu's logic. "We must correctly handle the relationship between economic construction and the programme to cure and rectify the economy; we must raise economic efficiency through the curing and rectification process," he said during a visit to Jilin in January 1991.[39]

However, remnant liberal economists had by early 1990 tried to stop the retrenchment policy, pointing out that conservatives were again taking advantage of the rectification process to roll back reform. This was the theme trumpeted by a gathering of avant-garde theorists in Hangzhou in mid-June 1990. The 50-odd social scientists came from CASS and the Economics Research Centre of the State Planning Commission. They argued that retrenchment should not be used as an excuse to throttle reform. Moreover, rectification should be carried out using economic levers, not administrative orders.

"The aim of curing and rectifying the economy is to create a favourable environment for further deepening reform, and it does not mean a retrogression or a halt to reform," NCNA quoted the participants as saying. The economists argued that instead of just resorting to government fiats, "efforts should be made to deal with [economic] problems by economic means". The news agency reported that while some at the conference stuck to the view that the austerity programme was necessary to correct dislocations such as inflation, "others held that rectification had been excessive in the control of the money supply, resulting in insufficient demand in the market." The latter group added they were worried about "a return to the traditional system".[40] It turned out that these mavericks had the support of Deng. In an internal speech of December 1990, the patriarch said that one way in which reform had been adulterated was the "curing and rectification" campaign. "The phenomenon of using the policy of curing and rectifying the economy to clamp down on reform is not correct," intimates quoted him as saying.[41]

It was not until the National Work Meeting on Economic Reform in March 1991 that Li Peng pronounced the curing and rectification over and that the reform phase could be switched on again. He said thanks to the austerity programme introduced since late 1988, the economy had become relatively relaxed and prosperous, making large-scale reform possible. "We must seize the opportunity to strengthen the leadership of reform and boost the proportions of reform," he said.[42] As we shall see, Deng gave a fairly negative assessment of the three-year retrenchment during his *nanxun* instructions.[43]

H. Controversy over Price Reform

Political considerations also impinged on the speed and scope of price reform in the difficult period of 1989 to 1991. Not surprisingly, prices were pretty much frozen in the first year after June 4. Stability was the order of the day. By mid-1990, however, the retrenchment policy had reduced inflation to below three per cent (according to official figures), and calls for price reform resurfaced. At a State Council meeting in July 1990, Premier Li said the country "must further restructure prices by gradually rationalising the relations between domestic market prices and foreign market prices". On another occasion, Li had this to say about the urgency of price reform: "The prices are not reasonable now and we must gradually rationalise the price [structure]. Only when the prices are rationalised can we give better play to the function of market adjustments."[44]

Beijing had to grasp the nettle mainly because of the enormity of price subventions. In 1978, the state provided 3.6 billion yuan in subsidies for grain and oil. The figure rose to 10.8 billion yuan in 1980 and 40 billion yuan in 1990.[45] While, in the light of the experience in Eastern Europe, and later in the dissolved Soviet Union, the wholesale cancellation of price subsidies seemed out of the question, selective steps were taken to re-orient prices towards the marketplace.

In early 1991, the prices of a host of products and services were unfrozen. On May 1, 1991, the price of flour rose by 54 per cent and vegetable oil by 108 per cent. Prices of goods made from these products, including cakes, noodles and soap, went up correspondingly.[46] Earlier, the prices of bus, subway and railway tickets, stamps, oil and steel were upwardly adjusted. For example, the wholesale price of crude oil was jacked up a hefty 34 yuan per tonne. The price of iron ore rose by at least 10 per cent. Pulp and paper, cement, and automobiles including the Liberation and East Wind models, were also affected.[47]

To soften the impact of inflation, urban workers were given a wage subsidy of 6 yuan a month from May 1991. Foreign correspondents had ample reports about the grumblings of workers. "The government has raised prices more than 100 per cent on some kinds of food, but I have been given less than a five per cent pay rise," the *Washington Post* quoted a manual worker in Beijing as saying. "How can we be anything but angry?"[48]

Because of the relatively circumscribed nature of these price adjustments, massive demonstrations of dissatisfaction that had taken place in 1988 did not recur. However, especially after the floods in the summer of 1991, a temporary moratorium was put on price changes. Western analysts said, however, that the spate of price rises in the first half of 1991 did not constitute real price reform. The market condition of prices determined solely by the forces of supply and demand had not yet been achieved.

The 1991 floods and their aftermath showed Beijing's macro-economic control was adequate enough to soften the impact of inflation. In July, when the deluge climaxed, the cost-of-living index in 35 cities in the country rose by 11.6 per cent against the same month in 1990. This compared with an average of 6.9 per cent in the first half of 1990. According to statistics released in early 1992, the overall national inflation figure in 1991 was a meagre three per cent — the lowest figure since the late 1970s.[49]

Most Western economists would presume that such a low rate of inflation would present a suitable climate for thorough-going price reform. As prominent economist Liu Guoguang argued, the government needed to adopt a forward-looking attitude towards cutting the Gordian knot. "A lot of thought was given to keeping [commodity] prices at low levels for the sake of maintaining short-term social stability," the Hong Kong China News Agency quoted the professor as saying in early 1991. "But instead, what we should have done is to take bolder steps of reform. It is wrong both to miss the opportunity or to

LIBRARY
BISHOP BURTON COLLEGE
BEVERLEY HU17 8QG

act too aggressively. But the former is probably more serious and its consequences could be disastrous."[50]

By early 1992, there was no indication that major surgery was on the cards.
The voice of caution seemed to have won the day. As Li Peng said at the NPC
report of April 1991, the prices of products that were scarce and that affected
national life must still be controlled by the state. The premier indicated on
another occasion that the party and government must "manage well the relationship between reform, development and [socio-political] stability and at
the same time bear in mind the ability of the state, the collective and the individual to cushion [the price shocks]".[51]

As with other aspects of economic liberalisation, it was along the coastal
belt that price reform saw the boldest advances. In mid-1991, Hainan
announced that it had by and large abrogated subsidies on grain. As a result,
the market prices of rice and wheat became on a par with what the state was
paying farmers. It also meant that grain prices in the nation's largest SEZ were
more than double those in other cities. Provincial authorities said the measure
had not produced "unstable signs" such as shortages, hyperinflation, or spec-
ulationary activities.[52]

III. Recollectivisation in Farming, 1989-1991

A. The Household Contract Responsibility System under Siege

From mid-1989 to early 1992, one of the fiercest battles between the two
dominant factions of the party was fought over the extent to which agriculture
should be recollectivised. Put another way, the debate was over how to retool
and "perfect" the household contract responsibility system (HCRS), which
had become synonymous with agrarian reform.

First tried out by then Anhui party secretary Wan Li in the eastern province
in late 1978, HCRS permitted individual households to engage in whatever
agricultural pursuits — or even non-agrarian activities — they liked after
guaranteeing to pay the authorities an agreed level of tax and other contributions. The communes and the work brigades were scrapped to make way for
family-based plots. And while land was still owned by the state, the households had "contracts" to use their plots for 20, 30 or more years. The net result
was the virtual privatisation of farming.

Long before the June 4 crisis, however, the household system had become
controversial. First of all, it meant less grain production as commercial crops
and industrial or commercial pursuits brought more money to the households.
Secondly, it discouraged mechanisation and collective works, particularly irri-

gation. The reason: land was now divided into minute portions and individual families had no incentive to pool resources for joint projects. As the semi-official Hong Kong China News Agency put it in October 1989: "Each family is fending for itself, with the result that water-conservation facilities cannot be systematised, and large-scale agrarian machinery cannot be used."[53]

Then there was the political consideration of the atrophy of CCP organisations. In the wake of the abolition of the commune, party cells were heading towards disintegration. In politics as well as in economics, recollectivisation would seem to make it possible for the CCP to reassert its control over the farm, deemed the party's traditional power base. In late 1990, the party began implementing a large-scale rural socialist education campaign, whose goal was to re-establish a tight network of CCP branches and associations (see Chapter 3).

Recollectivisation assumed a greater urgency after the Tiananmen Square crackdown. A top priority of the post-June 4 regime was to maintain socio-political stability. Nowhere was this more important than feeding 1.1 billion mouths. A HKCNA dispatch in September 1990 said that more than 50 million citizens had still not solved the problem of food and clothing.[54] In the eyes of the planners, only collectivisation could guarantee an adequate and sustained supply of grain.

Politics seemed to have brushed aside calculations based on purely agronomical considerations. Theoretically, China should, like any other country, follow the law of comparative advantage and grow commercial crops in addition to grain: cash crops can be exported and the foreign exchange earned can be used to buy wheat and rice.

This was precisely the argument used by liberal economists who before June 4 had openly questioned the Maoist doctrine of "taking grain as the key link". For example, in a March 1989 article in the *People's Daily*, CASS agronomist Liu Zhenbang said the emphasis on grain went against the principles of the commodity economy. Professor Liu cited the example of oranges on the plains near the tourist site of Guilin in Guangxi. In the past, oranges and mandarins from this area were able to enter the world market, allowing the locality to earn precious foreign exchange. After local cadres had adopted the principle of "taking grain as the key link", the plains were reserved for paddies, and the orchards were relocated to the hills. Because the climatic conditions were different, the oranges were no longer that juicy and could not find markets overseas. As a result, the income of the entire area suffered.[55]

Liu's arguments, however, became irrelevant after June 4. The hardliners, consumed by the mentality of the "war economy" could always say: what if the sanctions on China continue and nobody would take China's oranges and nobody would sell rice to China? As Yao Yilin put it soon after June 4:

"China's goal is self-reliance in the main, and to supplement it with foreign help." In a speech in late 1990, Li Peng openly praised the collective approach for "facilitating mechanisation and the building of infrastructure".[56]

After the devastating floods of the summer of 1991, which was partly blamed on failure to build and maintain water-conservation facilities, emotions against the HCRS climaxed. Chinese sources said that by late 1990, central planners had begun drafting a document that would declare a virtual end to the "privatisation" system. The masterminds behind the putsch were reported to be Premier Li and other Politburo hardliners including then Beijing party boss Li Ximing.

As we shall see, the "plot" never came to pass. However, that the hardliners almost pulled it off was evident from the media, which heaped praise on the collective approach. For example, a pioneer commune launched by Mao Zedong was eulogised by the press for its insistence on the "collective road". The village of Liuzhuang, near Zhengzhou, the provincial capital of Henan, was launched by the Chairman in 1958 as one of China's first communes. It was also one of the relatively few rural areas that had not adopted HCRS.

In a dispatch in October 1989, NCNA pointed out how, "when the responsibility system was sweeping the land, Liuzhuang did not follow the national example". Earlier the same month, Shi Laihe, head of Liuzhuang, was named a "model worker" by the State Council. Shi, who had been eclipsed by the media in the go-go days of reform, was lauded for "keeping the land under village control". In 1988, per capita income in Liuzhuang reached 2,000 yuan, three times the national average. Moreover, at a time when grain production nationwide had stagnated, Liuzhuang did not neglect the vital sector. Shi, a member of the NPC Standing Committee, was received by Mao nine times. And Liuzhuang, famous for its high-quality cotton, was an early model of China's first communes. "Chairman Mao visited Liuzhuang in the summer of 1958," a local cadre was quoted as saying. "After spending a day inspecting agriculture work, the chairman said, 'The people's commune is a good thing'."[57]

Recollectivisation was rampant in selected provinces such as Shandong. In a dispatch in October 1989, HKCNA explained why large districts of this province had not followed the household approach. The agency quoted local economists as saying that the evolution of Chinese agriculture had mainly followed three steps: the commune, the HCRS, and an "adequate degree" of large-scale production. "The great majority of farmers have accepted the household responsibility system," HKCNA said, adding there was a "division of opinion" on when China should enter the third stage. By late 1989, 1,000-odd "production mutual-help groups" had been formed among villages near the open city of Qingdao.[58]

B. The Compromise: A Dual Approach

The need to pacify the farmers, however, prevented the CCP from rolling back the reforms. As Jiang Zemin put it in late 1991, the party's priority was that stability be maintained in the rural areas. "Without progress in the village, there will be no comprehensive progress for society," the party boss said. "Without the modernisation of the village, there will be no national economic modernisation. Without the stability of the village, there will be no national stability."[59]

The debate on recollectivisation had so disturbed the nation's 800-odd million farmers that the party soon settled for a compromise: what became known as the dual approach to agriculture. On the one hand, party leaders reiterated that the HCRS would not be changed and that farmers could retain their individual plots. On the other, so-called "socialised service systems" would be set up to run communal projects, water conservation and other undertakings.

Efforts to reassure the peasants were manifested in a number of documents issued and national meetings held from late 1990 to early 1992. For example, in December 1990 the party and government issued an extraordinary "joint circular" on farming. The document pointed out in no uncertain terms that the HCRS would be "stabilised and perfected" but not changed. The document said the authorities "encouraged different localities to make every effort to stabilise and perfect the rural responsibility system and improve services for farmers...To perfect the system does not mean to change it."[60]

The circular stressed that land contracts given farmers should be "stabilised and improved", adding that as long as the terms of the contracts were basically reasonable and the masses were satisfied, the agreements should remain intact. The document also noted that "adjustments can be made in the land contract system according to the wish of the masses", hinting that recollectivisation should only be pursued if the farmers so wished.

In the same vein, then vice-premier Tian Jiyun pointed out in a national agriculture work meeting in Beijing in September 1991 that the HCRS should not be adulterated. "We must not come out with new-fangled ideas to dilute the system," he said. "We must earnestly, totally, and unremittingly implement the system. HCRS suits the production level of the Chinese village. Its potentials have been far from exhausted, and it will continue to push Chinese agriculture to new heights." As though anticipating the attack of hardliners, Tian added that the family system did not mean privatisation. "It is just a change of management methods. Land, the basic means of production, still belongs to the state."[61]

And while meeting a Hong Kong delegation in October 1991, Jiang Zemin recalled how he had tried to reassure farmers in the cotton fields in Henan Province. "The farmer told me that it would be best if the agrarian policy did not change during his lifetime," the General Secretary said. "I told him that the policy would not change in two lifetimes." [62]

The subtle reference to the necessity of "perfecting" the household system, however, meant it might be tempered by a degree of collectivisation. As Jiang put it as early as December 1989: "We must stabilise and perfect the contract responsibility system. At the same time, in areas with the necessary conditions, we should adequately encourage the development of large-scale production as well as various service systems." Similarly, then Politburo member Song Ping said on a tour of Inner Mongolia in July 1990 that while the HCRS would be "further stabilised", farmers should be encouraged to re-collectivise activities so as to "gradually strengthen the collective economy". [63]

Just how would the dual track system work? The June 1990 national meeting on agriculture said that areas where the household system had worked well should hang on to it. Other districts, however, should go for a "two-tier production system". Conference participants pointed out that this meant "strengthening the synthesis of unity and division: the combination between the superiority of the collective economy together with the enthusiasm of the rural household system". [64] The same message was sent by Jiang when he toured Henan in March 1991. "The party must ceaselessly perfect the synthesis of unification and decentralisation [in agriculture management]," he said. "It must develop a socialised service system in the villages and gradually strengthen the collectivist economy." [65]

By early 1992, it was by no means clear how this limited collectivisation would take place — or even whether it would be compulsory. As Tian Jiyun put it: "Socialised services means collectives and government units taking up things which cannot be done well by individual households." [66] Supposedly, this meant local governments units, for example, the Village Committees, would set up special teams for such communal efforts as digging irrigation dykes. While it is almost sure that households would have to contribute labour or money, the degree of compulsion was not spelt out.

In agriculture, then, the conservatives and the moderates reached a compromise. As Tian told Japanese television when he was touring Tokyo in late 1991, China would not return to the road of the commune. But neither would Beijing allow the privatisation of land. "Total privatisation would lead to a big disparity of income and social chaos," Tian said. [67] The key to development, however, still seemed to lie in individual counties and villages. Areas which enjoyed the "benign neglect" of Beijing could continue to develop along the lines of free-market farming.

IV. Debate over State Enterprises 1989-1992

A. Tackling the Dinosaurs

The forces of conservatism and reform were at loggerheads over the issue of re-tooling the state enterprises, long deemed the most intractable problem of the economy. The question was not properly addressed until April 1991 when the new vice-premier Zhu Rongji was assigned to tackle the "triangular debts" and allied issues. The time, however, was still not ripe for radical surgery, especially privatisation.

Zhu's "radical solution" consisted in foreclosing on the hopeless laggards and giving the robust companies enough autonomous powers to function as fully fledged economic entities that could respond to the forces of supply and demand. By early 1992, there were signs that Zhu's arguments had by and large carried the higher echelons of the party and government. However, it was still doubtful whether the State Council would go the whole hog in putting the dinosaurs out of action. In the first half of 1992, drastic steps such as closing poor-performing enterprises and granting autonomy to the star performers were only taken on a selective basis in several "experimental" cities.

There was a "bipartisan" consensus over the severity of the problem of government business units, once the pride of Chinese socialism. These products of Stalinism were in the 1950s lauded by Chairman Mao as the vehicle with which China would "catch up" with Britain in ten to 20 years. By the late 80s, however, the dinosaurs had become millstones around the neck of the economy. Losses incurred by government-owned units in 1991 were estimated at at least 84 billion yuan. Some 36.7 per cent of all state-owned enterprises were losing money in the first half of 1991.[68] The losses incurred were on top of the 56 billion yuan they drew from central coffers in the form of subsidies. Since these concerns were expected to surrender no more than 127.10 billion yuan in profits and taxes to the state, critics sarcastically remarked that Beijing stood to make 12.90 billion yuan a year if the entire sector was shut down.[69]

Remedial measures adopted by the State Council in 1990 and the first half of 1991, however, consisted of little more than pumping more funds into the chronic money-losers. The apparent hope was that the investments would help transform technology and make their products more attractive. In 1990, the State Council passed the policy of the so-called "double guarantees" for 234 government enterprises, giving these "daughters of the emperor" priority access to bank loans and raw materials. As Jiang Zemin made clear, the onus was on the government to help the enterprises modernise, not on the units to reform themselves. "We must further energise the large- and medium-scale enterprises," Jiang said in early 1991. "The government and local departments must enthusiastically create favourable conditions to enable them to deepen reform."[70]

As late as May 1991, when he chaired a State Council meeting, Li Peng pronounced this passive approach successful. "It looks like the 'double guarantee' policy has been effective and can continue to be implemented," the premier said. Spurning persistent calls to render the banking system independent of the CCP or the government, Beijing instructed financial institutions to make available in 1991 5 billion yuan of "modernisation funds" for the behemoths.[71]

Bolder steps were not taken until April 1991, when Zhu was put in charge of state enterprises, including the intractable problem of triangular debts, or money enterprises owed each other. The Vice-Premier soon served notice that the poor performers must wise up or their life support with the government would be cut off. A lightning tour of northeast and east China followed. On a trip to Jilin Province, Zhu called upon state-owned units to "improve internal management, retool the product mix and structure, and to raise economic efficiency." "They [enterprise owners] do not do market research, with the result that their products pile up [in warehouses] and efficiency is plummeting," Zhu scolded. In a radical departure from Li Peng, who had vowed to help state firms maintain their privileged positions, Zhu warned that he would close down units "whose hopes for becoming profitable are nil".[72]

Zhu had a hard time cutting the triangular debts, the exact amount of which could only be gauged. However, it was estimated they had mushroomed from 27 billion yuan in 1978, at the outset of the reform era, to more than 200 billion yuan in mid-1991. As the China-run *Wen Wei Po* put it in an editorial: "The bigger the amount of money enterprises owe each other, the worse hit will be the circulation funds available to them. What is even more damaging is that some business units borrow new debt to cover old ones, and the order of production and finance has been disrupted."[73]

During his tour of Jilin, Zhu cited three reasons for the growth of triangular debts. Firstly, the central coffers failed to honour earlier commitments of funds for capital construction and modernisation of technology, with the result that payment for equipment and raw materials was held up. Secondly, some enterprises went on producing goods even though the latter ended up in warehouses. Thirdly, some business units, including banks, failed to observe the laws of repayment.[74]

Zhu resorted to draconian measures to impose a solution. He forced local governments to come up with a fixed amount of money to settle the debts. Part of the money came from Beijing, but most of it from local sources. The target was that by September 20, 1991, 30 billion yuan had to be coughed up for this purpose. Each administration was obliged to report to Zhu whether enough money had been raised and how much of the debt had been cleared.

Also on September 20, Zhu took an unprecedented step in Communist-Chinese history: ordering massive work stoppages of factories whose products were spurned by the market. The first battle was waged in Liaoning Province, the famed redoubt of heavy industry which had by 1991 become a liability because of its loss-making factories. In the first eight months of 1991, 54.5 per cent of its state enterprises incurred losses. The Vice-Premier ordered that Liaoning factories which churned out 12 types of products that were no longer in demand to stop production: they included manufacturers of TV sets, small-scale tractors, low-grade paint, and rubber shoes. At the same time, production of 43 other categories of goods were subjected to strict controls.[75]

Iron rice bowls, too, were in jeopardy. Zhu gave a stern warning to the managers and workers of the dinosaurs at a conference on technological renovation of enterprises in late 1991. "If enterprises continue to lose money there will be no bonus for workers," he said. "If there are still deficits, the salary of cadres and workers will have to be cut." The Vice-Premier cited the dismissal and demotion of 32 factory managers and deputy managers in Xuzhou, Jiangsu Province. At the same time, the salaries of all the workers of 23 firms which lost money for six consecutive months were cut. And more than 20 of the worst-performing companies were temporarily closed.[76]

However, Zhu and his colleagues stopped short of the large-scale implementation of the bankruptcy law, which was passed in the mid-1980s. Instead, they pushed for the merger of inefficient enterprises with robust ones. One example cited in the national press in late 1991 was the "takeover" of the Chongqing Water Transport Co, a 34-year-old state unit which had 230 vessels and 6,000 employees. In 1990 and 1991, it was drawing state subsidies of 4 million yuan a year. In October, the dinosaur unit was merged with the Sichuan Chongqing Ferries Corporation, which was of similar size to the CWTC but a much more efficient concern.[77]

B. A New Dispensation for the State Sector

From late 1991 to early 1992, the party and government conducted a series of meetings on enlivening state enterprises. These included the Central Committee meeting on industrial units, which was held in September 1991, and the National Meeting on Economic Restructuring, which took place in January 1992. The recommendations of these conclaves could be summarised in one phrase: "re-orienting enterprises towards the marketplace".

As Li Peng put it after the January 1992 meeting: "Enterprises will gradually become economic entities that have autonomous management, that are financially self-sufficient and that are geared towards the market." The premier took a typically dialectical view towards the relation between business and government. He said that while "enterprises have to be supervised by the government, the government must create conditions whereby enterprises can be geared towards the market place."[78] The main ways in which enterprises would be "pushed" towards the market was to give them more autonomous powers. Severance of links with the government, that is, privatisation, was not an option.

In September 1991, three companies in Shanghai were given autonomy akin to that enjoyed by joint ventures. They were the Shanghai Tyre and Rubber Co, the Shanghai Industrial Sewing Machine Factory, and the Shanghai Analytical Equipment Co. They were vouchsafed a high degree of freedom in fixing their production plans. The same applied to the determination of the prices of those products which were not controlled by the State Price Administration Bureau. Other freedoms included investment for further development, personnel, and foreign trade. "The aim of this experiment is to give these enterprises the opportunity to compete on an equal footing with other enterprises, especially joint ventures," said Zhang E'ren, then head of the Economic Commission of Shanghai.[79]

Similar experiments were also conducted in 12 state enterprises in Shenyang and 32 units in Guangzhou. The 32 companies in the provincial capital of Guangdong included 16 factories and as many commercial units. The powers granted them included: design of their own management systems; hiring and firing of workers; control over cadres; the marketing of products; and the raising of funds, including the partial selling of stocks.[80]

The call for autonomy was most eloquently expressed by then party secretary of Chongqing, Xiao Yang, a former associate of Zhao Ziyang. "The way out for enterprises can be summarised by the word autonomy," he said in October 1991. Two major moves were mooted for the city by late 1991. First, as in Shanghai, the more robust enterprises were given autonomy akin to that enjoyed by foreign enterprises. Moreover, another batch of specially selected units would be given "five types of freedoms" in the areas of management, personnel, determination of product prices, use of profits, and technological transformation. Interestingly enough, Xiao did not have much to say about ideological and political work. "We check if there is gambling in our factories," he said. "We are not going to count how many times [commissars in] a factory have talked about the basic line [of the Central Committee]," the maverick said.[81]

Beijing's decision to loosen gradually the party and government's grip on enterprises spawned new calls for partial privatisation. Theorists were again saying that state companies should emulate private-sector units or joint ventures. "Recently, Guangzhou has carried out a series of measures to bring new life to our state-owned enterprises by borrowing experience from township enterprises and foreign joint ventures," HKCNA reported in a dispatch in October 1991. The news agency said there would be further reductions of state directives and less government interference in general. In many factories, professional managers were asked to double as party secretaries to minimise interference from the left.[82]

By early 1992, the most thorough-going "privatisation" proposed was permission for selected cities to convert a number of state companies into shareholding concerns. As we shall see later, however, these experiments were limited in nature. Up to late 1993, Beijing was not prepared to go the distance in privatisation.

In the mid-1980s, many members of avant-garde think-tanks such as the now-defunct Research Institute for the Reform of the Economic Structure contended that state enterprises were doomed unless basic structural changes took place. In other words, government business units must be converted into private or at least collectively-owned concerns. And so long as an enterprise remains state-owned, it is susceptible to triangular debts and allied ills. As the China-run Hong Kong paper *Wen Wei Po* put it: "the problem of triangular debts occurs mainly among state enterprises. It does not arise in private-sector units or those with foreign participation — or between these concerns and state-owned enterprises."[83]

V. The *Nanxun* Imperative of 1992: All the Way to the Marketplace

A. Breakthroughs Scored by the Nanxun *Talks*

(i) Deng Cleared More Theoretical Hurdles

Seldom has a series of instructions by a Communist-Chinese leader settled so many theoretical and practical questions as Deng Xiaoping's *nanxun* talks, which were first collected as Central Committee Document No. 2 of 1992 and subsequently, as the concluding chapter of the Third Volume of the patriarch's *Selected Works*. The philosophical significance of the talks was discussed in Chapter 1. Here we shall examine how the edicts affected the disputes over economic issues outlined previously.

On the key issue of the "surnames" of policies, Deng did not take a clear-cut stand on whether planning or market forces should have pride of place. "The difference between the nature of socialism and capitalism does not lie in [which system has] a higher proportion of planning or the marketplace," Deng said. "Planning and the market are both economic measures." The patriarch added that "the essence of socialism is to liberate productivity and to develop productivity." However, many observers, including members of the party's left wing, detected a pro-market bias here. If central planning — which was advocated by Mao and Chen Yun — had been able to develop productivity, there would have been no need to introduce market reforms.[84]

The patriarch's attitude towards the private sector was nebulous. Both before and after the *nanxun*, he never spoke out in favour of privatisation. Indeed, in trying to allay the fears of the opponents of the SEZs, he said during the *nanxun*: "We have superiority [on our side]; we have the large- and medium-scale state-run enterprises, as well as village and township enterprises. Even more important, the regime is in our hands." In his heart of hearts, however, Deng knew whether those state enterprises were indeed "superior". The philosophical pride of place accorded the state sector would be transferred on the practical level to an endorsement of the private sector when it was clear that the former was holding back, and the latter developing, productivity. As discussed in Chapter 1, for Deng, the ultimate rule was whether a policy or a sector was beneficial towards expediting productivity, strengthening national power and upgrading the people's standard of living.

By contrast, Deng's stand on the issues of the speed of growth and the tug-of-war between the centre and the regions was crystal clear. He defended his high-growth model, saying: "What I am worried about most is losing the opportunity." And since fast-paced growth could initially be achieved only in such resource-rich areas as Guangdong and Shanghai, the patriarch lent his support to the no-holds-barred development strategies of the regions. "Areas with relatively good development like Jiangsu should aim for a growth speed that is higher than the national mean," he said. "Shanghai has all the qualifications it needs to go faster." The senior leader also told Guangdong cadres they should outstrip the Four Dragons of Asia in 20 years.

Deng was at pains to point out that he was not after "an unrealistically high speed" or a repeat of the Great Leap Forward. The patriarch defended the high-growth model followed in the years 1984 to 1988, saying it was "not a small achievement" and one that facilitated the overall advancement of the economy. He grudgingly acknowledged the usefulness of the three-year retrenchment programme that ended in late 1991. However, he indicated the achievement of the austerity programme was confined to "restoring stability". He made it beyond doubt that the accent should be on periodic leaps forward, "crossing a new threshold once every few years". He encouraged places with the requisite resources to "go as fast as they can".[85]

(ii) Documents No. 4 and No. 5

In the wake of Document No. 2 came Central Committee Documents No. 4 and No. 5, which fleshed out many aspects of the spirit of the *nanxun* edicts.

If carried to the logical conclusions, the documents would have the effect often attributed to rebel astro-physicist Fang Lizhi: "changing the colour of the party". It would also revolutionise economics and politics by legitimising the country's march towards the quasi-capitalist road. As we shall see later, the developments of 1993 and 1994 showed that the two major documents lived up largely to their billing.

While Document No. 2 defined in broad conceptual terms Deng's call for a "new wave" of market reforms, No. 4 provided the concrete details of how this could be done. This magna carta for reform, entitled "Proposals of the Central Committee on speeding up reform, expanding the open door, and ensuring that the economy will enter a new stage in a faster and better manner", committed the party to "propagating and developing the market system".

First, practically the whole of China would by early next century be turned into one large Special Economic Zone. During the first phase of this radical transformation, some 30 cities along the Yangtze River and in the border regions — in addition to all provincial capitals — would be vouchsafed preferential policies on a par with the SEZs. For the first time since the start of the open-door policy in 1978, Hong Kong and foreign corporations would be allowed to go into sectors other than tourism, industry and certain sectors of infrastructure. Coastal as well as heartland cities were in 1992 luring overseas funds for hitherto taboo areas such as commerce, banking, insurance and real estate.

The booming private sector — including individual and rural enterprises — was given extra powers to expand its business, including absorbing foreign capital. In a bold statement in early June 1992, bourgeois-liberal theorist Du Runsheng endorsed efforts by peasant entrepreneurs along the coast to pool their resources to build entire new towns and industrial parks.[86]

The document said enterprises must be weaned off the government, in the process becoming "real producers and managers". The CCP pledged to give business units autonomy in personnel, investment and foreign trade as well as in determining wages and the prices of their products. The document encouraged enterprises to go into the service sector, and to form conglomerates and multinationals. Moreover, the go-ahead was given to more robust firms to convert themselves into stock companies and to sell their shares on the market. If this quasi-capitalist strategy was allowed to run its course, the public sector would before the end of the century have been displaced as the mainstay of the economy by private enterprises, stock companies and joint ventures. And "the socialist road" — the backbone of the Four Cardinal Principles — would be no more.

During Deng's visit to the Capital Iron and Steel Works on May 22, 1992, the patriarch gave his blessing to granting a higher degree of autonomy to large state corporations. After a tour of the plant by Zhu Rongji days later, the State Council promised Capital Steel new powers in investment, finance and foreign trade. The most controversial of these was authority to set up its own bank, to open a branch office in Hong Kong, and later to list part of the conglomerate in the British territory.[87]

The second thrust of Document No. 4 was "changing the function" of government departments, particularly the separation of government and business. The bloated and labyrinthine administrative structure would be trimmed, and a large number of sinecure posts slashed. Ministries including state planning, commerce, construction and raw material would witness a reduction of personnel by up to 400 per cent. Through a process of Chinese-style corporatisation, business units that used to be adjuncts of government departments would become quasi-independent, financially self-sufficient entities.

Specifically, the document said the functions of government units should not go beyond "planning, co-ordination, supervision and service". Economics-related departments in the party and central-government establishment would be divided into professional ministries and professional companies. The latter, which would function like business conglomerates or chambers of commerce, would have no executive powers. The authority of the State Planning Commission, the traditional power base of conservative bureaucrats, would be curtailed. The document demanded that the commission only concerned itself with "macro-economic adjustments" and not "concrete matters".

Perhaps the most controversial aspect of the magna carta was that it gave the green light to government units and cadres to run businesses on the side. The exceptions were security departments, even though quite a number of army and police units had by mid-1992 boosted a formidable record in capitalist-style wheeling and dealing.[88]

As Zhu Rongji put it at a mid-1992 economic conference, cadres must "emancipate their minds" in order to better transform the role of government. Zhu pledged that the structure and functions of the "next government" would be entirely different. The ideal first raised by Zhao Ziyang for Hainan Island — "small government, big business" — seemed to be coming to fruition. Document No. 4 showed Deng had been able to beat back sabotage from the conservative faction and to provide new momentum for his reforms.[89]

Especially after June 4, 1989, the CCP had become hardly distinguishable from the government. The fairly thorough-going divorce of government and business as recommended by Document No. 4 would inevitably spell the atrophy of "CCP leadership", another cornerstone of the Four Cardinal Principles. Was Deng Xiaoping, — whose uppermost priority was the preservation of the party — not aware that Documents No. 4 and 5 would chip away at the CCP's monopoly on power? The patriarch might not have a choice. Privatisation and the weaning of business away from government were perceived as the only way to ensure the viability of the economy, without which the party would be overwhelmed by popular revolt.

The major thrust of Document No. 5, which was also issued in mid-1992, was to encourage party and government units to open up and to develop the tertiary or services sector. The document underpinned the Resolution on Speeding up the Development of the Services Sector, announced by Beijing on June 29, 1992.[90]

The resolution committed the nation to expanding the services sector, which accounted for only 27 per cent of the economy. It said that the pace for the development of services should be faster than that for traditional areas such as industry and resources. The goal was for China to develop a market system that would provide urban and rural areas with services in areas such as commerce, finance, agriculture and tourism within the next ten years. Special emphasis was given to new areas such as the law, accountancy, auditing, real estate and business consultancy.

Equally important, Hong Kong, Taiwan and foreign companies were encouraged to pour investment into areas ranging from insurance to department stores. The resolution empowered party and government units to let collectives and shareholding entities run services-related businesses including information, consultancy, transport and communications. By late 1992, the nation's first private or semi-private law firms, clinics, real estate agents, and even stock brokers had been set up.

Again, the only restriction seemed to be that units in the newly revitalised services sector not violate the party's stringent regulations on state security and "state secrets". "We should enthusiastically encourage administrators to go out of [party and government] departments and into the services sector," the resolution said. "We should implement the reform of the personnel system, and enable business units in the services sector to have autonomy." Moreover, the services sector would also help expedite price reform because business units in this field would be allowed to determine their prices according to market forces, the resolution said.[91]

B. A Fillip for the Rural Sector

Deng Xiaoping's *nanxun* ideas also amounted to a "steady-the-heart" pill for farmers. The patriarch again lent his authority to the household contract responsibility system (HCRS), which in a number of provinces was in danger of being replaced by the old collective approach. After Deng had spoken, other liberal leaders including then vice-premier Tian Jiyun, also voiced their support for giving farmers a freer hand.

Deng said it was "natural" that there was opposition to reform from the very beginning. He said that the controversy over HCRS and the abolition of the commune was even bigger than that over the SEZs. "At first only one third of the provinces adopted it [the HCRS]," Deng revealed, referring to experiments first conducted by Wan Li in Anhui. "In the second year it was more than two-thirds. And in the third year, nearly all provinces followed suit. Yet at the beginning they [cadres] were not enthusiastic. And many people adopted a wait-and-see attitude."

Deng also seconded peasants who left traditional agriculture to get into the market through industrial or commercial activities. He cited the case of a *nouveau riche getihu* farmer in Wuhu, Anhui, who instead of growing grain, hired extra hands to mass-produce melon seeds. "At the time [late 70s] many people were uncomfortable with his having made a million yuan, and they wanted to do something to him," Deng recalled. "I said if we interfered, people would think the policy of the party centre had changed — and our losses would outweigh our gains."[92]

The patriarch's ideas were given concrete expression by Tian Jiyun in his now-celebrated speech to the Central Party School on April 25, 1992. Tian indicated that the HCRS had given farmers and labourers their "second liberation" because "peasants now have autonomy over the production and management of their land". The vice-premier, then in charge of agriculture, said the party must resolutely uphold the HCRS as well as the development of village and township enterprises. As discussed earlier, Tian also supported a dual-track system, meaning "the construction of a socialised service system" to ensure that such collective goals as irrigation would be properly looked after.[93]

Tian never expressed worries that farmers consumed by the profit motive might abandon the goal of "taking grain as the key link". He urged the synthesis of all forms of agriculture — farming, fishery, animal husbandry and forestry — as well as that between agriculture and aspects of the commodity economy such as commerce. Tian said the rural economy would be enlivened if 100 million out of the nearly 900 million peasants were engaged in distribution and sales work. The agriculture czar also asked farmers to look into the export market. [94]

C. The Phenomenon of Quanmin Jieshang

At the height of the Cultural Revolution, the Red Guards compared Mao Thought to an atomic bomb. Well, the sayings of the Great Helmsman did have the cataclysmic result of retarding China's collective brain for several years. Deng Thought, or at least his *nanxun* pronouncements, however, packed even more punch. It radically depoliticised the "overall climate" by making Marxism irrelevant, in the process also enabling the populace to make a few extra bucks. While the moral purist might decry the rise of the vilest philistinism, the materialism that began hitting China from 1992 at least had the "progressive" effect of weaning the people off those ungainly socialist ideals.

The year 1992 would be remembered for the socio-economic whirlwind of *quanmin jieshang* and *xiahai*: "everybody engaging in business" and "taking the plunge into the sea [of business]". People, even cadres and engineers who had comfortable and respectable jobs forsook their tenured positions for the market place. As the adage put it: "Those wielding the scalpel make less than those using the barber's scissors; those making the atomic bomb make less than those selling eggs soaked in tea." (In Chinese bomb and egg sound the same.) The catchphrase "900 million out of the 1 billion people are doing business" was being repeated everywhere.[95]

Others took on second or third jobs. As the Hong Kong China News Agency put it: "The first job is for filling the stomach; the second job is to get rich." [96] "While not giving up their iron rice bowl, many people also have a porcelain rice bowl, even a gold rice bowl." Most reprehensible for moralists and commissars alike was the phenomenon of female college students doubling as ballroom hostesses. Such collegiates made up to 10,000 yuan a month. The leftist magazine *Seeking Truth* (*Zhenli de zhuiqiu*) quoted a hostess as saying: "Dancing is a lofty affair. From the point of view of the market place, it is an exchange of labour [for money]. Each party gives up something in return for something."[97]

As we shall see, the wild chase for the fast buck unleashed by the *nanxun* made possible the unbridled development of the regions and of private business. It also engendered dubious practices that in other countries would be identified as corruption, what the leaders would later call "the exchange of power for money" (see Chapter 5).

Before the corruption crackdown of 1993, various provincial governments including Sichuan and Guizhou had passed internal documents allowing official organs and cadres there to take part in economic activities, including setting up business units. The Chinese media reported in mid-1992 that 200,000 party members had gone into business. Even party schools, considered high temples of the purest Marxism, had caught the bug of Mammonism. For example, the Hubei Party School initialled a co-production agreement with a Hong Kong firm to manufacture bamboo art objects.[98] In relatively conservative Hunan, more than 40,000 former government officials or employees established 10,000-odd business units on the side. In some party and government units, more than one-third of the staff was engaged in business.[99]

D. Economic Reforms at the 14th Party Congress

(i) The *Nanxun* Talks as State Creed

The thrust of the 14th Party Congress of October 1992 — another watershed event in post-June 4 China — was to lay down a leadership structure for the 21st century (see Chapter 6). In economic matters, the resolution of the 14th congress was less adventurous than that of the 13th, in that it broke no ground on issues such as privatisation. However, the conclave fulfilled the vital function of confirming the *nanxun* talks as state doctrine.

The gist of the 27,000-character report delivered by Jiang Zemin was that Deng Thought, particularly the part about taking economic construction as the key link, should be "upheld for 100 years and should never be shaken". The phoney debate about the "surnames" was buried forever. "Comrade Xiaoping particularly pointed out that a planned economy was not socialism; there was planning under capitalism too," Jiang said in his report. "Whether the emphasis was on planning or on market regulation was not the essential distinction between socialism and capitalism."

As a reflection of the fact that a party congress document tends to be a product of compromise, the 14th Congress resolution did not spell out bold or concrete reforms to be undertaken.[100] Jiang spoke in favour of using price reforms and boosting competitiveness so that "efficient [enterprises] will prosper and inefficient ones will be eliminated". On price reform, he said: "It is necessary to straighten out price relations and establish a system in which most prices are determined by market forces." Echoing Central Committee Document No. 4, the congress report urged the opening up of new regions to foreigners, in particular areas along major rivers and the border regions.

However, the Resolution had nothing new to offer on re-tooling state enterprises. The document merely said: "It is necessary to change the way in which state-owned enterprises operate . . . and push them towards the market to increase their vitality and efficiency." The functions of government and businesses would be separated. It added that "some small state-owned enterprises" might be leased or sold to collectives or individuals. No major surgery or restructuring was promised.

On the question of ownership, the 14th Party Congress report failed to go beyond that of the 13th Congress. It was adamant that the public sector should remain predominant, "with the private sector, which includes individually-owned and foreign-owned enterprises, as a supplement". There was no pledge for the large-scale development of the non-state-owned sector.

The congress report also laid down caveats against excessively ambitious goals or inordinately bold steps towards the marketplace. "We should not rush headlong into action, neglecting economic results, vying with each other in pursuit of a higher growth rate and seeking only increased output value," Jiang said. The Congress recommended a growth rate of eight to nine per cent, which was lower than the "ten per cent or more" recommended by Deng during the *nanxun* talks.[101]

(ii) A Pro-Reformist Constitution

A major decision of the 14th Congress was to revise the constitution of the party, the first time in a decade that such an exercise had been taken. The leadership pointed out the charter had been rewritten so that members could be better mobilised to make "bold experiments" in reform. "Party members should take the lead in taking part in reform and the open-door policy, and in the construction of socialist modernisation," the revised document said.

The revised constitution stated unequivocally that the primary pursuit of the party was economic construction. Specifically, the charter laid down four requirements for the task of "party construction". These included "upholding the party's basic line" of taking economic construction as the key link. Party affiliates were urged to "liberate their thoughts and to seek truth from facts". "Members should make positive explorations and bold experiments in order to creatively expand their work," the document said. "They should ceaselessly study new situations, sum up new experience, and solve new problems, in the process enriching and developing Marxism through practice."

Party cadres and members were allowed relative autonomy in applying the decisions of the party centre to local conditions. "Members should synthesise the goals and policies of the party with the actual conditions of their areas and departments," the document said. "They should tell the truth, do concrete things, seek real efficiency and oppose formalism."[102]

Most significantly, the document incorporated Deng's theory on the "preliminary stage of socialism", which was first spelled out by Zhao Ziyang at the 13th Party Congress. The theory said that under the premise of the means of production being held by the public sector, "multiple economic elements", including private ownership, should be allowed to co-exist. The revised constitution said in the course of this "preliminary stage", the fundamental task of the party was to "further liberate production forces and to develop productivity".

The charter also reinstated other relatively liberal ideals associated with Zhao and Hu Yaobang. The old party goal of "fighting class enemies" had been dropped. The new clause about "developing Marxism in line with new requirements" echoed a theme first struck by Hu in late 1985, when he said the party could not expect Marxism "to solve all the problems of today".[103]

VI. Re-definition of the "Socialist Market Economy" at the Third Plenum of the 14th Central Committee, 1993

The Third Plenum of the 14th Central Committee of November 1993 has been compared with the Third Plenum of the 11th Central Committee of late 1978, which confirmed Deng Xiaoping's powers and threw out the remnant Maoists. The plenum, which ended on November 14, 1993, endorsed a document on the construction of the "socialist market economy", which if carried to its logical conclusions, would have made China more market-oriented than socialist. However, the plenum resolution also made it clear that Beijing would not emulate Eastern Europe and take the plunge towards a Western-style market economy.

The measures recommended were a compromise between the political needs of the CCP to re-centralise economic powers and revenues on the one hand, and the requirements of the marketplace on the other. While bold strides were taken in areas such as restructuring the state enterprises and the banking system, many local leaders and managers felt after the plenum that their autonomous powers had been truncated.

The thrust of the socialist market economy was well defined by Premier Li Peng in a late October 1993 interview. "While on the one hand, the fundamental status of market mechanisms in the arrangement and distribution of economic [resources] has been stressed, on the other, we also stress that the state will institute macro-level adjustments and control," the conservative leader said. The major difference with the *ancien regime*, he said, was that "in the past we mainly used executive fiats to pursue adjustments and control; now we use more economic means and we have cut down on administrative interference."[104]

In general, however, the Third Plenum had the result of anchoring the country more firmly on to the path of reform. And when the old guard or central planning-oriented cadres were no longer around to look after the "socialist" aspect of the "socialist market economy", the march towards the marketplace would be greatly expedited.

A. The Question of Ownership and Rejuvenation of the State Sector

The boldest step towards liberalisation taken at the plenum was a re-think of perhaps the single most important of the Four Cardinal Principles: "the socialist road", usually interpreted as the fact that the "wholly people-owned sector" remained the mainstay of the economy. The "question of ownership" has been described as the stumbling block to real reform. By late 1993, however, the consensus seemed to be that different kinds of ownership systems, including the private sector, could vie for resplendence.

The resolution of the plenum said: "It is necessary to uphold the principle of taking the publicly-owned sector as the mainstay [of the economy] while striving for a simultaneous development of all economic sectors." However, there was an important rider that while nationwide, state-sector dominance should be maintained, the exact proportion of state ownership "may vary in different places and trades".

On the eve of the plenum, several influential media commentators and economists had come out with arguments that Beijing could be flexible on this score. In a commentary in early November, the *People's Daily* pointed out that the public ownership criterion need only manifest itself in the fact that publicly-held assets enjoyed a "superior position" in the total assets of society. The paper said that different kinds of ownership could hold dominance "in different areas, product sectors and enterprises". Moreover, public ownership could have different incarnations. The party mouthpiece cited the example of joint-stock companies in which the state held shares; or state companies run by managers hired through open competition.[105]

The *Economic Daily* also pointed out in a November commentary: "It is not necessary that public ownership takes a dominant position in every sector." "In quite a few sectors including commerce and the services, it is all right to let different forms of ownership to develop," it continued. The *Economic Daily* went so far as to argue that public ownership was a "means" and not an "end". "The ultimate goal of choosing the public ownership system is to boost productivity. The size of the public sector and how to realise its central role can only be determined by whether it increases productivity." The unspoken corollary of the *Economic Daily*'s argument was that if it were proven that public ownership was a millstone around the neck of productivity, the economy should take bigger steps towards privatisation.[106]

The decision about the change of ownership actually means quasi-privatisation of the state sector, which consists of 1.4 million business units having total assets of 2,000 billion yuan. More than 100,000 of these units suffered losses. Worse, the proportion of money-losing enterprises was much higher in what the Chinese call large- and medium-sized enterprises. One-third of them suffered clear-cut losses and another third would have been in the red had it not been for state subsidies.

Privatisation takes the following forms: outright sale of such units to the private sector or their transformation into joint ventures, limited liability companies and shareholding companies where non-state-owned entities including foreign companies can hold stakes. Even before the plenum, a large number of small-scale state units, especially those in the commercial sector, were auctioned off to private entrepreneurs.

By late 1993, 45 cities had set up "markets for transferring property rights and assets of enterprises". The NCNA reported in mid-November 1993 that 10,000 state enterprises, mostly those of a smaller scale, had been "reinvigorated" through auctions or through a transformation of ownership. In Fujian Province, 1,800 state commercial enterprises and 90 industrial enterprises had by late 1993 been "farmed out" to the private sector. In the city of Quanzhou, 80 per cent of the 381 small-scale state commercial units were "privatised" under the formula of "state ownership; private management".[107]

The auctioning off or management restructuring of large- and medium-sized enterprises, however, was more problematic. There were considerations of ideology, national security and state interests. Obviously, Beijing — or any government for that matter — would have qualms about privatising enterprises deemed vital to the national interest. The plenum resolution indicated that "companies that turn out special-category products and armaments should be held by the state alone".

An equally thorny problem was finding buyers. Even the profitable and efficient state enterprises were saddled with baggage including debt payments as well as welfare, medical and pension benefits for workers. The latter easily took up 30 to 40 per cent of the recurrent expenses of a majority of state concerns. By late 1993, Beijing bureaucrats were still debating whether, in order to make state enterprises more attractive to potential buyers, they should write off their debts or take over the welfare benefits.

At a meeting called by the State Commission for the Reform of the Economic Structure (SCRES) soon after the plenum, Commission Vice-Minister He Guanghui revealed that 100 large- and medium-sized state enterprises had been designated "pilot points" for "the establishment of modern management systems". He said that a "limited number of highly profitable and well-managed enterprises" would become state-owned stock companies. "Other state-owned enterprises in competitive industries will be turned into limited liability companies jointly owned by the state and other legal persons," the vice-minister added.[108]

Other officials and government advisers revealed that scores of the more efficient state companies would be converted into shareholding or joint-stock concerns. The shares would be split among other state concerns, collectives, private companies, and overseas corporations. What is more important, however, was that Beijing had decided that the state need not hold a majority stake.

As the Plenum Resolution said: "What amount of shares in the companies should be suitably held by the state can vary according to the different industries and the different degrees of distribution of the shares." A major restriction was that "the state should have controlling shares in key enterprises in 'backbone' and basic industries". According to Chinese officials and Western businessmen, however, Beijing was by early 1994 ready to lower the state's stake in "non-sensitive" categories of newly formed shareholding companies to just 15 to 20 per cent.[109]

In an apparent attempt to get rid of some of the chronic loss-making state enterprises, Beijing had in late 1993 also opened up hitherto taboo areas for equity participation by overseas companies. They included service sectors such as banking and insurance, relatively sensitive infrastructure projects, airports and airlines, even gold mines. In the latter half of the year, 20 or so companies from countries including the United States, Canada, Australia and South Africa expressed an interest in acquiring stakes in Chinese gold mines. "Gold production has always been a special trade in China and it has been a latecomer in the open-door policy," said Cui Dewen of the State Gold Administration Bureau. "However, the policy for the integration of the Chinese and the world gold markets has already been set."[110]

Liberal cadres and scholars also proposed various ways to turn wholly or partly government-owned units into "Western style corporations". For example, former SCRES vice-minister Gao Shangquan suggested in November 1993 the "corporatisation" of state concerns. Gao, a one-time adviser to Zhao Ziyang, argued that while state companies remained wholly or partly government-owned, such enterprises should be considered independent "legal persons" and should be responsible for their profits and losses. In other words, the shareholders and members of the board of directors, including representatives of state assets, would entrust the management with full autonomy in the running of the company.[111]

Other experts, including member of the CPPCC Standing Committee Li Lang, suggested that the state let government enterprises be "run by the people", that is, privately managed. This again entailed the radical separation of ownership and management. While a certain State Council unit would be charged with overseeing the growth or otherwise of state assets in different government concerns, their actual management would be in the hands of hired managers or private entrepreneurs.[112]

Again, however, Beijing made it clear privatisation would be tried out at a gradual pace. And while on the one hand it seemed eager to get rid of the dinosaurs, the central government was on the other hand decrying the speedy loss of state assets. The drain of state properties and assets was estimated to be 30 billion yuan in 1993. One source of the "drainage" was the large number of companies formed by party and government units as well as cadres. However, as the official *Outlook Weekly* revealed, in their anxiety to attract foreign investment, many central, and especially provincial, cadres had deliberately undervalued state properties.[113]

A set of regulations on the supervision and management of state assets was announced in early 1994 whose major goal was to ensure that the State Council retained control over national assets, including those in shareholding concerns. And the National Bureau for Administering State Assets was beefed up to plug the drainage.[114]

B. Tax Reform and the Recentralisation of Powers: Boosting Beijing's Share of National Income

Tax reforms — especially the establishment of a dual tax system for the centre and the regions — was a major preoccupation of the Third Plenum and economic policy-making in 1993. However, quite a number of foreign analysts doubted whether this "reform" constituted economic liberalisation at least in the Western sense of the word. The basis of this new measure was Beijing's urgent need to re-centralise fiscal power and boost its tax revenues. While this imperative was understandable in the Chinese context, it also had the effect of hurting the reform enthusiasm of localities as well as enterprises.

At least in the eyes of Beijing, beefing up the centre's share of revenue was a key to ensuring that the market economy would remain socialist. Statistics varied as to the extent to which the central treasury's share of national revenue or of the GDP had declined since Deng kicked off his reforms in late 1978. One official estimate was that the centre's share of the GDP declined from 37 per cent at the outset of reform to 19 per cent in 1992. Various projections said in 1993 that if the trend were not reversed, Beijing's slice of the pie could slip to less than 10 per cent by the year 2000. By 1993, the central coffers' share of total national tax revenues had also declined to about 35 per cent.[115]

The major thrust of tax "reform" at the plenum, not surprisingly, was to abrogate the so-called contract financial responsibility system (CFRS) which had held sway since the early 1980s. Under the system, the funds to be surrendered to national coffers varied from region to region: factors taken into consideration included the clout of the local leadership, and more important, the development priorities of Beijing. For example, under Zhao Ziyang, the south-eastern "gold coast" enjoyed unprecedentedly low tax rates because they were Beijing's favoured "growth and high-potential regions". In 1992, out of its tax revenues of 22.2 billion yuan, Guangdong paid 7.45 billion yuan to central coffers. By contrast, Shanghai, which collected 37 billion yuan worth of levies and other incomes in 1992, had to surrender nearly 27 billion yuan to Beijing.[116]

After the plenum, the CFRS was replaced by an assignment or dual-tax system, whereby tax bases would be drawn for the central and for local administrations. By late 1993, Beijing was poised to set up a central tax bureau to collect dues owed the central government, as well as a regional tax bureau, which oversaw tax collection processes for the regional and local authorities.

The Plenum Resolution was nebulous about the division of the spoils. "The categories of taxes required for safeguarding national rights and interests and the exercise of macro-economic control are assigned as central tax," it said. "The main categories of taxes directly related to economic development are assigned as sharing taxes," that is, taxes to be shared by both the central and local authorities. The Resolution added that "the range of items subject to local tax should be broadened to increase local revenue".[117]

As of late 1993, Beijing had reserved for itself 33 kinds of taxes, while 34 categories would fall within the regional net. Categories of central taxes included: customs duties; consumption tax; profits taxes from state enterprises; levies on financial services; duties on liquor and cigarettes. Regional administrations would be entitled to: personal profits taxes; city construction levies; several agriculture-related taxes; and business and profits taxes on local enterprises except those in banking, finance, insurance, mail, electricity, and railway transportation. In addition, there were taxes that would be split between Beijing and the regions. The most important of these were the value-added tax, duties on stock transactions, and taxes on resources. For the first two, the split between the centre and the regions was respectively 75 and 25; and then 50 and 50. In general, richer regions or those that had made the best go of the open-door policy, would be paying the most to Beijing.[118]

The plenum did not indicate how big a slice of the revenue pie Beijing wanted for itself. However, officials made clear that the centre was gunning for a 60 per cent share of total revenue, and that the goal should be attained within three years. Gao Qiang, a senior Finance Ministry official, indicated at the time of the plenum that "financial income directly organised by the centre" would account for about 60 per cent of national income. However, regional administrations would also be able to collect about the same proportion. The reason: aside from taxes and levies that would accrue to the localities, the latter would be entitled to tax transfers and other capital injections from central coffers.[119]

The division of the tax pie represented a major compromise between the *zhongyang* and the localities. The regions, especially provinces along the Gold Coast, were given the guarantee that their tax incomes would not be less than those of 1993. All localities would be entitled to transfer payments from Beijing at least to the year 2000. The number of taxes reserved for the provinces and cities — as well as those that could be shared between the centre and localities — was much more than initially envisaged.[120]

At the same time, both the NPC and the State Council were by late 1993 drafting regulations strictly forbidding individual party and government units

— especially local governments — from spending beyond their budgets. For example, according to the Regulations on the Management of the State Budgets promulgated in late 1993, local administrations would have to abide by severe restrictions on a wide range of spending and purchasing. These included "institutional purchases" of goods ranging from cars to consumer products. Spending on trips abroad, conferences and activities to attract investment was also restricted.[121]

Other aspects of taxation reform also had the purpose of augmenting revenue. For example, it was decided at the plenum that a uniform tax rate — 33 per cent — would from early 1994 be slapped on all kinds of domestic enterprises as well as foreign enterprises that did not qualify for exemptions. Accounting systems for all types of enterprises would also be unified. The eventual goal was for both domestic and foreign-participated concerns to pay the same level of taxes. There was a possibility, however, that at least at the initial stage, individual categories of enterprises would have to up the ante. For example, it was suggested that private enterprises might have to pay up to 35 per cent of profit taxes.[122]

The new, unified tax system meant in practice that the *caizheng baogan* or financial contract responsibility system for enterprises as exemplified by Capital Iron and Steel Works, had been scrapped. In a January 1994 article, the China-run *Wen Wei Po* of Hong Kong quoted an "authoritative figure" as saying that the new system would not spell higher taxes "for the great majority of enterprises". However, with the abolition of the *baogan* system, at least certain types of enterprises would cease to have the wherewithal to retain a bigger portion of their profits.[123]

Chinese economists also expressed worries that while the new taxes on property and stock transaction might curb speculation, they could dampen the enthusiasm of individual entrepreneurship. The unification of the tax rates also deprived local administrations of flexibility. A much-discussed case in point was VAT slapped on real estate, which could be up to 60 per cent. Guangdong and other coastal areas that marketed a large number of properties overseas had tried to lure back customers by making selective remissions to favoured clients. This was resolutely stopped by Finance Minister Li Zhongli, who said in early 1994 that "adjustments made on the tax rates by southern provinces would be rendered null and void".[124]

At the same time, taxation for individuals would be systematised. The initial ceiling for exemption was 800 yuan per month. However, in view of the fact that China already had by early 1993 a million millionaires, higher tax rates of up to 45 per cent would be slapped on top-bracket income earners. They included individual entrepreneurs, certain professionals, and stars in the entertainment business. The kinds of monetary gains that would become taxable increased from six to 11. Important new levies included those to be slapped on property and stock transactions and income from lotteries.[125]

C. Banking Reform and the Restoration of Financial Discipline

Zhu Rongji's lasting legacy could be at least the partial success he had in overhauling the financial system, perhaps the most intractable area of the economy. As we shall see, however, it is not certain whether all the financial reforms mapped out in late 1993 would favour the progress of the market economy.

After Zhu became Governor of the People's Bank of China (PBoC) in early July 1993, he moved swiftly to end the political interference in the money supply. By late that year, it was decided that the nation's financial institutions would be divided into policy banks and commercial banks. The latter would function like similar institutions in the West, meaning loans would be made strictly upon calculations of creditworthiness.

Three policy banks were contemplated for early 1994 to make available funds for sectors and companies that were either favoured by Beijing or that would have difficulty securing loans from the commercial banks. The three were the State Long-term Development Trust Bank, which would finance key state construction projects; the Import and Export Credit Bank, which would provide credit for exports; and the Agriculture Bank, which would ensure finances for what many leaders insisted was the economy's most important sector.[126]

The functions and powers of the PBoC as central bank would be vastly expanded. The main brief of the Bank, as Vice-Governor Chen Yuan explained, was to pursue Western-style monetary policy, especially the control of the money supply and the stabilisation of the currency. After all, a major reason for the runaway money supply in 1993 — and previous junctures of rapid economic expansion — was that powers to augment the money supply were scattered among different PBoC units and the specialist banks. Moreover, politicians in other government departments as well as local administrations had a big say in credit policy.[127]

From early 1994 onwards, only the headquarters of the PBoC would have authority over making loans. This, the authorities explained, was to ensure that politicians, especially regional cadres, would no longer have the wherewithal to interfere with the money supply. Moreover, inter-bank lending would be severely restricted, with the deadline for the settlement of such loans curtailed from three months to three days.[128] As we shall see, however, the recentralisation of credit could stymie the growth of a non-official or private financial system. It could also hurt the ability of quasi-private companies — or those in sectors not favoured by the state — to raise cash.

In currency and foreign-trade reform, the biggest step forward was the unification of the foreign exchange rate in preparation for the eventual convertibility of the yuan. On January 1, 1994, the official exchange rate (US$1 to 5.7 yuan) was abolished in favour of that prevalent in the swap market (US$1 to 8.7 yuan), resulting in a 34 per cent devaluation of the yuan. This was a big step forward for reform in the currency and foreign-trade sector. The yuan would be allowed to float within certain limits. Overseas corporations no longer needed to deal with two exchange rates. Foreign companies which had paid part of their costs or expenses using the official rate could now pay much less.[129]

Domestically, the system of forex dispensation and retainment was abolished. Prior to this reform, state enterprises in the foreign-trade sector had a quota of "cheap" US dollars (meaning US funds exchangeable through the official, not the swap rate) assigned to them by the banks; and they could also retain a portion of forex earnings acquired through exports. From January 1994 onwards, the twin measures were scrapped. The abolition of the quotas of "cheap" US dollars could be interpreted as a step ahead for reform because state enterprises would be rid of a valuable subsidy.

However, the autonomy of business units might also be adversely affected. By early 1994, the State Council had not laid down regulations as to the procedures through which enterprises could secure foreign currencies using the unified exchange rate. Moreover, enterprises were now obliged to immediately sell their forex earnings back to the official banking system.[130] Some analysts feared that enterprises would come up with all sorts of shenanigans to keep their US dollars earnings in "private gold coffers".

Again partly with a view to entering GATT, steps were taken towards the liberalisation of the foreign trade system. For example, the quota system for exports was all but abolished, with the number of commodities that required state export licences cut by about 50 per cent to just 138. The number of companies that had authority to handle foreign trade increased to more than 7,000. Beijing said its eventual goal was doing away with all kinds of state control in this sector. However, as a result of the record US$12.18 billion deficit for 1993, the central government also took strong steps to cut down on imports. For example, Beijing indicated that in early 1994 it hoped both imports and exports for the year would stay at the US$100 billion mark.[131] This "target" led to queries as to whether Beijing was really committed to foreign-trade liberalisation.

D. Price Reform before and after the Third Plenum

Great strides were taken in price reform in 1992 and 1993, to the extent that by late 1993, officials were claiming that in China, the number of commodities whose prices were controlled by the state was less than that in the West. The HKCNA reported in September 1993 that the retail prices of 95 per cent of all commodities had been unfrozen, while in the past, those of 97 per cent of commodities were fixed by the government. 90 per cent of the procurement prices for farm produce had been "opened up". And 85 per cent of the prices of raw materials and producer goods had also been unshackled. The semi-official agency said that in developed countries in the West, some 20 per cent of all prices were controlled by the state.[132]

Beijing decided soon after the Third Plenum that the prices of six major raw materials and farm produce — coal, electricity, natural gas, chemical fertilisers, grain and cotton — would be unfrozen to various extents. For example, the prices of coal and coal products would from January 1994 be entirely determined by the forces of the market. The prices of electricity and the procurement prices of grain and cotton would be raised substantially to reflect market forces, but they would not be totally decontrolled.[133]

While advances had been made to breach the fortress of price reform, Beijing failed to go the distance. The CCP leadership would still take administrative measures to control prices to ensure political and social stability. Thus, the Third Plenum document indicated that the state would "decontrol the prices of competitive commodities and services, and adjust government-set prices for some commodities and services to reasonable levels". Measures would also be taken to abolish the dual-pricing system for producer and factor goods and to "accelerate" the marketisation of their prices. However, such actions would be taken "under the premise of keeping the general price level relatively stable".

In a December 1993 dispatch, HKCNA quoted officials as saying that price changes in the coming few years would be "bearable". The news agency said that the goal of the full marketisation of prices would be reached "within several years". It said that the tolerance of the populace would be a key factor in considering the pace of price reform. "Next year's price reform should keep the level of price rises below the highest level of tolerance in society," the report said.[134]

Events in mid- and late 1993, however, showed that the authorities were willing to scale back price reform — and to re-impose price controls — in order to preserve stability. On both occasions, the clock was turned back because of signs of panic buying in the large cities. For example, in June, Shanghai authorities took steps to contain price rises by selective administrative measures. An NCNA dispatch quoted local officials as saying they would "further strengthen the supervision and management of the prices of commodities and scrutinise the order of market prices". Such steps included the "inspection" of the prices and fees charged by state-owned, collective and private enterprises, as well as joint ventures. Similar policies were adopted by other municipal governments along the coast.[135]

Price reform met a further setback in December 1993 and January 1994 when the prices of grain and other foodstuffs went up by 30 to 40 per cent. Moreover, panic buying in cities ranging from Beijing to Guangzhou took place over big-ticket consumer products including gold jewellery and imported TV sets.[136] At a State Council meeting on December 25, Zhu Rongji took steps to curb the spiral. "Stabilising grain prices and suppressing inflation were the key to smooth reforms next year," he said. National grain stores were obliged to lower prices to levels prescribed by state plans for 1994. Moreover, the prices of 27 major commodities would be stabilised.[137]

By early January, the State Planning Commission had re-imposed price controls by posting guidelines for the prices of rice and other produce. For example, the "recommended standard price" for a kilogram of rice was 1.3 yuan; flour, 1.1 yuan to 1.3 yuan; and 6.4 yuan to 7 yuan for rapeseed oil. In addition, "price ceilings" were fixed for a large number of foodstuffs, commodities and services. These included meat, eggs, vegetables as well as transportation, restaurants, hotels, movies, bathhouses, barber shops, parks and repair shops. Practically all the cities set up or reactivated price monitoring units to check on speculators and hoarders. New regulations for the labelling of prices and their "supervision" were announced in the spring.[138]

VII. The Non-State Sector, 1989-1994

Perhaps nothing illustrated more dramatically the progress of economic reform — and the ultimate hope for the entire modernisation enterprise — than the leaps-and-bounds growth of the private sector. We shall examine the deep freeze that the non-state sector, especially the *getihu* (individual entrepreneurs) and private managers, went through the first couple of years after June 4, leading up to their relatively unbridled development after the Third Plenum of 1993. The political implications of the expansion of the private sector will be discussed in Chapter 6.

By early 1994, there were signs that the state or the "wholly people's owned" sector might soon be displaced as the mainstay of the economy. Statistics in late 1993 showed that wholly people's owned units accounted for 48.4 per cent of the total value of industrial production, as against 38.2 per cent for collectives (business units with both government and private participation, including village and township enterprises), and 13.4 per cent for privately-owned units as well as units with foreign participation.[139]

In such an "advanced" economy as Jiangsu, for example, the non-government sector accounted for 60 per cent of the industrial production.[140] In Guangdong, the proportion between the registered capital of the state-owned sector and that of the non-state-owned sector was 1.7 to 1 in late 1993. In such "quasi-capitalist havens" as Shenzhen, Shishi (Fujian Province), and Wenzhou (Zhejiang), the private sector had become predominant.[141]

As of September 1993, there were 210,000 private enterprises which employed 3.31 million workers. They had a registered capital of more than 50 billion yuan. In 1993, the private sector paid a hefty 20 billion yuan worth of taxes, or 7.8 per cent of industrial and commercial levies nationwide.[142] With the quasi-privatisation of the state sector which started in early 1993, quite a number of private entrepreneurs started buying up small-scale government-owned units. Private concerns also started forming joint ventures with overseas companies, and the first "private multinationals" emerged in 1993.

However, as Zou Jun, the official in charge of private enterprises at the State Industrial and Commercial Bureau, said in late 1993, "the development of the private economy is far from enough". Zou revealed that in terms of numbers, total employees and registered assets, the private sector was respectively just 25 per cent, 1.1 per cent and 0.8 per cent that of the state and collective sectors combined.[143]

That, at least until 1991, the post-Zhao leadership was much less enthusiastic about the private sector is evident if we compare the 13th Party Congress document and the resolution of the Seventh Plenum of the 13th Committee. The 13th Party Congress report spoke glowingly of the contributions of the neophyte "red capitalists". "Practice has shown that a considerable degree of the development of the private economy is beneficial to speeding up production, enlivening the market and broadening employment," the document said. It added: "At the present moment, economic elements other than those of full public ownership are not over-developed but are far from sufficient." [144]

The seventh Central Committee plenum of 1990 agreed that Beijing should "develop the beneficial, supplementary functions that the individual, private or other economies provide for the public economy". In other words, activities of the private sector not deemed "beneficial" would be restricted. Indeed, the Proposal for the Eighth Five-Year Plan and the Ten-Year Blueprint particularly stressed the need to "strengthen the correct management of and guidance over" the non-government-run sectors.[145]

By the end of 1991, Beijing was again warming to the private entrepreneurs, who were regarded as "honest workers of socialism". And steps were made to convert state companies to joint-stock concerns. However, there seemed little doubt that in the minds of Li Peng and fellow central planners, the private sector was tolerated because it helped to ensure the longer-term viability of the public sector. As Li put it in a meeting on economic reform in March 1991, the experiments with shareholding companies should be conducted with the aim of "consolidating the socialist ownership system".[146]

A. War against the Private Sector, 1989-1991

The split personality of economic policy-makers after June 4, 1989, was evidenced by their ambivalent attitude towards the private sector. There was a general fear that the "red capitalists" would collude with the bourgeois-liberal elements in the party and government to demand political liberalisation, and to bring about "peaceful evolution". Premier Li Peng and other party elders issued internal documents warning that many dissidents had gone into business in the coastal economic zones — and that they were biding their time for a second democracy movement (see Chapter 6).[147]

Moreover, the size of the practitioners of the non-state-owned sector became too big for the comfort of the orthodox Communists. By the end of 1990, there were already 98,141 private concerns, which employed around 1.7 million workers. Their registered assets amounted to 9.52 billion yuan, and their total value of industrial production was a staggering 12.18 billion yuan.[148]

Orthodox planners also had reservations about the speedy growth of village and township enterprises (VTEs). While VTEs were in most instances "joint ventures" between households and local party or government units, they were products of private initiative rather than the "superiority of socialism". The value of industrial production of VTEs was estimated at 1.1 trillion yuan in 1991, or 23.3 per cent over that of 1990. This meant that these enterprises already accounted for 30 per cent of the country's total industrial — and 60 per cent of agricultural — production. Experts predicted that by the end of the century, VTEs would "evenly split up the sky" with the state sector.[149]

In the first year after Tiananmen Square, Beijing adopted measures to cramp the private sector. This was despite the fact that the policy of allowing non-government sectors to "supplement" the public sector was written into major charters like the Political Report of the 13th Party Congress. The case against the "red capitalists" was adequately made in a mid-1991 commentary by the quasi-official China News Service. CNS said China could not accept the theories of Nobel Laureate Milton Friedman, that a free-market economy with private ownership would be the country's panacea. Specifically, privatisation would create unbalanced development and bring about social instability. CNS said more and more economists had come to see that sole reliance on the market could not solve economic ills.

"People have to eat, get clothing and survive," CNS said. "As resources are limited and we want to provide as many jobs as possible, we have to give five people the job that can be done by three, and let five people share the food for three." The official news agency claimed that at least 30 million rural workers would lose their jobs if China privatised its enterprises. It also contended that if land were allowed to be freely traded on the market, at least 200 million farmers would lose their plots in ten years.[150]

Other State Council bureaucrats argued that VTEs, being not subjected to government fiat, had spoiled the state plan and posed unfair competition to state-run enterprises. As Li Peng pointed out in September 1989: "Rural enterprises must not fight for energy and raw materials" with government ones.[151] Moreover, VTEs and *getihu* concerns were attacked for being shady and unethical players in the economy. In another dispatch, CNS quoted officials as saying that private-sector concerns "evade taxes; take part in speculation and wheeling and dealing; monopolise markets and otherwise break up the order of circulation; and they [excessively] raise prices". And in a November 1989 issue, the *People's Daily* criticised individual entrepreneurs for crimes and activities including "having excessively high incomes, lacking legal concepts, cornering markets, and cheating customers".[152]

In the first year after June 4, a sizable number of VTEs and *getihu* units, including those in prosperous Jiangsu, were forced to close. The major reason: they were denied access to bank loans and raw materials. Uncertain about state policy, red capitalists who had already made their fortunes simply sold out. The money was then remitted to Hong Kong and overseas, or used for such conspicuous consumption as buying foreign passports and sending their children to study overseas.[153]

Various State Council departments were by late 1989 drafting long-term plans to constrict the private sector. For example, Ren Linzhong, Chief of the State Industrial and Commercial Bureau, said in October 1989 that Beijing was readying a set of rules specifying the kinds of trade from which *getihus* would be barred. Ren indicated various local administrations should determine the number of private companies that should be allowed in each product or service category. "Tax departments in various places should strengthen tax collection to relieve the contradictions of inequality in the distribution of income," he said.[154]

The State Council was in late 1989 drawing up a three-year programme to "cure and rectify" privately-held concerns. This would set the ceiling for the growth of the non-government-owned sector as well as put limits on the investment funds available to them. For example, in the two years before the June 4 crisis, the industrial production value of *getihu* and other private enterprises had expanded by 30 per cent. The rate would henceforth be restricted to at most 20 per cent. In actual fact, owing to difficulties in securing raw material and funds, the growth rate of the private sector was already down to 20.8 per cent in the first half of 1989.[155]

Capital construction in the private sector would be contained to 20 billion yuan a year. The planners were complaining that in 1987 and 1988, fixed-assets investments had already breached the 40 billion yuan mark, contributing to inflation and shortage of raw material. The Hong Kong-based left-wing journal, the *Economic Reporter*, quoted an official from the Agriculture Ministry as saying that the growth rate of the private business units "must be congruous with that of the state-owned and agricultural sectors".[156]

B. The Self-Redemption of the Red Capitalists, 1991-1993

The bulk of these strictures were never carried out. By early 1991, the CCP seemed ready to recognise fully the legitimacy of private-sector practitioners. At the National People's Congress in 1991, Premier Li confirmed that private entrepreneurs were "honest, socialist labourers". "They [non-government sectors] are beneficial additions to the publicly-owned economy of Chinese socialism," Li said. "The Eighth Five-Year Plan and Ten-Year Economic Blueprint have settled this point." The premier added that many operators of the individual economy were "patriotic" and that they had socialist awareness. "While there are still illegal elements, the majority are honest socialist labourers," he said.[157]

Bo Yibo, perhaps the elder closest to Deng Xiaoping, also went out of his way to allay the fears of the private entrepreneurs. "Some *getihu* workers and householders consider themselves 'third class' citizens," he told 500 private entrepreneurs in April 1991. "Their hearts are not at rest and they have fears." The then vice-chairman of the Central Advisory Commission said he could assure the red capitalists by saying they were definitely not third-class citizens. "The policy adopted by the central authorities about the co-existence of various types of ownership will not change over a considerably long period of time," he added. "The development of the individual economy suits the present needs of national conditions and are welcomed by the people. The individual economy can have even further development."[158]

By late 1991, the State Council had drafted the country's first regulation affirming in detail the status of private entrepreneurs. The red capitalists were formally recognised as "management workers" and as such entitled to the "full rights accorded citizens of the socialist state". The regulation spelled out that the business rights of private-sector practitioners would be protected. For example, it said: "The rate of their profits should not be less than the interest rates offered by banks."[159]

In a briefing for the nation's private entrepreneurs in early 1992, the nation's premier red capitalist, Rong Yiren, said that a recent Central Committee document had re-affirmed the "long-term existence" of the non-state economy. Rong, who headed China International Trust and Investment Corp until his elevation to the state vice-presidency in March 1993, said the private sector would "continue to be the beneficial supplement to the public sector, and that it would exist and be developed over a considerably long historical period". Vice-Premier Tian Jiyun told the same audience that the CCP's policy in the 1950s of trying to "reform" red capitalists would not be repeated. "We will try to unite the heads of private enterprises," he said. "We will help, guide, and educate them."[160]

By late 1991, party and government leaders seemed to be going out of their way to reassure the "red capitalists", especially the heads of VTEs. Beijing was, of course, bowing to the reality that private-sector enterprises had significantly outperformed their government counterparts. Moreover, they provided employment to the estimated 150 million farmers who would be displaced from traditional agriculture jobs by the mid-1990s. And non-state units accounted for more than a quarter of the foreign exchange earned by the entire industrial sector.

Even by late 1991, however, private-sector practitioners were still subjected to political discrimination of one kind or another. The rule barring "red capitalists" from CCP membership, first instituted in late 1989, seemed to be holding by early 1992. And party cadres and members who wanted to run businesses of their own were subjected to severe restrictions.[161]

C. The Private Sector After the Third Plenum of 1993

While the Third Plenum of the 14th Central Committee did not spell out a clear-cut policy towards the private sector, it practically administered a *coup de grâce* to the state sector by urging a "simultaneous development of all economic sectors". As the semi-official Hong Kong China News Agency pointed out in a commentary, the Third Plenum resolution had already breached "the palpable and unpalpable limits being put on the private sector". "The plenum has not laid down the proportions for the development for the various sectors," the commentary said, adding it was a "necessary trend" for the state and the private sectors to have an "organic synthesis".[162]

Just before the plenum opened, several well-known politicians and academics had called for the further development and protection of the private sector. While meeting a delegation of Hong Kong businessman, CPPCC Chairman Li Ruihuan praised the contributions of the non-state-owned sector. "A large number of facts have shown that the healthy development of the non-state-owned sector has a very important significance for rendering the economy prosperous and the market active, satisfying the daily needs of the people, and providing employment."[163]

Two noted scholars Xiao Zhuoji and Wang Liming lobbied for specific laws to protect private properties. Xiao, of Beijing University, called for a revision of the constitution to ensure the sanctity of private property. "The protection of private property by the state charter would provide assurance to private entrepreneurs," he said. Professor Xiao added, somewhat tongue in cheek, that if the policy of the CCP remained unchanged, the private economy would exist for at least another 100 years. Professor Wang, of the People's University, said the protection of private property was beneficial towards "encouraging exchanges [of commodities], developing markets, and encouraging fair competition and fair trading".[164]

At the same time, the central government pledged in late 1993 to boost investment in VTEs, a key component of the non-state-owned sector. Many VTEs had by 1993 become shareholding concerns whose major investors were households instead of party or government units. A late 1993 report in Hong Kong's *Wen Wei Po* said Beijing would commit an annual sum of 10 billion yuan to VTEs up to the year 2000, by which time it was anticipated that they would take up half the national economy and employ 170 million workers.[165] As we saw in Section IV, a pivotal contribution of the Third Plenum was to give a big push for the development of shareholding companies.

It is also important to note, however, that the private sector still suffered from inequality and discrimination. Firstly, the state banking system still favoured government concerns and collectives more than *getihu* or private companies. With the partial demise of the "underground banking system" in mid-1993, the cash flow of those private concerns which could not attract foreign investment became a serious problem. Secondly, in spite of new quasi-private chambers of commerce being set up in 1992 and 1993, private entrepreneurs did not have viable institutions through which they could lobby for economic and political rights from Beijing (see Chapter 6).[166]

D. The "Shareholding Economy", 1989-1994

(i) The Growth of the Shareholding System

A widely recommended mechanism for privatising state concerns was turning them into shareholding or joint-stock companies. Theorists working for Zhao Ziyang had by mid-1980s vigorously pushed for a "shareholding economy". They pointed out it was the only way to resolve the "ownership question" through radically severing the links between government and business.

Experiments with stocks and shares did not go very far under Zhao and were stopped soon after June 4. However, by mid-1991, liberal academics like Li Yining of Beijing University had revived the debate about ownership and the shareholding system. Li, sometimes known as the guru of the stock system, argued in an article in *Economic Daily* that Beijing should "develop the securities market as a way of freeing itself from the current financial predicament". Li said the shareholding system would promote the efficiency of enterprises and help increase government revenue. The liberal theorist added that a security market would also facilitate price reform and make it easier for ailing enterprises to be absorbed by more robust ones.[167]

On a theoretical level, a consensus had emerged by early 1991 that the shareholding system might be a "pro-market" alternative to the contract financial responsibility system. In an article in January 1991, the *China Daily* quoted a survey of the opinion of key entrepreneurs in Beijing, Shanghai, Liaoning, Hubei and Guangdong. The conclusion was that the CFRS was no longer an adequate reform tool because it had "failed to achieve its main goals of increasing the financial revenue and reducing the losses [of state units] or increasing their productivity". The official paper quoted Li Yining as saying the stock system was called for because enterprises were too closely linked to the government and "were unable to operate independently".[168]

The support for a stock economy seemed to be growing even among more official economists. A late 1991 survey among experts and social scientists who worked for direct subsidiaries of the State Council indicated 59.2 per cent favoured using the shareholding system to change the management of state concerns. Some 95.7 per cent of these experts thought that experiments with stock companies should be expanded and expedited.[169]

In terms of action, however, the pace of the conversion of state companies into stock units was cautious. The "stock economy" got a mere half a sentence in the Outlines for the Eighth Five-Year Plan and the Ten-Year Economic Blueprint released in January 1991. The document merely said that "experimental points" in promoting the shareholding system would continue to be established. The *China Daily* quoted Li Peng as saying that "the shareholding system, based on public ownership, can be tried out in selected places", most likely in open cities along the coast. The premier warned that the issuing of stocks and bonds "must take place under certain conditions and be restricted to a certain scale".[170]

It was not until mid-1991 that individual ministries and sectors began sounding more bullish on the stock economy. The most positive assessment was made in the "Main Points on the Reform of the Economic Structure in 1991", which was passed by the SCREC in June 1991. The document said under the general principle of public ownership remaining the bulwark of the economy, the number and sizes of stock companies should be "steadily" expanded. Three types of stock concerns — with shares being held by companies, by workers or by ordinary citizens — could be developed at the same time.[171]

By early 1992, it was in the coastal enclaves — and among relatively small-scale enterprises — that the shareholding system had seen its best development. A case in point is Wenzhou in Zhejiang Province, long known as "little Hong Kong". Its unorthodox practice of encouraging farmers and townsfolk to form small joint-stock companies had received official endorsement. By the end of 1990, the number of stock concerns in Wenzhou rose to 15,000, and they accounted for 70 per cent of the total number of rural enterprises. Some 12,000 of the stock companies were manufacturing units. They boasted an annual output value of 3.1 billion yuan, representing 35 per cent of the city's total industrial output value.

In May 1991, the Agriculture Ministry promulgated the country's first set of "Contemporary Regulations on Farmers' Joint Stock Enterprises", which were based on the "Wenzhou experience". The regulations stated that the joint-stock rural enterprise was a "new kind of socialist collective economy of the working people. It is an important component of rural enterprises." Party boss of Wenzhou, Liu Xirong, spoke in praise of the practice, saying that "compared with household-based industries, the shareholding system has explicit co-operative and social characteristics." "It is a new kind of socialist co-operative economy that should be protected and be further developed," he added.[172]

Partly in response to efforts by the government to "reinvigorate state enterprises", a sizeable number of business units along the coastal belt had by early 1992 been turned into stock companies. Cities and provinces which were pacesetters in the stock economy included Guangzhou, Shenzhen, Zhuhai, Shanghai and Hainan Province. However, in most instances, less than 50 per cent of the assets and equities of the companies could be openly transacted — and the issues were only available to employees of the concerns. And as we shall in the following section, barely a handful of companies had permission to be listed on the country's two stock exchanges.

It was not until December 19, 1990, that the Shanghai Stock Exchange officially opened for business. Trading was limited to 30 issues, mostly bonds. Only eight were corporate stocks, 1.6 billion yuan worth of which was transacted in 1991. The Shenzhen counterpart, which had unofficially opened for business in late 1990, was inaugurated in June 1991. Initially, only six types of corporate stocks were listed. However, by late 1991, Beijing had given authorisation to the Shanghai and Shenzhen facilities to take on respectively 18 and 17 types of issues in 1992.[173]

At the opening ceremony of the Shenzhen bourse, then acting governor of Guangdong Zhu Senlin said the "improved performance" of enterprises which had adopted the shareholding system proved its success. A Shenzhen official said he expected 2.04 billion yuan worth of shares to be traded by the end of

1991. In 1992, a selected few companies in Shanghai and Shenzhen were also allowed to issue "B shares" for foreign investors.[174]

Up to 1992, however, senior bureaucrats were adamant about restricting the scope of experiments with stocks and shares. In mid-1990, senior economist Liu Hongyu, then SCRES vice-minister, pointed out that the "key step in China's financial reform is the development of the security market". However, he went on to say that the scheme should be limited only to experiments in Shanghai and Shenzhen. Moreover, Liu was actually talking more in terms of a bond market, and he cautioned against undue speculation.

In a dispatch in mid-1990, the China News Service quoted Liu as warning against the massive issuance of stocks and shares as well as their free trading: "As for the issuing of stocks, the important thing for setting up a bond market is to make sure that the rules and regulations are in place for solving the problems of ownership and market operations and for maintaining investors' interests." CNS cited other official sources as saying that the "government-established securities market will be a bond market, dealing mainly in state bonds, although there would also be several other kinds of bonds handled, such as enterprise, financial and construction bonds."[175]

Li Peng, who had given his grudging approval to the Shenzhen bourse, tried to teach its wheeling-dealing brokers how to run a "socialist stock exchange" when he visited the facility in October 1991. "According to the practice of capitalist countries, the stock exchange brings with it a high degree of speculation," Li said. "We must prevent speculative activities."[176]

The message was repeated when the premier toured the Shanghai bourse in December the same year. "The trading of securities is new to China and we need to test it out in pilot areas," he said. "We must boost macro-economic guidance and adjustment. We must prevent massive speculation as well as the shortcoming of [stocks] being concentrated in the hands of a minority of people. We must also prevent big swings in prices in such a way that they would no longer reflect the worth of the stocks." Upon leaving the Shanghai facility, he inscribed: "The trading of securities is to serve socialist economic construction." Translation: no capitalist goings-on will be allowed.[177]

(ii) The Shareholding Economy after the Third Plenum of 1993

A significant leap forward had been taken by the "stock economy" by the end of 1993, when the number of shareholding corporations reached 3,800. In the latter half of that year, almost one shareholding company was born every week. Only a minority of these new entities was officially "floated" as most of the stocks were held either by the state, other legal persons, or workers. Beijing did not allow these three categories of stocks to be freely traded, although, as we shall see, there was a thriving market for shares theoretically restricted to employees of the enterprises concerned.

By late 1993, 192 kinds of A shares and 38 B shares were listed on the Shanghai and the Shenzhen bourses, compared with 52 A shares and 18 B shares for 1992. The A-share transactions for Shanghai and Shenzhen in the first ten months of 1993 were respectively 325.8 billion yuan and 99.27 billion yuan. Equally significant, the ambition of a number of stock conglomerates to go global had been realised. In 1993, nine major state corporations were permitted to issue so-called H shares in Hong Kong. The number of H shares would increase by 15 in 1994. Several types of Chinese stocks were also listed on American and European bourses in 1993.[178]

In spite of the fillip given by the Third Plenum, there were indications Beijing would continue to toe a cautious line on the shareholding question. A relatively paltry 5 billion yuan worth of stocks were sold to the public in the year. The quota for 1994 — 5.5 billion yuan — was only slightly higher. SCREC Vice-Minister Hong Hu pointed out in late 1993 that the stock system "was still at an experimental stage and it would not be implemented on a large scale".[179]

The State Council was also cautious on the public listing of stock companies. It was estimated that in 1994, no more than three shareholding companies in each province or major city could be listed in Shenzhen or Shanghai.[180] An unpublicised document of the watchdog State Securities Supervision and Management Commission indicated that Beijing would observe a "product sliding policy" when giving permission to shareholding units to be listed on the two exchanges. Stock companies in sectors including energy, transport, and raw materials would have priority in listing privileges, while applications from units in the real estate and financial sector would be put on the back-burner.[181]

Beijing's apparent footdragging did not prevent coastal cities from following in the footsteps of Shenzhen by trying to steal a march on the central authorities and set up operations even before the official green light was received. By 1992 and 1993, several major cities were lobbying to open the third bourse. They included Guangzhou, Xiamen, Tianjin, Wuhan, Hainan and Shenyang. In early 1992, the then Vice-Mayor of Guangzhou, Lei Yu, told foreign businessmen and newsmen that his city would "definitely" be chosen. And Hainan officials were disciplined for trying to start an illegal stock-trading facility.[182]

By late 1994, Beijing had no intention of setting up a third stock exchange. With computerisation and foreign techniques, however, brokers and *gumin* ("stocks-crazed investors or speculators") in practically all cities could hook up with the two bourses. The exponential growth of the "stocks speculation industry" showed beyond a doubt that the profit motive had not only overwhelmed official parameters but rendered them quite irrelevant.

By mid-1993, there were an estimated 2,600 brokerages and 69,400 "individual brokers", only 24,400 of whom were registered. About half the *getihu* brokers were farmers or jobless urban residents, and 38 per cent of them retirees or people who had newly quit their jobs.[183] Official estimates put the *gumin* population at the end of 1993 at 25 million, up from 2.1 million in 1992. Guangzhou alone boasted 800,000 fervent traders. About 10,000 Chinese joined the ranks of the *gumin* every day.[184]

The Shenzhen incidents of November 1991 and August 1982 were showcases of *gumin* irrationalism — and in general, the chaotic nature of the "primitive stage of capitalism". However, they also illustrated full well that the authorities could only channel but not stop the mass enthusiasm for taking part in the shareholding economy.

On November 10, 1991, an estimated 500,000 people, many of whom from neighbouring counties, flocked to the SEZ and lined the streets the night before the Shenzhen bourse put out applications for 11 types of securities. The municipality deployed 3,000 police and People's Armed Police to maintain order. The issues that day, worth around 200 million yuan, would later be distributed to the half a million would-be shareholders by lottery. The success rate: a mere 3.6 per cent. Fortunately, no serious injuries among overzealous *gumin* were reported. [185]

Then in August 1992 came the notorious Shenzhen stocks scandal, which also witnessed the first major rioting since the democracy movement of 1989. On August 10, at least 10,000 residents in the SEZ and from nearby counties converged on the streets to vent their anger at the corruption and gross government inefficiently over the sale of the application forms for 10 new issues. The day before, more than half a million would-be *gumin* had lined up before the sales outlets for the "lotteries". Tear gas cannon were fired, and 12 "ruffians" arrested. An investigation report published in December 1992 showed more than 4,000 municipal employees were implicated for graft and for pocketing the application forms themselves.[186]

Officially, speculative activities were limited to the 192 stocks listed on the two exchanges. However, *gumin* and brokers alike were making fortunes out of the sale and resale of stocks that were legally restricted to employees of the issuing companies. The relative backwater of Sichuan provided the best example of *gumin* fever boiling over. This is despite the fact that 80 per cent of the issues of a typical Sichuan shareholding company were classified as state or legal-person stocks, meaning they could not be traded.

In places including Chengdu, Chongqing and Leshan (dubbed the "biggest underground stock market" in China), nearly 100 types of stocks were "traded". In mid-1993, transaction of "black stocks" in Leshan ran into several hundreds of millions of yuan everyday. Most surprisingly, the Vice-Mayor of the medium-sized city claimed in an interview with the Hong Kong press that such activities were sanctioned by the state and he would at most "offer guidance" to the *gumin*.[187] By late 1993, Stocks guru Li Yining was advocating the establishment of official stocks transaction centres outside the bourses to give *gumin* who did not have access to a broker a legal alternative to black-market trading.[188]

By early 1994, it was clear that while Beijing still wanted to keep the "shareholding economy" on a tight leash, market forces and the profit motive were gaining the upper hand. The State Council indicated the value of stocks and shares to be issued in 1994 would be the same as 1993, or 5.5 billion yuan. And as the Securities Law went through its final drafts at the NPC, there were clear-cut indications that Beijing would not bow to widespread demands from gumin and allow state-held stocks or shares held be legal persons to be traded. However, judging by the explosion of stocks-crazed speculators — and of black-market transactions — it seemed apparent the floodgates could not be held back for long.[189]

VIII. The Challenge of the Regions, 1989-1994

The struggle between the *zhongyang* ("the centre") and the localities will likely top the economic and the political agenda throughout the 1990s. In the following sections, we will examine roughly three phases: first, the period of the aggressive reining in of centrifugal forces from 1989 to the end of 1991; second, the liberalising effect of the *nanxun* talks; and third, efforts at recentralisation in the latter half of 1993. By early 1994, it was obvious that contradictions between Beijing and the local "warlords" had not been resolved, and that the tug-of-war would intensify in the mid-1990s.

In the first half of the 1989-1994 period, it was primarily a contradiction between Beijing and the Gold Coast, or the southeast belt favoured by Zhao Ziyang and his liberal faction. Soon afterwards, however, it became a matter of Beijing against everybody else as the open-door policy spread to practically all of China, and various localities were gunning for autonomy at the expense of the central government. The difficulty the State Council encountered in putting together the dual tax system in late 1993 illustrated the inexorable decline of central power.

A. The Comprehensive Open-Door Policy vs. the Coastal Strategy

Immediately after the June 4 crisis, the impulse of the hardline leadership was to take back powers from the regions, especially the southeast quasi-capitalist belt. The three-year austerity programme that started in late 1988 was still very much in effect. There were political imperatives as well. *Nouveaux riches* areas such as Guangdong and Hainan threatened to become a law unto themselves. Guangdong, and to an extent, Fujian and Hainan, were not vocally supportive of the "resolute action" taken by the Centre to use military force to crush the pro-democracy movement. State Council bureaucrats were also critical of the Gold Coast for spawning dislocations in the economy such as inflation.[190]

In early 1990, Beijing announced three modifications to its open-door policy and its regional development strategy. First, as we saw in Section One, the "products sliding policy" — the state giving priority to certain sectors and product lines — would replace the "geographical sliding policy". Second, instead of favouring the southeast coast in terms of resource allocation and tax privileges, Beijing was gearing towards "overall and comprehensive development". This meant that all parts of the country that had the qualifications would have equal access to state investment as well as "special policies" to attract foreign investment. Third, Shanghai and its Pudong zone seemed to have displaced the southeast "Gold Coast" as the beachhead for the open-door policy in the 1990s.

However, as the "comprehensive" open-door policy ran its course, different parts of China — and not just Guangdong — were demanding more autonomy. Regional economic blocs, such as the "Southwest Cabal" consisting of Guangxi, Yunnan, Guizhou, Sichuan, Tibet and Hainan, were gaining influence and displaying signs of economic "warlordism".

It also transpired that the southeast, principally Guangdong and the zones, had weathered its post-Tiananmen Square setbacks very well. Up to late 1992, actual investment that had poured into Shanghai and Pudong were not substantial compared with Guangdong. Especially in the first two years after June 4, 1989, the southeast belt was helped by investment from Hong Kong — and was less affected by sanctions imposed by the West. And when Beijing pronounced in late 1991 an official end to the three-year retrenchment policy, it was obliged to again allow Guangdong, Hainan and their open cities to go on with their market experiments. Provided it did not require new cash injections from the central government, the Gold Coast could continue to spearhead the country's reform and open-door policy.

The focus of the "new open door" as introduced after the June 4 massacre was a multi-faceted opening to the outside world: not just the southeast coast but other parts of China could benefit from special policies to attract foreign capital. It was to some extent a bid for "egalitarianism": a response to the complaints of the heartland and other backwater provinces that they had been left out. The more "equitable" open-door policy was also a revision of Zhao's famous "trickle-down" theory: that as the eastern sector of the country gets developed, the benefits will gradually spill over, first to the central provinces and then to the impoverished west.

In an emotional address to the press in early 1990, the then vice-minister of the State Nationalities Affairs Commission, Jiang Jiafu, urged Beijing to abolish the so-called "East-Centre-West Strategy". "We are in favour of the strategy of balanced development, symbiotic links between east and west, and getting rich at the same time," said Jiang, who is a member of the Zhuang minority. "Already, areas inhabited by minority peoples have become the 'Third World' of China. If we proceed with the East-Centre-West Strategy, the discrepancy between the minority areas and the rich areas along the coast will become more pronounced."[191]

Even Xiang Nan, the former party boss of Fujian and a notable liberal, lobbied for a "balanced development strategy" in his capacity as President of the Chinese Foundation for Helping Poor Regions. He called on the developed coastal regions to show more concern for impoverished districts. "From now on, the focus for helping the poor should be on central and Western China, especially areas in the west," he said. "Without the support of the east, it will be difficult for western areas to shed their poverty. Conversely, when the west is developed, it will also support the development of the east."[192]

The new strategy also had political overtones. In the wake of the dissolution of the Soviet Union, Beijing had to use economic development to maintain its hold over the potentially restive minority peoples, the denizens of China's "Third World". The new dispensation was specially aimed at Uighurs in Xinjiang and Mongolians in Inner Mongolia. At a national conference on minority nationalities held in early 1992, Jiang Zemin announced that economic development in areas inhabited by the minorities would be expedited. "Development in areas with minority peoples should gradually be commensurate with national development," Jiang said, adding that favourable policies towards these regions would be boosted.[193]

A key component of the new developmental strategy was to spur economic growth of the northeastern, southwestern, and northwestern parts of China by promoting their links with the international marketplace. To this effect, three "open belts" along the border were set up to facilitate commerce and other economic ties with neighbouring countries and regions. The new dispensations included more autonomy for these outlying areas to engage in border trade, permission for which was first given in early 1991. Initially, border regions could only sell locally made products. Moreover, only a relatively few designated foreign-trade companies in these localities could engage in international commerce. The restrictions were lifted for areas bordering Yunnan, Burma and the Commonwealth of Independent States.[194]

The Northeast Zone incorporates the northern and northeastern provinces of Heilongjiang, Jilin, Liaoning and Inner Mongolia. They would do business mainly with neighbours such as Russia, North Korea and Mongolia. By 1991, the former USSR had become China's fifth largest trading partner after Hong Kong, Japan, the United States and Germany. The priority Beijing put on commerce with its giant neighbour was evidenced by the fact that in 1991, China extended to the Soviet Union commodity loans worth SFr150 million. Trade and other business ties with the former Soviet Union did not seem to have been affected by the failed coup in August 1991 and the dissolution of the USSR. Pilot zones for trade with Russia such as Heihe and Suifenhe in Heilongjiang had become boom towns by early 1992.[195]

The Northwest Zone was centred upon the Xinjiang Autonomous Region, which had a large concentration of Muslim Uighurs. Because of religious and cultural affinities, Xinjiang and neighbouring Qinghai could become part of the envisaged Islam Economic Circle, made up of Pakistan, the Muslim republics of the former USSR and other Near East nations. The future of the Northwest Zone, however, was dealt a body blow by the events in the Soviet Union. By late 1991, one of Beijing's priorities for the northwest was to curb potentially destabilising relationships between the Uighurs and their brethren in Kazakhstan and Turkey. [196]

The Southwest Zone envisaged hook-ups between such provinces as Yunnan, Guangxi, Sichuan, Guizhou, and Hainan on the one hand, and countries including Burma, Vietnam, Laos, Thailand, India, Nepal and Bangladesh, on the other. The Chinese also started work on the so-called Southwest Continental Bridge, which links Southwest China to other parts of Asia. The "bridge" comprises a railway system (Fangcheng in Guangxi, Nanning, Kunming and Burma), a highway system (between Yunnan and Burma), and a waterway (Lancan River and Mekong River).[197]

Partly because of the political consequences of the break-up of the USSR, the Southwest Zone emerged in early 1992 with the most potential. As top non-CCP politician and sociologist Professor Fei Xiaotong put it: "The international market for western China has more potential than the east. The outward-oriented economy of eastern China might be blocked by Japan, Hong Kong and the Asian dragons. Yet China has a degree of superiority when it thrusts westwards into Central Asia, West Asia, and the Middle East."[198]

By late 1992, an inchoate regionalism seemed to have taken hold in the Southwest Zone. In an apparent reversal of the "trade wars" that had erupted because of inter-provincial blockades set up in the late 1980s, members of this new bloc seemed ready to link their fates together. For example, they demonstrated a willingness to co-ordinate their investment and foreign-trade policies — and to band together to press for concessions from Beijing.

Since late 1990, leaders of the five provinces — and the 50-odd cities in the region — began holding Economic Co-ordination Meetings regularly. At one such conclave in September 1991, the local chieftains talked about the revival of the Southern Silk Road. As then Guizhou party boss Liu Zhengwei saw it, the goal of the co-operation among the five provinces was to "hack out a path" to southwest Asia. "The southwest areas [of China] should boost internal union in order to promote a comprehensive [open-door] policy," said then vice-mayor of Chengdu, Zhu Yongming. "We must implement favourable policies that will be as attractive as those along the [southeast] coast." In the same vein, the Vice-Governor of Sichuan, Ma Lin, envisaged the formation of a "southwest common market".[199]

By late 1991, early signs of a "common market" had emerged. For example, in the year ending October 1991, 55 cities in the area concluded more than 200 co-production and other economic agreements, 150 of which had started operations. These hook-ups were expected to generate GDP measuring more than 300 million yuan. The cities had also pooled funds or shared finances totalling 1.2 billion yuan.[200]

In late 1993, leaders of the five provinces, plus those of the three west Guangdong cities of Zhanjiang, Mouming and Zhaoqing announced China's first regional development blueprint. The "common market" would pool resources for such goals as exploiting hydro-electric power, mining, building transport networks, and developing tourism. The most eye-catching of their co-operative ventures was the construction of a 2,132-kilometre pipeline for transporting oil and gas to this energy-short area. The cost of 4.26 billion yuan would be borne by the provinces as well as overseas investors.[201]

By the time Deng Xiaoping embarked on his *nanxun* and Central Committee Document No. 4 was promulgated, the consensus for a comprehensive, open-door gameplan had been reached. The policy had also transcended the preoccupation of constricting Guangdong. The next question for relations between Beijing and the regions became whether the "warlords" would gang up on the *zhongyang*.

B. Shanghai and Pudong: An Emergent "Warlord" Zone?

The fast-paced development of Shanghai — and especially the new zone of Pudong — represented Deng Xiaoping's determination to engineer a "second wave" of reform in spite of the setback of the Tiananmen Square tragedy. It was a manifestation of his hope, expressed in the mid-1980s, that there would be a "string of new Hong Kongs" along the coast. And it is a tribute to Deng's power and stubbornness that he overcame the desire of conservative patriarch Chen Yun, who is a native of Shanghai, to turn Pudong into a "socialist zone".

According to Chen's thinking, Pudong would be subjected to tighter central control. And while it would make use of investment from Western countries, it would not display the signs of quasi-capitalism or centrifugalism Shenzhen did.

The "birth" of Pudong and the rejuvenation of Shanghai was also a classic case of the struggle between Beijing and the regions. Even given Deng's patronage and Shanghai's inherent strengths, Pudong had a hard time winning concessions from Beijing. The idea of the zone was raised in the early 1980s by former mayor Wang Daohan. Perhaps reflecting his relative mediocrity, the scheme did not go very far when Jiang Zemin was party secretary and mayor of the city in the mid-1980s. It would be simplistic to give the credit of Pudong to Zhu Rongji. However, the former Shanghai mayor did try hard to preserve the spirit of reform in Shanghai after the June 4 crackdown.[202]

"While there may be shortcomings in carrying out some concrete [reform] policies, readjustment [to the policies] should be made only on the basis of detailed studies and investigations," then mayor Zhu said in a municipal function soon after the June 4 crackdown. "Otherwise, no changes should be made. Maintaining the stability and continuity of the current policy is an important guarantee of the healthy development of reform and opening to the outside world in Shanghai." And Huang Ju, then executive vice-mayor, added: "The practice of the shareholding system and other economic reform experiments will be continued in Shanghai. Further development of the reform and open-door policies is the key to promoting our economy."[203]

The green light to Pudong was given after a visit to Shanghai by Deng in the Lunar New Year of 1990. However, when the Pudong project was first announced in mid-1990, Li Peng pointed out Pudong would only follow most — but not all — of the policies practised in the SEZs. "The party's Central Committee and State Council have agreed that, to speed up the development of Pudong District, the policies for an economic and technological development zone — and some policies for a SEZ — will be applied there," Li said. "This move is yet another major step China has taken to deepen reform and expand its open-door policy."[204]

From the start, of course, Zhu was anxious that Pudong acquire the same number of perks as Shenzhen, if not more. Zhu's lobbying efforts with the State Council ministries persisted right up to the night before September 10 1990, when he announced to a packed press conference in Shanghai the investment rules for the new zone. Zhu was having special difficulties with the mandarins in the People's Bank of China. A bone of contention was the remission of profits taxes — from 25 to 15 per cent — which would be accorded the branches of foreign banks to be set up in Pudong. It was not until the eve of the press conference that PBoC Governor Li Guixian gave him the nod.[205]

Pudong thus ended up having even more autonomous powers than Shenzhen. Permission for the establishment of the branches of foreign banks was one "special policy" denied Shenzhen. Other favourable conditions enjoyed by Pudong were similar to those of other SEZS. For example, the profits tax for joint ventures would be 15 per cent. Enterprises that agreed to remain for more than ten years would enjoy full exemption from profits taxes for their first two money-making years. There would also be a free-trade bonded area in the Waigaoqiao district.[206]

New impetus was given to Shanghai and Pudong after a second visit by the patriarch in the Lunar New Year of 1991. Deng laid down instructions for turning Shanghai-Pudong into another Hong Kong or Singapore. The patriarch expressed regret he had not made Shanghai-Pudong one of the zones in 1979. The patriarch pointed out that Shanghai should become a financial nexus. "Shanghai was a financial centre in the past, a place where currencies could be freely exchanged," he said. "It should be run along such lines in the future."[207]

A few months after Deng's 1991 visit, Shanghai announced that six foreign banks would be allowed to set up branches in Pudong. One more did so in late 1991. Other concessions for foreign businessmen were announced later the same year. For example, relatively lax foreign-exchange regulations would make it easy for overseas corporations to change renminbi into US dollars and remit them abroad. Land-use fee for the early period of investment would be lower than the cost of land development.[208]

Even as late as October 1991, however, the future for the Shanghai-Pudong metropolis was far from assured. That month, Pudong was surprisingly placed under the SEZ Office of the State Council. This was announced during the National Day gala in Shanghai by Mayor Huang Ju. Huang said this meant that the Shanghai and the Yangtze area would "occupy an even more important position and play a bigger role" in the open-door policy.[209] However, one would have expected such a vital "dragon head" as Pudong to report directly to the State Council.

Funds became a big problem for the "new Shenzhen". At the time Pudong was set up, Beijing agreed to give the zone 6.5 billion yuan in funds and loans for 1991-95. During the same period, Shanghai would be allowed to "reserve" out of its revenue 5 billion yuan for the development of the new area. However, according to Zhang Tan, then vice-chief of the Foreign Economic Relations and Trade Committee of Shanghai, Pudong required 25 to 30 billion yuan a year in recurrent expenses through to the early 21st century. Some 45 billion yuan was required to lay down the infrastructure.[210]

By the end of 1991, Zhu, now Vice-Premier, was desperately looking for new avenues of funds for Shanghai-Pudong. He proposed that as much as 80 billion yuan be pumped into the zone during 1991-95. In addition, 40 billion yuan would be earmarked for the redevelopment of old sections of Shanghai in the Ninth Five-Year Plan period of 1996-2000. Zhu hoped that the central government would make up for the shortfall in foreign investment by pouring money into Pudong to develop hi-tech industries in the areas of autos, aeronautics, telecommunications and electronics.[211]

The financial problems of Pudong were resolved not because of Beijing's largesse but through the influx of capital into China that came in the wake of the *nanxun*. Powerful Hong Kong and overseas-Chinese conglomerates such as Cheung Kong, New World, and Kerry properties had by 1993 made hefty investments in the new zone, making real estate in Shanghai-Pudong one of the most expensive in the country. One late 1993 estimate said that Pudong could become as big as Shanghai in 40 years.[212] Yet as Deng said during the *nanxun*: "With lots of money, one becomes bold." As we shall see, Shanghai put up surprisingly fierce opposition to the fiscal demands of Beijing in 1993. This is despite the fact that Zhu was by then running the economy and most of the Shanghai "warlords" had been his underlings and protégés.

C. The SEZs and Economic Development Zones (EDZs), 1989-1991

For about one year after June 4, the SEZs, including Hainan Island, came upon hard times. They were threatened on both the political and economic fronts. Considered by the extreme ideologues as the "tails" of capitalism, the SEZs were the target of the retrenchment and recentralisation policy. The cold political wind from Beijing was most evident in the first six months after the massacre, when Shenzhen and Zhuhai became the launching pad for dissidents who eventually escaped to Hong Kong and the West. The two zones were saturated with security personnel — and crackdowns on "bourgeois liberalisation", sometimes in the guise of stamping out pornography, were frequent.

The tense atmosphere was felt even in August 1990. At a ceremony marking the tenth anniversary of the zones, then-propaganda chief of Shenzhen Qin Wenjun expatiated on the virtues of "spiritual civilisation". Qin, who later became a Vice-Director of China's *de facto* mission in Hong Kong, the New China News Agency, said the zones must preserve a "good socialist spirit". "As central-level leaders have reiterated, what we are building up are special economic zones, not special political zones." He added that a major task of the zones was to "grasp socialist spiritual civilisation" by promoting ideological and political work.[213]

It was clear even before Tiananmen Square, however, that the SEZs would gradually lose their preferential policies with the advent of the "products sliding policy" and the comprehensive open-door policy. For example, beginning in 1989, the zones were no longer allowed a 100 per cent retention ratio for their foreign exchange earnings from exports. Premier Li pointed out at a National SEZ Work Conference in early 1990 that the zones must abide by "the principle of the combination of planning and market forces in socialist economic management". Li conceded, however, that given the export-oriented nature of their economies, the zones would be allowed a greater role in experimenting with market forces.[214]

An equally sinister threat to the propagation of more SEZs and EDZs was posed by economic retrenchment. In late 1990, Li Peng delivered a stern warning to the coastal areas not to start new zones, in the form of either fully fledged SEZs, open cities, EDZs or hi-tech industrial parks. "The fad to start new development zones must be stopped," he said. "After the Pudong Industrial Zone came into being, various localities are worried and they want to start their own development zones in order to attract foreign capital," the premier said. "If everybody goes about running his own zone, nothing will be accomplished."[215]

Li pointed out that even with foreign capital, the viability of new zones depended on hefty capital outlay from the central government. Moreover, as various localities cut taxes and offered "preferential treatment" to foreign companies, the income of both the central and local governments would be affected. Li warned local administrations against "usurping power" by unilaterally announcing their own "investment guidelines" to the foreign business community.

With the Zhao Ziyang faction apparently eclipsed, the zones and EDZs were left with few defenders. Former vice-premier Gu Mu, a godfather of the zones, however, felt duty-bound to say a few words. The CPPCC Vice-Chairman, who still made frequent trips to the south, warned at the height of the rectification campaign against the "universality of application". "It won't do for the zones to stop their operations in order to implement the programme of rectification," he said. "The policy of the central government to give special consideration to the SEZs and the open cities is correct."[216]

By mid-1991, however, the zones — as well as other open cities and EDZs along the southeast coast — had bounced back. As with the *getihu* and the village and township enterprises, what "saved" the zones was not any dispensation from on high but their solid track record. The policy of extending "the open-door treatment" to the entire country would take years to materialise, and the SEZs and EDZs still enjoyed a certain lustre. Moreover, their proximity to Hong Kong and Southeast Asia, as well as their much greater experience of industrialisation and exports, were major factors for their outperforming the hinterland.

Of the 29,052 companies with foreign participation that had been established in China up to the end of 1990, 85 per cent were based along the coast.

Their total investments totalled US$18.9 billion. Nearly 10,000 of these *sanzi* ("foreign-participation") enterprises were in operation, employing more than 2 million people. In the same year, Hong Kong companies alone provided work for an estimated 1.5 million Chinese employees in the Pearl River Estuary, a number that was doubled by the end of 1993.[217] In 1990, the per capita share of GDP in the five SEZs and 14 open cities was 3,042 yuan, nearly double the national average. In the 1989 to 1991 period, coastal joint ventures in the manufacturing sector registered a 50 per cent growth rate in their aggregate value of industrial production.[218]

More important, the zones and open cities regained their autonomous powers to experiment with Western-style business practices. By the end of 1991, five bonded areas or customs-free sub-zones were established in Shenzhen (in the Putian and Shatoujiao districts), Guangzhou, Pudong, Tianjin and Dalian. Fujian authorities announced that free-port policies would be tried out in the Xiamen SEZ and the Fuzhou Economic and Technological Development Zone. A bonded export processing zone and a bonded producer goods market would be established respectively in Xiamen and Fuzhou.[219]

Hainan as well as other zones and cities were by 1991 aggressively trying to "contract out" to foreign corporations large tracts of land for development along capitalist lines. Yangpu port in northwestern Hainan, which was "leased" to the Japanese construction giant Kumagai Gumi, was the first such "concession" granted to an overseas consortium. Within the 30 years provided for by the lease, the Japanese concern would have a free hand in developing Yangpu. In September of the same year, Fujian authorities invited overseas companies to "lease" ten islands off the coast of the province for long-term development. Local commentators said these islands would be Fujian's "new Hong Kongs." Coastal governments hoped that in the 1990s US$10 billion worth of investment could be raised through similar concessions.[220]

By late 1991, Beijing decided to lift the moratorium on new zones and open areas. During his much-publicised visit to Guangdong in October 1991, then vice-premier Tian Jiyun gave his go-ahead for more zones and EDZs provided that the centre did not have to foot the bills. "The strategy of economic development zones using different channels to secure their own finances to speed up development is correct," Tian said. The liberal leader toured such new EDZs as the West Zhuhai Economic Development Zone, the Guangzhou Nansha EDZ, and the Zhongshan Hi-tech Development Zone. Tian, who was accompanied by Hong Kong tycoon Henry Fok, heaped praise on the Nansha EDZ, the brainchild of the "patriotic businessman".[221] Sources in Guangzhou said that local authorities had originally been wary of naming Nansha a fully fledged EDZ in view of the earlier proscription against building new zones.

All together, 27 "hi-tech development zones" were announced in 1991.

Authorities said "experimental points" in management, investment, labour, and social insurance would be tried out in these coastal enclaves to facilitate "interchange and co-operation" with similar facilities in the West. Other new zones went by the name of industrial parks, open cities, hi-tech EDZs, and so forth.[222]

Even before the three-year retrenchment came to an official end in late 1991, individual zones had mapped out expansion plans that were clearly way beyond the national rate. For example, the Shantou SEZ was in mid-1991 granted permission to expand its area of jurisdiction by four times. When the SEZ was founded in 1981, it occupied a paltry 1.6 sq km. Three years later, it grew to 52.6 sq km and, by 1992, 234 sq km. The GDP of Shantou was also slated to grow by four times from 1990 to 2000. In late 1991, Shenzhen, too, was mapping out bold plans. Then mayor Zheng Liangyu said that a total of 16.1 billion yuan and US$4.7 billion would be spent on infrastructure development in the Eighth Five-Year Plan period. The city was gunning for US$8 billion of foreign investment in the 1990s. Total industrial growth was expected to rise at an annual rate of 16.5 per cent throughout the 1990s.[223]

D. Guangdong's Return to the Limelight

(i) Open Defiance by Guangdong Cadres

Guangdong officials were flabbergasted by the June 4 conflagration. They lost their most important patrons in Beijing, Zhao Ziyang and his aides. They also knew that the "get-rich-quick province" might also lose its status as the darling of the reform enterprise. However, the gung-ho cadres there put up a valiant fight to preserve their hard-earned autonomy.

Even after the hardline leadership in Beijing had reiterated its determination to pursue a recentralisation policy, Guangdong officials were still rooting for Zhao's goal of "letting Guangdong go one step ahead of the nation". At a management seminar in Guangzhou in September 1989, the province's leading entrepreneurs asked Beijing to modify its "indiscriminate, across-the-board" measures to restrict growth, especially that of non-government-run companies. "Leave one side of the dragnet [of government intervention] open," said the director of the award-winning Jianlibao Group, a mammoth food and beverage manufacturer. "At least let's have a hole in the dragnet."[224]

The defiant mood was best exemplified by Lin Ruo, the provincial party secretary who stepped down in 1990. In a talk to senior Guangdong officials in the autumn of 1989, Lin rigorously defended his province's record. "Practice in Guangdong has fully shown that the goal of reform and the open door has been completely correct," said Lin. He implied that Guangdong would not slow down, as the central planners had demanded. "At the moment, we must tightly grasp the idea of economic construction as the centre, and prevent the provincial economy from slipping," the party boss added. Lin, a Zhao ally, crafted an elaborate apologia for Guangdong in the official journal *Seeking Truth*. The party boss denied the generally held assumption that Guangdong had grown rich at the expense of the poorer, inland provinces. "Guangdong has mainly relied on self-procured funds for economic construction," he said.[225]

Lin also stressed the good things — contributing to state coffers and providing business opportunities and employment — his province had done for the whole country. "Guangdong's contribution to the nation has become larger and larger," he claimed. Lin cited the province's growth in the past ten years — 12.9 per cent per annum — in defence of what he considered its strong points: "A wide enough open-door policy, an energetic way of doing business, and quick growth." Lin also reminded Beijing that the past practice of the command economy — "doing everything according to plans and fixed proportions" — was obsolete. He pleaded with the central authorities to continue to allow Guangdong to "take one step ahead of the rest".[226]

The defiant spirit was also demonstrated by the "Emperor of the South" Ye Xuanping, who was governor until 1991. In 1990, as the CCP's Organisation Department went about "rotating" the chiefs of the provinces, Ye bucked the trend by insisting that his successor be a native son instead of a cadre transferred from other provinces. The candidate who won — Zhu Senlin, a former party secretary of Guangzhou — was not Ye's first choice. However, while Shanghai-born, Zhu had spent most of his career in Guangdong.

Significantly, even though Ye was given the honorary position of CPPCC Vice-Chairman in early 1991, he insisted that he be allowed to spend most of his time in Guangzhou. Chinese sources said that until 1993 Ye kept his old governor's mansion in the provincial capital and spent most of his time in the go-go province. "Ye wants to be Guangdong's Deng Xiaoping, pulling strings behind the scenes," a local source said.[227]

In spite of the grandstanding, Ye and company took care to massage the egos of the State Council mandarins. In an interview with the Chinese-run Hong Kong magazine *Bauhinia* in July 1991, the former governor described as "incorrect speculation based on certain superficial phenomena" widely circulated reports that under his tutelage, Guangdong had been at loggerheads with Beijing over the extent of autonomous powers that the "before-the-times" province could enjoy. Ye insisted that the reform programmes carried out in his province, including "not a few special policies and flexible measures", had all been approved by central authorities. [228]

As for his tarrying in Guangzhou, Ye said: "In the recent period, I have stayed in Guangdong and have toured its cities and counties. I am happy to concern myself with and to show support for concrete matters that are of benefit to local economic construction." The ex-governor, still the most powerful politician in Guangdong, continued to star in major government and business functions in the province after his elevation to the No. 2 position in the CPPCC in early 1993.[229]

(ii) The Revival of the "Fifth Dragon"

As was the case with the SEZs and EDZs, what "saved" Guangdong was not the bravado of its tough-talking cadres but its sterling economic performance. By early 1991, Guangdong had regained its status as the foremost province in the country. In 1990, the province's share of total national income was 7.8 per cent and that of GDP 8.3 per cent. This meant a progression from sixth position (on both counts) in 1978 to third and first place respectively. In the first eight months of 1991, the province's value of industrial production was 130 billion yuan, an astounding 27.7 per cent jump compared with the same period in 1990.[230]

More importantly, in terms of policy, Guangdong — like the five SEZs and the other open cities — also clawed back its freedom to experiment with market-oriented mechanisms. This is most evident during the high-profile visit to the province in October 1991 by Premier Li Peng and then vice-premier Tian Jiyun. On that occasion, then executive vice-mayor of Guangzhou Lei Yu lobbied Li to grant Guangdong more autonomy especially in financial matters. "All 16 technological EDZs in China are faced with the question of lack of finance and blockage in distribution of goods," Lei said. "We must have more thorough-going financial reform to facilitate funding." Among the things demanded by Lei, a "cowboy capitalist", was freedom to grant licences to overseas banks and to set up a stock exchange in the provincial capital. [231]

Sources said short of giving specific promises, Li indicated that Guangdong should regain much of its former status as an "ahead-of-the-times" experimental zone. The premier, not formerly known as a fan of Guangdong, praised the province for having acquitted itself well of the task of reform as well as "curing and restructuring" its economy. "Its economy has developed speedily and its efficiency is gradually on the rise," Li said. "Guangdong is approaching the level of a benevolent cycle." The premier further claimed Beijing was not necessarily biased in favour of Shanghai and Pudong. "The party centre decided to develop Pudong in order to develop the superiority of the economic and technological levels of Shanghai," he said. "At the same time, it wishes to run the SEZs, the economic and technological zones and other coastal open areas even better — and that they will have greater achievements."[232]

The status of Guangdong as national pacesetter was reinforced in the provincial People's Congress of January 1992. During the conclave, which confirmed Zhu as Governor, officials disclosed that foreign banks would be allowed to open full branches in Guangzhou, and that overseas capital would be used to develop real estate. At his post-election press conference, Zhu said that Guangdong would march towards a market economy. "We do not use words like a 'market economy'," he said. "But we will establish a strong market sense, and we will propagate and expand the market. In actual fact, since the start of reform, Guangdong has always used the market to orientate reform." The Governor indicated that Guangdong would take further advantage of its Hong Kong connection to diversify its market and integrate its economy with that of Hong Kong in addition to the international marketplace.[233]

As we saw in Section III, Guangdong got an extra lift from the *nanxun* talks, during which Deng urged the province to outstrip the Four Dragons in 20 years. However, by 1993, as practically all of China's 300-odd open cities could claim "preferential treatment" on a par with that of Guangzhou or Shenzhen, Guangdong's difficulty was in the area of comparative advantage. High land and labour costs meant that many labour-intensive or assembly-type operations were moved to the northern districts of the province — or out of the province altogether. It became clear that the province had to develop hi-tech industries and the services to retain its lead into the next century.[234]

E. Showdown between Beijing and the Regions, 1993

The year 1993 was a watershed in terms of relationship between the *zhongyang* and the regions. The CCP leadership figured that if they could not turn the tide, the seemingly relentless trend towards the depletion of central powers would become irreversible. By the end of the year, the scorecard was uncertain, with most analysts saying while Beijing had clawed back some territory, it failed to redress the overall trend of funds, talent and resources flowing from Beijing to the coast — or those parts of the country where money could be made quickest. In the wake of the untimely end of the three-month-old austerity programme, most localities were by early 1994 again following their own agendas for high growth.

(i) Recentralisation in the latter half of 1993

With the onset of the austerity programme in mid-1993, the following powers were taken back from the regions: finance, especially the granting of loans and the raising of funds; power over the setting up of EDZs; and, most importantly, as discussed in Section IV, the replacement of the contract financial responsibility system with the dual tax system.

The Third Plenum decision to centralise loan-making powers in the headquarters of the PBoC meant that local administrations would have much less leeway in raising funds. Powers for local governments and banks to grant loans and to implement inter-bank lending were curtailed. Moreover, by early 1994, it seemed likely that Beijing would, as far as was practical, continue the ban on fund-raising outside the banking system. This meant an end to "underground banks" as well as the practice of local administrations and enterprises "raising money in society" through offering customers "investment certificates" that bore interest rates significantly higher than those of the banking system.

After all, Beijing bureaucrats had made a "national negative example" out of the Changcheng Electronics, Electrical and High-Technology Corp, which raised more than 1 billion yuan in early 1993 through issuing investment certificates that bore interest rates of 34 per cent or more. After the start of the austerity programme, Hebei Province closed down more than 150 "illegal financial institutions". And in late 1993, Shenzhen set up a task force to look into illegal operations for "raising cash in society".[235]

In a throwback to 1990, Beijing also clamped down on the powers of local governments to start EDZs. Before the austerity programme, Beijing was very lax in granting permission for local administrations to set up such zones, to the point that application for central approval became almost perfunctory. Vetting procedures were stepped up after August 1993. On a trip to Guizhou in July, Zhu Rongji laid down restrictions for the establishment of "hi-tech development zones". The Vice-Premier pointed out that they must not take up too much farm land; moreover, only industries with genuinely high level of technological sophistication could be allowed into such zones.[236]

Soon after the 16-point austerity programme was announced, over 1,000 "illegal" EDZs were abolished. Head of the State Council's SEZ Office Hu Ping claimed in August 1993 that only 10 per cent of these rogue zones "turned out to be beneficial for the local economy". By the end of the year, 1,555 out of the 2,025 DEZs opened by administrations below the provincial-government level had been abolished. The remainder, plus the more than 100 zones sanctioned or established by central-level units, meant only 600 or so EDZs would be allowed to remain. Hu said in November that the number of such zones would remain more or less constant in the foreseeable future.[237]

At the end of 1993, Beijing also confirmed what had become very apparent in the past year or so: that the SEZs, and, by implications, the open cities, had "fulfilled their historical function as China's windows". "In the future, the SEZs must depend on their own qualifications — not preferential policies from Beijing — to develop," said a senior planning officer at the SCREC Lu Yonghua. Lu indicated, however, that as pioneers of the open-door policy, SEZs could still have a go at experimenting with new reforms. He also encouraged the zones to be "bridges" between SEZ enterprises, business units in the heartland, and multinationals.[238]

Moreover, as part of the financial reforms endorsed at the plenum, Beijing unified tax and other policies for development zones nationwide, thus depriving provincial or municipal authorities of the freedom to vary the terms of investment for favoured overseas clients. For example, the maximum percentage of profits-tax deductions by EDZ enterprises was set at 15 per cent, with the provision that reduction of a further 10 per cent was possible for units that exported more than 70 per cent of their products. Localities were forbidden from enacting special tax regulations to attract investors. To this end, Guangdong set up in late 1993 a Leading Group on the Eradication of the Improper Granting of Tax Remissions.[239]

On a micro-economic level, localities were asked to tighten restrictions on overheaded business activities such as real estate. For example, in August 1993, Guangdong laid down six regulations on land-use rights-related zoning. The granting of land-use rights or the re-zoning of plots must meet "the production strategy of the state", the regulations said. Other requirements included the need to preserve farm land, and guarantees that funds for the development of relevant plots must be secured through proper channels.[240]

The biggest "coup" by the central authorities in 1993 was, of course, the enshrinement of the dual tax system at the Third Plenum. While addressing the plenum, Zhu Rongji glowed over his triumph and even praised Guangdong Province for its co-operative spirit.[241] As discussed in Section IV, however, Beijing was forced to make numerous concessions on how the dual-tax system would be carried out, including a guarantee that all regions could at least maintain their 1993 level of tax revenues. These compromises were a good illustration of the *zhongyang*'s failure to claw back its old authority.

The compromises had been forced upon Beijing because of the ferocious resistance put up by the "warlords" in the course of Zhu's visit to 15-odd provinces and cities prior to the plenum.

His session with Guangdong's party secretary and governor Xie Fei and Zhu Senlin reportedly ended in a shouting match. It took some sweet-talking by Jiang Zemin when he met the two Guangdong chiefs in Beijing for the latter to accede to the compromise. Zhu encountered unexpected resistance from his old powerbase, Shanghai. Local leaders claimed that while touring the metropolis in early 1991 and 1992, Deng Xiaoping had pledged that Shanghai could stick to the CFRS.[242]

Jiangsu, another rich coastal province, also offered fiery resistance. Party secretary Shen Daren reportedly lost his job in October because of altercations with Zhu. Governor Chen Huanyou, however, continued to make counter-arguments to the dual tax system during the plenum itself. The Jiangsu cadres said the new tax arrangements would spell an end to the advantages enjoyed by the province's famed village and township enterprises. Provinces whose leaders also gave Zhu a hard time included Hainan, Liaoning, Shandong, Jiangxi, Ningxia and Shaanxi. For example, Hainan cadres insisted that the financial reforms were at variance with the 23-point dispensation Beijing had granted the island in the late 1980s.[243]

Immediately after the plenum, Finance Minister Liu Zhongli admitted that the central government was prepared to fine-tune its reforms to accommodate the demands of localities and enterprises. He said the introduction of the new taxation system for local administrations and enterprises would be a "gradual process" that could stretch to a few years. "In working out the fiscal and tax reform plan, the central government has taken into account the realities of enterprises and the interests of localities," Liu said, adding that the reforms "will not immediately affect local interests".[244]

More explicitly, a senior researcher at the ministry, Cong Anni, said the financial reforms would be carried out "under the premise of guaranteeing the vested interests of localities". She said tax bases for Beijing and the localities would only be carved out after a new delineation of responsibilities for central and regional authorities. Cong indicated that "at a mature time", revenues accruing to central coffers would be redistributed to the localities so that there would be a "rational balance" between the responsibilities and incomes of the various levels of government. In early 1994, Minister Liu gave more details about the "transfer payments". For example, while the VAT would in theory be split between Beijing and the localities in a 75:25 ratio, because of "kickbacks" to the latter, the actual proportion would be just 52 per cent for the *zhongyang*, and 48 per cent for the regions.[245]

By early 1994, various localities had taken steps to neutralise the effects of the dual-tax system. For example, to boost their 1993 tax threshold, various provinces had in the last months of the year began collecting taxes for 1994. In September 1993, tax revenues accruing to the localities were at least 52 per cent greater than the previous year. China economists said that local administrations would likely siphon resources away from those economic activities from which they could not collect taxes. These included the production of wine and cigarettes.[246]

(ii) Tug-of-War over Loans and the Growth Rate

In spite of apparent triumphs of the centre, that the initiative shifted to the regions is also evident from the short-lived nature of the austerity programme. With a duration of a mere three months, it was the briefest such exercise in the history of Communist China.

Let us first examine the most important of Zhu's 16-point drive: to collect loans that banks and local administrations had illegally or improperly lent to government units and enterprises for speculative and other questionable activities. In June 1993, the Vice-Premier set the deadline of August 15 by which all such funds should be surrendered to central coffers. Beginning in early July, the central government dispatched high-level investigation teams to at least 20 provinces and directly-administered cities to check on breaches of financial discipline. Zhu, who had repeatedly said he would "chop off the heads" of local cadres who disobeyed central edicts, indicated that offending officials would be cashiered on the spot.[247]

By mid-August, barely 72.7 billion yuan, or one third of the original target, had been surrendered to the national treasury. However, except for several officers of the People's Bank of China system, in particular the Agriculture Bank, Zhu failed to carry out his threat to make heads roll. Indeed, the fiery economic czar was forced to sweet-talk those warlords who had apparently spat in his face. After the Jiangsu bosses had openly defied him, Zhu told the media after his Nanjing tour that he had praised the provincial leadership for observing financial discipline by not engaging in real estate and stock market speculation as well as "chaotic attempts to raise capital from society". Significantly, Zhu extended the deadline for returning the money to Beijing to the end of 1993. And after the Third Plenum, the "December 31 deadline" mysteriously disappeared from the media and official speeches.[248]

The record of the localities for parting with "improper loans" was far from exemplary. By late August, Guangdong had only returned 13 billion yuan to Beijing, or 40 per cent of the funds it "owed" the banking system. Within two months of the austerity programme, Hainan coughed up 1.1 billion yuan, or half the requirement. The record for Hangzhou was 1 billion, also half what Beijing had demanded. The best performer seemed to have been Fujian, which by September had fulfilled 80 per cent of the corvee by surrendering 1.1 billion yuan to the central bank.[249]

Moreover, the central government was not entirely successful in its efforts to force the warlords to make one-time, emergency contributions to Beijing. At the onset of retrenchment, Beijing called upon many rich provinces and municipalities to bail out the depleted central coffers. Guangdong obliged with a one-off contribution of more than 10 billion yuan. However, many regions, including Shanghai, flatly refused.[250]

More importantly, regional resistance — and lobbying — explained why Zhu and other central leaders were obliged to relax the tight-money policy by late September. Hong Kong and Taiwan reports said that on a trip to Anhui in the summer, Zhu promised provincial cadres a fresh injection of central funds of 10.5 billion yuan, 1 billion yuan more than requested. In late September, Zhu personally authorised an injection of 100 billion yuan worth of credit into the banking system. This was followed by loans worth 260 billion yuan for the last quarter of 1993. The austerity programme of 1993 became history.[251]

By late 1993, there was evidence that many provinces and cities were again flouting fiscal prudence imposed by Beijing by gunning for double-digit growth. Aside from their growing clout, local leaders were able to force Beijing to abandon the tight-money policy because of the alarming stagnation of industry and other economic activities. The problem of the triangular debts had worsened to historic levels. One estimate said the scale of the debts had by early September nudged the 200 billion yuan mark. Moreover, as we shall see in the next section, Deng personally intervened in September to put a moratorium on retrenchment.[252]

That the tide had again shifted to the localities became evident during a trip made by Jiang Zemin to Guangzhou in late September, in which he repeated the edicts that Deng had delivered earlier that month. In a talk to leaders from ten provinces, Jiang focused not on austerity but the need to speed up reform and development by pursuing "sustained, high-speed and healthy development," Deng's new slogan. "It will not do if the development speed is too low, because this will mean the economy will not be able to take off," Jiang said. "Areas that have the wherewithal should go faster; those that can't do it yet should positively create the conditions and gradually speed up development."[253]

While touring Shanghai in early October, Vice-Premier Zou Jiahua reminded local leaders of the instructions Deng had given the metropolis both during the *nanxun* and in early 1991. The NCNA quoted Zou as repeating Deng's dictum about the need for Shanghai to "have a facelift once every year and to cross one threshold after the next". Zou said that the development in the metropolis had matched Beijing's requirement about boosting macro-level adjustments and controls.[254]

Also remarkable was an early November speech by PBoC Vice-Governor Chen Yuan, who seemed to be currying favour with the warlords. Chen said "the bank has not severely or comprehensively implemented the regulations on tightening up credit". "Because development in the south and along the coast has always been very fast, the austerity programme has not had much impact on them," he added. "The centre still encourages them to develop [further]."[255]

Needless to say, Deng's new edicts had won the support of the regional chieftains. In a late October dispatch, the NCNA quoted officials in Fujian as saying that efforts by the province to cure and restructure its financial order had reached a "definite stage of development". The news agency said the province now had a "relatively magnanimous financial environment" to pursue "sustained, high-speed and healthy development". China analysts pointed out that by saying that the austerity programme had scored a definite stage of achievement — and not just "initial achievement", as most leaders were saying up to October — Fujian cadres had skillfully used Deng's blessing to prevent Beijing from going the whole hog with retrenchment.[256]

Regional enthusiasm received a further fillip with the publication in November 1993 of the Third Volume of Deng's *Selected Works*, which gave another push for high growth. In talking about his reactions to the tome, Shanghai party boss Wu Bangguo waxed lyrical on the many occasions in which the patriarch urged the metropolis to go faster. Wu quoted Deng as saying that "Shanghai is the nation's strong suit; and the short cut [to development] is to develop Shanghai". Moreover, the party secretary also pointed out the patriarch had regretted the tardiness with which he had given Shanghai special zone status.[257]

By the end of 1993, Premier Li and other leaders indicated the growth rate for 1994 would be 9 per cent, or 4 per cent less than 1993. Most local leaders, however, unveiled development strategies that were noticeably more bullish than the national norm. For example, Hainan said it was going for a growth rate of 18 per cent; Shanghai 12 per cent; Pudong 30 per cent; Guangzhou 16 per cent; and Hebei, at least 14 per cent.[258]

IX. Conclusion: The Limits of Reform, 1992-1994

After touring China in October 1993, Nobel prize-winning economist Milton Friedman was not terribly happy with the way reform was going. He raised the familiar point about half-heartedness, the fact that the party and state were unwilling to part with their powers. "The answer to the question of how to go about getting a free market system is very straightforward — you get the government out of the way [and] privatise, privatise, privatise," the monetarist guru said. "I believe China needs some movement in the direction of reducing the role of government, of reducing the arbitrary power of individuals over others at the same time that it moves towards a free market," he noted, adding that there was no evidence that "there are any fewer bureaucrats than five years ago".[259]

In the run-up to the Third Plenum of late 1993, there were high expectations that Beijing might give up its old strategy of "crossing the river while feeling out for the boulders" — for the more radical course of "arriving at the goal in one jump". Before the conclave, the quasi-official HKCNA claimed the leadership had abandoned the trial-and-error approach of the past for that of "attaining goals in one step". The news agency also attacked "people who have a residual attachment to a planned economy". Former SCREC vice-minister and Zhao Ziyang aide Gao Shangquan also advocated "quick steps and big steps" for reforms for which there were already "mature conditions". "Reform has entered the historic period of storming the fortresses," he said. "We must make up our minds and seek breakthroughs over the deep-seated contradictions."[260]

Yet, reflecting the CCP's long-standing refusal to give up power, reforms introduced from the *nanxun* to the Third Plenum failed to "storm the fortress" of the old system thoroughly. This is despite arguments by liberal economists in and outside China that conditions were favourable for a major putsch. If we take official statistics at face value, China was by late 1993 not far away from a market model. For example, a September 1993 dispatch by the NCNA said that merely 6.5 per cent of the aggregate value of industrial production (AVIP) within the state sector was controlled by government plans, down 12 per cent from a year ago. And 25 per cent of the AVIP fell under non-mandatory, advisory "guidance". In 1993, the SPC only set specific targets for 62 industrial products, down from 91 a year ago.[261]

Beijing, however, lacked the will to go the whole hog. Deng's famed approach of "feeling out for the boulders" prevailed. As the Third Plenum Resolution made clear: "For some major reform measures, plans can be drawn up first and co-ordinated in related areas of the economic system, while some others should be tried out first in selected localities or areas and then extended after experience has been gained."

That Beijing had not delivered on its liberalisation plans was voiced in perhaps the most significant meeting of scholars in 1993: a gathering of 100-odd "bourgeois-liberal" academics and former cadres in Beijing in October to air their reservations about the all-too-visible hand of the state. While on a superficial level, the barbs of the liberals were aimed at the just-concluded austerity programme, their complaints went to the core of Beijing's residual attachment to the diktat economy. Speaking at the conference were officials and economists close to ousted party chiefs Hu Yaobang and Zhao Ziyang: Zhu Houze, Yu Guangyuan, Wang Jue, Wu Mingyu, and Tong Dalin.[262]

The avant-garde theorists pointed out that the "main current" of economic work was reform and development, and that "boosting macro-level adjustments and controls" was only a tributary. They railed against "using new slogans and old methods" and "the restoration of the old system". Wang Jue, a professor at the Central Party School, said: "While macro-level adjustments and controls were necessary, they must be based on market economics. If we depart from this foundation, we will inevitably return to the old system of planning." Wang also griped that whenever there was a tight-money policy, the state sector was given exemptions whereas "market elements" such as VTEs and private enterprises were hard hit.

Even more remarkable was the "reappearance" of Zhu Houze, who was Hu Yaobang's propaganda chief and head of the official trade union under Zhao Ziyang. "Reform must solve the problem of the fusion between party, government and enterprises — and return powers to the enterprises," he said. "Society can only have development when the state retreats from areas which it does not need to, should not, and cannot control." Paraphrasing Marx, Zhu hinted that the state should return to society its due powers and perquisites.

In the eyes of the liberal member of the CPPCC Standing Committee Li Gang, efforts to raise the state's macro-level control could only cure "superficial ills". "Macro-level adjustments and control should be gradual and not rapid, less and not more," he said. Li argued that Beijing's efforts should concentrate on deepening reform, especially transforming the functions of government, hinting that the latter should stop interfering in the economy.[263]

The CCP leadership, however, had opted for the safer course, an approach that would "synthesise" market forces with heavy-handed political and economic control by the *zhongyang*. We will examine here the major factors behind — and manifestations — of this approach. Its longer term consequences for the CCP and for China will be discussed in the conclusion of this book.

A. The East-Asiatic or Singapore Model

That the CCP leadership has set definite parameters to its free-market experiments is evident from its predilection for the so-called East-Asiatic model of market economics. It is also what various theorists have called the Singapore model, the Asia-Pacific model, or the neo-Confucian, neo-authoritarian approach to the marketplace.

According to Chinese sources, cadres and academics responsible for drafting the Third Plenum document distinguished between roughly three strains of market economics. They were: the Anglo-Saxon or American model, whose primacy is individual effort; the model prevailing in Germany and Northern Europe, which sets store by social welfare and worker participation; and the East-Asiatic or Asia-Pacific persuasion, which posits a "collectivist" approach to the marketplace.[264]

As economics guru Wu Jinglian put it in a late 1993 conference: "The market economic system that China is building will on the one hand have the general traits of market economics worldwide. On the other, it will have its own characteristics, and it will be relatively close to the market economic model in the Asia-Pacific region." Wu, who had the ear of President Jiang and Vice-Premier Zhu, cited the following attributes of the Asia-Pacific model: a big role for institutional investment, including that of banks, in the structure and behaviour of enterprises; avoidance of excessive polarisation of income; and a "more active function" of government in developing the market, helping new industries, and raising the country's global competitiveness.[265]

Politically, there is a mighty dose of new authoritarianism in the East-Asiatic, Singapore, or Taiwan model. Put simply, the theory says a developing country needs a strongman, coupled with one-party dictatorship, to help it make the jump from quasi-feudalism to the marketplace. Quite surprisingly, the theory was first made popular by the associates of Zhao Ziyang. In early 1989, Zhao apparently discussed it Deng, who agreed with it.[266] Out of fashion the first few years after the June 4 killings, the creed again found favour with such would-be "authoritarian" figures as Jiang and Zhu.

It is no accident that patriarch Deng re-hoisted the flag of new authoritarianism and that of the Singapore model during his *nanxun* talks. As former president Yang Shangkun recalled a few months later: "China puts a lot of stress on the Singapore experience. When Deng Xiaoping inspected the south in January [1992], he raised the point of learning from Singapore."[267]

In mid-1992, Deng dispatched the Executive Vice-Chief of the party's Propaganda Department, Xu Weicheng, a noted Maoist, to tour Singapore with a view to compiling a primer on how the country could benefit from the Singapore experience. Xu's book, which, unfortunately, was only for internal circulation, came out later that year, and it had nothing but praise for practically all aspects of the island republic's politics, economics, culture and social order.

Since then, high-level delegations have been dispatched to Thailand, Malaysia, Japan (Zhu's favourite), and South Korea (the apple in the eye of Deng's second son, businessman Deng Zhifang). Paradoxically, Deng's soft spot, aside from Singapore, was Taiwan. The patriarch had no end of admiration for the neo-authoritarian statecraft of the late president Chiang Ching-kuo — at least until the last years of the Taiwan leader's death, when he began to institute fairly radical political reforms.[268]

A key recommendation of the Third Plenum's 50-point programme was "to strengthen and improve party leadership" (see Chapter 5). For example, party organisations in enterprises would "play the role of the political core and supervise and guarantee the implementation of the principles and policies of the party and state". Moreover, the resolution said, party cells would also play a bigger role in the drafting of legislation. As we shall see in Chapter 3, throughout 1993, the CCP tightened its straitjacket on the ideological and propaganda sphere as well as the police-state apparatus.[269]

B. The Residual — But Still Significant — Role of Planning

In deference to the East-Asiatic model, the long arm of the state was still very much in evidence after the Third Plenum. After all, a key recommendation of the plenum resolution was to "strengthen and improve [the state's] macro-level adjustments and control" over the economy. Leaders including Li Peng were at pains to remind the world, especially foreign investors, that such adjustments and control were not the equivalent of Soviet-style state fiats. Li repeatedly said the central government's goals would be accomplished through non-mandatory guidelines, laws and regulations, and "executive means where necessary" but that such executive measures would be reduced to the minimum.[270]

Yet there is no question that state interference would be more pronounced than in a Western-style market economy — and that such interference would be a long-term phenomenon. The premier pointed out in October that "macro-level control [associated with the just-ended austerity programme] is not a temporary emergency measure but [one that] deserves our attention throughout the process of establishing a socialist market economy". More significantly, Li said that "market mechanisms depend on macro-level control [by the state] for exerting their functions", meaning that both were equally important.[271] And in his address to the Third Plenum, Jiang urged an "organic synthesis" between macro-level control mechanisms and market forces. "We will, in accordance with practical situations, give more emphasis to the market at some junctures, and more emphasis to macro-level adjustments and controls at others," he said.[272]

Such adjustments and control would mainly be exercised through the State Planning Commission, a Stalinist creation whose demise had been rumoured countless times since the mid-1980s. At a national conference on planning in December 1993, SPC officials said the role of the department had shifted from laying down mandatory fiats to making medium and long-term plans and forecasts through non-binding and "advisory" guidance, legal measures, and economic policies and levers. They disclosed that production still subject to the commission's mandatory plans in 1994 would drop from 6.8 per cent of total national industrial production to just 4 per cent. The officials noted, however, that "a minority of necessary mandatory plans" would remain.[273]

That the SPC and allied central-government agencies would still play a sizable role in resource allocation was evident from remarks made at the time by Vice-Premier Zou Jiahua and SPC chief Chen Jinhua. Addressing the December SPC conference, Zou, a former SPC chief, said the focus of planning in 1994 was to ensure a "sustained, high-speed and healthy" economic development. Top priority would be accorded to agriculture, particularly guaranteeing sufficient investment in the rural sector. Beijing would also try to ensure a significant increase in the income of farmers. The investment structure would be streamlined, with efforts being made by the central government to cut down outlay on fixed assets.

Zou, believed to be a "planner" at heart, hinted that in spite of price reforms, Beijing would use its influence to prevent hyperinflation. "We will give a high degree of attention to the question of prices, so that the degree of price increases will be controlled within the goals of [the policy of] macro-level adjustments and control," he said.[274] As we saw in Section IV, Beijing reintroduced price controls on at least 27 types of produce and commodities in December 1993.

In his October speech referred to above, Li Peng said market mechanisms would "form the basis of economic operations and the distribution of resources". However, in the real world, bureaucrats controlling state-planning mechanisms would continue to play a formidable role in the allocation of funds and raw materials. The SPC's Chen, for example, made clear that the bulk of the central government's resources would be devoted to ten favoured sectors, namely, agriculture, water conservation, transport, energy, major raw materials, machine-building, electronics, education, and science and technology. Chen underscored the importance that Zou and others had attached to farming, saying: "We must pay close attention to farmland protection, and to the stabilisation of cropland and the total output of grain crops and cotton."[275]

At an agriculture conference called in January 1994 in response to the crisis over grain prices a month earlier, senior officials made it clear state fiats would be back for some time. Agriculture Ministry Jiang Liu laid down fairly detailed plans to ensure sufficient production for grain, cotton and other produce. For example, the target for grain yields was 450 million tonnes, roughly the same as 1993. The nationwide acreage for wheat and rice was set at 1.65 billion *mu*, and cotton, 90 million *mu* (1 *mu* = 0.0667 hectare). Fairly industrialised Guangdong was told to earmark 3.33 million hectares for grain in 1994. To make it more attractive for farmers to stick to the staples, grain and cotton prices would be significantly raised in 1994. Per capita income for the agrarian sector would be increased by 5 per cent.[276]

China economists suspected that in spite of the revolutionary changes being wrought in the banking system, there would be a residual but still significant political interference in the allocation of funds. A major reform of the banking system involved the differentiation between policy banks, which would lend to the priority sectors listed above, and "Western-style" commercial banks. The economists said there seemed little question that in the foreseeable future, the commercial banks would still give favourable treatment to

Beijing's preferred clients. And state enterprises would still find it easier to secure loans from commercial banks than *getihu* or private concerns.

C. Beefing up Central Authority

As discussed in Section IV, a key "reform" of the Third Plenum was to centralise financial powers. However, the leadership's concern was not just boosting Beijing's share of national revenue but strengthening central power in general. This trend mirrored the rise of "neo-conservatism" among a large number of academics and advisers to party leaders. Echoing the theory of new authoritarianism, they argued that market reforms could only be carried out by a centre that had strong macro-economic clout.

In a now-famous paper written in mid-1993, two consultants to the Chinese Academy of Sciences, Hu Angang and Wang Shaoguang, contended that China could disintegrate *à la* Yugoslavia unless drastic steps were taken to recentralise economic authority. The pair, who had done post-doctoral research at Yale University, indicated that the first step was to retrieve the revenues. In the paper entitled "Strengthening the Central Government's Leading Role during the Shift to a Market Economy", the "neo-conservative" economists argued that even in well-developed capitalist countries, the centre's hold over financial resources was much greater. For example, they said, from 1972 to 1989, the income of the federal government of the US increased from 19.1 per cent of GNP to 23 per cent. Comparable figures for Japan in 1989 were 12.7 per cent and Germany, 16.5 per cent.

They warned that by the year 2000, Beijing's state revenue could diminish to unsustainable levels, accounting for just 11.3 per cent of the GNP, or one-third the amount when reform began in late 1978.[277] "In years, a few, or, at the latest, between 10 and 20, the country will move from economic collapse to political break-up, ending with its disintegration," the paper said. "If a 'political strongman' dies, it is possible that a situation like that in post-Tito Yugoslavia will emerge."[278]

Likewise, 36-year-old economist Wang Yizhou said China needed a "strong government that is oriented towards the market". "The government can interfere in the market, and even do so at a deep level," he said. "However, such interference must tally with the principles of the market and help in the propagation of the market economy." The scholar indicated the centre needed to have strong political and economic powers to help defuse contradictions and bottlenecks engendered by reform — and also to help China adjust to the challenges in the international scene.[279]

By late 1993, there were indications that even Deng, a veteran supporter of regional autonomy, had voiced concern about the need to recentralise powers.

This apparently was one of the key messages that he brought to Shanghai during a trip that lasted from December to February 1994. In an early 1994 speech, Zhu Rongji stressed those parts of Deng's old speeches that urged the centripetal imperative: "If the party Central Committee and the State Council lose their authority, the situation will go out of control." "Macro-level management must manifest the fact that what the *zhongyang* has said counts," he added.[280]

D. Political Interference from Neo-Authoritarian Figures

An integral part of the Singapore or the neo-authoritarian model is that authoritarian figures, or helmsmen and "architects", would exercise a personal role in policy-making. While Deng Xiaoping played a key role in reactivating reform after the June 4 disaster, his influence was often less than salutary. The same, to some extent, could be said of Zhu Rongji, whose imperial style, what Chinese propagandists called "fierce as the thunder and forceful as the wind", could warp the orderly progress of the economy towards the marketplace.

As discussed in Chapter 1, the patriarch, after the success of this *nanxun*, used his influence to postpone to the last possible moment — end of March 1993 — the austerity programme to rein in the overheated economy. In September, he again stepped in to tone down the tight-money crusade. The reasons were familiar: the fear that, as the liberal economists argued, the emphasis of policy-making had shifted from reform and development to retrenchment — and that conservatives were again taking advantage of the curing and restructuring exercise to roll back reform.[281]

In September 1993, Deng called a meeting of his intimates, including Jiang, to order to put a halt to the austerity programme and to announce another round of rapid growth. The Deng campaign gained extra momentum with the publication in early November of the Third Volume of his *Selected Works*, whose major drift was again fast-paced economic liberalisation.

The edicts spoken by or at least attributed to Deng consisted of the following: that the nation must aim for "sustained, high-speed and healthy development"; regions and localities that have the requisite resources should go as fast as they could; the nation must seize the opportunity for rapid growth; and that "only development passes the rigorous [test of] reason". The last slogan was actually mentioned by Deng in the course of the *nanxun*. For some strange reason, it was not included in Central Document No. 2 of 1992, an edited transcript of the *nanxun* talks. By the end of 1993, all senior cadres with the exception of Zhu Rongji had mouthed the same slogans.[282]

Chinese and Western observers feared, however, that Deng's new edicts —

and the readiness with which they were observed — might ignite a new round of inflation. This is despite the fact that in September 1993, the industrial growth rate dipped below 20 per cent for the first time in 14 months. The GNP growth for the entire year hit 13 per cent, which met Deng's oft-stated requirement that the economy grew annually by "ten per cent or more". This fast clip, however, was considerably greater than the 8 to 9 per cent that most economists thought was healthy.

After all, the austerity programme had been watered down if not stopped before most of its goals had been achieved. By year's end, the official figure for inflation in urban China remained at 19.5 per cent, with unofficial estimates much higher. Because of new credit made available, the industrial growth rate for December shot up to a staggering 29.8 per cent. The central government seemed to have lost control of the money supply. A total of 360 billion yuan worth of credit was pumped into the banking system in the last four months of the year. In 1993, the total amount of currency in circulation swelled by 180 billion yuan over the previous year. This compared with the year-on-year increase of 120 billion for 1992.[283]

As we shall see in the conclusion of this book, by early 1994, there were obvious signs that for political reasons — the need to maintain socio-political stability without political reform — the administration was ready to tone down those liberalisation measures deemed must likely to cause unrest.

3

The Maoist Restoration: Class Struggle and the Negation of Reform

I. Introduction

FOR the Chinese Communist Party (CCP), politics after June 4, 1989, largely consisted of one word: self-preservation. The sense of crisis was heightened by the dissolution of communism in Eastern Europe and the former Soviet Union. For at least one year after the Tiananmen Square bloodbath, the CCP revived Maoist class struggle as a surefire means to cut down its enemies and to maintain power. Purges of CCP ranks were carried out relentlessly in the name of party construction.

In an effort to hide its moral decrepitude, the party chose to call its enemies — actually, all Chinese who oppose Stalinist, one-party authoritarianism, and socialism —— "bourgeois liberals". For good measure, the CCP also invoked the bogey of neo-imperialists — meaning largely the United States — hell-bent on turning China into a capitalist country through "peaceful evolution".

The siege mentality became even stronger after the unsuccessful Soviet coup of August 1991 — and the dissolution of the Soviet empire by December that year. Deng Xiaoping, putative Architect of Reform, masterminded one of the most vehement anti-rightist campaigns in CCP history. Three days after Tiananmen, he had identified the US as well as remnant bourgeois elements in China as having plotted the overthrow of the socialist regime.

There is, however, a subtle difference between the anti-rightist gambit of Deng — and that of such stalwarts of the conservative or left-wing faction of the party as elders Chen Yun and Deng Liqun. (NB in China, unlike in the West, "left" means conservative, and "right" liberal.) While they agreed on the need to boost the "dictatorship of the proletariat", Deng did not want the anti-liberal pogrom to hurt economic construction. The hardliners were trying to use this opportunity to get rid of their enemies in the liberal wing — including the followers of Hu Yaobang and Zhao Ziyang — once and for all.

Moreover, the leftists wanted to roll back reform across the board. While Deng wanted to ensure iron-fisted communist rule on the political front, at the same time he hoped to revive economic reform. The hardliners, however, were busy killing economic-reform initiatives they deemed as the "tail of capitalism". They were also reinstating a key doctrine of Mao: that class struggle, not economic construction, was the "core" of national work.

Until about mid-1991, the leftists were by and large successful in their Maoist revival. Deng himself was subjected to heavy criticism for conniving at the mistakes of his former heirs-apparent Hu Yaobang and Zhao Ziyang. For if Hu and Zhao had been "soft-handed" towards bourgeois liberalisation, it meant Deng had to bear the responsibility. The following sections will describe how, after Tiananmen Square, reforms in the fields of politics, ideology, culture and propaganda were frozen. The agendas of heavyweight leftist politicians like Chen Yun and Deng Liqun will also be discussed.

The pendulum did not swing back towards the right till the second half of 1991. In the wake of the *nanxun*, the remnant Maoists were again on the defensive. Deng was able to reassert the "Third plenum line" of taking economic construction as the core of party and state work. Many economic liberalisation programmes championed by Zhao Ziyang were back in place. For about a year after the *nanxun*, a vigorous anti-leftist counterattack was staged by the bourgeois-liberal intellectuals. The last sections of this chapter will argue, however, that for reasons including propagating one-party dictatorship and fomenting blind loyalty in the party, elements of Deng's faction — as represented by Jiang Zemin — were willing to seek co-existence with the Maoists. By early 1994, the likes of Deng Liqun ("Little Deng") went on attacking the quasi-capitalist road championed by "China's Gorbachev". However, the days of the leftists are numbered. They are fast becoming irrelevant in the market economy. While they are not expected to be wiped out soon, Deng Liqun's anti-reformist tirades have become a voice in the wilderness.

II. The Crusade against Bourgeois Liberalisation and "Peaceful Evolution", 1989-1992

A. An Enemy Behind Every Tree

Call it "bourgeois liberalisation", "spiritual pollution", or "all-out Westernisation". Despite the fact that since the early 1980s, the propaganda machinery had churned out reams of material on the subject, "bourgeois liberalisation" meant only one thing: ideas and activities that attempt to deny the CCP its absolute monopoly on power. What the leadership called efforts by foreign and domestic enemies to "infiltrate and sabotage" the socialist system included the introduction of political pluralism and the quasi-capitalist system. In other words, whatever opposed the Four Cardinal Principles (the socialist road, Communist Party leadership, dictatorship of the proletariat, and Marxism-Leninism, Mao Zedong Thought) was deemed to be liberalisation or all-out Westernisation.

This was succinctly stated in an article in the *People's Daily* written by the commentator of *Contemporary Ideas*, a post-June 4 magazine sponsored by ultra-leftist ideologues. The commentator defined bourgeois liberalisation as "negating the socialist system and advocating the capitalist road". He went on: "Politically, it advocates the Western-style multi-party politics and the parliamentary system, negating the leadership of the Communist party and the dictatorship of the proletariat. Economically, it advocates private enterprise and the market, negating public ownership and the planned economy. Ideologically, it advocates multi-dimensionalism in ideas, negating the leading position of Marxism-Leninism and Mao Zedong Thought."[1]

Who are the domestic and foreign foes decried by the leftists? They comprised the remnants of the "unreformed" and unrepentant capitalist class; victims of past movements such as the Cultural Revolution; cadres and intellectuals smitten with Western ideals; the nascent capitalist and middle classes; and spies and agents planted in China by foreign countries, including news reporters who "blackened" China and its leadership by spreading rumours. And as we shall in the following section, the ideologues accused neo-imperialists in the West, particularly the US, of spearheading the move to bring about China's transition to capitalism through "peaceful evolution".

The new battle against the bourgeois liberals showed up the feudalist and Maoist strains in Deng. The "master-reformist" had consistently refused to admit his errors in helping Chairman Mao execute the Anti-Rightist Movement of the mid-1950s. Deng's *Selected Works* of 1983 brimmed with hostility against participants in the Democracy Wall Movement of 1979-80, who, the patriarch said, were full of desire to "kill" the CCP. After all, Deng

approved the short-lived Campaign Against Spiritual Pollution in 1983 and
the Campaign Against Bourgeois Liberalisation in 1987.[2]

There was a subtle but important difference between the leftists and the CCP's
moderate wing on how to wage the campaign against liberalisation or "peaceful
evolution". Deng — and such of his followers as Zhao — agreed that, for the
sake of economic progress, the CCP had to pay the price of fostering a potentially anti-socialist class of private entrepreneurs. As we shall see in Chapter 6,
however, the Maoist ideologues wanted to restrict the economic and political role
played by the "red capitalists", who they perceived as a "fifth column".

In a seminal talk to the Central Party School in December 1989, then Chief
of the Central Committee Propaganda Department Wang Renzhi pinpointed
the inchoate "middle class" as the economic force behind the political phenomenon of bourgeois liberalisation. "Advocates of bourgeois liberalisation
pin their hopes on the 'middle class'," Wang said, pointing out that the middle class was the same as the bourgeois class decried by Marx and Mao.

Wang then cited — out of context — statements by liberal intellectuals
Wen Yuankai, Liu Binyan and Wan Runnan on the growth of a new pro-
Western, pro-reform class in China. "We should let private entrepreneurs
become a sizable political force in China," Wen reportedly said. "A new social
force is on the rise," Wang quoted Liu as saying. "This is the middle class
which comprises individual entrepreneurs as well as the managers of collective enterprises. They are not content just with money but want to take part in
politics. They seek political agents and spokesmen."[3]

Instead of seeking material gain and bourgeois values, the commissars
urged the people to see the light: the Yan'an-era spirit of "plain living and hard
struggle". "Except for a long period of plain living and hard work, we have no
other choice," the *People's Daily* intoned in August 1989. The spirit of austerity and self-reliance must "suffuse the entire process of production, work,
and living," the paper added. It railed against the "economics first" and the
"high consumption" theories propagated by the likes of Zhao Ziyang and Hu
Yaobang throughout the 1980s.[4]

B. Threat from the "Neo-Imperialists"

During the previous anti-liberal campaigns, the ideologues largely targeted
free-thinking intellectuals or "all-out Westernisers" such as Bai Hua, Fang
Lizhi and Wang Ruowang for spreading Western ideals about political plural-
ism. While Gang of Four holdovers like Xiong Fu, the former editor of *Red
Flag*, had as early as 1987 pinpointed the plot by "neo-imperialists" to subvert
China through Fang and other "running-dog" intellectuals, it was only after
June 4 that the anti-imperialist drive became a *leitmotif* of the times.

Deng Xiaoping gave the theory of "peaceful evolution" its most eloquent expression when he met Martial Law Command troops in Beijing three days after the massacre. He blamed the "rebellion" on a combination of external and internal factors, highlighting "plots" by the "neo-imperialists" to expedite China's "degeneration into a vassal of imperialism".[5] Referring to the pro-democracy protests, Deng said: "The storm will come sooner or later. This is determined by the major international [political] climate and China's own minor climate." The patriarch said the foreign-instigated rebels had two slogans: "Down with the Communist Party" and "Overturn the socialist system". "Their goal is to establish a totally Westernised republic," Deng warned.

CCP leaders and ideologues thus came to see the world as dominated by the Manichean struggle between good and evil, socialism and capitalism. As theorist Xu Dasen saw it: "In the fast-changing international scene, 'peaceful evolution' and the fight against 'peaceful evolution' is the major form taken by the struggle between capitalism and socialism." He added that "defeating the peaceful-evolution tactics of imperialism is the historical task for consolidating and developing socialism".[6]

Like other conspiracy theorists, Xu insisted that the US had been going about its peaceful-evolution plot since the end of the Second World War. Xu pinpointed a US Government White Paper of 1949, which mentioned the prospect of bringing about liberalisation in China through "democratic individualists" in the country. Like other commissars, Xu identified John Foster Dulles, US Secretary of State in the mid-1950s, as the grand strategist of peaceful evolution. He cited especially a speech by Dulles in July 1957, in which the US official reportedly said: "If they [the first generation of socialist leaders] bear children, and if the latter have children, their offspring will one day enjoy freedom." "These words show that Dulles pinned his hope of peaceful evolution on the third and fourth generation of socialist countries," the ideologue said.[7]

The democracy protests of 1989 were repeatedly cited as "proof" of American infiltration into China. Deng Xiaoping told former president Richard Nixon in their meeting in the autumn of 1989 that "the US was too deeply involved" in the democracy movement. In his report on the "counter-revolutionary turmoil", Beijing Mayor Chen Xitong repeatedly cited American and other foreign "conspiracies" to overthrow the Communist order.[8]

In the same vein, ideologue Xu Dasen claimed that in the spring and summer of 1989, "anti-communist forces in the US, Hong Kong and Taiwan co-opted bourgeois-liberal 'élites' on the mainland and supported them to fabricate pro-bourgeois liberalisation propaganda." He added: "Anti-communist forces in the US and the US-based reactionary organisation 'China Democratic League' took part and plotted this rebellion."

Unfortunately, neither Chen Xitong nor Xu Dasen could produce the facts. What they came up with was circumstantial evidence of, for example, "anti-Chinese" reporting by the Voice of America and other US, Hong Kong, and Taiwan media. Chinese sources said a key area of investigation into the activities of ousted party chief Zhao Ziyang, his secretary Bao Tong, as well as members of Zhao's think tanks was their so-called "American connection".[9]

For example, for a few months after June 4, Zhao aides were hauled in for questioning over the activities in China of the US-based Soros Foundation, alleged in internal publications to be a source of "bourgeois liberalisation" and a "front" for the Central Intelligence Agency. In 1988, the Foundation had set up a fund in China to help research in the social sciences as well as to finance overseas study trips by Chinese intellectuals. Beneficiaries included researchers in such radical brains trusts as the Research Institute for the Reform of the Economic Structure and the International Research Institute under CITIC. No incriminating evidence was found.[10]

Judging by the pronouncements of a number of ideologues, their fears seemed real. "The question of peaceful evolution and counter-peaceful evolution is the new characteristic of class struggle under new historical circumstances," intoned Beijing Normal University ideologue Wang Ruihua. CASS's Hu Sheng warned that if China were to lower its guard, the great nation would "go the same way as aboriginals in America and Australia".[11]

In the first year or so after the June 4 bloodbath, an intense debate erupted within the leadership as to whether the country should scale down relations with the US. Academic and cultural exchanges almost ground to a halt as these were supposed to pave the way for "peaceful evolution". However, it seemed clear from the start that the propagandists were playing up a "foreign threat" to divert attention from the party's failure to enact meaningful reform.

C. "Peaceful Evolution" after the Gulf War

The Gulf crisis of late 1990 to early 1991 furnished the panicky souls in Zhongnanhai with more evidence about American "imperialism". Shocked by the speed with which Yankee weaponry had quashed the war machine of Saddam Hussein, the ideologues feared that Washington might next turn to the East and "tame China". The most outspoken theorist about this conspiracy was He Xin, the Chinese Academy of Social Sciences literary critic turned futurologist who had in late 1990 become the adviser to Li Peng on international strategy.[12]

He Xin's idea about US imperialism after the Gulf War was eloquently expressed in an internal paper "The Gulf War and China", which received wide circulation within the leadership in January and February 1991. It is worth quoting in some detail. For He, known as an advocate of "neo-conservatism" as well as the "New Cold War", Washington's goal in annihilating the Iraqi war machine was simple: world domination.[13]

"The US is trying to use the absolute military superiority which it commands at the present moment to annihilate the Iraqi regime and to intimidate and control the problem-plagued Arab Peninsula," he wrote. "Its ultimate goal is the control of 40 to 60 per cent of the world's energy resources, and to manipulate oil-generated excess capital through puppet regimes."

He argued that "Yankee imperialism" was all the more alarming given the seemingly inevitable decline of Soviet power. "The status of the USSR in today's world strategy fails even to match that of tiny Iraq," he wrote. The then fast-rising theoretician noted that Beijing would suffer from the Gulf War on two levels. First, oil prices would fall, directly eroding China's export earnings. Moreover, the war would exacerbate a recession in the country's major markets. Much more important, however, was the fear that Washington would move next to "tame" China.

He invoked an apocalyptic vision that after victory in the Gulf, the US would "move its forces eastwards" to establish an Asian-Pacific empire. "The potential adversaries on America's list are Japan and China: its competitor in the area of economics and technology is Japan. But what lies in the way of the American goal of world unification is China."

"Out of its global strategic goal and the needs of its own security, the US has decided that it must thoroughly destroy the existing order of China and retool China's power [structure]," He continued. "Isolating China, blockading China, disintegrating it through [instigating] internal disorder, and eventually rendering China innocuous through democratising it has been and will be a strategic goal that the US will steadfastly continue to implement," he said.

In a follow-up paper around mid-1991, He Xin upped the ante by predicting a US-inspired war against China "within the coming three years". The document, which was also widely disseminated, counselled the nation to "prepare for war" against the neo-imperialists. He argued that to stop China's successful economic and military developments in their tracks — and to remove the last obstacle to its goal of "global domination" — the US might launch a pre-emptive attack on China in the next three years.

The CASS futurologist also predicted that, in view of "deepening contradictions" between North and South, and also within the capitalist camp, a Third World War would break out within the coming decade. He argued that national policy, including economic construction, should be formulated with the prospect of war in mind. Analysts said He was again sponsoring Maoist "war economics", which entails a high priority for defence-related industries and "plain living and hard struggle" for the populace.[14]

D. "Peaceful Evolution" after the Soviet Break-up

Zhongnanhai was shocked by the failed Soviet coup of August 1991. Soon after the putsch took place on the 19th, there was ecstasy all around. The leftist-dominated propaganda machinery was about to issue a public statement declaring the "victory of the Soviet people" against the vile revisionism of Gorbachev. The then ambassador to Moscow Yu Hongliang lost no time in offering China's congratulations to the "Gang of Eight" pretenders.

Self-congratulatory feelings gave way to fear and loathing as the coup fizzled out after three days. In an emergency session called by Deng Xiaoping, the elders and Politburo members expressed dismay at the future of Chinese-style socialism. Pointing to attempts by Boris Yeltsin's radical coalition to banish the Communist party, Deng said: "If this happens, China will be the only [major] country that still practises socialism. Then what shall we do?"[15]

As we shall see, leftist elders including Deng Liqun, who were present at the emergency conclave, tried to take advantage of the occasion to revive the Maoist doctrine that "class struggle is the key link". Among those who supported "Little Deng" was Li Peng. The premier reportedly said: "If peaceful evolution succeeds, it will spell the end of us [the CCP] no matter how successful economic development is."

From late August to the end of the year, the CCP issued a steady stream of documents playing up the need to raise its guard against Western infiltration. Take, for example, a document dated September 23 entitled "Correctly understand the rapidly changing situation in the Soviet Union". "Officials must seriously study the lessons of the Soviet Union and guard against the forces of peaceful evolution," it said. "The West will now step up its pressure on China, and a small number of bourgeois-liberal elements in China could try to take advantage of the situation." The document concluded by calling upon party members to build up an "iron wall" to keep out the forces of Western-style democratisation.[16]

In an internal talk weeks after the failed coup, Foreign Minister Qian Qichen also warned against new threats from the Yeltsin camp. "Some foreign countries think the Soviet communists are close to collapse and so are the Chinese. But China will remain the last bastion [of socialism]," he said. Qian indicated while the powers of Gorbachev were waning, those of Yeltsin were on the rise. China's foremost expert on the Soviet Union said that Yeltsin might revive "Russian imperialism", and that, in view of the 7,000-odd kilometres of common boundary between the two neighbours, this could spell trouble for Chinese stability. Seen in this context, China had to build a double wall, one against the West, and one against the former Soviet camp.[17]

E. Perennial Class Struggle As The Key Link

The ideologues were convinced that given the sorry state of the communist movement in the world, the struggle with bourgeois liberalisation would not only continue but be exacerbated through to the next century. With one stroke, the commissars had revived Mao's ultra-leftist idea of "perennial class struggle". One of the underlying themes of the Cultural Revolution was Mao's perception that the party was under threat from "capitalist roaders" and that repeated purges and mass movements must be launched against enemy forces as well as party members who had succumbed to the lure of revisionism.

After the 1989 massacre and the fall of communism in the former Soviet bloc, class struggle assumed new urgency. In a key article in the theoretical journal *Qiushi*, then propaganda chief Wang Renzhi pointed out: "We must use the class viewpoint of Marxism, and the Marxist methodology of class analysis to assess the counter-revolutionary rebellion [of 1989]. Only then can we see clearly the profundity, seriousness and danger of the struggle between the two roads."[18]

The arguments of the leftists represented a stunning reversal of Deng's reforms. Soon after he grasped power, the patriarch especially called a farewell to arms: he announced that class struggle was no longer the "major contradiction" of the times or the "core" of national endeavour, and that the party and government must re-focus its attention on economic construction (See Chapter 1).

In his televised address on the 40th anniversary of the founding of the People's Republic on October 1, 1989, Jiang Zemin paid lip service to the Deng concept that "class struggle is no longer the primary contradiction of our society." In the same breath, however, the party chief said: "Class struggle will continue to exist within certain parameters, and it will even be exacerbated under certain conditions."[19]

How long will the class struggle go on? In his essay in *Qiushi*, Wang Renzhi said since bourgeois liberalisation "runs counter to the fundamental interest of the working class and the broad masses", its defeat and death was "inevitable". "We are full of confidence towards the eventual victory of socialism as well as the future of communism," he said. At the same time, however, the ideologues were preparing the people for a "long-term struggle". After all, soon after the December 1986 student demonstrations, then chief editor of *Red Flag* Xiong Fu quoted Deng Xiaoping and other party elders as saying the campaign against bourgeois liberalisation would last "50 to 70 years". That Deng had indeed raised the point of a 100-year-long struggle was evident from the Third Volume of his *Selected Works* published in late 1993.[20]

Ideologues like Little Deng did their level best to re-affirm the Cultural

LIBRARY
BISHOP BURTON COLLEGE
BEVERLEY HU17 8QG

Revolution in their efforts to justify Maoist class struggle. The former head of
the Propaganda Department told participants in an internal party meeting in
early 1991 that Chairman Mao was right in initiating the Ten Years of Chaos.
"We must have a new assessment of the Cultural Revolution," he said. "Parts
of the movement were correct and should be re-affirmed." For example, Little
Deng claimed: "Mao was right to bombard the capitalist roaders. It was only
in its execution that the [original] goals of the Revolution went astray." Little
Deng insisted that Maoist-style class struggles must be periodically launched.
At which point his protégés voiced vehement support. For example, Vice-
Head of Propaganda Nie Dajiang was overheard commenting: "Comrade
Liqun has voiced what has been on our minds for the past few years."[21]

In the final analysis, the ideologues were again propagating perennial class
struggle because they lacked confidence about the attractiveness — and the
"eventual victory" — of their creed. This was laid bare in a fairly frank article in *Contemporary Ideas* in April 1991. "The attitude of those who are resolutely opposed to liberalisation and the attitude of those who insist on liberalisation are very firm," said the commentator of the leftist journal. "The key
to the anti-liberalisation struggle lies in winning over middle-of-the-road people."[22] Given the bed of roses that bourgeois-liberals are promising the masses, the spartan Maoists need to hunker down for a century-long combat.

In explaining the "perennial nature" of the anti-bourgeois struggle, ideologue Guo Yubing said weeks after the Tiananmen Square crackdown: "An
extremely small minority of reactionary elements, who hate the Communist
Party and the socialist order, have never given up their political goal."[23] Guo
did not make it clear why a party of 51 million members needed to fear such
an "extremely small minority". The truth of the matter may be that power
struggles and "criticism and self-criticisms" are an integral part of CCP culture: As Mao and Deng knew, without such "struggles", party members would
spend their time making money and making merry, in the process making ideology, the *raison d'etre* of the party, totally irrelevant.

III. Leftists versus Deng Xiaoping, 1989-1992

A. Deng as "Soft-handed" towards Liberalisation

Before restoring their Maoist agenda, the leftists first had to negate a sizable
chunk of the reforms introduced since late 1978. In other words, they had to
cripple "Dengism" before they could rehoist the old standards. An effective
way for cutting down the New Helmsman was to imply that he had acquiesced
in the liberalising tendencies throughout the 1980s.

The leftists' critique of Deng Xiaoping was inherent in State Council Research Office Director Yuan Mu's summation of CCP history since 1949. "History and the experience of reality have repeatedly told us that when we are fighting rightism we must counter 'leftism,' and vice versa," said Yuan, Li Peng's right-hand man. "During the first 30 years, the country concentrated on ceaselessly combating the right, the result was it made a 'leftist' error. In the past 10 years, it concentrated its efforts on fighting 'leftism,' and neglected the growth of rightist tendencies. The result has been the inundation of bourgeois liberalisation."[24] The implication was that the New Helmsman did not acquit himself well in setting the ideal, "neither-left-nor-right" course for the country.

In the same vein, the *People's Daily* complained in an article in late 1990 that "in the past few years, under the new conditions of reform and the open-door policy, party construction, the construction of spiritual civilisation, and ideological and political work have been seriously neglected". It added that "because of this, many negative and corrupt phenomena have arisen and led to the strong dissatisfaction of the people."[25]

It is no secret that the ideologues had long blamed the liberal wing of the party — and by implication Deng Xiaoping — for conniving at the expansion of bourgeois-liberal influence of the past decade. They identified at least four or five instances of the "inundation" of Western values. The first was the Beijing Spring or Democracy Wall movement of 1979 and 1980, during which Wei Jingsheng and other liberals advanced the earth-shattering idea that "democratisation is the most important modernisation". Deng was then hardly "soft-handed": he was "resolute" enough to arrest Wei and lock him up for 15 years.

Then came the Campaign Against Spiritual Pollution of late 1983. Thanks to the intervention of Hu Yaobang and Zhao Ziyang, who threatened to resign on the grounds that the campaign was driving away Western investors, it lasted no more than 40 days. Zhao also managed to contain the scope of the Campaign Against Bourgeois Liberalisation (CABL), which raged for several months after the December 1986 student movement. In the case of the CABL especially, Deng fully supported the "fire-fighting" efforts of Zhao.[26]

Looking back on the years of reform, Deng Liqun came to the absurd conclusion that whenever it was an even year, the forces of liberalisation swelled. In an odd year, however, the empire struck back in the form of a determined clamp down on Western ideas. For Little Deng, there was no doubt that it was Deng who had failed to contain the inundation of spiritual poison.[27]

In a commentary in April 1991, the *People's Daily* appeared to exonerate Deng by claiming that his instructions about clamping down on rightism had not been followed. "For more than ten years, even though comrade Deng Xiaoping had very clearly insisted on the Four Cardinal Principles and on combating bourgeois liberalisation, the struggle against liberalisation had not been waged according to the instructions of Deng," the commentator said. "During many major rounds [of the struggle against bourgeois liberalisation] we injected enthusiasm and efforts; yet they all got nowhere and were aborted."[28] The arrow, of course, was aimed squarely at Deng. For without the patriarch's consent, how could these anti-rightist crusades have fizzled out?

B. Were Deng's Reforms Surnamed Capitalist?

For die-hard conservatives like Wang Renzhi, the dozen-year-long reform consisted of no more than a tilt to bourgeois-liberal values. As the Propaganda Chief put it in early 1990: "Ten years had elapsed from the Exploratory Theoretical Work Conference in the spring of 1979 to the political storm in the spring and summer of 1989. During this decade, the trend of bourgeois-liberal thoughts ebbed and flowed but it became more and more serious."[29]

The Exploratory Theoretical Work Conference, whose participants included such intellectual as giants Wang Ruoshui, Sun Changjiang, Yu Haocheng and Yan Jiaqi, laid the groundwork for reform, especially "thought liberation" and the "modernisation of Marxism". It was at this "conference of enlightenment" that the "whateverism" of Maoist party chief Hua Guofeng ("whatever the Chairman said was right") was shot down. Delegates also enshrined the key reformist slogan "practice is the sole criterion of truth". Not surprisingly, the conference was called at the behest of Deng Xiaoping and his protégé Hu Yaobang.

Going by their own standards, the leftists were certainly right in fingering the "crimes" of Zhao — and, by extension, Deng. It is true that albeit indirectly and subtly, Zhao and his followers had waged a campaign to emasculate the Four Cardinal Principles. In his private conversations, Zhao had admitted that for him, socialism was no more than "communist party leadership plus distribution according to labour". In one of the many anti-Zhao articles published after June 4, the liberal party chief was reported to have said that of the Four Cardinal Principles, only "CCP leadership" need to be upheld. "The other three can be downplayed or ignored," Zhao reportedly said. "Nobody is sure what exactly the socialist road is."[30]

In ideology, both Hu and Zhao encouraged the famous policy of "tolerance and harmony". In 1985 and 1986, Hu set off another round of "thought liberation" by announcing that "Marxism could not solve the problems of today". Zhao was in a sense less adventurous than his predecessor in terms of ideas. However, the former party chief and premier had tried to "reform" ideological and political work by in general playing down Marxist orthodoxy.[31]

Especially in the mid-1980s, Zhao had turned his attention exclusively to economic matters. He had in particular given support to the private sector, arguing that non-state-owned entities such as town and village enterprises should spearhead the transformation of the entire economy into an amalgam of public and private sectors. Zhao gave special favours to the private-sector units along the South and East coast, hoping that they would expedite the integration of the Chinese economy with that of the West.

The Deng-Zhao line was criticised for neglecting education in ideology. As CASS researcher Li Pengcheng said not long after the June 4 crackdown, the Zhaoists had encouraged "economicism and pragmatism" in policy-making, and they had forgotten that "the fundamental purpose of the CCP was to practise socialism and communism". Deng made an implicit self-criticism when he said about a year after the June 4 crackdown that China had for the past ten years neglected "education", meaning ideological education.[32]

In his self-defence at the end of June 1989, which was first published by the *Hong Kong Economic Journal* in June 1994, Zhao admitted that he had failed to grasp ideological and political work well enough. In the same breath, however, he indicated that problems of ideology could automatically be solved if economic reform succeeded. The former party chief questioned the effectiveness of old, Yan'an-style indoctrination. Zhao pointed out: "To solve the question in people's minds whether socialism is superior to capitalism. . . we must render reform successful and quickly develop a socialist democracy that is suitable for China."

Moreover, Zhao also quoted Deng's remarks that the success of the campaign against bourgeois liberalisation hinged on the success of reform. "We must not carry out mass movements," Zhao quoted Deng as saying. "We must rely on reforms and develop the economy well to show the superiority of socialism. We must use practical results to convince those who distrust the socialist system."[33] In other words, both Zhao and Deng were prime advocates of "economicism and pragmatism".

Equally devastating is the related charge that quasi-capitalist reforms sponsored by Deng and Zhao had shepherded the country down the capitalist road. The leftists had by 1990 revived the old argument about the "surnames" of a particular line or policy: that China should only adopt measures surnamed socialist. As the leftist *Guangming Daily* put it in an article in August 1991: "In actual life, there were reform concepts and reform measures surnamed socialist and surnamed capitalist," the commentator said. He added that the "capitalist" kind of reform and the open door would pave the way for "all-out" and "comprehensive" Westernisation. The *Daily* warned that if the country did not differentiate between the surnames, "the people's ideological armament will be dissolved" and "reform will go down the road of evil".[34]

In internal meetings, the central planners' critique against Zhao was balder. In a "dump Zhao" meeting even before the June 4 massacre, Li Peng and Yao

Yilin had listed four major crimes of the party boss. The first was: "Zhao has engendered a capitalist market economy, not a socialist commodity economy."[35] The charge that Deng and Zhao had not only failed to tell "capitalist" from "socialist" reform — but had advocated the former — raged anew with the dissolution of Soviet Communism. As we shall see, the quasi-capitalist tendencies unleashed by the *nanxun* did not deter the Maoists from bombarding what they saw as efforts to undermine socialism and the party's survival.[36]

C. Mao as a Weapon to Beat Deng

(i) Mao as the Prophet against "Peaceful Evolution"

In the eyes of the leftists, there was no question that, compared with the New Helmsman, the Great Helmsman was much more adept at discerning the challenge from bourgeois liberalism. From late 1989 to 1992, a veritable Mao craze was whipped up by the propaganda machinery. The mastermind of the campaign, not surprisingly, was Deng Liqun and his cohorts.

In a series of talks in late 1991, Deng Liqun claimed that if China had followed Mao's edicts, it could have snuffed out bourgeois as well as "revisionist" values long ago. The conclusion, of course, was that Deng Xiaoping was not "resolute" enough in cutting off the tail of capitalism. "It was Chairman Mao who first raised the warning against peaceful evolution and laid down strategic tasks on how to prevent it," Little Deng said, adding the Helmsman was also dead on target about Soviet revisionism. The leftist commissar said the Mao craze was a "healthy and progressive phenomenon that was full of hope".[37]

In the many conferences on Mao Thought organised during this period, other ideologues heaped praise on China's once-and-future philosopher king. Su Houzhong, who taught Marxism at the Beijing Municipal Party School, considered Maoism the "spiritual weapon for socialist reform". Su thought that the late Chairman's ideals guaranteed that China would not become "revisionist" or fall victim to "peaceful evolution". Referring to the liberalisation movement in the Eastern bloc, cultural commissar Wei Wei wrote in an article for the 97th birthday of Mao: "The series of changes in the international arena have proven how correct Mao's judgment was on matters like class struggle, the struggle between the two roads [socialism and capitalism] and the possibility of the revival of capitalism."[38]

Lecturer Su laid particular store by Mao's warnings against the "smokeless warfare" waged by the capitalist schemers. "Mao's many strategic ideas about the prevention of the 'peaceful-evolution' [tactics] perpetrated by our adversaries in the international scene must be upheld," he said. Ideologue Feng Xianzhi eulogised the Great Helmsman for "accurately foreseeing" the imperialist plot as early as 1964. Feng quoted a Mao speech of June 16, 1964, in which the great leader said: "The imperialists have said that they have lost hope in our first and second generation. But they see hope in the third and fourth generation. Will their prediction come true? I hope not. But it could yet be so."[39]

In a sense, there was mass support for the "Mao Phenomenon" although not for reasons the ideologues would have liked. There were indications that in cities and towns, ordinary Chinese were smitten with some form of Mao nostalgia. For example, in 1991 more than 1 million people — four times that of 1980 — visited Mao's hometown in Shaoshan, Hunan Province. In the same year, there were seven films based on different aspects of Mao's life. The new edition of Mao's collected works sold upwards of 1 million copies. Mao pictures were very much in demand for decorating homes as well as the windscreens of vans and buses.[40]

China analysts said that especially after the June 4 crackdown, disillusioned Chinese looked to the Mao era as halcyon days of relative purity, when there was "clean government" and guaranteed income. As the semi-official Hong Kong China News Agency pointed out in a late 1989 article: "The people thank Mao for helping the needy and stabilising the people's livelihood . . . they hope Mao's style of honesty, cleanliness in government and frugality in enterprise can be developed." In another dispatch, HKCNA said the people were nostalgic about the "unforgettable" 1950s, when "the cadres were uncorrupt, and the people were harmonious and loved each other".[41]

Other commissars praised Mao's marriage of ideology and the economy, as seen in the Great Helmsman's exhortation that the new proletariat men and women should forge a new heaven and earth through "plain living and hard struggle". A key Maoist slogan for building up heavy industry, "in industry, learn from Daqing [Oilfield]," was revived with gusto.[42]

A congratulatory message sent by the State Council on the occasion of the 30th anniversary of the founding of the oilfield said: "The Daqing spirit and experience is a valuable spiritual nugget and it must be further developed." According to the State Council, the Daqing spirit consisted of "patriotism, building up an enterprise through plain living and hard struggle, seeking after truth, and self-sacrifice". In other words, building up the country the Daqing way would ensure that phenomena of Western-style corruption — wheeling and dealing and "looking at everything with only money in mind" — could be avoided.[43]

(ii) Deng as the Humble Student of Mao

Another strategy used by Deng's enemies to negate reform was to portray him as but a humble student of the Helmsman. For if Deng Thought was seen as no more than an outgrowth of Mao Thought, there would be no need for bold

reforms. And liberal ideas on the "rightist" fringe of the Deng cosmology —
such as that advocated by Hu and Zhao — would be deemed heresy.

For example, in a late 1990 article in *People's Daily*, ideologue Wang
Hongmo argued that Deng's theories about party construction were "a continuation and development" of Chairman Mao's. "In the struggle against bourgeois liberalisation, Deng has strengthened the leadership function of the
party, in the process manifesting his resoluteness in defending Mao's theory
on party construction," Wang added. He also quoted such Deng aphorisms as
"we must completely and accurately comprehend Mao Thought" and "We
must scientifically establish the leading position of Mao Thought".[44]

At the same time, commissars within the PLA highlighted the linkage
between the military thinking of Mao and Deng, both of whom had been
chairmen of the Central Military Commission (CMC). For example, Chief
Political Commissar Yang Baibing pointed out in late 1990: "Chairman Mao,
Chairman Deng and other older generation of proletarian revolutionaries put
great emphasis on party construction in grassroots military units."[45]

That, at the height of the leftist restoration, Deng was talked about almost
in the past tense was evident from a China News Service report in October
1990 on a Conference on Deng Thought held in his native county of Guang'an
in Sichuan Province. A key item on the agenda of the conclave, CNS reported, was to "remember Deng's contributions to the Chinese revolution". There
was, of course, no cause to "remember" the patriarch if he could still move
mountains for reform.[46]

That the CCP's left wing would sooner or later re-hoist the Maoist standard
— or even claimed that Deng was nothing more than Mao's disciple — was
inevitable. After all, Deng never tried, or dared, to exorcise totally the
Chairman's ghost by repudiating his mentor's feudalistic world-view. This was
evident from the landmark *Resolution on Certain Questions of the History of
the Party since 1949*, which was passed in 1981.

Billed as the CCP's definitive assessment of its own post-Liberation record,
the *Resolution* actually boiled down to the appraisal of one man: Mao Zedong.
The key clause of the *Resolution* — "Chairman Mao's contributions are primary, his mistakes secondary" — was not unexpected. In spite of the horren-
dous failings of the Great Leap Forward and the Cultural Revolution, it was
obvious that the CCP leadership, including Deng Xiaoping, lacked the nerve
to sweep Mao into the dustbin of history. As Deng admitted while the
Resolution was being drafted: "If we go overboard and blacken comrade Mao
Zedong, we'll be blackening our party and our country."[47]

There were other reasons why, in spite of the atrocities he had committed,
the Great Helmsman's former associates dared not dump him. For example, in
the mid-1950s, Deng was Mao's key enforcer in the pogrom against liberal

intellectuals known as the Anti-Rightist Movement. Had Mao been unreservedly condemned, Deng, too, would have to be banished from the political stage. The wishy-washy verdict on Mao, however, provided the theoretical underpinning for Gang-of-Four holdovers to rehabilitate the reputation of the fallen demigod.[48]

IV. "Party Construction" as the Key to Survival

A. Crusade to Save the Party

As we have seen, the CCP concluded that the key to preventing "peaceful evolution" was weeding out disloyal elements from its ranks. Soon after the massacre, the party set about the task of "party construction". It meant first of all boosting the "cohesiveness" of the 50-million strong party affiliates through promoting ideological and political work (IPW). CCP cells and other party-related organisations would be re-established among local-administration units as well as in factories, farms and colleges. And "party life" meetings including indoctrination and "criticism and self-criticism" sessions would be back on stream. The ideologues believed if the party could become a "steel fortress", it could easily withstand the slings and arrows of liberalisation. Equally important, Maoist commissars saw in the promotion of IPW and party construction a way to reassert their powers and to claw back the turf lost to modernisation-minded cadres.

The goals of party construction were made clear by the then member of the Politburo Standing Committee Song Ping at a late 1989 meeting of cadres from central and local Organisation Departments. Song stated that the major reason why the 1989 protests went as far as they did was that organisation and discipline in the CCP had been weak and lax. The hardline elder pointed out that the "counter-revolutionary rebellion" of 1989 had "enabled us to see clearly that there are many problems in party organisation and among the rank and file. Some of these problems are extremely serious. There were many Communist party members among those who instigated, organised and directed the rebellion."[49]

Song then elaborated on the programme for "party construction". First and foremost, the leftist elder said the commissars must "ensure that the party organisation is pure" by "guaranteeing that various leadership positions and functions are taken up by true Marxists". Purges would periodically be conducted among cadres and party members: they would be appraised particularly on their behaviour during the spring and summer of 1989. Harking back to the Mao days, officials would be sent to the grassroots to "learn from the masses".

The second prong of the attack was to re-build the party cells. Party organisations in the government, factories and universities would be reinstated and strengthened in the wake of the "misguided" attempts by Zhao Ziyang at "separating the party and government". Since Zhao's crusade to "weaken" the party, CCP organisations in many government units had been abolished (see Chapter 5). As we shall see later, special emphasis was put on re-building party cells in the countryside, where 80 per cent of the population lived. A mid-1991 *People's Daily* analysis admitted that with the break-up of the commune, many farmers thought "there is no more need for the party cell [to exercise power]". And by late 1989, party and government organisations in 20 per cent of village administrations were considered close to paralysis.[50]

In his address, Song indicated that the party would also crack the whip on individual members' personal relationship with Western governments and institutions. "In their dealings with foreign countries and foreigners in the past few years, many party members only talked about 'friendship', 'bottoms up', and 'let the world be filled with love'," the then Politburo member scolded. "They have lowered their guard towards the peaceful evolution plot of the imperialists. Their ideological armament has totally disintegrated."[51]

At the same time, an unprecedented "spiritual civilisation" and "socialist education" campaign was launched in the cities and countryside. "We must stress education on the Four Cardinal Principles, combating bourgeois liberalisation, and rectifying ideological and theoretical questions that have been perverted by bourgeois liberalisation," Song said. "Through frequent education campaigns and IPW, we must ensure that ideological and propaganda fronts are occupied by socialist ideas."

It was left to Jiang Zemin, considered a crypto-Maoist by many Beijing intellectuals, to give vent to perhaps the most radical statement on IPW: that the party must start "patriotic education" with infants. While talking to Shanghai NPC deputies in 1990, Jiang indicated socialist education must start from the young. "This kind of education must start from kindergartens and primary schools," he said, adding that values about socialism and patriotism should "take root in the heart and soul of children".[52]

B. The Sorry State of the Party

Even before the 1989 democracy movement, it had become obvious that the CCP had lost not only its importance but its relevance in the large- and medium-sized cities. During the December 1986 student demonstrations — considered to be a "trial run" for the events in the spring of 1989 — there were anti-party protests in an estimated 150 cities. Such key Hu Yaobang aides as Hu Qili and Zhu Houze began talking about the urgency of tackling the "crisis of confidence" in the party as early as 1984. [53]

After the June 4 bloodbath, the prestige and legitimacy of the CCP plunged to new lows. Few college and middle-school graduates bothered to enroll in the party. Chinese sources said that those who were eager to sign up looked upon CCP affiliation as a ticket for professional advancement in government. What surprised many analysts, however, was the fact that even in the villages, considered the traditional strongholds of the party, faith in the CCP also reached a nadir.

The sorry state of the party in the countryside was graphically illustrated by a report given by then vice-president Wang Zhen to an internal meeting in February 1991, in which the arch-conservative warned that the nation's villages were in danger of being overrun by the forces of Western religion, capitalism and the clans.[54]

Wang said the prestige and vitality of the CCP had fallen to a record low, with practically no desire among young rural folk to become party members. The speech, entitled "The Challenge of Feudalist Forces in Villages", pointed out that in rural areas, party organisations and activities were being disrupted and broken up by the influence of religion, the inchoate "capitalist class", and clans.

"Fewer and fewer people want to be enrolled in the party or the Communist Youth League, yet more and more people want to join religious groups," Wang said. "Many people in the villages, particularly young people, have absolutely no desire to join the party or the league." For example, in Handan county, Hebei Province, 813 people became Catholics in 1990 while only 270 people joined the party. And from 1982 to 1990, the number of Christians in central Henan province swelled from 400,000 to more than 1 million. Many of these new converts made the unheard of decision to withdraw voluntarily from the party. Sixteen did so in the Langfang district in Hebei in 1990.

The vice-president particularly deplored the fact that "while political activities are cold-shouldered, religious ones are drawing large crowds". He said that the eight places of worship in a village in Cheng'an county in Hebei were bustling with life during the twice-daily Bible classes, weekly masses, as well as at major festivals such as Easter and Christmas. "We take part in church activities of our own free will. Nobody need notify us, and we want no recompense," Wang quoted one convert as saying. By comparison, attendance at meetings organised by party cells was unsatisfactory, despite the fact that proceedings were relayed to the masses by broadcast systems and each attendee was paid 1 yuan.

The vice-president said he was equally disturbed by the fact that "while the words of CCP cadres in the villages have little appeal, the response to religious figures is overwhelming". For example, in Cheng'an in late 1990, 500 people gave money and 600 donated their labour to the building of a 4,000 square-metre church, which was finished in one month. However, response to appeals for public duty by party units was tepid.

In the summer of 1990, party authorities in Ningjin county in Hebei resorted to asking a Catholic priest to persuade farmers to sell their grain to the government. In many counties in remote Qinghai province, party organisers practically depended on church networks to promote CCP activities. "The approval of church leaders is required before [party-related] mass meetings can be called," Wang reported. Some party officials even had to make use of the opportunity of a church gathering to talk to their people. The vice-president admitted that some people had joined the "religious army" to "absolve themselves of the pains of reality".

Even more alarming was the phenomenon that new capitalists in the villages — the bosses of private and co-operative rural enterprises — were buying power with money. (For a more detailed discussion of the rise of the "red capitalists", see Chapter 6). "To consolidate their positions and to make further advances, they [the capitalists] have an increasing motive in seeking political status," Wang said. For example, the so-called 10,000-yuan or 100,000-yuan householders engaged party cadres as consultants to their businesses. They gave generously to charities and built up their "masses network" by dispensing loans and creating jobs.

Quite a few of the *nouveaux riches* individual entrepreneurs had become deputies to people's congresses, and local units of the Chinese People's Political Consultative Conference. Some had even become village administrators. To supplement their meagre incomes, many cadres teamed up with the capitalists or otherwise offered them illegal protection and "conveniences".

Wang disclosed that one-third of the 611 party cadres in seven villages in Linxiang county, Hunan province, had become partners of or consultants to private entrepreneurs and had all but abandoned their party-related work. The rising clout of the "converts to Adam Smith" had further undermined the prestige of the party. As the vice-president testified: "Some peasants are openly saying, 'we would rather follow the money-splashing rich households than offer our allegiance to the poor government'."

The third evil decried by the vice-president was the revival of the influence of clans, which were supposed to have been wiped out by the communist revolution in 1949. He cited the popular adage: "We would rather depend on the clans than on village governments. We would rather salute the chief clansman than the village chief." One third of the villages in the outskirts of Yueyang city in Hunan had resuscitated clan organisations, he said.

The revival of the clans was confirmed by a late 1991 report in the Shanghai *Wen Hui Bao*. "Feudal-patriarchal forces are now gaining ground after disappearing from the scene for a long time," the report said. "Such forces are pounding at the stability and unity of the countryside." The news-paper said that in many cases, peasants were paying respect to clan laws and taking their problems to the clan elder instead of to the government.[55]

V. The Post-Tiananmen Square Purges

Draconian purges — the most extensive house-cleaning after the Cultural Revolution — were carried out in the first few months after June 4. There were no mass executions or *wudou* ("armed struggle") as in the Cultural Revolution. However, many aspects were reminiscent of the Ten Years of Chaos. "Work teams" were stationed in practically all central party and government departments in addition to many local units. Investigation units were assigned to prominent intellectuals ranging from officials such as Zhao Ziyang and Bao Tong to journalists including Dai Qing and Zhang Weiguo.

As Chinese sources said, during the first six months after June 4, party members in most central government units, and in some instances, even non-party cadres and officials, were asked to give a detailed, day-to-day account of their "involvement" in the democracy crusade. To satisfy the inquisitors, CCP members under investigation had to furnish evidence that they did not take part in demonstrations, that they did not express support to the students, and that they did not sign the numerous petitions to Beijing asking for democ-ratisation.[56]

In the first half of 1990, the CCP launched an unprecedented "re-registration" campaign: all party members automatically lost their affiliation until they were re-registered after satisfying the authorities of their total devotion to Marxism and the party. This variant of the purges had never been carried out before.

The rationale for the purges was given by Jiang Zemin in a late 1989 speech to the party organisation experts. "There were many party members who went out to take part in street demonstrations during the turmoil," the party boss said. "This is a serious problem." Jiang indicated that the most dangerous among the unfaithful party members were "opportunists and fence-sitters" who held leading cadre positions.[57]

The party chief also laid down guidelines for the recruitment of new members. In a throwback to the era of Mao, who considered intellectuals as members of the "stinking ninth category", Jiang said more proletarians — mainly workers and farmers — should be inducted. The party boss also ruled that people with "exploitative behaviour" should be barred from the party. By late 1989, the Organisation Department had issued specific orders barring private-sector practitioners from joining the CCP (see Chapter 6).

The results of the purges were announced by the *People's Daily* in mid-

1991. The total number of CCP members had reached 50.3 million. In 1990, 127,000 affiliates were either expelled, or persuaded to leave the CCP. In addition, 166,000 members were subjected to internal party discipline. All in all, however, the authorities were satisfied that the house-cleaning had engendered a crop of more loyal and "combat-ready" rank and file. Fully 70 per cent of the "model workers" in various fields were CCP members. More than 1.3 million new members were inducted in 1990.[58]

No new pogroms were announced after early 1991. However, it is a law of Stalinist politics that one purge leads to another. In spite of the CCP's avowed satisfaction with the results of the purges, the party did not feel one whit more secure. In June 1991, the Central Committee released yet another circular pointing out that the CCP was still under dire threat from within and without. The document said the party had been "subjected to the dual attacks of foreign-based subversion and anti-party forces from within". "Inner-party enemies" referred to bourgeois-liberal cadres who because of the party's neglect of discipline and education had penetrated the higher echelons.[59]

Chinese sources said that on instruction from the leadership, security departments, including the police and secret police, had beefed up "internal security". This meant increased surveillance of officials, including relatively senior cadres, who were suspected of having unsanctioned contact with the West. Cadres on the "lists of suspects" included former associates of Hu Yaobang and Zhao Ziyang, some of whom, like Hu Qili, Yan Mingfu and others, had been partially rehabilitated by mid-1991.[60]

In retrospect, the purges were not as severe as some intellectuals had feared in 1989. A surprisingly large number of pro-democracy party members or intellectuals received relatively light sentences of one to two years. However, markedly different sets of criteria were at work in the nationwide purge. For example, workers in the movement received a much harsher treatment than intellectuals, particularly those listed by Amnesty International and Asia Watch. Moreover, provincial administrations tended to mete out tougher sentences than Beijing did. Within the CCP, the house-cleaning had the effect of further alienating intellectuals, who realised in any case that a party membership was now worth next to nothing (see Chapter 5).[61]

VI. The Great Socialist Education Campaign

A. The Primacy of Spiritual Engineering

To arrest the decline of the party's prestige and to restore the the people's faith in socialism, the CCP went about reviving another Maoist canon: brainwashing. Sometimes called "spiritual engineering", Mao believed that a man's thoughts and beliefs — even his "class" nature — could be changed if he were subjected to the right education or indoctrination. Through psychological coercion or mass hysteria, a bloodthirsty capitalist can be turned into an eat-from-the-common-wok proletariat.

A major means of "spiritual engineering" was through the building up of "socialist spiritual civilisation", which would provide the norms of thought and behaviour for a worthy citizen of socialist China. For the first time since the Cultural Revolution, the CCP decided to put together a plan for spiritual civilisation that would match that of material civilisation, or economic development.

Thus, while the central planners were in 1990 and 1991 drafting the Eighth Five-Year Plan and the Ten-Year Economic Blueprint, the ideologues were also readying blueprints for constructing their "empire of the spirit". For example, at a national conference on building spiritual civilisation held in November 1990, Propaganda Chief Wang Renzhi spelled out the criteria for a Five-Year Plan for Spiritual Civilisation to propagate values including patriotism, total self-abnegation, and unthinking devotion to the CCP. "We must make a concerted effort to organise mass-oriented activities to construct spiritual civilisation," Wang said. "Relying on the participation of millions of people, we will ensure that the task of building socialist spiritual civilisation will be implemented at grassroots levels in towns and villages."[62]

The ideologues' efforts to reinstate Maoism were disturbing because they went against the promise, made by the CCP soon after the end of the Cultural Revolution, that mass movements would be a thing of the past. The emphasis on the "empire of the spirit" ran counter to Deng Xiaoping's insistence that economics should precede politics. As the patriarch put it in a 1983 speech: "For a long period in the past, we have neglected the development of production forces. That is why we now have to pay special attention to material civilisation."[63]

Deng's argument was based on the fundamental Marxist precept: that economics is the basic structure of society, while concepts such as culture and ideology are the "superstructure" that changes in accordance with the metamorphosis of the fundamental structure. Wang Renzhi, however, seemed to dispute this point. "The development of the commodity economy [alone] will not bring about a high degree of spiritual civilisation," he said.[64]

As we shall see, special attention was being paid to "socialist education" in the countryside, deemed the bastion of Communist rule. As the *People's Daily* put it: "Farmers make up more than 80 per cent of the population. Agriculture is the basis of the economy. The implementation of socialist education in the villages has a high significance for the consolidation of the socialist regime." In other words, the CCP ran the risk of losing power if proper remedial measures in thought control were not taken in the villages.[65]

B. The Big Lie

For neutral observers, a sizeable portion of the process of building "spiritual civilisation" consisted of painting a thick coat of whitewash over the imperfections of the Communist regime. The people were asked to study articles and speeches by a group of "élite Marxist intellectuals" who claimed socialist economics and politics were infinitely superior to those of capitalism.

A typical apologia for socialism was penned by He Xin in the *People's Daily* in December 1990. The CASS futurologist argued that "overall, the socialist economy has more life and energy than the capitalist economy". "Some Western economists have tried to convince us that the reason why underdeveloped countries are underdeveloped is because they have a bad, non-market economic system," He said. However, the academic pointed out, capital had in the past decade actually been flowing from the underdeveloped into the developed world. "Underdeveloped countries are poor because first, there is a problem with their developmental goal, and second, because developed countries are not willing to let them succeed," He contended.[66]

He, who had no training in economics, claimed that in the past 40 years, China's growth rate was not low but excessively fast. He even ventured that "many economic problems of China have been engendered precisely by the excessively fast development of production forces". The Li Peng protégé failed, however, to explain why, if the socialist system was so superior, China needed to adopt the reform policy in the first place.

Yuan Mu, considered Li Peng's alter ego, stuck to the same theme in a talk to a German reporter at about the same time. The State Council spokesman said China should be proud of its socialist economy. He asserted that since China was assured of a growth rate of at least six per cent throughout the 1990s, it was fast closing in on the Western world whose economy was forecast to expand at a much slower rate.[67] Yuan, however, forgot to explain why, if the Chinese way was so preferable, about 40 per cent of the state-run factories were perennially in the red.

The commissars revived much of the rhetoric and vocabulary of the 1950s when they tried to disparage the Western political system. For example, Vice-chief of Propaganda Xu Weichang argued in an article entitled "On the Fundamental Difference Between the Two Types of Democracy" that in "socialist democracies, power was held by the great majority of citizens with working people as the main [foundation]". In capitalist countries, Xu claimed, "a small minority of the representatives of the capitalist class" wielded all the power. The ideologue dismissed as a "sham" such Western institutions as elections. He ridiculed "press freedom" in the West as yet another bogus "bourgeois-liberal" institution.[68]

Even party elders who had long retired from the frontline felt compelled to lend their voice to bashing capitalism. "It is an objective law of the historical development of mankind that the socialist order will supplant the capitalist order," former NPC chairman Peng Zhen pointed out in an address to the nation's youth. "Chaos, defeat, further chaos, further defeat, until destruction, this is the logic facing imperialism and all reactionary forces in the world," Peng intoned. "I strongly believe you will bravely march forward along the road [of socialism] and make continual improvements until communism is reached."[69]

At the same time, the CCP re-launched Maoist-style "mass movements" to coax the masses into learning from a number of proletarian saints. Even intellectuals inured to the worst excesses of communist propaganda were shocked when, in March 1990, the CCP kicked off a full-scale campaign on Lei Feng, who was lionised by Mao in 1963. As Jiang Zemin put it when he met with former colleagues of the "unstinting screw of the revolution": "We must learn from Lei Feng's communist-style total self-abnegation. We must learn from Lei Feng's self-sacrificing spirit. We must learn from Lei Feng's spirit of total devotion to the people."[70]

In a commentary, *Seeking Truth* pointed out that the Lei Feng spirit was a crystallisation of the wisdom of Chinese socialism. "The Lei Feng spirit is the continuation and development of the superior moral tradition of the Chinese race as well as the lofty rectitude of the proletariats," the journal said. It blamed the liberal wing of the party for failing to implement the Study Lei Feng Campaign in the past few years. In the one year after the launch of the Lei Feng movement, more than 100 books on Lei Feng, amounting to more than 10 million copies, were issued.[71]

C. The Rural Socialist Education Campaign

By late 1990, the CCP had kicked off what must have been the world's largest indoctrination campaign: to turn nearly 1 billion people into loyal Marxists. The aim of the so-called "socialist ideological education movement" (*shejiao* in Chinese) was to ensure that "bourgeois-liberal values," which seemed to have inundated the cities, be kept out of the countryside. Aside from proselytising about Marxist values, a central focus of the campaign was to rebuild party cells and other CCP organisations.

The importance of securing the rural base was especially underscored after the crumbling of Communism in the Eastern bloc. As Song Ping indicated: "We must saturate the peasants with socialist thoughts. We must raise their socialist and patriotic consciousness and their love for the collective." During a series of tours to the countryside in mid-1991, top leaders upheld what Mao Zedong's revolution had demonstrated: heaven and earth are won in the countryside. For example, while visiting Hebei Province, Jiang repeated the Deng Xiaoping dictum: "Without stability in the villages, there will be no national stability."[72]

The extent of the "thought-reform" programme was revealed at a national work conference on rural ideological education held in November 1991. Jiang said at the conclave that alongside the promotion of the economy, the party must "implement socialist ideological education for its cadres and masses". "This is a long-term task that must be unceasingly upheld," he pointed out.[73]

Song Ping, who was present at the meeting, said that intensified indoctrination had been completed in 390,700 villages, or 53 per cent of the total. Good results were achieved, Song claimed. Jiang, however, betrayed signs of uneasiness. He said that rural cadres must "further consolidate the rural base of socialism and guard against merely going through the motions [of obeying party instructions]". Jiang's statement suggested that many local cadres were merely paying lip service to the re-hoisting of Maoist standards.

At the same time, a report by the Zhejiang Party Committee in late 1991 said that of the 68,000 party branches in the province, 6.7 per cent were considered not up to par. While this was a drop from 19 per cent in 1988, local authorities said, the "weakness and laxity" of the party cells remained a major cause for concern.[74]

A major thrust of the Resolution of the Eighth Plenum of the Central Committee held in late November 1991 was to strengthen rural party organisations, which was seen as the prerequisite for "consolidating the rural socialist base". "Party branches must be combat-ready, and resolute fortresses that will seriously implement the party's line and policies," the document said. The Central Committee pointed out that the rural education campaign would go on for at least two to three years. It called on various levels of party committees to set up leading groups to supervise the ideological campaign.[75]

The *shejiao* campaign was perhaps waged with even more intensity in the rich, coastal provinces, whose leaders were eager to show Beijing the development of their market economies was not incompatible with socialist norms. *Shejiao* committees were set up in many localities along the coast. For example, at the height of the mass movement, Guangdong dispatched 44,000 IPW workers to 1,682 counties and villages to propagate the faith.[76]

VII. The Left Wing's Bid for Power, 1989-1992

The 1989 democracy protests provided the various factions of the CCP's left wing with possibly their last chance to seize power. Previous attempts, symbolised by the Campaign Against Spiritual Pollution of 1983 and the Campaign Against Bourgeois Liberalisation of 1987, proved to be unsuccessful putsches against the moderate or "centrist" coalition led by Deng Xiaoping.

Perhaps seeing that their days were numbered, the leaders of the various left-wing factions joined forces almost immediately after June 4, 1989, to implement the Maoist restoration. Prominent among the leftist factions was the clique of hardline central planners represented by then Central Advisory Commission Chairman Chen Yun. While Chen, like Deng, had suffered persecution during the Cultural Revolution, he thought that basic parts of the Maoist canon including fostering "spiritual civilisation" and waging periodic battles against "bourgeois liberalisation" should be kept intact.

On economics, the conservative patriarch advocated a fairly rigid form of central planning. Chen's primary power base included State Council bureaucrats who had worked in such units as the State Planning Commission, the Finance Ministry and the People's Bank of China. Vice-Premiers Yao Yilin and Zou Jiahua, and to some extent, Premier Li Peng, were considered Chen protégés. Never having been to the West — or even to the Special Economic Zones — Chen had an ingrained antipathy towards anything capitalist.

A leftist clique closely allied to that led by Chen consisted of professional ideologues who wanted to make class struggle the "core" of national work. Their leader was the former head of the Propaganda Department Deng Liqun. Little Deng was a shade to the left of — or more "Maoist" than — Chen Yun. As we shall see, from the late 1980s onwards, the political thoughts of Little Deng, once quite close to Deng Xiaoping, became steadily more radical. Unlike Chen Yun, however, Little Deng did not have any distinct economic programme other than discriminating against private enterprise.

After Tiananmen Square, both the central planners and the ideologues also formed a coalition with the Gang of Four holdovers. Having been stigmatised for their association with Jiang Qing and company, these ultra-radicals laid low throughout most of the 1980s. By the early 1990s, however, their primary interest was not so much ideology as seizing power and perks. A key representative was Vice-Chief of the Propaganda Department, Xu Weicheng, who used to head a "writing team" under Madame Mao.

With the common aim of shoving aside the moderate wings of the party, including the fast-rising Shanghai Faction, all three cliques thought it convenient to use Mao's banner to undercut Deng and his protégés. However, most China watchers would think that these left-wingers were opportunists rather than *bona fide* Maoists.

A. The Challenge of Chen Yun

(i) The Attack on Deng's Politics

Chen Yun was the godfather behind the turn to the left of Chinese politics and economics. The former chairman of the Central Advisory Commission also masterminded the campaign to undermine Deng's influence. The challenge posed by Chen was all the more formidable because of his reputation as "Mr Clean". Unlike the other party elders, he did not suffer from an over-arching personal ambition. Analysts said that for the sake of stability, Chen would not mind Deng remaining as a figurehead patriarch. Yet the CAC chief certainly wanted his theories and protégés to carry the day.[77]

Since about 1987, Chen, who was believed to be seriously ill, had been spending the bulk of his time outside Beijing: mostly in his well-appointed dachas in Hangzhou and Shanghai. However, his key lieutenants, principally then Vice-Premier Yao Yilin, briefed him regularly on affairs of state. And through leaks and cryptic messages to the press such as re-issuing old speeches and articles Chen managed to stay very much in the frontline.

The focal point of Chen's attack on Deng was the latter's alleged failure to propagate "spiritual civilisation": that is, Deng was soft on the spread of liberalisation. As Chen made clear in a speech in the mid-1980s: "In the course of the open-door policy, the decadent thoughts and styles of capitalism would inevitably infiltrate China. If we neglect the construction of socialist spiritual civilisation, our whole enterprise will veer away from Marxism and from socialism."[78]

In April 1990, the national media re-issued a July 1987 speech in which the conservative patriarch underlined the "importance of studying philosophy". "To run our party and state well, the most important thing is to ensure that the thinking methodology of the leading cadres is correct," Chen said. "This means we need to learn Marxist philosophy." Chen argued that even when the country was undergoing modernisation, the views of Marx and Mao must be closely adhered to. "Under new conditions, the whole party is still faced with the task of learning how to use the standpoint, views and methods of Marxism and Mao Thought to analyse and solve problems," he said.[79]

In the eyes of Chen Yun, Deng had erred "on both the right and the left side" in his handling of events leading up to the June 4 crisis. First of all, the patriarch's soft treatment of the rightist dissidents engendered wave after wave of challenge to communist rule. Worse, when the party was almost overwhelmed by the "counter-revolutionaries", Deng resorted to the "ultra-leftist" tactics by turning the troops on the people and sullying the image of the party. Soon after the June 4 massacre, Chen told his intimates: "We must have a new verdict on the Tiananmen Square incident. When we old comrades are still around, we must clarify who is responsible for what. Otherwise, we would carry the stigma to our graves."[80]

Chen, who was no sucker for the "bourgeois-liberal" ideal of "inner-party democracy", nonetheless criticised Deng for running a "one-voice chamber". In the re-issued 1987 speech, Chen stressed that the leadership of the CCP must listen to different points of view on matters of state. "It is not a bad thing to be able to listen to different voices," Chen said. "Views different from that [of your own] can help you consider questions [more carefully]."[81]

Chen again launched an oblique attack on the alleged "dictatorialness" of Deng with the publication in January 1991 of a 15-character motto that the conservative patriarch cited to Zhejiang cadres a year earlier. The motto, which could be summarised as "seeking truth from facts" was, according to Chen, crystallised from his re-readings of Mao's "documents and telexes". "Policy-makers should make a decision based on truth after exchanging views with others, making comparisons and considering the matter over a period of time," Chen said.[82] Translation: Deng failed to exchange views with enough leaders and factions before making up his mind on major policies.

Later that year, the conservative elder even warned against the emergence of Gorbachev- or Yeltsin-like figures, an unsubtle attack on Deng and Zhu Rongji. "China must prevent the emergence of ringleaders like Yeltsin," he said. "We must draw the lesson from the Soviet Union and stress political principles and ideological purity."[83]

(ii) Attack on the Economy

In repeated internal talks, Chen Yun laid into what he considered to be the failings of the dozen-odd years of reform. First of all, Chen said, they lacked a "comprehensive theoretical system", with the result that the policies were rudderless, now going left, now going right. Secondly, the reforms in general had departed from the socialist norm. "We lack a comprehensive theoretical system to guide reform policies," Chen told a group of intimates in a talk in November 1990. As a result, he added, reform policies had undergone too many mutations and failed to hold a steady course.[84]

Chen said the reformist line as determined at the Third Plenum of the 12th Central Committee in 1984 was designed to "build a planned socialist commodity economy". "After the years of reform, however, the part about the economy being a planned and socialist one has been forgotten," Chen groused. "Only the part about building a commodity economy has remained." The former economic czar urged the party's ideologues and economists to put together a sound theoretical basis to ensure a "correct direction" for reform.

"We need a comprehensive theoretical system including theories on planning, the market, fiscal policy and tax," he said. "We must hoist high the flag of socialism in the hearts of the people. Our party must raise its voice and sing the praises of socialism."

Chinese sources said Chen's point that reform had veered away from the goals of socialism and central planning was an attack on the market-oriented experiments of Deng and Zhao Ziyang. Moreover, the economic czar's complaint about the lack of a steady course for reform also seemed a criticism of the famous dictum of Deng that exploring an economic path was like "crossing the river while feeling for the boulders".

Chen's influence peaked before Deng embarked on his *nanxun* in early 1992. A so-called Chen Yun Thought had come into being, which began to rival Deng as the arbiter of the direction of reform. At a late 1990 symposium devoted to the conservative patriarch, Chen Yun Thought was elevated at least to the same plane as Deng's theories. As the participants put it: "In the previous stage of reform, we pinned too much hope on the regulatory role of the market and relaxed planned control. This showed we had not made sufficient effort to study and master comrade Chen Yun's economic thinking about correctly handling the relationship between planning and the market."[85]

During his frequent trips to Shanghai, Chen told local cadres not to give in to Deng's "Great Leap Forward" mentality by seeking an excessively high growth rate or following a quasi-capitalist path. "You cannot allow the direction of your reform programme to be determined by capitalist ideas," he told Shanghai cadres in early 1991.[86] The elder also accused the reforms of Deng and his aides such as Zhao Ziyang of engendering unprecedented corruption, which would lead to "the death of the party".[87]

B. The Challenge of Little Deng and Allied Leftists

Until the Tiananmen Square bloodbath, China watchers used to make a distinction between "leftists" and the followers of Gang of Four. The latter were followers of Chairman Mao and Jiang Qing including the Red Guards and the "Three Types of People" who looted, smashed and beat up the innocent during the Ten Years of Chaos.

"Leftists", on the other hand, refers to politicians who occupied the conservative end of the broad coalition that Deng put together to topple the Gang of Four, and later, Hua Guofeng. Many leftists, including Little Deng, were victims of the Gang of Four hoodlums during the Revolution. While opposed to Deng's quasi-capitalist reforms, they were against the autarkist road of closing the nation's doors to foreign influence.

After the June 4 massacre, however, there was a marriage of minds and convenience between the two cabals. To put it simply, the leftists turned to the Gang of Four holdovers and re-hoisted the tattered standards of Maoism. One reason could be that the 1989 "turmoil" might have convinced them of the correctness of Mao's sponsorship of "perennial revolution" (see earlier section). More importantly, the two camps shared the common goal of wresting power from the Deng faction.[88]

Deng Liqun, 79 (in 1994), was the mastermind behind the Campaign against Spiritual Pollution in 1983 and the Campaign Against Bourgeois Liberalisation in 1987. He started out as a relatively liberal theorist in the late 1970s. The secretary of then-president Liu Shaoqi, Deng Liqun was one of Deng Xiaoping's principal advisers on ideology in the late 1970s.

Little Deng could claim credit for expediting market reforms in the early 1980s. As head of the Chinese Academy of Social Sciences, he sponsored research into the social sciences, including market economics. For example, Little Deng encouraged the setting up of the Rural Economic Development Research Institute, a forerunner of the Research Institute for the Reform of the Economic Structure, one of Zhao Ziyang's main think-tanks. RIRES director Chen Yizi, now in exile in the United States, was a protégé of Little Deng when the former was conducting research in Henan Province in the early 1980s.

It is not known when Little Deng crossed over to the opposition. By 1983, he had become an implacable enemy of Hu Yaobang and such other radical modernisers as Hu Qili and Zhu Houze. It could have been because of his reservations about the wholesale abandonment of classical socialism. But then again it could also have been jealousy: Little Deng had ambitions of becoming party General Secretary, and he thought he was much more qualified then either Hu or Zhao Ziyang. By allying himself with the remnant followers of the Gang of Four, Little Deng hoped he would have more chips in the showdown with Deng Xiaoping.

Little Deng lost two subsequent duels with Hu and Zhao. After the Campaign against Spiritual Pollution, he lost his position as propaganda chief. And at the 13th party congress in 1987, the veteran ideologue lost all major positions in the party save for ordinary membership of the Central Advisory Commission. Equally important, the Research Office of the Central Committee, which had long been his power base, was dissolved soon after the 13th congress.[89]

Two notable players among the Gang of Four holdovers were Xu Weicheng and He Jingzhi, respectively the Vice-Head of Propaganda and the Acting Culture Minister. (He retired from this position in early 1993.) At the young age of 53 (in 1994) Xu was tipped to go places. A veteran youth worker and journalist, Xu, a graduate of Daxia University in Shanghai, served with the

Shanghai Youth News and later, the *Liberation Daily*. He became the deputy editor of the latter paper at the tender age of 27. Xu was also an alternate member of the Central Committee of the Communist Youth League from 1964 to 1972. The inveterate opportunist hit the big time in the early 1970s, when he headed a "writing team" that churned out much of the propaganda for the Gang of Four.

It is proof of Xu's political acumen that he avoided being purged after the arrest of Jiang Qing. Chinese sources in Beijing said he made use of his CYL credentials to curry favour with Hu Yaobang, who apparently thought that as a former chief of the League, he had a responsibility to save lost sheep. By 1982, Xu had become chief editor of the influential *Beijing Daily*. In 1983, he became a member of the Beijing party committee and head of its propaganda department.

For a few years, Xu went through the motions of rendering support to the bold liberalisation programmes of Hu, and later, Zhao Ziyang. But he displayed his true colours during the student protests in December 1986. Editorials of the *Beijing Daily* — some of which were penned by Xu — were considered so reactionary that campus activists burnt copies of the paper, a high point during that round of protests.[90] Xu — or at least the *Beijing Daily* — was, however, praised by Deng for "resolutely countering bourgeois liberalisation" during the 1986 movement. Xu's behaviour during the 1989 protests was likewise meritorious in Deng's eyes. In September 1989, the unreconstructed Maoist was made No. 2 of the Propaganda Department.

Another crony of Mao and Jiang Qing who made good was poet He Jingzhi, apparently a good friend of the Great Helmsman. His wife, novelist Ke Yan, was close to the late vice-president Wang Zhen, who reportedly recommended He for a senior position. A veteran of the famous Lu Xin Art Academy in Yan'an, He was responsible for some of the most hackneyed propaganda pieces since 1949. They included the drama *White-Haired Girl*, which won a Stalin Prize in 1951. After becoming Acting Culture Minister in late 1989, He made use of his connections to Wang Zhen to frustrate efforts by Li Ruihuan to liberalise the cultural arena.[91]

VIII. The Anti-Leftist Campaign of 1992

A. Anti-Leftist Moves by the Deng Camp

For many Chinese, the most spectacular and crucial aspect of the nanxun was the promise that finally, the patriarch might have realised that the success of his economic reforms hinged upon the eradication of leftism. A number of edicts that Deng gave during his tour of southern China revolved around fighting leftism, now deemed the "main task" of the party (see Chapter 1).

As the Chinese-run Hong Kong magazine *Bauhinia* put it, a key lesson that the patriarch drew from the disintegration of the former Eastern bloc was that "leftism" would drive socialism into its grave. "Rightism can ruin socialism, but the same can be said of leftism," Deng reportedly said. *Bauhinia* explained: "During the few decades that Ceausescu reigned over Romania, he closed the nation's doors and refused to reform. He persevered with leftism, and the result was not only failing to maintain his regime but the loss of his life and properties."[92]

Deng's *nanxun* edicts, including his battle cries against leftism, were endorsed in a seminal Politburo meeting in mid-March 1992. "While keeping vigilance against rightist deviation, the main attention [of the party and nation] should be paid to guarding against 'leftist' deviation," the Politburo said in a communique. "It is necessary to further emancipate the mind and adhere to the principle of seeking truth from facts," it said.[93]

Most importantly, the party's moderate wing managed to force the conservatives to enshrine — at least for a few months anti-leftism as a "state doctrine". As the NPC opened in March 1992, Li Peng tried to buck the "*nanxun* whirlwind" by making no reference to the anti-Maoist crusade in his Government Work Report. But the Deng camp — and the deputies — would not let him get away with it. Li was forced to make more than 140 corrections to his report. And one key clause he was forced to add was: "While we must be on guard against rightism, our major task is to prevent 'leftism'." Li also put in the clause about upholding Deng's reform theories "for a hundred years".[94]

It would be left to Qiao Shi and Tian Jiyun to elaborate on the theory of anti-leftism. And they did so with elan and flair. As Qiao put it while speaking to cadres in Jiangsu Province in mid-1992: "Leftism is not an abstract concept, it is a concrete phenomenon which exists [in Chinese society]," he said. "If we do not truly eliminate leftist deviations, we will not be able to implement resolutely the basic line of the party or absorb the technology, management skills and foreign investment necessary for economic reform." [95]

Tian Jiyun, the right-hand man of Zhao Ziyang who was almost sidelined after June 4, earned an illustrious perch in Communist-Chinese history with a bugle call against leftism. The occasion was a speech on agriculture policy at the Central Party School. And it was no accident that it was Qiao, the principal of the school, who asked Tian to deliver his thunder of a speech.

Half an hour into his talk on the need to preserve the household responsibility system in agriculture, however, Tian laid into the leftists. He amazed his audience by using that most unfamiliar of Chinese genres — black humour — and proposing the establishment of a series of "leftist special zones" where the faithful followers of Maoism would be banished. At such a leftist Shangri-La, however, food would be rationed, cadres would not be allowed to run business and inhabitants would not be allowed to go abroad. In this pariahs' paradise, the leftists could spend all their time engaging in "struggles" and "criticisms and self-criticisms".[96]

Most significantly, Tian made a thinly-veiled attack against Jiang Zemin and other affiliates of the Wind Faction, who were willing to trade their principles for advancement. The then vice-premier hinted that they posed as great a threat to reform as the leftists. "In the course of weeding out leftist influence, we must be especially on guard against members of the Wind Faction. They use people's language when talking to people, and the language of ghosts when they consort with ghosts. They will jump out and oppose reform once they see an opportunity." As we shall see, Tian's bold speech managed to offend not just the party elders and the ideologues but also Jiang and his followers — and in effect guaranteed that he would be barred from promotion at the 14th Party Congress.

A couple of noted leftists then went through the motions of supporting Deng. While touring Yunnan in April 1992, Song Ping repeated the patriarch's message about the primacy of reform: that a policy should be pursued if it is beneficial towards reform and if it raises productivity. "We must further liberate our thoughts and seize the opportunity," Song said. However, he failed to mention the campaign against leftism.[97]

An in an apparent effort to save his job, then Beijing party secretary Li Ximing went on an anti-leftist rampage. In a speech in late 1992, Li said: "Fourteen years' experience of reform has shown that if we insist on the liberation of thought, our brain will be nimble and our methods flexible. If not we will feel hamstrung." Li indicated that cadres of all levels must cast out various mistaken tendencies, "especially interference from the left".[98]

Seasoned observers were quick to note, however, that the leftist camp had by no means capitulated. The most obvious signal: among the moderate wing of the party, Qiao and Tian were the only two senior cadres who joined the fray. Such other pillars of the post-June 4 order as Jiang Zemin and Zhu Rongji kept mum on this vital question. Moreover, it became very obvious that neither Qiao nor Tian had the authority to cashier or sideline the leftists. Everything still depended on Deng — and as we shall see, after the *nanxun*, the patriarch failed to keep up the momentum.

B. Anti-Leftist Manoeuvres by the Intelligentsia

Buoyed by the anti-leftist trend among officials, long-silent intellectuals began by mid-1992 to launch a series of anti-Maoist leftist conferences and

books. For the first time since June 4, semi-private "salons" on thought liberation and allied topics were called. And avant-garde books and journals hit the
streets to the consternation of the censors.

One cannot, however, over-estimate the fervour or effectiveness of the anti-
leftist crusade in 1992. First of all, the authorities did not relax control over
the freedom of expression of opinion. And the dissident intellectuals were
again taking advantage of a rift in the leadership — and the fact that one faction was making use of the intellectuals to fight another faction — to air their
views. Hence, as in many previous "thought liberation" movements, the lifes-
pan of this anti-leftist crusade depended on the durability of patronage by the
pro-liberal faction in the party. It has been reported that the Deng family, especially the patriarch's activist daughters Deng Rong and Deng Nan, had pro-
ferred assistance or at least protection to the avant-garde intellectuals who
dared open fire on the leftists.

The second constraint on the anti-leftist movement was its lack of a
mass base. Protagonists consisted of veteran "bourgeois-liberals" including *bona fide* rightists such as Wang Ruoshui, Hu Jiwei and Yu Haocheng,
as well as activists during the 1989 pro-democracy movement such as
Beijing University law lecturer Yuan Hongbin. There were relatively few
new recruits.

Thirdly, the scope of the anti-leftist campaign in 1992 was limited: to
defend Deng Xiaoping and to "make propaganda" for the continuation of
market reforms. The crusade did not seem to break new ground. The prevailing view of the activists was that it was not yet time to rock the boat.
Propagating Western political ideals on political reform would again provoke
a conservative backlash; and the best strategy was to "provide an imperial
escort" for Deng.[99]

The first anti-Maoist salvo was fired on June 14, 1992, at the Olympic
Hotel in northwestern Beijing, when nearly 100 intellectuals vented their
anger on the Maoist ideologues. Participants included Wang Ruoshui, Wu
Zuguang, Qin Chuan, Li Rui, Sun Changjiang and Lin Jingyao. The organiser of the private salon was Yuan Hongbin, a radical moderniser who put his
hope on another 1989-like mass movement to topple the dictatorship.

The focus of the discussion, however, was milder: rendering support to
Deng's reforms, and, in the words of Wang Ruoshui, the former *People's Daily*
theoretician, "to ensure that the anti-leftist movement does not become an
anti-rightist one, as has happened so many times in Communist-Chinese history". "Deng Xiaoping has pointed out that the major task is to counter leftism," Wang said. "Yet the conservatives still insist that the biggest danger is
posed by 'peaceful evolution'."[100]

The May meeting was followed by another conclave on October 27, 1992, whose goal was to propagate the reformist spirit of the 14th Party Congress. Participants included 50 liberal authors including former culture minister Wang Meng, Feng Mu, Chen Huangmei, Shao Yanxiang, and Lan Ling. Lan, a veteran literary theoretician, spoke for many when he intoned during the session: "The worst instance of a shoddy product now on the market is not some TV set but a self-styled Marxist."[101]

The year 1992 also saw the publication of several anti-leftist books, some of which were later banned by the censors. *The Tides of History* and *Memorandum on Anti-Leftism*, however, achieved a fairly large circulation in spite of sabotage by the commissars. The former was put together by Yuan Hongbin, and the latter by a cadre in the Culture Ministry Zhao Silin. As Zhao put it in his postscript to *Memorandum*: "The task of eradicating leftism ideologically and in terms of personnel is very difficult." Aside from authors cited above, big-name rightists who contributed to the two anthologies included Yu Guangyuan, Li Rui, Xia Yan, Liu Xinwu, Li Zehou, and Ba Jin.[102]

Among the most spectacular anti-leftist broadsides was one fired by Hu Jiwei, the former chief editor of *People's Daily* who was involved in a doomed petition to remove Li Peng in May 1989. In an essay that was anthologised in *The Tides of History*, Hu traced leftism back to the 1950s, and warned that the scourge had hardly waned after Deng assumed power in late 1978. "The controversy as to whether the [party's] main task is to fight rightism or 'leftism' has been very fierce since the Third Plenum [1978]," Hu wrote. "Leftist theoreticians have repeatedly made waves in order to seize the initiative [in combating rightism]." Implicit in Hu's argument was Deng's failure to banish the leftist challenge. And picking up where Tian Jiyun left off, Hu pinpointed the culprits. He accused ideologues holding sway in such publications as *People's Daily*, *Guangming Daily*, *Seeking Truth* and *Contemporary Thoughts* of sabotaging reform. These commissars, Hu said, also prevented the dissemination of Deng's ideas during the *nanxun*.[103]

By early 1993, however, the bourgeois-liberals had called off their anti-leftist crusade. In an interview with the author, Yuan Hongbin said: "It's time we turned our attention elsewhere, such as preparing for another mass movement to fight for political reform after Deng's death." Yuan and his colleagues and followers had begun building up a network of activists among labourers and even farmers. Yuan hinted that there was only so much the intelligentsia could achieve with an anti-leftist campaign. The success of such a movement depended on Deng, and by early 1993, it was clear to all that the patriarch was half-hearted about stamping out leftist influence. Intellectuals who wanted real change needed to forsake the perennial left versus right cycle in the party — and to stake out their own turf.[104]

IX. The Half-hearted Purge of Leftists, 1992-1993

At the height of the *nanxun*, Deng seemed to be resolute about weeding out the leftists. The New Helmsman listed a dozen-odd high-level leftists whom he wanted to get rid of. For example, he wanted to replace Wang Renzhi, He Jingzhi and Gao Di with, respectively, the Vice-Party Secretary of Shanghai Chen Zili, the then party secretary of Hebei Xing Chongzhi, and the then party boss of Tibet, Hu Jintao. Nothing came of these manoeuvres.[105]

At or around the 14th Party Congress, a relatively small number of influential leftists were forced out. They included the two members of the Politburo Standing Committee, Yao Yilin and Song Ping, both considered Chen Yun's henchmen. Vice-Minister of the State Education Commission He Dongchang and the Party Secretary of Beijing Li Ximing also retired. Both He and Li played a crucial role in persuading Deng to use force against the student demonstrators in 1989.

By mid-1993, however, many leftists, especially those in the ideological and propaganda establishments, either received a mere slap on the wrist or managed to hang on to their jobs. As veteran author Bai Hua put it, Deng was "not firm" in removing the remnant Maoists. "Deng seems not to have made up his mind over personnel issues," Bai said. "It was as though he were afraid that once the leftists had been wiped out, the [factional] balance would be upset and another wave of 'bourgeois liberalisation' would set in."[106]

Firstly, several well-known leftists remained in the Central Committee that was elected at the 14th Party Congress. The most notable was the "whateverist" former party chairman Hua Guofeng, whose popularity remained inexplicably high. Other Maoists and hardliners on the Central Committee included Organisation Chief Lu Feng, a protégé of Song Ping; former minister of water resources Qian Zhengying; party boss of Jiangxi province Mao Zhiyong; then Minister of Radio, Film and Television Ai Zhisheng; trade unionist Ni Zhifu; Vice-Party Secretary of Beijing Wang Jialiu; and Head of the Central Committee Research Office Wang Weicheng.

Secondly, Deng's avowed objective of revamping the ideological and propaganda establishment did not go far enough. The new line-up in this crucial sector, announced in late 1992, represented only a lily-livered effort at flushing out leftist influence. The Propaganda Department itself underwent a minimal facelift with the appointment of Ding Guan'gen and Zheng Bijiang as Head and Vice-Head of Department. In mid-1993, the veteran vice-chief of propaganda in Shanghai Gong Xinhan was promoted another Vice-Head of Propaganda. Xu Weicheng, the noted Gang of Four holdover, hung on to his position as Executive Vice-Chief of Propaganda. Many department- and bureau-level posts in the Department were still held by cadres loyal to Little Deng.[107]

Similar cosmetic changes took place in the Culture Ministry, another stronghold of leftism. The ailing Maoist poet, He Jingzhi retired as acting minister, making way for Liu Zhongde. Many departments of the Culture Ministry remained pockets of Maoist influence, according to former minister Wang Meng, the liberal writer.[108]

At the same time, former head of the propaganda department Wang Renzhi was compensated with the position of Party Secretary of the Chinese Academy of Social Sciences, deemed a "disaster zone" of bourgeois liberalisation. It was reported in intellectual circles in Beijing in early 1993 that Wang, still young at the age of 59, was manoeuvring to become CASS president, replacing conservative historian Hu Sheng. Other changes included the promotion of former vice-chief of propaganda Zeng Jianhui as Head of the Central Committee's Leading Group on Overseas Propaganda and Head of the Information Office of the State Council.

Analysts said it was unlikely the new line-up would make for a liberalisation of policies on ideology and the media. While not considered conservatives, cadres such as Ding Guan'gen, Liu Zhongde, Zheng Bijian, Gong Xinhan and Zeng Jianhui were reckoned as fence-sitters who would generally abide by Deng's precept of freeing the economy while constricting the ideological sector.

Compared with such former arbiters of the field as Hu Yaobang, Zhu Houze and Li Ruihuan, the likes of Zheng Bijian, Liu Zhongde and Gong Xinhan could be classified as conservatives. For example, while Zheng, whose last posting was CASS vice-president, was sometimes considered a liberal because of his having worked for Hu Yaobang, he played a role in the purge of CASS "miscreants" after the June 4 bloodbath.[109]

Likewise, the supposedly liberal credentials of Liu Zhongde were dubious. Liu was close to Premier Li Peng when both worked in the State Education Commission during the mid-1980s. The same was true of Gong Xinhan, who occupied the No. 2 position in the Shanghai propaganda department for nearly ten years. Considered a member of the Wind Faction, Gong was considerably less liberal than such former Shanghai propaganda chiefs as Wang Yuanhua or Pan Weiming. Chinese sources said it was mostly unlikely that Zheng, Liu or Gong would change the hardline agenda already set by Deng Liqun.[110]

Equally disturbing to the nation's intellectuals was the fact that, in return for stepping down, a number of noted leftists seemed to have earned the right to appoint their "successors". Take for example Song Ping, the former Politburo member in charge of organisation and head of the Gansu Faction. Among Song protégés who got far at the 14th Party Congress were Hu Jintao and Wei Jianxing, both of whom made the new Politburo. Likewise the successor to Li Ximing as party boss of Beijing was Li Qiyan, considered a soulmate of Li as far as their conservative ideology was concerned.

By the end of the 14th Congress, it was apparent Deng had called off his campaign against leftism. Qiao Shi and Tian Jiyun — about the only two senior cadres who had responded to Deng's call for undermining leftist influence — kept silent on the subject. Tian, who missed membership of the Politburo Standing Committee, was slated for the No. 2 slot in the NPC, which was a disappointment for supporters of the virulent fighter against Maoism.

By early 1993, Little Deng and his cohorts were celebrating the fact that they had emerged from Deng's "anti-leftist pogrom" relatively unscathed. They were seen holding boisterous banquets at the new Da San Yuan Restaurant near the Zhongnanhai party headquarters. The leftists had scuttled the prospects of Tian Jiyun. And another of their *bêtes noires*, Li Ruihuan, had given up his ideological and propaganda portfolio for the largely ceremonial post of Chairman of the Chinese People's Political Consultative Conference. Moreover, the leftists had blocked the elevation of Zheng Bijian to Head of the Propaganda Department. Four bureau chiefs of the department, who were appointees of Little Deng and Wang Renzhi, petitioned the Politburo about not elevating Zheng. This is doubly ironic given the fact that in the eyes of the Beijing intelligentsia, Zheng hardly qualified as a liberal.[111]

The leftist domination of the ideological and propaganda establishment was hardly changed with the elevation of more members of Jiang Zemin's Shanghai faction to this arena in late 1993 and early 1994. In the wake of Gong Xinhan's transfer to Beijing, the star journalist from *Liberation Daily* Zhou Ruijin was made a Vice-Chief Editor of *People's Daily*, and Shanghai social scientist Li Junru was promoted to Head of the Theoretical Bureau of the Propaganda Department. Zhou had a hand in the drafting of the ultra-liberal Huang Puping articles in 1991 (see Chapter 1).

Zhou and Li, however, were unable to halt the leftward drift of policy on ideology and propaganda. Li reportedly did not even hold regular office hours. The Propaganda Department was in many ways still dominated by Gang of Four sympathiser Xu Weicheng. In January 1994, Xu began another campaign to purge the "Hong Kong contents" from mainland cultural productions. In a talk to staff of the Ministry of Radio, Film and Television, Xu indicated that state television and radio stations should weed out songs and videos by or featuring Hong Kong and Taiwan artists. When asked what they should play instead, the ideologue said: "The one hundred patriotic movies or their theme songs." The commissar was referring to the 100 mostly old films the Propaganda Department had selected for their "patriotic and socialist" orientations.[112]

In mid-1994, Ai Zhisheng, one of the longest-serving ministers and a noted leftist, relinquished his portfolio of radio, film and television after nine years.

The removal of Ai, considered Li Peng's crony, however, was hardly good news for the liberals. The 65-year-old ideologue was compensated with the senior position of Vice-Chief of the Central Committee's Leading Group on Ideology and Propaganda, the party's highest organ in the area. Moreover, the new minister Sun Jiazheng was hardly a liberal. The NCNA described him as "strong in planning and relatively stable in tackling problems".[113]

X. Why the Leftists Were Needed

A. The Re-assertion of the "Twin-Fisted" Policy

It is paradoxical that as the reform and open-door policy grew by leaps and bounds in late 1992 and early 1993, the leadership still thought it imperative to hang on to the "two-hands" or twin-fisted policy: to grasp economic construction with one hand, and to ensure ideological purity with the other. It is not surprising that there was still a sizeable role for the Maoist ideologues.

First of all, moderate leaders like Deng Xiaoping and Jiang Zemin needed the leftist ideologues to stop Zhao Ziyang's followers from coming back. As we shall see in Chapter 6, there was even a sign of co-operation between Jiang's men and Little Deng's protégés. Secondly, the leadership had to play up conservative themes to blunt popular opposition against such imperfections of reform as the polarisation of income and corruption. Conservative ideals like nationalism and collectivism could also help to defuse challenges to the regime that would inevitably accompany the rapid development of the market economy. And who else would play up Maoist themes better than the ideologues?

By late 1993, Deng had entered one of his periodic "leftist" phases. The *People's Daily* quoted the patriarch as again giving his blessings to the re-hoisting of Yan'an-era values. The patriarch reportedly said that China's goal of "common prosperity" would be doomed if the party failed to maintain the "spiritual purity" of the people by combating negative influence from the West. "If a person does not love the new socialist China under the leadership of the Communist Party, what else can he love?" Deng was quoted as asking. "Ideological and cultural departments must produce more spiritual fruits for the people, and resolutely stop the production, import and circulation of poor quality products."[114]

With the departure of Li Ruihuan to the CPPCC, ideology and propaganda fell into the hands of Jiang Zemin and Ding Guan'gen, both considered relative conservatives. The pair lost no time in reviving the "two hands" policy. As Jiang put it in late 1992, China would never "blindly worship capitalism" and it would do whatever it could to stamp out the flies and the mosquitoes. By late that year, the party chief had characterised as the "*leitmotif* of the times" the following beliefs: "patriotism, collectivism and socialist ideals". No matter that these "isms" had become totally irrelevant outside the narrow world of the ideologues.[115]

In a meeting with leading commissars in mid-1993, Jiang claimed that "the development of the market economy requires the strengthening of ideological and political work". In a statement that would have done Little Deng proud, Jiang said that as China went further down the road of the socialist market economy, it must "all the more comprehensively boost and improve thought and political work". The party chief repeated the old tune: "While we must positively learn from the advanced technology, scientific management and progressive culture of Western countries, including capitalistic countries, we must at the same time resolutely combat the invasion of various types of corrupt thoughts."[116]

Such quasi-Maoist ideas were closely echoed by Ding Guan'gen who had a power base of his own thanks to close personal ties with Deng Xiaoping. Soon after taking over the Propaganda Department, Ding made it clear to those cadres who had worked for Li Ruihuan that he would pursue a different agenda, and that no "liberalisation" would be allowed.

Throughout 1993, Ding acquitted himself well with the "two hands policy". As he told cadres while touring Guangdong in April of that year: "Propaganda and ideological work are at the service of reform and economic construction. We must build up a spiritual civilisation and work on it constantly." Under Ding's tutelage, the commissars continued to run leftist campaigns such as Learning from Lei Feng and confiscating "pornographic" books and works that propagated decadent ideas.[117]

The imperative of ideological work got a boost in mid-1993 with the launch of the anti-corruption campaign, on the success of which, the leadership indicated, hinged the ability of the CCP to hang on to power. To placate anger against special privileges — particularly the phenomenon of senior cadres and their offspring making big bucks out of their connections — the CCP in July and August 1993 launched a Maoist-style *qunzhong yundong*, or mass movement, against corruption. Again, the filthy ideas of the capitalist West were blamed for the spread of graft.

Leaders including Jiang Zemin cleaved to the old theme that corruption was the result of the unsavoury aspects of the market economy, particularly the infiltration of evil, capitalist thoughts. In internal speeches in August, Jiang cited "hostile foreign forces" and "Western values" as the fountainhead of corruption in China. The campaign against peaceful evolution, which had lain dormant for two years or so, was again launched. "Some forces in the

West have never relaxed their peaceful-evolution plot against China," Jiang said. "They confuse people's minds and wreak havoc on our socialist construction. We will not change our insistence on taking economic construction as our core work. However, we must at any time counter peaceful evolution and combat corruption and wholesale Westernisation."[118]

The party also tried to score points by simply appealing to the people's sense of nationalism and patriotism, the primitive, xenophobic "my country, right or wrong". Perhaps mindful of the people's frustrations with communism and the CCP's record, the propagandists at times deliberately made no association between their patriotism campaign and ideological values. In an editorial on "Hoisting high the flag of patriotism", the *People's Daily* pointed out that patriotism was the "spiritual pillar" for the nation's various peoples. "In recent and contemporary history, patriotism has time and again harnessed the people's determination and combative spirit against foreign invasion," the paper said.[119]

A mammoth patriotic campaign was organised in the run-up to Beijing's bid to host the summer Olympics for the year 2000. The activities included parades and mass gatherings — as well as a media blitz. After the International Olympic Committee made its fateful decision in Monaco on September 23, 1993, however, the commissars tried to score ideological points out of the fiasco. According to Chinese sources, Chen Xitong, the Politburo member who headed the China delegation to Monaco, claimed in an internal speech soon afterwards that "neo-imperialist and hostile forces abroad" such as the US House of Representatives, had blocked China's advance on the international scene. A mini-campaign against the duplicitous West was launched within party cells upon the dissemination of Chen's tirade.

In late 1993, the Propaganda Department, the State Education Commission, the Ministry of Radio, Film and Television, and the Culture Ministry jointly launched a campaign to promote "patriotic" works of art. In a seminar on patriotic films organised in November 1993 by the *People's Daily* and *Guangming Daily*, patriotism was played up as the "*leitmotif* and spirit that will never change". Participants quoted unnamed parents of secondary-school students as complaining how the "invasion" of foreign, Hong Kong and Taiwan movies had led to "corrupt" ideas such as Mammonism, hedonism, nihilism and extreme individualism.[120]

B. The Cold Wind of 1993 and 1994

By the latter half of 1993, intellectuals all over the country were hit by yet another of the periodic swoops on "bourgeois liberals". At a time when Deng's health was precarious as ever, "moderates" led by Jiang Zemin were colluding with the remnant Maoists to keep the lid on the most basic level of the

expression of opinion. With the question of the succession looming, it benefited no faction of the party to have a loud voice of dissent.

The new straitjacket was laid down by Jiang Zemin in a speech to senior
propaganda officials in January 1994. Using Maoist lingo, the party chief said
the goal of propaganda and ideology work was the following: "To use scientific theories to arm people; correct opinion to guide people; and lofty spirit
to mould people." Jiang paid lip service to the bogus goal of "letting a hundred flowers bloom". However, the crypto-Maoist said workers in this field
must serve the overriding theme of patriotism, socialism and collectivism.[121]

Intellectuals active in the brief anti-leftist campaign of 1992 had become
quiescent — or at most gnashed their teeth in muted anger. Their ultimately
unsuccessful effort to publish a new, non-official magazine, *Elite*, said much
about the cold wind emanating from Zhongnanhai. Founders of, and contrib-
utors to, the avant-garde monthly included former *People's Daily* editor Qin
Chuan; former culture minister Wang Meng; liberal economists Yu Guangyuan and Wu Jinglian; liberal elders Li Rui and Xia Yan; and taboo-breaking
writers Shao Yanxiang and Zhang Kangkang.

They waged a year-long battle to secure for *Elite* a *shuhao*, or book and
periodical number. The problem was partly solved when the journal became a
semi-dependent entity under the China Strategic and Management Research
Society, a quasi-official unit in which Qin's son was a senior staffer. In late
1993, *Elite* was granted a temporary *shuhao*. However, the 3,000 copies of the
inaugural issue could not be circulated nationally through the regular distribution network. This was despite the inordinate precautions taken by the editors not to run foul of the censors. For example, the first page of *Elite* carried
a giant photograph of Deng. In his inaugural message, Qin cited Deng's name
four times, saying *Elite* "is willing to make propaganda for Deng Thought".
In early 1994, *Elite* was forced to cease publication because the temporary
shuhao had lapsed and a proper one could not be secured.[122]

For fear of rocking the boat before Deng's death, the Propaganda Department and the Press and Publications Administration were taking no chances.
Since mid-1993 these departments practically stopped giving permits for new
newspapers, periodicals and publishing houses. Worst hit were avant-garde
intellectuals who were unable to have their works published. For example, in
late 1993, the Beijing Yanshan Publishing House held up the distribution of
its series of books entitled *Life after 60*. What apparently went awry was that
two volumes of the autobiographical pieces contained retrospectives penned
by liberal philosophers and journalists Wang Ruoshui and Hu Jiwei. The authorities also put pressure on an American foundation to withdraw financial
support from a team led by Beijing University legal scholar Gong Xiangrui.
Gong was trying to put out a series of monographs on the constitutional his-

tory of Asian countries, including China.[123]

New *shuhao* were as a rule no longer issued. In May 1994, the cadres of 45 publications were penalised for trying to sell or lend their *shuhao* to new publishers. Journalists and cultural personages were only allowed to sing the *leitmotif* of patriotism, collectivism and socialism. Ding laid down the following sixfold criteria in early 1994: "Provide help [to the party] and do not add trouble; sing the *leitmotif* [of socialism] and stay away from cacophonous sounds; pay attention to "social productivity" and do not be lured by profits [alone]; observe orders in propaganda and do not go your own way; focus [on major party policies] and do not dissipate your energy; materialise your goals and do not fool around with superficial effects."[124]

The year 1994 saw record proscription of cultural and artistic productions, including the much-acclaimed films of Zhang Yimou. Draconian laws were put into place to stop or discourage joint ventures or co-production with Hong Kong and Taiwan companies in the areas of publications, video and movies. Big-name media companies in Hong Kong and Taiwan, including *Ming Pao*, the Sing Tao Group, *China Times* and *United Daily News* were frustrated in their attempts to penetrate the mainland market. This was despite millions of yuan these organisations had spent on cultivating the requisite *guanxi*.[125]

The censors were so nervous they were banning things that were quite apolitical. In June 1994, authorities in a number of cities proscribed movie star "flash cards" favoured by teenagers in Hong Kong and Taiwan. In the same month, two "behavioural artists", Ma Liuming and Zhu Min, were detained by police for performing artistic rituals in the nude. This is despite the fact that the two were staging their shows to a private audience, and that they were "merely showing one's helplessness towards life".[126]

XI. The Leftists' Last Stand against Reform, 1993-1994

For about two months after Deng Xiaoping first kicked off his *nanxun*, the inhabitants of what Chinese intellectuals call "the leftists' village" pretended nothing had happened. Since most media units were under their control, they tried to put off as far as they could the publication of Deng's edicts. Orders were also given to the national press not to reprint *nanxun*-related articles carried by the *Shenzhen Special Zone Daily* and the *Zhuhai Special Zone Daily* — which were the first media to give details of Deng's instructions.

Even the dissemination of Central Document No. 2 — which was supposed to be compulsory for all CCP units — was diluted and restricted. Cadres with lower than mid-echelon ranks were denied access to it. While reading out the document, commissars in such well-known leftist strongholds as the Beijing municipality and the State Education Commission made tactical omissions. Samples of what had been excised: the names of leftists Deng cited; and the fact that the "major task" of the party was to prevent and counter leftism.[127]

How *People's Daily* director Gao Di tried to sabotage the *nanxun* was graphically described in an open letter to the NPC that former *Daily* editor Qin Chuan penned in July 1992. Almost immediately after Gao got wind of the *nanxun* talks, the Maoist told his intimates: "Xiaoping's talks have led to confusion of thinking [on the part of cadres]. I again see the forebodings that struck us before June 4 [1989]." Gao made cunning revisions to Deng's instructions even as he relayed them to *Daily* staff. "Some departments should concentrate on fighting leftism, and other departments should concentrate on fighting rightism," he said. And in apparent contrast to Deng's exhortations about putting priority on economic work, Gao said: "Abnormalities in the larger climate have occurred in the land; [political] confusion could reign for some time."[128] Let us examine in more detail how Gao and other leftists tried their level best to deny Deng the centre stage.

A. Equating Reform with Mammonism

First of all, Little Deng cast doubt on the efficacy of the market — or at least its suitability for China. Soon after the 14th Party Congress, he began to rally the troops and to "make propaganda" against Deng's reforms. "The market economy enabled the capitalist system to be set up, and yet there is no scientific proof that the market economy can help socialist countries develop and prosper," the conservative patriarch said. "We must still raise the fundamental precepts of Marxism in economic work."[129]

On another occasion, Little Deng insinuated that economic growth under Deng Xiaoping was "superficial" and "ephemeral" because it was built on debt. He said that the growth during the Mao era was "real" because it was debt-free. In particular, Little Deng pointed out that agriculture, the "key link" of the economy, had grown faster under the collectivisation phase of Mao.[130]

Taking the cue from his ally Chen Yun, Little Deng trained his firepower on Zhu Rongji and other reformist officials promoted by Deng. "We must raise our guard against bourgeois-liberal officials and former rightists," he told his intimates. Beijing's intellectuals said Little Deng began collecting the speeches and internal sayings of Zhu and other reformers with a view to "nailing" them when the time was ripe.[131]

For those who were unconvinced by Little Deng's "economics", however, the leftist resorted to the familiar argument that the search for profit would lead to "Mammonism" and polarisation of incomes. This was, of course, nothing more than the same old gripe against "looking at everything with only money in mind". From spring 1993 onwards, the media ran stories galore about the new breed of *dakuan*, or big spenders, who splashed on everything from karaoke girls and concubines to 100,000-yuan banquets that featured gold-plated cuisine. A yacht club in Shanghai was charging membership fees of US$20,000, while golf clubs in Guangdong were charging many times more.[132]

A fairly emotional attack on Mammonism and conspicuous consumption was made by a signed commentary in the conservative *Guangming Daily* in May 1993. "There are people who, soon after amassing a little wealth, begin to spend extravagantly and to indulge their senses," the commentary said. "They will come to no good. Nor will there be any future for a country that indulges in reckless consumerism just when it has built up a small [economic] foundation."[133]

Song Ping, who became active again by mid-1993, fired a mighty volley against Mammonism when meeting representatives attending the Communist Youth League. "We must never engage in money worship," he said. "Youths should devote their boundless energy to studying theory and technology, especially the basic tenets of Marxism and Maoism."[134]

Even such a relatively liberal cadre as Li Ruihuan felt duty-bound to decry money worship. "Recently, unsavoury phenomena have appeared in the social atmosphere," he told a group of commissars in April 1993. "Money worship, selfishness and indulging in the senses have become popular. People look with admiration on how the *nouveaux riches* and deal-cutters make a big killing [on the market]. The psychology of big-spending has increased."[135]

B. Revival of the "Surnames" Debate and Attack on Privatisation

As we saw in Chapter 2, the party Central Committee was close to endorsing quasi-privatisation at the Third Plenum of late 1993: that the state sector need no longer be the mainstay of the economy; and that all loss-making enterprises should be restructured and privatised through the sale of state assets to private or foreign concerns. However, Chen Yun and his cohorts were quick to raise objections. And by mid-1994, the privatisation drive was temporarily held up.

Soon after the Third Plenum of 1993, leftists re-introduced the debate on the "surnames", arguing that rightists in the party were trying to wreck socialism by introducing reforms "surnamed capitalist". In 1990 and 1991, leftist articles in *Guangming Daily* and *Contemporary Thoughts* had argued that if the differentiation between the surnames was no longer upheld, "some people will lead reform towards the evil path of capitalism", and "the fundamental economic and political system of socialism will be adulterated".[136]

In late 1993, the quasi-privatisation of state enterprises was attacked as an effort to renege on China's "socialist surname". In a series of directives disseminated by his protégés, Chen indicated that the survival of the party and of socialism hinged upon the wholly-owned people's sector. "Major enterprises of the state can only be strengthened in the course of reform, and they must never be curtailed," he repeatedly said in late 1993 and early 1994. The conservative elder particularly warned against the loss of state assets. He indicated that certain vital sectors — ports, airports, railways, major mines and strategic resources — should be off limits to foreign participation. And in one of his frequent proposals to the Politburo, the conservative godhead discouraged "speculation on real estate and stocks".[137]

In a series of articles in the leftist theoretical journal *Seeking Truth* (*Zhenli de zhuiqiu*), the ideologues slammed Deng's old productivity theory. Deng contended during the Cultural Revolution that productivity, not whether a policy was "surnamed" capitalist or socialist, should determine whether that policy was correct. Since the *nanxun*, the patriarch hinted that questions concerning the "ownership system", for example, the size of the state sector as well as the extent of state fiats, should no longer be insisted upon in the course of constructing the socialist market system. Since 1993, a number of liberal social scientists argued that China should adopt whatever ownership system jacked up productivity.

In a much-noted article in *Seeking Truth*, Zhang Deqin, a rising star among the commissars, railed against the argument that the "ownership system" was just a means of production, not a national goal or state creed. "If an ownership system is just a means [of economic activities] and that means can be changed, the conclusion could arise that [values like] the primacy of the state-held sector as well as the entire socialist system can also be changed." Zhang reminded his readers that the "socialist road" was one of the Four Cardinal Principles, which were written into the party charter and the Chinese constitution. The ideologue also claimed that market economics should only be emphasised during a limited and specific time: "when the economy is underdeveloped and when the market is not yet mature or that it is unbalanced."[138]

In mid-1994, Little Deng and his disciples held a series of meetings decrying the lunge to quasi-capitalism. The master ideologue reportedly burst into tears at a conference commemorating Marx's birth. Other ideologues indicated that even if the debate on the surnames could be sidestepped, they must insist on the primacy of state ownership and prevent the drainage of assets.[139]

C. Using Mao to Undercut Deng, 1993-1994

Intellectuals in Beijing were sick to death of the flagrant reinstatement of Maoist norms in the run-up to the observation of the centenary of the Helmsman's birth in December 1993. No doubt there was a relatively high level of unanimity within the party on the need for a big fuss over the celebrations: after all, as Deng himself admitted, Mao created the CCP and in spite of his errors, Maoism was a unifying force for the party and for China, as well as a source for its legitimacy. However, there was no denying the fact that remnant Maoists and leftist ideologues were using the fete to undercut Deng.

The success with which the ideologues magnified the scale of the centenary took the Deng camp by surprise. In mid-1993, advisers to Deng had suggested that most of the celebrations be kept out of the capital, and that no politician with the ranking of Politburo member or above be allowed to attend. Propaganda officials were also asked to devote 60 per cent of their resources to propagating Deng Thought, and only 40 per cent for the centenary. Deng, who left Beijing in early December and did not attend any of the festivities, complained to his intimates about Little Deng's "plot" to use the Mao centenary to upstage the concurrent campaign to study the Third Volume of Deng's *Selected Works*. "Who is behind the festivities?" Deng reportedly asked. Sources revealed that Deng had, through his personal office, warned Little Deng not to go too far with the Mao celebrations. And while the latter had not shown his face throughout the activities, his behind-the-scenes manoeuvres were all too clear.[140]

At the very least, the leftists managed to turn out the crowds. On December 26, the day of the centenary, more than 10,000 lined up outside the Mausoleum to see Mao's waxen — and very unreal — body. A month earlier, police had to be deployed to enforce order among eager buyers fighting over US$1,500 diamond-studded Mao wristwatches. About 5,000 copies of Mao CDs, which featured original recordings of Mao making speeches at state meetings, sold out over three days. On a more popular level, new tape recordings of Cultural Revolution era ditties such as *The East is Red* sold more than 1 million copies in the three months before the birthday.[141]

No doubt crass commercialism was behind many of the galas and memorabilia. There is no denying, however, that as in previous celebrations of Mao, "anti-reformist" elements including those sectors of the population badly hurt by inflation, had used the occasion to vent their anti-Deng feelings. Particularly obvious was the fact that people remembered the 1950s for the relative lack of corruption and *guandao* ("officially-sponsored speculation").

The stature of Mao and Maoism also grew in the wake of the elaborate eulogies made by senior cadres including Jiang Zemin and Qian Qichen. This is despite the fact that toeing the general line laid down by the Deng Office, Jiang and Qian had put their emphasis on how Deng had developed, enriched or improved upon Mao Thought. For example, speaking in the Great Hall of the People the day before the centenary, the President contended that Maoism was a "scientific guiding thought that suits China's conditions". Jiang claimed that Mao's mistakes were "the mistakes made by a great revolutionary and a great Marxist". According to Foreign Minister Qian, Mao laid down the foundation of "the diplomacy of the New China", in the process making "indelible contributions".[142]

The praise heaped on Mao by other leftists and party elders was even more problematic from Deng's viewpoint. Elder Bo Yibo, usually considered a Deng ally, went overboard in arguing that it was Mao who had first spotted the shortcomings of the Soviet system. Bo also gave the Helmsman credit for putting agriculture before industry, and for urging the participation of workers in the management of factories. Some of these ideas ran counter to Deng's market reforms. CASS President Hu Sheng claimed that reforms since the late 1970s were "the continuation of Mao's unfinished explorations". The leftist historian highlighted Mao's uncorrupt lifestyle. "You not only belonged to the past but will forever belong to the future," he rhapsodised.[143]

Given the fact that Mao and Mao Thought had become all but irrelevant in China's daily life, the fact that Little Deng's ideologues could still generate some enthusiasm for the centenary was no mean feat. In isolated pockets of Maoism in Hunan and Hubei, ideologues and Mao converts openly railed against efforts by the Deng group to constrain the festivities. A month before the centenary, a group of party elders even wrote a petition to the Politburo casting doubt on the probity of elevating Deng to the same status as Mao or Marx. This was their way of protesting how the Deng camp had tried to use the campaign to study Deng Thought to upstage Mao worship. "If the writings and theories of comrade Xiaoping are raised to the same status as those of Chairman Mao, Marx and Lenin, we may need to change the party charter and the constitution," the conservatives said. None of the petitioners was disciplined.[144]

D. Little Deng's Final Attack, 1993-1994

The leftists' challenge to the entire Dengian order was best summed up in an intriguing piece called *A Peasant's Article* which was published in the May 1993 issue of *Study, Research, Reference*. Styled as the humble opinion of a farmer from Jiangsu Province, the diatribe represented the Maoist commissars' heartfelt views about where the Revolution had gone wrong.

The monthly journal was the mouthpiece of the nation's premier think-tanks, the Policy Research Office of the Central Committee and the State Council Research Office. Both units remained strongholds of leftist cadres loyal to Deng Liqun or Yuan Mu. That the ideologues were bold enough to mount a public challenge to Deng, however, said much about the political recovery they had made since the *nanxun*.[145]

The major point of *A Peasant's Article* was that reform undertaken by China's Gorbachev-like figures would precipitate the disintegration of the socialist state. The leftist ideologues behind the jeremiad began by lambasting the household responsibility system, the cornerstone of Deng's agrarian reforms. They argued that the "go-it-alone system of individual households [tending individual plots] has obstructed the development of agrarian productivity". "Because of the popularisation of mechanisation, the household approach is not advantageous to unified farming, planning and [production] arrangements," the article said. There seemed little doubt that the remnant Maoists were gunning for the reinstatement of the late chairman's communes, where total collectivisation supposedly made for efficiency.

Even more damaging to the reformist cause was the wholesale denigration of Deng's open-door policy — and the revival of Mao's autarkist tendencies. "We have introduced foreign capital on a large scale and run Sino-foreign joint ventures," *A Peasant's Article* said. "We have asked foreigners to come to China to start factories, mines and enterprises. What is the result? I think this will lead to the bankruptcy of our [native] industry. Our industry faces tremendous difficulties because foreign goods are occupying our markets." The ghost-writers behind the article hoisted high the famous Mao dictum: "We hope to have foreign aid, but we do not rely on it. We depend on our own hard work, the creativity of the whole army and the people."

At the same time, the ideologues were peddling Little Deng's theory that market reforms had spawned a new class of "exploiters". Referring to the patriarch's call for "letting parts of the population get rich first", the article said: "No matter how high sounding the slogans are, the result is that polarisation [of rich and poor] has become more and more severe." The *nouveaux riches*, it went on, had piled up ill-gotten gains through "exploiting workers, manufacturing and selling shoddy products to rip off customers, and profiteering in state assets".

Most alarmingly, Little Deng and his followers laid bare their deep-seated anti-business streak by asking: "Do they [the red capitalists] love the socialist motherland? Who were the people who actively supported the counter-revolutionary rebellion in Beijing in 1989?" As we discussed earlier, the leftists were convinced that the democracy activists of 1989 were acting in collusion with the nascent class of private-sector entrepreneurs.

Implicitly, Deng and his bold reformers were cast as Gorbachev-like traitors who were about to ruin the communist cause. "Shall we go the same mistaken way of the Soviet Union," *A Peasant's Article* asked. "Isn't it true that under the leadership of Mikhail Gorbachev, the USSR was transformed from a strong socialist country into a situation of splintered [sovereignty], where the people suffer extreme hardships?"

Little Deng and his ilk were taking advantage of the economic problems in mid-1993 to cast aspersions not only on reform but on Deng's personal integrity. Consider, for example, the mind-boggling article on Emperor Xuanzong of the Tang Dynasty, which appeared in *Beijing Daily* in June 1993. China watchers suspected that the piece was a thinly-veiled attack on the patriarch's personality and statecraft.[146]

The author, Beijing University historian Wu Zongguo, gave Xuanzong, who ruled in the 8th century, credit for reforms in the rural, military and administrative sectors. However, the monarch was faulted for picking inept ministers and for failing to rein in warlord-like provincial and military chiefs. These aberrations led to the revolution of An Lushan, which almost wrecked the dynasty.

Wu wrote that Xuanzong erred "in the nurturing and selection of talents", as evidenced by the fact that his ministers were "untutored in administrative theories and lacking in knowledge about history". The historian thought Xuanzong was a disaster in his last years. "Thinking that the world is at peace, he delegated all authority to his ministers and generals," Wu wrote. "He went in search of longevity and pleasure. His thoughts were no longer clear and he refused to listen to advice. He became dictatorial, which necessarily rendered his decision-making faulty."

Then there was a tell-tale piece in *China Daily* at about the same time about Ming dynasty monarch Xizong, who "enjoyed life to such an extent that his inattention to government crippled his empire". Again, there was a reference to the emperor relying on sycophants and spurning advice. "As a result, peasants throughout the country frequently rebelled."[147]

Were Xuanzong and Xizong foils for Deng? Were the evil ministers prototypes of such Deng protégés as former party chiefs Hu Yaobang and Zhao Ziyang — and Vice-Premier Zhu Rongji, another Gorbachev-like reformer much-maligned by the ideologues? And were *A Peasant's Article* and Xizong's peasant insurrections allusions to the 170 or so disturbances that hit the countryside in the first half of 1993?

XII. Conclusion: Leftists in Decline

As we saw in Chapter 1, Deng Xiaoping had by early 1992 succeeded in re-hoisting the flag of economic reform. His triumphant tour of Shenzhen and Zhuhai showed he could at least hammer together a consensus within the leadership concerning the need to "speed up" the use of market-oriented means to retool the economy. Furthermore, Deng, together with other members of the moderate wing such as Yang Shangkun and Jiang Zemin, succeeded in re-anchoring the ship of state on to the course of "taking economic construction as the core".

The left wing of the CCP was, of course, by no means finished. By early 1994, the central planners still controlled many State Council units. The ideologues' hold over the ideological and propaganda establishment remained solid. Such conservative elders as Chen Yun and Song Ping still had a large say over personnel. Most importantly, there was a symbiotic relationship between so-called moderates such as Deng and Jiang and the hardliners: the former needed the latter to act as "executioners" and bully boys on the ideological and political front. So long as the CCP refuses to take up political reform, "ideological policemen" will be required to snuff out the challenge posed by bourgeois-liberal intellectuals.

However, it seemed clear that the dream of Chen Yun and Deng Liqun of taking power seemed more and more remote by mid-1994. To maintain the people's standard of living — and to shore up its international status — the CCP had no choice but to proceed with economic reform as well as the integration of the Chinese economy into the international marketplace. At least on the economic front, Beijing had no choice but to proceed down a quasi-capitalist road. The force of "peaceful evolution" seemed invincible. And the leftists were heading towards irrelevance and obsolescence.

A. Erosion of the Powerbase

That, in spite of their sticking to a putative "mass line", the leftists had by 1993 lost large chunks of their mass support was clear from the meagre number of votes they secured during the limited ballots that took place at the 14th Party Congress of 1992 and the NPC and CPPCC of 1993.

Take for example, the voting for various positions in the CPPCC, for which many leftists received nominations as a "compensation" for retirement. Out of 1,862 valid votes, such relatively liberal or popular politicians as Li Ruihuan and Ye Xuanping received 1,837 and 1,851. The ballots for the following leftists were markedly lower: Yuan Mu, 1,421; He Dongchang, 1,483; Gao Di, 1,524; Xu Weicheng, 1,602; and He Jingzhi, 1,616.[148]

The conservative wing of the party, however, was unprepared for their massive loss of face during elections for state positions at the 1993 NPC. Li Tieying, the head of the SEC and the *bête noire* of Beijing's intellectuals, suffered the humiliation of his life during ballots for the position of State Councillor. Out of 2,896 valid ballots, 722 were negative votes and 137 abstentions. Former People's Bank president Li Guixian and State Council Secretary-General Luo Gan, both considered protégés of Li Peng, also did poorly. The negative and abstention ballots for Li Guixian were 323 and 86; and for Luo Gan, 161 and 51.[149]

Faced with the obvious discrepancy between their Marxist beliefs and the reality of everyday business, quite a few noted leftists were forced to recant on a *de facto* basis. In his message of condolence on the death of Li Xiannian, Chen Yun practically disowned his insistence on "pure upon pure" socialism. The patron saint of planning admitted he had "to learn new things" in order to catch up with the 1990s. "Some ways of doing things in the past no longer apply under the new situation of reform and the open door," Chen said. "We must ceaselessly explore and solve new problems." The leftist also said that while he had never been to the Special Economic Zones, he was concerned about their development.[150]

Mao's former secretary and the premier theorist of the Politburo, Hu Qiaomu, also reportedly made his peace with reform before he died in September 1992. Weeks earlier, Hu authorised the publication of a talk that he had delivered on a tour of the United States before the June 4 crackdown. While the piece criticised "rightist" errors committed by Hu and Zhao, it basically explored "why China incurred 'leftist' mistakes for 20 years". Chinese intellectuals in Beijing said that Hu left a will in which he pointed out that "it is now time to give up obsolete words, concepts and ideas".[151]

B. A Lack of Vision

By late 1993, it was obvious that Deng Xiaoping had weathered perhaps the last major challenge of the leftists. This was despite the fact that the economic dislocation that became apparent in the middle of the year had given the ideologues opportunities for a counter-attack. Even the moribund Chen Yun summoned enough energy to speak out on the need to rectify the economy and to crack down on corruption, again seen as a manifestation of the excessive reliance on the market. In early 1993, the conservative patriarch reportedly drew up a ten-point proposal for reining in credit and speculation on real estate and stocks. He asked Beijing to put more stress on sectors like transport and energy. Chen also pointed out it was "high time" to combat corruption as well as "infiltration of decadent, capitalist trends".[152]

It also became clear, however, that the left was a force without an agenda. Leftists could only point out what, according to them, had gone wrong. They could also try to dress up their monkish "empire of the spirit". However, the ideologues had nothing positive to offer, specially in the way of improving the people's standard of living. One recalls a January 1982 speech by Chen Yun, in which he warned against the danger of excessive material riches: "The people's livelihood has to improve. Food on the table must not be too meagre — but it must not be too abundant either." In an internal talk to CASS academics in late 1991, Little Deng admitted that he had failed to establish class struggle or "countering peaceful evolution" as the "core" of national work. "Talking about the dangers of peaceful revolution is easy, doing concrete things about it is difficult," the top ideologue muttered.[153]

Why the resistance? There was nothing much the ideologues could deliver in the age of McDonald's fast food, Ferrari sports cars, karaoke bars, and Yaohan department stores. Chen Yun's famous weapons — the "Bird Cage theory" and the theory of the four balances — date from the Yan'an caves. While the former economic czar could prescribe old formulas for rectifying the supposed "aberrations" of reformers such as Zhao Ziyang and later Zhu Rongji, Chen and his ilk were not tuned in to the 21st century.

That patriarch Chen was pathetically out of touch was evident from his talk to the leaders of Zhejiang Province in 1990. On that occasion, Chen mentioned how, "in the Yan'an days, I had carefully studied the documents and telegrams drafted by Chairman Mao. After I had read through all of them, I could see the basic guiding idea: seek truth from facts."[154] It was, however, difficult to imagine what kind of truth Chen — who steadfastly refused to go either to Western countries or to the SEZs — could be seeing from his hermit's hideout in Hangzhou.

Analysts have repeatedly noted that Chen's ideas were only good enough for the China of the 1930s to the 1950s. The self-sufficient nation at that time had no inflation and no budget deficit; but it was only because China had no need to do business with the outside world. At the same time, Chen's ideas have precluded China from fast-paced development and integration with the world economy.

In spite of his claim to theoretical brilliance, all Little Deng could serve up was some Mao memorabilia — maudlin nostalgia about the clean, good old days of the 1950s. "In the old days, Mao Zedong was very resolute in implementing the 'Campaign against the Three Evils' and the 'Campaign against the Five Evils'," Little Deng said in an internal talk in September 1991. "Mao's lifestyle was so frugal and hardworking. How good it was. We cannot stop people from remembering the past!" Little Deng then contended that the on-going "Mao craze" was tantamount to "an opinion poll having been taken" on the attitude of Chinese people towards Maoism.[155] How deluded can such a putative dialectical materialist be!

By late 1994, there was evidence that many leftist ideologues had caught the business bug and gone down the quasi-capitalist road with elements they had earlier condemned as "heretics" or "traitors". The Central Party School, considered the Mecca of communism, raised eyebrows when it decided to branch out into business. By 1993, it had set up more than a dozen enterprises, which ranged from publishing to import and export. And horror of horrors, the Lei Feng Memorial in Fushun, Liaoning, opened a nightclub and karaoke bar in early 1994.[156]

C. The Dearth of Talent

(i) Where is the Next Generation of Leftists?

A key priority of leftist commissars after the June 4 crackdown was to groom the next generation of talents who were both "red and expert". However, it soon became apparent that with the advance of the market economy, very few young and bright party members were tempted to assume the mantle from the likes of Little Deng or Song Ping. Reason: the leftists who stole the limelight in the first few years after the massacre were hardly role models younger cadres would look up to. The reputation of quite a few of the hottest leftists sank to new lows in 1992 and 1993.

Take, for example, Gao Di, the Director of the *People's Daily* who imposed a hard line on the paper until he was forced to retire in early 1993. A well-known ignoramus, Gao shocked his intellectual friends by once suggesting that there were 5 million prostitutes in Taiwan. Aside from bringing in his cronies to fill top positions in the paper, the former party secretary of Jilin Province became notorious for various moral and "lifestyle" problems. According to one story doing the rounds of the capital in 1992, Gao, who spent part of his school days in Japanese-occupied Manchuria, was a "fan of Japan" in his heart. On a visit to Tokyo that year, he reportedly sought out some of his old schoolmates and in a downtown club, sang songs glorifying the "East Asia Co-Prosperity Sphere". An equally damaging story had it that Gao shed his wife — who had been the household amah — and co-habited with a Chinese-French journalist. Which led to outcries of impropriety because as a member of the Central Committee, Gao was not supposed to live with a woman who had a foreign passport.[157]

And how about propaganda supremo, and later, CASS party secretary Wang Renzhi, the apparently holier-than-thou guardian of the faith. He was seen as an opportunist who tried to hedge his bets. In late 1991, the Central Commission for Disciplinary Inspection (CCDI) investigated his alleged involvement in a petition drawn up by his more liberal colleagues in May 1989. The letter to the Central Committee, which pleaded for more tolerance for the pro-democracy movement, was broadcast at Tiananmen Square by the students. The free-thinking staffers of the Propaganda Department apparently asked Wang to check the wording of the petition. Instead of tearing it up, Wang reportedly helped polish the missive.

More damaging was the accusation that Wang figured in the so-called

video scandal of 1990, in which a Shanghai entertainment company allegedly greased the palm of some Propaganda Department officials for its imprimatur on a series of audio and video products. One of Wang's underlings, who
was later fired, reportedly put 2,000 yuan in his boss's drawer. Wang reportedly received a reprimand from the CCDI.[158]

No less tarnished was the reputation of He Xin, the doyen of the neo-conservatives who, at the acme of his career in mid-1991, was seen as a successor of Yuan Mu or even Deng Liqun. At the time of the outbreak of the 1991
Gulf War, he was a strategic adviser to Li Peng and his internal reports were
required reading for senior cadres. It soon became apparent, however, that the
literary theorist turned futurologist had glaring feet of clay.

The downhill track of the Li Peng protégé began when he tried to sue Hong
Kong reporters — whom he called "liars and scum" — for libel. He even insisted they be "extradited" to Beijing for trial. However, this effort to impose the
mainland's moral and legal standards on Hong Kong reportedly incurred the ire
of moderate leaders including then president Yang Shangkun, who wanted to
highlight Beijing's commitment to the "one country, two systems" formula.
After the *nanxun*, He Xin was spurned even by Li Peng. He was practically
ostracised by colleagues in CASS. And the self-styled futurologist experienced
great difficulty trying to transfer himself to units including the CPPCC.[159]

(ii) The Vain Search for Talent

In the early 1990s, the leftists were desperately trying to groom successors.
There were mainly two avenues: relatively young commissars in the ideological and propaganda establishment under Little Deng; and the sons and daughters of party elders.

After the dissolution of the CAC in late 1992, Little Deng set up a ministerial-level PRC Historical Research Society as a base for leftists. Deng himself became the President. The Vice-Presidents included such leftists as He
Dongchang, You Lin and Sha Jianxun. A major objective of the society was
to propagate the next generation of Marxist ideologues.[160]

By 1994, however, it became apparent that Little Deng had not made much
headway. Middle-aged ideologues who had reasonable exposure in the media
included Sha, also Vice-Head of the Party History Research Office; author
and theorist Zhang Deqin; *People's Daily* ideologue Huang Meilai; and
Shanghai-based ideologue-journalist Luan Baojun. Most of these "second-
tier" leftists, however, were known as sycophantic hacks and dour pedlars of
dogma who lacked a mass appeal. Little Deng had a good track record of finding plum jobs for promising leftists. But not many young talents were prepared to take up the offers.[161]

Very few of the children of conservative elders such as Chen Yun, Wang Zhen, Peng Zhen and Little Deng made good as leftist ideologues. The most promising among them was Chen Yuan, the son of Chen Yun who was Vice-President of the People's Bank of China. The younger Chen (born 1945) made a name for himself for advocating a strict monetarism as well as state control of assets. Moreover, he was by the early 1990s able to gather together a mini-think-tank. The brains trust of mostly social scientists included the son of Deng Liqun, Deng Yingtao; the nephew of Hu Qiaomu, Du Ying; and the Party Secretary of Qinhuangdao, Tang Ruoxin. However, by 1993, Chen Yuan had trimmed his sails and made accommodations with market economics. For example, he repeatedly told foreign businessmen and reporters that his father was a keen supporter of Deng's market reforms.[162]

The majority of the offspring of conservative elders, however, have forsaken ideology for business. Being up-and-coming "red capitalists" who hobnobbed with Hong Kong and Western businessmen in hostess bars, they would certainly feel embarrassed about bringing up topics such as the virtues of "plain living and hard struggle" or fighting peaceful evolution.

4

The People's Liberation Army:
Deng's Great Wall of Steel

I. Introduction

BY mid-1994, five years after the Tiananmen Square shootout, most aspects of Chinese life had returned to normal. Maoist restoration in areas including ideology and the economy had by and large declined. New breakthroughs had been achieved in economic liberalisation. Superficially, the People's Liberation Army (PLA) also underwent multifarious transformations, as evidenced by the large number of mobile phone-toting "military businessmen" cutting deals in karaoke bars. Deep down, however, the "June 4 mentality" still held sway.

The role of the army as the Great Wall of Steel to preserve the party's monopoly on power continued in spite of drastic changes in the international and domestic arenas. In the post-Cold War era, the threats of foreign invasion had decreased. Within China, the challenge posed by dissidents had somewhat subsided. However, as the succession problem loomed larger than ever, Mao's old adage about the army — "Power grows out of the barrel of the gun" — rang as true as ever for Deng Xiaoping and his would-be successors.

To understand Deng's reluctance to implement defence modernisation in the Western sense of the word, let us look back at the history of party-military interaction. Until relatively recent times, the Red Army, later the PLA, was hardly distinguishable from the party. Even after "entering the cities" in 1949, it was the army that helped the Chinese Communist Party (CCP) impose "the dictatorship of the proletariat" by crushing the remnants of the "enemy classes". Internationally, Mao relied on his loyal troops to breach the blockade of the Western powers — and to withstand the slings and arrows of the "neo-imperialists".

Chroniclers of the June 4 crackdown would be mistaken if they thought the use of brute force to crush the democracy movement was an instance of panic or crisis management gone awry. There has not been a single crisis since the establishment of the CCP in 1921 when its leaders have not seriously considered the military option. During the small-scale student demonstrations in December 1986, the late party elder Wang Zhen suggested a military solution. "Give me a platoon of soldiers and I shall get rid of them [the student demonstrators]," the ex-general boasted. Wang had the backing of Deng. Chinese sources said if the student movement had not abated by January 1987, the patriarch would have declared martial law on the capital.[1]

The clout of the army was boosted by the widely held perception that it was the PLA that saved the CCP in May and June 1989. Deng made this clear in his celebrated briefing to the officers of the Martial Law Command three days after the Tiananmen Square bloodbath. The New Helmsman, then still chairman of the Central Military Commission (CMC), pointed out that the brass had "passed muster" in its role as the "Steel Great Wall" of the party. The patriarch praised the PLA as "the loveliest people of them all . . . The army is forever the defender of the country, forever the defender of socialism."[2] Deng's successor as CMC chief, President Jiang Zemin, also pointed out in November 1989 that "the people have nothing without the army. The PLA is a strong pillar for the people's democratic dictatorship."[3]

The fall of the Soviet Communist Party and the disintegration of the USSR in late 1991 further enhanced the resolve of the party to boost the powers of the army — and to ensure that the PLA remains under "the party's absolute leadership". Deng later told intimates that the key lesson from the USSR was to boost the party's control over key aspects of the polity including the army. According to Chinese sources, Beijing was aware of the political implications of army loyalty even before the collapse of the Kremlin. During his visit to Moscow in early 1991, Jiang advised Mikhail Gorbachev to bolster the party's control over the armed forces as well as his own relations with the generals.[4]

In mid-1992, the three departments of the PLA issued orders about the army's role in quelling internal dissent. "The objectives and goals of the PLA in defending [the party] against rebellion are: assist the people's government in swiftly cowing rebellions into submission and pacifying them; restore social order to normal; protect the lives and property of the people, preserve the unity and stability of the nation and guard the leadership role of the party and the socialist system."[5]

In the following sections, we shall look into the new powers being given the PLA as well as ways through which the Deng leadership tried to consolidate the party's grip over the army. These included major purges in mid-1990, late 1992 and late 1993.

However, by early 1994, the army remained riven by factionalism. And the ability of the PLA to acquit itself of its dual role of deterring foreign aggression and snuffing out internal dissent had been cast into doubt by the leaps-and-bounds expansion of military business. The chapter will end by looking at how "defence modernisation" suffered a setback — and how the army remained a wild card in the succession sweepstakes.

II. PLA Power Play: Army Intervention in Everyday Life

The reinstatement of Maoist military ideals went into high gear immediately after the June 4 killings. It came as no surprise to observers familiar with the party's military roots that the PLA would consume a substantial portion of national resources. Army leaders would play a major role in national policy-making. Students would take part in military training and ordinary Chinese would be kept in a "state of alert".[6]

Even as the threat of war had receded with the virtual end of the Cold War, both the PLA and the media played up the dangers of China being swallowed up by neo-imperialists — and the imperative of a strong army. In a commentary in late 1989, the *PLA Daily* warned that "the class struggle in the world has taken a very sharp turn", and that China must guard against efforts of capitalistic countries, "led by the US", to destroy it.[7]

What with class enemies colluding with neo-imperialists to subvert the socialist order, the people must be kept in a state of combat-readiness. From mid-1989 onwards, a comprehensive plan was hatched to boost the people's "national defence mentality". As Jiang Zemin put it, the people must "strengthen their concept of national defence and vigorously support and concern themselves with army building". Defence Minister General Chi Haotian also urged the populace "to think of danger in times of peace and to boost the consciousness of national defence to guard against unexpected turmoil".[8] Orthodox elders such as Chen Yun liked to say that "without grain, there would be no social stability". The post-June 4 top brass was saying that "without soldiers, there will be no peace of mind".[9]

Most provinces and large cities upgraded their reserve corps, and ordinary citizens were asked to sign up. The ranks of the reserves had swollen to about 1 million by late 1993. Starting the autumn of 1989, all college students had to undergo some form of military training. The *PLA Daily* went so far as to propose "revolutionary measures" to boost military awareness, including tea-ching national defence courses in primary schools. From late 1989, the entire freshman class of the "trouble-making" Beijing University spent one year at a military academy. In the autumn of 1990, this practice was extended to more than a dozen of the country's élite universities. It was not until mid-1993 that compulsory military education was scaled down.[10]

When Beijing slapped martial law on Beijing and Lhasa, Premier Li Peng was careful to point out that martial law did not mean "army control of civilian life" — just the deployment of soldiers to better maintain law and order. In fact, at least in the capital's central-level units, the army extended its tentacles into civilian life in subtle but important ways. For example, after martial law was declared in Beijing on May 20, 1989, military units were installed in major media organisations as well as "trouble spots" like the Chinese Academy of Social Sciences. Liberal-minded editors in influential propaganda units, including the *People's Daily*, were replaced by army-affiliated staffers. And even after martial law was lifted in 1990, army officers participated in a big way in civilian affairs.[11]

A. Army Participation in Civilian Affairs

In spite of calls for the continuation of political reform, the hand-in-glove relationship between the army on the one hand, and the party and government apparatus on the other, became more pronounced. It can even be argued that except for the chaotic days of the first phase of the Cultural Revolution, when the PLA was called in to re-establish order, the army never enjoyed so much clout as in the early 1990s.

The acme of military prowess could have been reached at the 14th Party Congress. Over 13 per cent of the 1,989 delegates to the watershed conclave were from the defence units. The army gained an unprecedentedly high level of representation on the Central Committee — 22 per cent — up from 18 per cent at the 13th Party Congress in 1987. For the first time since the Cultural Revolution, a Politburo Standing Committee seat was made available for a professional soldier, General Liu Huaqing.[12] General Liu's voice was deeply felt in matters including diplomacy and the economy.

The Political Report of the Congress made it clear the PLA would fulfil three major functions: to protect territorial integrity; to safeguard the socialist system; and to take part in socialist construction. The Central Committee vowed to "strengthen the army and to increase the country's defence capabilities so as to guarantee the smooth progress of reform, the open door policy and economic development". In other words, the military's brief ranged far beyond ordinary defence matters.[13]

That the PLA would play sizable civilian roles was evident from two secret orders issued by Deng soon after the Congress. Ten generals, including CMC members Zhang Zhen, Chi Haotian, Zhang Wannian, Yu Yongbo and Fu Quanyou were given permission to sit in on Politburo meetings. Besides, commanders and commissars of military regions and districts were allowed to join local party committees in policy-making.[14]

As we shall discuss in more detail in later sections, the most obvious manifestation of military influence in civilian life was in economics: a bigger budget for the PLA and a free hand to run businesses. The army's growing clout was also apparent in foreign affairs. Military elements were partially responsible for the tough stand the CCP took towards Taiwan's upgraded relations with countries including the United States and France. In November 1992, a dozen odd retired generals reportedly wrote a letter to Jiang Zemin and Li Peng urging a "stern reaction" against the sale of jet fighters to Taiwan by France and the US. Beijing subsequently closed Paris's consulate in Guangzhou and until early 1994, the French were frozen out of lucrative joint-venture opportunities.[15]

According to Western and Asian officials, the PLA was generally more hawkish than civilians — notably the diplomats — on the issue of "territorial integrity". Take, for example, the flash points in the South China Seas, including the Spratlys. The top brass was reportedly less inclined to abide by the principle, first laid down by Deng Xiaoping, of shelving the issue of territorial dispute for the joint development of the archipelago.[16]

General Liu Huaqing perhaps best exemplified the army's clout in civilian affairs. Chinese sources said he took part in the deliberations of many non-military issues. In April and May 1993, Liu toured Shanghai together with top local leaders. It is noteworthy that the CMC Vice-Chairman dabbled in economic matters when he inspected local factories and waxed eloquent on how "doing a good job in Shanghai has a major significance for national economic construction". He expressed satisfaction that the Shanghai party committee had set as its goal of "building up spiritual civilisation" the emulation of the Eighth Platoon on Nanjing Road in Shanghai, a long-standing model PLA unit.[17] Also in May 1993, Liu gave a speech to the Central Party School on the importance of defence modernisation. Analysts said it was rare that a general had been invited to take the podium at the party school, the traditional training ground for top cadres.[18]

Before his disgrace in late 1992 (see following sections), Yang Shangkun's half-brother, chief political commissar General Yang Baibing became perhaps the military officer who had the most say in civilian affairs after the June 4 crisis. In late 1989, the general, who was also CMC Secretary-General until October 1992, was inducted into the CCP Central Committee Secretariat. One of Yang's briefs seemed to be to ensure that PLA interests were looked after in the policies of both party and government. Yang was also charged with promoting close co-operation between the military and intelligence establishments in fighting "internal subversion".[19]

Judging by media reports and public functions, it was evident the relationship between ordinary cadres and PLA officers had become closer. On occasions such as New Year's day or National Day, civilian and military officials in central- or regional-level administrations held celebrations together. Politburo members who made trips to the regions invariably held brainstorming sessions with local cadres as well as military representatives. And army and civilian units jointly took part in many civilian engineering and irrigation projects.

Beijing also passed measures to substantiate concrete co-operation between the civilian and military sectors. For example, at the March 1992 session, the National People's Congress passed a law on National Defence Mobilisation. Besides facilitating conscription and the "mobilisation of the masses", the statute provided the basis for "co-ordination between the PLA and government departments, in particular, between the military and economic-planning departments".[20] As we shall see in the following section, in the wake of the Gulf War, officials including Jiang Zemin and then State Planning Commission minister Zou Jiahua talked about integrating the research and development functions of the military and industrial sectors.

B. The Army as "Guarantor" of Reform

Yang Baibing's place in history would likely consist in his having coined the slogan *baojia huhang* — the army providing an "imperial escort" for Deng and his reforms. The catch-phrase became popular soon after Deng's *nanxun* ("imperial tour to the south") in early 1992. As Yang put it in rather cumbersome language: "The people's army will resolutely, and from beginning to end, support, take part in, and safeguard reform and the open door."[21]

It is widely assumed that Yang Baibing and the Yang Clan in general started the *baojia huhang* campaign to elevate their status. However, it is also true that Deng encouraged if not masterminded the gambit. The army played a key role in ensuring the success of the *nanxun*. Suffice it to point out that the bulk of the *nanxun* talks was a replay of Deng's sayings in early 1991. Because of opposition within the party, however, those reform-minded instructions never became the dominant doctrine (see Chapter 3).[22] The subtle kind of "military intervention" engineered by Deng and the Yang Clan in early 1992 has been compared to the PLA's role during the Cultural Revolution: While Mao used the PLA to rein in the ultra-radicals, Deng used the army to ensure that the *nanxun* spirit would prevail over the Maoist ideologues and the central planners.

In the three months after the *nanxun*, General Yang's General Political Department organised three trips to the special economic zones of Shenzhen and Zhuhai for 61 top officers. As one officer put it about the army's renewed commitment to the Deng line of reform: "The people's army must from beginning to end maintain and protect this line. Our goal is to study it for 100 years and implement it for 100 years."[23]

At least for Western observers, the *baojia huhang* campaign has disturbing implications. However benignly the crusade was carried out, it amounted to military intervention in everyday life, including the economy. Consider Zhuhai Mayor Liang Guangda's response to the campaign: "With the army stationed here, they would fulfil the function of stabilising people's hearts and stabilising society. [They could accomplish this] without firing one shot."[24] One could not help but asking: why was it necessary for the PLA to fire a single shot within China if the country was not under threat of invasion?

In late 1992, ten retired generals who usually did not see eye to eye with General Yang Baibing also expressed their support for the *baojia huhang* campaign. In a letter addressed to the official journal *Chinese Talent*, Yang Dezhi, Chen Xilian, Yang Chengwu and others expressed their support for reform. "We will resolutely, and from beginning to end, support, take part in, and protect the reform and open-door policy," they wrote. "To provide an imperial escort for reform is a new task that has befallen the PLA under new circumstances."[25]

And in his speech to the Central Party School, General Liu practically put the state and the army on an equal basis as far as their contributions to reform is concerned. The theme of the address was that "the state posits economic construction as its centre; the army puts modernisation construction as its core." "Defence modernisation is an important, integral part of the Four Modernisations," the CMC strongman said. "It is an important guarantee for the materialisation of the three other modernisations."[26]

C. The Budget: A Bigger Slice of the Pie

From 1989 onwards, the status of the army as a "state within a state" was underscored by its growing share in the national budget. The preponderance of the PLA perhaps climaxed in the year or so after the Gulf War of January 1991, which demonstrated the importance of sophisticated weaponry in modern warfare. Thus, in addition to demanding "kickback" for helping defend the party, the PLA was asking for more funds for research and development of new weapons.

Let us examine the official budget as passed by the NPC from 1990 to

1994. In 1990, defence expenditure was 28.97 billion yuan, or 8.71 per cent of total national spending. The allocation was a hefty 15.20 per cent over that of 1989. The increase rates for the following four years were 12 per cent, 12 per cent, 13.5 per cent and 20 per cent. However, taking into view the low inflation rate before 1993, these were big hikes.[27]

Chinese sources said the yearly budget increase throughout the 1990s had been fixed at 10 per cent, discounting inflation. Quite independently of the party and government, the CMC held a budget meeting in 1991 for its own Eighth Five-Year Plan. Because of the growing clout of the navy and the new imperatives of strategy, a large portion of the budget for procurement was expected to go to the naval forces. This is despite the fact that the navy, with 260,000 men in arms, is the smallest of the three major branches of the PLA.[28] No other sector of the polity, including education and social welfare, got anywhere near this large a cut of the budget.

To defuse criticism both at home and abroad of the increase in the budget, PLA officers claimed that much of the increase was used for food and other basic necessities for the troops. "The bulk of the small increase in the military budget for 1993 will be used to compensate for the increase in the cost of living due to price adjustments and the introduction of reform measures," NCNA said. Likewise, Finance Minister Liu Zhongli claimed the 1994 budget increase was called for because of "price rises, army wage reform and higher living expenses".[29] Moreover, to dispel what Beijing called the bogey of the "China threat", the propaganda machinery made much of the fact that China's per capita spending on defence was one of the lowest in the world. The 1994 PLA budget took up 9.59 per cent of China's total government expenditure, compared with 23 per cent for Taiwan, 24.3 per cent for South Korea and 17.6 per cent for the US.[30]

Western military intelligence said actual army expenditure could be three to six times the amount alloted by the government. London-based sinologist David Shambaugh estimated that "hidden military spending" for 1993 was US$42 billion, almost six times the official budget. Much of this came from State Council allocations for defence-related ministries and R & D in the area of electronics and aerospace. Moreover, foreign-exchange earnings from arms sales — which are handled by PLA subsidiaries and front companies in Hong Kong, the US and elsewhere — went directly to military coffers.

From the early 1980s to 1991, China is reported to have sold arms overseas worth a total of US$8.3 billion. Armaments exports amounted to an estimated US$2 billion in 1991.[31] As we shall see in a later section, by 1993, some 70 per cent of the production value of military factories were destined for consumer markets in China and overseas. The bulk of the profits from these military-turned-civilian factories were vouchsafed PLA units.[32]

That the army was helping itself to a larger slice of the pie was a setback for a key reform credo: the army must subserve overall national interests, and PLA expenditures must be subsumed under the imperative of economic growth. From the early 1980s to the Tiananmen Square crackdown, the army budget had in real terms been pared year after year. However, at the 1991 NPC, then finance minister Wang Bingqian told the NPC that while state coffers were sustaining a record deficit of 15.04 billion yuan, the increasing outlay for the PLA was justified. "We must adapt ourselves to complicated and fast-changing international situations," he said. "We must be able to handle unexpected occurrences and safeguard national security and economic development."[33]

In an apparent reversal of Deng's arguments, then army chief of staff General Chi Haotian said that a strong army was needed "to defend the fruits of economic progress". The general told the NPC in 1991 that "the Gulf War reflected, to some extent, the characteristics and trend of modern wars and gave proof to the importance of strengthening China's defence while boosting its economic development". He claimed that a strong army could provide an "impetus" for economic development. "A strong sense of national defence can be converted into a binding force for the entire nation, a mighty fighting power for the armed forces and a great impetus to economic construction," the NCNA quoted him as saying.[34]

These views were endorsed by Jiang Zemin. Jiang indicated in a talk to PLA officers in late 1990 that economic construction was predicated upon a "peaceful and stable domestic and international environment", which could only be guaranteed by the PLA. "Army construction is beneficial to both stability and the reform and open-door [policy]," he said.[35]

D. The Marriage of Defence and Industry

It is, however, not just dollars and cents that the army was getting. Central planning-oriented cadres like Li Peng and Zou Jiahua were advocating the partial merger of defence and industry, in other words, a return to the order of the 1950s and 60s. Partly under the influence of the Soviet Union, and partly because China was the victim of the policy of containment by the "imperialists", Chairman Mao opted in that era for a quintessentially Stalinist strategy: putting all emphasis on defence and heavy industry.[36]

At least up to the late 1960s, much of national resources went to building the nuclear bomb, as is attested to by the adage "we'd rather have the bomb than trousers". Ordnance factories and steel mills had priority access to raw materials, energy and state investment. Research and development even in the civilian industrial sectors were called upon to serve the military juggernaut.

Deng reversed the trend when he took over in the late 1970s. The Four Modernisations Programme — industry, agriculture, science and technology, defence — made it clear that China must first develop the national economy and raise the living standard before attending to weaponry. Both Zhao Ziyang and Hu Yaobang were keen lobbyists for the light-industrial sector. Light and other consumer products satisfied the needs of the people and had the best export potentials.

The Gulf War provided a good excuse for the conservative faction in the party to put the Maoist agenda back on the table. In March 1991, Li Peng said the order of the Four Modernisations had been changed, with science and technology taking the lead.[37] Because of the diplomatic implications, Li refrained from mentioning defence. However, it is clear the premier was lumping together the development of technology and armament, which would have priority in the national perking order.

CMC Chairman Jiang Zemin made the same call when he met with military officers in Hunan Province in mid-1991. Again pointing to the Gulf War, Jiang said: "Modern warfare has gone hi-tech: it means three-dimensional, electronic and missile warfare." Jiang, a former minister of electronics industry, further asked the nation's industrial and technological departments to have military needs in mind when they mapped out developmental programmes. "Electronic technology occupies a decisive position in national economic construction and national defence," he said. "We should arouse the enthusiasm for national defence among comrades engaged in scientific and technological research."[38]

It was then State Planning Commission minister Zou Jiahua, however, who best invoked the Maoist credo of the "inter-changeability" between military and civilian pursuits. "We must raise the level of mutual compatibility between the army and the civilian sectors of the economy," he told the 1991 NPC. "We must boost the capacity of the economy to make drastic shifts between peaceful and wartime needs."[39]

III. The Drive for Loyalty

Because of the need throughout the 1989-1994 period to use the army to maintain the dictatorship of the proletariat, it is not surprising that the drive to ensure troop loyalty remained the CMC's priority. Army loyalty was cast into doubt in view of the large number of officers and soldiers who showed reservations about opening fire on Tiananmen Square. By 1994, centrifugal forces had become obvious within the ranks.

A full-scale inquisition was carried out within the PLA after the 1989 massacre. Standards of "absolute loyalty" reminiscent of the Yan'an caves were re-imposed, with various degrees of success. In a bizarre instance of dehumanisation, men in uniform were regarded as clones of "proletariat paragon" Lei Feng whose minds could be programmed by the General Political Department (GPD): they were not allowed to go near anything smacking of bourgeois liberalisation. For example, unlike ordinary citizens or party members, they were not permitted to join even officially approved religious bodies or the eight Beijing-sanctioned "democratic parties".[40]

The GPD, however, might be waging a losing battle. To keep the soldiers from "seeking truth from facts", Martial Law authorities in May 1989 prevented their rank and file from reading newspapers or conversing with citizens in the capital. However, the times were changing and not even the strictest censorship could ensure that military men would march to the old tunes of Yan'an. By late 1991, there were reports that young soldiers were taking a fancy to rock-and-roll music as well as Hong Kong- and Taiwan-originated novels. From mid-1992, satellite dishes for foreign broadcasts could be spotted in barracks even in relatively remote areas like Yunnan and Guizhou. And as we shall see, in the wake of the craze for doing business, morale became a big problem in the mid-1990s.[41]

A. June 4, 1989, and the Voices of Opposition in the Army

In an address to an enlarged CMC meeting on May 24, 1989, then Commission vice-chairman Yang Shangkun admitted that he had doubts about the loyalty of officers. On whether the army had the "right ideological inclination", Yang said he had no worries about the fealty of the heads of military regions and districts. "But will there be a problem with officers below the rank of army [commander]?" he asked. "There are still people who ask the question, 'Since the CMC has three chairmen, why is it that Deng Xiaoping alone can sign the order mobilising troops [to Beijing to enforce the Martial Law command]?'" Yang's statement referred to the fact that many officers seemed loyal to then CMC vice-chairman Zhao Ziyang.[42]

In a rare interview with the China News Service in November 1989, then chief of the general staff General Chi Haotian tried to deny rumours of dissension in the ranks, especially dissatisfaction among officers over the June 4 military suppression. Referring to the June 4 events, Chi said: "From beginning to end all commanding officers of the army maintained a high sense of unity with Chairman Deng Xiaoping and the CMC that he led." "Once the CMC gave the order, all military regions lived up to the [principles of] coming [to the help of the centre] once being called and obeying instructions," he added. [43] Chi also denied as "absolute nonsense" reports that various military units of the Martial Law Command fought each other in the run-up to and immediately after June 4, 1989, — or that there were cases of mutiny. He emphasised that "in the areas of thought, action and organisation", military officers were "from beginning to end as united as a seamless rock" over the need to crush the 1989 protests.

Chinese sources said, however, that the CMC — as well as Deng Xiaoping and the pro-crackdown group in general — did have to contend with divergent opinions in the run-up to the bloodbath. At least seven retired generals, including former defence minister Zhang Ziping, wrote open letters to the CMC and Deng to advise against the military option. Equally important, these seven military elders refused to own up to their "mistakes" after June 4.[44]

Among the so-called doves, the role of former defence minister Qin Jiwei was especially intriguing. A former commander of the Beijing Military Region and protégé of Deng Xiaoping, Qin was the only senior officer who could jockey for position with other supremos such as the Yang brothers. Chinese sources said that Qin not only opposed the crackdown but schemed to join forces with Zhao Ziyang. There were conflicting reports concerning Qin's gambit. One version said he attempted to organise a coup. Another said he tried to discourage the regional commanders from sending in troops to join the Martial Law Command. Zhao, however, did not lend his signature to the telegram that Qin tried to dispatch to the regional commands — and the "coup" fizzled out. Not surprisingly, there were many rumours about Qin's arrest and imprisonment immediately after June 4.[45]

The most palpable manifestation of dissent within the ranks was that at the height of the demonstrations in the latter half of May 1989, as many as 1,000 PLA officers and soldiers joined the students and other protesters. It is difficult to estimate which particular PLA unit had the largest number of pro-democracy sympathisers. However, eye-witnesses reported seeing large contingents of protesters coming from the National Defence University and the three headquarters.[46]

On May 18, 1989, the CNS ran a rare item on an open letter written by a group of middle-aged officers, which was publicised by the students' broadcasting station at Tiananmen Square that same day. The petition asked the CMC to ensure that "measures of using force to suppress students and the masses" would never be used. "The entire officers and soldiers of the PLA must be educated to love the people and protect the people," the letter said. This group of liberal officers, whose identities were never named, professed support for Zhao in his capacity as CMC vice-chairman. They pointed out that the whole army must observe the advice of general secretary Zhao Ziyang on "maintaining good relations with the masses on the basis of rationalism, cool-headedness, restraint and order". The petition also called on the CMC to "persuade government leaders to go into the midst of students, to accept the rational demands of students, and to bring about real unity and stability".[47]

Most important, the petitioners called upon army authorities to expedite military reform. "Various reform programmes in the army must be implemented," they said. "The military budget should be curtailed, PLA offices and divisions should be shrunk and the structure of the army reformed." The petition urged senior officers to get out of their imported limousines and to "eat bitterness together with the people". The money saved, it said, should be used for education.

The extent to which individual officers were willing to risk their careers — perhaps even their lives — to register opposition to the crackdown was evident from a classified document on the number of "rebel" military figures. The tally, made by the GPD, said the Commander of the 38th Group Army, 110 other officers and 1,400 soldiers refused to take orders or left their posts during the June action.[48]

The document, which also contained a long speech by Yang Baibing, was leaked to Hong Kong in late 1989. It said 21 officers and cadres with the ranks of divisional commander or above, 36 officers with ranks of regimental or battalion commander, and 54 officers with the rank of company chief, "breached discipline in a serious manner during the struggle to crush the counter-revolutionary rebellion". In addition, 1,400 soldiers "shed their weapons and ran away", General Yang said. He particularly cited Xu Qinxian, commander of the Beijing-based 38th Group Army, as one of the 21 senior officers who had disobeyed orders from the CMC. No other officers were named.

Failure of the 38th Army — many of whose soldiers were recruited from the capital and were allegedly friendly with students behind the 1989 protests — to clamp down on the protesters was a factor behind the rapid growth of the movement. Xu was reportedly court-martialled in the autumn of 1989 and given a stiff sentence. While the thousand-odd "rebels" were but a negligible percentage of the force, General Yang expressed doubts over the loyalty of the entire officer corps. He pointed out that during the rebellion, "if a group of army political commissars had not insisted on their political stand and stuck to their positions in times of difficulty, the outcome would have been unthinkable".[49]

B. "Absolute Loyalty" to the Party

(i) Primacy of Ideological Work Restored

After June 4, the first priority of the leftist commissars was to restore the Maoist doctrine that the "core" of PLA work was "politics", including ideological indoctrination and waging class struggle. The June 4 tragedy revived the long-standing debate on whether ideology on the one hand, and "expertise", training and technological modernisation, on the other, should have pride of place in resource allocation.

Speaking both out of his own beliefs — and out of a desire to boost the importance of his department — commissar *extraordinaire* Yang Baibing moved quickly to revive the Maoist ideal. "Politics is the commander-in-chief, the soul of the party and army," he said in late 1989. "Only through strengthening ideological and political work in the army can we guarantee its correct political orientation." While conceding that the army needed to modernise equipment, the ideologue stressed that "our priority concern is in whose hands the guns are being held, in which direction the guns are pointing". "More serious and higher political demands will be put on the army," the general said. "This is to ensure the party's absolute leadership over the army."[50]

In a December 1990 address, Jiang Zemin said ideological and political training was an integral portion of the "strict training and management" of the PLA. "The troops live in an environment of openness, and we must pay even more attention to ideological and political work," he said. A key slogan propagated by the CMC and GPD was: "Uphold the party's absolute leadership of the army, and ensure that the people's army will never change its nature."[51]

Aside from loyalty to the party, the basic precepts being drummed into the brains of soldiers included political and economic issues close to the heart of leftist ideologues such as Deng Liqun. As the *People's Daily* put it in a late 1991 article summarising the indoctrination campaign: "Officers and soldiers now understand that in economics, China cannot implement privatisation; in politics, we cannot have a multi-party system; ideology must never be multi-dimensional; and the army must not be weaned from the party or become depoliticised."[52]

At least in the first three years after the June 4 crackdown, hardliners and even moderates within the top brass saw the army as a major base for countering the "peaceful-evolution" tactics of the West. In this context, not only was it necessary for soldiers to steep themselves in ideology work; the army must spearhead the nation's fight against the corrupt influence of the West. In an early 1990 editorial, the *PLA Daily* said the army must "be a good leader in the construction of spiritual civilisation", meaning the crusade against "money worship, hedonism and looking at everything with only money in mind". As General Chi Haotian put it as late as August 1993: the army must help the party in "resisting corruption and preventing [peaceful] evolution".[53]

Efforts by Zhao Ziyang to depoliticise defence matters were also subjected to bitter attack. Echoing ideologues such as Deng Liqun and Wang Renzhi, Yang Baibing castigated Zhao for "neglecting" ideological work. Specifically,

Zhao was accused of trying to "transform" the nature of political work by playing down Marxist theories and promoting "Western" precepts such as the separation of party and army. "Ever since he became first vice-chairman of the CMC [in 1987], Zhao undermined and disrupted the work of the General Political Department with the result that army political work became leaderless," Yang said. "This [Zhao's conspiracy] was to meet the political needs of those who advocated bourgeois liberalisation. Their goal was to overthrow [the existing order] and to build up a new one."[54]

(ii) Promoting Iron Discipline

The message driven home in repeated indoctrination sessions the PLA organised the first two years after mid-1989 was the same: absolute loyalty to the party, which would ensure that the guns were pointed in the ideologically right direction. As CMC Chairman Jiang Zemin said in the first post-June 4 meeting of the Commission held from November 10 to 12, 1989: "We must insist on the party's absolute leadership over the army. This is the party's fundamental principle of army construction."[55]

The CMC Disciplinary Commission also listed six tasks that every officer and soldier had to follow in the post-Tiananmen Square era. As outlined by Guo Linxiang, then secretary of the Commission, they included "guaranteeing that the army remain in unison with the party Central Committee in thoughts and politics" and "using iron discipline to ensure that the orders of the party Central Committee and CMC are carried out".[56]

A major thrust of the indoctrination campaigns was to rehabilitate Mao's military thinking. For example, after seeing a training session held by the Beijing Military Region, Jiang said the PLA must implement Mao's thoughts to strengthen military construction. "The people's army led by the party is an army whose political quality has passed muster and which has a high combat ability," Jiang said. "With such an army, the party's heart is at rest. And so are the people."[57]

Momentum for ever-stringent ideological training sessions was provided by unexpected events in the former Eastern bloc. The fall of the Ceausescu Dynasty in Romania in December 1990 and the failed Moscow coup in August 1991 prompted urgent meetings by the GPD. Chinese sources said the main lesson the PLA drew from the Moscow event was that the coup would have succeeded if the "Gang of Eight" pretenders had secured the loyalty of the troops. At a much-noted conference in Guangzhou held in September 1991, Yang Baibing compared the "ideological purity" of Chinese officers with the dubious loyalty of their Soviet counterparts. Yang outlined secret plans the CMC and other leading bodies had hatched to prevent the "Soviet scenario" from happening in China.[58]

As we shall see in the next section, the most effective "institutional" means the PLA adopted to ensure loyalty was periodic purges. Other rules and regulations were passed. In February 1990, the CMC endorsed a 16-point document called "Outlines on Grassroots Construction of the Army". The main points included boosting the proportions of ideological and political education and "doing periodic political work well".[59] Party cells and other organisations would be revived and strengthened even in lower-level military units. And grassroots party cells would be given more authority to promote the ideological rectitude of soldiers. Other foci for the work of the commissars included "perfecting a democratic lifestyle and rendering cultural life more active". Foreign analysts estimated that 30 per cent of the education for new recruits and cadets was taken up by ideological training.[60]

In the two years after June 4, 1989, officers with ranks of regimental commander of above went to the grassroots and gave more than 2,000 talks on ideological topics. The army undertook 1,619 training and refresher courses, which were attended by 92 per cent of battalion-level officers.[61]

However, judging from empirical evidence, it seems the so-called Spirit of the Old Eighth Route Army was gone for good. At least until mid-1991, various army and PAP units offered shelter to dissidents or connived at attempts by them to flee the country. Famed student leader Chai Ling, for example, was reportedly given shelter by a military officer in Guangdong. The same was true for a number of high-profile dissidents who subsequently fled to the West. Moreover, the CMC was unable to ensure that all the officers and soldiers who displayed sympathy to the 1989 democracy movement were punished. In many instances, "bourgeois liberal" army men got off with a slap on the wrist.[62]

IV. The Great Purges, 1990-1994

A. The 1990 Purge: Loyalty Came First

The much-awaited reshuffle of the leadership of the seven military regions took place in late April and early May 1990. Officers proven to have toed the party line, specially those who distinguished themselves in crushing the 1989 protests, were given priority in promotion. By the same token, officers deemed to have been reluctant in supporting the centre were demoted or eased out.

A corollary of the "loyalty" criterion was the rise of the political commissars at the expense of commanders. In the reshuffle of both military regions and districts later in 1990, commissars accounted for more than half of the promotions. As distinguished from "professional" commanders, commissars are specialists in ideological work who have little or no experience in leading soldiers in combat. However, being experts of Marxism-Leninism as well as the military thoughts of Mao and Deng, they were deemed the guardians of the faith.[63]

Another indication of the new balance of power is that the GPD accumulated more power. It is a tradition since the early days of the Red Army for the Chief Political Commissar to vet the dossiers of all officers groomed for promotion. This system was enhanced under Yang Baibing. In 1990, the PLA Commission for Disciplinary Inspection — which is the military equivalent of the Central Committee's Central Commission for Disciplinary Inspection — came for the first time under the control of the GPD.[64]

The way the reshuffle was engineered, however, exposed clearly that much-ballyhooed efforts to lay down a legalistic, institutionalised framework for military decision-making was nothing more than propaganda. The change of leadership was essentially the initiative of at most four men: Deng Xiaoping, CMC vice-chairman Yang Shangkun, Yang Baibing, and, to a lesser extent, Jiang Zemin. Comparable regional reshuffles in 1983 and 1985 were the result of fairly detailed deliberations by enlarged CMCs, which were usually attended by retired generals as well.[65]

The personnel changes were announced over one week by Yang Baibing, who made a lightning tour of the seven regions. Chinese sources said the general briefed individual officers on why some of their colleagues had been promoted and others demoted or transferred. Western military analysts said it was likely Yang made the extraordinary trip to forestall opposition. At a full-scale CMC meeting, not only officers whose political fortunes were going downhill but retired generals might express reservations about the revamp.[66]

Analysts said the 1990 reshuffle had set a dangerous precedent because of the criteria on which it was based. In the past, officers were promoted for distinguishing themselves in wars to "protect the country and the people", for example, the Korean War and the "Self-Defence War" against the Vietnamese. This time around, laurels were dispensed for those who gunned down defenceless students, intellectuals and workers.

B. The Post-Tiananmen Square Line-up

The new line-up of the regional command was as follows: Beijing Military Region: Wang Chengbin (replacing Zhou Yibing) as commander, Zhang Gong (replacing Liu Zhenhua) as political commissar; Nanjing Military Region: Gu Hui as commander and Shi Yuxiao as commissar (replacing respectively Xiang Shouzhi and Fu Kuiqing); Shenyang MR: Liu Jingsong and Song Keda (no change); Chengdu MR: Zhang Taiheng and Gu Shanqing (replacing Fu Quanyou and Wan Haifeng); Guangzhou MR: Zhu Dunfa (replacing Zhang Wannian) and Zhang Zhongxian (no change); Jinan MR: Zhang Wannian (replacing Li Jiulong) and Song Qingwai (no change); and Lanzhou MR: Fu Quanyou and Cao Pengsheng (replacing Zhao Xianshun and Li Xuanhua).[67]

Let us look at the Beijing Military Region as an illustration of the new rules at work. The region is considered the most important of the seven because it guards the capital and has the largest troop strength. It also covers the provinces of Inner Mongolia, Shanxi, Hebei and the directly administered city of Tianjin. Since 1949, only officers proven to be loyal beyond the shadow of a doubt have been appointed commanders and military commissars of the Beijing MR.

General Zhou Yibing, 66 (in 1990) and General Liu Zhenhua, 67, were apparently retired because of their poor performance during the 1989 protests. While Zhou is known to be loyal to Deng, he was considered "not resolute enough" in crushing the pro-democracy movement. Zhou is also believed to have suffered from his close association with former defence minister Qin Jiwei, also former commander of the Beijing MR. Moreover, both Zhou and Liu had to take personal responsibility for the fact that the bulk of the 1,000-odd officers who failed to carry out orders in May and June 1989 came from the Beijing MR.[68]

Their replacements, Lieutenant-General Wang Chengbin and Major-General Zhang Gong were considered "loyalists" and protégés of the Yang brothers. A native of Shandong province, Wang joined the army and the party in 1945. He took part in warfare that "liberated" such key cities as Shanghai and Fuzhou. A 1981 graduate of the Army Military Academy, Wang was deputy commander of the Nanjing MR from 1985 until his promotion. Western military sources said General Wang personally led soldiers into Beijing to crush the student movement.[69]

Zhang Gong was considered one of the fastest rising stars of the PLA. A native of Shanxi province, Zhang, 54 (in 1990), joined the army in 1951 and the party in 1961. Most of Zhang's career as a specialist in ideological and political work was spent in the Beijing MR. He rose to become director of the region's Political Department in 1985. Zhang is considered a protégé of Yang Baibing, who had been political commissar of the Beijing MR. There is no doubt Zhang owed his meteoric rise to his contribution to the Martial Law Command, of which he was spokesman. Soon after June 4, Zhang told Chinese and foreign journalists that "not one student or Beijing resident was killed" during the crackdown.[70]

In addition, three of the newly promoted commanders and commissars —

General Zhu Dunfa of the Guangzhou MR, and Generals Gu Hui and Shi Yuxiao of the Nanjing MR — were identified by Western analysts as having personally led troops to Beijing in the run-up to the June 4 massacre.

However, it would be an overstatement to say that the reshuffle was entirely based on ideological or factional considerations. By and large, the changes satisfied other criteria for personnel changes in the army and party in general. Take the goal of "rejuvenation". The age of the post-reshuffle MR leaders ranged from 55 to 64 and averaged 60, which was significantly lower than the ceiling of 65 set by service regulations. Prior to the reshuffle, the age of the incumbents ranged from 57 to 73, the average being 65.

It could also be argued that the new corps of leaders was roughly as professionally qualified as their predecessors. All seven of the new commanders were graduates of military academies. For example, Beijing's General Wang Chengbin headed a junior command school from 1983 to 1985. However, only three of the new PCs could claim formal training in military academies. Compared with their predecessors, — six commanders and four PCs having had formal military schooling — the new group was more or less equally well qualified professionally.[71]

C. The Fall of the Yang Clan and the Late 1992 Reshuffle

(i) The Falling-out between Deng and the Yangs

Nothing more poignantly illustrated China's dynastic politics — and the setback for defence modernisation — than the removal of the Yang brothers from military influence. The *coup de grace* was administered by Deng in consultation with Jiang Zemin, old generals including Liu Huaqing, and Politburo members including Qiao Shi. The thunderbolt was delivered by Deng in a personal letter to the Politburo barely a week before the 14th Party Congress convened on October 12, 1992.[72]

Various theories have been put forward for Deng's decision to rid the Yang brothers — as well as the large corps of Yang loyalists — of their military powers. The main reason seems to be that the Yang clan, especially Yang Baibing, was exhibiting too overt a propensity for power grabbing. Resentment against the younger Yang, a mediocre officer who only made the big time with the help of his elder brother, seemed to be fairly widespread. Beijing was awash with rumours of the chief army ideologue lavishing huge sums on Maoist-style films and cultural productions — and even of the army strongman womanising. And firecrackers were let off in various PLA headquarters in Beijing the moment his downfall was announced.[73]

For Deng, the last straw appeared to have been a series of secret conferences the chief political commissar called in the summer to allegedly plan for a peaceful transition after Deng's death. It transpired that Deng had had a minor stroke in August 1992, which fed speculation about his imminent demise. The patriarch was not informed of the meetings. And the Yang Baibing caper was interpreted as the precursor to a coup. While Yang Shangkun apparently played no role in the "black meetings", he suffered as least guilt by association in the eyes of Deng and his advisers.[74]

Deng's letter to the Politburo, which has never been publicised, did not spell out the exact reasons for sidelining Yang Baibing. The missive did not mention Yang Shangkun. However, Deng pointed out specifically that while the younger Yang should be removed from all military positions, he should be inducted into the Politburo. Moreover, as we shall examine later, Deng cited the principle of the "five lakes and the four seas" — meaning factionalism should be eradicated. This was an indirect reference to the Yangs' blatant faction-building.[75]

The Yangs could not shirk their responsibility for empire-building. For example, they were reported to have taken advantage of their role in the mid-1990 reshuffle to install cronies and protégés in key positions. As chief political commissar, Yang Baibing controlled the dossiers of officers, and his office vetted the political rectitude of candidates marked for promotion. The older Yang, who began his career in military intelligence and was a long-time CMC secretary-general, enjoyed playing the role of a PLA godfather. One report said he used to offer patronage to the rising stars. For example, after graduating from military academies, élite officers on the make were often invited by the former president for a tête-à-tête or for small group meetings.[76]

There is probably some truth to the accusation that the brothers tried to block Jiang Zemin from exercising his authority. The Yangs also had a run-in with Qiao Shi over control of the People's Armed Police. Both Jiang and Qiao were apparently instrumental in persuading Deng to part ways with the Yangs.[77]

Apart from Deng's worries about their empire-building, an equally fundamental reason for the patriarch's decision to dump the Yangs was the fear of the overturning of the June 4 verdict. While the Yangs played a sizeable role in the Tiananmen Square killings, rumours began to circulate in 1992 that they were trying to put the blame on Deng. A widely reported story had it that the older Yang told intimates in the summer of 1992 that he had a tape recording "proving" who it was that gave the orders for opening fire on the demonstrators the night of June 3, 1989. While Yang named no names, it was assumed that the culprit was Deng. The patriarch reportedly flew into a rage upon learning this.[78]

Then there was the "syndrome of the No. 2" in Chinese politics. As in the relationship between Mao and Lin Biao, Deng found the Yangs threatening. This is despite the immense help the brothers rendered Deng in steadying the ship of state after the June 4 massacre, particularly in ensuring the success of the *nanxun*. The patriarch was convinced that to consolidate Jiang Zemin's position as the "core" of the post-Deng leadership, he must first shove aside other would-be helmsmen.[79]

The removal of the Yangs — just as the dumping of Zhao as CMC vice-chairman — was in effect unconstitutional in view of the fact that it was basically the decision of a retired CMC chief. Moreover, Deng acted with the advice of old generals like Xiao Ke, Zhang Aiping, Qin Jiwei and Yang Dezhi, retirees who should not have had any more say in policy-making. This group of "non-mainstream top brass" had opposed the use of force in June 1989 as well as the preponderance of the Yangs after the crackdown.[80]

(ii) The Post-Reshuffle Line-Up, early 1993

A thorough-going military reshuffle took place immediately before and after the 14th Party Congress. About 300 officers, many of whom were suspected to have ties to the Yang Clan, were removed, retired, or transferred to less sensitive positions. The composition of the new CMC was announced the day after the congress closed on October 18. Jiang, as expected, retained his position as Chairman of the commission. The two new vice-chairmen were Liu Huaqing and Zhang Zhen. Originally slated for retirement, the two members of the Central Advisory Commission — basically a "club of retirees" — were summoned to the front line and given memberships in the policy-setting Central Committee. Analysts could not recall another instance of such a transfer from the CAC to the Central Committee.[81]

General Zhang Wannian became the Chief of the General Staff, General Yu Yongbo, Chief of the General Political Department, and General Fu Quanyou, Chief of the General Logistics Department. The three, in addition to new Defence Minister General Chi Haotian, became ordinary members of the CMC. It is noteworthy that Deng and the other senior generals decided to do away with the position of CMC Secretary-General, which had been occupied by the two Yangs.

There were major reshuffles in the three departments at headquarters as well as the Air Force and Navy. The new regional line-up was as follows: Beijing Military Region (MR) Commander Wang Chengbin, Commissar Gu Shanqing (new); Chengdu MR Commander Li Jiulong, Commissar Zhang Gong (new); Guangzhou MR Commander Li Xilin (new), Commissar Shi Yuxiao (new); Jilin MR Commander Zhang Taiheng (new), Commissar Cao Pengsheng (new); Nanjing MR Commander Gu Hui, Commissar Liu Anyuan (new); Shenyang MR Commander Wang Ke (new), Commissar Song Keda.

According to a Hong Kong report, about 40 officers who were promoted by Yang into the General Political Department and other headquarters units in the weeks prior to his sacking had had their promotions revoked. They included the senior editors of the *PLA Daily*, long considered a Yang Baibing stronghold. Two deputies to Yang — vice-chiefs of the GPD Zhou Wenyuan and Li Jinai — were demoted. Zhou was made a deputy commissar in the Shenyang MR and Li a deputy commissar in the Commission for Science, Technology and Industry for National Defence (COSTIND).[82]

In more ways than one, the late 1992 reshuffle can be considered less brutal than that of mid-1990. Well-known Yang Baibing crony Zhang Gong, the Beijing MR commissar who gained notoriety for his pivotal role in the Martial Law Command of 1989, was not sacked but moved to the less sensitive position of commissar in Chengdu. The same lateral transfer took place for the vice-commander of the Beijing MR Zou Yuqi, who was given the same position in the Lanzhou MR. Vice-chief of Staff Xu Xin, who had been trying to curry favour with Yang Baibing, was eased out but not otherwise disciplined. Xu's colleague and fellow Yang sympathiser, vice chief of staff He Qizhong was demoted to be a Vice Commander of the Nanjing MR.[83]

It would be a mistake to think that settling scores with the Yang Clan was the sole motive of the reshuffle. Since many of the affiliates of the Yang Faction rose to power or gained promotions due to valiance displayed in tackling the 1989 "turmoil", their sidelining was, in a sense, Deng's way of showing the world his determination to turn over a new leaf.[84]

Moreover, the reshuffle was also a vote for modernisation. While the mid-1990 personnel changes represented a triumph of the commissars and the ideologues, professionals were favoured this time around. Such "stars" as the newly promoted Air Force Chief Cao Shuangming and the Vice Chief of Staff Li Jing were respected professionals. General Cao took part, together with Deng, in the famed Huai Hai Liberation Warfare. And General Li had 46 years of experience in all three branches of the forces.[85]

D. The Late 1993 Reshuffle

The series of house-cleaning that began around the 14th Party Congress continued throughout 1993 and climaxed with a fairly large-scale reshuffle in December of that year as well as January 1994. Up to 1,000 officers, including around 80 with the ranks of head of a group army or vice-commander, were retired, transferred or demoted.[86]

The year-end personnel changes were finalised at an enlarged CMC meeting held in the capital on December 18 and 19. Apart from rejuvenation and professionalisation, the CMC wanted to achieve a factional balance to ensure support for the post-Deng leadership with Jiang as its "core". While weeding out the Yang Clan affiliates continued to be on the agenda, the emphasis was on maintaining a rough equilibrium of forces among all the mountain strongholds.[87]

Commander of the Beijing MR General Wang Chengbin retired in favour of one of his deputies, Li Laizhu. Considered a modernisation-minded professional, General Li served in the Tianjin region before becoming vice-commander of the Beijing region in 1985. Tao Bojun was appointed a Vice-Commander of the Guangzhou MR. A chief of staff of the regional command since 1992, General Tao, also a seasoned professional, was considered a rising star. He accompanied CMC Vice-Chairman Liu Huaqing on his trip to Thailand and Indonesia in January 1994. In the Nanjing MR, Political Commissar Liu Anyuan was replaced by Major-General Fang Zuqi, Director of the Political Department of the Beijing MR.

The most politically charged move took place in the Chengdu MR, with the retirement of Political Commissar Zhang Gong, the well-known crony of Yang Baibing. General Zhang had occupied that position for just one year. His replacement was General Zhang Zhijiang, another vice-commander of the Beijing MR. In addition, analysts in late 1993 expected other Yang Baibing protégés to go. These included the vice-commander of the Jinan MR, General Dong Xuelin.[88]

Of the three PLA headquarter units, the most thorough-going changes hit the GPD, the bastion of General Yang's. Two assistant directors, Generals Du Tiehuan and Xu Caihou, were promoted Vice-Directors. It is believed that prior to and after the fall of General Yang, a number of his colleagues, including the incumbent Chief Political Commissar and Director of the Department General Yu Yongbo, switched allegiance and professed their loyalty to Jiang and the new CMC. At the General Logistics Department, which was headed by Jiang loyalist General Fu Quanyou, General Zhou Youliang replaced the retiring vice-director General Li Lun. General Zhou had since 1988 been head of the army's Department of Capital Construction and Barracks.[89]

It is not certain whether the ailing Deng could summon enough energy to supervise the December 1993 reshuffle. Moreover, it is very unlikely the patriarch would know in a personal capacity any officer who was aged below 55. Analysts said he probably left major personnel matters to Jiang, General Zhang Zhen, and General Wang Ruilin. However, Deng's primary wish was still to prop up the military influence of Jiang. As discussed earlier, however, Deng did not go whole hog with the anti-Yang purge for fear of upsetting the factional balance. Several officers who gained promotions, including General Fang Zuqi and General Zhang Zhijian, a former head of the Beijing garrison, were once close to Yang Baibing.[90]

By early 1994, it was clear that a kind of collective leadership had prevailed over the PLA. While Jiang seemed to have collected the reins of authority, power was exercised by the CMC Chairman, the two Vice-chairmen Liu Huaqing and Zhang Zhen, and Wang Ruilin. The power of General Wang, the head of the Deng Xiaoping Office, did not seem to have diminished after he had relinquished his position of Secretary of the PLA Commission for Disciplinary Inspection in late 1993. There was intense speculation that both General Wang and General Chi Haotian would gain promotions after the retirement of the two vice-chairmen.[91] While Deng had called on Liu, Zhang, Wang and Chi to support Jiang, the scenario could change drastically after the patriarch's demise.

V. Deng's "Military Thoughts" and the Construction of an Elite Corps

The eclipse of the Yang Clan opened the way for the CMC under Jiang to hoist high the flag of Deng's Military Thought. The study of Deng's military thinking was essentially a double-pronged exercise. On the one hand, Jiang and other PLA propagandists concentrated on those aspects of Mao's strategy "inherited" by Deng which were still useful for the early 1990s. A prime example was the Maoist concern for "willing to eat bitterness" and the party's leadership over the army. On the other hand, there was a pronounced shift of the focus of army work to training, professionalism, modernisation of weapons, and the building up of a streamlined, "élite corps".

The main ideological exercise of the PLA after the 14th Congress was to better equip themselves with Deng Thought, deemed the "general key" that would unlock all problems. A meeting of the GPD in Guangzhou in May 1993 recommended using "Deng Xiaoping's theory of Chinese-style socialism to arm the brains" of officers and soldiers.[92] The study of Deng Thought reached a new crescendo after the publication in November 1993 of the Third Volume of Deng's *Selected Works*, which became must reading for the entire army.

A. Deng's Military Thinking

What exactly was Deng's military thought in the context of 1993? Part of it seemed to be a mere regurgitation of Mao Thought such as the so-called "five kinds of revolutionary spirits of the PLA". They included "self-sacrifice" and "not fearing death while conquering insurmountable difficulties". One Hong Kong commentator even suggested that Deng had plagiarised Mao's teachings in this area. [93]

The new CMC re-emphasised the overriding concern of party leadership over the army. As the *PLA Daily* editorial after the 14th Party Congress indicated, the leadership would never allow "the gun to command the party". Officers were called upon to "listen to the words of the party and to uphold the party's absolute leadership". The same message peppered speeches made by Jiang Zemin, and Generals Liu Huaqing, Zhang Zhen and Yu Yongbo in the half year after the congress.[94]

The harsh requirements for the top brass were laid down by Jiang in the form of the five principles for seeking a qualitative leap forward: "The army must pass muster in politics; be tough in combat; go after a good working style; have clear-cut discipline; and possess guaranteed forcefulness."[95] However, it seems clear that combat-readiness enjoyed pride of place among the five ideals.

In spite of the Maoist packaging that individual officers had given Deng Thought, the thrust of the patriarch's military thinking was not ideological purity but professional standards. In a late 1993 dispatch, the NCNA highlighted some of the military teachings of Deng that had most impressed officers. They included "taking education and training as the centre [of PLA work]"; "stick to the road of [building up] an élite corps with Chinese characteristics"; and "science and technology are the most important productive force."[96] Earlier, a *People's Daily* commentator had extracted some of Deng's key concepts of army modernisation. "Deng mapped out the principles for reform of the army," the commentator said. "He pointed out that to suit the needs of modern warfare, the number of troops should be reduced and the organisation of the army be streamlined so that efficiency is raised. The money thus saved will be used for upgrading equipment."[97]

From late 1992 onwards, the focus of the CMC's endeavours was to build an élite corps: weapons would be modernised even as the number of soldiers be further pared down through the 1990s. The command structure would be rationalised. As Liu Huaqing, Deng's point man on modernisation, put it in March 1992: "We must speed up the pace of the modernisation of army equipment. We must render the PLA structure more superior, the organisation more scientific; we must streamline the number of troops and administration."[98]

At a CMC meeting soon after General Liu had spoken, ambitious plans were mapped out for the construction of élite corps through chopping away superfluous structures and units. For example, three field armies would be disbanded and merged with provincial military establishments. About 20 military academies and medical colleges would be dissolved. Four units under the General Staff Department — the armoured, artillery, anti-chemical warfare and engineering divisions — would be combined into a special unit. Most important, around half a million soldiers would be demobilised in the coming five years.[99]

The major principle underlying the construction of an élite corps was promoting organisational and technological skills needed for modern warfare. As the new Chief of Staff Zhang Wannian told NCNA in early 1993, the goal of training would be "streamlining, integration, and high efficiency". The three headquarters departments would exert a more direct control over the group armies through the establishment of an American-style Joint Tactical Command, Control and Communications Agency. Emphasis would be laid on the integration of the disparate elements of ground, sea and air forces — as well as their speedier mobilisation. The army media revealed that the PLA had expanded units including the artillery, intelligence and communications, engineering and armoured corps — as well as their integration with more regular units. According to General Zhang, the PLA had over a recent period held more than 2,000 seminars on modern warfare and organisational principles.[100]

The spring of 1993 saw a massive spate of war games by the three forces, many of which were overseen by members of the CMC. As the Chinese-run Hong Kong daily, *Wen Wei Po*, put it, "a major wave of training" had been unleashed. Quoting military sources, the paper said: "The new CMC clearly pointed out that boosting training during peace time was the only way to maintain and raise combat ability. This, and absolutely nothing else, was the core work of army construction."[101]

In the early 1990s, Deng and Liu also oversaw an aggressive arms procurement programme, principally from Russia and other former Eastern bloc members. Among the more eye-catching imports were the Su-27 jet fighters and the S300 missiles. By late 1993, Beijing and Moscow were also working on the possibility of co-production of such sophisticated aircraft as the MiG-31 on Chinese soil.[102]

Domestically, the Chinese munitions establishment also attained remarkable success in modernising their ageing equipment. The PLA substantially upgraded its missile production facilities in the early 1990s, which was a factor behind its increased exports to Pakistan and Iran. Missile production capacity grew by 53.9 per cent in 1993 over 1992, according to PLA figures.[103] In January 1994, the air force announced it had embarked on a "take-off strategy" which would make China "self-sufficient in advanced fighter planes" by the year 2000. In 1993, China produced 256 civilian and fighter aircraft, up 24 per cent from the year before.[104]

Underlying the patriarch's commitment to building an élite corps was his vision that, with the economy booming — and with China having re-asserted itself on the world stage in the wake of the June 4-related sanctions — China must acquire defence capabilities commensurate with it's geo-political and economic status. As Jiang Zemin put it in March 1993: "Only when building a strong army that is commensurate with our national status can we protect with assurance our national security and safeguard the smooth progress of socialist modernisation construction." "The Chinese army must be able to see its historical responsibility," he added. "It must work hard to strengthen its comprehensive construction and to boost its combat ability."[105]

B. The Construction of a Mini-Cult around Chairman Jiang

Apparently with the patriarch's blessings, the CMC propaganda machinery took advantage of the study-Deng campaign to boost the authority of Jiang. As was evident from the speeches of senior officers, the Mao-Deng-Jiang lineage was established. This is in spite of the well-known fact that Jiang had even less military credentials than former party chiefs Hu Yaobang or Zhao Ziyang.

While lecturing officers in Liaoning Province in September 1993, Defence Minister Chi Haotian spoke of Mao, Deng and Jiang in the same breath. First General Chi cited "Mao Zedong's military thought and Deng Xiaoping's thought on army construction". Then he upheld "Deng Xiaoping and [CMC] Chairman Jiang Zemin's instructions on putting military training in a strategic position". The minister, who is believed to be a Deng and Jiang loyalist, ended by highlighting "a series of important speeches" made by Jiang on the army withstanding the test of reform and the open door.[106]

In a late 1993 dispatch on how the top brass was studying Deng's *Selected Works*, the NCNA played up the supreme status of Jiang. "If the army were to listen to the instructions of the party, it must self-consciously uphold the authority of the party centre," NCNA quoted some officers as saying. "All actions must be in accordance with the guidance of the party centre and the CMC with comrade Jiang Zemin as its core."[107]

As we shall discuss in a later section, Jiang was reasonably effective in boosting his stature in the armed forces. His handlers also made him out to be a latter-day theoretician worthy of his forebears. In early 1993, the media spotlight was on Jiang's 64-character dictum on an enterprising style of running the army. It included such ideals as "thought liberation", "plain living and hard struggle", and "taking the national situation into consideration and selfless devotion".[108]

The media also made him out to be a "natural" among the rank and file. In a typical article in August 1993, the *PLA Daily* portrayed Jiang as going out of his way to mix with ordinary soldiers and concerning himself with their welfare. The army mouthpiece quoted the CMC chief as asking an army cook the price of vegetables. The *Daily* also reminded its readers of Deng Xiaoping's aphorism: "Eating is politics. Eating is a military affair." "Two generations of CMC chairmen deeply understand the same principle," the *Daily* continued. "Combat power also comes from the rice bowl." It then went on to claim that "the soldiers have put Jiang in their hearts".[109]

Under the plodding of Deng, Jiang belaboured the point of upholding unity among the different factions — in the process offering himself as a "compromise candidate" among all the mountain strongholds. It was the CMC Chairman who in 1990 initiated the ritual of singing the song "Unity is Strength" during morning drills and on major military functions.[110]

VI. The Curse of Factionalism

A. Maintaining a Factional Balance

While meeting the then president of Bangladesh, Hossain Mohammed Ershad, in the autumn of 1989, Deng admitted that the army was almost by its very nature prone to factionalism. "Turmoil in China will be unlike that in Eastern Europe or the Soviet Union," the patriarch reportedly said. "If it happens in China, one faction will control part of the army and the other, another part. A civil war could then erupt."[111] Despite propaganda about the fact that the PLA was "one whole piece of well-wrought iron", there were indications that internecine rivalry within top brass and the ranks had worsened after the June 4 crackdown.

Signs of disunity prompted Deng to intervene several times after mid-1989. In an internal speech to CMC members in May 1990, the patriarch asked the top brass to cut out the squabbling and to promote "the utmost level of unity". "The unity of the army is the lifeline of the Republic," Deng said. "If the army is unified, it signals that the entire country is stable."[112]

Deng, who until 1992 still held regular informal meetings with CMC members and senior commanders, stressed that the utmost unity had to be maintained in all echelons. "We must not have internal quarrels among officers," he admonished in 1990. Chinese sources said Deng's outburst was the result of occasions earlier that year when CMC members and other senior officers squabbled in public. The sources pinpointed two instances in the spring and summer of 1990 involving Yang Baibing. In April, Yang quarrelled with General Hong Xuezhi, the retired chief of logistics. On another occasion in May, he engaged in a heated exchange with another member of the CMC.

Chinese sources said after Deng's lecture, party committees of the various military regions held enlarged meetings to disseminate the patriarch's instructions and to promote unity. At the meeting of the party committee of the Beijing MR on May 18, 1990, Yang Shangkun repeated Deng's statement that "unity is the lifeline of the army".[113]

Factionalism was allegedly the reason for the downfall of the Yang brothers. This is despite the well-known fact that the Yangs would not have become so powerful had they not received the support of Deng. Again, we see a repetition of Deng's favourite trick: the New Helmsman first build up a faction — in this case the Yangs — to beat his enemies and then cut it down to size after his own purposes have been accomplished.

In the letter to the Politburo on October 8, 1992, revealing his decision to sack Yang Baibing, Deng referred to the principle of the "five lakes and the four seas", or the need to avoid factionalism. From October 30 to December 14, the *PLA Daily* published 12 commentaries on how the army leadership should handle itself under Deng's military ideals. The commentary on personnel matters stressed "appointing cadres who have both morality and ability — and solely on the merits [of the candidates]". "Leaders must not substitute this personnel criterion with their personal likes and dislikes and their prejudices," the *Daily* said. There can be little doubt the commentary was targeted at the empire-building efforts of the Yang Clan.[114]

To lay the ghost of factionalism to rest, Deng resorted to three measures in the reshuffles of late 1992 and early 1993. First, he inducted a large number of affiliates of the Third Field Army to top positions. In the dozen-odd years since Deng assumed power in 1978, it had been alumnae from the Second and Fourth Field Armies which had grabbed the lion's share of top jobs. In the post-14th Congress PLA, the top representative of the Third Field was Zhang Zhen, who was resurrected from semi-retirement to be the CMC Vice-chairman. Other Third-Field titans included Chi Haotian and the new commander of Shenyang MR General Wang Ke. Another godfather figure who had re-emerged in 1993, former defence minister Zhang Aiping, also hailed from the Third Field. [115]

The second principle was to bring in the navy as a counterpoise to the army. At the 14th Party Congress, six naval representatives were promoted full or alternate members of the Central Committee — more than any other branches of the PLA. While the aggrandisement of the navy reflected the growing clout of Liu Huaqing, it also mirrored the fact that much of the power projections of the country in the 1990s would take place over the deep blue seas.

Thirdly, a number of officers who won major promotions were well-respected professionals who did not have a "horizontal" personal network — or a potential "mountain stronghold", a clique of affiliates spread out over a region or a PLA branch. A good example is the new logistics chief Fu Quanyou. The much-decorated general began his career with the First Field Army, which was virtually dissolved soon after 1949. Fu is not known to have a power base of his own. Perhaps to a lesser extent, the same could be said of Chief of the General Staff Zhang Wannian.[116]

Another measure the CMC reportedly toyed with to curb factionalism was to strengthen centralised control. In late 1992, there was intense speculation that some or all of the seven military regions would be scrapped. Reports from Beijing said Deng and Jiang were considering setting up a unified command centre at the General Staff Department which would oversee the three forces, including the 24 group armies.[117] While this had not come to pass as of mid-1994, the GSD was expanded with the reinstatement of the position of assistant chief of staff. Three new assistant chiefs of staff, who were one rung below the vice-chiefs, were named in November 1992. They were the head of the GSD Operations Department, Kui Fulin; head of the Intelligence Department Xiong Guangkai; and the commander of the Nanjing-based First Group Army, Wu Quanxu.[118]

There were indications, however, that factionalism remained as serious after the supposed demise of the Yang brothers. In their joint essay heralding Army Day in 1993, Liu Huaqing and Zhang Zhen harked back to an old theme when they underscored the need to fight "mountain strongholds" and factionalism so as to boost unity and strength. They cited Deng on the fact that the army must "persevere with a cadre policy based on appointing officers on the grounds of merits".[119]

Aside from squabbles that arose because of factional affiliation such as the distribution of plum jobs, bones of contention were aplenty. They included funds and resources that were allocated different branches of the PLA — and which sections of the forces would be slashed in the name of streamlining. And as the army business empire mushroomed, conflicts multiplied over which units should have access to the best business opportunities.[120]

A heavy dose of pathos informed the remarks of Jiang as he gave out the insignia to six new full generals in mid-1993. "Leaders of various levels must live up to [the ideal of] being very strong politically," the CMC chief said. "They must resolutely listen to the words of the party at any time. In particular, they must seriously study and grasp Deng Xiaoping's theories on building socialism with Chinese characteristics and his ideas about army construction in the new era." Jiang cited famous Tang Dynasty poet Li Shangyin's adage: "Looking back at what the sages had to say about running the family and the country; Success comes from thrift and failure, extravagance." Obviously, Jiang could not but repeat the hackneyed slogans and exhortations used *ad nauseam* after June 4, 1989. Could he really be the new "core" around which the officers would rally?[121]

B. Case Study: Ideology vs Professionalism

To better understand PLA factionalism, let us study in detail one of the most ingrained bones of contention among the top brass. As we alluded to earlier, a major "contradiction" existed between advocates of ideology and partisans of professionalism. From June 4, 1989, to around the Gulf War of early 1991, Maoist military thinking was revived with gusto. Ideologues and commissars argued that the human factor — whether soldiers stay loyal to the party and whether they are armed with the "correct" worldview — was at least as important as weaponry in winning wars and boosting army superiority.

The ideas of the President of the Chinese Academy of Military Science (CAMS), Zheng Wenhan, were typical of the Maoist commissars. At a conference on military thinking in November 1989, Zheng said that although modern warfare was quite different from that of 40 years ago, the precepts of Mao Zedong's "dialectical military thinking" should still play a guiding role in the strategy of modern warfare. "Blindly copying foreign experience will not do any good," General Zheng said. "With its deep roots in the years of Chinese revolutionary experience, Chairman Mao's dialectical military thinking is particularly applicable to China's situation."[122]

Before the outbreak of the Gulf War, futurologist He Xin, then a strategic adviser to Li Peng, claimed in a widely disseminated internal document that Mao's "people's war" concept was "an invaluable heirloom". He, a former Chinese Academy of Social Sciences scholar, argued that the US-led imperialists were out to pillage the economic wealth and cultural heritage of Third World countries. The "neo-conservative" theorist contended that if Baghdad succeeded in using Mao's idea of the people's war to unify its own people as well as the other Muslims — and that it held out against American "imperialism" for just one month — "Washington would meet with its Waterloo".[123]

Generally speaking, Jiang Zemin seemed to favour the professionals. However, at least before the 14th Party Congress, his position in the army was so insecure he sometimes gave the impression of trimming his sails with the wind. For example, in a Maoist speech in early 1991, Jiang seemed to lend his authority to the "ideology first" persuasion. "We must respect science and respect weaponry, but weapons are not all," he said. Jiang indicated that the major determinants of past victories scored by the Chinese people were "spiritual forces" such as party leadership and the socialist road.[124]

The principal spokesmen for Maoist-style military thinking were the political commissars. As we have seen, under Yang Baibing, the "ideological and political workers" held the limelight in the first year after June 4, 1989. However, by late 1990, there were signs that the "professionals" — who thought the PLA's primary calling was improving combat skills and weapons, not Maoist dialectics — were clawing back lost territory.

The scales were tipped in favour of the professionals especially after the relatively quick US victory over Saddam Hussein's war machine. The CMC came to the speedy conclusion that the Gulf War was won by superior firepower and electronic wizardry — and that the Chinese army had to make up for lost time in the development of advanced weapons.[125]

The professionals won a sizeable battle in February 1991 when the CMC issued a circular calling on all military units to improve their professional and combat skills. The circular was based on the minutes of a December 1990 conference of the General Staff Department entitled "Uphold the Criterion of Combat Power, Open up a New Situation in Military Training and Management Work, and Diligently Ensure that the Military Passes Muster". The commission document said that the "basic requirement of military work" was combat power, or "making the grade" in fighting skills.[126]

"We must put emphasis on grasping military training and management work well," the circular said, adding that the minutes of the GSD conference was a "major document" for the future. "Based on existing conditions, we must build up the army thriftily," the document added. "We must reform and renovate, run the army seriously, pay attention to the materialisation [of theories], and unite our efforts in grasping military work well." Military analysts said it was significant that the CMC circular made no mention of ideological indoctrination. Jiang said specifically at the conference that "[professional] military training is the centre of army work". Even Yang Baibing was forced to concede that the emphasis on ideological indoctrination "in no way negates the central position of military training in army work".[127]

Western military analysts said that after the Gulf War, the top brass concluded that "control of the sky" was the key to victory in 21st century warfare. CMC Chief Jiang, while not a professional soldier, was said to have expressed admiration for American "smart bombs" and laser technology, which enabled US bombers to strike the Iraqi presidential palace without hitting luxury hotels nearby. Jiang urged the improvement of China's air defence, including radar and advance-warning systems, surface-to-air missiles, jet fighters, intelligence and telecommunications.[128]

The emphasis on a hi-tech force was voiced by Liu Huaqing in a speech to COSTIND cadres in June 1991. "High technology has changed the way of fighting," General Liu said. "Raising the technological level of the Chinese army has become an important strategic task." Liu said that Beijing should concentrate on know-how including nuclear weapons, aeronautics and astronautics, electronics, laser and infra-red systems. Liu, who had been in charge of R & D for decades, added that the army must accomplish "automation and unity of command controls, [and improved] intelligence, reconnaissance, and telecommunications networks".[129]

The Gulf War coincided with the deliberation and passage of the PLA's Eighth Five-Year Plan for 1991-95. Indications were that the goals of professionalism by and large had pride of place within the development gameplan.

In its mid-1991 issue, the Hong Kong-based journal *Wide Angle*, which has ties with the military, quoted Jiang as saying that the spirit of the plan was "orientation towards modernisation, world-class standards and futuristic [technologies]". "In the area of national defence know-how, we must concentrate on developing some key technologies and come up with a series of killer weapons," Jiang said.[130]

The modernisers' "victory" was assured by the fact that, even at the height of Yang Baibing's influence in 1989 and 1990, the PLA's upper echelons were still dominated by professionals. Key representatives included Liu Huaqing, then defence minister Qin Jiwei, as well as retired but still influential generals such as former chief of staff Yang Dezhi and former defence minister Zhang Aiping.[131] Interestingly enough, most of the "professionals" also harboured doubts about using the army to resolve a domestic political crisis such as June 4 "turmoil". A month or so before the 14th Party Congress, the old generals, especially Qin and Zhang, reportedly wrote to Deng asking him to shove the Yangs aside.[132]

At the regional level, the Shenyang MR could be considered a hold-out against the Maoist restoration that took place in the one year after the massacre. During the reshuffle of May 1990, Shenyang was the only region where no major personnel changes occurred. Commander Liu Jingsong and Commissar Song Keda reportedly opposed ways in which Yang Baibing had tried to boost his own power under the pretext of promoting ideological rectitude among the rank and file.

Witness the following article written by General Liu in early 1990 for the *PLA Daily*, in which he cast aspersions — albeit in a subtle way — on General Yang's revival of Maoism. "At the present moment, we put our stress on assiduously strengthening political construction," Liu wrote. "We put as our priority ways to ensure that the troops pass muster politically. Yet this does not mean that political work 'takes precedence over everything' or that it is 'most supreme'; nor should we say that other kinds of work need not be done or can be done less."[133]

C. Case Study: The Old Guard vs the Young Turks

If we take generational politics into account, the PLA was by the early 1990s divided between the holders of vested interests — who included Deng, Liu, Jiang and their cronies — and the up-and-coming officers. This is despite the fact that both camps could be classified as professionals as defined in the preceding section.

An influential faction among the young turks were "radical modernisers" who sympathised with the military-reform ideas proposed by the likes of Zhao

Ziyang. The rising stars were officers aged below 45, most of whom being graduates of military academies. In the heyday of reform in the mid- to late-1980s, they were known to have organised salons or discussion groups to brainstorm about army modernisation theories. Some of the firebrands advocated that the Chinese army should go along the Taiwan or South Korean models. Others wanted to pursue the Western ideal of the "separation of army and party" (see the conclusion). The number of officers who participated in these sessions were so numerous the CMC decided not to take disciplinary action for fear of arousing further instability.[134]

A powerful sub-set of the below-45 generation has been identified as members of the *laosanjie*: officers in their early 40s who were in the last years of high school or early years of college during 1966, 1967 and 1968, or the first phase of the Cultural Revolution (1966-76). Many of them joined the army during the Ten Years of Chaos and graduated from military academies. By the early 1990s, they had assumed ranking as high as battalion and divisional commanders. *Laosanjie* affiliates were exposed to the military thinking of the West, and they were eager to absorb Western know-how and military thinking to modernise defence.[135]

"A significant number of officers in the General Staff Department have been characterised as pro-American because of 'infiltration' by *laosanjie* affiliates," a Chinese source said. Indeed, after the Gulf War, there were many "professionals" among the officer corps who professed open admiration for the superiority of American firearms. Commentator Li Ziqiang wrote in the *PLA Daily* that the way the Patriot missile shot down the Scud was an instance of "beautiful and excellent" missile-to-missile combat. "We are seeing the warfare of the 21st century, used on the battlefield today," Li rhapsodised.[136] There was no doubt that the perceived need to catch up with American technology would render the professionals even more resentful of attempts to reinstate Maoist ideology in the army.

Yet another sub-group of young modernisers consisted of reserve corps that many provinces and cities had built up. While the central instructions on establishing reserve platoons were first issued in 1983, it was only after 1989 that locally based, "irregular" military units witnessed their major development. An NCNA dispatch in mid-1993 said that after ten years, reserve units had expanded to include platoons in the areas of infantry, artillery, armoured, anti-chemical and anti-tank operations.[137]

Most reserve corps were led by professional PLA officers and trained along normal army lines. Yet the bulk of the staff were young men who had regular jobs in factories or government departments — and they are considered less doctrinaire in their thinking. Since these units were financed by — and professed loyalty to — local administrations, some analysts believe they would play a role should power struggle break out between factions or geographical units.

A case in point was the reserve corps of Guangdong, some of whose crack units took part in the military parade just before National Day in 1991. Guangdong had lavished immense resources on building up the reserves, which enjoyed their own offices, quarters and even business operations.[138] It is an exaggeration to say that the "before-the-times" province was trying to use the reservists as a bargaining chip in its bureaucratic battles with Beijing. However, the "Guangdong army", made up mostly of cadres and soldiers steeped in the reformist spirit of the south, was a solid force for military modernisation.

VII. The Boom in Army Entrepreneurship

A. The PLA Business Craze

At a landmark CMC meeting in January 1993, Jiang Zemin gave the green light for the PLA to pursue business on a large scale. While the phenomenon of *junshang* or *bingshang* — the army going into the corporate world — started in the mid-1980s, this was the first time that official blessings for the aggressive commercialisation of PLA resources were given from the highest quarters. Moreover, earlier cases of *bingshang* were mostly the purchase and sale of weapons. In the wake of the *nanxun*, however, PLA companies were involved in business activities including real estate, manufacturing, retailing and the services.

Jiang's rationale was that PLA business activities, which reportedly raked in earnings of 30 billion yuan in 1992, were an essential means of ensuring army strength — mainly through supplementing the meagre state allocations. Responding to those members of the top brass who opposed *bingshang*, Jiang said: "If somebody could find me 30 billion yuan, I can stop the army from going into business."[139]

By mid-1993, civilian products accounted for 70 per cent of the production value of the military-industry complex, which had more than 50,000 factories. *Bingshang* had absorbed more than US$1 billion in foreign investment. During the 1991-1995 period, Beijing committed loans of over 6 billion yuan for 400 major projects undertaken by military production units.[140]

The biggest *bingshang* players were well-established companies that had cut their teeth in the arms trade. They included such renowned names as Polytechnologies, Norinco, and Xinxing, which were under the jurisdictions of major branches of the PLA including the General Staff Department and the

General Logistics Department. Xinxing Corp, for example, had by late 1992 launched 17 joint ventures with Western companies that were worth US$60 million. Sectors covered included steel, garments, real estate, cosmetics, and services. Xinxing had eight branches in the coastal cities and more than 100 factories which employed 100,000 people. By early 1993, *bingshang* behemoths had joined the influx of Chinese capital into Hong Kong and become budding multinationals. For example, the 999 Enterprise Grouping, which had fixed assets of 1.6 billion yuan, had investments in Germany, the US and Russia. [141]

Apart from the eye-catching few, however, it is doubtful how efficient *bingshang* factories really were. A mid-1993 report said military plants, which, after all, were state concerns, were among the biggest money losers in the public sector. Moreover, to survive, they were dependent on government orders. And less well-connected *bingshang* outfits had to lobby aggressively for funds for research and development.[142]

Much more disturbing, however, was the moral and political implications of the large-scale commercialisation of the PLA. Questions of corruption and conflict of interest arose even as morale was undermined: generals and corporals alike seemed to be spending more time monitoring the stock exchange or striking deals than on training.[143]

B. The Questionable Fallout of Bingshang

By late 1993, the public outcry against *bingshang* had swollen to the extent that the CMC had to take at least token steps to rein in the business craze. Let us first examine in detail the damage *bingshang* had done to the army's image and combat-readiness — as well as the entire modernisation enterprise.

Bingshang exacerbated the trend of the monopoly of business by the well-connected, especially the offspring of senior cadres. Even more so than in the party or government, the sons and daughters of first-generation revolutionaries had a monopoly of the top army jobs. The big bosses of the military-commercial complex — as well as those of military-civilian joint ventures — have illustrious pedigrees. The Commission of Science, Technology and Industry for National Defence (COSTIND), which co-ordinated army research and was a big player in army business, was practically a husband-and-wife team. Generals Ding Henggao and Nie Li, respectively the COSTIND minister and the vice-chief of its Science and Technology Committee, are the son-in-law and daughter of Marshal Nie Rongzhen, the father of China's Bomb. The offspring of elders including Deng Xiaoping, Wang Zhen, He Long, Ye Jianying, Chen Yun and Liu Huaqing are believed to be well-heeled practitioners of *bingshang*.[144]

Secondly, PLA businesses seemed to be beyond the pale of Beijing's very rudimentary watchdog apparatus — government units in the areas of auditing, tax, anti-corruption and anti-trust — as well as supervision by the National People's Congress. This became evident in the latter half of 1993, when civilian and PLA units launched separate anti-corruption campaigns.[145]

That army business was almost a law unto itself was evident from a number of high-profile deals. Take, for example, real estate. In the early 1990s, a large number of prime sites in Beijing, Shanghai and Guangzhou were developed by PLA companies or firms with army participation. 40-odd years ago, many of the urban plots were practically given away to the PLA as the peasant revolutionaries "entered the cities". In 1949, of course, the pieces of land were worth next to nothing and their being occupied by the army was a matter of strategic and logistic concern. However, given the drastic changes in politics and economics since 1949, should the PLA be enriching itself through the development of sites which, after all, were national property now worth billions of yuan?[146]

Equally disquieting was the fact that *bingshang* leaders often did not follow free-market practices. For instance, the partners they chose for property development were invariably "trusted comrades", meaning senior cadres or their children. It was widely reported that the 63 villas that Deng Zhifang, the second son of the patriarch, was hawking in Hong Kong in mid-1993 were built on military land close to the Shanghai airport. Western business analysts said the PLA would have been offered much higher prices if they had allowed ordinary Chinese, Hong Kong and overseas corporations to bid for the prime site.[147]

Then there is the question of whether *bingshang* concerns paid government levies such as customs dues and profit taxes. Or whether army business units were subject to the control and supervision of government auditors, graft-fighters, legislators or the judiciary. Existing regulations and practices seemed to indicate that *bingshang* outfits answered only to the party's secretive Central Military Commission as well as the military Commission for Disciplinary Inspection. And while even official organs like the *PLA Daily* had reported on growing corruption in military companies, they were outside the jurisdiction of the courts or procuratorates.[148]

C. Crackdown on Army Corruption and Restraints on Bingshang

By mid-1993, the PLA's own propaganda organs had sounded alarums over the proliferation of graft and questionable deals such as smuggling. In various commentaries, the *PLA Daily* warned against the rising tide of "mammonism, hedonism and individualism". "The tendencies of using power to seek economic gains, mammonism, going after the good life, and materialism, which exist within a minority of our social [sectors], will be reflected within the armed forces," the paper said in somewhat of an understatement. The official mouthpiece added that the army had to "propagate revolutionary soldiers who have ideals, morals, culture and discipline".[149]

While the PLA shied away from publishing data on internal crime, the army media revealed in July 1993 a "massive corruption scandal" in Liaoning which involved 43 army units and almost 300 personnel. The army's partner in the unspecified graft case was the provincial civil affairs bureau. US$500,000, one of the largest sums ever reported, was at stake. In addition, both army and civilian media alluded to the scandal of the smuggling of South Korean cars into the Shandong peninsula, which was perpetrated with the connivance of, if not the active participation by, army, naval as well as customs personnel.[150]

Western military attaches in Beijing claimed that military elements were involved in big-time smuggling. For example, they said, fully 60 per cent of the computer equipment on sale in the capital were handled through military suppliers and importers, many of whom brought in their wares without paying customs fees. The same applied to electronic and electrical appliances in the hi-tech area of Haidian in northwest Beijing. Army suppliers had the advantage that they could use military transport to bring in material from overseas, Hong Kong, or the coastal cities.[151]

It was not until the summer of 1993 that the CMC became serious about launching its anti-corruption campaign. The first salvoes were fired by leading officers including Jiang and Defence Minister Chi Haotian. In a speech given to cadres in Tianjin in August, General Chi warned against "corruption, graft-taking, smuggling, and profiting from public funds". He asked officers and soldiers not to "blindly make comparisons" between their standard of living and those of other sectors of society. The veteran said he hoped the rank and file would take into consideration comrades like those guarding Tibet, "where the oxygen level is low and where it is difficult even to cook rice".[152]

In July 1993, in tandem with efforts by the central government to reimpose macro-economic controls over the economy, the CMC mapped out ways to rein in the unhealthy if not illegal wheeling and dealing by army enterprises. The regulations, called "On Boosting Financial and Economic Management in the Army" imposed a partial ban on speculative activities. The rules forbade the use of budget allocations for business activities. "Army units cannot start financial businesses without permission," they said. "Speculation in foreign exchange is strictly forbidden."[153]

Concrete measures to tackle and prevent corruption were discussed at a CMC meeting in August 1993. Up to ten army-level officers were put under investigation for graft and other economic crimes. The ten reportedly included a Shandong-based general who had made millions importing automobiles from South Korea. The CMC decided in principle to cut down on the army's *bingshang* pursuits but stopped short of concrete recommendations that might hit the "tigers".[154]

In late 1993, the CMC finally agreed to pare down the army's business activities to curb corruption and unhealthy competition with the civilian sector. *Bingshang* units affected, however, were restricted to those below the level of military regions (MRs). These would be either absorbed by newly set up Army Enterprise Bureaus in each MR or taken over by civilian companies. The AEBs would ensure that PLA business units refrain from questionable deals such as smuggling. Independently, the CMC decided to surrender to civilian control a number of army economic units, mainly mines and transport facilities such as ports and airports.[155]

Negotiations for the containment of the PLA business empire were conducted in the autumn between Zhu Rongji and Liu Huaqing. The central government reportedly agreed to compensate the PLA by about 4 billion yuan at the initial stage. Western military analysts said, however, it was doubtful whether the move would significantly cut the army's commercial dealings. The bulk of PLA factories and business units were run by units above the level of MRs, such as the GSD, GLD and GPD. Departments that straddle the army and government, particularly COSTIND, also owned highly diversified business ventures. Moreover, some of the most lucrative business deals were consummated by joint ventures or shell companies formed with civilian and foreign companies, many of which were registered in tax havens in the South Pacific.[156] A mid-1994 report by *The Times* of London claimed that some 10,000 PLA business firms had been set up without central approval. They involved investments of 100 million pounds and were very active in the Hong Kong real-estate and stock markets.[157]

Analysts said as business integration between the army and the civilian sectors became more pronounced in the mid-1990s, it would be even more difficult for disciplinary or law-enforcement units to tell an army corporation from an ordinary one. However, such was the special clout of the army that neither the NPC nor liberal intellectuals dared to call publicly for mechanisms to monitor the PLA business empire.

VIII. Conclusion: A Step Back for Army Reform

A. Sophisticated Weapons vs Declining Morale

By early 1994, it was apparent that Deng and Co had achieved a large measure of success in weapons modernisation. Starting in early 1993, the PLA propaganda machinery gave out a series of figures illustrating the country's military prowess. For example, China boosted the world's third largest air force in terms of fighters. It was successful in procuring Russian aircraft such as the Su-27s and electronics defence systems. R & D experts persevered with an ambitious missile development programme. An early 1993 report said time needed for the Second Artillery Corps to fire its missiles had been shaved by 33 per cent to 50 per cent. And tests during the past four years showed the missiles never missed their targets.[158]

Another NCNA report in July 1993 said that the quality of officers had been significantly raised. Over 50 per cent of cadre-level staff had college degrees or above. The proportion of the rank and file that had education levels of senior middle school or intermediate technical school was "increasing unceasingly", the report said. From the mid-1980s to 1993, the PLA's own institutes produced more than 600,000 "experts".[159]

In spite of the hype, both Chinese and Western analysts testified to the declining quality — and morale — of the forces. This cast into doubt whether the goals laid down by Deng and Jiang — that officers must be able to pass muster on both ideological and professional scores — could materialise. And with the officers' overwhelming enthusiasm for the market economy, it is doubtful whether Yan'an-era morale could withstand the onslaught of the *bingshang* craze.

By early 1993, an increasing number of army leaders had expressed worries that, mired in Mammonism, officers and soldiers alike were putting wheeling and dealing before training and other traditional military pursuits. Surely, scenes of generals cutting deals with the vilest American, Taiwanese and Hong Kong capitalists in hostess clubs might cause Chairman Mao, founder of the Red Army, to turn in his Mausoleum. Senior cadres including CMC Vice-Chairman Zhang Zhen and the retired vice-chief of staff Xu Xin voiced opposition to the commercialisation of what Deng called the Great Wall of Steel. In an interview with the official China News Service, Xu decried *bingshang*'s "corrosive impact on fighting effectiveness".[160] It seemed, however, that Xu was a minority among the top brass, most of whom would look the other way at their colleagues or children making money.

Liu Huaqing and Zheng Zhen warned on the eve of Army Day in 1993 that many of the world's military powers had withered away because members of their forces "wallowed in luxury and pleasure" and were given to "frivolity". They decried the marriage of "the decadent thoughts and lifestyles of capitalism with the remnants of Chinese feudalism". "Money worship, hedonism, and extreme individualism may be engendered," they pointed out. "People's ideals and beliefs might be corroded and subjected to severe blows."[161]

During a meeting in May 1993, GPD commissars admitted with frankness that "the psychology of some officers and soldiers has become unbalanced" as a result of the onset of the socialist market economy. "Their thoughts had become confused", the commissars continued, with some being consumed by "individualism and money worship".[162] One source of "confusion" was, as mentioned in an earlier section, the growing disparity between the income of soldiers and businessmen. By late 1992, the compensation even for officers was abysmal by Chinese standards. The basic salary of a colonel-level officer was a mere 200 yuan. The other destabilising factor was ill feelings among the rank and file that their superiors were making millions without even giving them the crumbs.[163]

According to Western defence analysts in Beijing, military fat cats had by the early 1990s imported fleets of Mercedes and Lexuses. These cars, which carried military licence plates, could often be seen parked outside Western-style department stores, hotels and clubs. It was apparent, however, that very few of the riches had trickled down to ordinary soldiers. Western analysts said in some instances, funds originally allocated for raising the salaries and living conditions of soldiers had been used by the powers-that-be to do business.[164]

As a result of the national financial squeeze in 1993, long-expected salary rises for the rank and file had in many instances been postponed. Moreover, ordinary soldiers were suffering from the consequences of inflation — and the loss of special privileges in the wake of the arrival of the market economy. Army units were no longer guaranteed preferential pricing when they bought food and basic consumer products. This was despite an urgent circular issued in early 1993 by the State Council and the CMC urging that artificially low prices of grain and other staples be preserved for the army. "The PLA and the People's Armed Police shoulder the glorious task of protecting and building up the motherland," the circular said. "Army grain is a basic material condition for ensuring [a decent level of] army life."[165]

The fallout of all these demoralising developments was that the army experienced increasing difficulty in recruitment. In 1993, PLA and PAP conscription became an important task for military and civilian leaders of each province. Induction work for the year proved to be largely successful because of guarantees of improvements in income and other subsidies. During the winter recruitment exercise, 12.6 million youths applied nationwide, and 375,000 were taken on.[166] However, there was no guarantee that the new conscripts could withstand the twin assault of materialism and declining morale.

B. A Freeze in the Modernisation of Military Thinking

The tragedy about the modernisation of defence theory and structure is that while the weapons have become sophisticated as ever, the mentality behind the army remains the same. It can even be argued that many defence policies went against the reforms advocated by Deng — as well as Yang Shangkun and Zhao Ziyang — in the mid-1980s. At that time, Deng, or at least his "liberal persona", wanted to turn the PLA into a modern, professional force by weaning it from the party. Control of the PLA would gradually be shifted from the CMC to a civilian unit. Like armed forces in the West— and indeed, in more progressive countries in the former Eastern bloc — the PLA would be a branch of the government and subject to the scrutiny of the legislature.[167]

Deng's ideas were seconded by liberal academics in official think tanks. In a perceptive essay in 1988, Chinese Academy of Social Sciences economist Zheng Kaizhao levelled criticism at the "old-style army [philosophy]". "To bring about a new world in which there is no imperialism, capitalism or exploitation, the armed forces were constantly put on a state of alert," Zheng wrote. "This wasted amounts of human and financial resources that defied any calculation." Zheng said that the only way to resolve this problem was to end the special status of the army. "When national interest is put before ideology, it requires that the PLA be placed under the command of the government — and that the defence budget be subordinated to the national economic plan, instead of remaining independent of it," he argued.[168]

Deng kicked off his army-modernisation gameplan with a pivotal speech to the CMC in 1982. "The army's present structure and its leadership system and methods are not that good," he said. For example, Deng suggested ways to trim the authority of the CMC. This was indirectly accomplished through the establishment of the state-level CMC and through investing the Defence Ministry with a modicum of power. The appointment of Deng protégé General Qin Jiwei to the position of defence minister in 1984 was interpreted as a sign that his ministry might spearhead the "separation of party and army" and that the PLA would gradually come under state or governmental control.[169]

In the early 1980s, Deng also advocated the partial depoliticisation of the PLA. For example, professionalised training, technological pursuits and the procurement of weapons would take precedence over the study of Mao Thought. By 1987, Deng was giving behind-the-scenes backing to the call by Zhao Ziyang, who had become first vice-chairman of CMC, for the separation of party and government and the separation of party and army. In 1988, the Chinese Academy of Military Science completed a secret study on "The Chinese Military in the 21st Century". Among its main recommendations: beefing up the powers of the State CMC and the Defence Ministry; restructuring the command system along Western lines, for example, the French and West German models; and boosting army professionalism. The academy's recommendations were supposed to have been put into practice by late 1989.[170]

That, after June 4, 1989, the military leadership — including Deng himself

— had turned back the clock was attested to by a GPD circular that warned against "bourgeois-liberal" thoughts in the ranks. The late 1991 document cited three "dangerous" ideas for the modernisation of defence theory. They were: "the separation of army and party"; "that the army should be politically neutral and should not interfere in internal politics"; and "the army should be brought under the state".[171] Not surprisingly, these "heretical" thoughts had been propounded by Zhao and a corps of young professional officers.

By late 1993, it became obvious that things were moving in the opposite direction. Party and army became even more intertwined. In return for the support rendered by the PLA to both the party and their faction, Deng, Jiang and their cronies were willing to continue giving it special privileges. To boost their political fortunes in the post-Deng era, all contenders to the throne had to curry favour with the comrades who held the guns.

About the only progress made in terms of structural modernisation was the passage of a few laws to rationalise and standardise army procedures. For example, in September 1993, Jiang Zemin promulgated a "Stipulation on the Registry of Military Regulations and Regulations on Military Administration", which was an effort to systematise the 1,000-odd rules and regulations passed by the CMC and various senior army units.[172]

In early 1994, Beijing announced the drafting of a Defence Law that would be promulgated a year later. The statute, to be put together by the CMC and State Council experts and passed by the NPC, would according to the NCNA, "adjust and regulate national defence and army construction". There was no indication by mid-1994, however, that this legislation would put the PLA under the scrutiny of the NPC. Analysts said the Defence Law would likely touch on areas such as conscription, the relationship between the army and civilian sectors, and army business activities including PLA property rights. But it would also be a vehicle for boosting the people's "national defence consciousness" and for ensuring that enough resources be devoted to the PLA in peace and war.[173]

C. The PLA and the Succession Imbroglio

(i) The Generals as Kingmakers

Questions about modernisation theories are more than academic because of the intricate linkage between PLA modernisation and Chinese politics. The army will play a key role in the post-Deng transition. Deng's reversal on the principle of separation of party and army meant that the PLA would remain a "private army" of the Communist Party and — and of the Deng Faction. Put another way, aside from its traditional role of national defence and curbing internal dissent, the 3.2 million-strong force was maintained to safeguard the interests of Deng and Co.

One of Deng's last political acts was to dump the Yang brothers and to ensure that the PLA would funnel support to Jiang, Zhu Rongji and other protégés after his death. Such considerations of loyalty and political balance underlined Deng's military appointments at the 14th Congress. For example, Liu Huaqing and Zhang Zhen were "resurrected" for two reasons: they were loyal to Deng; and since they were already in their late 70s, neither was considered to have personal political ambitions or even a political agenda.

For the first time in his career, Deng placed its own family members and aides-de-camp in the army. General Wang Ruilin, the Head of the Deng Xiaoping Office who was practically a member of the Deng household, became the No. 2 person in the GPD. Since the department controlled promotions and disciplinary matters, Wang was in effect the army's personnel and discipline supremo. Yang Baibing's successor as head of GPD, Yu Yong-bo, was reportedly a former Yang protégé who gained his promotion by spilling the beans on the Yang Clan. It is generally assumed that General Yu deferred to General Wang in major matters.[174]

Members of Deng's immediate family also had an impact on military policy. A former bureau-level cadre in the GPD, Deng's third daughter and private secretary Deng Rong was in 1993 theoretically no more than a member of the military delegation to the NPC. However, she exercised influence by virtue of her control of the Deng Xiaoping Office. Two sons-in-law of the patriarch, He Ping and Wu Jianchang, were top-tier *bingshang* bosses. He, Deng Rong's husband and a one-time military attaché to the Chinese Embassy in Washington, was in 1994 considered a rising star in the PLA establishment because of his involvement in military intelligence and foreign affairs.[175]

China-watchers and allied conspiracy theorists have suspected a *quid pro quo* between the Deng household and Jiang. In return for their support, Jiang, who might become the next helmsman, would safeguard the political and economic interests of the Deng clan well into the next century. This is despite the fact that none of the Deng offspring held substantive political positions.

(ii) Can Jiang Zemin Hold the Fort?

The thrust of Deng's succession strategy was to prop up Jiang Zemin in both the political and military arenas (see Chapter 6). But can Jiang really hold up the sky? In the autumn of 1989, Deng was very conscious of the fact that he had picked a man with no military credentials as his successor as CMC chairman. The patriarch tried to defend his choice in a speech to an enlarged CMC meeting in November that year. "Jiang Zemin is a qualified chairman of the military commission because he is a qualified General Secretary of the party," Deng said. "The party Central Committee with Jiang as its nucleus is [the result of] a correct choice made by the whole party."[176]

Central to Deng's succession gameplan is whether the former party boss of Shanghai would continue to enjoy military support after the patriarch's demise. As discussed earlier, Jiang's military links were even more tenuous than those of his two predecessors: Hu Yaobang and Zhao Ziyang. For example, Zhao was concurrently the political commissar of the military districts of Sichuan and Guangdong when he served as first party secretaries of the two provinces in the 1970s.

Since his elevation to the top military post, Jiang tried his level best to establish his prestige in the army. And the party chief's efforts seemed more successful than people would give him credit for. For example, on his trips to the provinces, the CMC Chairman almost always took the opportunity of hob-nobbing with local officers and troops. "I don't have enough time, but if I did, I'd really like to lead a [PLA] company," he said during an inspection trip to a frontier outpost. The *PLA Daily* said in a report in August 1993 that when he toured the regions, Jiang paid a lot of attention to the living conditions of the rank and file. The army mouthpiece estimated that since becoming CMC Chairman in late 1991, he had made at least one visit a month to soldiers in the field.[177]

Jiang was adept at playing to the PLA's myriad factions. In the heyday of Yang Baibing's powers, Jiang apparently lent his authority to the chief politi-cal commissar's efforts in restoring Maoist norms. After the Gulf War, the party chief endeared himself to the professionals and the young turks by endorsing China's own Star Wars programme. Jiang was helped by the fact that as a former minister of electronics, he could speak with some authority on "electronic warfare". Moreover, thanks to the help of Deng and Liu, Jiang was able to cement his relationship with the anti-Yang faction, particularly old generals who felt slighted if not upstaged by the two brothers. As discussed earlier, Jiang improved his relations with the princelings within the PLA when he gave the green light for the unbridled development of *bingshang*.

As early as 1991, there were indications that Jiang had tightened his grip over the PLA apparatus. In a widely reported internal meeting in November of that year, then president Yang Shangkun took the trouble of asking senior officers to get Jiang's approval for major decisions. Moreover, Yang insisted that Jiang's signature be sought for all troop movements.[178] The President's military powers expanded dramatically after the departure of the Yang Clan. He played a pivotal role in the late 1992 reshuffle, which enabled him to in-stall several protégés in key slots.

It is not surprising that a number of the military officers Jiang elevated also had a Shanghai connection. A commonly cited example was the promotion of the head of the Shanghai garrison Ba Zhongtan as Commander of the quasi-military PAP in December 1992. Other officers said to be close to Jiang included Head of the GLD Fu Quanyou, who had served in the Zhejiang region. Since late 1992, Jiang also seemed to have cemented ties with affiliates of the Third Field Army, including Generals Zhang Zhen and Chi Haotian.[179]

By late 1993, there were even signs of an inchoate Jiang personality cult in the PLA. Officers openly sang the praise of the illustrious "twin-core" of the party and army leadership. For example, upon his return from the Seattle "summit" with US President Bill Clinton in November that year, the generals heaped lavish praise on the success of his diplomacy.

This is not to say, however, that Jiang had the loyalty of the top brass all sewn up. At least according to Western diplomats, many officers, specially the young turks, resented the Maoist elements underpinning the Deng-Jiang succession. Jiang came across to the radical modernisers as a Hua Guofeng-like figure who was a man of a past era. They disliked Jiang's intense conservatism even when compared with such ideologues as Yang Baibing. For example, during his tenure as GPD chief, Yang afforded protection to a number of liberal military artists and writers, including the author of the banned book *White Snow, Red Blood*, Colonel Zhang Zhenglong.[180]

Jiang, however, had the reputation of a conservative even within the army. And this became evident in the half-year period after the 14th Party Congress. During the NPC in March 1993, Jiang issued orders to ban the book *Elegy of the Barracks*, which was said to be disparaging about army life. Two months later, the CMC Chairman raised eyebrows in Beijing by sacking a few senior editors of the *PLA Daily* for failing to put his interview with the American network CNN on the front page. By mid-1993, of course, Deng's health was going steadily downhill. And even if the patriarch was offended and embarrassed, there was no way he could stop Jiang's handlers from building up a Jiang personality cult both within the party and the PLA.[181]

5

Political Reform on Hold: How the Party Consolidated its Dictatorship

I. Introduction

ONE of the most detrimental fall-outs of the June 4 crackdown was that Deng Xiaoping virtually put political reform on hold. Even going by the CCP's own definitions before Tiananmen Square, political reform means things like separation of the party and government — and more participation by experts, academics and non-Communist politicians in government and politics "under overall CCP leadership".[1] While it is true that no Communist leader would agree to a curtailment of the party's monopoly on power, liberal chieftains like Zhao Ziyang and Wan Li at least made efforts to co-opt into the party's higher councils intellectuals from disparate backgrounds. Such efforts, however, were since 1989 equated with conspiracies to dilute the authority of the party — and, in effect, with the most insidious form of bourgeois liberalisation and "peaceful evolution".

This outcome was tragic, as much as it is unforeseen, for both the party and China. It was Deng who singlehandedly laid out the contours of political liberalisation under CCP tutelage. Much of what the CCP regarded as liberalisation — or, as astro-physicist Fang Lizhi called, "changing the colour of the party" — could be traced to a speech that Deng gave to the Politburo in March 1980. Entitled "The Reform of the Party and the State Leadership Structure", it spelled out efforts in political liberalisation that, if followed to their logical conclusion, would lead to a degree of pluralism.[2]

That address was collected in the *Selected Works of Deng Xiaoping* of

1983. Most interestingly, the speech was reissued — on the front pages of newspapers — after the ouster of Hu Yaobang in January 1987 as a sign that Deng was still committed to reform.

In the talk, the patriarch called upon the CCP to rectify a plethora of institutional and practical problems that had not only stunted efficiency but alienated itself from the masses. The most important of these were: the "overconcentration of powers, which has impeded the implementation of the socialist democratic system and the democratic centralism of the party"; "the problem of not distinguishing between party and government, and using the party to substitute the government"; failure to implement "generational changes".[3]

Such considerations finally led to the watershed Political Report of the 13th Party Congress of late 1987, which represented the zenith of political reform. Zhao Ziyang, who delivered the report, said that "one long-standing problem has not yet been completely solved: the lack of distinction between the functions of the party and those of the government; and the substitution of the party by the government".

In words which fully reflected Deng's ideas, Zhao said: "It was under the leadership of the party that organs of state power, mass organisations and all kinds of economic and cultural associations were established." However, he went on to stress that the party "must ensure that these organs exercise their functions to the full". The then party boss said that only when the functions of party and government were separated could the CCP concentrate on party building and avoid being the "focal point of many contradictions", including mass opposition in the wake of a particularly unpopular policy. Zhao mentioned specifically that in enterprises, party organisations should, "instead of attempting to provide centralised leadership, support the [professional] directors and managers in their assumption of overall leadership".[4]

Chinese sources said that in private, Deng had actually gone further in his sponsorship of political change. He was the first among Yan'an-era revolutionaries to in effect advocate the diminution of the party's powers. In an unpublished 1941 article on the phenomenon of "the party taking the place of the nation", Deng lambasted those cadres who "use the party to rule the country", or who used the authority of the party to interfere with the affairs of the government and other social units. "Some comrades have misunderstood the principle of the leadership of the party, thinking that this means 'the party towering above everything'," he lamented.[5]

In the go-go years of 1978 and 1979, Deng also mentioned in private talks the possibility of the gradual abolition of party cells and other organisations in government, business and cultural units. These instances of relative radicalism, which were never put on the record, were rescinded in the wake of Deng's decision to close down the "Democracy Wall" in 1979. However, the idea of the separation of party and government, which was enshrined in the 13th Party Congress document, was seconded by Deng. After the June 4 crackdown, Deng repeatedly said that "not one word of the 13th Congress report need be changed".[6]

The CCP insisted after June 4, 1989, that political reform had not stopped. However, the party's definition of the "reform of the political structure" was changed to exclude separation of party and government and participation by non-party or non-mainstream politicians and intellectuals. Senior leaders would only commit themselves to improvements and developments in areas including the National People's Congress (NPC) system, consultation with the "democratic parties", fighting corruption, administrative reform, and trimming bureaucratic deadwood.[7]

However, as we shall see in the following sections, the CCP was going about these adulterated goals of "political reform" in a half-hearted fashion. Everything seemed to be mere public relations: to pacify in a superficial way international opinion and the demands of intellectuals. Many aspects of political liberalisation witnessed a retrogression. First of all, the party was obsessed with the over-riding need to preserve and enhance CCP domination of all sectors of the polity. Deng took over from Mao as the dictatorial patriarch; Deng Thought displaced Mao Thought as the state creed. The succession problem remained unchanged because the party elders — who retained almost mythical powers — were only interested in conferring power on their offspring or younger members of their own cliques.

While meeting the late American president Richard Nixon in October 1989, Deng claimed that "it is wrong to say we only pursue economic reform but not political reform". The patriarch made it clear, however, that the reform of the political structure must be implemented "under the principle of the Four Cardinal Principles". In an internal address reported in Hong Kong and Taiwan newspapers in 1993, Deng talked about fine-tuning and implementing "democratic centralism" within the party. This means that before a decision is made, party members could freely express their views. After a line had been laid down by the *zhongyang* (Party Centre), however, "the individual must obey the organisation; juniors must obey their superiors; and the entire party, the *zhongyang*". On other occasions, Deng talked about perfecting the system of consultation with the eight democratic parties, which had about 360,000 members. These were all hackneyed, conservative ideas that the CCP had first broached in the 1950s.[8]

This chapter will look at how the CCP maintained its monopoly on power through boosting the functions and powers of the party and beefing up its formidable police-state apparatus, which includes the judiciary. There will be sections on what the party claimed to be elements of Chinese-style political liberalisation, including the slowly changing roles of the Chinese People's Political Consultative Conference and the NPC. Failure to implement real political reform led to unprecedented corruption, which tore asunder the moral fabric of the party and state. The conclusion will explore the possibilities of some form of "inner-party democracy" for the rest of the 1990s.

II. Bogus Re-commitment to Political Reform

Political reform as defined by the 13th Party Congress Report and by liberal leaders like Zhao and Wan Li came to a halt after the June 4 crisis. Especially in view of the crumbling of Communism first in Eastern Europe and later in the former Soviet Union, the leadership was convinced they must put as their first priority the strengthening of party authority and the tools of the dictatorship of the proletariat (see Chapter 3).

However, to mollify Western investors and the restive intelligentsia, top leaders repeatedly stressed that political reform would continue in tandem with economic liberalisation and the open-door policy. This is apparent from statements made by Premier Li Peng and other hardline leaders.

For example, Li said in December 1989 that the reform of China's political structure should be carried out simultaneously with that of the economic structure. He indicated that "it is wrong to think that China carries out only economic reform, but not the reform of the political structure". Two years later, the premier was still plugging the same theme. As he said in October 1991: "China is implementing the reform of the economic and political structure. We think that the reform of the economic structure must be commensurate with that of the political system."[9]

The message was reiterated in the Chinese media. *Outlook Weekly*, the official organ of the Central Committee, said that Beijing had never given up political change. "Reform of the political structure has never stopped," it said. "Even after the political storm of June 4, political reform has still been going on." *Outlook* even blamed the foreign media for neglecting to report this "positive development". "For example, the CCP has held consultations over major matters of state with members of democratic parties as well as people with no political affiliation," *Outlook* asserted. "Yet many people outside China do not even know that China has eight democratic parties, let alone the functions they are performing in China's socialist-democratic politics."[10]

On closer examination, it becomes obvious that what Li Peng and others meant by "reform of the political structure" was little more than window dressing. Almost by definition, reform means far-reaching if not revolutionary changes, a disturbance to and transformation of the status quo.

As Chairman Mao put it in his inimitable shorthand: "Revolution is not a dinner party." Or as Deng said in 1982, streamlining the administrative structure was a "revolution".[11]

After 1989, however, all senior cadres were careful to point out that political reform must take place in the context of stability. In his December 1989 talk, Premier Li stressed that "political restructuring should be conducive to the stability and prosperity of the country rather than causing social disturbances". And in his October 1991 address, Li cautioned that "economic reform will only succeed when the political situation is stable". In other words, all reform efforts deemed potentially destabilising — that is, liable to chip away at the CCP's monopoly on power — would be proscribed. Or as former vice-foreign minister Yao Guang put it: "If we say that China is resolute in developing socialist democracy, it is also resolute in maintaining the stability of the situation."[12]

The leadership also spelled out clear boundaries for "political reform with Chinese characteristics". It was made crystal clear from the outset that "Westernised" concepts such as multi-party politics and the "tripartite division of powers" would be taboo. "The political system of a country should be determined by actual conditions in that country and not copied from other countries," said then president Yang Shangkun in 1991. "China resolutely opposes the bourgeois-liberal concept of attempting to copy the Western system, and to change China's existing system."[13]

The sentiment was echoed by party chief Jiang Zemin. "China should take as its model for reform not only the experience of countries that have a similar system [to China's] but also the worthy experience of capitalist countries," the party boss said in 1992. "But we cannot simplistically copy these experiences." "We cannot transplant to China the parliamentary democratic system, the multi-party system, and other political systems of the West," he added.[14]

On other occasions, Jiang stressed that political reform consisted in no more than the "perfection of socialist democracy". "The core of the reform of the political structure in China is to diligently perfect socialist democracy and the socialist legal system, and to earnestly guarantee and materialise the status and rights of citizens as masters of themselves," the General Secretary said in mid-1990. "China has chosen socialism not because of outside factors but because of China's own national conditions and needs." Jiang warned that there was no question of his people "making a new choice of their social system".

The Party General Secretary hinted that Western ideals of democracy and freedom were not compatible with China's "national conditions". "From the point of view of China, it can be said that democracy and freedom are relative," he added. "They must be commensurate with this country's tradition, history, culture, and the development levels of education and the economy."[15]

In other words, so long as China remained relatively underdeveloped, democracy would remain illusory.

Even a relative liberal such as Politburo member Li Ruihuan was convinced that, as he put it in May 1993, "the construction of Chinese democratic politics" must be based upon "the premise of unity and stability". He pointed to the relatively backward economic and cultural standards of the people, and the fact that "complicated questions and contradictions" would arise as the country made the switch to a market economy.[16]

By early 1994, the ideal of political reform was subsumed under the overall concern of building up a socialist market economy. In other words, political liberalisation was being pursued not for its own sake or its innate virtues but because it was good for the economy. As Politburo member and Guangdong Party Secretary Xie Fei put it in March 1994: "We must speed up the construction of the mechanism of the rule of law and the mechanism of democratic supervision." Xie added that political reform must be in lockstep with economic reform, so as "to guarantee the healthy development of the socialist market economy". The corollary of this argument is that if there were elements of political reform that might impede economic development, they must not be entertained.[17]

III. "The Party is Supreme"

A. The Party Looking After Everything

In apparent contravention to the ideals of the 13th Party Congress, a top priority of the CCP since the June 4 shootings was to beef up the powers of the party. After all, one of the key charges levelled against Zhao Ziyang and his fellow liberals was diluting the authority of the party. Conveniently forgetting what he had preached, Deng Xiaoping pointed out after the Tiananmen Square massacre that the "separation of party and government" was a manifestation of bourgeois liberalisation.[18]

According to the newly ascendant ideologues, "peaceful evolution" in Eastern Europe and the former Soviet Union was rooted in the idea that the Communist party had to give up its absolute monopoly on power. For the Maoist holdovers, the dissolution of the USSR began when Mikhail Gorbachev decided in the late 1980s that, for the sake of *perestroika* and other reforms, Moscow could play fast and loose with one-party dictatorship. In the post-Tiananmen Square era, "party building" — ridding the CCP of bourgeois-liberal elements and boosting the structure and "cohesiveness" of party cells and other organisations — became a matter of life and death.[19]

We saw in Chapter 4 how a major focus of ideological and political work in the army after June 4 was ensuring the party's "absolute leadership" over the PLA. Deng and other senior cadres also moved heaven and earth to strengthen CCP control over other sectors of society, including business. In an internal speech in early 1993, Deng indicated that the CCP must not follow the same fate as other communist parties through the neglect of business. "A key reason why the former Soviet party disintegrated is that it was divorced from the governmental process and business interests," he said. As we shall see, this philosophy explained the phenomenon of *guanshang bufen* ("the fusion of officialdom and business") — and massive corruption — after the *nanxun* talks of 1992.[20]

Much of the "political restructuring" after June 4 consisted in undoing the gingerly steps that Zhao Ziyang and such of his associates as Bao Tong had taken in the separation of party and government. The hardline leadership went about doing what Deng had decried as "the substitution of government by party" by reviving *dongzu* or party organisations in government, business and other units.

According to a report in the Beijing-run Hong Kong weekly, *Economic Reporter*, *dongzu* in the bulk of State Council commissions and ministries were abolished soon after the 13th Party Congress. The journal pointed out that by mid-1989, party organisations only remained in "special cases" like the State Education Commission and the People's Bank of China.[21]

Perhaps with tongue in cheek, *Economic Reporter* noted in an early 1990 dispatch: "As a result [of the reform under Zhao], the system of the minister-ial responsibility system was more pronounced. But at the same time, it has been reported that the concept of the leadership of the party and its leadership functions had been curtailed." The decision to revive the *dongzu* was made in late 1989. "Relevant authorities have pointed out that this has a bearing on guaranteeing that government departments will carry out the policies and goals of the party, and that the correct direction of governmental work will be maintained," the journal said.[22]

Apart from government departments, the resurgence of party organisations was specially felt in two areas: the university and the factory. Under the influ-ence of the ultra-leftist State Education Commission, which was until 1993 controlled by the remnant Maoist vice-minister He Dongchang, the "college president responsibility system" was all but abrogated by late 1989. Under this system, which was a major educational reform under Zhao Ziyang, the professional educator or academic at a university called the shots instead of the *dongzu* or party secretary.

Under the new regime, the head of the reinvigorated *dongzu* in a college once again dominated matters including curriculum, ideological indoctrination, and administration. For example, the party secretary now had a big say in promotion and demotion — and overall disciplinary matters — particularly towards professors and teachers deemed to have "bourgeois-liberal" tendencies. Under the influence of the apparatchiks, most colleges also increased the number of teachers of courses on Marxism-Leninism. The new system was called the "college president responsibility system under the leadership of the party". Until his retirement in 1993, ideologue Yu Wen, who was made Vice-President of CASS in late 1989, wrote several letters to Jiang Zemin lobbying for the revival of the "party leadership" system at that institute of higher learning.[23]

The rise of party authority was even more pronounced on the factory floor. A key reform of Deng Xiaoping in the mid-1980s was the factory manager responsibility system, meaning that authority in overall management should be vested with the professional manager or director, not the party secretary of the resident CCP cell. After mid-1989, however, the party secretaries in many business units seized the chance to resume power. Things went to the stage where, in many concerns, there were pitched battles between the "centre", meaning the professional managers, and the "core", meaning the party functionaries.[24]

By 1991, party organisations had also been set up in enterprises that were joint ventures, and in many instances, units with Taiwanese investment. According to the Vice-Chief of the Organisation Department of the CCP, Zhao Zongding, party branches or cells should be established in foreign-funded enterprises where there were more than three CCP members. "In those [joint ventures] that do not have many party members, we should recruit more employees to join the CCP," Zhao said in a conference on party work in foreign-funded firms that was held in Beijing in August 1991.[25]

Zhao indicated that party cells should promote the party line, policies and measures among workers who were CCP affiliates. Another task was to safeguard "national interest" and the employees' rights and benefits. The senior cadre admitted that foreign businessmen might become "suspicious" about the setting up of party branches in joint ventures. "We should first improve our work, the working style and the activities of party cells in enterprises" to allay the fears of the capitalists, he said.

An internal document issued in mid-1991 stated that 20 per cent among the nation's 26,400-odd foreign-funded enterprises had party cells or other kinds of party organisations. In Guangdong, the corresponding percentage among enterprises with foreign investment was 41 per cent, more than half of which operated openly. The document pointed out that a key task of the *dongzu* was to prevent the "infiltration" of capitalist ideology and lifestyle and to boost the Marxist consciousness of the workers.[26]

The anxiety among conservative elements in the CCP to maintain and even increase the role of party organisations in joint-venture enterprises, however, had an adverse effect particularly on Taiwan businessmen. The latter tried as much as they could to discourage party-related activities among their workers. In 1993, the New York-based Human Rights Watch also started a campaign to persuade American corporations with investments in China to prevent "compulsory ideological activities" within their enterprises.[27]

B. Centralisation of Party Power, 1992-1994

The Political Report of the 14th Party Congress of late 1992 confirmed the party's abandonment of the ideal of the separation of party and government. There was no mention whatsoever of the separation of party and government or party and business — just the separation of "government and business", meaning that administrative units, but not party cells, should cease to interfere with state-run companies.[28]

A major step was taken towards the pre-Liberation concept of the fusion of party and government, now called "cross leadership", a reference to the fact that Politburo members and other top cadres can concurrently take up positions in the party, government, legislature and the CPPCC. The ultimate expression of this Yan'an-era idiosyncracy was the many hats thrust upon Jiang Zemin, Deng's anointed successor. At the Congress, it was decided that Jiang should be head of state, the party and the army, in addition to other substantial and ceremonial titles (see also Chapter 6).[29]

Another step backwards was the transfer of Politburo members Qiao Shi, Tian Jiyun and Li Ruihuan to the NPC and the CPPCC. As we shall discuss later, the fact that they were headed by heavyweight politicians helped enhance the clout of the two bodies. However, from the point of view of power relations, it also meant that the party was keeping the parliament and the consultative body on a tighter leash. Throughout 1993, the phenomenon of "cross leadership" also manifested itself at the regional level, with numerous cases of party secretaries doubling as heads of local governments or legislatures. Notable examples included Hainan, Hubei, Fujian and Heilongjiang.[30]

After the *nanxun*, but especially from 1993 onwards, major developments were made in the principle of the fusion of party and business — or the party controlling the economy. The "theory of party ownership" had been developed with flair in a paper written by a group of young neo-conservative academics and cadres soon after the break-up of the Soviet Union in late 1991. The treatise, entitled "China's practical response and strategic choices after the drastic changes in the Soviet Union", was first published as a *neican* ("internal reference material") by the *China Youth Daily*. The theorists, including "princelings" Chen Yuan and Bo Xicheng, argued that the only way to maintain the party's supremacy was to ensure its control over the finances and the business empire.

"Some scholars think that a major reason why our party could grow and strengthen itself was that it held the gun, thereby ensuring the army's obedience towards the party," the paper said. "Yet an even more important aspect is that the party must control the finances and the economy." The neo-conservatives claimed that the fusion of party and business would facilitate political reform because it meant that the party would have the wherewithal to consolidate its power and implement reforms. Other theorists of the same persuasion cited the example of the Kuomintang. They said that one reason behind the success of the KMT's political and economic programmes on the island was the ruling party's control of a big business empire.[31]

The young theorists' point about the party "becoming an aggregate of [economic] interests" was best expressed after the *nanxun*, when Deng sanctioned the no-holds-barred development of cadre capitalism (See Chapter 2). As the putative reformist party secretary of Guangzhou Gao Qiren put it in mid-1993: "In a shareholding company, we can experiment with the system of the party secretary [of the CCP cell within the business unit] doubling as chairman of the board and general manager. We must further rationalise the system of the party and political leadership of enterprises." He added: "It is all right for the factory director and the party secretary to be the same person."[32]

Even in liberal Shenzhen, officials working on the structure of a new generation of shareholding companies in 1994 recommended the "fusion" of the board of directors and the resident party committees. The argument was that a fair amount of overlapping in the membership of the board of directors and the party committee would minimise internecine bickering between the two major "power organisations". Whether this political consideration would militate against efficiency, seemed another question.[33]

C. Geriatric Politics with Chinese Characteristics

(i) Long Live the Gang of Elders!

Chinese elders had a point when they repeatedly boasted that whatever had happened in Eastern Europe and the Soviet Union would not take place in China: unlike the former USSR, the "first generation" of revolutionaries were not only alive and well but calling the shots at least until 1994. The June 4 disaster and the dissolution of Communism in the Eastern bloc led to another setback in a key political reform — the handling of the baton to the younger generation. The need to preserve the party and to crack down on "class enemies" provided the veterans with an excuse to hang on to power.

That the retirement of the so-called Gang of Elders would be a distant prospect was evident from the statements of former vice-foreign minister Yao Guang at the 1990 NPC. When asked by Hong Kong reporters whether there was a programme to retire the octogenarians, Yao, then NPC spokesman, said: "I feel that Hong Kong compatriots are somewhat impetuous on the question of the process of democratisation. We must proceed orderly and gradually on such questions. This is why it is not strange that some old comrades are still occupying leadership positions."[34]

The Gang of Elders, also known as the White-Eyebrowed Cabal, is a reference to octogenarian elders who pulled strings behind the scenes at Zhongnanhai. They were the Long March generation, or "first-tier" leaders who had nominally retired from the centre of power. Eight of the veterans, known as the Eight Immortals, were particularly powerful immediately after the June 4 crackdown: Deng Xiaoping, Chen Yun, Yang Shangkun, Wang Zhen, Bo Yibo, Li Xiannian, Peng Zhen, and Song Renqiong.

The justification for the Gang of Elders clinging to their sceptres was given by patriarch Deng on June 9 1989, when he inspected the Martial Law Command officers in Beijing. Deng said that the "counter-revolutionary rebellion" would occur sooner or later. But the fact that it occurred then and not later was "relatively advantageous" because the CCP could still count upon its party elders to steady the ship of state. "We still have a large batch of senior comrades who are alive," Deng said. "They have experienced many storms and they know the cause and effect of things." According to Deng's logic, only senior comrades like himself could discern the tide of history. Hence, they should still be entrusted with major policy-making.[35]

The Gang of Elders looked upon China pretty much as their fiefdom. Vice-President Wang Zhen, who passed away in early 1993, said it all when he noted soon after "liberation" that "he who won heaven and earth has a right to rule over it". This "proprietary mentality" was expressed by Chen Yun, when on May 26 1989 he made a speech supporting the imposition of martial law. "We are all old comrades who have struggled for decades for the creation and construction of the socialist republic," he said. "At this critical juncture, we seniors must throw ourselves" into the effort to quell the "rebellion".[36]

After the new leadership was licked into shape in late June 1989, then vice-chairman of the CAC Song Renqiong said: "The existing young leadership with Jiang Zemin as its core is doing a very good job. We old comrades are very supportive of their work." Implicit in this remark was the caveat that if the third generation of leaders did not measure up, the elders were ready to withdraw their blessings.[37]

On the eve of the first Lunar New Year after Tiananmen, the then chief of the Organisation Department Song Ping went further by praising the White-

Eyebrowed Cabal as "the treasure of the party and government". "They have rich experience and are adept at handling complex contradictions," Song said. "They are a strong force in maintaining national stability." He added that the party should "develop the political superiority of the old comrades and make use of their rich political experience and their art of [political] struggle".[38]

Two years after June 4, the octogenarians' lust for power had hardly abated. At a meeting of retired elders in June 1991, then CAC vice-chairman Bo Yibo told them that the party Central Committee expected them to do four things: "Be concerned about major state affairs; boost their studies; have the goals of the party fully in mind; keep a clean working style."[39] Analysts said that "to be concerned about state affairs" meant that the elders would go on being the power behind the throne.

The elders' refusal to depart found its most scandalous — and ludicrous — expression in the late vice-president Wang Zhen, the retired general who played a key role in deposing Hu Yaobang and Zhao Ziyang. Wang's craving for publicity — preferably on national television — was legendary. As early as 1987, Chinese sources said that the secretary of the elder would often call up the press and other relevant units for opportunities in which Wang would receive full media attention. The Long March veteran's thirst for the limelight did not diminish after he was diagnosed to have prostrate cancer in 1990.[40]

Wang's obsession with publicity reached an apogee in the few weeks before the celebration of the CCP's 70th birthday on July 1, 1991. He was on TV at a function to launch the television serial *A Century of Travel*, a diatribe against "bourgeois-liberal poison" from the West. Almost immediately afterwards, Wang granted an audience to what other ideologues might construe as an emblem of the "sugar-coated bullets of capitalism": beauty queen Miss Narcissus from Hawaii, Chen Mei-Hua, together with the other Narcissus Queens. "You are all so beautiful and capable," Wang gushed.

As Honorary President of the China-Japan Friendship Association, Wang's door seemed always open to Tokyo-based politicians and businessmen, especially those willing to remind the general of his glorious past. In August 1991, for example, he met the head of the Desert Development Research Company of Japan, Sei'ei Toyama, who praised the elder for his success in conquering the sand dunes while being the honcho of Xinjiang Province in the 1950s. And while talking to an oil-exploration delegation from Japan a few days later, Wang himself boasted about his excellent connections in Xinjiang.[41]

That the vice-president considered himself a patriarch in the mode of Deng was clear from the way he gave his endorsement to Jiang Zemin in mid-1991. "Jiang Zemin is versed in the theory of Marxism and Mao Zedong Thought," Wang told an African delegation. "His belief in Communism is strong. He has a wide range of knowledge." By 1991, however, Wang's reputation had been tarnished by allegations of corruption: he reportedly kept luxuriously appointed villas in Xinjiang and Zhuhai and that local authorities picked up the tab whenever he travelled there with a large group of relatives and hangers-on. And when he finally succumbed to a combination of bronchial problems and other ailments in 1993, a number of dissident intellectuals in Beijing let off firecrackers.[42]

(ii) The Fortune of the Elders after the Dissolution of the CAC

The hold of the elders was such that by early 1992, there were still doubts as to whether their bastion, the Central Advisory Commission, would be dissolved at the 14th Party Congress. When the CAC was set up in 1982, Deng explicitly pointed out that the "transient body" would last no more than a decade. Chinese sources said that at a Politburo meeting in late 1991, it was suggested that the CAC would stay on until the 15th Party Congress in 1997. However, some modifications were suggested. There would be no new inductees to the council. Secondly, regional authorities would be free to decide whether to scrap their local-level commissions. Prior to this, a number of areas including Heilongjiang and Guangzhou had abolished their local advisory councils of elders.[43]

Chinese sources said that the debate about whether to scrap the CAC outright — or to replace it with a less powerful Advisory Committee that would be headed by Yang Shangkun — persisted to the eve of the 14th Party Congress. Deng, however, bit the bullet and abolished the council. This did not mean, however, that the elders would cease to be major power players.

Analysts have cited various reasons for Deng's failure to fulfil his earlier goal of expediting "generational change". Firstly, the patriarch himself wanted to continue exercising power to ensure the survival of economic reform in the face of a possible Maoist restoration. Deng's attitude about retirement had all along been ambivalent. One of the reasons behind the fall of Hu Yaobang was his suggestion in early 1986 that Deng step down at the 13th Party Congress.

Moreover, after mid-1989, Deng needed a coterie of high-powered elders to help him maintain control. The informal council included Yang Shangkun, Bo Yibo and Wang Zhen. Until the falling out between Deng and Yang in late 1992, the latter, together with his half-brother Yang Baibing, was instrumental in providing "imperial escort" for Deng's reforms (see Chapter 4). Bo also gave generous backing for Deng's introduction of the market economy by making speeches and penning articles. Deng needed Wang Zhen to do "dirty jobs" such as supervising the purge of bourgeois liberals.

After the dissolution of the CAC, there was little question that Deng was still in charge of overall policy. Other elders including Yang Shangkun, Bo Yibo and Wan Li kept their offices in Zhongnanhai and often issued instructions to Politburo members. Chen Yun, who spent most of his time in Shanghai and Hangzhou, received periodic "work reports" from Shanghai party secretary Wu Bangguo. As we saw in Chapters 2 and 3, Chen kept on airing his views on politics and economics until the Lunar New Year of 1994.

Moreover, there were numerous reports that in lieu of a formal body like the CAC, the elders formed semi-official groupings to influence policy and give a hand to their offspring or former underlings. For example, a "five-man group of elders" made up of Chen Yun, Yao Yilin, Yang Shangkun, Bo Yibo and Wan Li was reported to have been set up in mid-1993 to "provide economic advice" to Zhu Rongji. Remnant Maoists among the elders, led by former CAC titan Deng Liqun, were grouped under the Contemporary China Research Institute. And in the PLA, retired generals organised numerous private clubs along factional lines. A clique led by Generals Zhang Aiping, Xiao Ke and Qin Jiwei reportedly played a role in the ouster of the General Yang Baibing in late 1992.[44]

D. The Rise of the Gang of Princelings

(i) Institutionalising the Revolutionary Bloodline

A key goal of the pro-democracy movement of 1989 was wiping out nepotism. In May 1989, the noticeboards of the capital's major campuses were full of large-character posters citing the high positions monopolised by the offspring of senior cadres. For at least a few months after June 4, the propaganda machine put out repeated denials that nepotism had become the nation's premier institution. For example, official news services denied "rumours" about the blood links between Jiang Zemin and elder Li Xiannian or that between Yang Shangkun and the then Army Chief of Staff Chi Haotian.[45]

In spite of protestations about political reform, the CCP failed to make a dent on nepotism. The furthest it ever went was to institute cosmetic measures at the regional level. For example, provinces such as Guangdong began in 1990 to implement the so-called "system of bureaucratic avoidance". This means, among other things, that close relatives — husband and wife, father and son, and siblings in general — could not work within the "same leadership corps" of the same department. Under the regulation called "avoidance in executive work", cadres should refrain from handling affairs of their relatives including promotions, demotions, criminal investigations and permission to go abroad. Under "territorial avoidance", cadres at the county level could not remain in the same locality for more than two terms. As we shall see, this "avoidance" rule was incorporated in the Temporary Regulations on the Civil Service of August 1993.[46]

Talk about rooting out nepotism, however, abruptly ceased after the Communist dominoes began falling one after the other. Reason: the party elders wanted to institutionalise the principle of the "revolutionary bloodline". They were convinced that before seeing Marx, they had to pass the baton to their offspring, the *gaoganzidi*, deemed the least likely to betray their creed.

Since late 1990, a top priority of the leadership was to ensure that positions of influence in both the party, government and the army remain in the hands of cadres "totally trusted by the CCP". The elders made no secret of the fact that they considered their sons and daughters "more trustworthy than the others". As Chen Yun put it in 1991: "We have confidence in our offspring, who at least will not stage a rebellion against their fathers. Here, we also have the advantage over [the former] Soviet Union. Moreover, our children have passed through the test of the Cultural Revolution."[47]

China analysts said nepotism with Chinese characteristics was doubly disturbing because most affiliates of the so-called Gang of Princelings tended to be politically conservative. This has historical roots. In the 1950s, Beijing sent the best and the brightest of its young cadres — a sizeable portion of the princelings — to study in colleges in the USSR or Eastern Europe. These members of the Gang of the Graduates of Eastern Bloc Colleges were now the who's who of Chinese politics. Aside from Li Peng, who is the adopted son of Zhou Enlai, powerful princelings trained in the Soviet bloc included Vice-Premier Zou Jiahua, who is the son of veteran cadre Zou Taofen and son-in-law of the late Marshal Ye Jianying; and Politburo member Li Tieying, the son of party elder Li Weihan.

By contrast, those among the second- and third-generation princelings who furthered their studies in Japan, the US and Western Europe had yet to make their mark in politics. This is in spite of the fact that the fathers of many American or West European trained scholars were top leaders like Jiang Zemin, Qiao Shi and Zhu Rongji. One reason is that many graduates of Western universities decided to go into business instead of politics.

The most illustrious member of the "Gang of the Graduates of American Colleges" was Deng Zhifang, the second son of Deng Xiaoping. After earning a doctorate in physics from Rochester University, Deng worked for the China International Trust and Investment Corp — a bastion of princelings — before setting up his own business in 1993. Likewise, Wu Jie, the son of former vice-president Ulanfu, became a red capitalist for a few years. Quite a number of potential princelings were reportedly so disillusioned with the June 4 massacre that they decided to stay in the US for good. These included the grand-daughter of the late party chief Hu Yaobang.

At the 14th Party Congress, Deng and the headhunters bowed to domestic and international opinion and did not promote a large number of princelings to the Central Committee. This is despite reports that months earlier, Deng had personally vetted the dossiers of more than 20 sons and daughters of senior cadres with the purpose of elevating them to the supreme council.[48]

That the *gaoganzidi* did not make it to the Central Committee, however, mattered less than the fact that they still held a number of key positions, particularly in the PLA, where "trustworthiness" counted even more. In 1992, Deng set a bad example when he broke an earlier promise not to allow any of his children to occupy a senior posting. Second daughter Deng Nan was made a Vice-Minister at the State Commission of Science and Technology. Third daughter Deng Rong was an even more powerful figure because of her position as her father's private secretary and "imperial lip-reader".[49]

Other princelings on the rise included the following: Vice-President of the People's Bank of China Chen Yuan (son of Chen Yuan); Liu Yuan, a senior commissar at the People's Armed Police and a former vice-governor of Henan Province (son of former state president Liu Shaoqi); former head of the Beijing Tourism Bureau Bo Xicheng (son of elder Bo Yibo); Head of the Organisation Department of Guangdong Province Fu Rui (son of Peng Zhen); and Party Secretary of the open city of Fuzhou, Xi Jinping (son of elder Xi Zhongxun). On the military side, there was the husband and wife team of Ding Henggao and Nie Li at the Commission of Science, Technology, and Industry for National Defence (respectively the son-in-law and daughter of Marshal Nie Rongzhen); Vice-Commander of the Navy He Pengfei (son of Marshal He Long); and the super-salesman in the PLA business empire He Ping (son-in-law of Deng Xiaoping).

Many analysts were disturbed by this succession scenario because, ideology aside, quite a few of the princelings seemed to lack the right stuff to govern one fifth of mankind. Take, for example, Chen Yuan, the princeling who had generated the most interest among the Hong Kong and foreign press. Chinese sources in Beijing, where Chen spent most of his career, said he was a lacklustre administrator. In 1987, delegates to the Beijing municipal party congress voted Chen out of the ruling party committee.[50]

Other sons of senior cadres who had reputations of being mediocre at best — but who were still being groomed for heaven — included Liao Hui. In 1984, Liao "inherited" the directorship of the Office of Overseas Chinese Affairs from his father Liao Chengzhi, the late Politburo member in charge of overseas Chinese affairs. Analysts said the younger Liao would likely be given more responsibility in united front work.[51]

(ii) The Legitimisation of Nepotism

By late 1991, there were signs that the princeling phenomenon had almost been accepted as part of the CCP political culture. Nepotism — or at least the practice of sons inheriting the positions of their fathers — seemed to have ceased to be a stigma. On the contrary, *gaoganzidi* were flaunting their pedigree.

The case of Premier Li was particularly glaring. Immediately after the June 4 massacre, Li told the foreign press he was neither the foster nor adopted son of the late premier Zhou Enlai. Li said he was but one among a large group of orphans and other children who grew up in the "revolutionary cradle" of Yan'an. Since 1991, however, Li had apparently taken advantage of the "Zhou craze" — which manifested itself in poems, essays, movies and museums in honour of the "people's premier" — to boost his own standing. In a late 1991 interview with the mainland journal *Sons and Daughters of China*, Li played up his ties with the revered revolutionary. After Li's father, Li Shuoxun, became a martyr when the little boy was three, the late premier arranged to have the "heir to the revolution" educated in Chongqing, and from 1941 to 1945, in Yan'an. When the young Li fell sick from overwork, Zhou's wife Deng Yingchao gave their foster son her daily supply of half a pound of milk.[52]

Other cadres who bragged about their "revolutionary inheritance" included Li's competitor for pre-eminence in the post-Deng era, Jiang Zemin. The party chief was hardly shy about his illustrious lineage. The childhood of the supremo was detailed in a 1991 article in the left-wing Hong Kong monthly *Wide Angle*. Jiang is the son of martyr Jiang Shangqing. And he also enjoyed the patronage of elders including former finance minister Zhang Jingfu.[53]

Similarly, so-called fourth-generation revolutionaries, or princelings in their late 30s and 40s, also boasted about their high birth. Prime examples included Chen Yuan, Bo Xicheng, and Deng Yingtao, the economist son of leftist elder Deng Liqun. In meetings with intellectuals in Beijing and overseas after the June 4 crackdown, Chen and Deng tried to persuade the latter to "return to work for the motherland" by assuring them that they would adopt more moderate policies after taking the mantle of their famous forebears.[54]

Why were the cadres advertising the fact that the CCP had institutionalised the principle of the "revolutionary bloodline"? Firstly, as Chen Yun and others emphasised, the CCP had no choice but to ensure that power would stay in the hands of "trustworthy Marxists". And elders including Deng Xiaoping thought they could convince the people that, given their background and upbringing, the princelings were "more trustworthy" than ordinary party members.

The propaganda offensive mounted since 1990 about the virtues of first-generation revolutionaries like Mao, Zhou and Deng might have been geared towards promoting the acceptability of their descendants. Moreover, the CCP apologists wanted to persuade the people and overseas observers that the fourth-generation revolutionaries were "closet liberals". According to this theory, they represented the "Third Force" in Chinese politics. And once the Eight Immortals left the scene, the neophytes would usher in an era of reform.[55]

Secondly, princelings such as Li Peng were subtly using their claim to "in-born redness" to shove aside their "low-born" competitors. For example, in a talk to education officials in early 1992, the premier underscored the fact that the ideal cadre must be "both red and expert". Non-princelings were a minority at the CCP's higher echelons. Equally significant, most of the plebeian contenders for the very top rung happened to be members of the liberal and moderate camps. Zhu Rongji and Tian Jiyun fell into this category.

As we saw in Chapter 2, there were clear signs by 1994 that while many *gaoganzidi* still wanted to inherit their parents' kingdom, an even larger number saw a brighter future in the business world. In the wake of the decision in 1992 by Bo Xicheng to leave the Beijing Tourism Bureau to start a hotel- and restaurant-related business, the bulk of the princelings, including those who still held senior posts, had *xiahai*. Aside from Deng Zhifang and He Ping, prominent princeling-businessmen included CITIC General Manager Wang Jun (son of Wang Zhen); Venturetech senior manager Chen Weili (daughter of Chen Yun); and manager of a PAP-related company Li Xiaoyong (son of Li Peng).[56]

IV. Boosting the Police-State Apparatus

A major retreat for political reform manifested itself in Beijing's all-out effort to boost the "dictatorship of the proletariat", otherwise known as "the people's democratic dictatorship". Attempts to strengthen the police-state apparatus went on at full throttle even as the economy became liberalised in 1993 and 1994.

The basic rationale for the police state was laid down by Public Security Minister Tao Siju at the 18th National Public Security Meeting held in Beijing in November 1991. Tao indicated that the role of the police and other tools of the people's democratic dictatorship was to fight the enemies of the Four Cardinal Principles. "In the coming five to ten years, class struggle will manifest itself in the contention between those who uphold the Cardinal Principles and those who uphold bourgeois-liberal values," Tao said. "The heart of the struggle will be whether to insist upon the dictatorship of the proletariat."

Aside from cracking down on crime, a key task of the police was to "wage resolute struggle against enemy elements". The top cop added that the foes included advocates of "bourgeois liberalisation" and "peaceful evolution".[57] Apart from the regular police, other "law-enforcement" units were strengthened or created to help the CCP retain its monopoly on power. As we shall see, even the legal system — the courts and procuratorates — became potent weapons for instilling "dictatorship".

A. Beefing Up the Control Mechanisms

(i) Big Time for the Police Forces

The role of the People's Armed Police (PAP) as a tool for the dictatorship was enhanced after June 4. When it was established in 1983 as a supplement to the army, the PAP was placed under the joint administration of the PLA and the State Council. For example, the minister of public security, under the State Council, was always given the title of political commissar of the PAP. Soon after Tiananmen Square, however, the PAP came under the direct control of the Central Military Commission. The powers of the PAP were specially strengthened in Beijing and other large cities. After Martial Law was lifted in the capital in early 1990, at least a few tens of thousands of PLA officers were recommissioned as PAP officers.[58]

Nationwide, the establishment of the PAP and the regular police was boosted. At the November 1991 meeting mentioned above, Minister Tao said the national police force had doubled to 800,000 since the mid-1980s. The strength of the PAP stood at 600,000, or 100,000 more than the last available statistic given in the late 1980s. At the same time, anti-riot, anti-terrorist, and other crack units were formed in major cities. They often held exercises in downtown areas to instil fear in the hearts of potential "troublemakers".[59]

In late 1991, Beijing also laid down plans to boost its network of spies both domestically and overseas. The decision was taken at a national meeting of the heads of central- and regional-level security units. The size and powers of the Ministry of State Security — China's equivalent of the KGB — were expanded. For example, the Ministry could from then on freely plant agents in Chinese units abroad including embassies, business, media and cultural units. This was said to have met with opposition from other departments including the Ministry of Foreign Affairs.[60]

The extent and tentacles of China's security apparatus was revealed in an article in the Hong Kong-based China-watching magazine *Contemporary*. The journal reported in mid-1990 that police, secret police and other security officers made up 24 per cent of the personnel establishment of China's provinces and directly administered cities. *Contemporary* indicated that staff working in the police, national security, and reform-through-labour departments of the provinces and the three major cities (Beijing, Tianjin, Shanghai) exceeded 50,000 out of a total establishment of more than 210,000. These statistics only referred to personnel with cadre or officer ranking employed by the provincial and municipal governments. They did not include the PAP or lower-level employees such as policemen. Moreover, the figures excluded agents working at the national headquarters of the Ministries of Public Security and State Security.

"These statistics show that China can be called a police state, and that it has earmarked a startling amount of resources for the purpose of controlling its people," *Contemporary* said. The proportion of security staff was highest in the three directly administered cities. Beijing's municipal administration employed 18,288 staff cadres. Out of these, 6,520 worked in police, 4,334 in national security, and 408 in reform-through-labour departments. In other words, 61.6 per cent of Beijing's municipal personnel were "tools of the dictatorship of the proletariat".[61]

Police officers in the Shanghai municipality accounted for 30 per cent of the establishment. Outside of the three large cities, the coastal province of Guangdong had the highest concentration of security staff. 35.47 per cent of the 10,118 cadres on the payroll of Guangdong worked for the police and national security systems. The police and intelligence strength in Beijing, Shanghai, Tianjin, and Guangdong was highest not only because of their political and economic significance but because of the large number of foreigners resident there. The "dictatorship tools" were called upon to counteract "peaceful evolution" by so-called hostile overseas forces.

Aside from implementing the dictatorship of the proletariat, police organs tried to justify their self-aggrandisement in the name of "offering protection to reform". In an unusually frank report in 1992, NCNA indicated that police in Tianjin had been increased significantly. "Police in the port city of Tianjin say that their crackdown on crime has made the city one of the safest for foreign visitors and investors," NCNA reported.[62] Analysts pointed out that this was on a par with claims made by the PLA in early 1992 that it was providing an "imperial escort" for Deng Xiaoping and his reforms.

(ii) Police Deployment after the *Nanxun*

New security units came on to the scene even as the party anchored itself more solidly on the road to the market economy. This seems at first puzzling because, in theory, the deepening of reforms should render the regime more acceptable to the people. However, at least at the first stage of the "socialist market economy" in late 1993 and 1994, "contradictions" such as hyperinflation, unemployment and the unequal distribution of income were exacerbated. Failure of the CCP to consider political reform or to build bridges to the dissident community also meant the regime had to rely on police forces to defuse challenges to its supremacy.

The inter-departmental Central Commission for the Comprehensive Management of Social Order was established in 1992 to co-ordinate the anti-crime and anti-subversion efforts of units including State Security, Public Security, fire prevention, drugs, customs and border patrol. While the strength of the PAP surpassed the 800,000 mark in mid-1994, new units including patrol police in large urban areas and anti-*tufa* ("emergency incidents") squads sprang up like bamboo shoots in the spring.[63]

Chinese sources said that by mid-1993, the Public Security departments had drawn up a list of ten groups deemed to pose the most challenge to stability. Aside from remnants of the democracy movement dating from the late 1970s, they included "residual class enemies", underground organisations, triads and other secret societies, and intelligence operations from the West. Most indicative of Beijing's mentality of "seeing a soldier behind every stalk of grass", however, was its having designated the country's nascent "green movement" as a threat. In mid-1993, Beijing police denied permission by about 50 environmentalists to register as a "people's social group". State Security agents also investigated ties between China's green crusaders and radical groupings overseas.[64]

The year 1993 witnessed a record number of national conferences devoted to all aspects of security — crime, anti-espionage, as well as efforts to quell nationalistic movements in Tibet, Xinjiang and Qinghai. Fighting "intelligence organisations" of antagonistic foreign forces was the theme of a national security conference held in the capital in October. CNS quoted participants of the conclave as saying: "The international situation at the moment is marked by detente. Yet the world is hardly at peace. Spy and intelligence organisations overseas as well as certain hostile foreign forces continue to perpetrate disruptive activities against national security." The conference called on "the entire party and the entire nation to jointly safeguard national security". Addressing the meeting, President Jiang urged the people to "grasp economic reform on the one hand, and grasp the fight against criminal activities that hurt national security on the other".[65]

Summing up the security situation at the end of 1993, Jiang said that the country must persevere with a "merciless crackdown" on all crimes. Moreover, he added, law-enforcement forces must do more in "maintaining political stability and national security". "Officials of all levels must firmly rally around the main task of economic construction, realistically assess the destabilising influences, and adopt powerful measures to preserve political and social stability," he said.[66]

Another reason for the heightened vigilance was to forestall unrest that might break out because of negative side-effects of market reforms such as the laying off of redundant workers. With reference to the spate of panic buying in major cities in December 1993, State Council Secretary General Luo Gan said that the nation must raise its "consciousness of danger". "New contradictions will arise because of issues like the redistribution of wealth" and other radical reforms, he said. It is obvious that the paranoia and the siege mentality of the regime was hardly less serious four-and-a-half years after Tiananmen Square.[67]

The patrol police began their duties in the streets of major cities in early 1994. For example, the first such squadron in Beijing consisted of 664 officers, including 15 women, who had undergone training for eight months. Their beats were the Chongwen and Haidian districts, the latter being the hub of colleges including "bourgeois-liberal" Beijing University. Round-the-clock patrols were also introduced in cities including Shanghai, Guangzhou, Shenzhen and Zhuhai.[68] The frequency and size of police deployment also increased. In the run-up to the Chinese New Year in 1994, for example, Guangdong mobilised 18,000 officers to fight crime on the highways. And within a five-day period in late 1993, Shanghai police deployed more than 40,000 police to crack down on 300-odd gangs.[69]

(iii) The Questionable Effectiveness of Police Units

As with the PLA, the leadership did their level best to ensure that the guns of the various police forces were pointed in the right direction. The CCP took careful note of the fact that during the Romanian Revolution of December 1989, the secret police were more loyal to the Ceausescu dynasty than regular army units.

Ideological and other kinds of training were strengthened particularly for forces in the large cities. For example, police in Beijing conducted more than 1,000 training and refresher courses in 1991. Special classes were held in riot control and military-style body building to enable police to handle emergency. Other topics included political discipline, professionalism and "general culture", according to a dispatch by the official China News Service. CNS quoted a senior official as saying that the quality of the rank and file had "clearly been raised".[70]

Mirroring the purges in the PLA, the top echelon of the PAP was subjected to house-cleaning in the wake of the June 4 crackdown. A thorough-going round of reshuffle was announced in early 1990, when the bulk of the leadership was retired. Commander Li Lianxiu was removed largely for being "weak and lax" during the democracy movement in 1989. General Li had been a senior officer of the 38th Group Army before being transferred to the PAP in 1985. As we saw in Chapter 4, the 38th Army was repeatedly criticised for failure to effectively crush the student protests.[71]

Five of the six newly appointed leaders were picked from the PLA, not the PAP hierarchy. The new PAP Commander, Zhou Yushu, was formerly a commander of the 24th Group Army in the Beijing MR. The 24th army was commended for valour displayed during the crushing of the "counter-revolution-ary rebellion". In early 1990, many 24th-army officers were recommissioned as PAP staffers.

"Zhou's promotion reflects the anxiety of the leadership that the new PAP chief commands the personal allegiance of the PLA officers guarding the capital," a Western diplomat said. One the new vice commanders of the PAP, Zuo Yinsheng, was a vice commander of the Wuhan-based 15th Group Army, a unit of the Guangzhou MR. The 15th army was another military unit that played a big role in the June 4 bloodbath. The other new vice commander, Wang Wenli, formerly chief of staff of the PAP, was the only leader to have been promoted within PAP ranks.[72]

Another significant PAP reshuffle took place in early 1993 with the appointment of Generals Ba Zhongtan and Zhang Shutian as, respectively, Commander and Political Commissar. Both generals are believed to have links with Jiang Zemin. General Ba was head of the Shanghai garrison when Jiang served as party boss of the metropolis. Their appointments also reinforced the army control of the PAP.[73]

As an exercise in mass-psychological warfare, the Chinese media made Lei Fengs out of the "new-breed" policemen. Press reports played up the effectiveness of the police-state apparatus in quashing attempts by "class enemies" to overthrow the socialist order. A late 1991 dispatch by the official *Legal Daily* said that the PAP and its anti-riot squads suppressed 30 riots the same year. These disturbances included a gold mine incident in an unspecified locale, in which PAP officers clashed with thousands of illegal peasant gold prospectors that resulted in the death of three people.[74]

But were police forces really effective? In his address at the 18th National Public Security Conference, Minister Tao said his officers would target the following four areas in the 1990s: border areas; large state-run enterprises and mines; large and medium-sized cities; and coastal areas, including the economic zones and open cities. Tao indicated that a major concern of the police was organised crime, including triad activities and other underground organisations.[75]

Chinese sources and internal documents from 1989 to 1992 showed that the police could hardly cope with the growth of huge underground rings in both urban and rural areas. The police seemed more effective in cracking underground political units which had connections with the pro-democracy movement. This is evident from the large number of dissidents they arrested in 1992 and 1993 (see following sections). In this arena, State Security and police agents seemed to have recovered from their relative impotence in 1989 and 1990, when a large number of Tiananmen Square "agitators" escaped their dragnet and fled China.[76] Chinks in the armour of the police-state apparatus, however, were growing in view of its failure to stop the exponential growth of triads and other secret societies in urban and rural China.

Diplomats and journalists who visited cowboy towns along the coast had the impression that the triads had the run of the place after dark. In November 1993, the attention of international security experts was drawn by the Guangdong legislature's enactment of the nation's first anti-triad law. The statute empowered police to crack down on a dozen-odd triad-related activities which included extortion, running vice dens, cornering the market and recruitment of new members.[77]

Security sources said that a national network of triads ranging from Guangdong — which had the largest concentration — to the southwest and northeast had been formed. An early 1993 estimate said that there were 1,900-odd triad and other secret societies in the cities, up from 500 or so in 1990. According to a late 1993 report from the Hong Kong China News Agency, 17 triad units were discovered in two districts within Shenzhen. They had a total membership of 200. In the first seven months of the year, police in the Pearl River boom town of Foshan cracked more than 140 triad societies, which claimed a membership of over 700 ruffians.[78]

Western security sources said that Hong Kong triads had played a large role in the revival of secret societies in the motherland. The sources said that Hong Kong's ubiquitous underworld had extended its tentacles across the nation, and that its emissaries had no problem selling a mixture of glamour, derring-do and quick money to the big-spending youths of Guangdong.[79]

While triads tended to be active in the big- and medium-sized cities, rural areas were susceptible to the influence, and in many instances, control of secret societies. A late 1993 report by the *Economic Daily* said that there had been a re-emergence of feudalistic clans in the countryside. It said that "unstable elements" had surfaced in many villages as a result of "chaotic social order, backward economic development, and rampant growth of negative and evil phenomena". In a number of farm belts, such clans and secret societies had displaced party cells as the predominant socio-political organisations. *Economic Daily* alluded to the failure of many of the country's 800,000 rural party cells to "function as a fortress". It said that if the trend continued, "social stability will be endangered and the authority of party and government units in the villages will be undermined".[80]

There is disturbing evidence of collusion between party organisations and underworld elements. Some officials were simply "bought over" by gang leaders. Another reason is the CCP's strategic calculation that since the secret societies could not be rooted out, the party had no choice but to sue for peace by letting them run their little fiefdoms provided that the underground units accepted overall party leadership and did not pose a threat to the regime.[81]

Doubts about Beijing's policy of "if you can't wipe them out, co-opt them" were raised by Minister Tao's controversial statement at the 1992 NPC that there might be "patriotic" elements among the triads — and that the latter were welcome to start businesses in China. Many senior cadres are known to be good friends of Hong Kong triad bosses, who had investments in the mainland ranging from entertainment to real estate.[82]

B. The Judiciary as a Tool of Proletarian Dictatorship

A most ironic — some would say ludicrous — thing happened in the course of efforts by the leadership to convince Western opinion about the quality and impartiality of the Chinese judicial system. In the Chinese press as well as internal talks, top cadres made no secret of the fact that the courts, procuratorates and the prison system were primarily the CCP's weapons to ensure its monopoly on power. Yet in their conversations with foreign guests and media, Premier Li Peng and Foreign Ministry spokesmen tried to deflect questions concerning the heavy sentences meted out to dissidents by claiming that these were judicial matters with which the party and government could not interfere.[83]

The whitewash of the judicial system reached an apogee with the *White Paper on Human Rights* released in November 1991. The "manifesto" claimed that the "aim and task of China's judicial work is to protect the basic rights, freedoms and other legal rights and interests of the whole people in accordance with the law".[84] However, not even the White Paper dared claim that the judiciary was "independent". After all, leaders including Deng Xiaoping had reiterated that the Western ideal of the "tripartite division of power" and the independence of the judiciary belonged in the realm of bourgeois-liberal ideas.

(i) Boosting Party Control over the Courts

That the law courts had become a principal tool of the dictatorship of the proletariat became clear in the first major judicial conference after the June 4 massacre, a meeting of senior judges and court officials in January 1990. Supreme People's Court President, Ren Jianxin, also a member of the party Central Committee, made very explicit the "political" nature of the practice of law in China: to guarantee political stability, in other words, the supremacy of the party.[85]

Ren shocked audiences in both China and overseas when he said specifically that "judicial cadres" must abide by the instructions of the party as much as legal codes. The chief judge indicated that in addition to the law books, judges had to delve into "Marxist-Leninist theories on the state and law, as well as Chairman Mao's writings on class struggle". He pointed out that "courts at all levels must self-consciously follow party leadership". Apart from the statute books, Ren added, judicial officials must abide by party policies.

"All the trials conducted in China's courts of various levels should be beneficial to ensuring social stability," Ren said. "Courts should do their best to help foster a domestic political situation of unity and stability." He reminded judicial cadres that their brief was to safeguard party rule and "the people's democratic dictatorship". It was wrong, the chief judge said, to forget that "within certain parameters, class struggle will exist for a long time".

Ren's views were seconded by Liu Fuzhi, then head of the Supreme People's Procuratorate and a former minister of public security. In an early 1990 speech, Liu indicated that procuratorates, which are in charge of investigation and prosecution of crimes, must "take the initiative to fight for party leadership" of judicial work. "In important circumstances and difficult cases, we must report to the party and government leadership," he said.[86]

That the CCP had ironclad control over the judicial system was reinforced by conferences and speeches through the end of 1993. For example, at a late 1991 national conference on public security, Justice Minister Cai Cheng said that Chinese law must be at the service of "class struggle" and that judicial cadres must reject the theory that "the laws are supreme". Cai argued that China must jettison the principle of "the supremacy of the law" because the judicial code and system should be at the service of the proletariat class. "As a class tool, the law cannot be divorced from politics," he said. "It cannot but subserve the political needs of [a certain class]." "Since our law is socialist law, it will without question serve the politics of the proletariat class, socialist construction, reform and the open door, as well as the consolidation of the dictatorship of the proletariat," Cai added.[87]

At a meeting of the presidents of central and provincial high courts in early 1992, party chief Jiang Zemin and Premier Li Peng again asked the judicial organs to uphold the dictatorship of the proletariat. Jiang said that the more China undertook the reform and open-door policy, the more it should pursue the "people's democratic dictatorship" — and the judiciary should play a key role in both tasks. Li urged the courts to "keep a clear head" in the face of the complex international situation. "Court officials must stage a ceaseless struggle against criminals who disrupt national security and who damage normal social order," the premier said.[88]

At least on the surface, the role of the courts and procuratorates as tools of proletarian dictatorship was de-emphasised by the official media in 1993 and 1994. Instead, judicial officials chose to concentrate on how the legal system should help expedite the materialisation of the socialist market economy. At a speech in a legal conference at the end of 1993, Ren Jianxin upheld the principles of "egalitarianism before the law" and using laws to promote freedom of competition, combating improper competition and "establishing the concept of an open, mega-market". Ren railed against interference in legal work as a result of "regional protectionism and departmental protectionism".[89] However, the top court official did not dispute the fact that the entire judicial system remained under stern CCP leadership.

In the same vein, Li Peng said in late 1993 that "knowledge about the law and using legal means in management" had become a prerequisite for building a socialist market economy. The premier said that leaders of all levels must put emphasis on the construction of the legal system and that "administration must be based on the law".[90] Again, Li skirted the issue of the party's control of law-drafting as well as the entire juridical process.

As veteran dissident Yu Haocheng, a leading constitutional and legal scholar, put it in an interview, the party and government should simply leave the law and the courts alone. "The law should not serve any specific political agenda, be it class struggle or the construction of a socialist market economy," he said. "Just educate the people about the importance of the rule of law. Do not put any demands on the courts and the lawyers to toe the prevailing political line."[91]

(ii) Party-dominated Justice in Action

That the courts had become the regime's weapon to stigmatise and lock away its vocal opponents is clear from the hundreds of show trials and convictions of dissidents related to the 1989 democracy movement. Cases of abuse were exhaustively catalogued by international human rights organisations such as the New-York based Asia Watch (later called Human Rights Watch/Asia) and the London-based Amnesty International.

In its report "Trials and Punishments since 1989", which was released in April 1991, Amnesty International accused Beijing of mistrials and the overall travesty of justice. "Trial proceedings in China do not meet with internationally-recognised standards for fair trial, notably the right to have adequate time and facilities to prepare the defence, the right to be presumed innocent before being proven guilty, and the right to cross-examine prosecution witnesses and to call witnesses for the defence," Amnesty charged. "Furthermore, in practice, the verdict and the sentence are generally determined by those in authority before the trial even takes place."[92]

In a later study called "Punishment without Crime: Administrative Detention", Amnesty zeroed in on a much-maligned form of "rough justice": administrative punishment and detention of "criminals" through means such as "shelter and investigation" and "re-education through labour". The report said that police could keep suspects in detention for up to several years without going through the courts. This kind of draconian justice was often meted out for "vaguely defined forms of 'anti-social' and 'anti-socialist' behaviour or activities". The watchdog said the number of people being held under various forms of extra-judicial detention was believed to run into millions.[93]

In a report released in January 1992, Asia Watch charged that in spite of Beijing's claims that the bulk of the Tiananmen Square-related dissidents had been tried and released, more than 1,000 activists associated with the 1989 protests remained behind bars or were unaccounted for. The figure did not include underground religious activists or Tibetans. Asia Watch said the Chinese authorities "showed themselves even less willing in 1991 than in 1990 to ease up on the relentless repression that they have pursued" since June 4. It added that the trials and convictions in 1991 showed "only the extent to which criminal justice in China is administered at the fickle whim of the Communist Party".[94]

In a release in early 1994, Asia Watch said the number of arrests of dissidents, religious and "pro-separatist" figures in 1993 was the most since the massacre. The watchdog said it had documented 250 cases of political arrests and trials in the year, including 32 dissident-related trials that resulted in average sentences of four years in jail. There were also 216 new detentions. Concerning the judicial process, Asia Watch reiterated its earlier viewpoint: "Guilt has been predetermined [before the trials] and the verdicts decided upon in advance." "There is no meaningful independence of the judiciary in China, especially where political cases are concerned," it added.[95]

For reasons of space, let us just zero in on the show trials of the two most famous 1989 dissidents — Chen Ziming and Wang Juntao, which international watchdogs and Western diplomats characterised as a gross miscarriage of justice. Sources close to the families and the Beijing Intermediate Court, where they were each sentenced to 13 years in jail in February 1991, said the defence lawyers were denied access to key witnesses. Nor were the lawyers' charges that pieces of key evidence, including taped messages by the two, had been tampered with, adequately addressed during the trials.[96]

Sources present at the five-day trial of Chen said that three major pieces of evidence were cited by the prosecution to prove their having committed seditious and counter-revolutionary crimes: an April 13, 1989, speech on the future of reform delivered at a research institute; a May 15, 1989, speech on reform and work of the trade union; and 3,000 yuan Chen allegedly donated to student leader Wang Dan. Out of the two speeches, the prosecution extrapolated and pieced together nine sentences which, they claimed, proved that Chen had committed seditious acts. Samples: "Intellectuals are a newly rising force in society" and "Intellectuals should organise themselves."

Aside from the point that the pieces of evidence had been tampered with, Chen's lawyers insisted that at most, the statements cited had established a certain tendency in Chen's thinking, not a criminal action or conspiracy. Moreover, things like "organising intellectuals" were permitted by the Chinese constitution. Equally important, none of the written submissions by the 17 witnesses had characterised Chen's thoughts and actions as "seditious" or "counter-revolutionary". The authorities also denied the lawyers' requests to have the witnesses cross-examined in court.

Way before the trials opened, there was no doubt in anybody's mind that the two "black hands" would be given severe punishments. Li Peng had characterised Wang as a "tiger that must never be allowed to return to the hills". Another party elder had lambasted Wang for making trouble on at least three occasions: the Beijing Spring movement of the late 1970s, the December 1986 student movement, and the 1989 democracy movement.[97]

Both Amnesty International and Asia Watch published numerous accounts of harsh and inhumane treatment of dissidents in jail, including forced labour in penal production facilities. Prior to the visit to Beijing by then US Secretary of State James Baker in November 1991, six prisoners in an automobile assembly plant in the prison system in Lingyuan County, Liaoning Province, threatened to stage hunger strikes to dramatise their plight. The six included Liu Gang, a former physics student in Beijing University, as well as Tang Yuanjuan, an alleged labour organiser formerly with the Changchun No. 1 Automobile Factory.[98]

Throughout the early 1990s, the same disregard for "the fine points of the law" was evident in the trial of dissidents not directly related to the 1989 movement. A case in point was the sentences of ten and nine years slapped respectively on Yao Kaiwen and Gao Xiaoliang of Shanghai in December 1993. They were accused of organising an underground anti-government ring called the Mainland Headquarters of the Democratic China Front. Police seized a manifesto of the Front which allegedly called for "ending the dictatorial rule of the communist regime" through "peaceful and bloody, legal and illegal" means. Sources in Shanghai, however, said that the Front consisted of no more than a handful of radicals, and that they had never put their "ideals" into action. Yao and Kao had not even disseminated their manifesto or other beliefs in the form of an underground publication.[99]

The politicisation of justice was most evident in efforts by the administration to win Most Favoured Nation and other trading privileges from the US and other Western countries through the manipulative release of big-name dissidents. Beijing's very cynical "parole" of Wei Jingsheng — just five months before his 15-year term was up in March 1994 — to bolster its chances of hosting the summer Olympics for the year 2000 was universally condemned by human rights watchdogs and activists.[100]

(iii) Instructions to "Speed Up" Trials and Convictions

The CCP was slightly less secretive about party or administrative interference in justice if the cases concerned ordinary, not political, criminals. The offensive against the "Six Evils" — prostitution, pornography, abduction of women and children, drugs, gambling and superstition — which was kicked off in mid-November 1989, however, provided another illustration of the courts and the procuratorates being told what to do in the name of "national interest".

In a throwback to the days of Chairman Mao, Beijing used mass movement" techniques as a substitute for justice. Within a month of the campaign's launch, more than 350,000 criminals had come under investigation. Why the extra efficiency? Lin Zhun, Vice-President of the Supreme People's Court, indicated at the outset of the campaign that to facilitate prosecution and conviction, legal personnel need not be too squeamish about the fine points of the law. "Once the cases have reached the courts, the adjudication process should be expedited," Lin said. "If the basic facts are clear, the basic pieces of evidence are correct, and criminal cases can be established, judgments according to the law should be made in good time." "One should not be entangled by secondary matters which do not affect incrimination and the weighing of what punishment to mete out," he added.[101]

What Western jurists call "rough and ready justice" was also administered in the yearly *yanda* or "hit-them-hard" campaigns against felons, gangsters, and drug traffickers. Since late 1990, mass public trials — and sometimes executions — of major criminals and drug runners were constantly featured in the national media.

In a January 1992 article, the *People's Public Security* newspaper disclosed the philosophy of summary arrests, trials and execution as laid down by Deng Xiaoping. "We cannot let criminals become fearless," Deng said in the summer 1983, when Beijing kicked off its first *yanda* campaign. "*Yanda* means boosting the force of the dictatorship; it is the dictatorship itself. We are out to protect the safety of the majority of people. This is called humanitarianism."[102] The 1983 *yanda* campaign, which resulted in the execution of thousands of criminals, reportedly began when Deng's motorcade was briefly threatened by a group of ruffians on its way from Beijing to Beidaihe.

The same approach to "efficiency in justice" was preached by Ren Jianxin in late 1993 during yet another *yanda* campaign. "We must certainly be swift and severe when issuing punishments," Ren said during a meeting on fighting crime. "Our hands must not be allowed to be soft in the least." The administration also revived Mao's kangaroo-court justice by inviting the masses to take part in the national security campaign. Speaking in his capacity as Head of the Commission of Politics and Legal Affairs in early 1994, Ren said that the authorities must "mobilise and organise the masses to enthusiastically take part in the comprehensive curing of law and order".[103]

(iv) Who Controls the Courts?

The potent weapon of dictatorship called the judiciary is controlled by a supreme Central Committee unit called the Commission of Politics and Legal Affairs, which was headed by Qiao Shi, and since late 1992, Ren Jianxin. Members of the CPLA included the heads of the Ministry of State Security, the Ministry of Public Security, the Justice Ministry, the Supreme People's Court, the Supreme People's Procuratorate, and a representative from the General Political Department of the army.[104]

Aside from laying down yardsticks for the promotion of security, crime prevention and the punishments to be meted out, the Commission also met to discuss major cases. For "criminals" whose treatment might have international repercussions, the CPLA often referred the files to the full Politburo — and sometimes Deng Xiaoping himself. Chinese and diplomatic sources said the fate of Wang Juntao and Chen Ziming was almost certainly settled by the Politburo Standing Committee. Deng is known to have had the final say over the treatment accorded dissidents including Wei Jingsheng, Guo Luoji, Fang Lizhi and Bao Tong.[105]

The tradition of the Politburo and Central Committee being in effect China's "court of final appeal" goes back to the earliest days of the party. Stories abounded of Chairman Mao making fairly personal decisions on the handling of corrupt or disloyal party cadres.[106] It was not until 1988 that party chief Zhao Ziyang tried to modernise this feudalistic practice by phasing out the CPLA — as well as its regional equivalents — stage by stage.

In the interest of separation of party and government — and overall political reform — the CPLA was replaced in 1988 by a less authoritative organisation called the Leading Group on Politics and Law. Local-level CPLAs were replaced by Co-ordinating Committees on Politics and Law. The new bodies were much less powerful because their main role was confined to coordinating the work among departments including the police, internal security, and the judicial organs.[107]

Soon after the Tiananmen Square crackdown, the old structure returned with a vengeance. The dissolution of the CPLA became yet another of Zhao's crimes. And the re-established Commission resumed its old authority — and then some. With the feverish recruitment of various police units and more

extensive investigations into anti-party and anti-state activities, the power of
the entire security and legal establishment was boosted.

At a meeting of the staff of the CPLA and its regional branches in late
1993, Ren plugged the orthodox line about being tough on anti-state activities. "We must insist on grasping [the national situation] with two hands, and
the grip of both hands must be tough," he said. The new legal supremo was
referring to the fact that while the nation must persevere with economic construction, it must "strengthen the functions of the dictatorship of the proletariat". "New contradictions and problems will arise following the ceaseless
deepening of reform," he added. "We must correctly handle the people's inner
contradictions under new circumstances — and boost our ability to handle
tufa [emergency] events."[108]

Both 1993 and 1994 provided examples galore of the politicisation of justice — or the "rule of personality" infringing upon the judicial field. The decision to arrest Yu Zuomin, "the feudal monarch" of the Daqiuzhuang conglomerate near Tianjin, was taken by the Politburo, probably in view of Yu's
good connections with the Deng household. The entire investigation and adjudication of the junk-bond scandal involving Changcheng Electronics, Electricity, and High-Technology Corp were wrapped in secrecy. Changcheng
Chairman Shen Taifu, who is believed to be on good terms with a large number of senior cadres, was summarily executed in April 1994 (see later sections). The apparent reason: Beijing's fear that he might spill too many beans.
Senior cadres including Jiang Zemin and Zhu Rongji also played a role in the
heavy sentences given to mainland and Hong Kong journalists — including
Ming Pao reporter Xi Yang — for allegedly "leaking" state secrets.[109]

V. Stepping Up Control of Society

In a mid-1991 address to senior cadres on the role of trade unions, youth and
women organisations, then alternate member of the Politburo Ding Guan'gen
called for "total party control" of all fringe organisations and associations of
the party and government. He said the CCP must step up vigilance against tendencies in such units to "veer away from or undermine" CCP leadership. "We
will resolutely not allow the existence of political organisations which oppose
the Four Cardinal Principles and which pose threats to the administration," he
said.[110]

"Soon as they are discovered, [counter-revolutionary] units must be abolished," Ding pointed out. He reminded his audience that the "cardinal principle" of the "dictatorship of the proletariat" was as important as the other three
(party leadership, the socialist road, Marxism-Leninism and Mao Thought).

"We must uphold the dictatorship of the proletariat, protect the people's regime, safeguard national security, and maintain social stability," he said.

The control mechanism was expanded to the extent that even social organisations that apparently had nothing to do with politics were not immune to Big Brother's machinations. In 1990, a number of organisations of *qigong*, a kind of breathing exercise that gives some practitioners "supernatural" powers including healing, in Beijing and other large cities were closed. During the 1989 protests, members of *qigong* societies apparently lent their support to democracy activists. And in 1993, more than 1,000 martial arts schools in Fujian were required to re-register with the authorities because of their alleged threat to law and order.[111]

We shall examine the CCP's strategies for reining in workers and intellectuals, considered two forces most prone to destabilising the administration.

A. Promoting Stability Among Workers

(i) Quelling Labour Unrest, 1989-1992

Workers were a prime area of concern because the CCP knew that if it were to lose control over the "vanguard of the proletariat", the party and Chinese socialism would crumble. In spite of its fulminations against "all-out Westernisers" such as Fang Lizhi, Beijing never considered intellectuals a real threat. In December 1986 as well as May 1989, the CCP became alarmed only after the student demonstrators had been joined by workers.[112]

For Deng Xiaoping and the party elders, the history of the disintegration of socialism began with the Solidarity movement in Poland in the early 1980s and its victory in 1990. Deng made repeated references to Solidarity in internal talks on law and order. In his famous address on the December 1986 student movement, the patriarch praised Poland's then dictator General Jaruzelski for his "resolute" action against the underground worker movement.[113]

Workers played a sizeable role in the protest movement of 1989. However, even before Tiananmen Square, wild-cat or underground trade unions were reported in different parts of China. For example, a couple of such units in the northeast styled themselves after Poland's Solidarity. In most large cities that witnessed demonstrations in May and June 1989, there were autonomous workers' unions to go with autonomous students' unions. It is believed that the treatment meted out arrested labour activists was much harsher than that given dissident intellectuals.[114]

Beijing's post-June 4 strategy towards the labour sector was familiar: appease the majority through economic and political favours; and crack down hard on the "recalcitrant" minority. Economically, a top priority of the central government was to prevent unemployment and hyperinflation, which would almost certainly trigger social unrest.

Statistics released in September 1991 showed that the average income of workers had jumped from 668 yuan in 1979 to 2,140 yuan in 1990. The Labour Ministry claimed that discounting inflation, this represented a yearly increase of 3.8 per cent. A late 1991 report said that unemployment in China for the past eight years had remained below 2.6 per cent. Then labour minister Ruan Chongwu said he was confident the jobless rate could be kept within three per cent in the early 1990s.[115] Both sets of statistics are subject to dispute. For example, Beijing has traditionally understated inflation by as much as five to ten percentage points. Independent estimates of unemployment for 1990 was at least six per cent.

During the sharp economic downturn in late 1989 and early 1990, Beijing dispatched orders to local administrations on not laying off redundant labourers. State factories were asked to pay superfluous workers at least 50 to 70 per cent of their salaries, or just enough for subsistence. For example, in early 1990, unemployed workers in Shanghai were told they could get 75 per cent of their salaries. And Guangzhou decided to raise "unemployment benefits" to laid-off workers in the city. Dole for those with one to six years of working experience was raised from 45 yuan to 55 yuan. Benefits for workers with more than six years of experience were raised from 50 yuan to 60 yuan.[116]

Beijing's rationale for maintaining near-full employment was reflected in an article in the official *Guangming Daily* by Zuo Chunwen and Wen Haiying. The two social scientists argued that unemployment must be kept within 4 per cent — and that 5 per cent would constitute a "danger point". This ceiling, they said, had been "proven by history" to be the "limit of society's ability to absorb the shock" of joblessness. Zuo and Wen argued that the unemployed should if possible be absorbed by enterprises and not be "thrust upon society".[117]

The goal of full employment contradicted plans announced in 1991 to "reform" state-sector enterprises by rendering them into financially self-sufficient units. Obviously, a key way to improve the efficiency of government factories was to lay off superfluous workers. As far as possible, however, Beijing tried to keep the social disruptions to a minimum. For example, in the autumn of 1991, the central government announced relatively bold measures to close down chronic loss-making enterprises: at least ten of the worst-performing units in each province would be shut down. However, various levels of government took care to ensure that workers of the foreclosed units would still enjoy their basic salaries (minus their usual bonuses and other subsidies) before they could be transferred to other units.[118]

Until 1993, the dinosaurs among the state sector were not simply liquidated but merged with more robust companies — and the workers in the former taken over by the latter. For example, by the end of 1991, 210 loss-making business units in Beijing had been merged with better performing ones. The *People's Daily* reported that none of the 120,000 employees of the 210 had lost their jobs — and that they were getting salaries comparable to those of their old posts.[119]

In addition to pecuniary inducements, the party tried to win the workers' loyalty by apparently re-establishing their position as the "premier" class in China. In a December 1989 speech entitled "Struggle to build up the party as an even stronger vanguard of the working class", Jiang Zemin promised workers that their status would be enhanced. "Politically, the party must insist on maintaining the leading class position of the working class," Jiang said. "In our work, we must whole-heartedly rely on the working class." The party chief also pledged that more workers, especially those on the "production front-line", would be inducted into the party.[120]

Similarly, in an editorial in August 1991, the *People's Daily* called on the nation to "give their whole-hearted support to the working class", deemed the "ruling class" of the country. The *Daily* reaffirmed an appeal made by Mao in 1949 that "we must wholeheartedly rely on the working class". It added that the policy of "hoisting the flag of the working class" should be fully put into practice at various levels. Measures should be taken to ensure that workers be given a greater say and more opportunities to take part in national affairs.[121]

In spite of the economic and political blandishments, there was evidence that labour unrest had gone on unabated after the June 4 crackdown. Owing to tight censorship, it is difficult to get a complete picture of underground labour activities. A leaked 1991 document from the All China Federation of Trade Unions (ACFTU) — China's only official labour organisation — gave glimpses of the severity of the problem. According to the paper, about 37,450 workers took part in 1,620 protests in 1990 nationwide. These included strikes, go-slows, rallies, petitioning local governments, and sit-ins. "Some workers are in a predicament in which they have no money for medical care and no rice in their pots," the document said. Since China had some 140 million workers, only one out of every 3,740 had gone public with their dissatisfaction in 1990. ACFTU attributed the protests to material reasons: state factories losing money and unable to honour their paychecks.[122]

According to sources close to the labour movement, the Ministry of State Security was by late 1991 targeting 14 clandestine labour units in the capital. The organisations had memberships ranging from 20 to 300 workers. The ostensible goals of these groupings included raising the status of workers and promoting political reform.[123]

At least two of these "underground rings" patterned themselves after Poland's Solidarity. With memberships of about 100 each, the two groups vowed to form an alternative, workers-based party that championed "real democracy". While these units did not openly call for the CCP's downfall, the authorities took their challenge seriously. The MSS had according to the sources infiltrated many of the groups. However, they had very secretive organisations, and the police were not sure who the ringleaders were. The sources said the Ministry had by late 1991 collected impressive evidence, including underground publications put out by the clandestine units.

At the same time, the CCP continued to re-establish party cells and other indoctrination units in factories. After mid-1989, Beijing took draconian steps to re-assert control over the ACFTU, the official trade union which was deemed a "disaster area" of infiltration by bourgeois values. Federation staff had in May 1989 taken part in street demonstrations and made financial contributions of over 100,000 yuan to the students. After the June 4 bloodbath, about 40 ACFTU cadres were fired, demoted or kicked out of the party. The most famous of these was the Federation's party secretary Zhu Houze, a former chief of the propaganda department who was close to Hu Yaobang.[124]

In late 1989, the CCP Central Committee issued a circular on boosting control over the trade unions, the Communist Youth League, and women's federations. Then ACFTU president Ni Zhifu noted that the unions should help the party in making workers appreciate the importance of "national and social stability". Ni, a former Politburo member, said that labour organisations must keep close tabs on workers to ensure that "contradictions do not develop or become exacerbated".[125]

In late 1989, the CCP installed Yang Xingfu as ACFTU Vice-President with special responsibility for supervising the house-cleaning. A former head of the Shandong Branch of the ACFTU, Yang was known as a hardliner. One of his first moves was to expand the Federation's personnel bureau into an organisation department which had more authority over appointments and discipline. In general, however, the status of ACFTU as well as its subsidiaries and cells in state factories began to decline. Analysts said Beijing wanted to play down the role of unions, even those that were under the strict control of the party.[126]

(ii) The Threat of Urban Unrest, 1993-1994

In 1993, the flashpoints on the factory floor became highly volatile. Deeper stages of economic reform — particularly the restructuring of state factories — had directly cut into the income, and in many instances, the livelihood of workers. The massive lay-off of labourers also coincided with double-digit inflation, another result of accelerated growth. The CCP, however, failed to make any move to promote consultation with workers or otherwise to give them opportunities to take part in the political process. The result was that "the vanguard of the proletariat" felt marginalised in a society displaying more symptoms of the primitive stage of capitalism.

While the overall standard of living continued to rise in 1993, the proportion of urban residents who had difficulty making ends meet also increased. In late 1993, the Minister of Labour Li Boyang admitted that the problem of unemployment, estimated at 4 per cent early in the year, had worsened. Particularly worrisome was the drop in the re-employment rate of laid-off workers, down from 70 per cent in 1992 to just 20 per cent. Li vowed to bring the jobless rate back to 3 per cent in 1994. Yet given new freedoms granted many government-run factories to fire redundant staff, this looked like mission impossible.[127]

An early 1993 survey by the ACFTU said that 7 million workers — about 5 per cent of the national total — were in dire economic straits. In the first quarter of 1993, 850,000 workers applied for welfare benefits, more than the total of such cases in the past six years. Late that year, the official union dispatched ten "consolation teams" to hand out 3.45 million yuan to the neediest workers in 30 provinces and cities. An early 1993 dispatch by CNS said that 74 million workers in 470,000 state enterprises had some form of work insurance. Given the poor state of the central coffers, however, it would be several years before a national social insurance system could be licked into shape.[128]

Again because of the news blackout, there were no reliable figures on industrial incidents in 1993. However, work stoppages and other protests were reported in cities including Beijing, Shanghai, Shenzhen and Zhuhai. Significantly, a rash of strikes hit joint-venture business units in the SEZs, where pay and other conditions were already better than in state-run concerns. The Zhuhai municipal government set up a special tribunal to handle employer-employee relations in early 1993. Shenzhen, one of China's richest — and most expensive — cities, reported that in 1993 there were 4,000-odd cases of complaints and petitions from workers, who were owed salaries and benefits amounting to more than 5 million yuan. These incidents were responsible for 255 counts of work stoppages in the year. [129]

Aside from lay-offs and pay cuts, more workers were suffering from the Dickensian aspects of the "preliminary stage of socialism". In 1992, 15,000 labourers of various trades died because of atrocious safety standards in the work place. The 1993 record was estimated to be worse. Casualties from mining and fire accidents were particularly alarming. In 1993, 5,036 coal labourers died in the pits.[130]

By late 1993, the calls for setting up some form of legal and institutional mechanism for protecting worker welfare reached a crescendo. In an early 1994 dispatch, CNS disclosed that there had been 250,000 "labour dispute cases" since 1988. It quoted experts as saying that urgent legislation and other work had to be done to protect workers in four areas: obligatory overtime work; employers being tardy with pay cheques; poor living conditions; and unsafe working environments. Incidents like doing work in a 40-degree Celsius room and not allowed to go to the toilets more than three times a day were routine.[131]

There were also indications, however, that the authorities were trying to deflect attention and to shirk responsibility by pointing the accusing finger at foreign partners of joint-venture factories. In December 1993, the ACFTU sent a highly-publicised delegation to investigate the fire that killed 84 factory workers in Shenzhen a month earlier. The high casualty in the Hong Kong-owned unit was due to managers having locked up windows and doors to minimise thefts. A Guangdong government survey of local joint-venture factories said that more than 30 per cent of the workers had not been given a contract by their employers.[132]

During an address to the 12th ACFTU congress in October 1993, Politburo member Hu Jintao saluted the working class as the "masters of the country". His real message, however, was to ask the "masters" to tighten their belts as a sacrifice for reform. "It is inevitable that during the process of reform, [the positions of] different interest [blocs] will be readjusted," he said. "Workers should maintain their tradition of taking the overall interests of the state into consideration and subordinating their immediate interests to the long-term interests of the country as a whole." There was no mention of worker participation on the factory floor, in the legislature and on government boards, which seemed the only way to ensure that labour rights would be safeguarded.[133]

Failure of the CCP to handle the labour crisis adequately provided yet another example of the political process gone awry. At least in the cities, the Communists rose to power on the workers' coat-tails — and through organising underground unions. In the late 1980s and early 1990s, the CCP did nothing to build bridges to disgruntled labourers — or to co-opt the leaders of wild-cat unions. After nearly 30 revisions over 15 years, the NPC passed a Labour Law by the middle of 1994. Yet the long-awaited legislation did not allow workers to express themselves through industrial actions such as strikes or the formation of independent unions. Speaking at the 1994 NPC, Labour Minister Li Boyong said: "I do not think it is possible for China to have independent trade unions such as Solidarity."[134]

In 1993 and 1994, the CCP honed its time-honoured carrot-and-stick approach to pacifying worker discontent. Beijing decided to buy off the several million workers who were not paid — or partially paid — by state enterprises in the latter half of 1993 and the first quarter of 1994. For example, just before Lunar New Year in 1994, the State Council set aside 1.6 billion yuan in emergency funding to pay miners and other staff in the depressed coal industry. At least in the large cities, whenever strikes and demonstrations took place in protest against dishonoured pay cheques, local leaders were told by Beijing to pacify the labourers through whole or partial payment of salaries.[135]

At the same time, PAP and anti-riot police were mobilised to help restore order to cities and towns badly hit by industrial incidents. State Security units cracked down hard on a group of Beijing-based dissidents who tried to organise a petition to the NPC demanding worker rights including the freedom to form labour unions. Three of the leaders — Zhou Guoqiang, Yuan Hongbing and Wang Jiaqi — were arrested in March 1994. This did not prevent 120 of their comrades from establishing a League for the Protection of Working People in China (known as *Laomeng* in Chinese). One of its demands was a revision of the constitution to promote labour rights — and overall political reform. By mid-1994, police had arrested at least five other *Laomeng* stalwarts, and tracking down the rest of the activists became a high priority of the Ministry of Public Security.[136]

B. Keeping Intellectuals in Line

(i) The Post-1989 Clampdown on the Intelligentsia

The CCP used both threats and blandishments to keep the rebellious intelligentsia in line. Jiang Zemin made it clear in an address in July 1991 that only a very limited degree of the old "let a hundred flowers bloom" standard would be revived in the cultural arena. "We will never allow bourgeois-liberal things to poison the people, pollute society or counter socialism," he said.[137]

The colleges in particular became a battleground where the authorities tried to win over the soul of the next generation — most of whom would become cadres upon graduation. Aside from weeding out Western material from the curricula and boosting the proportions of ideological education, the most direct means was to tighten party control of the institutes of higher learning.

In a Politburo meeting in mid-1991, then minister of the State Education Commission Li Tieying baldly stated that "China must only have socialist universities". "The lectern must never be in the hands of bourgeois-liberal elements," he said. "Those teachers who do not want to propagate socialism can leave. Those students who do not believe in socialism can quit." College teachers who were also CCP affiliates were told that "in addition to being leaders in academic subjects, they must also be leaders in politics".[138]

Li, who before the June 4 massacre was considered a "reformist", further noted that universities must be run "with Chinese characteristics". He indi-

LIBRARY
BISHOP BURTON COLLEGE
BEVERLEY HU17 8QG

cated that Chinese colleges should not be compared with academic institutions in the West. "Talk no more about [China] running a world-class university," he said. "No matter how backward they may be, our colleges are still colleges with Chinese characteristics."

Military training, which was introduced after June 4, 1989, for the freshman class of Beijing University, was extended to more than a dozen colleges before the Maoist practice wound down in 1993. In a throwback to the Cultural Revolution, 1 million college students were asked to go to the countryside in the summer of 1991 to "learn from the masses". "They will do social research in rural areas, steep themselves in the national conditions, and increase their feelings for the masses of workers and peasants," CNS said.[139]

And when the students graduated, they must not only hand in their dissertations but pass a test on politics and ideology. Those who flunked the political examination might not get their degrees. In mid-1991, the SEC announced that they would examine the dissertations produced in key Beijing universities in the past five years for possible signs of "bourgeois liberalisation". The authors of "poisonous weeds" would be subjected to disciplinary action unless they recanted or at least demonstrated a "sincerity" towards rectifying their views.[140]

The new morality codes assumed a dimension of the absurd when it was announced in the summer of 1991 that Beijing students must not openly display their affection for the opposite sex. An official notice posted at Beijing University said that by October 5, 1991, collegiates must stop "uncivilised behaviour" like hugging, kissing, holding hands or putting their arms around each other's shoulders. And because the words "small bottle" sound the same in *putonghua* as "Xiaoping", smashing bottles would be strictly prohibited.[141]

In late 1991, the CCP announced that party units at the country's 1,075 institutes of higher learning would be reshuffled to ensure loyalty. Speaking at an internal meeting, then head of the party's Organisation Department Song Ping deplored that fewer and fewer college kids wanted to join the party. For example, before 1949, some 10 per cent of the students of élite Qinghua University were underground CCP members. It was down to barely three per cent in 1991. Less than one per cent of the students of 15 high schools in Hebei Province were party affiliates.[142]

Among the institutions that Beijing deemed hotbeds of "bourgeois liberalisation", the ministerial-level CASS underwent the most thorough house-cleaning. Chinese sources said at least 120 staffers and researchers received disciplinary actions, and six were imprisoned. Academics in the Political Science Institute and the Marxism-Leninism Institute were particularly hard hit. For example, nine out of the 70 researchers in the latter unit were penalised in one way or another. The ideologues even threatened to close down the Marxism-Leninism Institute and to replace it with an Institute of Contemporary Marxism.[143]

As with other cultural and academic units, the leftists managed to install their trusted comrades in the CASS. By late 1989, two ideologues had become Vice-Presidents of the institute. They were Yu Wen and Jiang Liu. Yu had been deputy secretary-general of the NPC, and Jiang, a deputy dean of education at the Central Party School. Both were considered protégés of conservative elder Deng Liqun. At the same time, two relatively liberal Vice-Presidents, Ding Weizhi and Li Shenzhi, were forced to make self-criticisms for conniving at "bourgeois-liberal" activities in the academy. As we saw earlier, remnant Maoists within CASS tried very hard to restore the "party secretary responsibility system" at the institute. It was not until late 1993 that leftists like Yu and Jiang were forced to retire (see Chapter 3).[144]

(ii) Campaign to Woo Intellectuals

By early 1991, however, the CCP also set into motion a campaign to woo intellectuals, particularly scientists and researchers in technology who were in a position to make direct contributions to the economy. In the spring of 1991, Deng Xiaoping kicked off a new campaign to "save the nation through technology". Partly inspired by the wonders that high technology had done for the Americans in the Gulf War, Deng revived another of his reform slogans: "Science and technology are the premier production force."[145]

A corollary of this "technology first" gameplan was to raise the status of the intellectual class in general, and scientists and researchers in particular. A milestone was reached in November 1991 when 1,200 top cadres began attending the first of a series of lectures on technology at the Zhongnanhai party headquarters. Rocket wizard Qian Xuesen and other world-class scientists expatiated on topics including the technological revolution and the Chinese economy, and "the Gulf War and high technology".[146]

Not only the spiritual but the material status of intellectuals was raised as Beijing unveiled a new deal for researchers. For example, the Chinese Academy of Sciences announced in late 1991 that 553 of its top scientists, one of whom was barely 28 years of age, would qualify for special subsidies in salary and housing. The SEC also made known that nearly 10,000 scholars and researchers would get cost-of-living subsidies of 100 yuan a month. By the end of 1992, some 110,000 teachers and intellectuals were recipients of special subsidies and awards from the government.[147] Intellectuals who had the slightest dealings with the 1989 democracy movement, however, were excluded from the dispensation.

By late 1992, the party and government also turned to wooing the thousands of students and professionals who had settled in the US and other Western countries since the mid-1980s. A State Council circular in October

1992 said that even those who had "taken part in activities detrimental to national security" could return provided that once on Chinese soil, they would refrain from actions deemed "anti-government" and "against the constitution". In some instances, researchers who had returned were given special funding for their professional pursuits.[148]

Official largesse, however, began to matter much less after the *nanxun*, when private enterprises — and later state factories — were luring professionals, managers, technicians, and salesmen with packages many times that of Li Peng. Zhuhai factories made a name for themselves by offering automobiles and even apartments for distinguished scientists and managers. Intellectuals, therefore, would thank the new spirit of entrepreneurship rather than the party for the better compensation.

In spite of Beijing's avowed re-commitment to the ideal of "rendering decision-making more scientific and democratic" (see later section), merely a token number of intellectuals were inducted into the advisory boards of central and local units. The chances of intellectuals having a say in politics remained minimal unless they happened to be appointed to the think tanks of the clique or politician who was on the rise. Again, the question of the independence of the intelligentsia became the topic of the day. At a time of a deep freeze in politics, many intellectuals decided to first build up their fortunes — and economic clout — before they took on the CCP monolith.

VI. A New-look Cadre System

A. Loyalty as the Key to Promotion

In the days of former party chiefs Hu Yaobang and Zhao Ziyang, the CCP observed four criteria for choosing potential leaders: "rejuvenation, knowledge and expertise, professionalism, and revolutionary fervour." Zhao tried hard to play down the "revolutionary" component of the formula. He stressed that *zhengji* or "concrete achievements" should be the touchstone of excellence. Since June 4, however, the balance between "redness" and "expertise" tipped in favour of the former. During his *nanxun* talks, Deng laid emphasis on finding young cadres who had both "morality and ability" — thus putting Marxist rectitude first. Reminding party members that neo-imperialists were pinning their hope on the new generation, he underscored the need to propagate cadres who would not "fail to make the grade on the question of countering liberalisation".[149]

Conservative patriarch Chen Yun pointed out soon after the June 4 crisis that "leadership powers should be vested in the hands of people who have a true and correct understanding of Marxism-Leninism". The stress on "redness" remained unchanged until the selection of cadres to be elevated during the 14th Party Congress in late 1992. The leadership was convinced that officials who would set the country's course through to the 2010s, — the so-called "cross-century cadres" — must be "trustworthy" Marxists. As then Politburo member Li Ximing put it: "If we have done well the job of propagating cross-century successors, our [socialist] enterprise will be greatly developed. If we fail in this, we [the party] will collapse even if we succeed in other kinds of work."[150]

Or as then Organisation Department head Song Ping put it, a prevailing concern of the CCP was who would take up leadership positions in various levels of party and government 10 or 20 years later. "People who are in their 30s and 40s will occupy senior positions in the party and government 10 to 20 years later," Song said. "Some of them may even enter leadership positions at the very top. If we do not seize the opportunity to propagate a corps of officials who are really loyal to Marxism, it is difficult to predict what will happen a certain number of years later."[151]

Beginning in 1991, the Organisation Department started compiling lists of "potential leaders" aged between 30 to 40 for special grooming. Each province was asked to select 200 to 300 cadres who already occupied senior slots at the county level; and each government ministry was asked to pick 100 to 200 officials who were at present chiefs of bureaux or departments.

"For the next eight to 10 years, we must nurture, train and test them in a planned and methodical manner," Song said. In their search for "tried-and-true" Marxists, of course, the CCP was automatically disqualifying a large number of competent and talented people. "Red" and "trustworthy" candidates in the eyes of Chen or Song meant, above all, officials in the mould of "proletarian martyr" Lei Feng, who obeyed party edicts unquestioningly.[152]

The emphasis on "redness" was heightened after the failed Soviet coup in Moscow. In an article in the *People's Daily* in September 1991, former vice-chief of the Organisation Department Chen Yeping recycled a 1940 slogan of Chen Yun: "Cadres should both have ability and morality, but morality is the main consideration." "Morality" meant, of course, knowledge of Marxism-Leninism and total devotion to the party. Chen Yeping also criticised Zhao Ziyang for having promoted "capable but morally suspect" officials, saying the latter would lead China down the capitalist road. And in an internal talk soon after the Soviet coup in August, Chen Yun said the party must be careful to throw out "Yeltsin-like figures". "China must draw the lesson from the Soviet Union and stress political principles and ideological purity when we promote cadres," he said.[153]

In view of the large number of university students and college-educated officials who took part in the 1989 protests, both the CCP and the army decided soon after June 4 to recruit more workers and farmers as cadres or officials. In internal speeches, Song Ping affirmed the practice of inducting "superior workers and peasants" into the upper echelons. In their search for undiluted "redness", Song and his fellow headhunters were at least conniving at a host of abuses. As discussed earlier, many party elders were taking advantage of the criterion of the "revolutionary bloodline" to elevate their offspring to top positions.

The second abuse concerned "rejuvenation". Because of their certified "trustworthiness", veterans way past the mandatory retirement age of 65 were allowed to stay on. Song Ping tried his level best to defend this phenomenon by saying that the party's decision to retain a number of old cadres "does not mean a change in the retirement system". "For the time being, some areas and departments have faced difficulty in finding the appropriate successors," he said. "Individual leading cadres can stay on the job for a period of time [after normal retirement age]."[154]

More moderate cadres also raised doubts about the "redness" criterion. In mid-1991, the official *Organisation and Personnel Newspaper* interviewed a "responsible cadre" in the State Council on the criteria for the appraisal of officials' performance. "We examine in the main their performance on the job," he said. "We will promote cadres who have both ability and morals — those who uphold the Four Cardinal Principles and who at the same time can do their job well and whose *zhengji* is outstanding." When pressed on whether "ability" or "morals" was the more important, the "responsible cadre" said: "When we test cadres, we should mainly appraise his *zhengji*. This includes whether he can improve the economy [of the locality under his jurisdiction], and whether the standard of living of the people has improved."[155]

Politburo member Li Ruihuan openly opposed the return to Maoist norms. In a talk in early 1991, Li outlined his own ten rules for picking the new generation of leaders. "People should be judged on concrete achievements," he said. "Cadres who are enterprising should be promoted, and those who are only interested in building networks of relationships should be demoted." Other criteria Li cited included knowledge, intelligence, ability and most importantly, the willingness to hold democratic consultation and to accept different views. And while Li said he preferred "upright people with high moral qualities and high awareness in their thoughts", he made no reference to "revolutionary ideals".[156]

B. Rustication and Rotation of Cadres

To whip its labyrinthine system of cadres into line, the CCP adopted two Maoist institutions: rustication and rotation. In the name of carrying out the "mass line", cadres, especially new college graduates, were asked to spend several months to a year in the villages. In the two years after June 4, around one million cadres were dispatched to grassroots units to learn from the masses. They took part in physical labour and do Maoist-style "investigation and research" work in an attempt to "solve problems on the spot".[157] Very often, however, rustication became a means for the commissars to punish cadres with bourgeois-liberal tendencies.

The rotation of cadres was practised by Mao even before 1949. The major purpose was to prevent the growth of regionalism, warlordism, or what the Chairman called "mountain strongholds". If a cadre's tenure in a city or county was limited to two to three years, it would be difficult for him to build up strong local networks with which to challenge central authority.

In the period from late 1989 to mid-1990, nearly 100 cadres of the rank of vice-minister, vice-governor or above were shifted from province to province.[158] Rotation also took place in the military regions and districts in the middle of 1990 (see Chapter 4). By late 1990, the party and government leaderships of all provinces, autonomous regions and major open cities had been reshuffled. And with just a few exceptions, notably Guangdong, the newcomers were not native sons but officials transferred from other provinces.

The theory of rotation was most dramatically illustrated in July 1990, when the governors of three major provinces changed places. Thus Li Zhangchun from industrial Liaoning in the northeast went to central, agricultural Henan. Henan's Zheng Weigao moved to Hebei, whose governor Yue Zhifeng was posted to Liaoning.[159]

In a meeting in Shijiazhuang to bid farewell to Yue Zhifeng and to welcome Zheng Weigao, Politburo member Song Ping heaped praise on the system of rotation. "Transfers of cadres enable them to be trained and tested within wider parameters, to expand their vistas, and to boost their ability and experience," Song said. "This is a good way to facilitate the maturity of cadres." Aside from territorial rotation, Song said cadres would also be transferred to jobs of a different nature.[160]

The then Politburo member, however, also hinted at political motives behind rotation. "Transfers of cadres enable them boldly and unreservedly to do their jobs in a new environment," Song said. "After a cadre has spent a long time in a certain location, he may have become very familiar with the local situation. However, he may also become less curious about new things. And he may succumb to bureaucratism and subjectivism. At the same time, it will be difficult for him to avoid being entangled by complex human relationships." By "complex human relationships", Song actually meant the phenomenon of "mountain strongholds": a local cadre becoming a warlord. The rotation of cadres thus became a major means for Beijing to take back power from the regions.

Beijing, however, was apparently unsuccessful in implementing the rotation credo in two areas, Guangdong and Shanghai. In April 1991, the central authorities managed to "transfer" a most important "warlord", Guangdong governor Ye Xuanping, to the capital to fill the post of Vice-Chairman of the CPPCC. However, as discussed earlier, Ye managed to spend most of his time in Guangdong, where he was seen as a Deng Xiaoping-like figure.

And contrary to the "rotation rule", Ye's successor in Guangzhou was Zhu Senlin, the former party secretary of the provincial capital. Likewise, in mid-1991, the cadres who succeeded Zhu Rongji — another potent "warlord" — as party boss and mayor of Shanghai were also "native sons". Mayor Huang Ju had spent most of his career in Shanghai. And while new Party Secretary Wu Bangguo was not a Shanghai native, he had worked in the metropolis since the early 1960s.[161]

C. The Cadre System, 1993-1994

With the advancement of the "socialist market economy" in 1993 and 1994, the party seemed to be putting more store by performance and *zhengji* as against Marxist orthodoxy. However, it is also apparent that "political rectitude" still figured prominently, and that the cadre system was far from depoliticised.

In a speech in early 1993, Jiang Zemin still stuck to the old tune about the need for cadres being groomed for top positions to be "well-endowed in both morality and ability." "Politically, they [up-and-coming cadres] must be real Communists," Jiang said. "They must resolutely uphold the party's basic principles, and have a firm belief in socialism and Communism." The President then mentioned other qualifications such as knowledge, professional ability and leadership.[162]

And in the wake of a series of squabbles between the Party Centre and local cadres, the Organisation Department began to put more emphasis on the fact that the new generation of leaders must toe the Beijing line. "We must further raise the consciousness of various leadership corps in the principle of democratic centralism," said Vice-Chief of Organisation Zhang Quanqing in early 1994. He called upon the cadres undergoing training to "handle well the relationship between localities and the centre", and in particular, to "safeguard the authority of the centre".[163]

Even more than before, the Central Party School (CPS) played a key role in ensuring the ideological correctness of cadres. Frequency of the Organisation Department sending promising cadres to be trained in the CPS increased. At a 1993 conference of the national party school systems, the new CPS Principal Hu Jintao pointed out "the need to deepen the reform of party-school education so as to raise it to a new height". "In this vital period of historical development, the ideological construction of the party should be put high on the agenda," he said.[164]

In 1993, the party Central Committee formed a Leading Group on the Work of New Cadres, a kind of co-ordinating agent for the propagation of new leaders. Head and Vice-Head of the Group were Jiang Zemin and Hu Jintao. Government ministries and commissions as well as provincial administrations were asked to pick 20 to 50 young cadres with potential for special training at the CPS for future promotion. Foremost among the qualifications the Group was looking for was: "loyalty to the enterprise of the party and socialism". Moreover, cadres who were active during the Cultural Revolution or the June 4 pro-democracy crusade would be disqualified.[165]

At the same time, the organisation department in each province devised its own programme for propagating local talent. In Guangdong, for example, there was by early 1994 a "reserve corps" of more than 400 officials ready to assume leadership positions at county level or above. In the early 1990s, seven rising stars groomed by the Guangdong Organisation Department were elevated to top party and government positions in the province — while 340-odd cadres with potential made it into the leadership corps of municipal and department-level units. While the Guangdong Organisation Department put a lot of store by the economic performance of cadres, its way of picking leaders could hardly be called democratic.[166]

Late 1993 and early 1994 was another high season for the rotation of cadres with new leaders installed in more than half the provinces and autonomous regions (see Chapter 6). A major reason for the shift was to ensure loyalty particularly in the face of unprecedented opposition posed by local leaders towards Zhu Rongji's austerity programme in the latter half of 1993. By mid-1994, however, it had become apparent that the "rotation card" was losing its lustre. The atrophy of central authority had become irrevocable. And for their own survival and prosperity, whoever might be posted by the Organisation Department to the provinces would after a brief period be "brainwashed" by local customs and ways of doing business.[167]

VII. Streamlining the Civil Service

Li Peng and other top cadres repeatedly cited "administrative reform" in the governmental system as a major if not the most important facet of "political reform" after Tiananmen Square. And judging by the accounts of officials and the media, it seemed some action was taken from 1989 to 1994 in areas such as curtailing the scale of government, cutting down the establishment and, most importantly, the construction of a Western-style civil service.

Such apparent progress, however, has to be seen in this perspective: the modernisation of the civil service, especially the trimming of bureaucratic fat, proceeded in fits and starts. And if, by 1993 and 1994, the ranks of the civil service were indeed cut, it was due to a large number of officials going into business as much as the success of the central government in promoting administrative efficiency.

Moreover, how modern or "Western-style" China's civil service could become has also been cast into doubt given the discussion above on the archaic cadre system of the CCP. The fact of the matter is that, at the higher levels, there is a large degree of overlap between the cadre system and the civil service. Up to the end of 1994, Beijing only committed itself to overhauling the civil service — meaning officials and other staff in the governmental set-up. Much more ambiguous was the pledge to streamline the personnel establishment of the party. However, practically all senior officials in the government were also cadres. And the majority of the cadres that the Central Party School was grooming would serve as administrative officers in the government.

Civil service reform first began in 1990 through pilot schemes in individual cities under the guidance of the State Council Secretary-General Luo Gan, a protégé of Li Peng. At least until the spring of 1993, however, the administrative reform seemed restricted to local-level governments. Nationally, the bureaucracy, especially those branches that were considered tools of the dictatorship of the proletariat, was spared the slim-down campaign.

A. The Bloated Bureaucracy

A natural consequence of boosting party authority and recentralisation was bigger government. While every Chinese leader from Deng Xiaoping onwards had talked about trimming bureaucratic fat, the goal became more and more illusory. A survey in late 1990 of 1,200 urban residents showed that they cited "streamlining of governmental structure" as the question that needed to be solved most urgently. In 1990, the staff of party and government offices was a startling 500,000 over its approved establishment. In 1978, there were about 4.1 million cadres and workers in governmental offices under the State Council. The figure jumped to 9 million in 1991. Every year, the ranks of cadre-level staff swelled by 1.1 million, while only 400,000 departed.[168]

Beginning in the late 1980s, the number of governmental units increased by 9,000 a year. For example, there were 16,000 units under provincial-level administrations in 1985. The figure skyrocketed to 26,000 in 1989. In that year, the number of relatively senior cadres at departmental level in provincial administrations was 6 per cent over that of 1986 — and the corresponding percentage was 26.4 per cent for bureau-level cadres. NCNA reported in early 1992 that the country's 2,181 counties were saddled with 1.94 million cadres, or 230,000 more than the permitted establishment. And there were 598,000 superfluous cadre-level staff in regional party and governmental set-ups.[169]

The fastest growth was registered in the area of professional party functionaries, especially commissars and other ideological police. After all, a key goal of the unprecedented rural socialist education campaign was to rebuild or consolidate party cells and other organisations in the nation's nearly 1 million villages.

On the governmental level, the establishment for the police and other security branches, including the courts and procuratorates, also witnessed quantum jumps. Judging by official statistics alone, the size of the police force had by late 1991 doubled to 800,000 from the late 1980s (see previous sections). Security staff in provinces that had experienced racial strife, including Tibet, Xinjiang and Inner Mongolia, mushroomed at an alarming rate.

In spite of the dire warnings about the nation's dwindling forests, the propaganda industry was on a bull run. Party and government units took on thousand upon thousand of professional propagandists to churn out reams of material on matters ranging from "countering peaceful evolution" to human rights with Chinese characteristics. In 1990, the party Central Committee added an Overseas Propaganda Office to try to project a new-look image abroad. And the State Council set up a press office to exercise spin control over China reporting by the foreign media. The Hong Kong press reported that the party authorities had even established an Office to Track Down Rumours.[170]

In the summer of 1991, police in the capital employed extra hands to chase down wearers of T-shirts which carried such apparently innocuous messages as "I'm bored" and "Leave me alone". A few months later, the campuses took on extra security guards to stop students from openly displaying their affection for the opposite sex, by kissing or holding hands. Even the official China News Service admitted that many of the new offices being set up bordered on the absurd. It noted in a dispatch that "ad hoc offices" had sprung up dealing with killing rats, beating dogs, saving electricity and water. "As a result, the bosses are everywhere. A document, important or not, has to go through numerous officials at various levels for a chop."[171]

Half the budget deficit in 1990 was due to administrative costs. The budget for this area in 1991 was 31.7 billion yuan, or 25 billion yuan more than ten years ago. Chinese sources said that starting in 1990, administrations in many poor counties had had difficulty paying their staff, with the result that cadres in these places often eked out a living as "consultants" to private businesses.[172]

B. Half-Hearted Trimming: The "Small Government" Campaign of 1992

In early 1992, the Chinese media announced that Premier Li had waged a campaign for "small government" to trim the deadwood in local-level administrations. On a trip to Shandong Province in late 1991, Li coined the slogan "small government, big service". He pointed out that economic and technological departments should be "separated" from county- and village-level governments, and that the former should "gradually metamorphose into economic entities". "They should become financially self-sufficient and eventually be transformed into enterprises," Li said.[173]

The NCNA dispatch reporting Li's instructions also disclosed that not only governmental but party organs would be turned into quasi-business units. The latter would be "severed from the CCP and [various levels of] governments as well as [public] funds, and depend on themselves for subsistence". The news agency disclosed that as early as 1989, nine counties in eight provinces had been picked as pilot zones for the "small government" experiment. Since then, 30 provinces and directly administered cities had selected more counties and districts for the conversion of party and governmental units into enterprise-like entities.

Zhuozi County in Inner Mongolia was cited as the national paragon for this streamlining exercise. After the "reforms", the county-level party structure consisted of no more than a general office, an organisation department, a propaganda department, and a "party work committee". And the slim-look county government was made up of barely a general office, an economic and administrative bureau, a finance and tax bureau, a social affairs bureau, the police, and a legal affairs bureau. All told, 30-odd party and government units in Zhuozi were slashed. The number of cadres and other civil servants was cut from more than 700 to 300, making possible savings of 3 million yuan a year.[174]

It is not surprising, however, that the leadership failed to announce commensurate "small government" campaigns at the national — or even the provincial — level. In 1991, then vice-minister of personnel Zhang Zhijiang said explicitly that the battle against over-staffing would only be waged at the local, not national level. Zhang, who was also Director of the Office of the Commission on the Personnel Establishment of State Departments — which, ironically, was also an addition to the bureaucracy — said the streamlining of the central government offices had been "completed" in 1990, and that in 1991 and beyond, similar exercises would only be tried out at local units "to facilitate convergence of work between upper and lower levels".[175]

The only step that had been taken on the national scale seemed to be a moratorium on the establishment of new, non-party or non-governmental organs. Thus in August 1991, the party Central Committee and State Council issued an internal document freezing the number of academic and research organisations, foundations, and social organisations that were "unofficial" in name but actually dependent on government subvention.

At the provincial level, Guangdong seemed to be the only province that had adopted concrete measures in this arena. In mid-1991, Guangzhou announced a four-pronged attack against the bloated bureaucracy. Firstly, units that had superfluous staff had to start trimming them at the rate of 30 to 35 per cent a year. Secondly, budgets had to be strictly enforced to stop overspending. Thirdly, subventions for things ranging from conferences to the private telephone sets for cadres would be slashed. Lastly, units that had realised savings could earmark 50 to 80 per cent of the money saved for collective welfare.[176]

C. "Major" Administrative Streamlining in 1993

Perhaps the most radical steps towards administrative streamlining took place at and after the NPC in the spring of 1993. The fairly deep surgery was taken in tandem with efforts to change the functions of government. Most government and party units that were affected, however, were involved in economic services. No shrinking of staff establishment took place in departments dealing with ideology, politics, or security.

Different officials and departments gave disparate figures on the exact percentage of staff to be cut. Then minister of personnel Zhao Dongwan said during the NPC of 1993 that 25 per cent of the 9.2 million staff serving party and government units would be trimmed over three years. "This administrative reform involves not only government units but departments directly under the CCP," Zhao said. "Various departments in the provincial, municipal, county and village administrations will also be affected."[177]

It was announced in mid-1993 that provinces and municipalities would be asked to follow the example of the central government. Provinces and directly administered cities would be required to limit the number of departments to 55 and 75 respectively — and to shrink their staff establishment by 20 per cent and 15 per cent respectively. Administrations directly reporting to Beijing would be asked to cut their staff by 30 per cent. It is interesting, however, that the establishment of security and finance departments at the regional level would be looked after by personnel units at the central-government level. Again, Shandong seemed to have acquitted itself best in the slimming exercise. In 1993, some 6,801 units within the province were closed and 56,000 personnel struck off the government payroll. Most of these found jobs in the market place, enabling the province to save 120 million yuan a year in salaries.[178]

Within the State Council itself, which had about 50,000 officials, 20 per cent would be laid off within the year. The number of central government organisations, administrative offices and ad hoc units was slashed from 171 to 85. However, the number of cabinet-level ministries and commissions was cut from 42 to just 41. Secretary-General Luo Gan said superfluous staff would be encouraged to find work in business or to shift to the fast-expanding government sectors such as tax and legal administration. In an internal talk, Jiang Zemin, who gave the number of party and government staff at more than 30 million, said that those made redundant should be encouraged to go into the services sector.[179]

Much of the trimming was accomplished through simply loping off redundant staff. For example, personnel at the Ministry of Coal Industries was cut from 1,200-odd to around 300. Staff in the Ministry of Machine-Building Industry (which was hived off from the Ministry of Machine-Building and Electronics Industry), was slashed from 869 to 340.[180]

However, the bulk of the streamlining was made possible by the conversion of government ministries, departments or units into economic entities such as corporations and trade associations. For example, the Ministry of Aeronautics and Astronautics became the Aeronautical Industries Corp and the Astronautical Industries Corp. The Ministry of Light Industry and the Ministry of Textile Industry (MTI) metamorphosed into respectively, the General Association of Chinese Light Industry and the General Association of Chinese Textile Industry (GACTI). GACTI had around 200 staff, against the 580 in the original MTI.[181]

Analysts said the administrative reform had not been too far-reaching because of opposition from vested interests. The former minister of textile industry Wu Wenying confessed to experiencing "a sense of loss" about the conversion of her ministry into the GACTI. Wu, however, was "compensated" with the presidency of the new association. A lot of cadres who lacked the skills to go into business saw their iron rice bowls being smashed. The Hong Kong-based *Wen Wei Po* quoted a number of MTI staff as saying they "could not accept the change emotionally", and that they worried about whether they could continue to enjoy subsidies such as medical funds. According to the CNS, personnel in the Ministry of Coal Industries were asked to fill in a form indicating whether they would like to stay on as cadres or to be transferred to non-governmental entities. Most preferred the former, and apparently safer, option.[182]

Moreover, some departments would likely swell through the rest of the 1990s. Aside from the security units, the new State Economic and Trade Commission saw a rapid increase in its staff establishment in 1993. The financial departments, especially the banks and tax units, would experience a large increase in personnel. There were 500,000 tax collectors in the beginning of

1993, and their ranks were projected to grow by 10,000 to 15,000 every year.[183]

More important, there were doubts among both Chinese cadres and analysts as to whether the newly-formed economic corporations had really severed their links with government. Wu Wenying admitted that the GACTI would continue to assume "some government functions". In many instances, even after a certain government department had taken on the name of a corporation, its functions, powers and personnel remained unchanged. The Chinese called these *fanpai* ("turning the plaque over") concerns. Not only did this practice make a mockery of the streamlining exercise, it also discouraged fair competition and spawned corruption. The new economic entities made use of their old connections to procure scarce resources or to corner the market.[184]

In a hard-hitting speech in March 1993, Zhu Rongji said the phenomenon of *fanpai* companies meant "using power to do business". In a commentary, the *Economic Daily* said that the phenomenon of *fanpai* companies was a "retrogression, not reform because this runs counter to the construction of the socialist market economy".[185]

D. A Civil Service with Chinese Characteristics

In August 1993, Beijing announced temporary regulations for setting up a civil service within three years. The new Personnel Minister Song Defu, the reformist-oriented former head of the Communist Youth League, said the new system would provide a more logical management structure based on job classification; promote clean government; facilitate checks and balances; and be based on a sound legal system.[186]

Clear-cut criteria were set forth regarding recruitment by open examination, the classification of grades, grounds for promotion and demotion, as well as the rights and duties of government employees. The salaries of cadres ranging up to the premier (1,200 yuan a month) were laid out. The differential between the highest- and lowest-paid civil servants would be 6.1 to 1. Western analysts said that while the propaganda machinery would like to persuade the public — and international opinion — that a "Western-style civil service" was being set up, the new structure also had distinct Chinese characteristics.[187]

"Building a civil service system is a major item in the reform of the political structure," said Li Peng in a September 1993 conference. "The Chinese civil service system has succeeded and developed the superior tradition of the cadre system which has been formed over many years. It has at the same time absorbed certain reasonable aspects of the civil service system of some developed countries." [188]

While the CCP was not mentioned even once in the temporary regulations, there could be no denying the fact that the party maintained tight control over the civil service. For example, the temporary rules stated that "the promotion of state civil servants should be based on the principle of the dual qualifications of morality and competence as well as the elevation of the capable". Clearly "morality" was a reference to Marxist precepts as well as loyalty to the CCP. Moreover, there were draconian clauses forbidding civil servants from "spreading opinions detrimental to the reputation of the government" and from "organising and taking part in illegal activities", including "anti-government assembly and demonstrations". Nor were they allowed to organise or take part in strikes.[189] Very clearly, the principle of total CCP leadership and the dictatorship of the proletariat was very much in the mind of the drafters of the civil service codes.

In late 1993, some informed observers suggested that the party hierarchy would follow a civil service system. "The organs of the CCP Central Committee and departments within the party throughout the country should also implement the civil service system of the state," the *Wen Wei Po* quoted an "authoritative figure" as saying.[190] Aside from the classification of job titles, functions and salaries, as well as the general principles for promotion and demotion, it was difficult to see how the "organisation principles" of the CCP as outlined earlier could be reconciled with the principles of a modern civil service. For example, the Organisation Department, which controlled all senior party and government appointments, remained a secretive body accountable only to the Politburo.

VIII. Reviving the Mass Line

A. *"Popular Participation in Politics"*

While the CCP has always claimed to be the party of the people, the ideal of the "mass participation" in politics was seriously raised only once: in the heyday of reform that immediately preceded the December 1986 student movement. For example, in 1985 and 1986, avant-garde social scientists including Yan Jiaqi were bold enough to theorise about popular participation in politics. As the *Guangming Daily* put it in mid-1986: "Letting the masses participate in the running and overseeing of national affairs . . . and in criticising and supervising [the government] is the best way to develop their enthusiasm and creativity."[191]

Given the huge population of peasants and the generally low education standards of the populace, of course, "masses" essentially referred to the well-educated élite. In the now-famous conference on "soft science" held in Beijing in August 1986, then NPC chairman Wan Li said the party and government should induct into its leading councils and think-tanks a wide variety of intellectuals and experts. Wan's ideal of the "democratisation of the decision-making process" was to some extent achieved in the three years or so before the Tiananmen Square crackdown. Social scientists and other intellectuals working in such think-tanks as CASS and the Research Institute for the Reform of the Economic Structure represented a broad spectrum of political views.[192]

"Mass-line politics", however, received a body-blow with the December 1986 demonstrations. Zhao Ziyang's 13th Party Congress report represented a watered-down version of what many of his closest advisers, including Bao Tong, head of the now-defunct Political Reform Research Office of the Central Committee, had recommended. Under the section entitled "Establishing a System of Consultation and Dialogue", the 13th Congress report advocated a form of *noblesse oblige*: letting the people know what those higher up are doing. "Only when the leading bodies at all levels listen attentively to the views of the masses can they gear their work towards actual conditions and avoid mistakes," the document said. "And only when they let the people know what they are doing and what difficulties they face can they secure the people's understanding." In other words, the people only had the right to offer their opinions and to know what is going on: they had no active role to play.[193]

It took a party with a thick skin to proclaim after the Tiananmen Square killings that it was still committed to mass-line politics. However, that was what the propaganda machinery set out to do. In an apparent attempt to heal the wounds of June 4, the CCP tried to tell the people that it understood their dissatisfaction and would be prepared to hear their voice.

The revival of mass-line politics was made at the behest of Deng Xiaoping and Politburo Standing Committee member Li Ruihuan. The "new" approach saw its concrete manifestation in the Sixth Plenum of the 13th Central Committee, which ended in March 1990. The plenum endorsed a resolution entitled "Strengthening the Ties Between the Party and the People". Reaffirming a cardinal principle of Chairman Mao, the Central Committee vowed to "tighten the ties between the party and the masses" by "asking party organisations at all levels to pay special attention to the solution of the problems with which the masses are most concerned". Cadres of all levels were asked to "go to the masses", and the latter would be given a chance at "real, earnest supervision over leading party organisations and leading cadres".[194]

Rekindling the ideal first raised by Zhao Ziyang and Wan Li, the Plenum Resolution vowed to "establish and perfect a democratic and scientific process of policy-making and implementation, so as to ensure that they are in line with the interests of the people". The Central Committee also appeared to breathe new life into political change by re-committing the party to "deepening the reform of the political structure" and "making vigorous efforts to broaden the party's channels of ties with the people". As the *People's Daily* put it in an editorial soon afterwards: "The people and the masses are the fountainhead of the party's strength. The fundamental goal of the party is to serve the people".[195]

Analysts said the plenum was impressive to the extent that the resolution made no reference to leftist stockphrases like "class struggle" or "weeding out bourgeois liberalisation". However, the plenum document merely upheld the *noblesse oblige* approach to the mass line: the CCP was asking the people to trust that it would do good for them, but not letting them participate.

By mid-1994, however, there was no indication that the party was ready to let the people "supervise" various levels of government. The most that various levels of authorities had done was superficial. The best example was perhaps setting up "hot lines" to mayors. By 1994, more than half of all large- and medium-scale cities had established them. In Taiyuan, capital of Shanxi, for example, the enquiry service helped treat more than 70,000 problems raised by citizens in the five years ending 1993.[196] Other cities also ran consumer complaints services. In early 1993, the quasi-private Dongfang Radio and Dongfang TV in Shanghai caused a stir when they hosted programmes where municipal leaders answered questions on the spot. These, however, did not amount to political participation.

Post-Tiananmen Square mass-line politics was also illustrated by the "populist style" of politicians including Jiang Zemin. The media were full of stories about how Jiang was "close to the people". At the Lunar New Year of 1990, for example, the party chief visited coal mine workers in Shanxi Province. Donning a safety helmet, Jiang went down a 160-metre pit and shook the blackened hands of the miners. "If cadres of various levels always maintain a flesh-and-blood relationship with the masses, we [the party] will be on impregnable ground," he said. The President also liked to match his skills with athletes before the Asian Games and the Olympics. On his return flight from a visit to the United States and Europe in late 1993, the self-styled statesman sang karaoke with flight attendants.[197]

B. "Doing Concrete Things for the People"

Liberal cadres like Li Ruihuan used the ideal of mass line politics to beat back the challenge of the left wing. For Li, the mass line meant "doing concrete things" for the people, especially promoting economic gains, rather than persuading people to become another Lei Feng-like "screw of the revolution".

This attitude was reflected in the *People's Daily* editorial in August 1990, in which the party paper called for more emphasis on the promotion of the livelihood of the people, saying it was a major component of political and ideological work. "Any political party that fails to bring practical gains to the masses will fail to get the support of the people," it said. "Under the premise of not violating state policies, we must think of ways to do good and concrete things for the people." The party organ also cited Deng's dictum that "leadership means service". It stressed that providing concrete service to the masses "goes hand in hand with political and ideological work". "It can be said that showing concern for the livelihood of the people is an inalienable part of ideological and political work," the *Daily* added.[198]

Li's philosophy was elegantly expressed in the book *On Doing Concrete Things For The People*, which, characteristically, was published in his power base, Tianjin, and not by a national-level publishing house in the capital. "The intimate relationship with the masses is one of the most important markers that distinguishes our party from other parties," Li, a former Tianjin mayor, wrote. Perhaps better than most of his Politburo colleagues, Li, then in charge of ideology and propaganda, was able to cite most of the social ills tormenting the people: corruption, crime, bureaucracy, and the "unfair distribution of income". He particularly warned about possible disorder because of "the increase in the number of enterprises that have ceased production or that are just producing at half capacity". "We must not take lightly all the destabilising factors that really exist," Li warned.[199]

By early 1993, Li was to some degree sidelined when he was transferred to the CPPCC. Yet his "prophecy" proved right to the extent that as more radical reforms were introduced in the year, social tensions — particularly lay-offs of workers coupled with hyperinflation — were exacerbated. By late 1993 and early 1994, the party was forced, at least on a temporary basis, to fine-tune or slow down a number of reforms in order to defuse the "destabilising factors".

As we shall see in Chapter 7, the major reason why the CCP did not dare to push through the radical reforms in the face of social disruption was its declining legitimacy and its utter refusal to share power with other social sectors. However, the excuse that the leadership gave in late 1993 and early 1994 for soft-pedalling on the reforms was its "concern for the people".

In a speech to a conference on grain, cotton and oil in early 1994, Premier Li played the "people's card" when he explained why price control still had to be imposed on these staples — and why old-style production targets for these basic foodstuffs must still be slapped on farmers. "The goal of the people's government are to serve the people with all their hearts and minds," Li said. "We must at all times show our concern for the personal interests of the masses." As an example, Li pointed to the "vegetable basket operation", in which the head of every city and county was personally held responsible that his charges could get abundant, relatively cheap food. [200]

In a similar vein, Jiang Zemin told workers while touring Shanxi Province in January 1994 that Beijing was "sympathetic" towards state enterprises that were in financial difficulties. He implied that the state would be cautious in allowing the units to lay off workers, saying: "The government will stay in the same boat with the broad masses of the workers of state enterprises." Li, Jiang and Vice-Premier Zhu Rongji reiterated that individual reforms for 1994 would only be waged "bearing in mind the ability of the state, enterprises and the people to cushion their shocks".[201]

In a commentary on the relation between reform and stability, CNS said: "How high a price that citizens — who are society's active agents — are willing to pay for reform has become a major issue."[202] None of the senior officials, however, was willing to address the question of letting these "active agents" play a bigger role in the formulation of policies. Analysts suspected that the "mass line card" was being brandished by Jiang and Li for political and factional reasons — to justify a certain pace and direction of reform and development — more than out of a genuine concern for the people's livelihood or grievances. Such a card was also handy for justifying the party's refusal to embrace changes.

IX. "Multi-party Co-operation" and the Role of the CPPCC

A. Real Power Sharing?

In 1990 and 1991, the party took some steps towards its avowed goal of promoting "mass participation in politics" by upgrading the status of the eight "democratic parties" and that of well-known non-communist politicians. These efforts had added significance because since late 1989, the institution of one-party dictatorship had begun to crumble, in Eastern Europe and then in the former USSR.

In internal speeches on countering "peaceful evolution", Deng Xiaoping reiterated that China would never adopt multi-party politics. However, to pacify foreign critics and conciliate with potential enemies at home, the CCP went through the motions of raising the stature of the non-CCP parties. This saw its most concrete manifestation in the document "On Upholding and Perfecting the System of Multi-party Co-operation and Political Consultation under CCP Leadership", which was published on February 7, 1990. The document, drafted under the supervision of Jiang Zemin, bore the personal imprint of Deng Xiaoping. It said that the eight democratic parties might be allowed to "take part in politics" and that the CCP would "explain" its policies to them at regular intervals.[203]

Unfortunately, aside from vague promises of elevating non-communist politicians and experts to high government positions, the document — and subsequent statements by leaders — did not indicate just how the democratic-party leaders might "take part" in politics. This is in spite of the boast by the *People's Daily* that the system of multi-party co-operation was a "characteristic and superior point" of the Chinese socialist system, a "creation born out of the synthesis of Marxism-Leninism and the Chinese revolution and socialist construction".[204]

For example, the document said that a certain proportion of the positions of the NPC and its Standing Committee — as well as local-level people's congresses — should be "set aside" for members of the eight parties. And when the State Council or local governments held plenary sessions and other meetings to discuss policy, they could, according to the needs and circumstances, invite non-CCP personages to sit in. But as we shall see, by early 1994 no non-communists had been put in a position of real power.

More importantly, there was never any doubt that it was the CCP which would call the shots. "The CCP is the leading core of the socialist enterprise and the ruling party," the early 1990 document made clear. "The democratic parties accept the leadership of the CCP and work closely with it at socialist projects." "The political foundation of co-operation between the CCP and the democratic parties is insistence on CCP leadership and the Four Cardinal Principles," the document added. "The basic principle of their co-operation is 'long-term co-existence, mutual supervision, be frank and forthright, and the sharing of honour as well as misfortune'."

That the "new" initiative did not augur well for real political reform was evident during a meeting on united front work held in June 1990. At the conclave, Jiang Zemin stated in no uncertain terms that the CCP's on-going efforts to "unite" different parties, sectors, and groups was not to further democracy as such but to preserve political stability and frustrate efforts by "hostile domestic and foreign" forces to subvert CCP rule.

"To develop the patriotic united front, we must pay attention to expanding and boosting unity," Jiang said. "We must unite whoever can be united. We will unite no matter what class, sector, party, grouping or individual provided that it is advantageous towards national unity, social progress and the happiness of the people — and if it is advantageous towards frustrating efforts by domestic and foreign forces to infiltrate and subvert [the socialist system] and to promote peaceful evolution."[205]

In fact, the role of the non-communist forces had already been spelt out by Deng Xiaoping soon after the fall of the Ceausescu regime in Romania. In an informal gathering with party elders and Politburo members in December 1989, Deng said: "The democratic parties should be turned from flower-vase parties into ones that take part in politics. The CCP should boost the relationship of friendly co-operation with the parties."

However, Deng went on to say that the flower-vase or "decorative" entities should never become opposition parties. "We [the CCP] will never allow democratic parties to become opposition parties," he said. "The ban on [opposition] parties should be maintained." The patriarch also held forth on reasons behind the fall of communism in Eastern Europe. "Why has the situation in Eastern Europe changed so rapidly?" he asked. "It happened first of all in Poland. As a result of the spread of the Solidarity Movement, a viable force of opposition took root. This quickly led to the loss of power of the Polish Communist Party. We must draw a lesson from the Polish experience. We should absolutely not allow an opposition party to take shape in China."[206]

B. Flower-Vase Politicians in Action

On the occasion of the 70th birthday of the CCP on July 1, 1991, Professor Fei Xiaotong heaped high praise on the multi-party co-operation system. "The system suits Chinese conditions, and is full of life and vigour," he said. "It is a system anchored in the soil of China and has the support of the people." The London-trained sociologist further claimed that the multi-party system or two-party system in Western countries "would fundamentally not work in China".[207]

Aside from offering support — and occasionally providing apologia — for the CCP, have non-communist politicians actually served any useful purposes? In his speech at the conference on the United Front, Jiang Zemin asked party leaders to induct qualified non-CCP elements into different levels of government. "The number of non-party people holding positions of substance has been on the decrease," he said. Since early 1990, the CCP had asked the eight parties to submit short-lists of suitable candidates for promotion to high government office.

By late 1991, the number of non-communist politicians seemed to have increased. The *White Paper on Human Rights* claimed that there were 1,200 "government leaders", including three vice-ministers, who were not CCP affiliates. Moreover, in 11 provinces and directly administered cities, including Beijing and Shanghai, there was at least one member of the democratic parties who was a vice-governor or vice-mayor.[208]

In terms of actual power wielded, however, the democratic parties remained what Deng wanted them to be: stage props and decorations. It can be argued that the non-communists had more power in the early 1950s, when there were a few full ministers who were not Communists. A notable example was the late novelist Mao Dun, who was Culture Minister. Before the June 4 crackdown, the CCP had plans to elevate 11 prominent members of democratic party members to ministerial or vice-ministerial positions. Both sociologist Fei Xiaotong, Chairman of the China Democratic League, and "red capitalist" Rong Yiren, then Chairman of the All-China Federation of Industry and Commerce, were seriously mentioned as candidates for the vice-presidency in 1989. This did not come to pass.[209]

Equally important, what critics called the political degeneration of the eight parties had become more pronounced. Every time that the CCP had announced a policy, leaders of these flower-vase entities, which were after all financed by the CCP, would go through the ritual of putting up their hands in support. This was exacerbated by the fact that quite a few of the so-called mavericks among the non-communist politicians left the country after June 4, 1989. They included economist Qian Jiaqu and painter Fan Zeng. In general, the prestige of the eight parties was at an all-time low.

Zhu Chuang, Vice-Chairman of the Chinese Association for Promoting Democracy, admitted that the eight democratic parties were faced with a dearth of talent, especially young and well-educated politicians. "Because of the rupture of almost 20 years before the end of the Cultural Revolution [in 1976], it is relatively difficult for democratic parties to find people of the right age to recommend to the CCP [for top government jobs]," Zhu said. "It requires a gradual process for non-CCP people to take part in politics. First we must let members of democratic parties become familiar with society, and let society get to know them better."[210]

C. The CPPCC & Democratic Parties under Li Ruihuan, 1993-94

Hopes in some quarters that the ethereal goals of the "mass line" and "multi-party co-operation" might grow into something more concrete were raised with the appointment of Li Ruihuan to the CPPCC in the spring of 1993. It was the first time since the consultative body's inception that a serving Politburo member had taken the chair. The status of the CPPCC chairman was also elevated when Li set out on a tour of India, Pakistan and Nepal in November 1993. It was the first time that a senior politician had gone on an official overseas trip as leader of the consultative body.[211]

Internal documents leaked to the Hong Kong press in 1993 quoted Deng's great expectations for the consultative body: "The CPPCC should have a considerable say and decision-making powers in government"; it should provide the channel for non-Chinese Communist Party politicians to play a bigger role in policy; and CPPCC of all levels should have more "independence and representativeness".[212]

In the speech marking the closure of the plenary CPPCC session, Li committed the conference to boosting "democratic supervision". "We will pursue supervision over the implementation of the constitution and the laws; over how major goals and policies are being carried out; and over how government units and staff are doing their jobs," Li said. The former Tianjin mayor vowed the CPPCC would "create a democratic and harmonious environment" so that "freedom in raising criticism [of the party and government] and freedom in expressing different opinions can be guaranteed". [213]

In a late 1993 address, Li added that the CPPCC had "an irreplaceable superiority in its role in giving opinions and suggestions to the decision-making stratum", in the process "rendering decision-making more scientific and democratic". Moreover, CPPCC members should also play a bigger role in the "democratic supervision" of the administration. He asked various party and government departments to respect the body's "rights and prerogatives in taking part and deliberating in politics".[214]

At the 1994 plenary session, the CPPCC indicated it would amend its constitution to enable the body to "fulfil its major functions in the country's political, economic and cultural life". Individual members indicated to the semi-official CNS that they must have "serious and practical, not superficial, functions of democratic supervision over the government and over society". On a private basis, the younger generation among the deputies hoped the CPPCC could be converted into an "upper house of parliament" similar to the House of Lords in England.[215]

To a degree, the CPPCC after Li Ruihuan had had its status upgraded. Of its Standing Committee, 65.6 per cent were either non-communist members or affiliates of the eight so-called democratic parties. For the first time in the body's history, a special "economic sector" was added to reserve seats for 100-odd economists, state- and private-sector entrepreneurs.

In 1993 and 1994, the status of non-communist politicians seemed to have risen. "Patriotic capitalist" Rong Yiren finally made the state vice presidency. In an interview in early 1994, he claimed he was "often consulted" on weighty matters of state by Jiang Zemin. For the first time, two non-communist officials were given senior positions in the Supreme People's Court and the Supreme People's Procuratorate. Various regional administrations also set aside senior positions for non-communist politicians. For example, within the Beijing municipality, up to 20 such figures were slated for posts at the bureau-level or above in 1994. [216]

At least on the surface, political participation by non-CCP personages seemed to have increased. For the first time, they were allowed to join high-level overseas delegations. The pro-Chinese Hong Kong daily *Wen Wei Po* quoted "authoritative sources" in Beijing as saying the "top echelon" thought participation by non-party politicians in diplomatic activities would "have tremendous meaning in political democracy".[217] In November 1993, eyebrows were raised when Professor Ding Shisun, a liberal non-communist politician, formed part of Li Ruihuan's entourage to South Asia. At the onset of the anti-corruption campaign in August the same year, members of the democratic parties were inducted into "investigation teams" dispatched by Beijing to a dozen-odd provinces to check on graft and other economic malfeasance.

Various municipal governments also formed senior think-tanks to fulfil Li Ruihuan's ideal of "making decision-making scientific and democratic". In December 1993, the liberal mayor of Guangzhou Li Ziliu set up a group of 20-odd consultants — mostly professionals and academics — to advise him on governmental affairs. Earlier in the year, Shanghai appointed a 43-member brains trust for the local government. Chairman Lee seemed particularly anxious to boost the political status of entrepreneurs. In late 1993, one of the eight democratic parties, the All-China Federation of Industry and Commerce (ACFIC), which used to be headed by Rong Yiren, was turned into a "non-official chamber of commerce". In early 1994, Li asked the ACFIC to air their views on "new economic questions", particularly the expanding role of the private sector (see Chapter 6).[218]

The problem with this series of gingerly-paced political reforms, however, was that it smacked too much of CCP patronage — and *noblesse oblige*. Rong Yiren being the Vice-President (after all, an honorary position) notwithstanding, no non-communist had been appointed to a substantial position by mid-1994. Latest statistics showed that 16 such figures occupied senior positions, such as vice-minister, in ministries and commissions in the State Council. Yet none was a fully-fledged minister.[219]

Participation by non-communist figures in the investigation of corruption had not changed the overall picture of "the flies, not the tigers [among the graft-takers] being hit". There had not been a single instance of the CCP changing a major policy because of the dissenting views of CPPCC affiliates. An example that was well documented in Hong Kong concerned efforts by Xu Simin, who had become a member of the Standing Committee in 1993, to lobby for a more open government. In late 1991, Xu said he and a group of NPC deputies had proposed a limited amnesty for June 4-related dissidents to be announced at the NPC session in 1992. The Hong Kong deputy, who published the influential *Mirror* monthly, claimed that he had the support of NPC Chairman Wan Li and other liberal leaders. However, Beijing had by early 1992 indicated that an amnesty was out of the question.[220]

The lack of concrete achievement of the CPPCC has fed widespread cynicism that it is mere window dressing for democracy. This view was indirectly confirmed by the opinion of the head of the Shenzhen's CPPCC, Zhou Ciwu.

For Zhou, "supervision [by the CPPCC] does not mean singing rival tunes but channelling people's opinion." The Shenzhen leader's concept of the CPPCC was merely a "talent bank" — a group of advisers to the party and government whose brief did not include challenging major policies. Indeed, in a dispatch in early 1994, the English-language service of the NCNA described the CPPCC as a think-tank.[221]

Even such a liberal and outspoken leader as the First Vice Chairman of the CPPCC, Ye Xuanping, was careful to point out the limits to the work of his body. In a mid-1993 speech, Ye talked about "letting a lot of people speak out" and ensuring that "they can say whatever they like". However, he threw in caveats aplenty. "We [CPPCC cadres] should do our best but not go beyond our frame of reference. We should strengthen the unity of people from various sectors." In other words, any action deemed prejudicial to the overall interests of unity and stability would be scuppered.[222]

The role and work of the CPPCC were also affected by the somewhat lacklustre performance of Li Ruihuan. While a liberal, Li was not deemed as effective as NPC counterpart Qiao Shi in expanding the "supervisory" role of the consultative body. Up to mid-1994, CPPCC members and intellectuals only credited him with promoting environmental consciousness and in preserving Chinese culture and artefacts such as the Beijing opera.[223]

X. Gearing up the National People's Congress System

By 1994, China had slightly higher expectations of the National People's Congress rather than the CPPCC, not as a means to introduce "multi-party politics" but as a vehicle for promoting a modicum of competition and give-and-take among the CCP's disparate factions.

A. "A Showcase of Democracy"? — the NPC, 1989-1992

After the hailstorm of criticism in the wake of June 4, the CCP was eager to turn the NPC system into a showcase of "proletarian democracy". The people's congress system, the Chinese media insisted, was superior to the parliamentary system in the West, which ensured the perennial domination of the rich and powerful. "In the aftermath of the Opium War of the early 1840s, enlightened Chinese sought a political system which would save the nation", the *People's Daily* said in late 1990. "But they were repeatedly frustrated until Marxism showed them the way. The congress system reflects the supremacy of the people's rights and hence enables the people to run the state."[224]

In his report to the NPC of 1990, then executive vice-chairman Peng

Chong indicated in no uncertain terms that the people's congress system would not be changed even though similar parliaments or congresses in Eastern Europe had been liberalised to accommodate different political parties. Peng called for a "continued battle against bourgeois liberalisation which negates the system of the people's congresses, and for efforts to overcome erroneous views that try to weaken the congress system".[225]

Peng, a former Shanghai party chief who had the reputation of a hardliner, warned that on-going political reform should not adulterate the legislative system, which observed the party's Four Cardinal Principles. "In China's political restructuring, a clear demarcation line must be drawn between socialist democracy on the one hand and capitalist democracy, anarchism and ultra-democracy on the other," he said. "The NPC Standing Committee will insist on being guided by the basic line of the CCP." Peng pledged that the people's congress system should be boosted to enable it to express the true wishes of the people. "Efforts will be made to establish procedures and systems for the NPC to enact laws, exercise supervision, and to make major decisions, appointment and removal [of government officials]," he said.

The propagandists made much of the fact that there were "universal elections" to the NPC, and that those were *cha'er* ballotings, meaning there were more candidates than positions up for grabs. Moreover, the voter turn-out rate was more than 90 per cent. In a dispatch in early 1991, the official China News Service claimed that during elections at the time, 85 per cent of the candidates for the municipal people's congress in Beijing were nominated by ordinary citizens, and the remaining 15 per cent by parties, presumably including the "democratic parties".[226]

However, as of mid-1994, direct election was only held for members of local people's congresses, for example, those of counties or municipal districts. These local deputies then elected NPC legislators by "indirect election". In both levels of elections, the CCP exercised extremely careful control. The majority of NPC delegates consisted of two categories: senior cadres, including state leaders, ministers and provincial chieftains; and "trusted proletarians" such as model workers and farmers who would unquestioningly toe the party line.

More importantly, even before June 4, 1989, the CCP had tightened its grip over the Congress. The authorities have never released the percentage of NPC delegates who are Communist party members, even though an educated guess would put it at more than 65 per cent. Apologists for the party like to cite the fact that of the 2,970 deputies to the 7th Congress (1988 to 1993), there were 684 workers and peasants, 697 intellectuals, 733 cadres, 267 military men, and 49 overseas Chinese who had resettled in the mainland. This set of figures was supposed to demonstrate the "representative nature" of the legislature.[227]

Beginning in the mid-1980s, the CCP began forming and consolidating *dongzu*, or party organisations, to "unify the views" of those deputies who were party members. The role of "party whips" was performed by professional commissars as well as NPC leaders, most of whom were also senior party cadres. This is despite the fact that the CCP has never admitted that it is exercising tight control over NPC members.

Political sources in Beijing said after June 4, the prospects for the modernisation of the people's congress system were not bright. This can be gauged if we look at proposals put forward by bourgeois-liberal intellectuals, many of whom fled the country in late 1989. For example, former Chinese Academy of Social Sciences political scientist Yan Jiaqi suggested that NPC deputies be "fully trained professional legislators" along Western lines. Yan, now living in exile in New York, also wanted national-level deputies to be directly elected by the people.[228]

Educationist Ng Hong-man, a Hong Kong-based deputy, proposed that the number of legislators be whittled down to make scrutiny of the government possible. "If the number of deputies is slashed to around 1,000, the efficiency of the NPC will be increased," he said. Other suggestions included giving individual legislators freedom to address the full congress on whatever topics they wanted. To avoid criticisms from being aired, the authorities in recent years favoured "small group discussions" among the deputies.[229]

The growing impotence of the NPC was ably demonstrated by the failure of individual deputies to supervise — or challenge — the party and government. In May 1989, some 40 of the 135-member NPC Standing Committee put down their names in a signature campaign for the convention of a special NPC session to repeal martial law and to remove Li Peng. Several of these brave souls, including a deputy from Sichuan, veteran journalist Hu Jiwei, were subsequently expelled from the body.

At the first meeting of the NPC Standing Committee after June 4, three members proposed setting up an NPC "Supervision Structure" within the Standing Committee to monitor and assess governmental work. The deputies were Yang Lieyu, Zhang Siming and Yao Jun. Yang, a Vice-Chairman of the Chinese Peasants and Workers Democratic Party, said that according to the Constitution, the NPC had powers to interpret the charter and supervise units including the State Council, the Central Military Commission and the courts. "But in this matter of supervision, we are not sure what the Congress or its members have done," they said. The trio added that the resolutions of the NPC were often taken as "formulae", or *pro forma* statements, hinting that they were not treated seriously by the CCP.[230] The proposal by Yang and company never came into fruition.

That the CCP had exercised "censorship" over the more outspoken NPC members was evident from how the authorities had muzzled firebrand representatives from Hong Kong and Taiwan. This came to a head at the plenary session in 1991, when Hong Kong deputy and lawyer Liu Yiu-chu, made applications to address the full session on how to lay the ghost of June 4 to rest. Liu said that while she was not out to overturn the verdict, she wanted to express Hong Kong's concern and sorrow for the people who died during the tragedy. As a gesture, she wanted the chamber to observe five minutes' silence out of respect for the victims. Liu was only allowed to speak at a "small-group discussion", the conclave for fellow deputies from Hong Kong and Macau, when her suggestion was shot down.[231]

B. Case Study: The Three Gorges Project

The multi-billion Three Gorges Project became the most graphic example of how the NPC — and to an equal extent, the CPPCC — had failed to maintain "checks and balances" on the party, or to reflect the views of the nation's intellectuals and the general populace.

Objections to the mega-project had been made on a number of grounds since the 1970s. The government indicated in late 1991 that the hydro-electric scheme at the Yangtze River would cost 57 billion yuan. Most neutral experts said the project, which would have to be built over 15 or more years, would cost at least 100 billion yuan at 1990 prices. In 1993, even senior officials admitted the latter was a more realistic assessment. Aside from costs, there were environmental concerns: for example, the massive flooding would kill off animal and plant species and displace more than a million residents in Sichuan and Hubei. Experts said that merely 10 per cent of the priceless cultural and historic relics in the area could be preserved. Geologists cited the fact that the dam would sit on a seismic fault.[232]

The pro-dam lobby mainly consisted of central planners and bureaucrats who had worked in the Water Conservancy and Hydroelectric Ministry and other heavy engineering departments. Foremost among them: Li Peng and former minister of water conservancy, Qian Zhengying. The anti-dam lobby comprised liberal intellectuals, including quite a few NPC and CPPCC members.

Before the June 4 crackdown, a famous physicist who was also a CPPCC member had lamented the lack of consultation over China's largest-ever civil engineering project. At a session of the CPPCC in March 1989, Ma Dayou, who has a doctorate from Harvard, said the Three Gorges Project would be a "test of whether the country will really render decision-making on major issues democratic and scientific". Professor Ma criticised departments charged with appraisal of the scheme of "taking in only views that are in favour of the project".[233]

It became obvious after June 4 that the pro-dam lobby would carry the day. After all, when the CCP was putting utmost stress on "stability" and party leadership, challenges to the wisdom of the powers-that-be were snuffed out. It is instructive that after mid-1989, the only major dissenting voice was raised by Professor Qian Weichang, another physicist who was Vice-Chair-man of the CPPCC. Qian took advantage of the debate on geo-politics and other strategic issues after the Gulf War to point out that the project would be a major target if China were under air attack. Qian's views originally appeared as an article in a small-circulation magazine called *Qunyan*, or *Words of the Masses*. Li Peng reportedly blocked the wider circulation of the story. It was only at the intercession of Deng Xiaoping and Chen Yun that Qian's viewpoint grabbed the attention of intellectuals in the capital.[234]

The massive flooding in the summer of 1991, however, clinched the deal for the pro-dam lobby. Premier Li and others argued that damming the Yang-tze was the only long-term solution to periodic deluges. And in spite of its commitment to "mass line politics", the CCP Central Committee decided in its Eighth Plenum in November 1991 to go ahead with the preliminary work. Resettlement of some of the estimated 1.3 million peasants whose homes would be flooded had begun that August.

Cadres who gave the go-ahead for the first stages of the Three Gorges Project, of course, were unperturbed by the fact that they had no legal autho-risation: the scheme was not contained in the Eighth Five-Year Plan of 1991-95. More important, it had not been approved by the NPC. For the sake of appearances, the party did not publicise the Eighth Plenum decision on the project. The pro-dam lobby, however, deployed the full force of the propa-ganda machinery to lend legitimacy to their gambit. [235]

In the second half of 1991, some 3,500 NPC and CPPCC members as well as other experts went on more than 20 all-expenses-paid "investigative mis-sions" to Sichuan and Hubei provinces. It came as no surprise they came out in support of the mega-project. That the NPC had not exercised its "supervi-sory" functions was clear from the statement made by one of its conservative vice-chairmen, former central banker Ms Chen Muhua. After a tour to the project site, Chen called on the people to "unify their thoughts and their understanding" on the scheme. The influential legislator called on the gov-ernment to "boost propaganda" on the project because a delay of one year could cost Beijing as much as 600 million yuan.[236]

Chen, of course, was oblivious of the fact that, at least theoretically, the 3,000 deputies to the NPC were supposed to deliberate on the Three Gorges question in March and April 1992. Her insistence that everything was settled — and the hint that the anti-dam lobbyists should be educated by official pro-paganda — made a total mockery of the institution of the NPC. At the 1992

NPC, barely 1,767 out of the 2,633 deputies voted in favour of the scheme, considered a surprising show of defiance by Chinese standards. And Taiwan-born deputy, Huang Shunxing, was not permitted to make his case against the scheme publicly.[237]

In 1993 and 1994, opposition was mainly voiced overseas by such veteran environmentalists as Li Rui and Dai Qing, who published their anti-dam tracts in the United States and Hong Kong. Within China, private expressions of dissent continued to be made as more discoveries were made about the awesome sacrifice the nation had to make.[238]

C. The NPC under Qiao Shi and Tian Jiyun, 1993-1994

The status and powers of the NPC received a dramatic boost when Qiao Shi and Tian Jiyun were appointed respectively as Chairman and First Vice-Chairman at its plenary session in March-April 1993. The two leaders of the relatively liberal wing of the CCP reiterated that they would strengthen the NPC's function as both the spokesman of the masses and the "supervisor" of the government.

Qiao and Tian took advantage of the two major items on the national agenda — to build a "socialist market economy" and to fight corruption — to enhance the clout of the legislature. They persuasively argued that a comprehensive set of laws was a prerequisite for both a market economy and a clean government.

More significant, the NPC leaders professed to some extent a "pro-West bias" in legislative work. Qiao said while touring Germany in early 1994 that "China will broadly learn from foreign experience in law-making" and that "all of China's reforms should dovetail with international norms".[239]

Qiao, who seemed to have lost one round in the power-play with rivals including Jiang Zemin and Li Peng, lost no time in converting the NPC into a formidable power-base for the relatively liberal wing of the party. In a major speech in April 1993, Qiao played the public opinion card when he hinted that the NPC embodied the power of the people. "Supervision by the NPC is an important part of the entire country's supervisory system," he said. "As a representative of the state and the people, the NPC is pursuing a kind of supervision which has the highest legal efficacy." Qiao, who remained a member of the Politburo Standing Committee, added: "The NPC's point of departure is the people's fundamental interests and common will. The NPC Standing Committee will further boost its links with the people."[240]

Qiao also vowed to defend the Chinese constitution, which afforded the legislature large supervisory powers. "We must safeguard the solemnity of the constitution and the unity of the legal system," he said, adding that the constitution had given the NPC and its Standing Committee the powers to supervise how the charter and other laws were being implemented — and to supervise the powers of the government, the courts and the procuratorate.[241]

Perhaps for the first time since 1949, Qiao underscored the role of the NPC in stamping out government inefficiency — especially corruption. Increased supervision, he said, was "beneficial to correct decision-making, to the avoidance of errors, and to the prevention and curtailment of corrupt phenomena". A possible hidden message: the party and government have made so many mistakes and become so mired in corruption that the NPC has to clean them up. The role of the NPC became even more important as the CCP launched the anti-graft campaign in August 1993. Qiao was again prominent in defending the role of the NPC in nailing the culprits. Predictably, he attributed what he called the "spreading of the negative and corrupt phenomena" to party and government units not observing the codes.[242]

In a speech on corruption delivered to the NPC Standing Committee in September, Qiao said the question of graft had arisen because existing laws against corruption had been observed more in the breach. "The problem is, these [anti-corruption] laws have not been well implemented," he said. "The phenomena of not observing the laws, not seriously implementing the laws, not punishing illegal actions — and even using powers to suppress the law — are very serious in some areas and departments."[243]

Qiao indicated on the same occasion that the NPC was in the process of enacting a law against "unfair competition". "This will regulate the behaviour of the market and ensure free competition," he said. "This is beneficial towards stopping the collusion between government and business; using power and special privilege for doing business; and region-based protectionism. This is also good for fighting corruption."

Indeed, the development of the socialist market economy gave the NPC a whole new universe of discourse — if not yet a solid power-base. The NPC pledged in 1993 to enact an unprecedented number of economics-connected laws to ensure the health of the economic system. Qiao said at the end of the NPC plenary session in 1993 that a market economy required a "sound and comprehensive" legal system.

"There is a fundamental difference between a market economy and a highly centralised economy which relies primarily on administrative means for management," the NPC chief said. "The history of economic development in modern states has proven that without sound legal standards or guarantees, various social and economic activities will have no guidelines." On a later occasion, Qiao said laws were essential to demarcate the economic rights and prerogatives of various regions and interest groups.[244]

In 1993, the NPC passed a record 67 laws and regulations, half of which dealt with the economy. For the first time since 1949, a number of policy initiatives had gone from the party and government to the legislature. Major statutes either passed or closed to being enacted in the 1993-94 period included a company law, statutes on banking and securities, anti-trust laws and legislation against insider-trading.

Qiao's bid for more power — for the NPC if not for himself and his faction — was helped along by Tian, who worked closely with Qiao in the short-lived campaign against leftism in the spring of 1992. Throughout 1993, Tian, the former right-hand man of Zhao Ziyang, fired mighty salvoes to boost the NPC's role of supervision. For example, Tian said in April: "We must further develop democracy and further boost the people's supervision. This is very important for improving government work." Tian even called on the media to expose cases of party and government officials violating the constitution and the laws.[245]

Qiao and Tian made two bold departures from tradition. They boosted the law-making capacities of the legislature by assembling a team of professional drafters. Before this, the NPC had never had a law-drafting team, and most of the bills had been put together by administrative departments for routine endorsement by the rubber-stamp congress. Chinese sources said that in instances like the statute on stocks and shares — slated for late 1994 — there were conflicts between NPC law-drafters and State Council bureaucrats.[246]

Equally important, Qiao and Tian played the "regional card" by encouraging provincial and municipal legislatures to "go one step ahead of the NPC" by enacting statutes that were in some instances more liberal than national ones. During a trip to Guangdong in mid-1993, Qiao said "while national laws are still not comprehensive, regions could do initial explorations and formulate local regulations". He added that with its experience in reform, Guangdong could be a "testing field for legislative work".[247]

In 1993 and 1994, the Guangdong and Shenzhen legislatures deliberated on laws on business practices and anti-corruption that were partly based on the Hong Kong experience. Bills on social security and the protection of the rights of labourers were also drafted. In late 1993, the Guangdong congress started work on a journalism and publication law, while the NPC had stalled on a similar statute for several years.[248]

It would be foolhardy to expect that the NPC would promote Western-style democracy in the foreseeable future. Indeed, partly because of the overall tightening of the political atmosphere in early 1994, the plenary session that year proved a disappointment for the progress of democracy. For example, a number of liberal deputies privately complained that *deng'er* ballotings (in which the number of candidates is the same as that of positions available) were used for the "election" of two members of the NPC Standing Committee.

Moreover, the NPC presidium and the party authorities continued to turn a blind eye to the controversial suggestions of maverick NPC members, including those from Hong Kong. This is the case with the idea of a "sunshine law" which would require senior officials to disclose their income and assets as well as those of their children.[249]

Indeed, both Qiao and Tian were members of the CCP Politburo and the party's hold over the NPC was stronger than that over the CPPCC. However, the two came from a different faction than that of the "mainstream clique" headed by President Jiang Zemin and Premier Li Peng. And as we shall discuss in the conclusion of this chapter, the expansion of the NPC's clout could mean a step forward for the ideal of "inner-party democracy", the full flowering of which was a *sine qua non* for the much more illusive goal of "multi-party politics".[250]

XI. The Stench of Corruption: The Anti-Graft Crusade

Nothing illustrated better the feudalistic and archaic nature of the political system than the mushrooming problem of corruption: there were no checks and balances; no input by intellectuals or the people; no awareness by the powers-that-be that greed would feed upon itself. This is despite repeated warnings by Deng Xiaoping, Chen Yun, Yang Shangkun, Wan Li and other elders that if the CCP should crumble, "it would not be because of invasion from abroad but atrophy from within through corruption".

After Tiananmen Square, Deng and his disciples were ready to admit that some of the demands made by the pro-democracy movement in early 1989 were legitimate. As Jiang Zemin put it one year after the massacre: "Young students [in early 1989] raised issues about correcting mistakes in our work and the crusade against corruption," he said in a letter addressed to nine American students in June 1990. "This was in unison with the views of our party and government."[251]

Indeed, almost immediately after June 4 1989, Deng Xiaoping laid down instructions on curbing corruption. "A major mistake made by the two former party general secretaries Hu Yaobang and Zhao Ziyang was their failure to combat corruption," the patriarch said in an internal meeting. "Fighting corruption is like raining [and nourishing the earth]. It is not enough just to do it in one to two days. The campaign must permeate the entire process of reform and the open door. Secondly, we must seriously grasp the task of combating graft, and investigations must be made even into the crimes of senior cadres."[252]

The fight against corruption was featured on a daily basis in the mass media. From 1989 to 1991, the courts and procuratorates handled about 50,000 corruption cases annually. For example, from January to October of 1991, judicial bodies made investigations into more than 40,000 cases, which involved ill-gotten gains of 354 million yuan. Quite a few of the exposed suspects were well-known politicians. They reportedly included the Governor of Hainan Liang Xiang; Vice-Minister of Railway Luo Yun'guang; Vice-Chairman of the Qinghai People's Congress Han Fucai; Minister of Construction Lin Hanxiong; and Minister of Communications Qian Yongchang.[253]

By late 1991, the leadership had mapped out plans to set up Anti-Corruption Bureaux in the regions and cities. Ironically, it was Zhao Ziyang who had urged that China establish bodies similar to Hong Kong's Independent Commission Against Corruption, whose track record was highly praised by the ousted leader. In December 1991, the Vice-Chief of the Supreme People's Procuratorate Zhang Siqing said that anti-graft bureaux would soon be set up in various levels of government. Zhang disclosed that a major focus of the investigations would be large companies which had run up huge deficits. Guangdong and Hainan were among the first provinces to announce plans for local anti-graft units.[254] However, by mid-1994, there was no sign the bulk of the provinces and major cities had set up these agencies.

A. Failure of the Anti-Corruption Exercise, 1990-92

After the multiple pledges and measures, had probity in government significantly improved? It became more obvious that as the economy opened up, officials and *gaoganzidi* were the principal culprits behind corruption. While it is not scientific to draw the conclusion that princeling-businessmen are necessarily prone to malfeasance, observers cite the fact that in 1988, Deng Xiaoping personally gave orders to close down Kanghua Corp, the company of Deng Pufang, as the first step to crack down on big-time graft. Such bold actions were not repeated after 1989.

In an article soon after June 4, 1989, the China News Service cited a few reasons why the anti-corruption drive had not scored significant results even though similar crusades had been launched almost annually since 1949. First of all, CNS said, there was loud thunder and lightning, but no rain. The anti-corruption drive became a classic mass movement that saw a lot of media exposure and mass gatherings. Once the campaign was over, everything went back to normal. Secondly, there was no supervision by the news media. Newspapers that concentrated on corruption cases were accused of waging "smear campaigns" and "dwelling too much on the negative side of social phenomena".[255]

A more important reason, however, has to do with Lord Acton's adage, which has repeatedly been cited by legal scholars such as dissident Yu Haocheng: "Power corrupts; absolute power corrupts absolutely." Could the CCP — or any political party in the world — be entrusted with supervising itself? The CCP's track record in the 1950s was relatively better only because as a party newly swept to power — and when the "revolutionary fervour" was still running high — senior cadres exercised a relatively high degree of self-restraint.[256]

The familiar charge that the clean-up-the-government squads "get the flies but not the tigers" still rang true. The arbitrariness of the administration of justice was most evident in the fact that, very often, it was only senior officials whose political fortunes were going downhill who were nabbed. Liang Xiang, Lin Hanxiong and others were obvious instances. Liang was, of course, a protégé of Zhao Ziyang and one of the few regional cadres who refused to support Beijing's military action in June 1989. And Lin was said to have been lukewarm in conducting purges immediately after the massacre. Other examples included the sons of Zhao Ziyang, at least one of whom came under investigation after June 4 for alleged wheeling and dealing. Before Tiananmen Square, there was no question of casting aspersions on, let alone arresting, the offspring of the party boss.[257]

The arbitrary way in which graft cases were handled was also illustrated by the following set of statistics, which seemed to suggest that a large number of corrupt cadres merely received a slap on the wrist. According to the NCNA, the authorities in the first half of 1991 launched investigations into 19,406 cases, 15,347 of which were completed. As a result, "administrative punishments" were meted out to 16,832 officials, out of which 1,695 lost their jobs. It is important to note that a mere 1,034 suspects were actually subjected to criminal proceedings in the procuratorate and the courts. Among those penalised were 42 department-level cadres and 537 officials with the rank of county chief or above.[258]

Chinese sources said that for major corruption cases, it was the Central Committee's Commission for Political and Legal Affairs as well as the Central Commission for Disciplinary Inspection that laid down the final decisions. Both councils were headed by member of the Politburo Standing Committee Qiao Shi, and after 1993, Ren Jianxin (CPLA) and Wei Jianxing (CCDI). Since 1949, many of the most serious cases of graft were settled merely through internal party channels and not in law courts. And suspects who for one reason or another were politically well connected merely received "inner-party" punishments which could mean a mere mark of disgrace on their dossiers or temporary expulsion from the party.

After the June 4 bloodbath, the only effort to provide a semblance of "non-CCP supervision" on the investigation of corruption cases was made at the

NPC of 1990, when 36 Shanghai-based deputies suggested the setting up of a Clean Government Committee within the legislature. The purpose was to "supervise the anti-corruption work of state organs and justice departments". The sponsor of the motion, opera star Yuan Xuefen said: "Many NPC members are concerned with this suggestion, which I first raised last year. I hope it can be accepted this time." The motion was not even mentioned in the domestic media, let alone passed into law.[259]

B. The Great Anti-Corruption Crusade of 1993

The floodgates of corruption were opened in the wake of the leaps-and-bounds growth of the economy after the *nanxun* (see Chapter 2). In a report on economic crimes of 1993, the new President of the Supreme People's Procuratorate Zhang Siqing said the wantonness of corruption and other related felonies was "rare since nation-building" in 1949. Sixty per cent of the cases handled by the procuratorate system in the first nine months of the year involved sums of more than 10,000 yuan. There were 77 cases of economic, mainly graft-related, crimes, that involved more than half a million yuan, and 157 cases involving more than 1 million yuan. The last two figures were respectively double and triple comparable statistics for 1992. "The graft takers are mostly people who administer finances and accounts, or who wield specific powers over human, material and monetary resources," Zhang said.[260]

The NPC report on judicial work in 1993 said the procuratorate system investigated 45,491 cases of economic crime that year, which included corruption cases. Suspects included 1,037 cadres with the ranking of heads of counties and *chu* ("offices") or above. In the last four months of 1993, officials handled 8,538 major corruption cases, or 5,883 more than those in the same period in 1992. Earlier, an official report said 30 per cent of all the cadres in Anhui Province had been implicated in taking bribes.[261]

An anti-graft crusade, officially known as the Large-Scale Anti-Corruption Struggle, was launched in August 1993 and ran through the rest of the year. In a throwback to the Struggle Against the Five Evils Campaign of the 1950s, Jiang Zemin committed the party to "grasping major and important cases, arresting a group of people and killing a group of people". Jiang said the party was targeting the phenomenon of "the exchange of power for money". In October, the Central Committee and State Council issued a national circular on the crusade. The gist of the exhortation was: official units and cadres must take the lead in implementing a clean government; cadres would be barred from business activities, including stock transactions; a group of big cases would be cracked; and "corrupt trends" with which the masses were most dissatisfied must be curbed.[262]

For the first time since the Cultural Revolution, marathon investigation teams were sent out to government departments and localities. In October 1993, 20 central-level departments were subjected to "inspections" by investigators over a period of five days. These included such sensitive units as the Ministry of Public Security, the Finance Ministry, the People's Bank, and the Tax Bureau. Investigation squads were also dispatched to the regions and cities.

Perhaps in view of the intractable nature of the problem, the leadership in fact started a Maoist-style *qunzhong yundong*, or mass movement, to eradicate the black spots. "We must take to heart Chairman Mao's instructions at the beginning of nation-building about using democratic means to counter corruption," Jiang said in an internal speech that was originally intended to be broadcast nationwide in August. By democratic means, the president meant whipping up the "enthusiasm" of the masses to take a whack at "feudal remnants" and "residual class enemies". In Maoist fashion, Jiang linked "infiltration by hostile foreign forces" to the corruption plague, saying the former had "confused people's minds and wreaked havoc on socialist construction".

In justifying the *qunzhong yundong*, Hong Kong's *Wen Wei Po* said: "In the course of building up the system of the socialist market economy, and before a social supervisory mechanism has been established, it is necessary to organise a large-scale anti-corruption struggle." Quoting "authoritative figures", the paper said the "struggle" would not go against the party's earlier decision to "take economic construction as its core work and to forswear *qunzhong yundong*".[263]

In the last quarter of 1993, the *yundong* manifested itself in mass meetings as well as the encouragement of people to report big-time offenders. The official media reported mass movements in areas including Hebei, Yunnan, Zhejiang, Hainan and the Beijing municipality. From September 1 to 20, Hebei authorities received 1,610 tip-off letters and telephone calls from residents. The Hainan government set up a Command Centre to Co-ordinate Work on Anti-Corruption and Bribery as well as an anti-graft hotline. The chief of the local procuratorate was personally involved in seeing the whistle blowers and petitioners.[264]

C. Failure of the Anti-Corruption Exercise, 1993-1994

It was apparent even from the start of this "unprecedented tiger-killing campaign" that there could be no real eradication of corruption: the party lacked the will, and perhaps a real desire, to root it out. During his *nanxun*, Deng acquiesced in if not encouraged party and government officials to *xiahai* ("take the plunge into business"). The leadership recognised that at least in the "preliminary stage of socialism", a certain degree of *guanshang bufen* ("the lack of distinction between officialdom and business") was needed to expedite economic development. As the *People's Daily* put it in an October 1993 commentary: "Since the concrete steps and measures of reform and opening up cannot be expected to always be perfect, loopholes and weak points are inevitable. Corruption is hard to avoid."265

Moreover, *quanmin jieshang* and *guanshang bufen* were the price Deng had to pay for party unity. The patriarch realised that conservative party elders would stop second-guessing his market reforms if their sons and daughters were reaping millions everyday "swimming in the sea of the market place". As discussed earlier, Deng wanted the party to control the business arena in order to ensure its monopoly on the polity.

The anti-corruption regulation of October 5, 1993, appeared to have banned the fusion of political power and business. For example, the decision forbade cadres to "engage in business or to run enterprises; to act as go-betweens; or to provide favourable conditions to the business activities of relatives and friends". Moreover, party and government officials were also forbidden to moonlight in business. No selling of stocks and shares would be allowed. This regulation summed up similar ones adopted by regional authorities in Sichuan and Shanghai earlier in the year.266

Yet ask any Hong Kong or Western China trader and he would tell you that by late 1993, the cognac was flowing as briskly and the karaoke scene was as rowdy. The crackdown on *guanshang bufen* did not seem to have made a dent on the "private gold coffers" of central or regional cadres. Yue Xiang, Secretary-General of the Legal Work Committee of the NPC Standing Committee, said in late 1993 there would be no formal legislation on the separation of officialdom and business. Yue said business units could only be cut off from the party and government apparatus "when the financial system and economic conditions completely dovetail with the operations of the market place".267

When the anti-corruption investigation teams were dispatched to the provinces in October 1993, a pro-Chinese newspaper in Hong Kong hinted that a list of the big-name offenders would be made public by the end of 1993. Nothing happened. As with past campaigns, the media played up certain cases as examples of the anti-graft crusaders having acquitted themselves well. A number of offenders were summarily executed or given life sentences. The "tigers" cited in the press included the police chief of Huizhou, Hong Yonglin; the head of the public security department in Guizhou Province, Guo Zhengmin; the director of the planning department of Hainan, Jiang Wei; and the vice-mayor of Xiamen, Chen Zhihan. Hong Kong's *Ta Kung Pao* daily claimed that Guizhou's Guo was an eye-catching "big tiger". The truth is, of course, that none of these "black hands" was a cadre with more than mid-echelon rank.268

In early 1994, the media played up the case of the Changcheng Electronics, Machinery and High Technology Corp as an example of Beijing's determination to handle big-time offenders. Chairman Shen Taifu was sentenced to death — and summarily executed — for taking bribes worth 2 million yuan. Vice-Minister of Science and Technology Li Xiaoshi was given a 20-year term for taking a relatively paltry 72,000 yuan.[269] The authorities, however, failed to give a clear explanation on the connections of a large number of senior cadres to the Changcheng case. Ministerial-level cadres including Li Peng, Song Jian, Deng Nan, and Fei Xiaotong were reported in Hong Kong and Taiwan papers to have given moral and other kinds of support to Shen and Li.

The law-and-order and judicial establishment had lost so much of its credibility that senior politicians had to lend their personal authority to the handling of particularly nettlesome problems. For example, Vice-Premiers Zhu Rongji and Li Lanqing personally oversaw the crackdown on the smuggling of cars in Guangxi, which involved 798 vehicles worth nearly 100 million yuan. In summing up the anti-graft drive, Politburo member Wei Jianxing said in December 1993: "Some leading cadres are not serious enough about clean government and self-discipline; some merely go through the motions; there have been cases of departments not reporting corrupt cases."[270]

In a September 1993 report, *Ta Kung Pao* quoted an unnamed "central leader" as ascribing the increase in smuggling to "political weakness and short-sightedness" on the part of cadres in localities, especially coastal areas. The leader said the officials "turned a blind eye to smuggling activities for their own petty interests". The central government was obliged to give a pay rise to officers in units including public security, customs, and industry and commerce. At an anti-smuggling conference called in October, Li Lanqing pointed his finger at officials who had teamed up with the smugglers. "That some of our enterprises and law enforcement units are behind the smugglers is a main reason why we have seen such a dramatic increase in smuggling," he said.[271]

An October 1993 commentary by the HKCNA accused black sheep in the police of being godfathers of drugs, vice, gambling and extortion operations. One of the culprits cited, police chief Hong from Huizhou, had such a secure power-base that local sources said provincial authorities had to deploy the PAP to nab him. Anti-corruption units were set up within police departments in a number of provinces. As HKCNA reported: "The anti-graft operations within the public security system has not proceeded very well. Officers in some areas are irresolute in fighting corruption and the measures they take are not effective... In just a few short years, not a few law officers became very rich. The masses are very bitter about this."[272]

XII. Conclusion: Failure to Institute a Rational Political Process

No regime in history has given up power voluntarily. This applies to all ruling élites, be they ancient or modern, Communist or capitalist. After the June 4 trauma, the dissolution of the Eastern bloc, and the "exacerbation of social contradictions" as a result of intensified reform in 1993, it was perhaps too much to expect the CCP to quicken its gingerly pace of political reform. It was also naive and unrealistic to expect the Deng leadership to institute multi-party politics. As the previous sections have made clear, the party took a step backward in areas including the issue of succession, special privileges for the party elders and *gaoganzidi*, strengthening the dictatorship of the proletariat, the fusion of the functions of the party and government and those of the party and the judiciary.

Yet as both Chapters 6 and 7 will argue, forces and trends were in place by 1993 and 1994 to indicate that non-mainstream elements within the party (for example, the liberal cliques) — as well as those outside the party (for example, the non-state economic sector) — might soon overwhelm if not significantly water down the CCP's 45-year-old stranglehold on power.

Here, we shall only examine what the CCP could have done — but unfortunately failed to do — to promote inner-party democracy. We will also look into those kinds of political changes that were possible even under overall "one party dictatorship".

A. The NPC and "Inner Party Democracy"

By early 1993, there were signs that the NPC system had made initial headway towards promoting inner-party democracy. This, however, took place not because of an initiative from on high but because of a general "revolt" against the extreme conservativism at the very top. Dissenting voices made themselves heard at the First Session of the Eighth NPC in March 1993 as well as at the elections of the heads of provincial and county-level administrations.[273] A dozen-odd conservatives got a surprising number of negative votes at the NPC. And in regional elections, a few Beijing-designated candidates were spurned.

In January, the CCP leadership was flabbergasted when two Beijing-backed gubernatorial candidates where thrown out in elections at the provincial people's congresses of Zhejiang and Guizhou. These incidents were extremely rare because most provincial congresses merely voted into office candidates for governor designated by the party's Organisation Department. However, since late 1992, *cha'er* elections (where there are more candidates than positions up for grabs) were generally introduced in the provinces. And a would-be governor merely needed the signatures of ten local deputies to stand.

In Zhejiang, the incumbent Ge Hongsheng lost to the most junior of the vice-governors, Wan Xueyuan. It was largely a protest vote against the fact that Beijing had soon after June 4 1989 removed Ge's predecessor Shen Zulun, reputedly a sympathiser of the student movement. The Zhejiang deputies were thus expressing their anger at Shen's dismissal by throwing out his replacement, Ge. Wan, a former secretary-general of the Shanghai municipal government who had arrived in Zhejiang in late 1992, was actually an unknown quantity to most members of the Zhejiang PC.[274]

The same dynamics were at work during the ousting of the Guizhou governor Wang Chaowen, who had occupied his position for nearly ten years without distinguishing himself in reform. Guizhou PC legislators gave a convincing victory to vice-governor Chen Shineng, a former vice-minister of light industry. Chen was "exiled" to backward Guizhou largely because of his display of support for the pro-democracy demonstrators in 1989.[275]

Chinese sources said Beijing was shocked by the contretemps in Zhejiang and Guizhou. In the former province, the election results were held up for a day as local party authorities consulted the Beijing leadership. During those tense hours, the deputies were asked to watch specially programmed movies. Jiang Zemin, however, decided that the non-recognition of the ballotings would provoke an outcry — and the Organisation Department grudgingly accepted the results. As Hong Kong's *Wen Wei Po* reported, Jiang indicated: "We must respect the opinion and choice of the people's representatives."[276]

The Organisation Department and other units, however, lost no time in ensuring that no similar mishaps took place in elections in other provinces and cities. The central leadership was especially nervous about their candidate for Beijing mayor, Li Qiyan, a noted conservative and protégé of the hated former Beijing party boss Li Ximing. Owing to intense lobbying and arm-twisting by the leadership, however, the younger Li was voted into office without embarrassment. And upon coming into office in early 1993, the new mayor lost no time in declaring he would "uphold the party's basic line without wavering".[277]

In 1993, there were other cases of incumbent county chiefs or Beijing-designated candidates for these positions being rejected by local congresses. It is a measure of Beijing's attitude towards such expression of inchoate "inner-party democracy" that no Chinese media except the quasi-official *China Business Times* in Beijing ran reports about the incidents.

NPC elections for the new cabinet in early 1993 proved a profound loss of face for conservatives. Somewhat deservingly, Li Tieying was given the thumbs-down by nearly one third of the 2,896 deputies present during ballotings for the position of state councillor: 722 voted against him and 137 abstained. Considering the rubber-stamp nature of the NPC, this was quite a rebellion. Another conservative, then People's Bank of China Governor Li Guixian, was hit by 323 negative votes and 86 abstentions during the same category of elections. Li Peng fared slightly better. There were 330 no votes and abstentions, meaning he failed to win the trust of 11 per cent of the deputies.[278]

There were also isolated displays of democracy. In late 1993, the "capitalist enclave" of Shishi on the Fujian coast conducted an "open election" for vice-mayor. At least according to the official CNS, the only conditions laid down by the authorities were that candidates be female and under 35. Fifty-nine "strongwomen" ran for the "elections", which included debates with other candidates. A doctoral candidate at Xiamen University, Zhou Zhenping, 28, was chosen by 128 local deputies, against just nine votes for her closest rival. After her victory, Zhou vowed to remain a non-communist.[279]

However, the democratic consciousness of national or local deputies could not be called strong. Partly owing to the heavy hand of Beijing, very few deputies stuck their necks out to clamour for a higher degree of choice in existing elections. For example, at the March 1993 NPC, the extent of the *cha'er* factor in ballotings for the Standing Committee was minimal: candidates merely outnumbered the available number of seats by 5 per cent. Raidi, head of the Tibet legislature, insisted, however, that such a limited degree of choice "still constituted democracy".[280]

Lower down the pecking order, some headway seemed to have been achieved in what Chinese propagandists called "village self-rule". A dispatch by the NCNA said that by early 1993, one-third of the country's 1 million villages and 56,000 towns had set up village and township committees vested with some autonomous powers. Such committees, which were in theory elected by villagers, had the power of appointing and removing officials, discussing local affairs, and supervising the village governments. "The system is designed to enable farmers to manage, educate and help themselves according to the law and to grant them the right to manage their village affairs," NCNA said.[281] However, this tendency towards "self-rule" also coincided with efforts by the party to boost the powers of its 800,000 cells in the villages. And observers were not sure how much real power the village or township committees could really have.

B. The Illusive Goal of "Inner Party Democracy"

Failing the introduction of real democratisation, the CCP could at least have promoted healthy factional politics: that is, to establish rational mechanisms and institutions for various cabals within the party to air and resolve differ-

ences through open debate and contention, and not through *coups d'etat* or
naked power struggles. Before the Liberal Democratic Party in Japan lost its
stranglehold on power in 1993, the so-called "LDP model" — which envisaged an open and rigorous competition among the party's disparate factions
— was seen as a positive example for Chinese-style democracy.

This fairly primitive ideal of democracy, however, would face tremendous
obstacles in the CCP context. First of all, the CCP never admitted to having factions. This is despite the fact that Chairman Mao long ago said that without
"mountain strongholds", the party would be as lifeless as a stagnant pool. And
one of the key tasks of patriarchs of the party from Mao to Deng was precisely
to maintain a balance among the disparate cliques. Outsiders only know about
the extent of factional strife after a crisis. For example, in early 1987, we knew
about the back-stabbing between Li Peng, Hu Yaobang and Zhao Ziyang — and
the cabals they led — only after Hu was ousted in an unconstitutional power-
play that virtually amounted to a coup. The same goes for the downfall of Zhao.

Factional dynamics were as intense as ever after the June 4 bloodbath. To
counterbalance the conservative cabal that played such a key role in throwing
out Zhao and the other liberals, Deng tried his level best to propagate the so-
called Shanghai Faction led by Jiang Zemin and Zhu Rongji. The patriarch
hoped this clique of politicians would be able to carry forward the reform
enterprise after his own demise. And by late 1993, the Shanghai Clique had
become the Mainstream Faction of the party.

Realistic prospects for some form of "LDP model" coming to pass in
China, however, did not become obvious until the transfer of Qiao Shi, Tian
Jiyun and Li Ruihuan to the NPC and the CPPCC in early 1993. As we discussed earlier, the trio, who could be identified as "moderate liberals", were
keen to use their new power-base to exercise "supervision" over not just the
government but the ruling faction within the CCP.

And as we shall discuss in Chapter 6, there is also the possibility of a coming together of the liberal forces in society: the old associates of Hu Yaobang
and Zhao Ziyang; regional cadres; and representatives of the private sector. In
the event of a confluence of interests, this group could form a strategic
alliance with the "Faction of Supervisors" led by Qiao Shi and Li Ruihuan to
impose some "Western-style" checks and balances within the CCP. Moreover,
there is a likelihood that such "flowering and contention" might be more institutionalised and open than before.

C. Public Demands for Democracy

The goals discussed above concerning "inner-party democracy" or the "LDP
model" were a far cry from the demands of the students — as well as those of

"bourgeois-liberal" cadres in 1988 and 1989. After the *nanxun*, a "revision-ism" had set in both among Chinese and foreigners concerning ordinary peo-ple's pursuit of democracy. The new conventional wisdom was that most Chinese were putting money before democracy — and that so long as the administration could keep on expanding the economic pie, it could keep demands for liberalisation at bay. At least for the near term.

While this might be true among some sectors of society, there is no denying that by 1993 and 1994, demands for a faster pace of political reform again emerged from the shadows. An early 1993 survey of urban residents by the Beijing-based People's University and the quasi-official *Public Relations Journal* showed that more than 80 per cent of respondents believed "economic reform cannot progress without reforming the political system". *China Daily*, which reported the survey, said "the residents [surveyed] also hope to open up more channels of communication between the government and the public."[282]

There were also isolated calls for political reform in the official media. A signed article in the *Beijing Review* in mid-1993 said China and other devel-oping countries could not ignore the political rights of their citizens. "As the UN resolution concerning new human rights concepts points out, the imple-mentation, promotion and protection of civil and political rights as well as economic, social and cultural rights should be given equal attention and urgent consideration," the weekly said. The author, Gu Chunde, argued that low economic and cultural standards did not mean "developing countries can ignore individual civil and political rights."[283]

A commentary in the official journal *Xinhua Digest* about the same time even hinted that democracy — not iron-fisted rule — was the best way to guarantee stability as radical economic reforms were pursued. "Western nations have built democratic and legal systems which provide the social and political stability as well as the individual freedom and equality to develop the market economy and social production forces," the article said.[284]

6

Succession Politics and the
Post-Deng Leadership

I. Introduction

THE strategy of succession of Deng Xiaoping and the Mainstream Faction of the Chinese Communist Party was simple: to groom and consolidate a leadership that would pursue market reforms at a steady pace while preserving the party's monopoly on power. As was evidenced by personnel reshuffle at the 14th Party Congress of October 1992 and throughout 1993 and 1994, Deng's gameplan was as follows:

a) Prop up the moderate technocrats, including the so-called Shanghai Faction. These politicians, led by party chief Jiang Zemin and Executive Vice-Premier Zhu Rongji, could be counted upon to pursue cautious market reform while putting a freeze on political liberalisation.

b) Promote a younger generation of politicians and cadres who had both "expertise and redness", that is, technocrats who can be trusted by the party. Again, this meant cadres with attributes similar to those of the Shanghai Faction.

c) Leftists or Maoist ideologues would be sidelined. As outlined in Chapter 3, however, the leftists remained a force to be reckoned with because Deng and Jiang needed them to rein in the "bourgeois liberals" as well as other challenges to the regime posted by dissidents.

d) Beef up the wielders of the tools of the proletariat dictatorship, principally the army and the police apparatus (see Chapters 4 and 5). Army leaders, in particular, would play the role of kingmakers in the post-Deng order.

e) Reserve a role for the radical modernisers who used to work under Hu Yaobang and Zhao Ziyang. Their mission would strictly be to give a boost to economic reform, particularly to facilitate the Chinese economy's integration with that of the Western world. However, at least before Deng's rendezvous with Marx, these "bourgeois-liberal" elements would be barred from the top echelon because of the patriarch's fear that they might ignite another round of political liberalisation.

f) A delicate balance of power would be maintained between central and regional authorities. More economic authority would be vested with local chieftains provided that this would facilitate economic development — and not lead to the growth of "warlordism" at the expense of Beijing's prerogatives.

g) Above all, in line with Deng's time-honoured statecraft, a balance would be struck among the disparate forces so that no power struggle would break out upon the patriarch's death. Jiang, as the "core of the third-generation leadership", would hold the the fort of communism — and proceed with market reforms with Chinese-socialist characteristics.

There is, of course, a major contradiction between the requirements of market reform and those of safeguarding the CCP's monopoly on power. This explains the extent to which the leadership endorsed by the 14th Party Congress and in 1993 and 1994 seemed to lag behind economic realities, the aspirations of the people, and indeed, criteria set forth in Deng's own speeches during his *nanxun* ("imperial tour to southern China") in early 1992.

Put simply, a solid majority of Chinese — not just the free-wheeling, irreverent denizens along the Gold Coast — wanted leaders who no longer spouted Marxist-Leninist platitudes and who dared take radical steps down the quasi-capitalist road. When he was in Shenzhen, Zhuhai and Shanghai in 1992, didn't the New Helmsman tell cadres who resisted reform "to go to sleep?"[1]

As the following will argue, however, the leadership line-up that Deng hoped would steer the nation into the Asia-Pacific century did not seem to pass muster. The collective leadership with Jiang as its "core" was in general committed to market reforms. However, in terms of economic policy it was a cautious team that was always ready to rein in the centrifugal tendencies of the regions and the non-state-sector entrepreneurs, two of the most dynamic forces in society.

In politics, Deng managed to shove aside a token number of Maoist ideologues. However, the political straitjacket remained. In addition, the CCP yielded too much to the security apparatus: representatives of the People's Liberation Army and the legal and security establishment gained ground *vis-à-vis* the other sectors.

Was this leadership structure at variance with the vision evoked by Deng at his *nanxun*? As had happened so often in recent CCP history, however, the survival and vested interests of the *zhongyang* or Party Centre towered above everything. A long-standing *leitmotif* of Deng's statecraft was to check and balance the various forces in the polity — in such a way that the Chief Architect of Reform could hold the balance and maintain his supremacy.

From the point of view of the survival of the entire party, it seemed that it was much better to proceed cautiously rather than risk being overwhelmed by the unpredictable, potentially chaotic forces that the marketplace might unleash. Having moved heaven to lay out his radical reform plans, Deng proceeded to move earth to confine the new forces within what the party would consider safe channels. The size of the bird cage increased significantly; but the bird still could not fly free. For the near term.

The genie, however, was out of the bottle. The logic of the marketplace dictated that the subjectivist wishes of the octogenarians could not hold sway forever. By late 1994, there were unmistakable signs of the emergence of a different power élite that would reflect the new balance of forces in Chinese society and economics — and the needs of the 21st century.

II. Balance of Power after the 14th Party Congress

A. Deng's Goal: To Reconcile Market Reforms with Political Stability

Improbable as it might seem, the rapidly ageing Deng took a hands-on approach to the preparation of the 14th Party Congress, especially the licking into shape of what he called a "cross-century leadership". As the patriarch made it clear in the *nanxun* talks, he wanted to groom and elevate young leaders who had concrete track records in reform. "We must choose those who the people think will resolutely insist on the line of reform and the open door, and who have solid accomplishments [in reform]," he said. "We must induct more young people [to high office]."[2]

The emphasis on youth and reformist credentials was repeated many times by both moderate and conservative leaders, especially at the 14th Congress. Even conservative Organisation Chief Lu Feng, a protégé of hardline elder Song Ping, waxed eloquent about "being bold in picking talent". "We must break through the old concept of just respecting seniority, making special provisions [for people with connections], and being too perfectionist," he said. "We must liberate our thoughts and go through various channels in selecting people from different modes."[3]

The 14th Congress, which ended on October 18, 1992, saw the removal of several diehard conservatives and the elevation of a relatively large number of young technocrats, including those from the regions. However, the over-riding concern of Deng was the maintenance of stability through a time-honoured balancing of the various factions.

By late 1992, the increasingly frail and senile patriarch was a lion in winter. With the generally solid support of the army and regional leaders — as well as that of the intelligentsia, entrepreneurs and international opinion — the patriarch could have manoeuvred for the kill and wiped out the leftists led by elders and ideologues such as Chen Yun and Deng Liqun. Yet, as had happened so many times since Deng grasped power in late 1978, the self-styled Great Balancer did not go the whole hog.

Firstly, in spite of the media hype surrounding the *nanxun* — and the apparent support that Deng's Second Wave of Reform had garnered among moderates and liberals alike — Deng had to sue for compromise with the conservative octogenarians as well as the bureaucrats in the Party Central and the State Council. As in past party congresses, there was a fair amount of give and take among the sectors and cliques of the CCP.

More important, however, Deng consciously gunned for a balance of power among the various "mountain strongholds". As he made clear in a message to the Politburo four days before the Congress opened on October 12, the leadership should reflect the "five lakes and four seas", meaning that none of the factions should assume a preponderant position.[4]

The obsession with stability was fully reflected in the line-up that was endorsed by the Congress. In his anxiety to pre-empt the emergence of a new strongman, Deng removed the military powers of the Yang Clan — the then president Yang Shangkun and General Yang Baibing — just days before the Congress opened.[5]

In spite of his reservations about Jiang's commitment to reform, Deng continued to shore up the latter's "core" status. The New Helmsman was aiming for a collective leadership with Jiang as its putative standard bearer. While the party chief would be first among equals, power would be shared among the other members of the Politburo, particularly its Standing Committee. Again, Deng hoped that the built-in checks and balances within the new team would minimise destabilising factors.

Politics being what it is, however, it is obvious that the octogenarian's subjectivist — and very non-Marxist — concern for stability would be shattered by fast-shifting reality. Already at the 14th Congress, we saw certain political forces — and personalities — gaining at the expense of others. New alliances were being formed as factions and cliques that no longer matched the requirements of the "socialist market economy" fell by the wayside.

Power blocs and socio-economic forces on the ascendancy included the

following: modernisation-minded technocrats; the army and security establishment; local-level leaders; and the cadres-turned-businessmen and private
entrepreneurs. It is likely that the leaders of these factions and social blocs —
many of whom did not fall within Deng's category of "cross-century cadres"
— would guide China into the early 21st century. Before we examine how
these trends and currents played themselves out at the 14th Party Congress
and after, however, let us look at the composition of the post-Congress pecking order.

B. The Leadership Structure after the 14th Party Congress

The following line-up was announced for the party and army at the Congress
and immediately after. The 1,989 delegates endorsed a 20-member Politburo
in addition to two Alternate Members of the supreme body. The Politburo
Standing Committee was expanded from six to seven members. In order of
seniority, they were: Jiang Zemin (66 at the time of the Congress); Li Peng
(64); Qiao Shi (68); Li Ruihuan (58); Zhu Rongji (64); Liu Huaqing (76); and
Hu Jintao (49). Senior Vice-Premier Yao Yilin and organisation chief Song
Ping, both 75, retired from the top council.

The rest of the Politburo was made up of the following members: Tian
Jiyun (63); Li Tieying (56); Ding Guan'gen (63); Li Lanqing (60); Yang
Baibing (72); Wu Bangguo (50); Zou Jiahua (66); Chen Xitong (62); Jiang
Chunyun (62); Qian Qichen (64); Wei Jianxing (61); Xie Fei (60); and Tan
Shaowen (63). The two Alternate Members were Wen Jiabao (50); and Wang
Hanbin (67).

Aside from Yao and Song, quite a number of heavyweights departed from
the Politburo. They either left active politics then and there — or stepped
down at the First Session of the Eighth National People's Congress (NPC) in
March 1993. The retirees were: Yang Shangkun (85); Wan Li (76); Qin Jiwei
(78); Wu Xueqian (71); Li Ximing (65); and Yang Rudai (65).[6]

An equally radical change of personnel took place at the Central
Committee Secretariat. The new line-up was, in order of precedence: Hu
Jintao, Ding Guan'gen, Wei Jianxing, Wen Jiabao and Ren Jianxin. Hu Jintao
replaced Qiao Shi as the *de facto* head of the Secretariat, which runs the party
apparatus and issues major documents. The "top morality squad", the Central
Commission for Disciplinary Inspection (CCDI) also had a facelift. The fast-
rising star in the Politburo, Wei Jianxing, took the place of Qiao Shi as Chief
of CCDI. His deputies were Hou Zongbin, Chen Zuolin, Cao Qingze, Wang
Deying and Xu Qing.

As we saw in Chapter 4, Deng masterminded a veritable purge of the so-
called Yang Clan both at and soon after the Congress. The Central Military

Commission (CMC), which is the country's highest military body, experienced a thorough changing of the guard. The Chairman remained Jiang Zemin. The two Vice-Chairmen were incumbent General Liu Huaqing (76) and newcomer General Zhang Zhen (78). There were four ordinary CMC members: Generals Chi Haotian (63), Zhang Wannian (64), Yu Yongbo (61), and Fu Quanyou (62).

Before we proceed with a full-scale analysis of this élite, let us briefly examine whether the new team satisfies Deng's imperative about the elevation of young and reformist-minded cadres. After all, Jiang Zemin's Political Report to the Congress also underlined "the principle of making cadres more revolutionary, younger, better educated and more competent, with both professional ability and political integrity".[7]

It is obvious that Deng and the "headhunting committee", which included Bo Yibo, Jiang Zemin, Song Ping and Hu Jintao, had only satisfied parts of their own criteria on youth. The much-maligned Central Advisory Commission (CAC), long regarded as a bastion of conservatism, was finally abolished. Out of the 189 full members of the Central Committee, 81 or 43.9 per cent were newcomers. 61 per cent of these inductees were under 55 years of age. However, the average age of the Committee was 56.3, which was slightly higher than the figure of 55.2 for the 13th Central Committee. Moreover, the re-appointment of septuagenarians Liu Huaqing and Zhang Zhen — who had gone into semi-retirement with their earlier appointment to the CAC — to the Central Committee looked very jarring.[8]

Aside from the youth criterion, Deng and his headhunters apparently made good on another promise: that the "princelings", or offspring of senior cadres, be barred from the Central Committee. To the surprise of analysts, odds-on favourites for the top such as Deng Nan (daughter of Deng Xiaoping), Chen Yuan (son of Chen Yun), Fu Rui (son of Peng Zhen), Wang Jun (son of Wang Zhen) and Bo Xicheng (son of Bo Yibo), failed to gain promotions at the Congress. Deng was quoted by insiders as having given specific instructions that the sons and daughters of party veterans not be considered for high positions.[9]

However, it would be naive to assume that the overall political influence of the princelings was on the wane. They still held some of the most senior positions in both Beijing and the regions. As discussed in Chapter 5, a major reason why the princelings did not seem to be doing particularly well in politics was because most had shifted their interest to business.

Summing up the post-14th Congress leadership, the Chinese media claimed that in terms of education, professionalism and experience, the new team was reformist in nature. Thus 83.7 per cent of the 189 most powerful men and women in China had college education or professional training; 44.5 per cent had mid- or upper-ranking professional qualifications in engineering or economics. "The great majority of the new Central Committee members are backbone cadres in different positions, including experts and scholars," the Chinese-affiliated *Mirror* magazine in Hong Kong pointed out at the time. "There are numerous cadres who have proven themselves in the reform and open-door policy."[10]

Above all, the 14th Party Congress paved the way for the dominance of the moderate or Mainstream Faction: middle-of-the-roaders in the mode of Shanghai Faction stalwarts Jiang Zemin and Zhu Rongji. As we shall see, Deng was putting his bets on the moderates to give the party a new lease on life.

C. Personnel Developments in 1993

Personnel developments throughout 1993 tended to reinforce Deng's obsession with stability and balance among the various "mountain strongholds" on the one hand, and economic reform on the other. The most salient feature was the replacement of the Jiang-Li axis with the so-called Jiang-Zhu axis, with Zhu Rongji, the former Shanghai mayor, and his technocrats gaining dominance over not just the economy but the central government.

The stability criterion was ensured by the principle of "cross leadership" — the party controlling all branches of the polity and senior cadres simultaneously occupying positions in different sectors such as the government, the army and the legislature. The most obvious example was Jiang Zemin. At the 1993 NPC, the party General Secretary gained the additional position of state president, displacing the partially disgraced Yang Shangkun. Jiang also took over the largely ceremonial position of Chairman of the State Central Military Commission.

Two other members of the Politburo Standing Committee were given major responsibilities. Qiao Shi, the former head of the secret police, became the chairman of the legislature, taking over from Wan Li. And Li Ruihuan, a leader of the liberal faction, now ran united front work through his concurrent post of Chairman of the Chinese People's Political Consultative Conference.

In an internal speech shortly before the Congress, which was held from March 15 to 31, Deng explained why he had given up his cherished goal of the separation of party and government. The patriarch said he had instead opted for the ideal of "cross leadership" because of the "lesson of the Eastern bloc". According to the astute analyst of the Communist world, a major reason for the fall of the USSR was that the party was divorced from the government, the army and other sectors, including the economy. As the new State Councillor Peng Peiyun put it: the fusion of party and government would be "beneficial towards the goal of the ideals of the party becoming the ideals of the people".[11]

Apart from safeguarding the party's supremacy, Deng acquiesced in if not ensured that Jiang's power base would be expanded. About the time of the NPC, the Central Committee's Leading Group on Finance and Economics (LGFE) was revived, with Jiang becoming its chief. The two vice-chiefs were Li Peng and Zhu Rongji. While the LGFE, which was practically dissolved after June 4, did not meet regularly, it was the party's highest authority on economic policymaking.[12]

Jiang was successful in consolidating his hold over the party apparatus with the elevation of a large number of like-minded "moderates" from Shanghai, who came to be known as the Shanghai Faction. For example, Zeng Qinghong, who served with Jiang in Shanghai as vice party secretary of the CCP committee, was in early 1993 promoted Director of the Central Committee General Office, the party's nerve centre.[13]

As we shall see in the next section, with the physical and political "illness" of Li Peng in much of 1993, Jiang also took on responsibilities in foreign affairs. First of all, he became head of the Central Committee's Leading Group on Taiwan Affairs. And there were indications that during Li's absence, Jiang chaired the Leading Group on Foreign Affairs, the party's highest authority on diplomacy.

·The year 1993 saw the inexorable decline of traditional central planners — led by Li Peng and the retired vice-premier Yao Yilin — and the rise of modernisation-minded technocrats led by Zhu Rongji. However, the power shift took place gradually. Immediately after the NPC, it was by no means clear that Zhu's influence had supplanted that of Li.

Zhu, who enjoyed the support of Deng Xiaoping, was expected to dominate economic policymaking through the super-agency, the State Economic and Trade Commission (SETC), which was comparable to Japan's Ministry of International Trade and Industry. The SETC, which was also an expanded version of the defunct State Economic Commission, was headed by a Zhu protégé, Wang Zhongyu. A former governor of Jilin Province and director of a paper-making mill, Wang first won Zhu's trust when the latter went to the northeast to clear up triangular debts in late 1991. The new Minister at the State Planning Commission, Chen Jinhua, is also considered Zhu's man. The former vice-mayor of Shanghai was a cautious technocrat in the Zhu mode. In addition, Zhu promoted a number of neutralist technocrats into vice-ministerial positions at the SETC.[14]

The cabinet that was confirmed by the 1993 NPC saw a rise in the influence of technocrats, even though most of them were cautious rather than radical modernisers. 42 out of the 46 cabinet members had college education, and 24 professional qualifications such as engineer or economist. Only two of them — the new Labour Minister Song Defu and Electronics Minister Hu Qili

— had affiliations with Hu Yaobang or Zhao Ziyang. Both Song and Hu, however, had clearly forsworn their political liberalism.[15]

A majority of the new ministers were moderate technocrats. Some among these had headed industry or commercial enterprises in their specialties. They included the Minister of Power Industry Shi Dazhen; Minister of Coal Industry Wang Senhao; Minister of Machine-Building Industry He Guangyuan; Minister of Posts and Telecommunications Wu Jichuan; Minister of Water Resources Niu Maosheng; Minister of Agriculture Liu Jiang; Minister of Forestry Xu Youfang; and the Minister of Foreign Trade and Economic Co-operation Wu Yi.[16]

It would be simplistic to assume that these technocrats were converts of the market economy. Very few of them were affiliated with Zhu Rongji's group in terms of personnel or ideology. Many were also time-tested bureaucrats whose first priority was preserving the privileges of their ministries. However, it would be fair to assume that they were realists who did not see their future in further identification with the diktat economy of the central planners. As we saw in Chapter 5, during ballots at the 1993 NPC, Soviet-school politicians such as Li Tieying and Li Guixian, respectively Education Minister and People's Bank of China (PBoC) Governor at the time, were humiliated by rebel parliamentarians.[17]

Li Peng and his so-called pro-Soviet clique, however, retained a formidable perch. Until late June 1993, Premier Li had a dominant say in finance and banking. Key leaders in this area, including Finance Minister Liu Zhongli and the then PBoC supremo Li Guixian, were deemed Li allies. Some analysts even argued that the power balance within the post-NPC State Council still favoured Li Peng. For example, among the eight State Councillors confirmed in March 1993, five were clearly closer to the Soviet-trained premier than to Zhu. They were State Council Secretary General Luo Gan; Minister for Restructuring the Economy Li Tieying; Science and Technology Minister Song Jian; Family Planning Chief Peng Peiyun, and Li Guixian. Luo, in particular, assumed greater powers in the key area of personnel and security. In July 1993, the Li Peng confidant became a vice-head of the Commission on the Establishment of Central Committee Organs.[18]

The tug-of-war between Li and Zhu shifted to the latter's favour with the onset of the austerity programme and Zhu's concurrent assumption in July of the post of PBoC Governor. This move broke the tradition of central planners — stretching from Chen Yun and Li Xiannian to Yao Yilin and Li Peng — having a stranglehold over the financial portfolio.

Soon after taking over the PBoC job, Zhu appointed three vice-governors: president of the Shanghai-based Bank of Communications Dai Xianglong; vice-president of the Shanghai Branch of the Bank of China Zhu Xiaohua;

and vice-president of the People's Construction Bank of China Wang Qishan. All three are moderate technocrats. Dai and Zhu are considered close to Zhu, while the political affiliation of Wang, a son-in-law of Yao Yilin, is dubious.[19]

Another major personnel development in 1993 was the further sidelining of leftists as well as opportunists who gained power through displaying "valiance and resoluteness" in the June 4 massacre. As we saw in Chapter 4, the PLA reshuffle that began from late 1992 to early 1994 weeded out members of the Yang Clan, including a number of officers who gained promotions through distinguishing themselves in the 1989 suppression of the democracy movement.

A number of leftists on the civilian side were also removed. Prominent among them was the much-maligned director of the *People's Daily*, Gao Di. Executive Vice-Chief of the Propaganda Department, Xu Weicheng, was slated for retirement. The Gang of Four holdover was in March 1993 given a membership on the Standing Committee of the CPPCC, a prelude to his departure from active duty. Two remnant Maoists promoted to leading positions in Chinese Academy of Social Sciences in late 1989, Yu Wen and Jiang Liu, called it quits in late 1993.[20]

III. Jiang Zemin, Zhu Rongji and the Shanghai Faction: The Rise of the Moderate Technocrats

A. The Rise of the Moderates or Middle-of-the-Roaders

By early 1994, the contours of the Mainstream Faction, which was built along a Jiang-Zhu axis, had become clear. The Mainstream clique consisted of moderates or middle-of-the-roaders, cadres who were neither left (remnant Maoists) nor right (bourgeois liberals). They were modernisation-minded technocrats not given to all-out Westernisation, relatively liberal in economic matters but conservative in the ideological arena. In terms of factional affiliation, these moderate leaders as well as rising stars under their wing were neither followers of conservative patriarchs Chen Yun and Deng Liqun, nor protégés of ousted party chief Zhao Ziyang. While they favoured market reforms in general, the moderates also heeded the imperative of beefing up the powers of the *zhongyang* or Party Centre. And while they were convinced that the Stalinist command economy should be dismantled and that most economic activities should be guided by the market, they believed in the perseverance of indirect, macro-economic control by the state.

It is not difficult to understand why "moderate" or "neutralist" figures should see a rise in their political fortunes. Stability being very much the priority of Deng, politicians who occupied the centre of the spectrum were seen as least likely to rock the boat particularly in the unpredictable first years of the post-Deng era. Since 1992, two blocs of neutralist politicians continued to make a steady ascent up the hierarchy. One was the Shanghai Faction whose titular head was Jiang Zeming: they were politicians either born in Shanghai or who spent at least part of their careers in the East China metropolis. The other consisted of moderate technocrats led by Zhu Rongji, many of whom could also be identified as members of the Shanghai Faction.[21]

There was a considerable amount of overlapping between the two groups. Both Jiang and Zhu had worked in Shanghai, and a large number of technocrats elevated by Zhu had associations with the city. It is not surprising, therefore, that Zhu was also referred to as the head of the Shanghai Faction. However, there is a clear difference between Jiang and Zhu, and between their respective cliques. Most of Jiang's associates were party functionaries who were at least a shade conservative in ideological matters. Zhu's technocrats, on the other hand, tried as much as possible to stay away from ideological and political issues. Moreover, the Zhu affiliates came from a broader base than Shanghai: many were known as members of the Qinghua Faction because of the fact that they were, like Zhu, graduates of the distinguished institute of engineering and the sciences.[22]

By mid-1993, the Shanghai Faction, including a number of Zhu's technocrats, had gained such an ascendancy in the rarefied halls of Zhongnanhai that Shanghainese seemed to have become the power dialect in party headquarters. In the mid-1980s, Deng Xiaoping liked to tell visitors that former party chief Hu Yaobang and former premier Zhao Ziyang were the "twin pillars that hold up the sky". Those roles were now being assumed by Jiang and Zhu.

A remarkable difference between the Hu-Zhao axis and the Jiang-Zhu axis is that while Hu and Zhao came from disparate backgrounds, Jiang and Zhu had close ties to Shanghai. Deng thus broke a long-standing taboo in Chinese politics not to let one faction — whether ideologically or geographically defined — dominate the Politburo and other top-level councils.

Why the Shanghai Faction? Why the moderate technocrats? As theorist Lu Jiamin saw it, at the 14th Congress, Deng elevated a large corps of "middle-of-the-roaders whose political orientation is blurred". "They are not connected with the June 4 incident and they assume low [ideological] profiles," Lu said.[23] Unlike the followers of Hu Yaobang or Zhao Ziyang, they had no agenda for political liberalisation.

Geo-political factors were also at work. Immediately after June 4, 1989, the following cliques held sway in Zhongnanhai politics: the Soviet Faction led by Li Peng and other graduates of East bloc universities; the Beijing Faction that was represented by the State Council planners and ideologues in the capital such as the then Beijing party secretary and mayor, respectively Li Ximing and Chen Xitong; and the Gansu Faction of conservative party functionaries under Organisation Chief Song Ping. These cabals, which played a big role in the Tiananmen Square suppression, also wanted to take advantage of the post-June 4 purge to roll back Deng Xiaoping's reforms.[24]

By contrast, Shanghai-related cadres were a breath of fresh air. At least superficially, they were not tainted with the blood of Tiananmen Square. Equally important for Deng, while Shanghai Faction affiliates were able practitioners of the open-door policy, they were less "Westernised" and independent-minded than cadres in Guangdong, Fujian or Hainan. Members of the Shanghai Faction were considered more amenable to central control than regional "warlords" from the southeast, including many affiliates of Zhao Ziyang, whose power base was Guangdong.[25]

"Being a victim of the Gang of Four, Deng was at the beginning of his tenure very wary of politicians with a Shanghai connection," a Chinese source said in 1992. "Yet after June 4, the patriarch had no choice but to rely on the Shanghai Faction, which provided a viable alternative to the central planners and the ideologues in the capital."[26] Referring to the Kuomintang chief Chiang Kai-shek's efforts in the late 1920s to crush the northern warlords with Guangzhou-based troops, Deng indicated privately in 1991 that the reformist faction must embark on a "northern expedition" by making use of "new ideas" and political forces in the south, particularly Shanghai, to smash the "ossified thinking" of the capital.[27]

The clout of the Shanghai cabal also swelled because of the new-found emphasis on the Shanghai-Pudong area and the Yangtze River Estuary, destined to be the focus of the open-door policy in the late 1990s. Every Lunar New Year after the massacre, Deng spent at least a month in Shanghai briefing local leaders on the new spirit of reform. At the height of the austerity programme in mid-1993, Shanghai politicians were assured that the area would still enjoy "priority status" in the allocation of state funds (see Chapter 2). [28]

The rise of the Shanghai Faction signified in a way that Chinese politics had come full circle. Shanghai always had a disproportionately large representation in the nation's top echelon. The Gang of Four and many other principal players of the Cultural Revolution hailed from Shanghai. In the 1930s and 40s, the East China Metropolis was the nexus of the underground anti-KMT movement, thus explaining why so many of today's leaders first earned their spurs in Shanghai. However, the post-June 4 dominance by the Shanghai Faction was unprecedented in Communist-Chinese history.[29]

Apart from politicians with direct ties of Jiang and Zhu, other heavyweights in the post-14th Party Congress order also had connections to

Shanghai. They included National People's Congress Chairman Qiao Shi, who was a leader of the underground student movement in Shanghai, and Vice-Premiers Zou Jiahua and Qian Qichen.

Then there were politicians who were gravitating towards the Jiang-Zhu axis — and adopting middle-of-the-road political stands — for opportunistic reasons. By late 1993, it was clear that Jiang had co-opted into his inner circles two new members of the Politburo: Ding Guan'gen and Hu Jintao. This is despite the fact that until 1992, neither Ding·nor Hu were linked with Jiang from a factional perspective.

Originally a reformist-oriented technocrat, Ding became Head of the Propaganda Department after the 14th Party Congress. As we saw in Chapter 3, Ding slapped a straitjacket on the media and cultural fields. Hu Jintao also adopted middle-of-the-road colours after taking over the crucial organisation portfolio in late 1992. While usually known as a protégé of the late Hu Yaobang, the youngest member of the Politburo enjoyed the patronage of Song Ping and as such could be considered a member of Song's Gansu Faction. In 1993 and 1994, Hu apparently acquiesced in Jiang's requests for the promotion of a large number of the President's cronies.[30]

B. Jiang Zemin as the "Core" of the Leadership

(i) Jiang's Expanding Power Base

In his talk to Li Peng and Yao Yilin five days before the June 4, 1989, crackdown, Deng asked the two heavyweights to throw their support behind Jiang, whom the patriarch had already identified as party chief. "I hope we can very well consider comrade Jiang Zemin as the core of the leadership, and we can unite behind Jiang," Deng said. "We must not be jealous [of the powers and authority] of each other. We must not waste energy on internecine bickering. If we fail to trust each other and make compromises, we cannot work in unison and minor differences will become major conflicts."[31] Very clearly, the patriarch was aware that since Jiang was more junior in party ranking than either Li or Yao, his meteoric rise might provoke opposition. When Jiang was made CMC Chairman in September the same year, Deng made a similar appeal to military officers to rally behind the new chief.

In spite of the fact that Jiang was considered a figurehead like Hua Guofeng, his performance in the five years after mid-1989 was better than most analysts had expected. Deng's expectations of Jiang was simple: to hold together the party, nation, and army — and to continue with economic reform. To a certain extent, Jiang acquitted himself well in these jobs, although, as we shall see, he tended to lean towards the conservative side soon after he became party boss. More importantly, Jiang probably spent more time jockeying for position and "vote-buying" than tending affairs of state.

Aside from Deng's blessings, what was Jiang's power base? Jiang was first notified of his move to Beijing a month or so before the Tiananmen Square gunshots, and he lost no time in trying to transfer favoured Shanghai aides to the capital. Shanghai-faction affiliates trusted by Jiang were noticeably more conservative than those allied with Zhu Rongji.

The most obvious attempt by Jiang to augment his power base took place in late 1990, when the General Secretary requested that a few dozens of his former associates be posted to party and State Council headquarters. At the time, Jiang sent 50-odd mid- and senior-ranking officials from the East China metropolis to a spell in the Central Party School. Jiang's idea was that they would stay behind in the capital after the special training. However, mostly due to opposition from party elders, the plan fizzled out.[32]

It is a measure of Jiang's success in empire building that, by mid-1993, he had succeeded in moving a considerable number of his protégés to the capital. Zeng Qinghong, the former vice party secretary of Shanghai who is his alter ego, was the first to go to Beijing. He was made head of the Jiang Zemin Office in late 1989 — in addition to Deputy Director of the General Office of the Central Committee. In early 1993, Zeng displaced Wen Jiabao as Director of the General Office, a post once occupied by Hu Qili, Qiao Shi, Wang Zhao-guo and Yang Shangkun.[33]

Other Shanghai cronies who joined Jiang at Zhongnanhai included Gong Xinhan and Liu Ji, both senior members of the Shanghai municipal propaganda office. In 1993, Gong became a Vice-Chief of Propaganda and Liu a Vice-President of CASS. Liu acted as Jiang's personal representative when he visited the US and Taiwan in 1992 and 1993. During these trips, Liu talked with politicians from different ends of the political spectrum, including dissidents and KMT cadres. Chinese sources said the party chief was particularly careful in posting trusted aides to the Central Guard Bureau, or the élite security officers who patrolled the Zhongnanhai headquarters and offered protection to the top leaders.[34]

Many denigrators of Jiang would be surprised by his versatility: the engineering graduate of famed Jiaotong University could claim impressive technocratic credentials. Moreover, especially given the authority over the economy that Deng had given him, Jiang was able, somewhat like Zhu, to gather under his wing a group of technocrats. Jiang's involvement in economic work first manifested itself in his having laid down the general directions for the Eighth Five-Year Plan and the Ten-Year Economic Blueprint. More importantly, the former electronics minister was able to use his old *guanxi* or connections to establish a foothold in the central-government apparatus. By early

1991, Jiang had become a keen lobbyist for the fast-paced development of electronics and information technology. "We must develop electronics as eagerly as we developed atomic bombs [in the 1950s and 60s]," he said.[35]

The former electronics minister was behind the surprising move in April 1993 by the central government to re-divide the Ministry of Electronics and Machine-Building Industries (MEMBI) into the Ministry of Electronics and the Ministry of Machine-Building. The two had been merged in 1988 in the name of administrative streamlining. Soon after his ascendancy to the post of party chief, however, Jiang was subjected to intensive lobbying by his former colleagues in the Ministry of Electronics to split up the MEMBI. That Jiang was able to do so during the NPC of 1993 was a testimony of his clout. Analysts said he could draw upon the support of bureaucrats from the two "new" ministries.[36]

Immediately after the Gulf War, Jiang was one of the first leaders to observe that modern warfare had become "three-dimensional, electronic" combat. In response to American preponderance in this arena, Jiang advocated the partial merger of the R & D of the industrial and military sectors, which he said should be anchored on breakthroughs in electronics and computers. Moreover, the CMC Chairman was a prime spokesman for putting technology, including military know-how, as the spearhead of the entire modernisation drive (see Chapter 4). "Jiang is using electronics as the 'key link' that will pull together and enhance his powers in the party, government and military," said a Chinese source in 1992.[37]

Unlike Shanghai-faction affiliates loyal to Zhu, those who were in Jiang's camp tended to be more interested in ideological matters. Their brief was to help the party chief maintain his dominance over the Zhongnanhai party apparatus — and to shoot down challenges to the regime that might be mounted by the right wing. Jiang proved to be adept at co-opting the Maoist ideologues, including the followers of Deng Liqun ("Little Deng" to Chinese intellectuals). As we saw in Chapter 3, there was almost a symbiotic relationship between Jiang's men and the leftists.

For example, Jiang retained many of Little Deng's followers in the Policy Research Office of the Central Committee (PROCC), which was headed by Wang Weicheng, a conservative cadre and former secretary of the late state president Li Xiannian. Wang's deputy, Teng Wensheng, a hardline commissar, became Jiang's chief speechwriter. As the party's premier think-tank, the PROCC drafted major party documents and Politburo papers.[38]

Beijing intellectuals, however, criticised Jiang for picking conservatives. By mid-1993, there was evidence that Jiang had made use of the services of one-time Li Peng protégé and Director of the State Council Research Office Yuan Mu — the *bête noire* of the liberals — for drafting the "socialist market economy document" for the Third Plenum of the 14th Central Committee. Yuan's deputy Wang Mengkui, who put together Li Peng's Government Work Report for the 1994 NPC, also offered economic advice to Jiang. Even He Xin, the much-maligned futurologist, became an adviser to Jiang on strategic affairs. He accompanied Jiang to the US for the "summit" with Bill Clinton in late 1993.[39]

Compared with either Hu Yaobang or Zhao Ziyang, Jiang was much better at currying favour with the leftist party elders. After all, Jiang's first and most important patron was the late Li Xiannian, who spent the bulk of his final days in Shanghai. Jiang also got on very well with such other conservative elders as Chen Yun.[40]

Upon becoming party boss, Jiang lost no time in making his pilgrimage to Yan'an, the "cradle of the revolution". Talking to cadres at the Marxist Mecca in September 1989, Jiang said: "The Yan'an spirit of self-reliance, hard struggle and plain living has not become obsolete." Jiang followed this up a few months later with a trip to the Minxi Revolutionary base area in Fujian Province, where Chairman Mao had held forth on the art of army building at the famous Guting Conference of 1929. Jiang told Red Army veterans that they must live up to the "revolutionary ideals" of the Great Helmsman by "promoting army ideological work".[41]

As we shall discuss presently, the widespread perception of Jiang as a "roly-poly" politician who was prepared to cut deals with the devil did little to change his reputation as head of the "wind faction", namely, a lightweight politician who would bend with the wind emanating from the powerful clans in Zhongnanhai.

(ii) Can Jiang Zemin Hold Up the Sky?

After more than three years of observation, Deng was by late 1992 apparently persuaded that Jiang was the best — or at least the least objectionable — cadre to hold the fort. While conservative by nature, Jiang was quick to profess loyalty to Deng's market-oriented gambit. Most importantly, the party chief could be trusted to put the supremacy of the CCP before everything. The former Shanghai party boss would not commit the same errors of Hu Yaobang or Zhao Ziyang by "succumbing to bourgeois liberalisation." [42]

What Deng seemed willing to overlook, however, was that in terms of economics, Jiang was closer to the central planners led by Li Peng than to the moderate technocrats led by Zhu Rongji. Moreover, he had more than once openly sided with Deng's nemesis, the leftists. Deng, however, was a hostage to history. Having already dumped two of his chosen successors, the patriarch would be hard put to replace Jiang with another heir apparent.

After the 14th Party Congress, Deng again indicated his total support for Jiang as the centre of the new leadership. In a meeting with Jiang soon after the Congress, Deng vowed that he would use whatever resources and energy he had to ensure his protégé's "core" status. "What more can I do for you in the next few years?" Deng reportedly asked Jiang. While Jiang was not effusive in his demands, the paramount leader apparently said that the party and military chief would have more say in the personnel reshuffles that were going on in both the civilian and military sectors.[43]

However, Jiang would seem to have serious flaws that might preclude him from becoming a *bona fide* Helmsman. And this has less to do with the fact that in Communist-Chinese history, none of the anointed successors — be it Lin Biao or Hua Guofeng — managed to last long after the demise of their patron.

First of all, Jiang had dubious credentials as a reformer. During Deng's *nanxun*, the patriarch criticised what he called the "formalism" of the top echelon, principally Jiang and Li Peng. This was a reference to the failure of the two to carry out fast-paced reform. The critique was repeated during the paramount leader's tour of the Capital Iron and Steel Works in May 1992, when he complained that certain leaders in Zhongnanhai failed to implement the spirit of the *nanxun*. He even hinted that the so-called Jiang-Li axis might have to be fine-tuned.[44] Indeed, Jiang, who had an unfortunate propensity for showing off his ungrammatical and accented English and Russian, was often ridiculed by Beijing intellectuals for his "empty words, foreign words, and nonsensical words".

The debate on how to achieve the "socialist market economy" was focused on whether one should emphasise market forces or "non-mandatory" macro-level control by the state. While liberal economists almost made a fetish out of the market, there was no mistaking the fact that the party boss wanted stronger macro-level regulations. In spite of its homage to the Invisible Hand of Adam Smith, Jiang's Political Report to the 14th Party Congress highlighted the need for "macro-level regulation and control" to rectify the "innate weaknesses" of the market.[45]

In a later context, Jiang also revealed his largely conservative approach to "synthesising" market forces and non-mandatory planning. He said in a December 1992 speech that "[various] markets had to be propagated and their functions developed". However, the party chief added: "We must use economic, legal and whatever executive means as are required, to strengthen the macro-level regulation and control by the state."[46] By the end of 1992, there were signs Jiang had joined the chorus of Li Peng and Yao Yilin in decrying Deng's high-growth model.

Jiang was able to win over the octogenarian leadership, including Deng, with his uncompromising stand against "liberalisation". As we saw in Chapter 5, the President played a key role in turning back the clock on political reform. Suffice it to say that Jiang was most lukewarm in carrying forward the reformist ideas — particularly the anti-leftist crusade — raised by Deng during the *nanxun*. In his much-hyped speech to the Central Party School on June 9, 1992, the party boss repeated the orthodox viewpoint that "leftism" was a matter of cognisance while "rightism" was a matter of political standpoint.[47]

According to the party boss, leftism manifested itself in taking an "orthodox", "bookish" approach to certain Marxist tenets, and in sticking to "unscientific and warped" interpretations of Marxism. "Rightism", however, meant negating the Four Cardinal Principles. In other words, Jiang was toeing the conservative line that while leftist cadres could be won back to the fold after their misunderstanding of the Marxist gospel had been corrected, rightist cadres should be punished for siding with "class enemies".

Perhaps reflecting the views of the patriarch, the party chief stopped making references to "anti-leftism" soon after the 14th Party Congress. During a visit to Shanghai in November 1992, he scandalised the intelligentsia by apparently departing from the criterion of "taking economic construction as the core of national work". "The leitmotif of our society should be patriotism, socialism and collectivism," he said.[48] This dictum was repeated *ad nauseam* in ideological and propaganda sessions held throughout 1993 and 1994.

To the dismay of liberal intellectuals, Jiang sided with the Maoists time after time after the *nanxun*. For example, on questions of ideology and propaganda, he funnelled support to *People's Daily* director Gao Di against Deng protégé Li Ruihuan. The party boss was instrumental in blocking the promotion of the vice-president of CASS, Zheng Bijian, to head of the Propaganda Department. Within the army, Jiang masterminded the purge of a number of so-called anti-PLA historical novels, including *Elegy of the Barracks* by Li Peiyang. Five years after the June 4 massacre, the intelligentsia could still not forgive Jiang for closing down the liberal *World Economic Herald* in May 1993.[49]

There were, however, indications aplenty that the mantle thrust on him by Deng was way too large for Jiang's ability. As we discussed in Chapter 4, the CMC Chairman was largely successful in ingratiating himself with the top brass. However, Jiang's blatant power grab might have cost him his popularity. As was evident from the case of the fallen chief political commissar Yang Baibing, PLA officers looked down upon leaders who named too many of their cronies to plum jobs. Such was the case with Jiang's appointment of General Ba Zhongtan as Commander of the PAP in early 1993. In early 1994, Ba openly said that the most important task of the PAP was to "protect party and state leaders", a not too subtle reference to his determination to shore up Jiang.[50]

Most fatal for Jiang's prospects of becoming a real supremo, however, was his abiding mediocrity. Not for nothing was Jiang compared to Hua Guofeng, a lacklustre minister of public security before he was named chairman of the party by a dying Mao. A look at his career shows that Jiang was a most undistinguished minister of electronics in the early 1980s. His track record in Shanghai was inferior to that of such other Shanghai mayors or party secretaries as Wang Daohan and Zhu Rongji.[51]

In 1993 and 1994, Jiang seemed to have formed a "power pact" with the likes of Zhu Rongji and Hu Jintao against such other pretenders to the throne as Li Peng, and, particularly, Qiao Shi and Tian Jiyun. While Jiang and Zhu were torn by rivalry when they both worked in Shanghai, the former realised that he had to depend on Zhu to take charge of the economy. The Jiang-Zhu symbiosis worked out particularly well for Jiang. While Zhu took the flak for pushing through the unpopular retrenchment programme of late 1993 and 1994, Jiang took the credit for the reforms introduced. For example, just before the Third Plenum of late 1993, the Chinese-run Hong Kong daily *Wen Wei Po* claimed that it was Jiang who had advocated the large-scale transformation of state enterprises into shareholding companies. The paper said Jiang displayed flexibility on the fact that government-held economic entities need not be the predominant sector in all trades and product lines.[52]

Apparently in return for his support, Jiang helped Hu Jintao gain the additional title of Principal of the Central Party School in mid-1993, displacing Qiao Shi. The party boss also tried his best to chip away at Qiao's hold over the security and legal establishment. Jiang was clearly disturbed by the fact that when they were both in the Shanghai underground student movement in the late 1940s, Qiao was his superior.

By 1993 and 1994, however, there were indications that Jiang was getting a little giddy with his power. Somewhat like Wang Zhen, his preoccupation with the limelight became pathological. In mid-1993, he fired a few senior editors of the *PLA Daily* for putting his interview with CNN on the back page, an incident which scandalised the top brass.[53] The support that Jiang seemed to enjoy in the civilian and military sectors seemed to have been bought rather than earned through years of hard work or achievements. Such a dubious base could quickly unravel when his "supporters" saw that it had become more to their advantage to profess their loyalties elsewhere.

C. Zhu Rongji's Go-Go Technocrats

(i) The Inchoate Zhu Rongji Faction

Especially after Li Peng's protracted illness in mid-1993 and Zhu's assumption of the role of Executive Vice-Premier and Governor of the People's Bank of China (PBoC) in early July, the former Shanghai mayor became the *de facto* head of the nation's technocrats. The latter included not just members of the Shanghai Faction but a large corps of modernisation-minded professionals, managers and civil servants.

The moderate technocrats took up a large chunk of "cross-century cadres", officials in their 40s and 50s on whose shoulders fell the task of ushering China into the 21st century. Unlike Soviet-trained central planners, the bulk of the technocrats were educated in local universities. Qinghua University is the alma mater of "first-tier" leaders such as Zhu Rongji and Hu Jintao and regional honchos such as Shanghai Party Secretary Wu Bangguo, Jiangxi Governor Wu Guanzheng, and Qinghai Governor Tian Chengping. "China's MIT" has produced such a large amount of technocrats that a Qinghua Faction is said to have come into being.[54]

Two of Zhu's strongholds in the central government were the State Economic and Trade Commission (formerly the Economic and Trade Office, which was set up in 1992) and the PBoC. The SETC was heavily staffed with Zhu-style technocrats some of whom hailed from Shanghai. Being the only central-government unit which saw major expansion in 1993 and 1994, the SETC had 11 Vice-Directors and as many departments looking after most aspects of the economy. As we saw earlier, upon becoming head of the central bank, Zhu installed a number of his protégés at both PBoC headquarters and branches.[55]

By the end of 1993, it was evident that Zhu had put together a think tank not unlike those assembled by Zhao Ziyang in 1987 and 1988. It is no coincidence that quite a few members of Zhu's brains trust had worked for Zhao. Compared with Zhao's "closet-capitalist" lieutenants, Zhu's young advisers put more store by maintaining the prerogatives of the central government.

Four rising stars who seemed to have a particularly strong influence on Zhu were identified in 1993. They were Lou Jiwei, a member of Zhu's personal office; Li Jiange, an economist with the Development Research Centre of the State Council who became Zhu's secretary; Wu Xiaoling, a PBoC researcher and former staffer of the Beijing-based *Financial Times*; and Guo Shuqing, a former associate of the Economic Research Centre of the SPC.[56]

Lou, considered one of Zhu's right-hand men, worked in the State Commission for the Reform of the Economic Structure, one of Zhao Ziyang's premier think tanks. He was a vice-chief of Shanghai's Bureau for Restructuring the Economy when Zhu was mayor of the city. Lou moved to the capital following his mentor's promotion to Vice-Premier in 1991. Guo, a radical reformer who had worked for Zhao, studied economics for two years at Oxford University. Guo was briefly sidelined after the June 4, 1989, crackdown. The four young turks were disciples of economics guru Wu Jinglian, a cautious reformer who wanted the coexistence of central authority and market reforms. Not surprisingly, Professor Wu did not find favour with Zhao Ziyang, who preferred more radical economists such as Li Yining.[57]

The philosophy and methodology of Zhu and his SETC yielded a good insight into the statecraft of the moderate technocrats. In general, the "mini-State Council" would concentrate on macro-economic guidance such as the drafting of industrial policies, trade strategies, and the coordination of the harnessing of key resources such as oil and transport. Zhu and his cohorts repeatedly made it clear that China would not go down the capitalist road. While talking to Swedish businessmen in Stockholm in late 1992, Zhu denied that China would embrace capitalism. He said Beijing would hold on to such socialist trappings as "public ownership as the mainstay, safeguarding social justice and egalitarian prosperity".[58]

In contrast to the avant-garde advisers of Zhao — who regarded the United States as the mecca of market-style economics — Zhu had more qualms about copying the West. Consider, for example, his remarks when, upon visiting the US in the summer of 1990, Zhu was briefed on the ways in which the American government regulated the economy. "So it is true that central planning plays an important role in capitalist countries," Zhu's hosts quoted him as saying.[59]

Befitting a technocrat of the "East Asiatic model", Zhu looked to Japan and Singapore instead of the West for inspiration. While briefing delegates to the 14th Party Congress, the Vice-Premier heaped praise on the "Japanese model". He was talking about a synthesis of free-wheeling market forces and a relatively tight control by the government, meaning patriarchal clans within Jap-an's Liberal Democratic Party. "We can learn a lot from Japanese institutions," Zhu said. "On the one hand, there is market economics; on the other, a very strict macro-economic control." The Vice-Premier pointed out that the SETC could be modelled on Japan's famous Ministry of International Trade and Industry. "MITI alone is a match for a dozen-odd of our ministries," he said.[60]

The way the SETC handled the development of the "stocks system" in the second half of 1992 illustrated well the approach of the technocrats. Zhu and his colleagues shot down applications by Guangzhou, Tianjin, and a host of other cities to set up the country's third stock exchange. Moreover, the State Securities Commission, which Zhu established in late 1992, laid down severe restrictions on the type and number of companies that could publicly sell or float their issues (see Chapter 2).

The political fortune of the Zhu-style technocrats was tipped to expand because they suited the golden rule of moderation espoused by Deng and other party elders. Moreover, even hard-core central planners and ideologues would find them more acceptable than the "all-out Westernisers" who worked for Zhao Ziyang. And the technocrats' innate cautiousness particularly in carrying out economic reform would make them less prone to the kind of mistakes committed by the Zhaoists in 1988.

(ii) Is Zhu Rongji a Reformer? An Efficient Administrator?

At least in the economics department, Zhu Rongji was Deng's fourth chosen successor after Hu, Zhao and Jiang. During his visit to the Capital Iron and Steel Works in May 1992, the patriarch openly praised Zhu's ability to propagate the market economy. He even expressed regrets about "not having elevated comrade Rongji sooner".[61] For if Jiang Zemin and Li Peng had somehow let him down in economic reform, Deng was convinced that the former Shanghai mayor would more than make amends.

Even before the 14th Party Congress, Zhu had assumed effective control over most aspects of the economy, including the distribution of resources; production; circulation of products; foreign trade; the transformation of state enterprises; and the development of shareholding companies and stock exchanges. In 1992, the Vice-Premier presided over the drafting of State Council regulations that gave unprecedented autonomous powers to public-sector business units. The main goal of such regulations was "pushing state enterprises to the marketplace". Zhu played a key role in speeding up the development of shareholding firms. He urged entrepreneurs to learn modern management techniques in both China and overseas and to attune themselves to market and technological conditions. This so-called "Zhu's definition of entrepreneurship" was refreshingly free of ideology.[62]

The Vice-Premier played a large role in the drafting of documents and policies that led to the breakthrough at the Third Plenum of the 14th Central Committee in late 1993 (see Chapter 2). It is to Zhu's credit that in spite of the overwhelming pressure being put to bear on the State Council in late 1993 and early 1994, he never wavered in his commitment to market mechanisms. While touring Hainan Island in late 1993, Zhu made propaganda for Deng's famous adage that cadres "must change their brains". "Resistance to our work mainly comes from our way of thinking," he said. "Old concepts and doctrines still exist among different leadership bodies." The Vice-Premier added that cadres must make a "thorough break" with old concepts and styles.[63]

Even in the face of potential instability triggered by the rising number of strikes and industrial incidents, Zhu insisted upon market reforms, particularly the restructuring the state enterprises. He defended the policy of "killing them and then bringing them back to life", that is, gradually declaring the most inefficient enterprises bankrupt while ensuring a subsistence livelihood for laid-off workers. "It will not do to try out the bankruptcy experiment too rashly as social stability is at stake," he said in early 1994. "Yet we can at least declare one enterprise bankrupt in every county."[64]

The major difference between Zhu and the Zhaoists is that he was not committed to the privatisation of the economy. Reflecting his predilections as a cautious technocrat, Zhu's calling had by late 1992 turned from offence to defence. In some speeches, the "Master Reformer" began sounding somewhat like Li Peng when the former cracked the whip on "excessively ambitious" cadres and entrepreneurs in the localities. In the last months of 1992, Zhu practically issued an ultimatum to regional cadres and managers to cool off their investment binge. The Vice-Premier pointed out at a State Council meeting that bank loans for the year had gone up by 20 per cent and currency in circulation an incredible 200 per cent. He particularly criticised excessive expansion in three areas: real estate, the issuing of stocks, and the start-up of development zones. "The extent of loans and credit and the issuing of currency should be restricted within prescribed limits," he said. "Whoever goes beyond these limits have to be held responsible."[65]

Zhu displayed a cool-headed approach to policy when he decried the imbalances and dislocations in the economy. He convincingly showed in early 1993 that the localities had started too many development zones, because as much as 4,400 billion yuan would be needed to complete the basic infrastructure for the 15,000 sq km of land that had been earmarked for such purposes. The economic czar also argued that China should not regard the issuing of stocks as the main means of raising capital. "We do not have a comprehensive legal system and experience to protect the people [who have bought stocks]," he said. "Moreover, a class of professional speculators will soon emerge."[66]

Zhu showed his real colours as the Great Rectifier during the "campaign to boost macro-economic adjustments and controls" in 1993. As we saw in Chapter 2, a number of the measures he adopted — particularly the 16-point programme to impose financial disciple — smacked of draconian means to reinstate state fiats. One of Zhu's most memorable remarks during the rectification campaign was his threat to "chop off the head" of any cadre who used public funds to wheel and deal — and who issued IOUs to farmers instead of paying them cash.[67] The austerity programme cost Zhu a great deal of popularity especially among State Council bureaucrats and regional leaders, a blow which the czar would take some time to recover. Being the party leader who negotiated with the PLA top brass on the curtailment of the army business empire, it is also inevitable that Zhu would not be the apple in the eyes of the military kingmakers.

Zhu was of course justifiable in taking harsh remedial measures. Excessive capital investment and inflation were real dangers. Moreover, as in 1988, there were signals that the central planners were taking advantage of the need to "cure and restructure the economy" to choke off Deng's fast-paced reforms. However, Zhu and other moderate technocrats were also doing their Li Peng act for political reasons: the regions and the entrepreneurs were whizzing away from the orbit of central party authorities.

In late 1993, Zhu received flak from a large number of liberal economists and former associates of Hu Yaobang and Zhao Ziyang for restoring elements of the command economy. The short-lived anti-Zhu crusade climaxed at a meeting of 100-odd social scientists and free-thinking cadres in Beijing in October, in which liberals like Xiao Zhuoji and Zhu Houze spoke about the imperative of keeping up the momentum of fast-paced reform (see Chapter 2). The conference was not mentioned in the official media in China — but a fairly detailed report came out in the semi-official China News Service, whose dispatches were widely used in Hong Kong and Taiwan. Zhu was so furious that he reportedly ordered an investigation into the CNS's "motives" for carrying the piece.[68]

Zhu had a solid reputation among many Chinese bureaucrats and foreign businessman as a "can do" administrator. During his tenure in Shanghai, he was known as "one chop Zhu" for simplifying ways in which foreign companies could set up shop in the metropolis. However, it is also true that like the average CCP cadre, he was prone to giving up his principles in the face of political obstacles. Zhu's career was strewn with half-finished projects. In late 1991 and 1992, the official media made much of the fact that the Vice-Premier had "solved" the problem of the triangular debts, or money enterprises owed each other. In actual fact, the imbroglio had never been thoroughly tackled — and it reared its head again in 1993 and 1994. By early 1994, such debts had reached the unprecedented level of 300 billion yuan.[69]

In September 1993, less than three months after starting the austerity programme, Zhu sued for peace in the face of stiff opposition from the regional warlords. In many instances, the Great Rectifier even volunteered to boost the amount of bank loans to the provinces (see Chapter 2). Nor did Zhu carry out his threat of cashiering officials deemed guilty of misconduct or failure to toe the central line. For example, no local official was punished for failing to meet the August 15 deadline for returning improperly secured funds to central coffers.[70]

Upon assuming the leadership of the PBoC, Zhu threatened to fire the large number of central and regional bankers who had illegally used deposits to speculate in the real estate and stock markets. As he told an internal meeting of the Standing Committee members of the CPPCC in late 1993, however, Zhu did not carry out his threat because "I need these staff to keep the banking system running". Those who had been suspected of misusing state funds apparently were allowed to go scot-free.[71]

(iii) The Enigma of Zhu's Political Persona

Somewhat like Qiao Shi, Zhu was adept at hiding his political persona — to the point that very few observers knew what his ideological positions were. Various incidents since the mid-1980s, however, would place him slightly left of centre in the political spectrum, meaning he was a shade on the conservative side. This is despite the fact that in the late 1950s, Zhu was classified a "rightist" for allegedly singing the praises of Yugoslav "revisionism" after taking part in an official trip to that country.[72]

Take, for example, the issue of human rights. Indications were that Zhu was stricter and less "Westernised" in outlook in this area than liberals such as Hu Yaobang and Zhao Ziyang — or even Li Ruihuan and Qiao Shi. While touring Denmark in 1992 and Canada in 1993, Zhu toed the standard line that criticism of Beijing's human rights records amounted to "gross interference in the internal affairs of China". "There are no serious human rights questions in China," he said in Canada. "Socialist democracy is superior to capitalistic democracy."[73]

Zhu won the admiration of many Chinese and foreign journalists for his "sensitive" and "bloodless" handling of the June 4 crisis in Shanghai. In early June, the mayor mobilised workers — not soldiers — to restore order to the city. In a much-noted television broadcast immediately after the Beijing massacre, Zhu told city folk that "history will one day shed light on the real circumstances behind the [June 4] events". This would seem to suggest that Zhu was at that time asking the people to think twice about party propaganda on the "counter-revolutionary turmoil". However, in an apparent effort to avoid antagonising Beijing, Zhu changed the script of the TV footage that would be aired nationwide. He added the following caveat: "We must trust and follow the Party Centre's conclusions on the events."[74]

Shanghai was the first city to have executed "hoodlums" and "counter-revolutionaries" for involvement in the pro-democracy crusade. A few days after the massacre, three young Shanghai "workers" were put to death for blocking and torching a train. It turned out that at least one of the trio was mentally handicapped. By mid-1994, there was no sign that Shanghai's intellectuals were prepared to forgive him for this.[75]

Shortly before Zhu took up the vice-premiership in April 1991, he wrapped up the case of the former propaganda chief of Shanghai, Pan Weiming. A radical liberal and protégé of Hu Yaobang, Pan was arrested a month earlier for patronising prostitutes in Sichuan. However, the circumstances of the arrest, particularly the fact that Pan's apartment was searched and his papers taken away, gave rise to the suspicion that it might have been a political set-up and vendetta. In an internal speech on Pan, Zhu lambasted the "decrepit morality" of the former liberal cadre, noting that he had succumbed to "the vilest bourgeois liberalisation".[76]

While Hu Yaobang and Zhao Ziyang were famous for recruiting aides with near-heretical beliefs, Zhu preferred efficient but strait-laced technocrats. His only known instance of innovative personnel management took place when, as Shanghai mayor, he set up a council of foreign businessmen to advise him on investment policies.[77]

Few Zhu watchers, however, doubted his good PR sense, his charisma, and considerable diplomatic skills. The former rightist had an eye for modish tailoring as well as Western-style etiquette. Sources close to the Zhu camp said during trips abroad, the first thing the Vice-Premier did each morning was to scan the local papers for reports of his activities the day before.

On home ground, however, Zhu was notorious for being abrasive — to the point of scolding senior cadres in the midst of large conferences. Official NCNA biographies invariably highlighted the way in which he "executed policies like thunder and tornadoes". A story making the rounds of Beijing in 1992 said he made a self-criticism for failing to promote unity among his colleagues. Zhu said he had alienated his underlings by being "too quick and forthright in pointing out their mistakes".[78]

As we saw earlier, Zhu's relationship with the media was hardly a model of tolerance. Soon after the 1993 NPC, he scolded a relatively small-circulation paper for reporting the threat he had made in an internal speech about "chopping off the head" of officials who continued to pay farmers with IOUs. Analysts believed that Zhu was behind the harsh treatment meted out Hong Kong reporter Xi Yang for "leaking" an internal speech that he made while inspecting PBoC headquarters in mid-1993.[79]

Apart from Deng's patronage, Zhu's meteoric rise in the hierarchy testified to his ability to survive the rough-and-tumble of Zhongnanhai politics. Unlike either Hu and Zhao, Zhu was a street-fighter who had a shrewd, sometimes ruthless edge. He also knew how to negotiate the cunning corridors of CCP politics. Take, for example, the birth of Pudong as the nation's premier open zone for the 1990s. Deng Xiaoping first gave theoretical approval to the Pudong Project — which was proposed by Shanghai theorists in the early 1980s — during a visit to Shanghai in the Lunar New Year in 1990. Thanks to Zhu's frantic lobbying, high-level visits by Yao Yilin and Li Peng followed in the spring. Pudong became a reality soon afterwards — and Zhu was able to take much of the credit for it.[80]

Zhu acquitted himself well as a super-salesman of first Shanghai and then Pudong. When he was in Hong Kong in the summer of 1990, the mayor was asked by reporters whether he considered the territory a "base of subversion". (Officials handling Hong Kong affairs, including Zhou Nan and Lu Ping, had given the enclave that derogatory label). "I'd love to visit Hong Kong no matter what kind of a base it is," was Zhu's very diplomatic answer.[81]

Not unlike Jiang Zemin, Zhu was a pastmaster at massaging the ego of party elders. Soon after becoming mayor of Shanghai, he set up a municipal advisory commission to seek the advice of — and to ingratiate himself with — retired municipal elders, many of whom still had an inside track with conservative patriarch Chen Yun. Taking advantage of the fact that Shanghai was a favourite vacation spot for senior leaders, Zhu was able to curry favour with elders from different ends of the political spectrum. Aside from Deng, they included Li Xiannian, Chen Yun, Song Renqiong, and Peng Zhen. Zhu was instrumental in arranging special medical care for the veterans as well as their offspring.[82]

Given the fact that China is still at the early stage of socialism — or quasi-capitalism — few would fault Zhu for charting a steady, cautious course. That Zhu lacked *bona fide* reformist credentials and inclinations, however, probably meant that he would be a transitional figure after Deng's death. Owing to factors including the galloping growth of the coast and the rapid advancement of "peaceful evolution", China will be a very different place ten years down the road. It takes a leader who has a heartfelt empathy for the marketplace — and who is able to tolerate and harness society's discordant voices — to lead the sprawling nation into the new century.[83]

IV. The Decline of the Central Planners

A. End-game for the Planners?

The 14th Party Congress confirmed the inexorable decline of the political bloc that, perhaps next to the PLA, had wielded the most power since 1949. While political stars and ideological gurus like Chairman Mao, Jiang Qing, and Deng Liqun might have hogged the limelight at one time or another, it was the bureaucrats in the State Council who oversaw the running of the economy — and the country. Disciples of heavyweights such as Chen Yun and Li Xiannian, these central planning-oriented cadres marched to the tune of Stalinist or "bird-cage" economics.

No more. With the advent of the "socialist market economy", the role of the diktat school of planners was being drastically cut. A key decision of the 14th Party Congress was "the separation of government and business", which would be accomplished through the large-scale curtailment of the size and power of government departments. In the wake of the growing importance of the marketplace, the state would only exercise "macro-economic control" over the economy. At least in theory, the functions of government departments of various levels would change from control and regulation to providing non-mandatory guidance and services.[84]

"The main work of economic departments should be transformed to strengthening macro-level regulations and adjustments," the Congress document said. "Professional economic departments whose functions overlap or whose jurisdictions are similar should be dismantled or merged. Staff establishments should be streamlined." The shrinkage of government and reorientation of its functions would be accomplished in three years.[85]

It was reported that at least one-third of the 30-million strong staff establishment of the party and government apparatus would be cut. Hardest hit was the State Planning Commission (SPC) — the stronghold of Stalinist statecraft — in addition to the Ministry of Foreign Economic Relations and Trade (MOFERT), the Ministry of Light Industry, the Ministry of Textile Industry, and the Ministry of Radio, Film and Television (see Chapter 5).[86]

Most illustrative of the shrinking leverage of the central planners was the uncertain fate besetting the SPC, traditionally the most important organ of the central government. Right after the Congress, the scope and quantity of its directives and production quotas began to be whittled down. For example, in 1993, 37 per cent of state fiats were reportedly abolished in fields including agriculture, industry and commerce. The role of the SPC would shift from direct control over production and distribution to laying down long-term plans and forecasts for economic activities.[87]

In an article in November 1992, the official *China Daily* described the SPC as a "think-tank". SPC Vice-Minister Wang Chunzheng indicated that instead of "administrative intervention", his unit would "mainly adopt economic levers to attain its goals of effective macro-regulation over the nation's economic performance". He claimed that by late 1992, only 10 per cent of state enterprises were still subjected to mandatory plans imposed by the commission.[88]

Given the CCP's determination to play up market forces, the handwriting was on the wall for central planners. However, it would be naive to assume that they would just fade away. Unlike Eastern Europe, China's transition to a market economy would be a long drawn-out process marked by U-turns and tergiversations. For example, by late 1992, two central planners supposed to be on their way out — Yao Yilin and Wang Bingqian — exploited the need to cool down the overheated economy to claw back some territory. At State Council meetings in December 1992, they compared the "high growth model" advocated by Deng to Chairman Mao's disastrous Great Leap Forward. Their conclusion, of course, was that the country still needed level-headed planners to rectify economic ills.[89]

In a late 1992 speech, Premier Li Peng surprised observers when he pointed out that the SPC, "in conjunction with other ministries and commissions", would be put in charge of revising the Eighth Five-Year Plan and the Ten-Year Economic Blueprint. The re-tooling of the plan and the blueprint — which had already been approved by the NPC in 1991 — had been ordered by Deng during his *nanxun* in view of their conservative nature. Up to mid-1992, it had been assumed that two ministries dominated by moderate cadres — the Economic and Trade Office (precursor of SETC) and the State Commission for the Reform of the Economic Structure (SCRES) — would be authorised to handle this vital task.[90]

And as we saw in Chapter 2, both the austerity programme of late 1993 and the socialist market economy blueprint announced at the Third Party Plenum meant that "macro-level economic adjustments and controls" would co-exist with market forces for the foreseeable future. There were signs in 1994 that the role of the SPC would again be beefed up in areas including the policing of illegal price rises (see Chapters 2 and 7).

Another factor behind the staying power of the central planners is that there was a certain degree of affiliation between them and Zhu Rongji's technocrats. A number of cadres promoted by Zhu had leanings towards central planning. They included, for example, SETC Minister Wang Zhongyu and SPC Minister Chen Jinhua. Both had headed major state corporations before joining the State Council. At a time when the overall climate favoured retrenchment, they were ready to de-emphasise market mechanisms and play up central control.[91]

At least in the short term, an important reason for the decimation of central planners was not streamlining but their plunge into business. By late 1993, a large number of State-Council bureaucrats had taken on new incarnations as the heads of the thousands of corporations that had been set up to "take over" the functions of the economic departments. Theoretically, these business units were supposed to be independent of the government and to be run like Western-style corporations. In reality, there was a high degree of fusion between government and business, and many so-called cadre-businessmen still ran these Chinese-style crown corporations along traditional lines, in the process obstructing the progress towards a market economy.

B. Li Peng's Reluctant Adieu

In mid-1993, partisans of reform among both Chinese citizens and foreign observers were elated by the prospect of Premier Li Peng's fall from power. After major heart surgery in April and May, Li looked set to vacate his position by the end of the year. However, having made a satisfactory recovery, it seemed probable that the symbol of the Tiananmen Square crackdown would be around as long as Deng Xiaoping was alive. By the autumn of 1993, the premier had more or less resumed his active duties — while his antagonist and competitor, Zhu Rongji, had taken an uncharacteristically low profile.[92]

Many China observers were convinced, however, that while Li might be able to remain titular head of government until the death of Deng, his powers would be truncated. In spite of Li's long-standing opposition to the "high-speed growth model", Deng had acquiesced in his continued stewardship of the central government. Li still enjoyed the support of the conservative elders as well as central planning-oriented bureaucrats. Moreover, Deng found it possible to stomach the foster son of Zhou Enlai for the familiar reason: the premier had a fairly good record for promoting stability.[93]

As was the case with his duels with Hu Yaobang and Zhao Ziyang in the mid- and late-1980s, Li saw a break for himself whenever the economy went wrong. In December 1992, Li got a new lease on life thanks to signs of the economy overheating. In a speech at a year-end economic conference, Li repeated the familiar arguments that the economy must grow under the premise of "stability, balance and harmony". While referring to Deng Xiaoping's plea at the *nanxun*, that "the economy should enter a new threshold once every few years", the premier warned: "The speed that we are after should be a speed that is based on a rational structure, that matches the needs of the market, and that is high in efficiency." On price reform, Li said it would only be implemented bearing in mind "the ability of society to cushion [the shocks]".[94]

Because of his heart problem and other political considerations, Li largely stayed away from the austerity drive in the latter half of 1993. Western diplomats surmised that, seeing how difficult the task was, the premier wanted Zhu to take the blame should the very unpopular programme falter.

However, as the retrenchment exercise was winding down towards the end of October, Li reassured the world that macro-level adjustments and controls would be "regularised" throughout the course of the socialist market economy. "Boosting and improving the state's macro-level adjustments and controls is a long-term task," he told the Hong Kong journal *Wide Angle*. "The system of the socialist market economy that we are constructing is to ensure that, under the macro-level adjustments and controls of the socialist state, the market will play a fundamental function in the distribution of resources."[95]

Moreover, in 1993, Li largely managed to retain his hold on foreign policy, including policy towards Hong Kong. His position as the Head of the Central Committee's Leading Group on Foreign Affairs seemed secure. In spite of his relatively poor image overseas, Li earned the respect of Deng and other elders for successfully enhancing China's diplomatic leverage.

As the successor of such central planners as Chen Yun and Yao Yilin, the premier would at least up to the mid-1990s continue to be the spokesman of central planning-oriented bureaucrats. Li also carried the brief of the so-called

Soviet Faction in the State Council, or cadres trained in the Eastern bloc in the 1950s. By early 1994, Li Faction affiliates in the State Council remained a force to be reckoned with. This was true of Li Tieying in spite of his humiliation at the hands of NPC deputies in 1993. For example, in 1994, the younger Li was put in charge of the task of working out ways to integrate the economies — and to some extent, the political systems — of Shenzhen and Hong Kong.[96] Even Li Guixian, who was relieved of his PBoC job by Zhu, was reasonably active. He retained his post of State Councillor and played a role in the anti-corruption campaign and the promotion of auditing in government.[97]

By early 1994, it was clear that Li Peng's political fortune was heading towards a downward spiral. The "socialist market economy" as defined by Li and Jiang would likely be short-lived given the fact that the wave of quasi-capitalism that began sweeping the nation in 1992 seemed unstoppable. Five years after the June 4 bloodbath, Li remained intensely unpopular. In mid-1993, there was widespread innuendo about members of the Li household being involved in the junk-bond scam perpetuated by the Changcheng Electronics, Electrical and High-Tech Corp. The accusations were so intense that Li had to assert through an interview later that year that neither he nor his family members owned any stocks and shares. One of Li's protégés, Vice-Minister of Science and Technology Li Xiaoshi, was implicated in the scandal and received a hefty sentence in early 1994.[98]

After Deng's death, Li would likely be among the first to go: as a scapegoat for the June 4 suppression and for more than four decades of productivity-killing central planning. According to sources close to the premier, he told intimates in late 1993 that he had no other ambition than serving out the rest of his term, which runs until 1998. Li also indicated that he would be happier concentrating on engineering projects such as the Three Gorges hydroelectric scheme, which would be his contribution to history. In 1993, the qualified hydroelectric engineer became head of the State Council's Three Gorges Engineering Construction Commission.[99]

V. The Zhao Ziyang Faction of Radical Reformers: Conserving Their Strength

A. The Vicissitudes of the Remnant Zhao Camp

Broadly speaking, the Zhao Ziyang faction or "Zhaoists" refers not just to cadres and intellectuals who worked for Zhao but the legions of "bourgeois-liberal" officials and scholars in and out of the CCP establishment. On economical matters, they were "closet capitalists" who clamoured for the quasi-capitalist road. They wanted the problematic qualifier "socialist" taken out of the 14th Party Congress ideal of the "socialist market economy". Politically, they could at least live with, if not enthusiastically support, political reform in the sense of "power sharing" between the CCP and other sectors of society.

The seemingly effortless way in which Deng Xiaoping and the conservative cliques dumped Zhao after the massacre might give the impression that the Zhao faction was lightweight at best. However, one must be reminded that at the height of the pro-democracy crusade in late May 1989, thousands of party and government functionaries — in addition to a sizeable number of military officers and soldiers — hit the streets in support of radical reforms.[100]

Moreover, Zhao's economic and political programmes generally found favour with intellectuals in Beijing and other large cities. The Zhaoists were able to co-opt the bulk of "right wingers" in the party as well as the intelligentsia. They seemed poised to play a significant role in the post-Deng order.

Even during the *nanxun*, it became obvious that there would be no rehabilitation for Zhao Ziyang — or large-scale reinstatement of his faction. In his talk to cadres in Guangdong, Deng praised Zhao for making contributions to fast-paced reform. However, he pointed out that former party general secretaries Zhao and Hu Yaobang had erred in the area of ideology: both failed to stem the tide of bourgeois liberalisation.[101]

More specifically, Deng could not have reinstated Zhao for reasons of political exigency. And this was not just due to the fact that rehabilitating Zhao would send the wrong signal that the party was ready to overturn the verdict on June 4. Deng knew that since the *nanxun*, he had in effect been advocating "a Zhao Ziyang policy without Zhao Ziyang". If Zhao were cleared of his "guilt", it should be he, not Deng, who should be leading the nation.

It therefore came as no surprise that at the Ninth Plenum of the 13th Central Committee on October 9, 1992, the party decided to uphold the Fourth Plenum verdict of late June 1989: "Zhao Ziyang made the mistake of supporting the turmoil and splitting the party; he bore unshirkable responsibilities for the shaping-up of the turmoil." However, the Ninth Plenum also said that "the examination and investigation" relating to Zhao had closed. The former party boss was allowed to keep his ordinary party membership and there would be no criminal proceedings against him.[102]

As a harbinger of Zhao's fate, his right-hand-man Bao Tong was sentenced to seven years in jail earlier that summer. This is despite the fact that influential party elders, who reportedly included Yang Shangkun, had argued against a harsh treatment of the former head of the Central Committee's Office for the Restructuring of the Political System. Chinese sources said that investigators had failed to unearth incriminating evidence that might have linked Bao with the student protesters. Bao's family members insisted that it was Deng who had laid down instructions on the heavy jail term to be slapped on Zhao's principal adviser.[103]

By 1994, it was obvious that the Zhaoists were by no means a spent force. As the economy continued to lurch towards the right, many in the country, particularly regional leaders and entrepreneurs, were picking up the threads of Zhao's quasi-capitalist experiments. The followers of Zhao were particularly well represented in middle and upper echelons in Guangdong, Hainan and other coastal provinces.

B. The Appeal of Zhao Ziyang

It is a strange phenomenon of Chinese politics that leaders always look better after their fall from grace. This was true of the late president Liu Shaoqi and the late defence minister Peng Dehuai. It was also true of Deng Xiaoping immediately after his three falls from power. The Tiananmen Incident of April 1976 was triggered to a certain extent by popular desire for the reinstatement of Deng. Then we have Hu Yaobang, who was by no means universally popular during his tenure. After his unceremonious fall in January 1987 — and especially after his death on April 15, 1989 — however, Hu took on the aura of a saint.

After the massacre, people were pining for Zhao's comeback because they could not see any member of the post-June 4 leadership qualified enough to put China back on track for reform. While some intellectuals and private entrepreneurs might be looking to Zhu Rongji and other relative reformers, Zhao's lustre did not seem to have faded. This is despite the fact that by early 1994, Zhao was regarded less as an active player than an elder statesman and kingmaker who might be an arbiter in the post-Deng power struggle.[104]

The staying power of Zhao was evident from the debate that had broken out within the CCP leadership on the extent to which the fallen leader should be rehabilitated. For a time after June 4, 1989, it was believed that Deng Xiaoping wanted a partial rehabilitation of his former protégé on condition that he owned up to his "mistakes". Chinese intellectuals said that Deng wanted Zhao — and his followers — to continue to act as a counterweight against the party's leftist factions.[105]

Immediately after the massacre, a special investigation team was set up by the CCDI to look into the Zhao "conspiracy". The group was headed by the late party elder Wang Renzhong. Its members reportedly included the son of party elder Peng Zhen, Fu Rui, who later became head of the Organisation Department of Guangdong Province. The group completed its investigations in the latter half of 1990. It never publicised its findings, but informed sources said no dirt had been uncovered. There was no evidence linking Zhao to the student leaders and other intellectuals behind the 1989 movement.[106]

The conservatives, however, were anxious to nail Zhao. In August 1991, Yuan Mu told a Japanese delegation that investigations into Zhao's "crimes" were still continuing. Li Peng dropped hints that Zhao might be put on trial and sentenced. Sources said that Li and other conservatives wanted to frame Zhao as the head of an "anti-party clique". If Zhao was convicted as such, he could be locked away for life.[107]

Deng, on the other hand, had since the autumn of 1989 been manoeuvring for a partial Zhao comeback. The patriarch refused to "blacken" the reputation of his erstwhile protégé, insisting that the latter had made economic contributions. In an internal speech in the autumn of 1989, Deng said that "Zhao had supported reform and the open-door policy". "When I transferred him [from Guangdong] to Sichuan in 1975, there were people in the province who were starving to death," Deng said. "He carried out reforms there, which bore fruit after three years. People [in Sichuan] now have no problem with food, clothing and shelter. Rural reform was begun by him and Wan Li."[108]

To avoid splitting the party, Deng ordered in late 1989 that the Zhao question be shelved for at least two years. The patriarch laid down four criteria to ensure that the anti-Zhao campaign did not degenerate into an overall attack on reform. They were: one must distinguish between the erroneous personal views of Zhao and reform theories and policies which were the correct decision of the Central Committee and the State Council; one must distinguish between the erroneous personal statements and policies of Zhao and those mistakes which the broad masses of cadres committed because they lacked experience in pursuing reform; one must distinguish between the erroneous thoughts and pronouncements of Zhao and the bold explorations made by theoretical workers in reform; in criticising Zhao, one must be careful not to lay into policies passed by the Central Committee and the State Council. Deng also urged that care be taken to protect the enthusiasm with which cadres and theoreticians continued their explorations in the reform enterprise.[109]

In mid-1990, in their first meeting after the June 4 bloodbath, Deng sounded out Zhao on his willingness to take up an honorary position. The patriarch also asked Zhao to make use of his idle time to conduct research on economic matters in the provinces. In the summer of 1990, Zhao and his wife were spotted playing golf in a facility near the Ming tombs just outside Beijing.

Deng tried again in mid-1991 to persuade Zhao to agree to a partial comeback. This time, Deng sent his close aide Ding Guan'gen, who told Zhao that his name would be cleared if he were willing to make an "indirect admission of guilt". Ding, who had succeeded Yan Mingfu as head of the United Front Department, told the former party chief that Deng would be satisfied if the latter were merely to concede that his actions in the run-up to June 4 had "the objective consequences of splitting the party". In return, Zhao would be offered honorary posts such as an adviser to the State Council or head of the Archives Bureau, a ministerial-level position.[110]

Zhao, however, saw no reason to yield on a matter of principle — and for an insubstantial consolation prize. After all, intellectuals still blamed Hu Yaobang for succumbing to the firepower of the elders in January 1987 and putting down his signature to a confession of guilt.[111]

Events in 1993 largely proved Zhao right. In spite of the harsh judgment of the Ninth Plenum of the 13th Central Committee, Zhao was in that year allowed to go on a tour of Guangxi and Hunan. There, he received a hero's welcome from local cadres, who accorded him a reception on a par with that of a Politburo member. The authorities, however, did not allow him to go to Guangdong, his old power base. However, pictures of Zhao in Hunan, which made it into the Hong Kong press — and then subsequently circulated back into China — caused a stir in the mainland, a testimony to the high regard with which the progenitor of reform was still held among the intelligentsia.[112] The enthusiasm for Zhao was such that in late 1993, the Central Committee General Office issued an instruction that local officials should treat Zhao as "no more than a ordinary party member". Such cadres should also refrain from seeing the former party chief.[113]

In 1993 and 1994, Zhao was hurt by reports in the Hong Kong and Taiwan press about the role he played in dumping Hu Yaobang — and his failure to join forces with such potential competitors as Wan Li to banish the leftists. The ex-party chief was also criticised as a weak leader who did not pay enough attention to such crucial matters as building up his own network.[114] However, there was little question that while Zhao was getting on in years — he was 75 in 1994 — he was still in a position to provide spiritual and moral leadership to reform. It is conceivable that, like Yang Shangkun and other party elders, Zhao would play a role after Deng's death in picking a successor and in steadying the course of economic reform.[115]

C. The Remnants of the Zhao Clique

The followers of Zhao Ziyang clawed back some territory after the 14th Party Congress of late 1992. Several former Zhao associates gained promotions, retained their influence, or achieved some form of rehabilitation. Moreover, as we shall see later, many ex-Zhao protégés made waves in the localities. It can be argued that the Zhao associates who kept their positions after June 4 1989 had "sold out" to the Jiang-Zhu axis. In the amorphous world of Chinese politics, however, it is true that when the tide turns, a number of Zhaoists in the Jiang-Zhu camp would re-hoist the old banner of radical reforms.

A former right hand man of Zhao, Wen Jiabao, was promoted an Alternate

Member of the Politburo at the 14th Congress. Wen, 50, came into the media limelight as the young cadre who accompanied Zhao to Tiananmen Square to see the students moments before the declaration of martial law on May 20 1989. In early 1993, Wen lost his position as head of the General Office of the Central Committee; but he was put in charge of the newly created Leading Group on Agriculture.[116]

A long-time Zhao protégé, Wen made his mark in Gansu Province and in the Ministry of Geology and Mineral Resources. While, like Hu Jintao, he might have owed his rise to conservative elder Song Ping, who is head of the Gansu Faction, Wen is generally considered a liberal. During the year before the June 4 massacre, he, together with Bao Tong, was one of Zhao's key liaison men with liberal intellectuals.

Another high-profile ex-Zhao protégé who made good was the party boss of Chongqing, Xiao Xang, who became Governor of Sichuan in early 1993 (see later section). In late 1992, Xiao was a candidate for party secretary of Sichuan as well as a Politburo membership. However, owing to sabotage by his own colleagues from Sichuan — mainly the "Chengdu clan", or politicians based in the provincial capital — Xiao failed to make it into the Central Committee at the 14th Congress and thus was disqualified for both posts.[117]

However, Xiao continued the Zhao tradition of no-holds-barred market reforms. He impressed many Western businessmen with this dictum on reforming state enterprises: "To study well how the boards of directors of capitalistic companies stem wastage and losses." More importantly, Xiao was not afraid of defending Zhao's reputation. He told reporters at the 1993 NPC that Zhao should take the credit for the economic development of Sichuan and the nation. "Sichuan still remembers Zhao's contributions to local reforms," Xiao said. "He had achievements in both rural and urban reforms."[118]

Other Zhao associates who were at least partially rehabilitated were the famous trio: former member of the Politburo Standing Committee Hu Qili; former member of the Central Committee Secretariat Rui Xingwen; and former head of the United Front Department Yan Mingfu. All lost their positions immediately after June 4, 1989. However, the three were partially reinstated in mid-1991 when they were given respectively the positions of Vice-Minister of Electronics; Vice-Minister of State Planning; and Vice-Minister of Civil Affairs.[119]

Immediately before the 14th Party Congress, there was speculation that the trio might gain further promotions. For example, it was strongly rumoured that Hu Qili, also a former right hand man of Hu Yaobang, would be re-inducted into either the Politburo or the Party Secretariat. This did not come to pass. However, Hu, whose reputation had somewhat been dented because of his apparent willingness to work with the conservative faction, was promoted Minister of Electronics at the 1993 NPC.

Hu, still relatively young at 66, remained intensely popular with both the bureaucrats and intellectuals. A late October 1992 article in the mass-circulation *China Youth Daily* seemed to attest to his staying power. "You can say that the hero has a place to exercise his martial skills," the paper said, adding that Hu was generally known as the "hardest-working minister". The homage was unusual given the fact that until early 1992, hardline ideologues had ruled that Hu be "banned" from the national media.[120]

The partial rehabilitation of Hu, Rui and Yan must also be seen in the context of intense opposition from conservative elements such as Li Peng and Yao Yilin. Take the example of Yan, 62, who had acted as Russian translator for Yang Shangkun and Deng Xiaoping when he worked in the Central Committee General Office in the 1960s. Given his good connections with Deng and Yang, Yan was before June 4, 1989, seen as a rising star. He was popular and effective as United Front chief from 1985 to 1989, particularly with intellectuals and Taiwan politicians and businessmen. However, while Yang had as early as 1990 raised the question of Yan's rehabilitation, it was shot down by the late president Li Xiannian.[121]

The partial comeback of Rui Xingwen, a former party secretary of Shanghai, was also sabotaged by hardline elders. Rui had the additional problem of rivalry with Jiang Zemin, who was his subordinate when they both worked in Shanghai. By mid-1993, Rui had stopped taking full duties at the State Planning Commission. He became the head of a real estate company under the commission.[122]

The real strength of the "Zhaoists", however, could not be gauged by the number of ex-Zhao protégés who remained in office. Zhao's influence was reflected in the sizeable corps of entrepreneurs and social scientists in their 30s, 40s, and 50s who agreed with his approach to reform. And while a quite a few of these radical reformists were shunted aside in the two years after June 4, most had made a comeback of one way or another, for example, as regional officials or as businessmen. Thus, especially at a time of leadership vacuum, Zhaoists (together with such of their soul-mates as the followers of Hu Yaobang) remained a very significant pool of talent that could notch the nation towards the requirements of the 21st century.[123]

VI. Remnants of the Communist Youth League and Followers of Hu Yaobang

A. The Communist Youth League Old Boys' Network

It is a tribute to the clout and organisational gizmo of Hu Yaobang (who was once head of the party's Organisation Department) that the Communist Youth

League faction he headed since the early 1970s remained a formidable political force after June 4. The CYL faction refers to politicians who spent at least part of their careers in the league. Because of their liberal leanings, CYL affiliates were considered a vital component of the party's reformist wing.

Owing to the relatively large number of CYL officials and ex-leaguers who took part in the pro-democracy movement in 1989, the political fortune of the faction took a nosedive in late 1989 and 1990. Media coverage of the league decreased. During the *nanxun*, however, Deng again gave instructions that the CYL regain its status as the training ground for new leaders. At a Politburo meeting soon afterwards, it was decided that the party should again "elevate CYL cadres as leaders". By early 1993, the CYL old boys' network had staged some form of a comeback. An estimated one quarter of the ministers endorsed by the NPC that year had league connections. Leading the pack was CYL party secretary Song Defu, who was made Labour Minister.[124]

At the CYL's 13th Congress in May 1993, protégés of such former League bosses as Hu Yaobang and Hu Qili swept all the leadership positions. The seven-member CYL party committee was headed by Li Keqiang, 37, a relatively liberal cadre. Li, who was pursuing a doctorate in economics under "stocks guru" Professor Li Yining at Beijing University (Beida), was considered a rising star. A native of Anhui Province, Li joined the Communist Party in 1976. He distinguished himself in the league organisation at Beida and at CYL headquarters. Li is believed to be a protégé of Hu Qili, a former head of the Beida league. Other members of the new CYL committee had similar backgrounds to Li's. In mid-1994, analysts were surprised when Li Qibao, 41, a member of the CYL party committee since 1985, was made a Deputy Secretary-General of the State Council. Also an Anhui native, Li spent most of his career in the league.[125]

Rather than getting back to the mainstream of the post-Tiananmen Square leadership, many CYL affiliates were expected to exert their influence by joining hands with liberal groupings such as the Zhaoists and regional "warlords". In spite of the thorough-going rotations of regional leadership that took place in 1991, 1993 and 1994, quite a number of provincial secretaries and governors had close CYL affiliations.[126]

By 1992 and 1993, many former aides of Hu Yaobang were exercising a strong "moral" influence on the political debate. They included the retired party boss of Fujian Xiang Nan, former propaganda chief Zhu Houze, and Hu's former private secretary Sun Changjiang. Both Zhu and Sun, who was chief editor of the *Science and Technology Daily* in 1989, were sidelined after the June 4 killings. However, the two liberal theorists were active in intellectual circles. They were instrumental in funnelling support to liberal intellectuals who staged anti-leftist crusades in 1992-94 (see Chapter 3).

For example, at the "anti-Zhu Rongji" conclave of October 1993 referred to above, a number of well-known Hu supporters voiced their support for yet another phase of radical reforms. Intellectuals who spoke on that occasion included Zhu Houze, Wu Mingyu, and Tong Dalin. They endorsed Deng's new slogan that "only [fast-paced] development passes the rigorous test of reason". All warned against the danger of central planners taking advantage of the austerity programme of late 1993 to roll back reform and to "go back to the old road of the command economy".[127]

By late 1993 and early 1994, there were signs that, like a number of Zhaoists, veteran CYL members were playing the "regional" card by allying themselves with the "warlords". In 1993, Xiang Nan and Zhu Houze formed a foundation for helping the poor provinces, through which they boosted ties with heartland provinces ranging from Gansu to Guizhou. The two were also at the forefront of the campaign to ensure coastal provinces such as Guangdong, Fujian and Hainan retain their status as "ahead-of-the-times" zones. In February 1994, they travelled to Xiamen to help local leaders lobby for the free-port status Deng Xiaoping had vouchsafed the SEZ ten years ago.[128]

It is a mark of the influence of the CYL that Jiang Zemin had by 1993 tried to subtly build bridges to such of its leaders as Zhu Houze. Chinese sources said that Jiang had more than once asked Zhu to advise him on agricultural matters. Jiang also used his influence to ensure that Hu Yaobang's son, Hu Deping, retain his senior posting in the United Front Department.[129]

B. The Emergence of Li Ruihuan

One of the unexpected rising stars — and possible standard bearer of the CYL liberal tradition — after the June 4 suppression was Li Ruihuan, a close associate of Hu Yaobang. A member of the CYL Central Committee Secretariat from 1979 to 1981, Li was also a protégé of Hu Qili, his immediate predecessor as Tianjin mayor. Li had emerged as a leader of the liberal faction two years after the massacre. His brave words and deeds offered the intelligentsia the hope he could one day wear the mantle of Hu Yaobang or Zhao Ziyang.

Moreover, Li, who was until the 14th Party Congress the party's highest arbiter in ideology and propaganda, enjoyed the support of Deng. Together with Qiao Shi, Li was seen as a counterweight against the conservative coalition in the Central Committee and Politburo.[130]

Li's ideas were reminiscent of such CYL veterans as the two Hus and Zhu Houze, who were active in the "thought liberation movement" of the mid-1980s. Li's post-Tiananmen Square statecraft could be summarised thus: the CCP must do concrete things to win back the trust of the masses. It must revive the "mass line" and soothe the people's feelings. In ideology and propaganda, avoid hackneyed stereotypes and tasteless, dry indoctrination. In economics, the reform and open-door policy must be developed further (see also Chapter 5).[131]

"Reform has brought actual benefits to the Chinese people," Li told a delegation of American academics in June 1990. "It is the wish of the Chinese people to persevere with reform. It is a necessary trend of history, not the idea of a particular leader." Taking a sly dig at those of his conservative colleagues who were paying lip service to reform, Li added: "Whether we are committed to reform does not depend on talking about it everyday. It depends on solving one difficult problem after another."[132]

Li was an exemplary practitioner of the philosophy first propounded by Deng: "Practice is the criterion of truth." After the June 4 massacre, it was the former Tianjin mayor who first suggested that the CCP revive the time-honoured policy of the "mass line" and "doing concrete things for the people". "The party must do solid things to improve its image," he said in an internal speech in early 1990. "It would not do just to put old wine in new bottles." "Mass line" politics — in the sense of "soothing the feelings of the people" — was viewed by Li as the only way to heal the wounds of June 4. In an address to Tianjin cadres in May 1990, Li said: "We must depend on the broad masses, unite whatever forces that can be united, and mobilise positive factors on all fronts."[133]

It was, however, the apparent success with which Li browbeat Gang of Four holdovers that had made him the "best liberal hope" after June 4. In speech after speech, Li lambasted hardline ideologues for resurrecting Mao's "kingdom of the spirit". Li accused the commissars of "substituting the existing economic policy [of reform] with moral standards and beliefs" that were outdated. Specifically, he disparaged the dubious ideal of unthinking devotion to the party, as embodied in the annual campaign to learn from Lei Feng.[134]

In his talk to the American academics, Li indirectly criticised the remnant Maoists for "sidelining the private economy". "We must affirm the positive significance of this type of economy," he said. "We must be on guard against the fact that the individual economy — in particular the enthusiasm with which farmers develop the individual economy — will be affected by improper propaganda and work."

Li took the orthodox scribes to task for penning tedious commentaries and editorials on the Marxist canon. Dogmatic indoctrination, he bluntly warned, "will turn people away". In a near-heretical address in June 1990, Li told a conference of journalists that "readability and interest in news reporting should not be neglected because of the emphasis on [the media's] loyalty to the party".[135]

China analysts have drawn parallels between Li's attempts to raise the liberal standard and efforts by Zhao Ziyang to put a damper on the Campaign Against Bourgeois Liberalisation in early 1987. Immediately after Hu Yao-bang's fall from grace, Zhao told the party's ideologues that their diatribes against liberalisation "resemble articles written during the Cultural Revolution and have a high dosage of *dong bagu* [party-dictated stereotypes] in them". However, for reasons including the need to conciliate the party's left wing, Deng was not prepared to let Li have a shot at power. His transfer to the CPPCC in March 1993 proved a disappointment to those intellectuals who hoped that Li might spearhead another liberalisation movement.[136]

However, as we saw in Chapter 5, together with Qiao Shi and Tian Jiyun, Li continued to boost the clout of the party's liberal wing by playing up the imperative of political reform. In his memorable address to the CPPCC in March 1993, Li picked up on the liberal themes upon which he had elaborated since 1989. For example, the CPPCC Chairman vowed to use his organisation to canvass the views of different sectors of society and to act as a supervisor of the party and government. "Consultation [with the democratic parties and other elements in society] and supervision are beneficial towards allowing people to speak out and collecting different viewpoints," he said. "Rendering decision-making scientific and democratic will help to discover problems and rectify mistakes."[137]

VII. More Muscle to the Regions

A. The Centrifugal Forces Runneth Over

The political aggrandisement of regional leaders — and to some extent, entrepreneurs — began with Deng's *nanxun*. Taking a leaf from Mao's book, Deng was mobilising local cadres to "bombard the headquarters", that is, to clobber mandarins in the central party and government headquarters. At the 1992 NPC, Li Peng and other central planners were subjected to the merciless "bombardment" of provincial deputies, who demanded, among other things, that the premier upwardly adjust the growth rate and enshrine "anti-leftism" as a national task. Very humiliatingly, the foster son of Zhou Enlai was forced to make nearly 150 amendments to his NPC Government Work Report. [138]

Representatives from the provinces and the cities won big at the 14th Party Congress. This was assured from the very beginning: 1,401 or 70.43 per cent of the 1,989 delegates to the conclave were from the regions. This compared with merely 329 delegates — or 16.54 per cent of the total — who spoke for central authorities. The unprecedented predominance of local cadres at the Congress was made possible at Deng's behest. Before the *nanxun*, the authorities had decided to allocate as many as 50 per cent of the delegate slots to central-level bureaucrats.[139]

After the ballotings at the 14th Party Congress, provincial and municipal chiefs took home 62, or 33 per cent, of the 189 seats on the Central Committee. Also at the insistence of Deng, the "warlords" had an unprecedentedly heavy representation on the Politburo. In additional to the seats traditionally assigned to the party bosses of the three centrally administered cities of Beijing, Tianjin and Shanghai, Politburo memberships were offered Xie Fei and Jiang Chunyun, the secretaries of respectively Guangdong and Shandong. As discussed earlier, Xiao Yang narrowly missed being elected Politburo member representing Sichuan. Reflecting the fast-shifting economic realities of the country, politicians from Guangdong and Shanghai did particularly well at the conclave. Seven Guangdong cadres became either full or alternate members of the Central Committee. Shanghai's share was six.[140]

The regions' new clout was best reflected in economic policy: autonomous powers that provinces and cities gained at the expense of central authorities. The turning of the tide in favour of the regions began very soon after the *nanxun*. For example, the now-famous Central Party Document No. 4 of April 1992 extended the open-door policy from the coast to the heartland and border regions. This meant that around 100 cities and zones all over the country would acquire autonomous powers akin to those enjoyed by the SEZs.

Emboldened by the patriarch's instructions, various localities took the unheard-of step of unilaterally abrogating national policies they deemed to be behind the times. A case in point was Wuhan, which in July 1992 invalidated 13 "out-of-date" regulations imposed by Beijing. These strictures had to do with financial and business activities, such as the ability of enterprises to acquire loans and to be transformed into shareholding companies.[141]

The bones of contention between the regions and the centre consisted largely of two areas: the speed of growth and the freedom to "do their own thing", especially raising funds locally and from overseas sources. Citing the instructions of the patriarch, many localities were by late 1992 revising their own Eighth Five-Year Plan and Ten-Year Economic Blueprint to reflect their particular needs and aspirations.[142]

The year 1992 could be a watershed: the central government began losing the power to regulate the pace of growth of localities, especially cities along the Gold Coast. After all, Deng indicated during the *nanxun* that if it was based on efficiency, a high rate of growth was desirable. This dictum was repeated by almost every local party secretary and mayor to justify their rapid expansion programmes. The "high-speed model", at least for Guangdong, was defended by such national leaders as Zou Jiahua, Ye Xuanping and Ren Zhongyi.[143]

A pitched battle was fought between practically all the open cities and the central leadership over the right to issue and float stocks. This became a matter of life and death for the nation's most dynamic cities and enterprises. The right to sell shares publicly meant the power to tap into the vast savings of 1.15 billion people, estimated at over 1.20 trillion yuan in 1993.[144] Moreover, the freedom to issue B-shares and to be listed on stock exchanges in Hong Kong and elsewhere meant the ability to raise money overseas.

The success with which the regions had clawed back the initiative was attested to by the dire warnings Beijing gave the localities for having gone too far. For example, the State Council issued an order in August 1993 saying that the levels of taxes to be imposed on foreign companies would be determined by Beijing alone — and local governments must not try to lower them in a bid to attract investment.[145] In November, Vice-Premier Zhu Rongji called on the regions and cities to cool the runaway development of stock companies as well as real estate speculation. "Areas of the economy which should be hot have not heated up; those that should not be hot have boiled over," he said. [146] The tug-of-war between central and local authorities reached an acme during the rectification campaign in 1993. A major thrust of the Third Plenum of the 14th Central Committee in November 1993 was to reverse the decline of Beijing's share of national income (see Chapter 2).

In theory, Beijing could still brandish a couple or so of trump cards. It retained the all-important power of personnel. This was manifested in the reshuffle of both regional and military leaders in 1993, whose main goal was to check the phenomenon of "warlordism".

In late 1993 and early 1994, new party and government chiefs were installed in at least 15 provinces and centrally administered cities. Appointments that were publicised included Jiangsu, Zhejiang, Hunan, Henan, Shanxi, Guizhou, Gansu, Liaoning, Heilongjiang, Xinjiang, Fujian and Hubei. While a number of these personnel shifts were tied to normal retirement, the bulk were motivated by Beijing's desire to impose a uniform line. Moreover, the party's Organisation Department tried to arrogate to itself the power of propagating the next generation of regional leaders. This is despite the fact that in an interview in late 1993, Li Peng urged foreign observers "not to engage in speculation that they [the personnel moves] had to do with curbing regionalism".[147]

The personnel card, however, could only be used sparingly. Too-frequent changes of administrators not only made for inefficiency but caused morale problems in the grassroots and raised questions about the efficacy of central authority. At least on the surface, therefore, the top-down command structure which had held sway since 1949 remained in place as of mid-1994. After all, the full Politburo did not meet very often, and the Central Committee was only convened once or twice every year. In spite of the gradual atrophy of central authority, regional politicians had yet to pose a frontal threat to Beijing's powers in formulating national policies.

However, the balance might already have tipped — irrevocably — in favour of the regions. Regional powerhouses like Shanghai, Guangzhou, Shenzhen and Dalian had by early 1993 surpassed Beijing in the ability to work the market place. A major reason why the austerity programme of late 1993 was so short-lived was that regional centres of commerce had independent means of finance, particularly credit lines from Hong Kong, Taiwan, and abroad.[148] As we shall see in the following section, this new-found economic clout would soon translate into political prowess — all at the expense of central authority.

B. The Maturing of Regional Leaders

By early 1993, regional leaders, especially those along the coast, had started openly gainsaying Beijing's edicts. The most vociferous protests were made by Guangdong leaders. For example, during the 1993 NPC, Shenzhen mayor Li Youwei and other cadres said that excessive control by Beijing would stymie local growth. Li claimed that Shenzhen would lose its competitive edge unless Beijing granted the zone more preferential policies. "Various central government departments should now consider granting Shenzhen the necessary authority," he said. Demands for more autonomy were also lodged at the legislative session by leaders from Anhui, Hainan and Heilongjiang.[149] As discussed earlier, the austerity programme of 1993 showed that local leaders were ganging up on the centre. For the first time since 1949, the central government was forced to yield on major issues such as tax contributions.

It is incorrect to assume that all or most regional leaders were "reformers". However, it is true that especially after the passage of Document No. 4 — which permitted cadres and party units to set up businesses — the fast-paced development of the local economy was intimately tied to the personal well-being of regional cadres. By 1993, many provincial, municipal and county-level cadres had become concurrently heads of corporations or advisers to private entrepreneurs; these businesses tended to prosper if Beijing would leave the localities alone in formulating investment policies.[150]

Partly as a check and balance mechanism, however, Beijing has a tradition of appointing cautious, unambitious leaders to vibrant areas. The reason is obvious: consider what would happen if a dynamic cadre were posted to a free-wheeling province like Guangdong or Hainan. While that region might develop by leaps and bounds, it could also (as in the case of Hainan under Lei Yu) zoom out of the CCP's purview. Ren Zhongyi and Xiang Nan, the former party boss of respectively Guangdong and Fujian, were very liberal and pop-ular. They both had inordinately short reigns. Former Guangdong Governor Ye Xuanping, one of the few local leaders who dared openly confront the planners in Beijing, had a relatively long tenure because of the special rela-tionship between his father, Marshal Ye Jianying, and Deng Xiaoping.[151]

It is not surprising that the leaders of Guangdong were, from Beijing's point of view, safe bets who could be trusted not to rock the boat. Both party boss Xie Fei and Governor Zhu Senlin were not known for their bush-whack-ing style of reform. In policy speeches, they had a tendency of repeating what had already appeared in central documents. The only exception among the top echelon in the province might be the Mayor of Guangzhou, Li Ziliu.

A gung-ho reformer and a star in karaoke bars because of his near-profes-sional singing skills, Liu impressed Hong Kong investors with his familiarity with the mores of the British colony. It was Liu who took care to brighten up Guangzhou's streets at night, an outwardly minor matter that had immense symbolic significance. The former chief of the city of Jiangmen was a firm advocate of the transformation of the planned economy to the market place. "We must grasp the nettle in reforming state enterprises and gradually bring about the shareholding system," he said in mid-1993. In early 1994, Liu play-ed a key role in persuading Beijing to postpone — and lower — new capital gains taxes so as not to deal a blow to Hong Kong property investors. The mayor also showed his mettle in attracting foreign investments to the Guang-zhou subway as well as the highways linking his fast-growing city to Hong Kong and Macau.[152]

Economic realities, particularly the need to fight increasingly tough com-petition from such other open cities as Shanghai, however, might prevail and lead to the phasing out of the inept top rung. The successors of Xie Fei or Zhu Senlin could well be mid-echelon cadres in Guangdong and Guangzhou — as well as the mayors of cities in the free-wheeling Pearl River Delta — who had enviable track records as bold reformers.

A case in point is the former party secretary of the boom city of Foshan, Ou Guangyuan, who was praised by Deng when the latter toured the Pearl River Refrigerator Factory during the *nanxun*. Ou, 44, was the youngest among the seven Guangdong cadres elevated to the Central Committee in late 1992. He won fame for implementing the stocks system and transforming the government from being a "mother-in-law-type *yamen*" to a centre of services for enterprises. Ou became a Vice-Governor of the Province in 1993.[153]

The Special Economic Zone of Shenzhen threw much light on the dichoto-my between a crust of cautious, even conservative cadres at the top and a corps of radical reformers occupying positions just one or two rungs below. At the apex were officials in the old mode like Party Secretary Li Hao, Mayor

Zheng Liangyu, and since October 1992, Mayor Li Youwei. (Liang Xiang, the former Shenzhen party secretary and Hainan governor who is an unrepentant Zhaoist, had weathered corruption investigations and spent his retirement in Shenzhen. He lived in a house in the CCP compound and still exerted a "moral influence".) Below Zheng and Li were a group of radical modernisers. They included the head of the Shenzhen Office for Restructuring the Economy, Xu Jing'an; the Secretary General of the municipal party committee, Ren Kelei (who is the son of Ren Zhongyi); and the Secretary General of the municipal government, Li Luoli. Both Xu and Li had worked in think tanks close to Zhao Ziyang.[154]

By mid-1994, analysts were at a loss to pinpoint regional leaders who had the right stuff for the very top. However, a number of former associates of Hu Yaobang and Zhao Ziyang went on making splashes — and they might yet play significant roles in the post-Deng era. We shall here discuss two major lieutenants of reform, Xiao Yang and Lei Yu. According to existing rules, Xiao, 64, and Lei, 59, were close to retirement age. Yet this should not detract from their ability to make waves in post-Deng politics.

Xiao Yang continued to blaze new trails in the open-door policy after his failure to make it into the Politburo in late 1992. As Governor of Sichuan, Xiao was noted for innovative ways in luring foreign capital not just from Hong Kong and the West but ASEAN countries. He retained a liberal American lawyer, Jerome Cohen, as his business adviser. "We are willing to yield parts of the vast Sichuan market for foreign investors," he said.

On many occasions, the Governor laid bare his pro-market bias. "No matter what we do we must first ask ourselves whether there is a need for it in the market," he told his subordinates. "If there is such a need, the project should go ahead." The Governor was an early proponent of changing the ownership system of state factories, saying that government firms could be run like village and township enterprises. Xiao also played a role in the conversion of PLA-owned factories into civilian production.[155]

Outside economics, Xiao was noted for the promotion of clean government. Sichuan was among the first areas to forbid cadres from engaging in business. In mid-1993, Chengdu passed regulations that prevented officials from dappling in the stock market, holding a second job, or foisting their expenses on subordinate units. Xiao, however, also had a more traditionalist persona. Soon after his election as Sichuan Governor in 1993, he alienated some intellectuals by vowing to "give a facelift to the home town of comrade Xiaoping". Why the special preference for Guang'an county, the birthplace of the New Helmsman? The intellectuals also cited other instances of Xiao currying favour with the Deng daughters.[156]

Lei Yu, whose career was for a long period dimmed by his association with the ill-fated Hainan car scandal of the early 1980s, remained as irrepressible as ever after his transfer to Guangxi as Executive Vice-Governor in late 1992. Soon after Deng's *nanxun*, Lei, then First Vice-Mayor of Guangzhou, was at the forefront of the anti-leftist campaign. "Anti-leftism means abandoning outdated ideas and we have to take a surgical approach to [ridding] ossified thinking," he said in mid-1992. Lei's economics had a high dose of Hong Kong flavour: "Do not be scrimpy about spending; be bold in borrowing; learn how to use funds [effectively]; be shrewd in earning money."[157]

The vice-governor was not afraid to rub the mandarins in Beijing the wrong way. At the height of the 1993 austerity programme, Lei said that there was no problem of overheating in the Guangxi Autonomous Region. "We must prevent overheating [of the economy] but we need not be afraid of it," he said. "We must base ourselves on practical facts, and maintain the good momentum we have already developed." To attract tourists, he gave his imprimatur to "socialist nightclubs" in Guangxi cities, where at least in theory there would be no prostitution, drugs or gambling.[158]

While it is difficult to exhaustively list the rising stars among regional leaders, the following brief biographies of notable local cadres in their 40s and 50s yield some insight into the question of leadership in the post-Deng era. While several are *gaoganzidi* (sons and daughters of party elders), all are noted for their pragmatism and non-ideological approach to doing business.[159]

Bo Xilai. The son of party elder and "immortal" Bo Yibo, Bo, (born 1949) helped transform Dalian, of which he was mayor, into an international port. Soon after Deng's *nanxun*, Bo vowed to turn his city into a "northern Hong Kong" in 20 years. Apart from investments by Hong Kong tycoons such as Henry Fok, Dalian benefited from cash injections from Japan and South Korea.

Chen Huanyou. The Governor of Jiangsu made a name for himself in late 1993 for resisting efforts by Zhu Rongji to impose a tight-money policy on his province. Chen insisted that the austerity measures would cripple township industries. The slogan of Chen (born 1934) was to internationalise Jiangsu further through "boosting foreign trade; using more foreign capital; and increasing technological transfer from foreign countries".

Chi Fulin. In his mid-40s, Chi was Head of the Office for Reforming the Economic Structure in Hainan Island. One of the think-tank *wunderkinder* of Zhao Ziyang, Chi continued to conduct market experiments in Hainan in the early 1990s. In the summer of 1993, Chi helped host an economic conference whose participants included intellectuals who went into exile after the June 4 massacre. One of his goals was to make Hainan a free port and a special customs area. Chi was also publisher of the popular news weekly *New Century*. In mid-1994, the ex-Zhao adviser was criticised by the leftist journal *In*

Search of Truth for advocating the quasi-privatisation of state enterprises through the "sale" of state assets.

Fu Rui. Head of the Organisation Department of Guangdong, Fu, son of party elder Peng Zhen, benefited from his *gaoganzidi* status. Fu (born 1941) also spent long years in the public security system, which his father once headed. While his ideological views were murky, Fu was regarded as an efficient technocrat with a bright future. In 1994, he was rumoured to be a candidate for Shenzhen mayor.

Liu Chengye. The mayor of Shishi, Fujian Province, raised eyebrows by turning his coastal city into a little Hong Kong. Innuendo abounded about corruption and smuggling in the quasi-capitalist haven. Yet the enclave was one of the country's leaders in garments and other light industries. Liu's philosophy was "small government; big society" and "stop the government from meddling [in business]." Liu (born 1943) was picked as mayor in 1988 in an indirect election featuring eight candidates.

Liu Mingkang. Liu became Vice-Governor of Fujian Province in early 1993, and was immediately recognised for his expertise in finance and banking. A veteran official of the Bank of China, Liu (born 1947) gained an MBA from London University while stationed in the British capital. He was instrumental in promoting links between enterprises in Fujian and the emerging money market.

Tang Ruoxin. Mayor of the industrial city of Handan in Hebei Province, Tang (born 1956) used to be in charge of policy research in the Shekou region in Shenzhen. During his tenure there in the mid-1980s, Tang helped put together the potentially revolutionary system of the election of Shekou leaders by cadre-level staff. Tang also maintained close ties to the sons of party elders, including Chen Yuan.

Wu Guanzheng. Wu (born 1938) was one of China's youngest governors when he became head of Jiangxi Province in 1986. Previously, he was Mayor of Wuhan, where he pioneered such elements of populist politics as a phone-in service for his citizens. While Jiangxi was a laggard in the modernisation drive, Wu improved its links with the Yangtze River economic zone as well as the southeast coast.

Xi Jinping. The son of party elder Xi Zhongxun, Xi (born 1954) became Party Secretary of Fuzhou in 1990. Xi indicated in an interview with a Hong Kong paper that Fuzhou, the provincial capital of Fujian, would be run according to market norms. "Now, the market economy is aeroplanes and big guns," he said. "It will not do to say that since it is capitalism, we should stick with swords and spears." Xi played a key role in setting up the Golden Triangle investment zone at the mouth of the Minjiang River.

Yu Zhengsheng. The veteran government and party leader of the picturesque city of Qingdao in Shandong Province, Yu used to work with Zhao Ziyang on urban and industrial reforms. Yu (born 1946) is the son of party elder Huang Jing, the first husband of Madame Mao. Yu was mentioned shortly before the 14th Party Congress as a possible candidate for the party secretariat. By 1994, Qingdao had become one of China's most successful open cities largely due to the influx of South Korean and Japanese investments.

Zhao Baojiang. The mayor of Wuhan is credited with luring investment to the landlocked city, now the hub of the Yangtze River development zone. Zhao (born 1941) had more than 20 years of experience in the Wuhan area. A technocrat, Zhao kept a low profile on ideological issues. He was noted for his public relations sense and his flare with foreign entrepreneurs.[160]

Especially after the June 4, 1989, trauma, most regional cadres learnt how to bend with the wind, and it is difficult to make out their ideological affiliations. Most of the "rising stars" were adept at paying lip service to the predominant faction in Zhongnanhai while pursuing their own agendas. After Deng's death, however, Beijing's authority will undergo a further drubbing. How the regional "warlords" align themselves will have a pivotal influence on which faction and politicians would come up on top.[161]

VIII. The Non-state Sector: Power Play by the "Red Capitalists"

A. Political Power for Private Entrepreneurs

Both the economic and the political powers of the non-state-sector are poised for marked expansion with the gradual maturation of the "socialist market economy". By late 1992, Beijing had promulgated regulations which made possible the untrammelled development of the private sector. Political discrimination against private-sector practitioners introduced soon after the June 4 crackdown were gradually being lifted. However, "red bosses" still had a long way to go in their bid for social status and political clout.

At the time of the 14th Party Congress, China boasted over 14.27 million *getihu*, or "individual entrepreneur households", which provided employment for some 23 million workers. There were 120,000 fully-fledged private companies, which had more than 2 million staffers. More than 11,000 of these private concerns were companies with limited liabilities, a jump of 71.65 per cent over the 1991 figure. The fixed assets of the private businesses were mushrooming, with the largest ones valued at 45 million yuan.[162]

In December 1992, the State Council passed measures that amounted to a new deal for the private sector. For example, aside from "strategic" product

lines and raw materials that the state must go on monopolising, private entrepreneurs could engage in every kind of industrial and commercial production
and management. Private companies were allowed to take up border trade and
overseas commerce, including setting up branches overseas. Earlier, different
provinces and cities had given permission to private concerns to form joint
ventures with foreign corporations.[163]

On the political level, the party rescinded a late 1989 order which forbade
getihu and private entrepreneurs from becoming CCP members. By the end of
1992, there were nearly 2 million CCP affiliates who were either the bosses
or employees of private enterprises.[164]

The biggest break for the non-state sector, however, had occurred with the
passage of Central Committee Document No. 4, which gave the green light to
party units and cadres to operate businesses. As discussed earlier, a number of
officials merely formed quasi-governmental corporations that were in practice
no different from state companies. However, many set up private companies
or joint ventures to take advantage of the new opportunities of the market
place. Some 300,000 new companies came into being in 1992 and 1993, the
bulk of which were non-governmental concerns. On a massive scale, people
with clout and high-level connections, including a host of "princelings," were
joining the ranks of private businessmen.[165]

In mid-1992, Bo Xicheng, the son of influential elder Bo Yibo, raised eyebrows when he resigned from his post of Head of the Beijing Tourism Bureau
to start a semi-private hotel management company in the capital. "In reform,
someone has to take the lead," said the 41-year-old "princeling". "We must
learn to be independent and to earn our own bread," he said.[166] By late 1992,
it was common knowledge that the sons, daughters and in-laws of the following CCP elders and senior ministers had, to use the Chinese expression, taken
the plunge into the sea of business: Deng Xiaoping, Chen Yun, Bo Yibo, Ye
Jianying, Yang Shangkun, Wang Zhen, Peng Zhen, and so on. So many cadres
had been lured to the exciting world of Adam Smith that the Organisation
Department reportedly had difficulty filling leadership positions in poor and
remote areas.[167]

By early 1993, there was no palpable evidence that private entrepreneurs
might be inducted into policy-making bodies. No "red capitalists" made it into
the Central Committee. They were not even invited into advisory or consultative councils. One of the most talked about innovations during Zhu Rongji's
tenure as Shanghai mayor was his having formed a council of business advisers, which was made up of foreign executives based in the metropolis. Zhu did
not think of picking the brains of the private entrepreneurs.[168]

However, it was becoming obvious that if, as most projections say, the non-
state sector would take up at least half of the economy by 2000, the red boss-

es, middle and professional classes would assume a political clout that is commensurate with their economic power. By 1992, the share of national industrial production by "totally people's owned enterprises" had fallen to 48.3 per cent from 77.6 per cent in 1978. By contrast, the share of collectives and private-sector concerns in 1992 were 38.2 per cent and 13.5 per cent, up respectively from 22.4 per cent and 0 per cent in 1978. In some provinces including Guangdong, the private sector had by 1994 displaced the public sector as the mainstay of commerce and industry.[169]

Somewhat echoing democratic developments in 19th-century Western Europe, groups and associations of businessmen would first clamour for a share of political power to ensure fair competition in the fledgling market place.[170] The process, however, would likely be slower in China. In 19th-century Europe, the emergent mercantile interests were battling a monarchical establishment whose power and reach were not as comprehensive and overwhelming as the CCP.

B. The Political Agenda of the New Bosses

At least in the embryonic phase, the red capitalists were expected to demand a fair share of political power not for its own sake but to ensure equal competition with the state sector. As author Xi Zhi wrote in Hong Kong's pro-Beijing magazine *Wide Angle* in early 1993: "Representatives of non-state enterprises will be fighting for power and jockeying for position" to ensure the legitimacy and expansion of their businesses. This is apparent from official and unofficial reports about the second-class citizenship of the non-state-owned sector.[171]

A survey of 117 private businesses reported by the New China News Agency in late 1992 showed that the entrepreneurs were full of gripes about "discrimination". They had difficulty getting credit, finding sales outlets, and hiring well-trained people. They suffered from an inferior social status as well as a negative press image. Worst, the red capitalists were subjected to "unfair taxes". Only 11.1 per cent among those surveyed who had assets of over 1 million yuan said they were optimistic about the prospects of their businesses. The figure was higher — 41.8 per cent — for bosses with assets of over 10 million yuan.[172]

Another study by the pro-Beijing Hong Kong daily, *Ta Kung Pao*, showed that private businesses laboured under severe handicaps. Many managers were worried about their status and future, to the extent that they wanted to re-register their concerns under a state unit. Others were subjected to taxes, levies and "forced contributions" of up to 70 categories. They generally had difficulty getting raw materials, credit and technological help.[173]

The semi-official Hong Kong China News Agency quoted managers in the Beijing-based Nande Economic Group — one of the country's largest private enterprises — as saying that the government should scrap the distinction between public-sector and private-sector business units. "For reform and economic measures, we have stopped asking whether they are surnamed socialist or capitalist," one Nande executive said. "Similarly, we should no longer classify enterprises as government or private ones."[174]

In its report on the plight of "red capitalists", *Ta Kung Pao* added: "There is not one administrative department or organisation to harmonise the relationship between [private] enterprises and government units in the areas of industry, commerce, tax or planning and construction, in such a way as to safeguard the proper and legal rights of private enterprises." It is therefore not surprising that private businessmen started banding together to lobby for economic — and political — privileges.

By early 1994, a budding group of private entrepreneurs — and sympathetic economists and politicians — was demanding improvements in socioeconomic conditions. As CPPCC member and law professor Wang Junyan pointed out at the time, the constitution and the laws should be amended to "make clear the fact that in the commodity economy, everybody is equal". Professor Wang added that the same principle should apply to "legal persons", meaning companies of all categories. "Every person should be equal before the law," he said.[175]

Other demands by private businessmen and their lobbyists included a change of the constitution to protect private property. "The nation's highest charter should protect private property," said Beijing University economics professor Xiao Zhuoji. "So long as it is legal, the incomes of citizens, no matter how much, should be protected by the law." Professor Xiao said that the lack of a constitutional guarantee was a factor behind the conspicuous consumption of private bosses: better spend the money on luxuries before it is confiscated by the government.[176]

More specifically, private entrepreneurs wanted business rights on a par with the state sector. The deprivations suffered by the non-state sector on a national basis were evident if we examine the generous terms offered them by individual municipalities. For example, in late 1993, Shaoguan in Guangdong gave the red bosses four dispensations. Put simply, there would be no limits on their scale of operation, the speed of their growth, and the nature of their product lines. Favourable tax and credit policies would be granted selective private units, for example, those that specialised in high technology or were in the preferred sectors of energy and transportation. In Jinan, the relative backwater city in Shandong, private enterprises with the requisite qualifications could issue stocks and shares.[177]

The restrictions imposed on private firms in general were also illustrated by the 19-point "dispensation" announced by Shanghai in early 1994. The new ruling said that non-state firms could handle all types of product lines save automobiles, oil, coal and some other energy products. Moreover, those that met certain requirements could engage in wholesale as well as retail businesses. The criteria were: *getihu* units must have working capital of not less than 30,000 yuan, and private companies, 100,000 yuan.[178]

These isolated examples demonstrated the norm: that private firms, including the highly successful village and township enterprises (VTEs), still suffered from daunting discrimination. Most of their gripes centred on lack of access to state credit and lack of freedom in foreign trade, in raising shares, and in opening branches overseas. As a group of entrepreneurs attending the 1994 NPC indicated, many red bosses even had difficulty securing passports to go on business trips. By early 1994, some legislators and private-sector practitioners were demanding a law to protect the rights of VTEs. "State enterprises are like children who have the right to inheritance while VTEs are like bastard kids," one NPC member pointed out. Shandong legislator Li Zhen argued that laws must have the ability "to anticipate and transcend events". In this case, there should be statutes to protect weak sectors of the economy and help them flourish.[179]

C. Token Political Representation, 1993-1994

Influential economist Yang Peixin pointed out the inevitable trend of history when he advocated "electing" more entrepreneurs and managers to the NPC, the putative "organ of the highest power". Yang said in 1993 that a larger corps of entrepreneurs in the NPC would ensure the orderly progress of the socialist market economy. "What the NPC discusses in the main is economic legislation and policies in order to pull down the obstacles for enterprises," he said. "It will not do if we do not invite entrepreneurs [to join the legislature]."[180] One thing, however, could lead to another. If there was a justifiable need to induct entrepreneurs into the legislature, why not the councils of government?

It is clear, however, that the CCP leadership still had doubts about the "trustworthiness" and "obedience" of the private sector. A token concession that the party granted *getihu* businessmen was to give them some of the 82 slots reserved for the "economic sector" at the 1993 CPPCC. However, the bulk of the seats under this category were vouchsafed cadres and theoreticians like Rui Xingwen, He Xin, Yang Qixian and Chen Daisun.[181]

The utmost that a number of administrations of various levels were willing to do was to "consult" businessmen whenever a new economic policy was being mooted. For example, in early 1994, Guangdong Governor Zhu Senlin and other senior provincial officials discussed ways to reform the enterprise system with a group of state- and private-sector entrepreneurs. In Quanzhou, Fujian Province, the heads of private-enterprise groupings were consulted on a regular basis by the municipal leadership. In early 1993, the bosses of 300-odd public and private enterprises in Wuhan conducted an opinion poll on and "assessment" of the relative efficiency of 53 municipal government departments. Vice-Mayor Wu Houfu said the assessment and survey were useful in helping government units improve productivity.[182]

The nation's first business — though not yet political — organisations were set up in the early 1990s. In line with such Western institutions as chambers of commerce, practitioners in different sectors and product lines began forming trade associations. By 1993, there were at least several hundreds of such outfits. Shanghai boasted 37 associations based on trade and product lines, and 13 based on geographical affiliations. Chambers of commerce of private entrepreneurs were also established in Guangdong and Sichuan. For example, the Guangzhou Chamber of Private Industry and Commerce represented 4,000-odd companies in the city, some of which boasted assets of over 100 million yuan.[183]

In late 1993, a big step was taken when the All-China Federation of Industry and Commerce (ACFIC) was turned into a "private" chamber of commerce called the China Non-Governmental Chamber of Commerce (CNGCC). The goal of the CNGCC was to "provide guidance to the non-state economic sector towards sustained and healthy development". Set up in 1953, the ACFIC had 670,000 members. Some 53.7 per cent of its 300,000-odd affiliates absorbed from 1988 to 1993 were non-public-sector businessmen. It is clear, however, that the CNGCC would be under heavy "guidance" by the Communist party.[184]

At the same time, a group of CPPCC members in Tianjin proposed a "law on the chambers of commerce" to regulate their activities and functions. The deputies said that the chambers could provide a "social support system" for the socialist market economy, and that they could "represent the interests of commerce and citizens and help maintain order in the market and in society".[185] By mid-1994, however, there was no evidence that the CNGCC and other chambers of commerce had won any advantages or concessions for the red bosses.

Even as they grew and prospered, the red bosses continued to be subjected to attack by hardliners within the party for "exploiting" the proletariats (see Chapter 3). At the 1994 NPC, Premier Li apparently found it expeditious to pin the blame of hyperinflation and other social ills on the expanding private sector. The conservative leader warned that a small number of private entrepreneurs had "become degenerate and some have even committed crimes". "Without being supervised by the party and the masses, some people may easily make big mistakes when they have power and money," he told regional NPC members. The premier urged party committees of all levels to "protect the masses and help them supervise the entrepreneurs".[186]

IX. Conclusion: Can a Rightist Coalition Seize Power?

A. The Contours of a Rightist Coalition

Before his exile to the US in 1988, rebel writer and journalist Liu Binyan said he still believed in what he called the "healthy forces" within the party. After June 4, 1989, Liu lost hope in the party's intrinsic ability to save itself.[187] However, it is conceivable that the more progressive and "upwardly mobile" sectors of the party — and society — could band together to take over the country after Deng's death. By which time, of course, the CCP itself might have undergone a sea-change, and metamorphosed into something similar to a socialist party in the former Eastern bloc.

The "healthy" forces mentioned in the previous two sections could, for economic if not political reasons, put together temporary or long-term alliances to bid for power. For example, it is possible that the Zhaoists and "Huists" — or cadres who identified themselves with the radical economic and political reforms of 1987 and 1988 — might form the core of a fairly broad-based coalition that included regional leaders and private entrepreneurs.

Broadly speaking, private entrepreneurs were sympathetic to the economic and political reforms of Zhao Ziyang and his followers. A trial run of the Zhaoists co-operating with private-sector practitioners took place during the pro-democracy crusade of 1989. Non-state-owned companies such as the Stone computer group of Beijing and individual entrepreneurs contributed heavily to the movement.[188]

As discussed in the last section, the "new class" of entrepreneurs, managers, and professionals were far from able to gain the political power that was commensurate with their economic clout. However, the picture could change dramatically if we look at the statistics — as well as the experience of developing countries not just in Asia but around the world.

In mid-1993, the size of the middle class in China was estimated at 60 million. This powerful bloc was forecast to reach 200 million by the end of the century. A nationwide survey among private enterprises published in early 1994 showed that 17.2 per cent of the "red capitalists" possessed college degrees while 72 per cent had had secondary-school education. Moreover, the assets of the entrepreneurs were in direct proportion to their educational level. The average holdings of a college-educated entrepreneur were 800,000 yuan.[189]

A national poll of 2,620 entrepreneurs completed in late 1993 showed that Chinese managers, including those in the private sector, were a driving force for reform. As the official China News Service put it: "Since the policy of reform and the open door, the overall quality of entrepreneurs has steadily improved. The independence and initiatives of the entrepreneurs have ceaselessly increased. They have become a major force for pushing reform forward." Two-thirds of entrepreneurs surveyed said the top item on the agenda should be "changing the function of government departments", meaning the separation of government and business.[190]

The years 1992 to 1994 witnessed further signs of a fledgling "coalition" between liberal cadres and intellectuals on the one hand, and entrepreneurs on the other. It was the bosses of both state and private corporations who sponsored the growing number of private conferences held by rightist intellectuals. Topics in these unsanctioned meetings included "fighting leftism", the strategies for market reform, and modernisation in general.

It was no accident that by late 1992, the élite among rightist cadres and intellectuals had openly called for the improvement in the status of private entrepreneurs, seen as a "new class" that could expedite the nation's modernisation. In two major meetings held in the capital in December 1992, liberal scholars and cadres heaped praise on efforts by private businessmen Chen Jinyi and Wang Xianglin to amass capital and to take over government concerns. They argued that the state should no longer monopolise production — and that the socio-political status of private entrepreneurs must be enhanced. Participants in these conferences included Zhu Houze, Yu Guangyuan, Hu Jiwei, Li Chang, Wu Jinglian, Wu Mingyu, Wu Xiang and Dong Fureng.[191] As discussed earlier, liberal cadres were at the forefront of the campaign to enshrine the rights of the private sector in the constitution and the laws.

The relationship between regional cadres on the one hand, and Zhaoists and private entrepreneurs on the other was also close. The southeast coast had a concentration of radical-liberal officials some of whom had worked for Zhao. Moreover, it is obvious that officials along the Gold Coast saw their future inextricably linked with how well private-sector businessmen were doing.

It is also probable that, depending on the development of the market economy, members of the "twilight sectors" mentioned above might join the action through ways including a pro-market self-transformation. For example, by the second half of 1992, quite a number of central planning-oriented cadres had emulated their more free-wheeling counterparts along the coast and become private-sector taipans.

B. Towards a More Pluralistic System

By mid-1994, analysts agreed that what was known as peaceful evolution was succeeding in spite of the CCP's determined efforts to wipe out the seeds of liberalisation. In the Pearl River Delta region, peaceful evolution had by early 1993 well-nigh run its course. As dissident Wang Ruowang pointed out, however, it would be naive to think that the materialisation of the market economy would necessarily bring about political liberalisation.[192] At this stage, the prospect of China peacefully evolving into a "Western-style" multi-party system seemed remote.

It is, however, not unrealistic to expect the flowering of some form of inner-party democracy. What Liu Binyan called the "healthy forces" within the CCP — and within Chinese society — seemed to be growing by 1993 and 1994. A large number of regional cadres and non-public sector entrepreneurs were for the first time tasting economic, and some political, power.

It is improbable that members of this "new class" would clamour for the end of the CCP. However, if only to ensure the viability of the socialist market economy, they might favour a more pluralistic approach to politics. For example, they would lobby for the inclusion of more disparate elements — entrepreneurs, professionals, and liberal intellectuals in general — into the party's higher echelons. The CCP's liberal wing — which incorporates the remnant followers of Hu Yaobang and Zhao Ziyang — might by the mid-1990s have another shot at power. And over time, to use the memorable clause of rebel astro-physicist Fang Lizhi, the colour of the party and the entire regime would be changed.

(i) Private Entrepreneurs and Bourgeois-Liberal Elements, 1993-1994

The year 1994 offered more evidence that the "liberal coalition" might be picking up steam. First, there were signs of closer ties between private entrepreneurs and the liberal faction of the party. In the first two years after the massacre, a large number of dissidents and liberal cadres — especially those under 45 years of age — went into business. Thanks to the leaps-and-bounds growth in the prices of property and stocks, at least a few scores of these former avant-garde cadres had become multi-millionaires by mid-1994.

Among big-name dissidents who turned entrepreneurs after their release from prison were Democracy Wall activists Wang Xizhi and Zhang Xianliang; Tiananmen Square activists Wang Dan and Zhou Duo; and two officials from the now-defunct Central Committee Research Office for the Reform of the Political Structure, Gao Shan and Wu Jiaxiang. However, because they were under tight police surveillance, dissidents-turned-businessmen were hard put to make a splash in the "sea of the marketplace."[193]

A number of the multi-millionaires were former bourgeois-liberal officials or intellectuals who were sympathetic to the 1989 movement but who did not participate personally. These disillusioned and in many instances sidelined cadres almost immediately *xiahai* after June 1989. Several members of the Research Institute for the Reform of the Economic Structure, which was closed in 1990, had by 1993 become millionaires many times over. Such RIRES alumnae included Zhang Shaojie and Bai Lanfeng, the senior executives of the Heng Tong Conglomerate, which had massive real estate holdings in cities ranging from Zhuhai to Shanghai. Other big players in business included the son of the later marshal Chen Yi, Chen Xiaolu. While not a full time democracy activist, the younger Chen saw no future in officialdom after the June 4 crackdown. By 1993, he had formed a large tourism company based in Hainan Island.[194]

Beijing was aware that many ex-dissidents who had made good as businessmen had not abandoned their democracy ideals. Wang Dan and his comrade at Beijing University Ma Shaofang suffered from repeated harassment in the course of setting up a small company. In August 1993, police stopped a gathering of *getihu* merchants in the North China seaside resort of Qingdao. The conclave, which would have been attended by luminaries such as Wang Xizhe and Zhang Xianliang, was, at least ostensibly, a business-networking event among small entrepreneurs from different provinces. Later the same year, security officers also prevented an American delegation of businessmen from meeting Wang and Zhang even though the Americans indicated that they only wanted to exchange business information with the dissidents-turned-*getihu*.[195]

However, except for those on black lists, Beijing had by mid-1993 slowly opened the door to bourgeois-liberal intellectuals who had settled in the US and Europe — and who were eager to return to China to do business. Open cities including Tianjin and Yangzhou, near Shanghai, had set up special industrial and hi-tech zones for such returnees. In the summer of 1993, Beijing gave the green light for a large-scale economic conference held in Hainan under the auspices of the Hainan Academy of Economic Research. Participants included a number of avant-garde scholars who had returned to China for the first time since June 1989.[196]

It is a mistake to assume that all or most of the liberal intellectuals turned private entrepreneurs were still interested in the crusade. A large number had totally forsaken politics and started blaming pro-democracy elements for disturbing social stability and preventing them from making more money. However, the new bosses were at least socially conscious enough to make contributions to research in market economics. A huge donation by various corporations including Heng Tong enabled Beijing University to open a centre for economic research in late 1993. The private entrepreneurs also contributed to the Sun Yefang Foundation for economic studies.[197]

There is no escaping the conclusion of Wang Dan that "the pursuit of wealth is a healthy trend in China". The phenomenon of *quanmin jieshang* ("everybody going into business"), he wrote in an article for a Hong Kong paper in mid-1993, "is not only beneficial towards economic prosperity. It will necessarily expedite democratic politics". "With wealth, individuals no longer need to be economically dependent on a party-dominated government," he added, pointing out that in the quasi-capitalist south, the control of Beijing had already been diluted. "Using wealth to check power and achieving the checks and balance of power on the basis of wealth has become a major trend in the development of democracy in China."[198]

(ii) Partial Improvement in the Fortunes of Zhaoists, 1993-1994

By mid-1994, there was no sign that the Zhaoists had a real chance of coming back to power. However, signals were aplenty that the clout of the right wing of the party had expanded. The political fortunes of a few seminal Zhaoists had improved markedly.

Police surveillance on Zhao relaxed noticeably towards the end of 1993 and 1994. While he was troubled at times by an unspecified lung ailment, Zhao, 74 in early 1994, continued to enjoy good health. According to intimates who saw him at that time, his mood varied with the vicissitudes of market reforms. But the liberal leader was generally optimistic about the future of the country. And he quietly expressed a wish to make further contributions to reform.

According to a businessman who met him in late 1993, Zhao paid close attention to progress in the economy. "Zhao is heartened that most of the reforms he advocated before June 4, 1989, have been revived," the business-man said. "He believes that the reforms will succeed." The source added that Zhao had in a subtle fashion expressed a desire to resume work, at least on the economy. He was convinced that he had a role to play after Deng Xiaoping left the scene. In 1993 and 1994, Zhao was allowed to see most of his former associates, including retired ministers and other influential politicians.[199]

Of equal significance was the sudden elevation in early 1994 of Wan Li, an old Zhao associate. Wan was nearly disgraced after the June 4 massacre for his failure to endorse the armed suppression. And since retiring from the Nat-ional People's Congress in 1993, the former vice-premier generally assumed a low profile. By 1994, however, it had become clear that Wan had been inducted into the ranks of the "immortals", or party veterans pulling strings from behind the scenes. The new pecking order of the elders was: Deng

Xiaoping, Chen Yun, Peng Zhen, Wan Li, Bo Yibo, Song Ping, Song Ren-qiong, Yang Shangkun and Yao Yilin. Since both conservative patriarch Chen Yun and Peng Zhen, another former NPC chairman, were near death, Wan, 77, had become a key adviser to Deng.[200]

Chinese sources in Beijing said that the elevation of Wan was Deng's idea, part of his familiar strategy of effecting a balance of power among the disparate factions. After the falling out between Deng and former president Yang in late 1992, the former needed Wan to play the old role of Yang, that is, to act as a countervail against conservative elders such as Chen Yun, the two Songs, and Yao Yilin. One must be reminded, however, that in spite of Li's dubious support of Deng during the June 4 crisis, their comradeship goes back a long way. It was Wan, not Li Peng, who was Deng's first choice for the post of premier in 1988. The relative expansion of Wan's clout also meant a sizeable improvement in the political fortune of politicians closely aligned with Wan: Zhao, Hu Qili and Li Ruihuan.

The career of another key ally of Zhao, former vice-premier Tian Jiyun, had also picked up steam by early 1994. During a swing of Guangdong in January and February, Tian, now the First Vice-Chairman of the NPC, played the regional card by seconding attempts by local cadres to "go as fast as they can" in economic development. He indirectly criticised Jiang Zemin's Mainstream Faction for trying to re-centralise powers under the guise of the campaign to boost macro-level controls. "We must never depart from the reform and open-door policy," he told cadres in Zhuhai. "There is no other road aside from reform." "Closing the door will lead to falling behind [the times]," he added. "Re-centralisation will lead to the death of the economy. We must mobilise the enthusiasm of the localities to creatively implement the spirit of the superior organs by bearing in mind local realities."[201]

7

Conclusion: China after
Deng Xiaoping

I. Introduction

I T'S way past midnight. The sun is coming out in a couple of hours. The
dancers and spectators are dead tired. But Cinderella, with her badly
soiled glass shoes, refuses to part the stage. By late 1994, it had become
apparent that the heavenly mandate for the Chinese Communist Party (CCP)
— Cinderella with advanced-stage Parkinson's disease — was about to ex-
pire. Deng Xiaoping was a candle in the wind. The patriarch was apparently
convinced of the efficacy of the police-state apparatus and of economic reform with socialist Chinese characteristics to prolong the "heavenly lease"
forever.

The CCP's Mainstream Faction — Deng Xiaoping, Jiang Zemin, Li Peng
and Zhu Rongji — had not only run out of new ideas. They had even stopped
trying to let on that they were capable of novel solutions. In a mid-1994
speech to cadres, Li Peng echoed the theme he had struck immediately after
June 4, 1989. "We must implement reform and construction in the midst of
stability," he said. "And we will maintain society's long-term stability through
reform and construction."[1] In a speech in Moscow later that year, Jiang vowed
to "change aspects of [China's] production relations and superstructure that
fail to meet the requirements of the development of productivity and overall
social progress". The President went on to dwell on the need to preserve the
supremacy of the state sector and Communist party suzerainty.[2]

Deng and Co's theory of stasis was totally contrary to Marx's — or Mao's

— theory of social change: contradiction followed by contention and the negation of contradiction, resulting in progress. But what will happen after Deng's rendezvous with Marx? This chapter will make projections of the post-Deng China in several major aspects: the party; the army; the economy; relationship between the centre and the regions; the growth of the entrepreneurial class and the *shimin shehui* ("civil society" or the "people's society").

It is a mark of Deng's stature that even in his dotage, the New Helmsman cast a long shadow over his 1.18 billion charges, and in almost all arenas. Deng, however, is the last of mainland China's helmsman-like, "charismatic" leaders. Like other helmsmen before him, Deng has been unable to propagate a successor who could remotely measure up to his genius. He was also unable to show the nation the way into the 21st century.

This chapter will argue that much as the CCP seemed to have achieved solid economic growth and consolidated its hold over the army and the police-state apparatus, drastic change would be inevitable. The ideal of stasis — as well as the *wanshi* ("stubborn rock") that the party had become — would prove no match for fast-shifting economic factors, the pull of the regions, and the leaps-and-bounds growth of the "people's society".[3]

Different sections will look at the possibility of the CCP — and the body politic in general — evolving into a more pluralistic entity. For example, will the CCP metamorphose into a democratic socialist party like those in Eastern Europe in the mid-1990s? Even if the CCP refuses to budge, however, the much-ravaged nation seems headed for a new and brighter era.

II. The Dearth of Political Change and the Uncertain Future of Reform

It is unlikely that China's rulers immediately after Deng will achieve much in the way of real political and economic change. Deng's theory — that so long as the standard of living keeps perking up (that is, the *shengcunquan*, or "livelihood rights", of Chinese is solved), the CCP can rule forever — has found wide acceptance within the party. The Mainstream Faction, represented by Jiang Zemin, Zhu Rongji and Li Peng, would go on making token modifications to the political structure without changing the basic nature of the dictatorship. Short of the radical wing of the party taking power, it was doubtful whether other elites within the CCP would go beyond the gingerly steps prescribed by Deng.

A. Deng Xiaoping's Last Recommendations for Political Change

Deng's philosophy was behind Li Peng's rather surprising claim during his tour of Germany and Austria in July 1994 that China observed a "tripartite division of power". "China is a country with rule of law," the premier told reporters in Vienna. "In China, judicial, executive and legislative powers are being exercised separately. It is the responsibility of judicial departments to implement the law."[4]

The only "new" thing that Deng proposed in 1994 was to put into place a degree of a "balance of power" among different branches of the polity. What the patriarch espoused was that under the premise of party suzerainty, there could be some checks and balances among cadres in government, the legislature and the judiciary.[5] Deng's motive was not different from that of Mao at the start of the Cultural Revolution: to prevent the party from stagnating and dying slowly. While the Great Helmsman tried to eradicate "bureaucratic tendencies" through "bombarding the headquarters", Deng wanted to stem corruption through some form of institutional change.

Deng's ideas were expressed in a roundabout way by Xie Fei, the Politburo member and Guangdong party secretary. The usually colourless apparatchik gave vent to surprisingly "progressive" views while attending the provincial commission for disciplinary inspection in the spring of 1994. "At the moment some areas and units do not follow the law or do not carry out the law properly," he said. "This is because the supervision mechanism is not strict enough." Xie proposed a fivefold system: a supervision mechanism within the party; a similar unit based in the NPC; "democratic supervision system" by the CPPCC and "people's bodies"; "democratic supervision by the masses"; and legal supervision.[6]

In early 1994, some party-affiliated experts also suggested setting up multiple layers of "supervision committees" within the party to ensure the probity of cadres and members. Such committees would be elected into office by various levels of party congresses. As such they reported to both the congresses — which had a degree of "popular mandate" — as well as the Central Committee and the local party committees. The experts argued that such committees would have more power than the CCDI, which proved ineffective in hunting down "real tigers" among graft-takers.[7]

Unfortunately, almost nothing was accomplished. Deng's motive — be it to cut down bureaucracy or to stem corruption — was to strengthen the CCP. The principle of "cross leadership", or senior party cadres holding major positions in the government and legislature, remained. The party's monopoly of power guaranteed that no meaningful political reform or "popular supervision" could be implemented.

Deng's possibly last instructions on domestic politics were given in mid-1994, when he toured Qingdao with protégé General Liu Huaqing. These recommendations, however, were concerned more with stasis than change, preservation of privilege rather than reform. "The policy of taking economic construction as the key link must never be changed; the reform and open-door policy must never be altered. The party's basic line must not be shaken for 100 years," he said. "We must properly draw the lesson from the former Soviet Union and handle well the relationship between the party centre and localities. We must uphold the leadership of the CCP. The CCP's status as the ruling party must never be challenged. China cannot adopt a multi-party system."[8]

Shortly before his 90th birthday on August 22, 1994, Deng was also quoted as urging "the correct handling of the relationship between the rule of personality and rule of law, as well as that between party and government". His main point, however, was still that "CCP leadership is unshakeable".[9]

B. Beefing up the Legislature

CCP leaders after Deng would likely do most in the area of strengthening the legislature and rationalising the legislative process. Legal reform was a key to ensuring the materialisation of a market economy — and ensuring a steady flow of foreign investment. Moreover, this could be attained under party supervision; legal modernisation must not affect the CCP's powers.

In February 1994, the Guangdong People's Congress passed a set of regulations on supervision over the "one government and two councils". This meant that provincial, municipal and county-level congresses would have power to supervise the government, the judiciary and the procuratorate of the same level. Chief of the Guangdong congress Lin Ruo said that this represented a "perfection of the people's congress system". Hong Kong NPC deputy Cheng Yiu-tong expressed the hope that the ideal of supervision would be extended to the entire country.[10] It is important to note, however, that the Guangdong law was murky about the legislators' prerogatives. There was no "Westminster-style" system of officials regularly appearing before the chambers to explain their policies. Nor did the deputies have the power to impeach senior cadres.

On a national level, the NPC began in 1994 to draft various laws that would in theory curb executive power or at least ensure the probity of officials. It was expected to pass a "government purchasing law" and a "law on bidding" in 1995 whose goal was to curtail corruption by government officials. Also in the pipeline were an "anti-corruption and bribery law" and statutes that would oblige cadres of certain levels to declare their assets. It was not expected, however, that a "Western-style" conflict of interest law would come into being.[11]

From mid-1993 onwards, the NPC and the CPPCC were slightly more active than before. Deputies blasted the government on issues including the runaway capital construction, neglect of farming and failure to accomplish enterprise reform. For example, the Finance and Economic Committee of the NPC published a hard-hitting report on the poor performance of state enterprises. It urged the government to send investigation teams to "major loss-making units" in industry, commerce and foreign trade "to find out the reason behind the losses".[12]

In an editorial entitled "A call for 'judicial independence,'" the *Legal Daily* said that free courts were essential for the development of a market economy. "The courts have become administrative tools of the government," the editorial quoted an unnamed court official as saying. "Judicial rights and administrative rights are combined into one." The *Daily*, which was later in the year disciplined for its liberalism, failed to spell out ways to cut the party's domination over the courts.[13]

The prognosis for the future is that while the NPC and local people's congresses would grow in power, their ability to check or balance the overweening authority of the party would be limited. The day when the leadership would allow the NPC or the courts to set up an "independent commission" to investigate the misdemeanours of a Politburo member seemed far off. To use a Chinese proverb, NPC supervision was like "scratching an itchy foot with the boot on".

C. The Exacerbation of Party Corruption

The failure of party reforms was evident from the worsening scourge of corruption. Judicial officials claimed that barely 0.04 per cent of officials had committed crimes in the early 1990s, a figure that was deemed a wild understatement by China analysts. In August 1994, the CCDI and the Supervision Ministry held a national meeting on laws and regulations on disciplinary inspection and supervision. CCDI cadres agreed that the problem of graft could not be cracked "unless there are well-defined laws, and unless the laws are enforced". The upshot was that the CCDI and relevant authorities would draft the CCP Regulations on Supervision Within the Party as well as Regulations on Disciplinary and Inspection Work in the CCP.[14]

The problem, of course, was that officials responsible for interpreting and enforcing the laws and meting out punishments to culprits would still be party functionaries. The NPC and other "people's organisations" would have no role in ensuring the probity of party officials.

The results of the anti-corruption campaign remained dismal as of late 1994. In June, almost one year after the kick-off of what was billed as the party's largest anti-graft campaign, the CCDI dispatched 20 teams to check things out in 24 ministries and as many provinces. CCDI secretary Wei Jianxin was relatively frank about the difficulties. "Deep-rooted problems affecting the anti-corruption struggle still await resolution," he said. "The prospect of the anti-corruption struggle is fairly grim." No results were announced upon the return of these 20 teams to the capital in August. Equally inexplicably, the authorities announced in the same month that yet another 20-odd teams would be dispatched to the provinces. The effort was Sisyphean.[15]

As of late 1994, the fattest "tiger" netted was still the Vice-Minister of Science and Technology Li Xiaoshi, widely believed to be a scapegoat in the Changcheng case (see Chapter 5). As Deng Xiaoping and Chen Yun rightly saw it, corruption struck at the very heart and soul of the party. It also erected a high wall between the CCP and the people, further curtailing the former's ability to cure itself.

D. The Retardation of Reform and the Impending Crisis

Judging by the superficial prosperity of Chinese society in the mid-1990s, the CCP as well as the casual observer might be forgiven for thinking that this anomaly might last forever: progress towards a quasi-market economy coupled with an obsolete Stalinist system.

However, the warning lights were flashing, and were ignored by the leadership. After June 4, 1989, and the collapse of the Soviet Union, the CCP's *raison d'être* was reform. Even reform in the narrow sense of the word — economic reform as understood by the CCP — however, presupposed some adjustments on the political front. The party was unwilling to make those movements. The result: a retardation of reform, and a further erosion of the CCP's "heavenly mandate".

The inflation crisis that hit the nation in late 1993 and early 1994 provided a good example of how, because of its failure to change, the CCP would rather slow reform or even turn back the clock. In the final weeks of 1993, panic buying hit a number of cities as the prices of grain, other food and consumer products soared by up to 40 per cent. The irrational turn of consumer behaviour took the leadership by surprise. As the semi-official Hong Kong China News Agency pointed out: "The storm of the panic buying of grain at the end of last year [1993] exceeded the expectations of officials."[16]

After all, China had a bountiful harvest of 450 million tonnes of grain in 1993. The storage of rice and wheat was considered sufficient to meet demand for another year. Much of the panic buying was fuelled by fear of new levies, particularly the 17 per cent value-added tax, as well as the 33 per cent devaluation. However, VAT in the Chinese context did not mean consumers having to pay 17 per cent extra. The levy was mostly slapped on manufacturers in place of other taxes. And while devaluation would make some imports more expensive, it had no direct bearing on domestic products or those imports that were formerly procured through the swap, or non-official foreign exchange rate. As mainland experts indicated, the main reason behind the buying spree was psychological: the anticipation of a price spiral.

And Beijing's abject failure to gauge — and defuse — the people's strong feelings about the radical reforms it was introducing superbly illustrated how the Leninist government set-up, including its vaunted propaganda machinery, had lost touch with reality. Beijing's first reaction to the price crisis was to bring out the People's Armed Police. It was not until late January, or more than two weeks after the climax of the panic buying, that the then Chief of the State Tax Administration Jin Xin and Agriculture Minister Liu Jiang were trotted out to explain the facts to the consumer.[17]

As we shall see, Beijing's inability to deal with unemployment — the inevitable result of the reform of the state sector — also forced it to soft-pedal enterprise reform in 1994 and 1995. We should perhaps have some pity for the cadre-mandarins in Beijing. They had no elected legislators, people's representatives, or consultative and advisory boards to tap popular opinion — or to explain the party's case to the people. To persuade a *blase* public that the CCP was fit for the 21st century, the Third Plenum of the Central Committee in November 1993 recommended policies such as fast-paced growth, deeper price reforms, restructuring state enterprises, and laying off redundant workers. These radical steps, however, immediately exacerbated destabilising factors like hyperinflation and unemployment.

The CCP could have minimised this adverse social impact — and forged full steam ahead with reform — if it had rendered the political system more transparent and pluralistic through measures including lifting press censorship, legitimising wild-cat trade unions, and allowing the people to form social if not political associations. It could have permitted intellectuals, consumer advocates, and non-official labour representatives to sit on the NPC and the CPPCC. None of these came to pass as the party opted for "socialist-style market reforms".

E. The Leadership Vacuum

In August 1994, Beijing closed down a retail outlet of the Hong Kong fashion-garment chain Giordano apparently because its chairman, Jimmy Lai, had penned an article that asked Premier Li to "drop dead". In the "personal letter to Li Peng", carried in Lai's trendy, Hong Kong-based news magazine *Next*, the maverick businessman also said: "[Li] is not just a *wangbadan* [bastard] but a *wangbadan* with zero IQ."[18]

What provoked Lai to call Li a "disgrace of the Chinese race" was the premier's tour of Germany a month earlier. As expected, Li made the standard defence of the June 4 massacre, saying that "in 10 or 20 years you will come to realise that these measures were necessary for the stability of China and for world peace". Yet the premier exposed himself to unnecessary ridicule by going overboard in self-righteousness. He made a point of touring the homes of Mozart and Goethe to show off his putatively liberal inclinations. On German television, the premier challenged his critics to go run China. "If some Western politician claims he is in a position to use normal Western methods to feed and clothe 1.2 billion Chinese, we would be happily prepared to elect him president of China."[19]

The premier, who had forgotten to mention that there were no elections in China, was full of confidence in himself and his colleagues. In his New Year's address for 1994, Li Peng boasted that the "third-generation leadership with Jiang Zemin as its core" had become "gradually more mature". "We now have organisational guarantees for modernisation construction," he said.[20]

The dearth of real leadership at a time of cataclysmic change, however, would militate against the longevity of CCP's reign. None of the third-generation leaders — those in their 60s — seemed to fit the bill. The cadre most often touted as a force for change — Zhu Rongji — was held in high regard for his intelligence and integrity by foreign diplomats and businessmen. As we discussed in Chapter 6, however, Zhu lacked a vision for the new century. In 1994, he displayed signs of lack of tolerance and "neo-authoritarianism" that did not square with his reformist reputation.

In a July briefing to cadres at Zhongnanhai, Zhu hinted that he should win the Nobel Prize for Economics for righting the Chinese economy. Such self-righteousness masked a heavy dose of authoritarianism. Zhu lambasted the views of liberal economists, including Beijing University economics professor Li Yining, that the country had to pay the price of inflation to maintain the momentum of growth and reform, as well as to cut unemployment. "I am opposed to Professor Li Yining's contention that unemployment is a bigger evil than inflation," Zhu said. He told the media to concentrate their firepower on the "aberrant theory about the harmlessness of inflation". The Vice-Premier also indicated that the nation's economic policy should not be swayed by the individual views of liberal economists. He largely supported the effort by the Propaganda Department to banish "cacophonous noises" from the media.[21]

Zhu also managed to put together a team of like-minded technocrats who subscribed to the neo-authoritarian creed. Many of his older subordinates and advisers had been managers in state factories. The young turks among them, however, were rated quite high by Chinese and foreign observers. In 1994, two young economists close to the czar, Guo Shuqing and Lou Jiwei, were promoted to respectively Head of the Department of General Planning at the

Ministry for Restructuring the Economy, and Head of the Department of Macro-economics of the same unit. Wu Xiaoling was made head of policy research at the People's Bank of China. These and other Zhu aides believed in using state fiats to push through market reforms (see Chapter 6).[22]

The quality of cadres below the very top echelon seemed even more dubious: to the point that Jiang Zemin, hardly an expert on the market economy, faulted cadres for their lack of understanding of modern economics. He asked senior economists to compile textbooks on the subject. Immersion courses were held at the Central Party School and other places. In April 1994, for example, 60 or so mayors took part in a 50-day course partly sponsored by the party's Organisation Department. Pace-setting cities such as Guangzhou even had timetables for making senior officials computer literate. [23]

In the run-up to the "dynastic change", however, what the party wanted to inculcate most among its cadres was still *ruzhong* ("Confucianist fealty"). In his talk to the new class at the Central Party School in September 1994, Politburo member Hu Jintao admonished them to learn "new knowledge". However, the 51-year-old rising star spent most of his time talking about boosting the cadres' "party nature", or loyalty and remaining faithful to Deng and Jiang.[24]

It is not surprising that some among the cream of the 54 million-strong party — those who know how to play the stock market and speak English — had left for the greener pastures of business. Starting in late 1992, the Organisation Department had encountered cases of short-listed candidates — particularly those who were heads of state corporations — refusing to take up positions of governors or mayors in remote and poor areas. In some cities, male cadres left for the business world, contributing to the rising proportion of female officials. By 1993, foreign corporations setting up branches in China had started poaching senior officials. Well-connected cadres who had taken up the offers of multinationals included Li Qingyuan, a former member of the State Commission for the Reform of the Economic Structure; and Ding Yuchen, the Western-educated son of Ding Guan'gen.[25]

F. The CCP in the late 1990s: A Projection

In a perceptive essay in 1994, Wu Dacheng, a little-known political scientist from the Jiangsu Public Security Specialist School, asked the overwhelming question: how long can the CCP-dominated society remain stable? "We cannot arrive at the conclusion that politics will be stable when the economy is developed," he said. "Nor can political authority be maintained for a long time based [solely] on personal charisma."[26]

What will happen after Deng's death? Will demonstrations *à la* 1989 break out? Most projections in late 1994 said that the leadership could withstand the disturbances that would inevitably break out after the Helmsman's demise. Firstly, most of the real or potential ringleaders of demonstrations would be locked up the moment Deng's condition took a nosedive. More importantly, the nation was not in the mood for political agitation. The "party nature" or "communistness" of the CCP manifested itself in little more than its Stalinist-style control mechanisms. Most citizens believed that this would be adulterated over time. They were reluctant to sacrifice their standard of living by supporting a movement similar to the 1989 crusade.

Thanks to this inertia, the leadership troika of Jiang, Li and Zhu is expected to stay in power for the short term — maybe 12 to 18 months. However, while the revolutionary path seems out of favour, the pressure put to bear on the regime to make drastic changes will be overwhelming. For reasons discussed above, it is most unlikely that the Jiang-dominated clique can withstand the pressure. A new line-up towards the end of the decade is therefore very probable.

Moreover, change could come from within the party. Jockeying for position had reached fever pitch in 1994. And the question of who was responsible for the June 4 massacre might become the pretext for removing Jiang and Li. After all, in the post-Deng order, overturning the verdict on June 4 could be the easiest way to win popular support and legitimacy.

Seeing the writing on the wall, Jiang took action in early 1994 to dissociate himself from the massacre. His strategy was to claim that he had stayed in Shanghai throughout, and that he was responsible for the bloodless handling of the "turmoil" in the metropolis. In an internal talk in the spring, Jiang said: "The central leadership must be careful and judicious in handling national disturbances." Referring to June 4, he added: "We in Shanghai were able to neutralise the trouble-making elements without upsetting stability." Chinese sources said, however, that it was well known that Deng had in late May 1989 called Jiang to Beijing to help handle the crisis. Moreover, the then Shanghai party boss became head of a secret body called the Emergency Committee to Handle the Tiananmen Square Turmoil.[27]

It would, however, be next to impossible for well-known "Tiananmen Square butchers" including Li Peng and Beijing municipal leaders such as Li Ximing and Chen Xitong to wash the blood from their hands. Li Ximing, then party secretary of the capital, also tried to exonerate himself. In a meeting on party history in early 1994, Li said: "Historical events, including those in the party, were never caused by a small group of people."[28] It is anticipated that politicians not tainted by the bloodshed, for example, NPC chairman Qiao Shi, would use the Tiananmen Square issue to bludgeon their political enemies. The departure of the "June 4 culprits" could open new vistas for the party and the nation.

According to the former secretary of Zhao Ziyang, Chen Yizi, there was a "very high possibility" that members of the old liberal wing would make a comeback after Deng's death. Chen thought they included Qiao Shi, Tian Jiyun, Li Ruihuan, Ye Xuanping, Yang Shangkun and Wan Li. Chen said they might "join hands to transform the existing power structure" in order to minimise the post-Deng political crisis.[29]

Another scenario is that the more moderate among the existing power elite — including the younger advisers of Zhu Rongji — might throw their weight behind faster change. While outwardly dour and conservative, Chinese cadres have a long tradition of trimming their sails. The proportion of officials with exposure to the outside world — through education, inspection tours, business, or handling foreigners regularly — had increased dramatically. Even the relatively open-minded cadres, however, must come to terms with the fact that to survive, the CCP has to share power with other sectors of society.[30]

III. The PLA: A Time-bomb Ticking Away

A. The Problematic Identity and Role of the Army

The PLA, which underpinned Deng Xiaoping's three comebacks from disgrace, could prove the patriarch's undoing, as least so far as his place in history is concerned. For a combination of reasons including selfishness and stubbornness, Deng chickened out of the daunting task of modernising the 3.2 million-strong army as well as the 800,000 para-military People's Armed Police (PAP).

By late 1994, it was obvious that Deng would leave the scene without solving one of the most crucial problems of modernisation: the identity and role of the army and its relationship with other aspects of the polity. Is the army that of the CCP, or more particularly, its dominant clique? Or should it be responsible to the country and to its 1.18 billion people? Should it be subject to the scrutiny of the National People's Congress, or just the secretive, politicised Central Military Commission?[31] Oblivious of the clarion calls for reform, Deng chose to stay with the Yan'an "ideal" of Mao Zedong: the PLA will only serve the interests of the powers-that-be.

(i) The PLA as the Private Army of the Deng-Jiang Clique

One of Deng Xiaoping's most valuable pieces of advice to Jiang Zemin was that to hold on to power, he must "grasp the PLA tightly". "Make frequent trips to the troops to get a handle on things," Deng reportedly told Jiang. The patriarch also gave his successor as CMC Chairman *carte blanche* to consolidate his position among the senior officers.[32]

The most important PLA-related event in 1994 — the appointment of 19 full generals in June — confirmed the unsavoury fact that the Deng-Jiang clique wanted the PLA to be their private garrison. On one level, as with all such high-level personnel moves, the promotions tended to reinforce the prestige and popularity of the commander-in-chief, in this case, Jiang. It is significant that 11 new generals were from the regions, a sign that the CMC chief wanted to cement personal links with potential warlords. Analysts could not recall another instance of such a large-scale elevation of local army bosses. [33]

Of most significance to the game plan of both Deng and Jiang was the promotion to full general of Vice Chief Political Commissar Wang Ruilin and the head of the garrison of the Zhongnanhai party headquarters, Yang Dezhong. The move stood the theories of Sun Zi and practically all other military thinkers — including Mao and Deng — on their head. Wang, Head of the Deng Xiaoping Office since the early 1980s, had, since the 1960s, been the confidant, secretary, and aide-de-camp of Deng. Yang Dezhong was a latter-day Wang Dongxing, the well-known chief palace guard and commander of the so-called 8341 Zhongnanhai guards. The "coup" against the Gang of Four in late 1976 would not have been successful if Wang had not hitched his wagon to Marshal Ye Jianying and Deng Xiaoping.[34]

But did Generals Wang and Yang deserve the helicopter ride to the top? Most likely not, judging by the widespread resentment the manoeuvre caused among officers, the rank and file and retired generals. Neither Wang nor Yang were career soldiers. According to internal publications, Wang's military credentials consisted of little more than a few years as a secretary in a platoon in his native Zhaoyuan county, Shandong, and later, a telegraph transcriber in the confidential office of the Northeast Military District.[35]

As early as the mid-1980s, Deng was criticised for bestowing too much power on Wang: he sat in on CMC meetings and helped Deng with personnel matters. Wang's clout expanded further upon his becoming Head of the army's Commission for Disciplinary Inspection. By mid-1994, the Deng protégé was widely expected to be promoted to the post of CMC Secretary-General, which had become vacant upon the disgrace of General Yang Baibing.

General Yang's experience was almost totally in military intelligence. His unexpected elevation betrayed a darker side of the succession slugfest. Jiang was apparently so fearful of a coup that he had to buy the support of the latter-day Wang Dongxing. In fact, soon after becoming party General Secretary in late June 1989, Jiang was distrustful of the military spook *par excellence*. For a year or so, he tried to replace Yang with Zeng Qinghong, his former aide in Shanghai who was Head of the Jiang Zemin Office.[36]

Another manifestation of Deng's feudalist approach to personnel was the elevation of Defence Minister Chi Haotian. While General Chi had been Chief of the General Staff, he was a career commissar and had never distinguished himself in combat, a previous criterion for promotion. PLA sources said Chi owed his rise to his well-known docility and loyalty to the Deng family — as well as recommendations by fellow Zhaoyuan native Wang Ruilin. Chi was regarded as a shoo-in to succeed Zhang Zhen as CMC Vice-Chairman in late 1994 or 1995.[37]

Yet aside from his febrile loyalty to the Deng household, Chi would seem to have little to commend himself. In mid-1994, the general raised eyebrows with a series of newspaper articles intended to massage the ego of Deng. In a short piece on a group of handicapped athletes and performers, Chi heaped praise on their "moving exploits and lofty feelings". One should not forget that the disabled sportsmen and artists were associates of an organisation headed by Deng Pufang. In late July, Chi wrote a long newspaper article commemorating the Tangshan earthquake. Nor surprisingly, the high point of the piece was that "the working class of Tangshan resolutely embraced [the] Deng Xiaoping [line]".[38]

According to Western military attaches, Deng's two daughters, Deng Nan and Deng Rong, had by early 1994 begun playing hefty roles in helping the patriarch read PLA documents and make army-related decisions. In mid-1994, Beijing was awash with rumours that Deng Nan, a Vice-Minister of Science and Technology, was a candidate to take Wang Ruilin's job at the GPD upon the latter's promotion to the CMC.

In their frequent salons, retired generals openly groused about the Deng- and Jiang-inspired "nepotism". They also lambasted alleged attempts by the Deng household to make use of their connections to finance army corporations. Even the relatively meagre royalties that Deng Rong raked in for *My Father, Deng Xiaoping*, were grist for the anti-Deng mill. Some officers accused Ms Deng of "stealing" portions of unpublicised army archives on the Second Field Army — and on Deng — and putting them in her biography of her father.[39]

(ii) Intensification of the Fusion of Army and Civilian Sectors

The dangerous practice of the fusion of army and civilian life became exacerbated in 1994. The political reason behind this was clear: to win the support of the officers for his post-Deng career, Jiang had to secure enough military votes. And the "interchangeability" of the two sectors tended to boost PLA powers.

As in the past, parts of the PLA budget were covered by the State Council.

The campaign of *yongjun youshu* ("Support Soldiers and Give Privileged Treatment to their Relatives") went into new heights of frenzy. The top brass was given an unprecedented say in non-military affairs, in particular, diplomacy. This "fusion" almost guaranteed that in the post-Deng power struggle, the PLA would become embroiled in party politics. The reason: only by playing a bigger role in national politics could the generals safeguard their vested interests.

The army's new-found clout was illustrated by a function in July 1994 to honour model cities and counties, "where the people support the army and their relatives, and where soldiers support the government and love the people". To underscore the close relations between the PLA, the party and government, all seven members of the Politburo Standing Committee including General Liu Huaqing, took part in the gala. Jiang Zemin pointed out that the "mutual support of the army and the people" was a great tradition of the new China. "Particularly at critical junctures, the broad masses of PLA officers and soldiers rush to the frontline and make brave sacrifices for the people," Jiang said.[40]

In July 1994, the *People's Daily* reported that the majority of provinces and cities had taken measures to ensure the quantity and quality of grain and other foodstuffs for the army. This meant that in many instances, PLA units were able to get priority supplies at subvented prices. Areas including Fujian, Hainan, Tibet and Xinjiang also helped army units start a so-called "vegetable basket engineering project", so that, the People's Daily reported, "the livelihood of the garrisons will improve at a time of major fluctuations in market prices".[41]

In various reports, the official and semi-official media hinted that the central government had underwritten army-related activities. In an August 1994 report, the New China News Agency disclosed that "central authorities" had in the past few years earmarked more than 100 million yuan to improve life in the Spratly garrisons. The NCNA said the money had been used for infrastructure projects such as forts, reservoirs and desalination plants. Presumably the "central authorities" included the central government, not just the CMC. In its August 1994 issue, the Chinese-affiliated Hong Kong journal, *Mirror*, reported that the State Council had set aside US$5 billion of foreign exchange for the purchase of Russian military hardware and technology.[42]

Despite pledges for introducing a "Western-style" civil service, most provinces and localities were obliged to absorb demobilised officers and soldiers. More than 30 large cities had introduced preferential policies in job placement for former soldiers. Some 58,000 PLA rank and file, together with 25,000 of their kinsfolk, were relocated in 1993. In some instances, the transplanted soldiers were able to win promotion. For example, 6,520 officers became cadres in Shenzhen in the 14 years ending 1994. 22 per cent of these worked in administrative departments and five became "municipal leaders" or their equivalents.[43]

(iii) The Worsening of PLA Corruption

No dent had been made in the fight against graft. The party and army authorities failed to check the mushrooming PLA business empire — or to install a proper supervision and anti-corruption mechanism.

In February 1992, Liu Huaqing issued a speech that was widely seen as a warning against army business-related corruption. "The construction of a [righteous] party style and clean administration is an important aspect of spiritual civilisation," General Liu said. "The army should of course do even better in this area."[44] It was widely reported that the CMC had decided to stem corruption by raising the salaries of officers. This was in the Chinese tradition of "nurturing cleanliness through adequate pay". As top think-tank theorists Hu Angang and Kang Xiaoguang put it, the PLA should ban all businesses. And the government should foot all army expenses. In time of war, special taxes could be levied to pay for additional outlay. Hu added on another occasion that even if the PLA were allowed to do business, their companies should only be under one unit, for example, the General Logistics Department.[45]

In June 1994, the CMC convened in Beijing a Conference on the Restructuring and Reform of Army Production and Management. The thrust of the conclave, at which Jiang and Logistics Chief Fu Quanyou spoke, was to cut PLA businesses run by regional army units — as well as those that ran foul of regulations. These illicit units would be "chopped off, stopped, cleaned up, or merged with civilian units". Some more army concerns such as the coal mines in Shanxi Province, were transferred to civilian authorities.[46]

In actual fact, Jiang and General Fu were powerless to stop the activities of the big players. *Bingshang* units were as aggressive as civilian companies in "privatising" and taking over state assets, an estimated 1 billion yuan of which was "lost" everyday in the early 1990s (see later section). Moreover, the trend of large PLA corporations becoming multinationals increased in 1994. Subsidiaries or "associate companies" of behemoths such as Polytechnologies and Norinco were by 1994 listed on Hong Kong and overseas stock exchanges. They were also vital components of the mutual funds offered by major Western banks.[47]

(iv) "Military-style diplomacy"

In the first half of 1994, the PLA established "effective links" with armies in more than 30 countries. It hosted visits by more than 60 military delegations and groups from almost 30 countries, 22 more cent more than in the first half of 1993. "The PLA's active exchanges and effective co-operation with foreign countries have proved conducive to enhancing mutual understanding, strengthening friendship, and helping promote relations between countries," General Chi said. Aside from the numbers and frequency, it was also notable that for the first time since 1949, regional commanders conducted a fair amount of "military-style diplomacy". In June 1994, Chengdu Military Region commander Li Jiulong made high-profile visits to Burma and Laos. Even more significant was the trip made by Shenyang Military Region Commander Wang Ke to Pyongyang in the same month.[48]

Defence analysts said they could not recall any precedent for such frequent travels by the top brass. They said it was clear that aside from cementing links with foreign armies, the itinerant generals played a big role in diplomacy. Examples cited included Taiwan, North Korea and the Spratlys.

Sabre-rattling rhetoric by Generals Chi and Zhang Zhen on the Taiwan issue — namely, that Beijing would never tolerate the "plot of two Chinas; or one China, one Taiwan" — confirmed widespread suspicions that the top brass backed a more hawkish policy towards the "breakaway province". During visits to ASEAN nations, the generals tried to persuade their hosts to bar Taipei from regional and international functions. Generals Chi and Wang were instrumental in persuading Pyongyang to adopt a more conciliatory attitude towards the US over the inspection of its nuclear facilities.[49]

Not surprisingly, the top brass took a hard line on the Spratly islands, whose sovereignty was being contested by Asian countries and regions including Vietnam and Taiwan. PLA sources said that beginning in early 1994, the generals had put pressure on the party and government to increase funding for troops deployed in the archipelago. The sources said PLA officers had groused that because of lack of funds and a long supply line, Chinese naval units had lagged behind the Vietnamese in the game of stationing at least symbolic garrisons on the islets.[50]

B. The Roots of Instability

Will the PLA play a sizeable role in the post-Deng factional struggle? Some analysts did not think so. In an interview with the Hong Kong press, London-based sinologist Gerald Segal said that "the PLA might well prefer to sit on the sidelines". Among the reasons given by Dr Segal was that "[while] it is clear that the PLA played an important role [in succession politics] in the past, now the PLA is itself divided. It is hard to see it as one institution."[51]

An even more persuasive argument along the same lines is that the army will not be involved in politics — provided that the post-Deng leadership will ensure the PLA's privileged status, which includes an over-sized share of the economic pie. There are, however, contrary theories. Only two of these will be cited. Firstly, in 1994, there were powerful factions within the PLA which were jealous of the supremacy and empire-building of the Deng-Jiang axis. They would take advantage of the first crisis faced by Jiang to unseat him.

The second concerns the longer term. Whoever takes over from Deng has to forge ahead with market reforms in order to stay in power. Such market reforms will necessarily cut into the perks of the PLA. For example, special, hidden subsidies will have to be curtailed. In the name of promoting political and governmental changes required by a market economy, the new leadership may also decrease the number of PLA representatives in high-level party and government councils. This will provoke opposition from the army, thereby sowing the seeds of instability.

(i) Identity of the Anti-Jiang Factions

The 67th anniversary of the founding of the PLA on August 1, 1994, could mark the zenith of Jiang's influence. At least superficially, there was not a cloud on the horizon for Jiang and his cohorts. In fire-spitting speeches marking Army Day, Chi Haotian saluted Deng's "ideas on army construction in the new era", and pledged the army's fealty to "the party Central Committee with Jiang Zemin as its core". Chi promised to "strengthen the building of an all-round army" in accordance to Jiang's requirements. The Defence Minister and Zhang Zhen went through the familiar routine about the army toeing the party line and "taking into consideration the overall situation of the nation".[52]

As in the case of other Third World countries, we do not often hear about a "malcontented army faction" or a bunch of coup leaders until after their putsch. The attempt to oust the Gang of Four in October 1976 was very close to a coup. As discussed in Chapter 4, Deng and Jiang were in the summer of 1992 persuaded that the Yang Clan was brewing an anti-Deng plot. If there had been a groundswell of discontent against the Yangs' empire-building, Jiang's self-aggrandisement would have provoked a similarly virulent reaction.

Anti-Jiang officers ranged from retired generals jealous of Deng's machinations to young turks who wanted to pursue real military modernisation (see Chapter 4). In late 1992, the retired generals wrote letters to Deng complaining about Yang Baibing. While they would not air their gripes against Deng or Jiang, it did not mean that they were contented with the status quo.

The discontent was indirectly mirrored in Deng's repeated stress on the "five lakes and four seas" principle. Since late 1992, Deng had also tried to strike a balance by promoting affiliates of the Third Field Army. This was reflected in the background of the 19 full generals elevated in June 1994. At least nine of them were Third Field affiliates. While this might be a function of the influence of CMC Vice-Chairman Zhang Zhen and General Wang Ruilin, both Third Field alumni, it also showed Deng's anxiety to placate the powerful cabal.[53]

The "Deng-Jiang axis" seemed, however, to have a harder time mollifying affiliates of the Fourth Field Army, once led by the disgraced defence minister Lin Biao. Western military analysts discounted stories circulated in Hong Kong and China that there was an effort to "restore Lin Biao's reputation" among the younger officers, many of whom were said to be "Lin fans".[54]

However, in July 1994, many PLA analysts were taken by surprise when it was announced that a high-level committee had been set up to compile the War History of the Fourth Field Army. The "general consultants" for the tome were Chen Yun and Peng Zhen. Retired general Hong Xuezhi was the head of the leading group on editorial work.[55] Chen and Peng were old foes of Deng. However, both had been almost incapacitated by illness. Analysts said their names could have been used by anti-Jiang elements to air their grievances.

(ii) Possibilities of a Coup

By late 1994, the PLA had gained First World trappings. According to findings of the London-based International Institute of Strategic Studies (IISS), the "actual" PLA budget for 1994 ranged between US$28.5 billion to US$45 billion, several times that of the "official" budget of US$6 billion. If the higher figure was taken into account, the outlay of the Chinese army surpassed that of Japan, whose 1994 budget was a mere US$39.7 billion.[56]

At the same time, however, Jiang Zemin tried to perpetrate what his minions called a "psychological engineering campaign" in the PLA that smacked of Lin Biao's ideological education crusades during the Cultural Revolution. The CMC chief continued to urge the army "to provide a reliable, safe guarantee for reform, development and stability".[57]

Such machinations, however, might invite instability in the post-Deng era. They also reflected the extent to which Jiang and Co were scared of being stabbed in the back. It is instructive to learn that the PLA top brass set up a secret research committee to prevent *coups d'état* in 1991. The outfit, which operated under the guise of a research institute on Asian security matters, was involved in detecting roots of challenge to the CCP ruling elite that might be posed by disgruntled units or "dissident rings" in the army and PAP.[58]

Leader of the group was CMC Vice-Chairman Liu Huaqing. Aside from senior officers and researchers in military think-tanks, the committee drew on the expertise of diplomats, academics and journalists. Senior Colonel Liu

Yazhou, son-in-law of the late president Li Xiannian, was a leading member of the committee. Sources close to the secretive unit said that Deng first became interested in coup research after the ignominious fall of the Ceausescu regime in Romania in late 1990. The "coup committee" had studied in detail every major military-inspired insurrection in Third World countries in the past decade. Deng's aides were said to be particularly interested in those that had taken place in Thailand.[59]

IV. Rocky Ride to the Market Place

That, in the first couple of years after Deng's death, China will not adopt "instant capitalism" or "shock therapy" *à la* Eastern Europe seems obvious. By 1994, a broad spectrum of the CCP leadership was committed to a so-called East Asiatic approach to economic reform: market elements coupled with "macro-level adjustments and controls", which was the theme of the fourth plenum of the 14th Central Committee late that year. As Jiang Zemin told the Third Plenum in November 1993, the party would opt for an organic synthesis between state interference and market forces. "We will, in accordance with practical situations, give more emphasis to the market at some junctures, and more emphasis to macro-level adjustments and controls at other junctures."[60] This policy looked set to continue through the rest of the decade.

Unless the radical, "closet-capitalist wing" of the party takes over, it does not seem that a post-Deng administration will adopt radical steps to privatise the economy. The uneasy coexistence between a "wholly people's owned sector" that is about to lose its dominant status and the upstart private sector could well go on to the late 1990s. Aside from the ideological need to stick to the label of "socialism", Beijing was convinced of the need for a significant degree of state control over the economy: it helped ensure the centre's hold over the disparate country; certain categories of revenues would be ensured; and social stability would be maintained.

During his European tour of July 1994, Li Peng reiterated that economic reform would only be continued under conditions of stability. "The transition from a planned to a market economy takes a long time," he said. "For example, market reform in China has taken 15 years."[61] What Li did not say was that Beijing had turned the clock back on price liberalisation throughout 1994. After Deng, however, the pressure on Beijing to move faster could mount — and overwhelm the CCP leadership. This process would accelerate as it became obvious that the mish-mash called the socialist market economy might slow productivity and make corruption worse.

A. The Staying Power of State Fiats

(i) Revival of the *Ancien Regime* of Planners

In March 1994, the State Council promulgated a document entitled "Outlines of China's Production Policy in the 1990s". It contained in some detail the nation's strategies for industry, commerce, finance and other sectors for the coming decade. The document said such a policy was necessary to "boost and improve macro-level adjustments and controls and to fine-tune and rationalise effectively the production structure". Conspicuous in its absence was any indication about expanding the role of the market or the private sector.[62]

Economic Czar Zhu Rongji had by early 1994 crossed over to the camp of the neo-conservative "rectifiers". Without commensurate political and social reforms, economic reform had entered a bad patch if not a blind alley. Tough central guidance was seen as indispensable to strike the balance among the disparate requirements of economic change, social stability and CCP suzerainty. As we saw earlier, Zhu put together a team of born-again planners to help re-impose control.

The once-moribund State Planning Commission roared back to life. In theory its power should have been diminished in 1993, when its staff was cut from 1,500 to 900 people. In 1994, however, the SPC was again given the responsibility of keeping an overall balance of the supply and demand of funds and "harmonising" their allocation. It would set the timetable for major development projects and vet applications for capital construction expenditures. Additional briefs included "supervising the orders, reserves and distribution of major commodities".[63] Other policy roles were performed by the State Economic and Trade Commission and the China Securities Regulatory Commission.

In mid-1994, Beijing revived another element of traditionalist planning. More than 10 ministries formed a Conference on the Comprehensive Co-ordination and Adjustment of Economic Operations. The body, which met periodically, would, according to senior officials, beef up state control and "ceaselessly fine-tune" the economy. The Conference reported to the SETC. "Only when we ceaselessly go about minute and micro-level adjustments [of the economy] can we avoid large-scale adjustments and prevent pronounced ups-and-downs in the economy," NCNA said. The ministries came from units in the areas of taxation, statistics, domestic and foreign trade, transport, electronics, machinery, and light industry.[64]

(ii) No to Privatisation

The bold calls for privatisation of the lumbering state enterprises, which emerged in the semi-official and provincial media in late 1993, were suppressed. Zhu and Co apparently succumbed to the hard sell by one of the most important power blocs within the party: state-sector managers and those among State Council bureaucrats who were their lobbyists and former colleagues. Moreover, the issue of unemployment benefits had become paramount. Late 1994 projections said that by the year 2000, there would be 200 million peasants and 68 million urbanites "waiting to be placed". Privatising the publicly held concerns, 11,000 of the largest of which accounted for 40 per cent of industrial production, might mean massive lay-offs and social disorder.[65]

SETC Minister Wang Zhongyu, the former manager of a state-owned paper mill, was unambiguous about the administration's dubious attitude towards privatisation. "Whether it is today or tomorrow, privatisation is not the necessary trend for the reform of China's state-held enterprises," he said in mid-1994. "It is also impossible for the state-owned sector to be replaced by other economic elements — or for it to undergo major structural changes."[66]

Conservative economist Sun Shangqing, Head of the Economic, Social and Technological Research Centre of the State Council, even theorised about the "expanding" role of the public sector. Sun was not adverse to the conversion of state corporations to shareholding companies because, for him, the question of non-governmental concerns gaining control of these new units was out of the question. The former professor indicated that the state would remain majority shareholders. "State-owned companies will hold the stocks of each other," he said. "The powers of state-owned enterprises will increase. State assets will appreciate."[67]

By mid-1994, remnant Maoists and "neo-conservatives" such as the followers of Zhu Rongji had joined hands to lambast the "pro-West" lobby among cadres and economists. In an article in the leftist mouthpiece *Seeking Truth* (*Zhenli de zhuiqiu*), Gao Hongye criticised "the blind worship of theories which have not been affirmed in the West, such as the omnipotence of the marketplace". The People's University economist asserted that the free-marketeers were out to "implement privatisation and dissolve the public ownership system". In an economic seminar in Beijing, the neo-conservatives attacked the "common trend" of worshipping Western economics. "Some people apparently thought that once China had become a market economy, it could be entirely run by the Invisible Hand."[68]

B. State Corporations and State Assets

(i) The Losing Battle against the Dinosaurs

While the leadership had apparently decided to postpone privatising the state enterprises indefinitely, how to restructure or modernise the dinosaurs became a big headache. Perhaps reflecting the need to "buy votes" for the power struggle that would ensue after Deng's death, leaders including Jiang Zemin, Li Peng and Zhu Rongji refused to grasp the nettle. Instead, a feel-good campaign about the public sector was mounted.

"Just because the state enterprises have met with difficulties, we should not shake our confidence in our ability to make them better," Zhu said. "We should not regard the enterprises as our baggage." He said the dinosaurs, the extent of whose losses was shrinking, would "continue to play a leading role" in the socialist market economy. Wang Zhongyu surprised most analysts when he claimed in May 1994 that state enterprises had made "progress". Wang asserted that only 10 per cent of enterprises had either stopped operations or were working below capacity. "At the moment, the profit levels of state enterprises are rising, and their losses have decreased," he claimed. When confronted with reports that the enterprises were doing much worse, he said: "This is a misunderstanding."[69]

Numerous accounts, however, indicated that in the first quarter of 1994, losses incurred by state-sector units increased by nearly 80 per cent and that 45 per cent of the concerns were in the red. The semi-official HKCNA reported in mid-1994 that the percentage of state enterprises losing money were double that of private ones. HKCNA said that "in the recent year", 46.2 per cent of enterprises in Liaoning were losing money, and 700,000 workers went without pay. The percentage of loss-makers was 35 even in prosperous Shanghai.[70]

The pro-state propaganda mounted by Zhu and Co seemed aimed at parrying the arguments of shock therapy. HKCNA quoted some radical economists as saying: "Increasing investment or subventions to those enterprises that are perennially losing money is a waste of resources. The new funds used cannot be converted to new productivity. They barely contribute to the budget deficit."[71]

(ii) Retreat from Radical Surgery

Measures to retool the enterprises — originally scheduled for 1994 — were postponed to 1995. Moreover, those will not be structural, "macro-economic" moves. The official or semi-official media in late 1994 quoted the leadership as saying that state-enterprise reform in 1995 would focus on "micro-economic measures" such as "modernising the management system".[72] Liberal economists suspected that the term "micro-economic changes" was a euphemism for steps that would not affect the ownership system of enterprises. The economists doubted whether such fairly superficial tinkering would be useful. After all, efforts to "modernise the management system" had already been tried out in the early 1990s.

Since the mid-1980s, liberal economists had proposed two "radical" methods to shake up or mercy-kill the dinosaurs. One was to close them or declare them bankrupt. The other was to sell off assets to non-state parties or foreign companies. In the six year since the passage of the Bankruptcy Law in November 1988, more than 1,000 enterprises had closed their doors. Most of these, however, were small-scale units.[73]

Zhu Rongji was said to be personally sympathetic to the bankruptcy approach. However, by mid-1994, he only proposed limited trials in 18 cities, where two or three companies "which have no hope to be turned around" would be declared bankrupt. Beijing had earmarked 7 billion yuan for the banks to write off the bad debts. This was a step back from the measure he had suggested in early 1993. Then Zhu had indicated that one enterprise or more in each city and county be foreclosed.[74]

Under the pretext of plugging the loss or drainage of state assets, Beijing exercised a tight control over the transaction of state enterprises in early 1994. The central government claimed that in the decade before 1994, 500 billion yuan of state assets had been "lost", mostly to collectives, private entities or foreigners. This is despite the contention of radical economists that the clean sale of state assets was the most efficient way of privatisation and attracting foreign funds and expertise.[75]

Aside from the familiar concern about "diluting socialism", State Council bureaucrats expressed fear about being cheated. Many departments undervalued state assets when they "sold" a certain company or factory to foreigners. A survey of 6,000 joint ventures that involved state enterprises showed that more than 60 billion yuan of state assets were "lost" in this way. Moreover, massive corruption had arisen. The cadres responsible either took kickbacks or became the bosses of the new entities. State assets were also transformed into private property — including stocks owned by employees — when state concerns were turned into shareholding companies. In other cases, officials used state properties to secure mortgages or loans to finance their business deals.[76]

In the latter half of 1994, the State Assets Management Bureau (SAMB) cracked down hard on the sale or transfer of assets and property rights. All such sales and transfers had to be approved by the central authorities. When a state-owned company wanted to set up a joint venture with a foreign corporation, it had to report the value of its state assets to the SAMB, which would do the requisite assessment and verification. Moreover, when a state concern sold assets to other firms, the "profits" realised must first be used to pay bank debts or unemployment and welfare benefits to workers.[77]

C. Monetary and Banking Policy

Zhu and his go-go technocrats wanted to go down in the history of economic reform as the trail-blazers for a quasi-independent banking system and monetary policy that would be free from political interference. This had not come to pass by the end of 1994. Analysts said such a "Western-style" monetary system would only be slowly licked into shape in the late 1990s. They expressed fears that through the mid-1990s, monetary and credit policy would be subordinate to the party's political agenda.

Soon after taking over the governorship of the PBoC, Zhu said that he would depoliticise banking and that credit policies would be based entirely on commercial considerations (see Chapter 2). He said that if local bankers were fired because they refused to heed the unreasonable demands of party and government cadres, he would penalise the latter.[78] However, in late 1993 and throughout 1994, the central bankers made the political decision of subsidising and bailing out loss-making factories and unemployed workers.

In a lightning tour of the northeast in April 1994, Zhu fired the party secretary and the governor of Heilongjiang Province, Sun Weiben and Shao Qihui respectively, for mishandling the state sector. On a second trip there two months later, however, Zhu agreed to pump loans into Heilongjiang and Jilin "to help them revive their economies".[79] Both Sun and Shao could supposedly argue that if they had secured the loans earlier, state enterprises under their watch would have fared better.

Zhu himself did a fair amount of tampering with banking neutrality when he asked local governments and banks to chip in to save factories and to pay subsistence wages of workers. In some instances, the central government ordered local banks to lend even to enterprises that had no collateral. Local authorities were asked to bear the interest. At least several municipal administrations and banks refused to go along with this.[80]

In spite of the fierce rhetoric throughout 1994 about a tight-money policy, Beijing had made selective but still significant modifications to its austerity programme. Senior banking officials disclosed that in the first six months of that year, banks and credit co-operatives had extended loans of 238.9 billion yuan, or 96.6 billion yuan more than the same period in 1993. Another figure put the loans at more than 250 billion yuan.[81]

By mid-year however, the spigot was removed at both the central and local levels. Shanghai announced in August 1994 that it would take 10 measures to "invigorate loss-making state-owned enterprises". Foremost among them was the provision of loans. The Shanghai Branch of the Industrial and Commercial Bank made loans worth 100 million yuan in June and July, and 90 million yuan was promised for August and September. Shenzhen banks indicated that they would make loans of more than 10 billion yuan in the second half of the year.[82]

Beijing had its excuses ready for the revival of old-style credit policy. For example, so many bad debts had piled up that they had to be written off or the banking system would be hopelessly snarled. Senior economist Dong Fureng estimated that bad debts incurred by loss-making state enterprises accounted for 45 per cent of the ledgers of specialised banks. Professor Dong said in mid-1994 that losses incurred by the state sector totalled 450 billion yuan, three times the registered capital of the banks.[83]

A related problem was the notorious triangular debts (money that enterprises owe each other or the banks), estimates of which ranged from 360 to 600 billion yuan. If the banking system did not cut the Gordian knot, activities of enterprises would grind to a halt. In early 1994, the troubled metallurgical industry — which was responsible for some of the strikes that Zhu saw during his swing through the northeast — was owed 60.7 billion yuan even as its own debts came up to 41 billion yuan. Liaoning was owed 34 billion yuan and it owed others 26 billion yuan.[84]

Zhu's favourite excuse for partially relaxing the tight-money policy was that money would only be lent to "enterprises with potential". The Bank of China indicated that loans would only go to efficient enterprises, preferably those with guaranteed export earnings. Units also qualified if their losses were due to "factors beyond their control", for example, adverse government policies or sudden shifts in the market place including the prices of raw materials. Moreover, such loans would only cover the working capital of enterprises.[85]

At the same time, the PBoC failed to come up with policies to ensure that non-public enterprises would have equal access to loans. This was made worse by the fact that the State Council refused to consider legalising non-official financial institutions such as private banks and trust companies. Such quasi-private financial institutions had provided much-needed help to private enterprises and VTEs.

Lack of a policy, however, did not stop the leaps-and-bounds growth of underground banks and activities relating to "collecting funds in society". In coastal provinces including Guangdong and Fujian, even state financial institutions and enterprises were partners or patrons of such institutions, which paid much higher interest rates than PBoC units. Fujian reported a large number of "foundations", rural co-operative foundations, and fund-swapping societies. In quasi-capitalist Wenzhou, there were 100 such outfits, some operating openly. The practice of official banks and business units raising funds in factories and universities also increased. In early 1994, staff in Guangdong Engineering College and Zhongshan University were offered deposit interest rates of up to 30 per cent.[86]

D. The Renewed Accent on Farming

The "tilt" towards agriculture would likely persist through the 1990s. Chen Yun's theory about "taking grain as the key link" would continue to take precedence over the law of comparative advantage. As the Central Committee circular of June 1994 put it: "Grain is a special commodity with strategic importance. The stability of the grain market has an important bearing on the overall situation."[87]

Jiang expatiated on the imperative of self-sufficiency in grain in a major speech in July 1994. The neo-conservative president spelled out his theory of the "three stabilities": "Acreage devoted to grain, the grain production volume, and the level of storage must all be stable." In a swing through the provinces in the middle of the year, Jiang said: "We must safeguard arable land. Coastal provinces that have well-developed industries and services should pay special attention to this." The president said that in spite of the advent of the socialist market economy, grain development "must still depend on [government] protection and efforts".[88]

Guangdong and Zhejiang were ordered to grow more grain. Guangzhou was told that even if it could afford it, the province must not import rice from other provinces or abroad. Guizhou was asked to switch from tobacco to wheat and rice. Guangdong and other coastal provinces had repeatedly incurred the wrath of Jiang and Zhu for neglecting agriculture. To help conserve arable land, acreage for real-estate development in Guangdong was set at 100,000 *mu* in 1994. Fujian was ordered to close 20 economic development zones in order to save 102 sq km of land.[89]

Apart from ensuring high yields, Beijing also cracked the whip on "speculative activities" on the grain market. By mid-1994, the central government had practically stopped private wholesale activities in grain and cotton. Procurement of produce again became very much a state monopoly. "Grain prices are the core of the party's agrarian policy," said Zhu Rongji. "The grain market must not be chaotic . . . What would happen if we let people who speculate in the stocks and real-estate markets also speculate in the grain market?" asked the official *Fortnightly Chat*.[90]

E. Re-imposition of Price Control

Price control is tipped to remain in place through the 1990s. Chinese politics is so volatile — and the relation between inflation and social unrest so intimate — that the post-Deng administration would not easily let go of control over this crucial arena. This is despite the fact that before the end of 1993, even the Jiang administration had cited price reform as a success story of China's economic liberalisation.

According to State Planning Commission Minister Chen Jinhua, state administration of prices did not contradict market reforms. "The [introduction of] the market economy does not mean that we [the central government] will take our hands away," he said. Chen was also head of the Leading Group on National Inspection of Prices which was set up in late 1993. "The operation of the national economy is gravitating towards boosting macro-level adjustments and controls, whose major task is to stabilise prices," Chen added.[91] Chen indicated that three categories of goods and services would remain under state control over the long haul: grain, cotton and basic staples; major producer goods such as petrochemicals and rural electricity; and "basic services". Other officials laid down five types of commodities and services, some of which overlapped with Chen's list. They were: commodities essential to "social stability and long-term economic development" such as oil and gas; drugs and weaponry; housing for civil servants and residents in low-income brackets; utilities such as water and gas; major services such as education and health. No timetable was given on when the controls might be lifted.[92]

In an August 1994 address, Zhu Rongji made it clear that long-term government interference in pricing did not constitute a return to the diktat economy. Zhu had just publicised ways and means to depress the prices of fertilisers and other raw materials. One of his directives was that the number of distributors would be cut, and that they must lower their prices within a specified time. "Practice in developed countries has shown that they do not just let the market have free rein and adopt a total hands-off policy towards prices," he said. "We cannot regard efforts by the government to regulate the market and to supervise prices as 'restoring the planned economy'."[93]

F. A Rough Ride for the Stocks and Futures Markets

Given Beijing's dubious commitment to building a "shareholding economy", it is not surprising that it was slow to put into place a body of rules and regulations governing activities such as the flotation of shares or their transactions. As with other aspects of the market economy, the central government was soon overtaken by events, in this case speculators exploiting the lack of laws or loopholes to make a fast buck. The need to rein in speculators then became an excuse for reintroducing central control.

Doing his Li Peng act, economic czar Zhu began in 1994 to slam on the brakes. Permission for new shareholding companies as well as their public listing remained cautious. Approval for a third stock exchange was again postponed. "The shareholding system is still at the experimental stage," Vice-Minister for Restructuring the Economy He Guanghui said in March 1994, adding that it was "unnecessary" to turn all enterprises into joint-stock ones. He also indicated that "there should be a small number of listed companies in China, as in developed western countries". While there were 11,560 shareholding companies with total assets of 314.7 billion yuan, 63 per cent of them were relatively small-scale collective enterprises and only 22 per cent were state companies. Only 217 were listed on the bourses.[94]

The year 1994 saw a depression on both the Shanghai and the Shenzhen stock exchanges. In mid-year, the Shanghai and the Shenzhen indexes were hovering around 400 and 100 respectively, down from their respective high points of 1,536 and 368 in early 1993. Zhu's initial response was reportedly that of jubilation: he indicated that "it was a good thing" because the low index figures were a realistic reflection of the real worth of the companies listed. By July and August, however, Beijing was forced to take draconian measures to rescue the market: declaring an end to the listing of new shares; and allowing some foreign investors to buy A shares.[95]

In mid-1994, the State Council levelled its big guns on the futures markets, which were allegedly responsible for the loss of hundreds of millions of dollars of foreign exchange. Futures trading facilities in the areas of steel, sugar and coal were closed. No new licences would be granted. Underground markets were raided and their bosses punished. Most of the 40-odd exchanges were turned into wholesale markets. Index-linked futures trading was banned, as were currency rate-linked futures.[96]

For many liberal economists, however, the key to combating speculative activities was not to restrict the growth of the various markets but an end to government interference. As economist Dai Yuanchen, who was also a CPPCC member, put it: "Speculation on the stock market is based upon speculation upon government policy . . . *Gumin* enter or leave the market in accordance with their projections about the next government move." He argued that if Beijing was committed to a hands-off policy, the effect of government policy on the behaviour of *gumin* would be minimised, and "the stock market would start to discipline itself".[97]

G. Economic Policy after Deng Xiaoping

A powerful source of pressure being brought to bear on the post-Deng administration will be the international market. Global bodies such as General Agreement on Tariffs and Trade (the World Trade Organisation after 1995) and the World Bank will reward China for adopting real market reforms. Major trading partners, particularly the US, will take reprisals against Beijing if it continues to hang on to Stalinist planning.

An equally potent factor will be the Chinese partners of the droves of foreign corporations setting up shop in the country. Because of their own interests, these Chinese partners — including many of the who's who in the Chinese political and business world — will lobby the government to adopt Western or international norms. Moreover, a number of foreign companies had by mid-1994 hired full-time lobbyists, who included the offspring of senior cadres, to force China to open the door wider.[98]

Moreover, the attractiveness of the "socialist market economy" may be ephemeral. Within a few years, it enabled senior officials and their offspring to make a fast buck. At least superficially, it also allowed the CCP to maintain its monopoly on power. Yet in the longer run, this contraption may prove detrimental to the interests of all. The trouble with "boosting macro-level adjustments and controls" is that it does not make for a fair and open environment for doing business. Who is to make the decisions on what to adjust and control? Political and personal elements invariably come into the picture. As we saw, the emphasis on agriculture and on "reinvigorating the state sector" reflected ideological as much as economic considerations.

Beijing's credit policy remained susceptible to the influence of politics — and corruption. Very often, beneficiaries of the "selective loosening of the austerity policy" happened to be politically well-connected sectors or companies. There was widespread innuendo about businesses run by the members and hangers-on of the Deng clan getting cheap and abundant loans.[99] By the early 1990s, Japan, whose patriarchal approach to the market place was much admired by Zhu, was bursting at the seams with scandals. And the leadership would be very naive if it lost sight of the fact that the Singapore version of the "East-Asiatic market economy" worked partly because the Island Republic had a very efficient — and independent — anti-corruption operation.

For all its shortcomings, the free-market economy provides a relatively level playing field for everybody. Very slowly, China may gravitate towards such a system. International investors are demanding this. Private entrepreneurs and the growing "civil society" (see following section) are clamouring for it. And a few years after Deng's death, even the members of the privileged classes, including *gaoganzidi* who set up the country's first "red business empires", may realise that it is in their best interests to shed the all-too visible — and clumsy — hand of the state.

V. The Centre vs the Regions: Will the Country Split Up?

Relations between Beijing and the regions are set to worsen through the 1990s. There is, on the one hand, the tug-of-war between the *zhongyang* ("the centre") and the localities. On the other hand, the relationship between "First

World China", meaning the southeast coast, and "Third World China", meaning the central and western parts of the nation, could also become more
strained. In general, Beijing's policy continues to be to squeeze the coastal
provinces and cities such as Guangdong to claw back lost power and revenues.
To redress the regional imbalance and to "divide and rule" the provinces, the
zhongyang is expected to boost its preferential treatment of the heartland and
western areas.

As we saw earlier, even Deng Xiaoping, the erstwhile patron saint of
regional autonomy, began cracking hard on centrifugalism in 1993. In an
internal meeting in early 1994, Zhu Rongji stated the problem very baldly.
"Some regional leadership bodies refuse to toe the central line," he complained. "They cast doubt on the correctness of the central policy or whether it suited local conditions. This has set off a chain reaction in some places."[100]

The problem of regional imbalance was addressed with clarity by Li Peng
during the landmark conference on Tibet in the summer of 1994, which
pledged unprecedented amounts of aid to the autonomous region. "We must
recognise the disparity [between rich and poor areas] and encourage areas
with the necessary conditions to develop faster," Li said. "We must also adopt
effective measures to help areas that have fallen behind to speed up development in order to expedite [the goal of] common prosperity."[101] *Fupin* ("help
the poor areas") became a major political slogan that echoed the Maoist ideal
of "common prosperity".

A. Squeezing the Coast to Benefit the Hinterland

(i) Killing Two Birds with One Stone

In a sense, the goals of arresting centrifugal forces and narrowing regional
disparity could be attained simultaneously: hitting out at the *nouveaux riches*
provinces and areas. In the spring of 1994, the Politburo Standing Committee
issued an eight-point circular to clip the wings of the "warlords". They were:

to take agriculture as the key link; stop using arable land for real-estate purposes or for building industrial parks; depress inflation and promote social
stability; limit fixed-assets investments and avoid collecting funds outside the
official banking system; stop using government funds to speculate in the real
estate, stocks and futures markets; stop issuing stocks and bonds or opening
financial exchanges; stop selling assets of state enterprises; to secure central
government permission for the transaction of the property rights of state
enterprises.[102]

Needless to say, the coast, particularly Guangdong, was guilty of neglecting agriculture and overheating the economy with "speculative" activities in

the real estate, stock and futures markets. Throughout 1994, Vice-Premier Zhu continued to hit hard at "overheated" activities. He was quoted more than once as saying that the slump that had hit the Shenzhen and Shanghai markets in the year was "just what we wanted". Particularly explosive was Beijing's insistence on toning down the sale of state assets, a speciality of administrations in both eastern, central and western China.

Provinces and cities including Sichuan, Guangdong and Wuhan were keen advocates of quasi-privatisation through the sale of property rights to foreign concerns. In June 1994, at the height of the crackdown on the sale of state assets, Wuhan's Economics Commission Chief Duan Lunyi said his city encouraged foreign enterprises to make a "clean buy-out" of state enterprises, one third of which were losing money. Duan indicated that this would not only pull in investment but help local governments get rid of chronic loss-making factories.[103]

Beijing also announced that during the Eighth Five-Year Plan (1991-95) and "a period of time afterwards", central and western areas would receive preferential treatment in the allocation of funds and resources. This included central investments in infrastructure projects; the opening up of resources; and investment policies. The bulk of the development loans that Beijing acquired from Western countries and Japan would be spent on the poorer provinces. It was estimated that at least 75 per cent of the yen loans Tokyo granted China in the late 1990s would go to central and western areas.[104]

These preferential policies clearly ran foul of market economics. In a reversal of the philosophy behind the special economic zones, Beijing said it would give "special treatment" to Western or overseas Chinese firms that invested in the heartland and peripheral areas. Spokesman for the Ministry of Foreign Trade and Economic Co-operation, Miao Fuchun, said in July 1994 that foreign investors in the central and western areas would enjoy preferential terms in the areas of "macro-level balance", transport facilities, raw materials and credit. "These concessions will be more than those [available] on the southeast coast," he said.[105]

"Transfer payments" to the impoverished regions were also increased. State Councillor Chen Junsheng indicated that the 80 million Chinese still below the poverty line would be able to achieve the level of "small-scale prosperity" by the year 2000. The *People's Daily* disclosed in August 1994 that in "recent years" Beijing had allocated nearly 10 billion yuan of aid to central and western areas. A total of 86 per cent of the 592 counties classified as "in major need of central help" were in the same parts of the country. From 1994 to 2000, investments and credit totalling 10 billion yuan would be made available annually to village and township enterprises in Third-World China.[106]

(ii) The Case of Guangdong: Deepening of the Contradiction

While Beijing was in theory asking all well-off areas in the eastern and south-
ern areas to make *fupin* sacrifices, the burden was not spread evenly: the
Yangtze Delta zone headed by Shanghai was doing better than the Zhujiang
Delta zone led by Guangzhou. Friction between Beijing and Guangdong,
China's most dynamic region, is expected to worsen in the coming decade.

In a high-profile tour of Guangdong in June 1994, Jiang Zemin tried to
pacify the disgruntled cadres of the southern province. He said that the relationship among the Yangtze Delta, the Zhujiang Delta and the Bohai Bay area
(centred on Tianjin and Dalian) should be characterised by mutual co-operation, symbiosis and synergy. "It is not as though one would substitute the
other; or that one should shut the other out," he said.[107]

In reality, Guangdong had been overtaken by Shanghai as Beijing's designated "dragon head" for the open-door policy (see Chapter 2). Many observers noted that during the 1994 NPC, the Guangdong delegation was
among the few that had not been visited by a member of the Politburo
Standing Committee. More to the point was the availability of credit and central investment. In 1990, Guangdong enterprises were able to secure loans of
30 million yuan for every 100 million yuan of increase in industrial production. The comparable figure was down to 13 million yuan in 1993, and a little over 7 million yuan in the first half of 1994. In the first six months of 1994,
loans to Guangdong firms for use as working capital were 1.6 billion yuan
lower than in the same period the year before.[108]

Shenzhen in particular had borne the brunt of the "squeeze Guangdong"
policy. The special economic zone's GDP growth rate in the first half of 1994
was the lowest among cities in Guangdong. "The sparrows have been chased
away but the phoenixes have not been enticed," was the complaint of local
cadres. Already burdened by high labour and land costs, Shenzhen risked losing everything since its "special" investment climate had already been dupli-
cated in scores of other open cities.[109]

On his trip to Guangdong, Jiang dispensed the proverbial "steady the heart
pills" to Shenzhen and Zhuhai. "Shenzhen's specialness must be further developed," Jiang said. "The special economic zone must continue to be special."
The party chief admonished local cadres to develop the SEZ's role as a "window", "laboratory", and "pace-setter". According to local cadres, however,
Shenzhen was looking to "integration" with Hong Kong after 1997 rather than
favours from Beijing as the wherewithal for a new lease of life. Jiang, however, warned Shenzhen against too intimate a relationship with Hong Kong.
"Shenzhen is a socialist SEZ. It cannot at any time become an extension or
continuation of Hong Kong," the party chief said.[110]

B. The Worsening Struggle over the Purse-strings

During its first year at least, the vaunted dual-tax system (which was introduced on January 1, 1994, see Chapter 2) did not achieve the goal of significantly raising Beijing's share of national revenue. Central revenue in the first six months of 1994 grew by 11.5 per cent against the same period in 1993. However, the comparable figure for the regions was 39 per cent. The only obvious gain for Beijing was that there were sizeable increases in the value-added tax and in the profits taxes, 35.7 per cent and 45.7 per cent respectively over 1993. Finance Minister Liu Zhongli said this showed that Beijing was successful in preventing business units and regional governments from evading taxes or illegally remitting the levies.[111]

Chinese economists said it was quite certain that Beijing could not achieve the goal of a 60 per cent share of national income by the end of 1996. While announcing the above figures in August, Liu castigated unnamed local officials for using "transitional, stop-gap measures" in handling tax matters, in the process failing to surrender to Beijing funds mandated by law.[112]

By mid-1994, various levels of government, including all provinces and major cities save Tibet, had set up their own tax administrations. This was to facilitate the implementation of the dual tax system. However, the problem of localities cutting taxes unilaterally to attract investments was expected to continue through the rest of the decade. In early 1994, Beijing and Guangdong had an ugly fight over the proposed capital gains tax for property. While Guangzhou seemed to have backed off somewhat, it was clear that provincial officials were in cahoots with local and foreign developers in exploiting the many loopholes that the new tax would afford.[113]

In late 1993, a central official was quoted by Hong Kong's *Wen Wei Po* as saying that as a result of illegal tax remissions, the actual tax that a foreign company had to pay was less than half the usual 20-odd per cent. Deputy Tax Chief Xiang Huizheng complained in late 1994 that in some localities, listed companies were paying 15 per cent instead of 33 per cent. And some village and township enterprises were able to enjoy the low rates accorded enterprises belonging to welfare institutions.[114]

The year 1994 marked the beginning of the central government routinely asking localities to contribute to projects that had formerly been bankrolled totally by Beijing. In July, Beijing unveiled an unprecedented aid package to Tibet. This consisted of 62 major infrastructural projects in the areas of energy, transport, telecommunications, and farming. The total bill of 2.38 billion yuan would be split three to one between Beijing and the localities. The NCNA said that all well-off provinces and cities, including the six cities with "independent budgets", would have to join in the altruistic effort.[115]

Another big-ticket item was helping the more than 1 million people in Sichuan and Hubei provinces who would be displaced by the Three Gorges hydroelectric project. By August, 12 provinces and cities had made contributions of 6.82 million yuan. It is significant that Guangdong entities made up three of the 12 donors: the provincial government and the cities of Guangzhou and Shenzhen. The semi-official China News Agency quoted relevant authorities as saying that aid to the displaced inhabitants was made "under the conditions of the market economy and the principle of mutual benefit."[116] The big question was: what did the 12 areas get back in return?

Moreover, Beijing's demands seemed insatiable. Local contributions were mandated for national sports games and arts festivals; celebrations of the October 1 National Day; and for special galas and commemorative activities. For cities like Shanghai and Shenzhen, the forced contribution that was hardest to stomach was perhaps the pay-off to provinces such as Sichuan in return for stopping the exodus of *mingong*, or superfluous rural labourers. With *mingong* tipped to swell to 200 million by the end of the century, the bill, which many thought should fall in Beijing's laps, could be staggering.[117]

C. Near-Open Rebellion by the Regions

At a conference on regional economic disparity held by governors and mayors in Beijing in May 1994, Guangdong turned down requests by the State Council that it funnel more financial aid to western and heartland areas. "Guangdong cadres expressed reluctance to bail out the poor regions, citing the fact that they had been badly hurt by the on-going tight-money policy," said a conference source. "The cadres insisted that their priority was helping impoverished counties in northern Guangdong, whose inhabitants still have problems with food and clothing."[118]

The leaders of Jiangsu and Shanghai tried to get around the problem by promising a dubious kind of aid. Instead of cash, the cadres pledged to relocate plants and technicians to the central and western areas. This was, of course, a qualified act of altruism. What would be transplanted to the heartland were low-technology and labour-intensive — and in many instances, loss-making — industries such as textiles.

Local leaders also took exception to the increasing frequency with which Beijing asked them to make "extra-legal" or "emergency" contributions to the central treasury. These were in addition to the regular tax and levies. The practice started in the mid-1980s, when the central government's budget deficits began to increase dramatically. Up to the late 1980s, Deng Xiaoping made personal appeals to local leaders for these special contributions. The reluctant donors included Shanghai, Jiangsu and Guangdong.

Guangzhou began to say no to these demands in 1994. In July of that year, Zhu Rongji was rebuffed in his attempt to persuade Guangzhou to make an extra contribution of 16 billion to 18 billion yuan to central funds. Guangdong cadres said Guangzhou had been making such "emergency donations" since the early 1990s. They were estimated at 5 billion yuan in 1992 and between 14 billion to 16 billion yuan in 1993. This time, Zhu was bluntly told that Guangzhou was in no mood to oblige. The province had been badly hurt by the austerity programme. Moreover, in view of the serious flooding that summer, Guangzhou needed extra cash to rebuild dams and highways. Local cadres said that while Hunan and Guangxi had received funds for flood relief, Guangdong got nothing.[119]

Regional defiance was on the rise. A ferocious give-and-take took place prior to Beijing's announcement of the Tibet aid package. Informed sources said the central government had originally stipulated that all the 62 infrastructural projects be bankrolled by the localities.[120] The concessions that Beijing had to make in this and other instances were unheard of in the days of Chairman Mao.

D. Zhongyang-*Regional Relations in the late 1990s and Beyond*

"The sword is out of its blade; the bow is fully strung." This Chinese saying aptly describes how open warfare is about to break out between Beijing and the regions. Most analysts do not anticipate the break-up of the Chinese "empire" soon. Beijing still holds certain trump cards, including the ability to fire recalcitrant "warlords". Moreover, the central government is not above using highly questionable means such as arbitrarily taking money from accounts that provinces maintain with the central banking system.[121]

Chinese intellectuals do not see any possibility of a political fragmentation of the nation in the coming decade or two. After all, unlike the former Soviet Union, the sense of nationhood in China — or "Chinese identity" — is still relatively strong. So-called "splittist" activities in Tibet, Xinjiang and Inner Mongolia seem to be under the control of the army and the police-state apparatus. However, schisms along economic lines are clearly visible — and are poised to grow through the 1990s. Aside from the now-familiar situation of the coastal provinces ganging up on Beijing, there is an additional phenomenon of blocs of provinces and cities doing battle with each other. For example, in a frank interview with the Guangzhou-based *Chinese Business Times* in September 1994, former Guangdong governor Liang Ningguang anticipated a ferocious struggle between a northerners-dominated Beijing-Tianjin-Shanghai axis and a southern Guangdong-Hong Kong axis.

After the death of Deng Xiaoping — perhaps the last figure who could command the respect of all regional chieftains — the depletion of central authority will accelerate. Jiang, Zhu, or other senior cadres after Deng will have to secure the support of the regional cadres to stay in power. Both 1993 and 1994 witnessed numerous occasions when leaders from various factions played the regional card. Heavyweights in the liberal camp such as Qiao Shi backed efforts by local cadres to have a say in their own development speed and in boosting their legislative powers (see Chapter 5 and 6).

Even the head of the Mainstream Faction, Jiang Zemin, had a knack for being conciliatory towards the warlords. It was during his trip to Guangdong in September 1993 that the first hints about the end of the austerity pro-gramme were given. Jiang repeated Deng's dictum that "it will not do for the speed of development to be too slow". Equally important, the party chief coined this new slogan: "Localities must obey the national situation; the entire country must take care of the localities." And when he revisited Guangdong in the summer of 1994, he told cadres in the city of Meizhou to proceed full steam ahead. "I have always advocated that areas that have the prerequisites should speed up [their development]," he said. "Areas that do not yet have the conditions should create those conditions."[122]

For the longer term, many believe that only way out of the problem of regionalism is a federal system. Since leaving China after the June 4 mas-sacre, ex-Zhao Ziyang adviser and prominent political scientist Yan Jiaqi has written profusely about a federal system that will comprise the mainland, Taiwan, Hong Kong, Tibet and Xinjiang. Surprisingly, however, the issue of federalism has also been studied, on an internal basis, by academics in official think-tanks in Beijing.[123]

The mandate of the think-tanks, which also studied the consequences of the break-up of Yugoslavia and the Soviet empire, was how to prevent China from having to adopt a federal-like system. Times, however, are changing fast. One of the first tasks of whoever takes over from Deng will be to work out a new deal for the regions. And this has to go beyond token gestures such as giving more Central Committee seats to provincial and municipal leaders.

VI. The Private Entrepreneurs and the Civil Society

A. The Contours of a Civil Society

By late 1994, social scientists in China and abroad were pinning their hopes for the transformation of the country on an inchoate civil society. By the time of the *nanxun*, China had ceased to be a monolithic society. The CCP's appar-ent confidence in maintaining a monopoly on power did not mean that power and influence were not being ceded to sectors outside Beijing's control.

Challenging Beijing's concept of the "dictatorship of the proletariat" were voices calling for the retreat of the party-state. Quite a few radical economists paraphrased Marx thus: "Render to society whatever belongs to society." Demands for a greater non-state-controlled sphere coincided with the urge for a market economy where the Visible Hand of the state took a back seat.

As American sinologist Dali Yang contended in a paper on the emergent civil society: "The expansion of market relations has . . . enlarged the scope for the expression of individual and group interests in areas that may diverge from those sanctioned by the political establishment."[124] Or as social scientist Gordon White put it in early 1994: "A gradual shift in the balance of power between state and society has been under way, which has provided greater opportunities for social forces to exert influence over party-state institutions, has opened up greater space for new socio-economic institutions and interests and led to increasingly open discontent and friction between the party-state and society."[125]

The most assertive component of the civil society is the fast-growing class of private or quasi-private entrepreneurs, businessmen, and professionals — as well as the attendant middle class (see Chapter 6). Their political clout is poised to expand throughout the decade. Other constituents of the civil society include the underground churches and a quasi-independent intelligentsia.

Most important of all, however, is the fact that ordinary Chinese citizens have begun to see the need to cut the umbilical cord with the authoritarian state. They want to realise their economic and personal ambitions — and very often, independence — by seizing their fate. Even the *People's Daily* got the message. A commentary in June 1994 warned: "Since the 1980s, a new class has been formed that is outside the direct control of the government work units, the beginning of a civil society."[126]

B. The Inexorable Rise of the Private Entrepreneurs

In spite of gallant attempts by Zhu Rongji and Co to resuscitate the state sector, the loss of its "dominant" position in the economy had become imminent. By the mid-1990s, the non-state sector — including village and township enterprises (VTEs), which were an amalgamation of public and private capital run along the lines of private enterprises — pretty much split the sky with state enterprises in industry. In coastal Zhejiang, VTEs accounted for 70.9 per cent of total industrial output value.[127]

The momentum was going the way of the non-state sector. In the first half of 1994, industrial production of state-owned industrial enterprises grew by 4.4 per cent, against 20.3 per cent for VTEs and 28.9 per cent for private enterprises and those with foreign participation. In early 1994, the number of workers employed by non-state units — 120 million — matched that of the state sector for the first time. Of these, 112 million worked in the 20 million-odd VTEs and 1 million in the 40,000-odd private concerns.[128]

By mid-1994, there were unmistakable signs of private-sector practitioners going up the political ladder — sometimes through the back door. A small essay in the mouthpiece of the Central Party School, *Party School Forum*, encapsulated the phenomenon. It reported that *nouveaux riches* bosses were buying positions at local level. The journal said a number of cadres with powers over appointments had succumbed to three types of pressure when nominating or endorsing positions such as head of a county and village government or local parliamentary leaders: pressure from senior cadres; *guanxi* or connections; and money. *Forum* blamed unnamed parties for using "loads of cash" to bribe cadres for cushy posts.[129]

"Five thousand yuan for a title; 10,000 yuan to show off your prominence; 20,000 yuan for a mandarin's cap," the journal quoted a popular aphorism. Most of the fat cats were millionaire private entrepreneurs who, according to numerous internal reports, had "infiltrated" thousands of lower-level party administrations. The problem raised by *Forum* was an indication that, bent on maintaining its monopoly on power, the CCP leadership had refused to propagate a "new class" of independent-minded entrepreneur-politicians through legal and institutional channels.

It was a tribute to the clout of would-be businessman-politicians that CCP strategists had tried to co-opt, neutralise, and then tame them by welcoming them into quasi-official bodies. Since 1993, Beijing had presided over the large-scale expansion of the All-China Federation of Industry and Commerce (ACFIC). Late that year, a large chunk of the ACFIC became the China Non-Governmental Chamber of Commerce (CNGCC) (see Chapter 6).

Sources close to the chamber said the CCP hoped that the CNGCC could absorb the bulk of the quasi-private trade associations that had sprung up in most cities. By early 1994, there were more than 50 each of such "businessmen's clubs" in Shanghai and Guangzhou. Those in Shanghai were known for their solid networking and those in Guangzhou for their wealth. The authorities were afraid that some of these entities might pursue heretical economic and political goals.[130]

Both before and after the elections of a new CNGCC leadership in late 1993, the CCP leadership installed party heavyweights in senior positions. A few of these, including Hu Deping, came from the United Front Department. The elevation of Hu, a son of the late party chief Hu Yaobang, to a CNGCC vice-chairmanship was significant given his popularity and liberal reputation. In addition, a number of "politically reliable" private entrepreneurs, such as the "Poultry Feed King of the Southwest", billionaire Liu Yonghao, were given vice-chairmanships.

It is doubtful whether members of the nation's richest and most dynamic class will be content with party patronage. With the re-emphasis in 1994 on "the primacy of state ownership", economic policies still lopsidedly favoured fully-owned government companies. Apart from outright vote-buying, methods used by the bosses to gain political influence included donations to charity and government projects; employment of senior cadres as board members or consultants of companies; and "collusion" with Hong Kong and foreign businessmen to press for favourable legislation and policies.

The clout of the private sector was most pronounced in the coastal belts, where capitalist-roader cadres and millionaires had struck up a "lips-and-teeth relationship". Their common enemy was the central leadership, which was committed to safeguarding the privileged position of state enterprises and central planners. The tug-of-war between Beijing and the coastal administrations on the controversial capital gains tax on real estate was but one illustration of these dynamics. Guangzhou cadres, backed by business interests that included the "red bosses" and Hong Kong tycoons, aggressively lobbied Beijing for a lower tax rate.

Many township and village governments gave at least qualified support to state and private firms engaging in questionable practices such as "underground banking". Apart from a minority of entrepreneurs who were former dissidents — they were closely watched by state security — red capitalists had openly forsworn political ambitions. However, they sought the wherewithal to influence policy-making on how resources, and the economic pie in general, would be divided.[131]

C. Intellectual Groupings and the Effect of Telecommunications

An important sub-theme of the "1989 turmoil" was the intelligentsia's crusade for independence: the educated class must cease to be an adjunct of the party apparatus. By late 1994, many urban intellectuals had claimed membership of the civil society. As is the case even in Western countries, these intellectuals became associated with particular business and interest groups.

Instead of being the mouthpieces of certain party factions, many influential economists and social scientists had become spokesmen of and lobbyists for certain economic theories, social trends or business groupings. This was best illustrated by the controversy over the growth rate and inflation that hit theoretical and political circles in 1993 and 1994. Zhu Rongji's tight money policy had dealt a severe blow to businessmen. Some observers believed that state and private businesses had urged "friendly economists" — including paid consultants among them — to press for an end to the austerity programme.

Liberal economists who insisted that the nation should pay the price of inflation for fast growth and reform were attacked by Zhu Rongji's aides. In an article in *Economic News,* conservative economist Zuo Dapei accused un-named economists of "representing the interests of business groupings" when they advocated a high-growth model. Another economist Yang Fan seemed to agree. "The essence of inflation is the transfer of interests," he said. "The losers in hyperinflation are citizens. The beneficiaries are enterprises."[132]

There was a larger number of social scientists who claimed to speak for neither the party nor big business. They vowed to promote social change through organising a series of non-official journals and academic functions. One group was centred upon the *Chinese Social Sciences Quarterly*, a Hong Kong-based journal that had a large readership in China. The *Quarterly* was edited by an elite corps of mainland scholars who wanted to bring about evo-lutionary changes by fostering a "non-official academic tradition". "We believe in people-based academic research as distinguished from one that is officially sponsored," said Chief Editor Deng Zhenglai, one of China's first private publishers. "Academic activities should not be tied to any ideology, policy or slogan." The 39-member editorial board represented top researchers such as economists Lin Yifu, Fan Gang and Bai Nansheng.[133]

The maturity of a civil society was hastened by the arrival of the age of the mass media and telecommunications. In spite of a strict censorship, including the annual closure of scores of publications in the early 1990s, the media con-tinued to thrive. In early 1994, there were more than 2,000 newspapers, 7,500 periodicals, and 540 publishing presses. Some 2,500 poetry societies were registered with the Ministry of Culture. About 50,000 poems appeared in print each year in dozens of official literary journals and countless unofficial mimeographed pamphlets.[134]

More importantly, an information revolution was finally sweeping the nation as Chinese became denizens of the global village. By early 1994, there were 21 million households with telephones. Projections were for a five-fold increase by the year 2000. The increase in IDD was equally astounding. The Ministry of Post and Telecommunications said it would use US$5 billion of foreign capital to modernise this area in the second half of the decade.[135]

Deemed most politically sensitive was the popularity of fax machines, mobile phones and modems. The number of cellular phones had more than doubled every year in the mid-1990s. In 1994 alone, there were 1.2 million new owners. In Guangzhou, a mobile phone cost 20,000 yuan, which was within the reach of *getihu* or middle-class families. By early 1994, computer users in the large cities were in a position to hook up to the Internet. What was holding them back was economic factors such as stiff IDD charges.[136]

The political fallout of the leaps-and-bounds growth of a non-state-controlled culture was obvious. First Guangdong and then practically the rest of the country were hooked on Hong Kong television and pop culture. A survey in late 1993 found that Hong Kong Governor Chris Patten, once called a "sinner of a thousand antiquities", was more popular among Guangdong residents than Governor Zhu Senlin. The empire struck back in late 1993 with a ban on the private satellite dishes. The Propaganda Department also mounted a campaign against "vulgar" Hong Kong and Taiwan pop artists. Sino-Hong Kong or Sino-foreign joint ventures in the area of television and publishing were stopped. Surveillance of the IDD and fax lines of dissidents was beefed up. The world, however, was getting smaller. Only a fool would believe that it was possible to hold back the floodgates for long.[137]

D. People Power with Chinese Characteristics

(i) The Basis of People Power

In China, a common synonym for the people is "the hundred surnames". This phrase denotes diversity and splendour. After 45 years of Mao's one-voice chamber, the chances for the revival of people power with Chinese characteristics were reasonably high.

By early 1994, the assets of Chinese citizens had exceeded 2 trillion yuan. They had bank savings of 1.4 trillion yuan, in addition to 500 billion yuan of cash, 400 billion yuan of stocks and bonds, and more than US$10 billion of foreign currency. According to social scientist Li Lianjin, material abundance could predispose the individual towards taking a more active part in social, if not political, events. "The growth of the economic freedom of citizens and the increase in the assets of individuals have expanded the parameters of the social activities of the individual," he said. "This has provided the material basis for the individual to develop his self-worth to the full."[138]

Wang Hui, Vice-President of the China Sociological Society, said that as a direct result of economic change, "the market has become the main source for people to get their raw materials and material for living". "The chances for self-development [for the individual] and the room for materialising his self-worth have expanded," he added. Professor Wang said that with wealth, the lifestyle of people became "individualistic and multifarious".[139]

Somewhat like private entrepreneurs, citizens would want to have constitutional and legal protection of their property. They might also demand equality before the law. As late as the mid- to late-1980s, the *nouveaux riches* merely indulged in conspicuous consumption. Otherwise, they deposited money abroad or sent their kids overseas as a hedge against political uncertainty. The next fad might be some form of social — and later political — participation.[140]

In 1993 and 1994, "social activism" manifested itself in individuals taking government departments and state enterprises to court. In July 1994, a Beijing court awarded Li Qiang, a college lecturer, 3,440 yuan in damages. Li had been detained illegally by the Guizhou police. A month later, a young man lodged an appeal to overrule a 960 yuan fine that had been slapped on him by a military registration committee for failing to register for army service. At about the same time, a group of Chinese farmers were given compensation of 700,000 yuan by a factory found guilty of polluting their crops. While these cases might seem trivial, they were unmistakable signals of a people slowly awakening to their heaven-given rights.[141]

(ii) *Gumin* Power in Action

Gumin ("stocks-crazed citizens") of China, unite! Primitive as the tools of their trade might be, the country's first generation of stock speculators — estimated at a few tens of millions in 1994 — were a major constituent of the civil society. After all, *gumin* were making decisions and planning their future solely in accordance with the rules of the market. For the first time since 1949, ideology and propaganda had fallen by the wayside, and the bourse-driven brethren had gained a measure of independence — and liberation from the socialist straitjacket.

While few *gumin* had articulated their economic and political demands, it was not difficult to divine what they might be. First of all, the party must scrap its long-standing practice of monopolising resources and put into place regulations and laws in line with Western norms. *Gumin* had complained about the large number of officials who had made giant killings based on *guanxi* and inside information. The notorious Shenzhen riots of August 1992 were triggered by *gumin* anger at local cadres jumping the queue in acquiring lottery certificates for choice stocks. Then there was the spate of national protests in the summer of 1994 lodged by speculators who had invested billions of yuan in scores of "underground" futures trading companies. Some had collapsed because of big losses and others had been closed down by the government.[142]

Whether the CCP liked it or not, it would soon be obliged to enact legislation to ban insider trading, and to promote some form of separation of party and government from business. Many illegal or rowdy stocks and futures trading companies had excellent connections with the ministries. Should this come to pass, the *gumin* would have succeeded where the pro-democracy demonstrators had failed: to force the CCP to truncate its own power.

Economic liberation might spawn a demand for civil rights and other political liberties. Both millionaires and paupers among the *gumin* realised that suddenly, they had achieved a modicum of individuality, equality, and freedom. Stock traders were proud individuals who had seized control over their own destiny. After they had succeeded in ensuring their right to "equal opportunity" at the bourse, the *gumin* might demand freedoms of speech and publication. Already private "financial newspapers" had sprung up in Shanghai and Guangzhou despite periodic efforts by authorities to close them down.

The stock market might become an institution for checking and balancing the powers of the CCP. Political actions that could cause major upheavals at the bourse were now out of the question. In mid-1989, hundreds of fasting students did not deter the CCP from taking the military option. Thanks to the stocks craze, such barbaric measures seemed to be ruled out. The reason: a repeat of Tiananmen Square — or simply the declaration of martial law in a major city — would precipitate a market collapse. *Gumin* — senior cadres among them — would see their riches wiped out in hours. Millions would take to the streets and riot.

The *gumin* were so obsessed with the prospects of their own investment that they would put pressure on Beijing to churn out the kind of news that would bring out the bull. Such a psychology was bad news for conservatives or neo-conservatives such as Li Peng and Zhu Rongji. The *gumin* knew they could somehow hold the CCP hostage by driving up the stock prices — or deserting the bourses *en masse*.[143]

VII. Conclusion

A. The End of the Old Road

(i) The Near-Bankruptcy of Deng's Dynastic Politics

By late 1994, it was obvious that the Deng solution to succession was in deep trouble. One of the last recorded instructions from the Chief Architect of Reform was hardly reformist or progressive: it was to use brute force to maintain the Communist-Chinese dynasty. In a secret talk to about 20 senior generals early in the year, Deng spelled out a multi-pronged strategy for guaranteeing a trouble-free succession: "Rally round comrade Jiang Zemin as the core of the new leadership. Uphold stability at all costs. Provide help to the party and the government in maintaining social order. Bolster central authority and check the growth of regionalism."[144]

About half a year later, however, Deng — now very much in the mode of

Mao in his final days — expressed doubts about his own formula. In what was an oblique criticism of Jiang, Deng cast doubt on the president's ability to maintain a factional balance. He hinted that Jiang had been too preoccupied with empire-building.

"Leadership in the new era must reflect the five lakes and the four seas," members of the Deng household quoted the patriarch as saying. "There are too many members of the Shanghai faction holding top party and army positions." There can be little doubt that this critique was aimed at Jiang, the putative head of the Shanghai clique. The patriarch also said he "had not been consulted enough" during the marathon reshuffles of the PLA leadership in the past year. He also cited the unexpected promotion in early 1993 of the head of the Shanghai garrison, Ba Zhongtan, to commander of the 800,000-strong People's Armed Police. The elevation of Ba was, of course, crucial to Jiang's bid for power.[145]

One recalls, of course, that Deng also cited the principle of the "five lakes and and four seas" when he dumped the "empire-building" Yang brothers in late 1992. Yet by late 1994, it was doubtful whether Deng could consummate what would almost certainly be his last purge. His health was rapidly failing. And in spite of his faults, Jiang was still seen as the best bet to maintain stability.

Should this come to pass, Jiang would only be a temporary beneficiary — and the Chinese nation a victim of a much longer duration. With his credibility dented, it was unlikely that Jiang could hang on for long after the departure of his reluctant patron. With the New Helmsman gone, however, the would-be Helmsman would not easily yield power. The internecine bickering that would ensue would be unnecessarily brutal.

(ii) Reforms No Longer Keeping Pace with the Contradictions

Leaders including Deng Xiaoping liked to harp on how an authoritarian regime was necessary to feed 1.18 billion mouths. However, the same argument could be used for a much speedier pace of political change. The reason is obvious. The CCP's old methods were no longer sufficient to defuse the mounting pressure put to bear upon the government.

Of particular relevance for political unrest was the rural "army of the jobless", estimated to exceed 200 million by the end of the century. Another late 1994 estimate said that "superfluous rural labour" had already reached 200 million. The "floating" or underground population in the cities — mostly migrant workers from the countryside — neared 60 million.[146]

Migrant population was one of the subjects of the hottest book in China in 1994, *Looking at China with a Third Eye*. Its description of the rural problem won the praise of Jiang Zemin. *Third Eye's* thesis was simple. The 800 million-odd peasants were China's "active volcano": "Without an exception, China's dynasties were wrecked by uprooted, migrant workers."[147]

Mao's solution, the book said, was to chain the peasants to the soil through institutions such as the people's commune and round-the-clock indoctrination by ideological workers. The system worked for 30 years. Deng, however, tried to "liberate the production forces" by dismantling the commune and popularising the individualistic "household contract responsibility system". Arguing that "we should allow a part of the population to get rich first", the New Helmsman gave *carte blanche* to peasants to go into industry and commerce.

For the pseudonymous author of the book, the "get rich first" ideal "spelled the beginning of the collapse of the Great Wall [of socialism] . . . The genie is out of the bottle." The genie was none other than every farmer's "lust for development" and "search for money and opportunity", his desire to hold his fate in his own hands. The book criticised Deng's neglect of party construction, so that "the authority of grassroots party cells has been curtailed".

Third Eye conjured up a "social cataclysm" with millions of lawless, anarchic peasants swarming the cities. "Once farmers have left the fields, all their actions become uncontrolled," it said. "Their relationship with society is in a state of total haphazardness." As a remedy, the author recommended that "the army be expanded to handle social warfare". He suggested a return to Mao's old method of "locking up the peasants": "Let the [Maoist] work brigades once again take over the village administration."

As we saw earlier, Beijing tried to tackle the problems by raising the standard of living of farmers. After the spate of rural riots in early 1993, Beijing abolished or slashed 50-odd taxes and other levies. The authorities claimed this helped the peasants to save 10.3 billion yuan. Beijing also raised the procurement prices for some kinds of produce by up to 30 per cent in mid-1994.[148]

However, the genie could no longer be bottled. Limping towards the end of its heavenly mandate, the CCP lacked the fiscal muscle and moral authority to persuade farmers to go on tilling the fields. However, it was clear that Beijing was also not in a position to embrace the "totalitarian temptation" offered by *Third Eye*.

B. The Beginning of a New Road

Less than three months before the June 4 fiasco, then member of the Politburo Standing Committee, Hu Qili, expressed confidence in the ability of the nation to weather the crisis that might come from the "complicated problems" engendered by reform. "Have trust in the broad masses of the people," Hu said during the 1989 NPC. "Our people, our intellectuals are very, very good. This concept cannot be shaken." The former head of the Communist Youth League further cautioned: "Contradictions" in the course of reform must be solved "through scientific, democratic decision-making." "They cannot be solved through a certain leader uttering one or two words," he said, apparently referring to Deng's one-voice chamber.[149]

After Deng's death, the Chinese people might be given a new opportunity to live up to the expectations of Hu Qili. As discussed earlier, it is by no means certain that there would be a replay of the street demonstrations of 1989. Or that, unlike last time, the post-Deng "revolution" would succeed and bring about a democratisation of the system. But the agitation for change will be faster with the death of perhaps China's very last patriarch. (After Deng's death, the only Helmsman figure in the ethnic Chinese world would be Lee Kuan Yew of Singapore).

A comparison with Taiwanese politics is in order. After the death of Chiang Ching-kuo, the last authoritarian figure in Taiwanese politics, the floodgates for change were thrown open. Taiwan's achievement in democratisation, though flawed in many areas, had planted hope in a large number of June 4 dissidents. After touring Taiwan in late 1992, rebel writer Wang Ruowang was moved to point out that one solution for the mainland was "to learn politics from Taiwan, economics from Hong Kong".[150]

The agents of change — a gradual evolution in the eyes of this author — were already in place in the mid-1990s. These changes would be facilitated if the post-Deng CCP were to take the initiative and evolve towards a post-1990 East European-style socialist party, one that permitted real elections and other elements of pluralistic politics.

The possibility of such a gradual evolution could not be ruled out. The CCP was reassured by the fact that such a change need not mean a loss of power. After all, in East European countries such as Romania and Hungary, transformed communist parties were by 1994 again holding power. Li Peng checked this out for himself during his trip to Romania in July 1994. The premier's host was President Ion Iliescu, a remnant of the *ancien regime* in addition to a classmate of Li in Moscow in the 1950s. And Li and his wife stayed in a castle formerly owned by the fallen dictator Nicolae Ceausescu. It is expected that the transfigured CCP could win at least the first couple of elections. As a Guangdong leader told a Hong Kong stockbroker in 1994: "We in Guangdong are not afraid of multi-party politics and the universal suffrage. The CCP will win in any case."[151]

"Western-style democracy" need not take place simultaneously all over China. Particularly with the 1997 integration of Hong Kong in mind, it would be unrealistic to rule out the possibility of special political zones (SPZs). With multi-party contention in full swing and with parts of its legislature directly elected, the Special Administrative Region of Hong Kong will have many elements of "Western-style democracy" and multi-party politics. It seems beyond doubt that "progressive" elements in China would demand that similar freedoms be granted cities or districts that have economic and education levels comparable to those of Hong Kong.

It is possible that the powers-that-be in Beijing would carve out SPZs in areas that were ripe for higher degrees of political participation. One must not lose sight of the fact that in the mid-1980s, a quasi-SPZ was conceived for the Shekou area in Shenzhen. At that time, the administrative committee running Shekou was elected to office by officials with cadre-level rank.[152]

With the example of Russia and Eastern Europe in mind, it is probable that leaders coming after the Jiang clique will eschew shock therapy. But they will be forced to adopt a faster pace towards market reforms and integration with the world economy. The central authorities will also be obliged to work out a more equitable and systematic form of power-sharing with the regions.

It is not difficult to trace the trajectory that political modernisation might take place in what some analysts have already called the "post-Jiang Zemin order". There will be more and more non-communist elements — and non-yesmen — in the NPC and CPPCC. Elections of government ministers by NPC deputies will become more "Westernised", meaning that legislators will at least have a choice among different candidates. Ministers will have to appear regularly before the NPC and the CPPCC to explain policy. An independent graft-fighting unit will come into being. Beijing will gradually legitimise non-party social organisations such as labour unions and "pressure groups". Such groupings, which include "private" chambers of commerce, will have a larger input in policy-making. The CCP administration will allow non-official bodies to run newspapers and other media. Tolerance for the non-violent expression of dissident opinion will increase.

The speed with which these manifestations of pluralism metamorphose into fully-fledged "party politics" will depend on domestic and international developments many of which have been discussed earlier. Modernisers in the post-Deng era are expected to take inspiration from the Taiwan, Singapore, Hong Kong and Eastern bloc models.

There will, of course, be strong forces blocking such changes. Some factions of the PLA and the major political and business clans stand to loose because the new system might wipe out the old guarantees to special privilege. However, even holders of vested interests might realise that it would be to their long-term advantage to follow the trend of history. After all, yielding to the pressure brought to bear on them by elements such as the private entrepreneurs entails sacrificing only parts of their perquisites. For example, the major clans would lose some political powers. But it is possible that they could retain big chunks of their economic and social clout. Not budging, however, might provoke a revolution — and the overnight liquidation of their political and economic assets.

Abbreviations and Glossary

ASEAN Association of Southeast Asian Nations
bingshang also *junshang* army businesses
CAC Central Advisory Commission
CASS Chinese Academy of Social Sciences
CCP Chinese Communist Party
CCDI Central Commission for Disciplinary Inspection
CMC Central Military Commission (of the Communist Party)
CNS the semi-official China News Service
CPLA Commission for Political and Legal Affairs
CPPCC Chinese People's Political Consultative Conference
CYL Communist Youth League
diktat economy also **command economy** an economy driven by state planning and
    government fiats
FCRS financial contract responsibility system, whereby provinces and cities — and
    in the industrial sector, state enterprises — fulfil their tax obligations by paying
    Beijing an annual sum that has been fixed after mutual negotiations
gaoganzidi also **princelings** sons and daughters of senior cadres
getihu "individual" or household entrepreneurs
GLD General Logistics Department of the army
GNP gross national product
Gold Coast the *nouveau riche* coastal provinces and cities

GDP gross domestic product; also General Political Department of the army

GSD General Staff Department of the army

guandao "officially-run speculations" in the marketplace

guanshang bufen "fusion of officialdom and business"

guanxi "connections"

gumin "stocks-crazed" people

HCRS household contract responsibility system; see RS

HKCNA the semi-official Hong Kong China News Agency

IPW ideological and political work

June 4 the massacre that took place in Beijing in the early hours of June 4, 1989

MR military regions

mu a unit of measurement that is equal to 0.0667 hectare

nanxun Deng Xiaoping's "imperial tour of the south" in early 1992

NCNA New China News Agency

PAP People's Armed Police

PLA People's Liberation Army

PSB Public Security Bureau

quanmin jieshang "everybody going into business"

RMB renminbi or **yuan**, the Chinese currency. Before "currency reunification" of January 1994, the exchange rate was approximately US$1 to 5.7 yuan, and after that, 8.7 yuan.

RIRES Research Institute for the Reform of the Economic Structure

RS responsibility system also known as **rural household contract responsibility system** the system whereby an agrarian household can engage in whatever economic activities it likes after surrendering to the government an agreed contribution

SCRES State Commission for the Reform of the Economic Structure

SETC State Economic and Trade Commission

SPC State Planning Commission

Tiananmen also **Tiananmen Square** a shorthand for the June 4 massacre

VTEs village and township enterprises

xiahai "take the plunge into the sea (of business)"

Xinhua same as **NCNA**

yindizhiyi "to each locality according to its characteristics"; the principle for the devolution of powers to the regions

yuan see **renminbi**

zhengji the administrative track record for a cadre

zhongnanhai party headquarters in Beijing

zhongyang "the centre", the Communist Party Central Committee. More often than not, the clique in power; Deng & Co.

Notes

Chapter 1

1. Author's interview with Hu Qili.
2. *Oriental Daily News* (Hong Kong), July 14, 1989.
3. New China News Agency (NCNA), September 17, 1989.
4. *South China Morning Post* (SCMP), Hong Kong, November 20, 1990; February 21, 1992.
5. *People's Daily*, August 30, 1989.
6. SCMP, March 6, 1991.
7. Reuters, January 3, 1991.
8. *People's Daily*, November 19, 1990.
9. For a discussion of Deng's "productivity" theory, see, for example, *Deng Xiaoping and his Enterprise*, ed. Lu Xingdou, (Beijing: CCP History Press, 1993), pp.366-490.
10. SCMP, September 27, 1991.
11. *Wen Wei Po* (Hong Kong), December 3, 1991.
12. NCNA, October 12, 1991.
13. *Wen Wei Po*, May 21, 1991.
14. SCMP, April 24, 1991.
15. *People's Daily*, April 23, 1991.
16. *Ta Kung Pao* (Hong Kong), August 15, 1991.

17. SCMP, May 22, 1991.

18. Deng Xiaoping and Deng Liqun, a former secretary of the late president Liu Shaoqi, used to be allies in the 1970s. One reason Deng could not exactly banish the leftists was his own role in the party's various anti-rightist campaigns.

19. *People's Daily*, August 16, 1989.

20. *People's Daily*, March 10, 1991.

21. Quoted by Chinese sources in Beijing.

22. SCMP, October 23, 1991.

23. *Wen Wei Po*, January 23, 1992.

24. Reuters, January 3, 1991.

25. SCMP, November 20, 1990.

26. *Wen Wei Po*, November 19, 1990.

27. NCNA, November 12, 1991.

28. China News Service (CNS), July 4, 1991.

29. *Ta Kung Pao*, January 26, 1992.

30. NCNA, June 13, 1990.

31. Many ideas raised by liberal cadres and intellectuals during the first two years of Deng's reign, from late 1978 to 1980, went much further than Deng would later be prepared to accept. Examples included the separation of party and government and a role for the intelligentsia.

32. Author's interviews with Chinese sources in Beijing and Shanghai.

33. *Liberation Daily* (Shanghai), March 2, 1991; March 22, 1991.

34. ibid.

35. The vendetta against the Huangpu Ping commentaries did not stop until Deng Xiaoping made it clear through his personal office that he was behind the ideas celebrated in the *Liberation Daily* articles.

36. NCNA, April 9, 1991.

37. SCMP, May 24, 1991.

38. SCMP, December 31, 1990.

39. NCNA, November 19, 1991.

40. NCNA, March 5, 1991.

41. For a discussion of the controversies over the speed of reform and development, see, for example, *China Review*, ed. Kuan Hsin-chi & Maurice Brosseau, (Hong Kong: Chinese University of Hong Kong Press, 1991), pp.20.15-20.17.

42. NCNA, October 22, 1990.

43. SCMP, December 11, 1991.

44. SCMP, February 1, 1992.

45. SCMP, August 3, 1990.

46. *The Mirror* monthly (Hong Kong), March 1991.

47. NCNA, May 23, 1991.

48. SCMP, May 8, 1990.

49. The official *nanxun* speeches, known as Central Committee Document No. 2 of 1992, are contained in the last chapter of *The Third Volume of Deng Xiaoping's Selected Works*, (Beijing: The People's Press, 1993). However, the official text was an edited version. In early 1992, newspapers in Hong Kong, Taiwan, Shenzhen and Zhuhai carried possibly more authentic versions of the speeches. See, for example, *Zhuhai Special Zone Daily*, April 17, 1992; *Wah Kiu Yat Po* (Hong Kong), March 15, 1992; *United Daily News* (Taipei), March 2, 1992; and *Hong Kong Economic Times* (HKET), March 12, 1992.

50. For a discussion of Documents No. 4 and No. 5, see SCMP, June 23, 1992.

51. *Wen Wei Po*, May 27, 1992; *United Daily News*, August 30, 1992.

52. SCMP, March 12, 1992.

53. Other leftists whom Deng criticised either by name or subtly included Deng Liqun and his ideologues.

54. *Pai Shing* weekly (Hong Kong), June 16, 1992.

55. A number of liberal intellectuals who responded to the *nanxun*, including Beijing University law lecturer Yuan Hongbing, were detained in 1994's anti-dissident drive.

56. SCMP, March 31, 1992.

57. *Ta Kung Pao*, February 1, 1992.

58. CNS, August 13, 1992.

59. Deng's desire to visit Hong Kong and Taiwan was reported by his children many times from 1992 to 1994. See, for example, *United Daily News*, April 27, 1993.

60. Vol. III of Deng Xiaoping's *Selected Works*, p. 373.

61. Even during the *nanxun*, Deng warned that the SEZs could "collapse within a night" should China fall prey to "the inundation of bourgeois liberalisation." See Volume III of *Selected Works*, p.379.

62. *New Evening Post* (Hong Kong), January 25, 1993; SCMP, January 26, 1993.

63. *The Mirror*, January 1994.

64. SCMP, March 18, 1993.

65. SCMP, November 30, 1993; December 29, 1993.

66. *Ming Pao* (Hong Kong), February 11, 1993; *Hong Kong Economic Journal* (HKEJ), January 8, 1993.

67. For a discussion of Deng's attitude towards the problem in inflation in late 1992, see, for example, SCMP, March 17, 1993; HKEJ, January 1, 1993.

68. ibid.

69. SCMP, March 3, 1993.

70. HKEJ, December 24, 1993.

71. HKEJ, January 21, 1994.

72. *The Mirror*, March 1994.

73. For a discussion of Deng's warnings against centrifugalism in late 1993, see

Cheng Ming magazine, (Hong Kong), January 1994.

74. For a discussion of Deng's hard-line statements towards Hong Kong, see, for example, *The Mirror*, April 1994; *Wide Angle* magazine, (Hong Kong), April 1994.

75. Vol III of *Selected Works*, p. 379.

76. SCMP, April 1, 1993.

. 77. Deng's reference to his "great invention" about not being bogged down by ideological controversies was left out in the official version of the *nanxun* talks.

78. *United Daily News*, February 24, 1993.

79. PLA Daily, July 25, 1993.

80. *The Mirror*, April 1994.

81. *China Times* (Taipei), December 25, 1992.

82. SCMP, February 27, 1993.

83. For a discussion of the fall of the Yang Clan, see, for example, *Ming Pao*, October 27, 1992.

84. Quoted by Chinese sources in Beijing.

85. For a discussion of Beijing's politics of driving dissidents into exile, see, for example, SCMP, April 27, 1994.

86. HKEJ, May 7, 1993.

87. *Selected Works of Deng Xiaoping, 1975-1982,* (Beijing: People's Press, 1983), p.207; p.258.

88. *People's Daily*, April 27, 1992.

89. SCMP, April 28, 1992.

90. *Wen Wei Po*, March 21, 1992.

91. NCNA, May 22, 1993.

92. HKET, May 14, 1993.

93. NCNA, June 15, 1993.

94. SCMP, April 16, 1993; September 30, 1993.

95. For Deng Rong's explanation on the motives behind her book, see *Commercial Daily* (Hong Kong), September 8, 1993.

96. *Bauhinia* monthly, (Hong Kong), October 1993.

97. Analysts said there was a special meaning in Deng's putting the *nanxun* talks as the last piece of his *Selected Works*. Other speeches and writings by Deng would presumably be put out after his death.

98. For a discussion of Deng's failure in political reform, see, for example, SCMP, November 10, 1993; *Ming Pao*, November 6, 1993.

99. *People's Daily*, November 10, 1993; SCMP, December 8, 1993.

100. *People's Daily*, December 7, 1993.

101. CNS, November 29, 1993.

102. CNS, July 23, 1993.

103. *Ming Pao*, March 23, 1994.

104. *United Daily News*, March 21, 1993.
105. *The Mirror*, May 1994.
106. CNS, May 11, 1994.
107. Vol III of *Selected Works*, pp. 344-345.
108. HKEJ, May 3, 1994.
109. HKEJ, February 4, 1994.
110. HKEJ, March 26, 1993.
111. HKEJ, September 11, 1992.
112. *People's Daily*, July 1, 1993; HKEJ, February 4, 1994.
113. *Next* magazine (Hong Kong), December 24, 1993; *Open* magazine (Hong Kong), July 1993.
114. For a discussion of the relationship between Deng Xiaoping and Yu Zuomin, see, for example, UPI, July 30, 1992.
115. For a discussion of Deng's earlier statements on anti-corruption, see *Deng Xiaoping on the Construction of Party Style and Clean Government in the New Era*, ed. by the Research Office of the Central Commission for Disciplinary Inspection of the CCP, (Beijing: Chinese Fangzheng Press, 1993).
116. Under the aegis of Deng and Zhao, several members of Zhao's think tanks went in early 1988 to do on-the-spot investigation of inflation in countries such as Mexico and Brazil. Their conclusion was that China could weather similarly high levels of price spirals.
117. *United Daily News*, June 16, 1993.
118. HKEJ, July 30, 1993.
119. HKEJ, July 15, 1993.
120. Author's interview with Sun Changjiang.
121. Hong Kong China News Agency, June 3, 1990.
122. *Pai Shing*, January 1, 1992.

Chapter 2

1. China News Service (CNS), October 30, 1989; January 6, 1992.
2. For a study of the debate of the surnames, see, for example, "On Countering 'Leftism' as the Main Task," by Hu Jiwei, in *The Last Chance for Deng Xiaoping*, ed. Lu Keng, (Hong Kong: Pai Shing Cultural Enterprise Ltd, 1992), pp.184-199.
3. CNS, January 11, 1992.
4. For a discussion of the leftists' worries about peaceful evolution, see, for example, "On Peaceful Evolution and the Struggle against Peaceful Evolution" by Xu Dashen, in *Discussion on Certain Questions of Socialism*, ed. Contemporary Thoughts Magazine, (Beijing: Hongqi Publishers, 1990) pp. 61-87; CNS, January 3, 1990; November 21, 1989.

5. For an exegesis of Chen Yun's ideas, see, for example, *Chen Yun's Economic Theories*, ed. Leung Chi-yan and Thomas Chan, (Hong Kong: CERD Consultants, 1985).

6. There is evidence the new formulation of the organic synthesis of planning and the market place had become state doctrine soon after the June 4 crackdown. Li Peng cited it in a speech reported in CNS, October 30, 1989.

7. *Economic Daily* (Beijing), July 12, 1990.

8. New China News Agency (NCNA), May 22, 1991.

9. *Wen Wei Po* (Hong Kong), October 18, 1991.

10. *People's Daily*, June 26, 1990.

11. Hong Kong China News Agency (HKCNA), December 11, 1989.

12. NCNA, October 25, 1987.

13. *Economic Reporter* weekly (Hong Kong), November 5, 1990.

14. *People's Daily*, March 6, 1991.

15. *South China Morning Post* (SCMP) (Hong Kong), August 1, 1990.

16. *Wen Wei Po*, April 17, 1991.

17. *Wen Wei Po*, September 12, 1991.

18. SCMP, August 1, 1990.

19. CNS, September 11, 1991.

20. SCMP, September 7, 1990; *Far Eastern Economic Review* (FEER) (Hong Kong), April 4, 1991.

21. ibid.

22. Same as note 12.

23. SCMP, November 5, 1990.

24. Same as note 16.

25. NCNA, February 12, 1991.

26. CNS, November 16, 1989.

27. *People's Daily*, June 26, 1990.

28. CNS, December 4, 1991.

29. For a discussion of the controversy surrounding the decision on the Three Gorges project, see, for example, SCMP, June 6, 1990; *Ming Pao* (Hong Kong), July 23, 1991.

30. The slogan about developing the economy in a "stable, sustained and harmonious fashion" was repeated by Li Peng and such of his allies as Zou Jiahua in 1990 and 1991. See, for example, NCNA, May 29, 1991; March 28, 1991.

31. SCMP, January 9, 1991.

32. NCNA, January 16, 1991.

33. SCMP, January 9, 1991. Almost exactly the same views were echoed in his *nanxun* talks.

34. HKCNA, November 12, 1990.

35. SCMP, November 7, 1990.

36. SCMP, January 9, 1990.
37. CNS, January 8, 1990.
38. SCMP, January 11, 1991.
39. NCNA, January 14, 1991.
40. NCNA, June 18, 1991.
41. SCMP, January 9, 1991.
42. *People's Daily*, March 3, 1991.
43. Deng's *nanxun* talks would reveal that the patriarch had only grudgingly acquiesced in the three-year austerity programme, which was actually aimed at rectifying "mistakes" caused by his high-growth model. At that time, however,
politicians like Chen Yun and Yao Yilin had the upper hand.
44. *People's Daily*, August 1, 1990; NCNA, May 29, 1991.
45. SCMP, April 29, 1991.
46. Reuters, April 28, 1991.
47. SCMP, May 13, 1991.
48. *International Herald Tribune*, April 29, 1991.
49. NCNA, January 20, 1992.
50. HKCNA, February 22, 1991.
51. SCMP, March 4, 1991.
52. NCNA, December 31, 1991.
53. HKCNA, October 18, 1989.
54. SCMP, September 6, 1990.
55. CNS, March 23, 1989.
56. CNS, November 21, 1989; SCMP, December 5, 1990.
57. NCNA, October 19, 1989.
58. HKCNA, January 3, 1990.
59. NCNA, September 22, 1991.
60. NCNA, December 25, 1991.
61. *Ming Pao*, September 17, 1991.
62. *Wen Wei Po*, October 15, 1991.
63. CNS, December 2, 1989; SCMP, August 1, 1990.
64. NCNA, June 25, 1990.
65. SCMP, March 21, 1991.
66. ibid.
67. Reuters, December 10, 1991.
68. *Wen Wei Po*, September 21, 1991.
69. SCMP, June 26, 1991.
70. *People's Daily*, January 15, 1991.
71. SCMP, September 30, 1991; CNS, October 20, 1991.
72. *Wen Wei Po*, September 21, 1991.
73. *Wen Wei Po*, August 16, 1991.

74. SCMP, September 25, 1991.

75. *Ta Kung Pao* (Hong Kong), September 21, 1991.

76. *Wen Wei Po*, December 23, 1991.

77. *Ming Pao*, October 12, 1991.

78. *People's Daily*, January 12, 1991.

79. *Ming Pao*, September 28, 1991.

80. *Ta Kung Pao*, September 12, 1991; NCNA, October 10, 1991.

81. *Wen Wei Po*, October 16, 1991.

82. HKCNA, October 9, 1991.

83. *Wen Wei Po*, August 16, 1991.

84. Various versions of the *nanxun* talks have been given. However, the most authoritative one was contained in the Third Volume of his *Selected Works*, (Beijing: People's Publishing Press, 1993), pp.370-383.

85. ibid. Similar statements defending his high-growth model were also made by Deng in Shanghai in early 1991 and early 1993.

86. *Ta Kung Pao*, June 18, 1992; SCMP, June 19, 1992.

87. For a discussion of Deng's talks in Shougang, see, for example, *The Mirror* monthly (Hong Kong), August 1992.

88. For a discussion of wheeling and dealing by PLA companies, see, for example, *Washington Post*, May 8, 1994.

89. SCMP, June 10, 1992.

90. SCMP, June 30, 1992.

91. ibid.

92. Same as note 84.

93. *Pai Shing* bi-weekly, (Hong Kong), June 16, 1992.

94. ibid.

95. For a discussion of the *quanmin jieshang* phenomenon, see, for example, *1992: A New Start, A New Way of Thinking*, ed. Tang Youlun and Xie Zhiqiang, (Beijing: Great China Encyclopedia Press, 1992), pp. 161-166.

96. HKCNA, November 22, 1993.

97. *Seeking Truth* monthly (Beijing), November 1993.

98. SCMP, August 5, 1992.

99. See *1992: A New Start, A New Way of Thinking*, op. cit., p. 163.

100. The team responsible for drafting the 14th Party Congress documents was largely put together by Jiang Zemin. It included a mixture of conservative and moderate cadres and academics, but very few liberals.

101. *People's Daily*, October 13, 1992; SCMP, October, 13, 1992.

102. NCNA, October 21, 1992; SCMP, October 22, 1992.

103. ibid.

104. *Wide Angle* monthly, (Hong Kong), November 1993.

105. *People's Daily*, November 2, 1993.

106. *Economic Daily*, November 2, 1993; SCMP, November 3, 1993.

107. NCNA, November 14, 1993; CNS, October 12, 1993; January 12, 1994.

108. NCNA, December 5, 1993.

109. SCMP, December 8, 1993.

110. *Ming Pao*, December 8, 1993.

111. *Ming Pao*, November 3, 1993.

112. NCNA, October 9, 1993.

113. *Ming Pao*, October 29, 1993.

114. SCMP, December 9, 1993; HKCNA, May 10, 1993.

115. *Wen Wei Po*, September 18, 1993; October 5, 1993; December 23, 1993.

116. SCMP, December 11, 1993; *Ming Pao*, November 29, 1993; *Wen Wei Po*, February 1, 1994.

117. The initial reaction of economists in Beijing was that the exact demarcation of tax bases for the centre and the regions would not be resolved till the mid-1990s.

118. As of early 1994, Beijing had not publicised full details about which types of taxes should go to Beijing or the localities, or which types should be shared. However, individual cadres gave a preliminary picture in interviews with the Hong Kong and foreign press. See, for example, *Wen Wei Po*, November 10, 1993; *Ming Pao*, January 14, 1994; *China Times Weekly* (Taipei), January 16, 1994; *United Daily News* (Taipei), August 14, 1993.

119. CNS, October 26, 1993; Reuters, January 12, 1994.

120. Beijing also promised to return to the localities parts of the revenues it would get from taxes that were to be shared by both the centre and the regions.

121. *Wen Wei Po*, November 10, 1993.

122. AFP, October 25, 1993.

123. *Wen Wei Po*, January 15, 1994.

124. *Wen Wei Po*, February 2, 1992; February 5, 1992.

125. *Ta Kung Pao*, November 6, 1993.

126. *Wen Wei Po*, November 24, 1993.

127. For a discussion of the authority of local administrations over credit policy, see, for example, Radio Television Hong Kong's report on Guangdong, February 6, 1994.

128. *Wen Wei Po*, October 31, 1993.

129. *Ming Pao*, October 22, 1993; *Wen Wei Po*, November 4, 1993.

130. *Wen Wei Po*, December 9, 1993; January 4, 1994; *Ming Pao*, December 28, 1993.

131. *Hong Kong Economic Journal* (HKEJ), January 28, 1994; NCNA, February 3, 1994; *Wen Wei Po*, February 2, 1994.

132. HKCNA, September 16, 1993.

133. *Ming Pao*, December 19, 1993.

134. SCMP, December 10, 1993.

135. SCMP, June 10, 1993.

136. AP, December 27, 1993; UPI, January 5, 1994.

137. *Wen Wei Po*, December 27, 1993; SCMP, December 28, 1993.

138. *People's Daily*, December 29, 1993; SCMP, January 6, 1994.

139. For a discussion of the expansion of the private sector, see, for example, *Ming Pao*, October 27, 1993; HKEJ, December 2, 1993.

140. *Ming Pao*, August 12, 1993.

141. CNS, October 21, 1993.

142. HKCNA, October 5, 1993; NCNA, December 13, 1993.

143. NCNA, December 13, 1993.

144. NCNA, October 25, 1987.

145. *Wen Wei Po*, April 17, 1991.

146. SCMP, March 4, 1991.

147. The attitude of the party towards dissidents becoming businessmen did not change until 1993, when some newly released prisoners of conscience including Wang Xizhe and Wang Dan were encouraged to get into business. Still, they were subjected to close surveillance.

148. CNS, August 31, 1991.

149. *Wen Wei Po*, November 10, 1991.

150. CNS, July 20, 1991.

151. *People's Daily*, September 27, 1989.

152. CNS, October 21, 1989; *People's Daily*, November 5, 1989.

153. As early as 1989, China's first generation of private-capital moguls were divesting their capital elsewhere. Wenzhou *getihu* merchants, for example, began setting up branches in as far as Europe, especially in Italy.

154. CNS, October 21, 1989.

155. Cited in internal party documents.

156. *Economic Reporter*, November 12, 1989.

157. SCMP, March 28, 1991.

158. CNS, April 15, 1991.

159. SCMP, November 4, 1991.

160. NCNA, January 11, 1992.

161. *Ming Pao*, November 8, 1991.

162. HKCNA, December 20, 1993.

163. NCNA, October 19, 1993.

164. *United Daily News*, November 5, 1993; HKCNA, September 15, 1993.

165. *Wen Wei Po*, October 27, 1993.

166. For a discussion of the political and economic handicaps still bedevilling the private sector, see, for example, SCMP, January 6, 1993.

167. *Economic Daily*, July 19, 1990.

168. *China Daily*, January 7, 1991.

169. *Hong Kong Economic Times* (HKET), January 2, 1992.

170. *People's Daily*, January 29, 1991; SCMP, January 7, 1991.

171. SCMP, June 22, 1991.

172. NCNA, May 28, 1991.

173. *China Daily*, November 18, 1991; HKET, January 7, 1992.

174. In 1993 and 1994, a large number of H shares were listed in Hong Kong. Chinese companies were also looking to bourses in Europe and the United States for listing.

175. CNS, June 9, 1990.

176. SCMP, December 11, 1991.

177. *Wen Wei Po*, January 1, 1992.

178. HKEJ, January 11, 1994; *China Business Weekly* (Beijing), December 19, 1993.

179. HKCNA, October 19, 1993; *Wen Wei Po*, January 15, 1994.

180. *Ming Pao*, November 20, 1993.

181. *Ming Pao*, August 12, 1993.

182. SCMP, January 7, 1992.

183. NCNA, May 10, 1993.

184. CNS, December 27, 1993; August 23, 1993; *Economic Daily*, January 14, 1994; *Shenzhen Special Zone Daily*, February 3, 1994.

185. *Ta Kung Pao*, November 11, 1991; *Ming Pao*, November 11, 1991.

186. *Ming Pao*, August 11, 1992; SCMP, August 11, 1992.

187. HKEJ, May 21, 1993; May 27, 1993.

188. *Ta Kung Pao*, December 30, 1993.

189. *Ming Pao*, January 27, 1994; HKCNA, January 12, 1994.

190. The leaders of Guangdong and Hainan were not enthusiastic supporter of the *zhongyang* just prior to the June 4 crackdown. For an inside look, see, for example, *The Memoirs of Xu Jiatun*, by Xu Jiatun, (Taipei: United Daily News Press, 1993).

191. SCMP, March 27, 1990.

192. CNS, May 29, 1990.

193. CNS, January 14, 1992.

194. HKCNA, September 24, 1991.

195. *Ta Kung Pao*, September 24, 1991.

196. Uighur nationalism got worse in 1993 with help going into Xinjiang and Qinghai from supporters in Turkey and former Soviet republics. For a discussion, see, for example, the *New York Times*, August 15, 1993; SCMP, October 16, 1993.

197. CNS, February 11, 1991.

198. CNS, March 9, 1989.

199. *Wen Wei Po*, September 9, 1991.

200. *Wen Wei Po*, October 21, 1991.

201. *United Daily News*, November 16, 1993; NCNA December 28, 1993.

202. For a discussion of Zhu's role in the "founding" of Pudong, see, for example, Zhu's biography by Ho Pin and Gao Xin, as excerpted in *United Daily News*, October 3, 1993.

203. NCNA, October 25, 1989.

204. SCMP, April 19, 1990.

205. SCMP, September 11, 1990.

206. *Asian Wall Street Journal*, September 11, 1990.

207. Volume III of Deng's *Selected Works*, op. cit., p. 366.

208. CNS, August 28, 1991.

209. *Wen Wei Po*, October 2, 1991.

210. *Ta Kung Pao*, September 27, 1991.

211. SCMP, September 26, 1991.

212. For an analysis of Pudong's future, see, for example, *Contemporary*, December 1993.

213. SCMP, August 27, 1990.

214. *People's Daily*, February 10, 1990. For an analysis of the changes in the SEZ policy, see, for example, Thomas Chan, "The Policy of Opening and Special Economic Zones," in *China Review*, ed. Kuan Hsin-chi and Maurice Brosseau, (Hong Kong: Chinese University Press, 1991) pp. 11.6-11.9.

215. *Economic Reporter*, October 23, 1990.

216. CNS, March 4, 1990.

217. HKET, August 7, 1992.

218. NCNA, September 26, 1991; *People's Daily* (Overseas Edition), September 24, 1991.

219. NCNA, May 5, 1991.

220. NCNA, September 12, 1991; September 29, 1991.

221. NCNA, October 21, 1991.

222. By 1991 and 1992, localities had secured autonomous rights to designate new development zones with minimal requirements of approval from Beijing. Those powers were withdrawn in late 1993.

223. NCNA, October 24, 1991; SCMP, September 23, 1991.

224. SCMP, September 27, 1989.

225. *Seeking Truth*, Beijing, September 1989.

226. ibid.

227. Cited by author's Chinese sources in Guangdong.

228. SCMP, July 4, 1991.

229. ibid.

230. CNS, September 28, 1991.

231. *United Daily News*, October 19, 1991.

232. NCNA, October 16, 1991.

233. *Ming Pao*, January 18, 1992.

234. Cited by Chinese economists in Guangdong.

235. CNS, August 1, 1993; HKET, November 20, 1993.

236. *Economic Reporter*, August 2, 1993; CNS, July 25, 1993.

237. *Ming Pao*, August 13, 1993; CNS, November 22, 1993.

238. HKCNA, December 31, 1993.

239. *Ming Pao*, November 4, 1993.

240. NCNA, August 17, 1993.

241. *Wen Wei Po*, December 22, 1993.

242. Cited by Chinese sources in Beijing.

243. For a discussion of regional resistance to the dual tax system, see, for example, SCMP, December 8, 1993; *The Mirror*, December 1993.

244. SCMP, November 18, 1993.

245. CNS, November 19, 1993; *Wen Wei Po*, February 2, 1994.

246. *Ming Pao*, December 24, 1993.

247. Owing to fears about his own position, Zhu did not carry out his threat of punishing recalcitrant local cadres.

248. *Ming Pao*, August 12, 1993.

249. *United Daily News*, September 7, 1993.

250. *Ta Kung Pao*, August 23, 1993; *Contemporary*, August 1993.

251. SCMP, October 20, 1993.

252. Cited in SCMP, December 8, 1993.

253. CNS, October 3, 1993.

254. NCNA, October 10, 1993.

255. *Wen Wei Po*, November 6, 1993.

256. NCNA, October 25, 1993; SCMP, October 27, 1993.

257. CNS, November 4, 1993.

258. CNS, January 4, 1994; SCMP, December 11, 1993; HKEJ, January 11, 1994.

259. SCMP, October 30, 1993; HKEJ, October 30, 1993.

260. CNS, October 18, 1993.

261. NCNA, August 9, 1993.

262. *China Business Times*, November 1, 1993.

263. *Ming Pao*, October 7, 1993.

264. HKEJ, November 5, 1993.

265. CNS, October 19, 1993.

266. Cited in SCMP, December 14, 1993.

267. *Ming Pao*, May 15, 1993.

268. Deng was an ardent admirer of the statecraft of Chiang Ching-kuo, at least until the last phase of the the Taiwan president's life, when he began introducing

political reform. The two briefly studied together in Moscow. For political reasons, of course, Beijing could not say it was learning from the Taiwan experience.

269. In 1993 and 1994, the CCP carried out yet another campaign to build party
cells in enterprises, even joint-venture factories.

270. *Ming Pao*, December 2, 1993.

271. NCNA, October 22, 1993.

272. *Wen Wei Po*, November 29, 1993.

273. NCNA, November 22, 1993.

274. NCNA, December 8, 1993; SCMP, December 9, 1993.

275. NCNA, December 6, 1993.

276. NCNA, January 5, 1994; CNS, January 6, 1994; *Wen Wei Po*, January 24,
1994.

277. NCNA, July 29, 1993; CNS, June 22, 1993.

278. NCNA, July 29, 1993; AFP, September 21, 1993.

279. CNS, November 13, 1993.

280. NCNA, January 28, 1994.

281. Cited by Chinese sources in Beijing.

282. SCMP, October 27, 1993.

283. SCMP, December 6, 1993; CNS, January 8, 1994.

Chapter 3

1. *People's Daily*, April 24, 1991.

2. For Deng's view on the bourgeois liberals, see, for example, *Selected Works of
Deng Xiaoping*, 1975-1982, (Beijing: People's Press, 1983), p. 258.

3. Cited in the semi-official China News Service (CNS), February 14, 1990.

4. *People's Daily*, August 15, 1989.

5. New China News Agency (NCNA), June 16, 1989.

6. *Study Socialist Theory; Increase Faith in Socialism*, ed. by *Contemporary
Thoughts* Magazine, (Beijing: Guangming Daily Press, 1991), pp. 165-167.

7. ibid.

8. *People's Daily*, July 7, 1989.

9. *Hong Kong Economic Times* (HKET), February 17, 1992.

10. Internal documents after June 4, 1989, accused American units such as the CIA
for large-scale involvement in the "turmoil".

11. *South China Morning Post* (SCMP), September 11, 1990.

12. SCMP, February 27, 1991.

13. ibid.

14. SCMP, July 13, 1991.

15. SCMP, August 26, 1991.

16. United Press International, October 28, 1991.

17. *Ming Pao* (Hong Kong), October 2, 1991.

18. CNS, February 14, 1990.

19. *People's Daily*, October 2, 1989.

20. Author's interview with Xiong Fu.

21. SCMP, July 13, 1991.

22. *People's Daily*, April 24, 1991.

23. *People's Daily*, June 15, 1989.

24. *People's Daily*, October 10, 1989.

25. *People's Daily*, November 5, 1990.

26. For a discussion by Zhao's attempt to contain the leftists' anti-liberalisation campaign, see, for example, *The Era of Zhao Ziyang*, by Willy Wo-Lap Lam, (Hong Kong: A. B. Books & Stationery, 1989), pp. 123-162.

27. SCMP, June 24, 1992.

28. *People's Daily*, April 22, 1991.

29. CNS, February 14, 1990.

30. *People's Daily*, August 9, 1989.

31. Zhao believed economic development was much more effective in promoting people's faith in socialism than indoctrination. See, for example, his self-defence after the June 4 massacre, cited in *Hong Kong Economic Journal* (HKEJ), June 4, 1994.

32. *People's Daily*, July 18, 1989.

33. HKEJ, June 4, 1994.

34. *Guangming Daily* (Beijing), August 10, 1991.

35. HKET, February 17, 1992.

36. In internal discussions and publications, leftists had a field day attacking the so-called Chinese Gorbachev or Yeltsin.

37. HKET, May 6, 1992.

38. *Guangming Daily*, December 27, 1990.

39. ibid.

40. NCNA, December 26, 1991; *Ming Pao*, January 14, 1992.

41. Cited in SCMP, January 2, 1991.

42. SCMP, September 28, 1989.

43. ibid.

44. SCMP, December 11, 1990.

45. ibid.

46. SCMP, October 24, 1990.

47. *Selected Works of Deng Xiaoping, 1975-1982*, (Beijing: People's Press, 1983), p.255.

48. Relatively liberal cadres also shared Deng's feelings about the inviolability of Mao's image. See, for example, Hu Yaobang's essay on Mao, *People's Daily*,

December 26, 1985.
49. NCNA, August 22, 1989.
50. *People's Daily*, June 25, 1991.
51. ibid.
52. *Wen Wei Po*, March 30, 1991.
53. For a discussion of the confidence crisis facing the party in the mid-1980s, see, for example, *The Era of Zhao Ziyang*, op. cit., pp.254-257.
54. SCMP, March 12, 1991.
55. *Wen Hui Bao* (Shanghai), December 4, 1991.
56. Quoted by author's Chinese sources.
57. SCMP, October 18, 1989.
58. NCNA, May 30, 1991.
59. Cited by Chinese sources in Beijing.
60. Cited by Chinese sources in Beijing.
61. The purge of intellectuals and CCP members was less severe partly due to the intervention of liberal Politburo members including Qiao Shi and Li Ruihuan.
62. *People's Daily*, November 21, 1990.
63. *Volume III of the Selected Works of Deng Xiaoping*, (Beijing: People's Press, 1993), p.10.
64. *People's Daily*, November 21, 1990.
65. *People's Daily*, January 15, 1991.
66. *People's Daily*, December 12, 1990.
67. *People's Daily*, December 19, 1990.
68. *People's Daily*, October 26, 1989.
69. *People's Daily*, June 5, 1990.
70. *People's Daily*, March 5, 1990.
71. ibid.
72. SCMP, August 16, 1990.
73. *People's Daily*, October 24, 1991.
74. *People's Daily* Overseas Edition, February 14, 1994.
75. SCMP, August 11, 1991.
76. *Shenzhen Special Zone Daily*, January 6, 1992.
77. For a discussion of Chen's career and ambitions, see, for example, AFP, August 27, 1993; *Far Eastern Economic Review* (FEER), May 10, 1990.
78. See "Grasping both civilisations at the same time," by Chen Yun, in *Selected Readings of Important Works since the Third Plenum of the 11th Central Committee*, (Beijing, People's Press, 1987) p. 897.
79. *People's Daily*, April 15, 1990.
80. SCMP, September 5, 1990.
81. *People's Daily*, April 16, 1990.
82. *People's Daily*, January 18, 1991.

83. SCMP, September 4, 1991.
84. SCMP, December 20, 1990.
85. FEER, November 8, 1990.
86. SCMP, May 20, 1991.
87. *The Mirror* monthly (Hong Kong), September 1990.
88. Most intellectuals in Beijing think the leftist commissars and the "three types of people" are after power and economic benefits rather than ideological ideals.
89. For a discussion of the political fortune of Deng Liqun and his allies in the mid-1980s, see, *The Era of Zhao Ziyang*, op. cit., 206-210.
90. Cited by Chinese sources in Beijing.
91. *Sing Tao Jih Pao*, (Hong Kong), April 26, 1992; HKEJ, December 16, 1992.
92. *Bauhinia* monthly, (Hong Kong), April 1992.
93. *People's Daily*, March 13, 1992.
94. *Ming Pao*, April 2, 1992.
95. NCNA, June 21, 1992.
96. SCMP, May 7, 1992.
97. NCNA, April 12, 1992.
98. CNS, December 13, 1992.
99. For a discussion of the mentality of intellectuals waging the anti-leftist campaign, see, for example, *Pai Shing* bi-weekly, (Hong Kong), November 16, 1992; CNS, October 25, 1992; *United Daily News*, October 8, 1992.
100. *Ming Pao*, June 15, 1992.
101. *Ming Pao*, October 28, 1992.
102. *Memorandum on Anti-Leftism* by Zhao Silin, (Taiyuan: Shuhai Press, 1992), p. 438.
103. Cited in *The Last Chance of Deng Xiaoping*, by Lu Keng, (Hong Kong: Pai Shing Cultural Enterprises, 1992). p. 199.
104. Author's interview with Yuan Hongbing.
105. Cited by Chinese sources. It must be noted, however, that Chen Zili and Hu Jintao are by no means liberals.
106. SCMP, September 4, 1992.
107. HKEJ, December 16, 1992.
108. *Ming Pao*, September 8, 1992.
109. HKEJ, December 16, 1992.
110. Cited by author's sources in Shanghai.
111. *Hong Kong Standard*, November 28, 1992.
112. SCMP, January 12, 1994.
113. HKEJ, May 26, 1994; HKEJ, May 24, 1994.
114. *People's Daily*, January 21, 1994.
115. SCMP, May 19, 1992.
116. NCNA, May 5, 1993; HKET, May 6, 1993.

LIBRARY
BISHOP BURTON COLLEGE
BEVERLEY HU17 8QG

117. HKET, April 11, 1993.
118. *Wen Wei Po* (Hong Kong), August 10, 1993.
119. *People's Daily*, January 29, 1993.
120. *People's Daily*, November 30, 1991.
121. NCNA, January 24, 1994.
122. SCMP, January 12, 1994; SCMP, May 5, 1994.
123. ibid.
124. *Ming Pao*, May 12, 1994; *The Mirror*, June 1994.
125. SCMP, May 10, 1994; *Wen Wei Po*, May 31, 1994.
126. *Ming Pao*, June 16, 1994.
127. SCMP, April 27, 1992.
128. *United Daily News* (Taipei), July 2, 1992.
129. SCMP, January 5, 1993.
130. *Hong Kong Standard*, May 10, 1993.
131. SCMP, January 5, 1993.
132. *Ming Pao*, June 1, 1993.
133. *Guangming Daily*, May 9, 1993.
134. NCNA, May 9, 1993.
135. *Ming Pao*, May 7, 1993.
136. *Ming Pao*, August 10, 1991; *Contemporary Thoughts* monthly (Beijing), April 1991.
137. *The Mirror*, March 1994; HKEJ, April 5, 1994.
138. *Seeking Truth* monthly (Beijing), February and March 1994.
139. *China Times Business Weekly* (Taipei), June 12, 1994.
140. SCMP, December 24, 1993; SCMP, January 12, 1994.
141. Reuters, November 15, 1993; *Wen Wei Po*, December 14, 1993.
142. CNS, December 26, 1993.
143. *People's Daily*, December 26, 1993.
144. HKEJ, December 24, 1993.
145. *Xuexi, Yanjiu, Cankao* monthly journal (*Study, Research, Reference*) (Beijing), May 1993.
146. *Beijing Daily*, June 23, 1993.
147. *China Daily*, June 25, 1993.
148. *Ming Pao*, March 27, 1993.
149. *Wen Wei Po*, March 30, 1993.
150. Reuters, July 24, 1992.
151. *Wah Kiu Yat Po* (Hong Kong), October 5, 1992; SCMP, September 22, 1992.
152. AFP, August 26, 1993.
153. Chen Yun remarks cited in *Important Works since the Third Plenum* ("Internal circulation" edition), (Beijing: People's Press, 1982), p. 1062; SCMP, December 14, 1991.

154. Quoted by Chinese sources.
155. SCMP, September 7, 1991.
156. *Ming Pao*, January 3, 1994; *Wen Wei Po*, May 4, 1993.
157. For the exploits of Gao Di, see, for example, *Wah Kiu Yat Po*, July 3, 1992; SCMP, November 27, 1992.
158. *United Daily News*, December 25, 1992.
159. SCMP, December 18, 1991.
160. *Pai Shing*, January 1, 1993.
161. For a discussion of the ideas of Luan Baojun, see HKEJ, December 22, 1992.
162. SCMP, May 19, 1992. For Chen Yuan's economic thoughts, see *The Works of Chen Yuan, by Chen Yuan*, (Harbin: Heilongjiang Education Press, 1990).

Chapter 4

1. Chinese sources reported that on the question of not being "soft-handed" towards the pro-democracy movement, there was essentially no difference between Deng Xiaoping and Wang Zhen.
2. For Deng's instructions to the Martial Law Command officers, see the Third Volume of his *Selected Works*, (Beijing: The People's Press, 1993), pp. 302-308.
3. *South China Morning Post* (SCMP) (Hong Kong), November 3, 1989.
4. Cited by the author's sources in Beijing and Moscow.
5. Reuters, September 15, 1992.
6. SCMP, November 22, 1989. There were reports of a few students attempting to commit suicide to protest against the military training.
7. ibid.
8. New China News Agency (NCNA), July 28, 1993.
9. Hong Kong Economic Journal (HKEJ), April 18, 1993.
10. *Ming Pao* (Hong Kong), May 30, 1993.
11. For a discussion of the army's role in politics, see, for example, interview with Dr Lin Chong-pin in *United Daily News* (Taipei), January 24-25, 1994.
12. See *Ta Kung Pao* (Hong Kong), October 20, 1992; also Michael D. Swaine, *The Military and Political Succession in China*, (Santa Monica: Rand Corp, 1993), pp 253-256.
13. HKEJ, November 29, 1992.
14. HKEJ, December 11, 1992.
15. ibid. For a general discussion of the role of the PLA in foreign affairs, see Benjamin Ostrov, "The PLA in the Foreign Policy Arena in 1993", in *China Review* 1994, ed. Maurice Brosseau and Lo Chi-Kin, (Hong Kong: Chinese University of Hong Kong Press, 1994), pp. 8.1-8.19.
16. *Ming Pao*, April 28, 1993.
17. NCNA, May 3, 1992.

18. *People's Daily*, May 21, 1993.
19. General Yang Baibing was arguably the most powerful CMC secretary-general ever. Aside from the Cultural Revolution period, there were few precedents of a general taking a key position in the Party Secretariat and playing a big role in civilian affairs.
20. SCMP, October 30, 1989.
21. For General Yang's role in *baojia huhang*, see, for example, *Ta Kung Pao*, February 25, 1992; China News Service (CNS), March 23, 1992.
22. Much of what Deng said during the *nanxun* he had uttered before during his outing to Shanghai in early 1991. The Shanghai talks, however, were not disseminated nationally due to opposition from the leftists.
23. NCNA, May 19, 1992.
24. NCNA, May 24, 1992.
25. CNS, October 1, 1992.
26. ibid.
27. For a discussion of the army's budget, see, for example, SCMP, March 24, 1992; *Outlook Weekly* (Beijing), July 27, 1992.
28. SCMP, November 19, 1992.
29. NCNA, March 8, 1993.
30. *Wen Wei Po* (Hong Kong), February 4, 1993.
31. *United Daily News*, November 19, 1992.
32. Reuters, December 9, 1990.
33. NCNA, March 25, 1991.
34. SCMP, April 1, 1991.
35. *People's Daily*, December 4, 1990.
36. For a discussion of the revival of Mao's military ideals, see, for example, SCMP, November 17, 1989.
37. *Wen Wei Po*, March 12, 1991.
38. SCMP, April 1, 1991.
39. NCNA March 25, 1991.
40. For a discussion of possible dissension among the ranks prior to the suppression of the democracy movement in June 1989, see, for example, Michael T. Byrnes, "The Death of a People's Army", in *The Broken Mirror*, ed. George Hicks, (Chicago: St James Press, 1990), pp 132-151; and Tai Ming Cheung, "The PLA and its Role between April to June 1989", in *The Chinese Military: The PLA in 1990/91*, ed. Richard H. Yang, (Boulder, Colorado: Westview Press, 1991), pp. 1-17.
41. In 1992 and 1993, PLA headquarters issued numerous directives against soldiers tuning in to hotlines about sex on some racier radio shows. Soldiers "speculating" in stocks also became a big problem. See, for example, *Ming Pao*, August 13, 1992.

42. Yang's speech, never published, was distributed by students on many campuses prior to the June 4 crackdown.

43. CNS, November 12, 1989.

44. *International Herald Tribune* (IHT), March 2, 1990.

45. For a discussion of Qin's role from 1989 to 1990, see, for example, *Far Eastern Economic Review* (FEER) (Hong Kong), April 12, 1990.

46. See Note 40.

47. CNS, May 18, 1989.

48. SCMP, December 28, 1989.

49. ibid.

50. For an overall analysis of General Yang's thoughts, see *Pai Shing* magazine, (Hong Kong), September 16, 1991.

51. *People's Daily*, December 7, 1991.

52. SCMP, December 6, 1991.

53. *People's Liberation Army Daily* (PLA Daily), March 8, 1990; HKEJ, September 6, 1993.

54. Cited by Chinese sources close to the PLA.

55. NCNA, November 14, 1989.

56. SCMP, November 17, 1989.

57. *People's Daily*, September 10, 1991.

58. SCMP, September 6, 1991; *Ming Pao*, September 1, 1991.

59. NCNA, February 20, 1990.

60. IHT, March 2, 1990.

61. *People's Daily*, December 6, 1991.

62. According to internal reference material, many officers known to have sympathies for the democracy movement were let off lightly. This is not to provoke further internecine bickering.

63. The importance of commissars as a whole declined towards the beginning of 1994, as was evident in the December 1993 reshuffle. Aside from his own problematic qualifications, the one reason why General Yang could never become a strongman was he had never led soldiers.

64. The army's Commission for Disciplinary Inspection was a parallel unit to the party's Central Commission for Disciplinary Inspection. After June 1989, the former was run for a few years by General Wan Ruilin.

65. For a discussion of the role played by General Yang in the 1990 reshuffle, see, for example, SCMP, May 4, 1990; June 6, 1990.

66. For an analysis of the criteria for the mid-1990 reshuffle, see, for example, SCMP, June 6, 1990.

67. See *China Review*, ed. Kuan Hsin-chi and Maurice Brosseau, (Hong Kong: Chinese University of Hong Kong Press, 1991), pp. xix-xx.

68. For an analysis of the political affiliation of leading members of the Beijing

MR, see Swaine, op. cit., pp. 80-87.

69. Cited by author's sources in Beijing.

70. SCMP, May 29, 1990.

71. Author's interviews with Chinese and Western military experts.

72. For an analysis of the fall of the Yang brothers, see, for example, *United Daily News*, November 17, 1992 and *Ming Pao*, October 27, 1992.

73. *Ming Pao*, November 19, 1992; December 1, 1992.

74. *China Times* (Taipei), November 14, 1992.

75. SCMP, October 16, 1992.

76. SCMP, November 11, 1992.

77. *Ming Pao*, October 27, 1992.

78. Cited by Chinese sources in Beijing.

79. For a discussion of Deng's differences with General Yang, see, for example, *Ming Pao*, December 1, 1992.

80. For a discussion of the differences between the Yang faction and the retired generals, see, for example, SCMP, June 28, 1990; *Cheng Ming* magazine (Hong Kong), April 1993.

81. For a discussion of the careers of Liu Huaqing and Zhang Zhen, see, for example, Swaine, op. cit., p. 197.

82. FEER, December 10, 1992.

83. In spite of his age, General Xu (born 1921) had great personal ambitions. His attempts to curry favour with Yang Baibing, however, put a premature end to his career.

84. There was a parallel development on the civilian side. By 1993, a fair number of cadres who gained promotions solely because of "valiance" displayed towards suppression the democracy movement had been sidelined. See Chapter 6.

85. *United Daily News*, November 19, 1992.

86. SCMP, October 21, 1993; November 1, 1993.

87. SCMP, January 13, 1994.

88. SCMP, October 21, 1993.

89. SCMP, September 21, 1993.

90. SCMP, January 13, 1994; *United Daily News*, January 14, 1994.

91. *People's Daily*, August 28, 1993.

92. NCNA, May 11, 1993.

93. HKEJ, May 19, 1993.

94. See, for example, *United Daily News*, November 11, 1993; NCNA, May 11, 1993.

95. NCNA, July 27, 1993.

96. NCNA, November 29, 1993.

97. *China Daily*, September 17, 1990.

98. CNS, March 25, 1992.

99. SCMP, April 27, 1992.

100. *United Daily News*, September 14, 1992.

101. *Wen Wei Po*, May 3, 1993.

102. SCMP, December 14, 1992.

103. AFP, January 19, 1994.

104. NCNA, January 18, 1994; Reuters, January 19, 1993.

105. NCNA, March 22, 1993.

106. CNS, September 21, 1993.

107. NCNA, September 19, 1993.

108. *Ming Pao*, March 28, 1993; NCNA, May 9, 1993.

109. *PLA Daily*, August 2, 1993.

110. SCMP, June 19, 1990.

111. *Asian Wall Street Journal* (AWSJ), October 9, 1991.

112. SCMP, June 28, 1990.

113. *Beijing Daily*, May 19, 1990.

114. *PLA Daily*, December 14, 1992.

115. For an analysis of the potentials of the alumni of the Third Field Army, see, for example, HKEJ, October 12, 1993.

116. Author's interviews with PLA sources in Beijing.

117. *United Daily News*, September 14, 1992.

118. For a discussion of the new-look GSD, see, for example, Tai Ming Cheung, "The PLA in 1992: Political Power Plays and Power Projection", in *China Review* 1993, ed. Joseph Cheng Yu-shek and Maurice Brosseau, (Hong Kong: Chinese University of Hong Kong Press, 1993), p. 6.11.

119. *Ming Pao*, July 27, 1993.

120. For a discussion of the factional dimensions of the PLA's business empire, see, for example, FEER, October 14, 1993.

121. *People's Daily*, June 7, 1993.

122. *People's Daily*, November 16, 1989.

123. He Xin's speech first appeared in an internal publication of the *People's Daily*. It was circulated among cadres but never published.

124. CNS, March 30, 1991.

125. For a discussion of the army's strategic change after the Gulf War, see, for example, SCMP, April 27, 1991; June 16, 1991.

126. NCNA, February 5, 1991.

127. ibid.

128. *Wide Angle* monthly (Hong Kong), June 15, 1991.

129. SCMP, June 14, 1991.

130. Same as note 128.

131. For a discussion of the profile of the professionals, see. e.g., Lee Ngok, "The PLA: Dynamics of Strategy and Politics", in *China Review*, op. cit., p. 5.21.

132. For a discussion of the traits of the Shenyang region, see, for example, Swaine, op. cit., pp. 87-92.

133. *PLA Daily*, March 9, 1990.

134. For a discussion of this facet of PLA factional dynamics, see, for example, *United Daily News*, January 25-26, 1994.

135. SCMP, August 8, 1992.

136. SCMP, February 6, 1991.

137. NCNA, May 29, 1993.

138. *Contemporary* magazine (Hong Kong), October 15, 1991.

139. SCMP, February 3, 1993.

140. For a discussion of the scale of the PLA business empire and the conversion of military factories for civilian use, see, for example, *China Times Weekly* (Hong Kong), July 18, 1993.

141. NCNA, October 22, 1992.

142. *Ming Pao*, May 15, 1993.

143. Whether the army should engage in business never became a public issue of discussion in the PLA. The CMC leadership must have been embarrassed by the fact that all the heroes it was setting up for the rank and file to emulate were altruists with very spartan lifestyles.

144. For a discussion of the PLA-related businesses of the princelings, see, for example, *The Nineties* monthly (Hong Kong), November 1991.

145. The anti-corruption crusade within the PLA was launched by Generals Liu Huaqing and Chi Haotian around August, the same time that the comparable anti-graft campaign on the civilian side was launched by such leaders as Jiang Zemin (in his capacity as party General Secretary) and Wei Jianxing.

146. Altercations over land-use rights were easily the most common among the mushrooming number of disputes between military and civilian authorities in 1992 and 1993.

147. SCMP, July 7, 1993.

148. By early 1994, the authorities imposed a ban on the reporting of PLA-related corruption in the official media.

149. *PLA Daily*, April 17, 1993.

150. AFP, July 6, 1993.

151. SCMP, July 7, 1993.

152. CNS, August 17, 1993.

153. NCNA, July 21, 1993.

154. SCMP, September 10, 1993.

155. SCMP, December 9, 1993.

156. For a discussion of multinational PLA concerns, see, for example, the *Washington Post*, May 8, 1994.

157. *The Times* (London), May 9, 1994.

158. *Wen Wei Po*, March 29, 1994.

159. NCNA, July 27, 1993.

160. CNS, March 1, 1993.

161. *People's Daily*, July 26, 1993.

162. SCMP, May 12, 1993.

163. *United Daily News*, September 8, 1992.

164. AFP, March 3, 1993.

165. AFP, May 13, 1993.

166. *Nanfang Daily* (Guangzhou), November 9, 1993; HKEJ, December 31, 1993.

167. Most of the liberal views on army modernisation by Yang Shangkun and Zhao Ziyang were contained in internal speeches which might never see the light of day.

168. *China Daily*, October 17, 1988.

169. See The *Selected Works of Deng Xiaoping, 1975-1982*, (Beijing: The People's Press, 1983), p. 364.

170. Cited in SCMP, June 6, 1990.

171. *Contemporary*, January 15, 1992.

172. NCNA, September 8, 1993.

173. NCNA, January 13, 1994; SCMP, January 14, 1994.

174. For a discussion of the career of Yu Yongbo, see *Wah Kiu Yat Po* (Hong Kong), October 22, 1992.

175. Practically all senior cadres — particularly those close to Deng — had children who were active in the PLA or the PAP. They included Yang Shangkun, Nie Rongzhen, Wang Zhen, Zhao Ziyang and Li Peng.

176. NCNA, November 12, 1989.

177. *PLA Daily*, August 2, 1993.

178. Cited by the author's Chinese sources.

179. HKEJ, April 18, 1993; *Wide Angle*, February 1993.

180. Partly due to Yang Baibing's intercession, Colonel Zhang was not court-martialled and was only put under surveillance. His book, reprinted in Hong Kong and Taiwan, had a wide following in the overseas-Chinese community.

181. *The Mirror*, June 1993.

Chapter 5

1. For a discussion of Deng Xiaoping's reform ideals before the June 4 crackdown, see, for example, *Ming Pao* (Hong Kong), November 6, 1993.

2. *Selected Works of Deng Xiaoping 1975-1982*, (Beijing: People's Press, 1983), pp. 280-302.

3. *People's Daily*, July 1, 1987.

4. New China News Agency (NCNA), October 25, 1987.

5. *Contemporary* magazine (Hong Kong), February 17, 1990.

6. *Oriental Daily News* (Hong Kong), July 14, 1989.

7. Quoted by author's Chinese sources in Beijing.

8. *United Daily News* (Taipei), May 3, 1993; *Volume III of the Selected Works of Deng Xiaoping*, (Beijing: People's Press, 1993), p. 332.

9. *South China Morning Post* (SCMP) (Hong Kong), December 14, 1989.

10. SCMP, April 8, 1991.

11. *Selected Works*, pp. 351-356.

12. China News Service (CNS), March 19, 1990.

13. CNS, May 9, 1991.

14. CNS June 12, 1990; *Ming Pao*, March 23, 1992.

15. CNS, June 27, 1990.

16. NCNA, May 21, 1993.

17. CNS, March 11, 1994.

18. Deng regarded Zhao's premier fault as diluting "party leadership", see Vol. III of *Selected Works*, p. 324.

19. In internal documents, the party's ideologues repeatedly slammed Gorbachev and Boris Yeltsin for betraying socialism.

20. Corruption became a big stick with which the remnant Maoists tried to beat the Deng Faction, even though, ironically, the fusion of party and business dovetailed with the leftists' agenda about promoting party supremacy.

21. *Economic Reporter* weekly (Hong Kong), January 8, 1990.

22. ibid.

23. SCMP, January 28, 1994.

24. Author's interviews with officials and factory managers in the Pearl River Estuary.

25. SCMP, September 12, 1991.

26. *Ming Pao*, June 13, 1991.

27. Author's interview with officials of the Human Rights Watch/Asia (formerly Asia Watch), New York.

28. *China Daily*, October 19, 1992.

29. *Ming Pao*, March 28, 1993.

30. Instances of "cross leadership" in 1993 and 1994 were even more numerous than during the reign of Mao Zedong.

31. *Frontline* monthly (Hong Kong), January 1992.

32. *Ming Pao*, May 14, 1993.

33. Author's interview with officials in Shenzhen.

34. CNS, March 19, 1990.

35. NCNA, June 10, 1989.

36. NCNA, May 26, 1989.

37. SCMP, January 22, 1990.

38. SCMP, July 3, 1991.
39. NCNA, July 2, 1991.
40. Quoted by author's Chinese sources in Beijing.
41. *People's Daily*, October 23, 1991; NCNA, June 28, 1991.
42. For a discussion of Wang Zhen's career, see, for example, SCMP, February 19, 1992.
43. *Hong Kong Economic Times* (HKET), January 16, 1992; *Wide Angle* monthly (Hong Kong), January 1992.
44. Hong Hong Economic Journal (HKEJ), August 26, 1993.
45. The official media, however, seldom identified the high-born parents of the *gaoganzidi*, some of whom adopt different surnames than that of their fathers.
46. CNS, February 16, 1990.
47. *China Times Weekly* (Taipei), January 26, 1992.
48. *The Mirror* monthly (Hong Kong), August 1991.
49. Most Chinese are ignorant about the high positions or business activities of the sons-in-law and other less prominent relatives of Deng Xiaoping.
50. For a discussion of the career of Chen Yuan, see, for example, *Archives of Senior Cadres*, by Gao Xin and Ho Pin, (Taipei: The Journalist Press, 1993), pp. 247-250.
51. Author's interviews with Chinese sources in Beijing.
52. SCMP, January 15, 1992.
53. *Wide Angle*, December 1991.
54. Author's interview with dissidents in the US.
55. The so-called theory of the "third force" died out in 1993 and 1994 as it became apparent most *gaoganzidi* would not necessarily adopt liberal policies after the demise of the octogenarians.
56. For a discussion of the business activities of the *gaoganzidi*, see, for example, *Next* magazine (Hong Kong), October 29, 1993.
57. *Ming Pao*, November 6, 1991.
58. The new commander of the PAP, Ba Zhongtan, talked candidly about the role of his troops in maintaining internal order, see CNS, March 12, 1994.
59. SCMP, November 6, 1991.
60. Reuters, September 17, 1991.
61. SCMP, April 21, 1990.
62. NCNA June 1, 1992.
63. For a discussion of the new police units, see, NCNA, November 24, 1993; CNS, March 1, 1994.
64. SCMP, July 7, 1993; Associated Press, April 1, 1994.
65. CNS, October 17, 1993.
66. CNS, December 15, 1993.
67. CNS, January 9, 1994.

68. CNS, December 28, 1993; *Wen Wei Po* newspaper (Hong Kong), December 28, 1993.
69. *Wen Wei Po*, January 21, 1994; *Ming Pao*, December 1, 1993.
70. CNS, November 23, 1991.
71. NCNA, February 15, 1990; SCMP, February 16, 1990.
72. SCMP, February 14, 1990.
73. *China Review* 1994, ed. Maurice Brosseau and C.K. Lo, (Hong Kong: Chinese University Press, 1994) p.xx.
74. *Legal Daily* (Beijing), December 26, 1991.
75. *Ming Pao*, November 6, 1991.
76. In spite of their boosted establishment, state security officials still complained about a lack of funds and personnel. Classified documents in 1993 and 1994 revealed the leadership's fear of leaks of political and economic material to the West.
77. *Wen Wei Po*, November 8, 1993.
78. Hong Kong China News Agency (HKCNA), December 8, 1993; CNS, November 15, 1993.
79. SCMP, November 24, 1993.
80. *Economic Daily* (Beijing), December 4, 1993.
81. State-level leaders have officiated at the opening ceremony of joint ventures with Hong Kong triad elements.
82. The Public Security Ministry later retracted the statement about "co-operation" with Hong Kong triads. In 1994, it invited Hong Kong Police Chief Li Kwan-ha to Beijing to help jointly fight Hong Kong underworld crimes, see *Next* magazine, April 15, 1994.
83. For example, in the case of Hong Kong reporter Xi Yang, who was given a 12-year sentence for "spying", various leaders indicated it was a matter for the judiciary, not the party or government. See, for instance, CCTV (Beijing), April 28, 1994.
84. *China Daily*, November 4, 1991.
85. SCMP, January 10, 1990.
86. CNS, February 4, 1990.
87. SCMP, November 12, 1991.
88. SCMP, January 8, 1992.
89. CNS, December 31, 1993.
90. NCNA, September 14, 1993.
91. Author's interview with Yu Haocheng in Beijing.
92. *Trial and Punishment since 1989*, Amnesty International, April 1991, p. 3.
93. *Punishment without Crime: Administrative Detention*, Amnesty International, September 1991.
94. SCMP, January 4, 1992.

95. AP, February 20, 1994.

96. SCMP, February 26, 1991.

97. SCMP, January 16, 1991.

98. For a detailed discussion of Liu Gang and other cases, see the Asia Watch cumulative report, *Detained in China and Tibet*, New York, 1994.

99. AP, January 4, 1994.

100. For a discussion of the interplay between pressure from the West and Beijing's human rights policy, see, for example, "Influencing Human Rights in China," by Andrew Nathan, in *Beyond MFN*, ed. James R. Lilley & Wendell L. Willkie II, (Washington, AEI Press, 1994), pp. 77-90.

101. CNS, November 18, 1989.

102. *Ming Pao*, January 22, 1992.

103. *People's Daily*, February 2, 1994.

104. For a discussion of the background of the CPLA and the party's control of the judiciary, see, for example, SCMP, December 16, 1992; January 8, 1992.

105. For example, Deng laid down the instructions about the nature of Bao Tong's crime and the length of the sentence. Author's interview with Bao's son, Bao Pu.

106. During the Cultural Revolution, which was partially Mao's vendetta against his enemies, the Chairman openly boasted about his philosophy of *wufa wutian* ("no laws; no heavenly justice").

107. SCMP, April 4, 1990.

108. CNS, December 21, 1993.

109. For a discussion of Jiang Zemin's role in the Xi Yang case, see, for example, *Eastern Express* (Hong Kong), April 21, 1994; HKEJ, April 29, 1994.

110. SCMP, July 13, 1991.

111. CNS, January 11, 1994.

112. Counter-espionage organisations including the Ministry of State Security have been on guard against infiltration of underground trade unions by such foreign counterparts as Solidarity and the AFL-CIO of the US.

113. Deng's speeches on the impact of Solidarity have never been made public.

114. For example, the first executions of June-4 related crimes involved three workers in Shanghai a week after the massacre. In general, punishment for intellectuals and students was less severe.

115. CNS, September 3, 1991; AP, February 23, 1991; AP, May 19, 1991.

116. HKCNA, May 2, 1990.

117. *Guangming Daily* (Beijing), March 17, 1990.

118. HKCNA, November 11, 1991.

119. *People's Daily*, December 14, 1991.

120. NCNA, December 20, 1989.

121. *People's Daily*, August 12, 1991.

122. AFP, August 29, 1991.

123. SCMP, December 12, 1991.
124. Author's interview with sources close to the ACFTU.
125. CNS, April 12, 1990.
126. SCMP, December 12, 1991.
127. *Ming Pao*, January 14, 1994.
128. CNS, January 13, 1994.
129. For a discussion of labour disputes and incidents in Shenzhen and other SEZs, see, for example, *Ming Pao*, January 19, 1994; SCMP, January 21, 1994.
130. *Ming Pao*, January 20, 1994.
131. *Ming Pao*, January 11, 1994; CNS, February 4, 1994.
132. *Ming Pao*, January 11, 1994.
133. NCNA, October 12, 1993.
134. SCMP, March 22, 1994.
135. SCMP, March 2, 1994; April 23, 1994.
136. *Asia Watch Report*, New York, March 11, 1994; AP, July 19, 1994.
137. *People's Daily*, July 2, 1991.
138. *Ming Pao*, July 9, 1991.
139. *Beijing Daily*, December 3, 1991; CNS, April 25, 1991.
140. *Ming Pao*, July 9, 1991.
141. *Ming Pao*, October 5, 1991.
142. SCMP, November 14, 1991.
143. SCMP, March 1, 1991; July 20, 1991.
144. SCMP, March 1, 1991.
145. For a discussion of Deng's theory on technology and productivity, see, *Deng Xiaoping and his Enterprise*, ed. Lu Xingdou, (Beijing: CCP History Press, 1993), pp. 366-403.
146. HKET, November 7, 1991.
147. *Ta Kung Pao* newspaper (Hong Kong), December 9, 1991; NCNA, November 12, 1991.
148. NCNA, October 13, 1992.
149. Vol III of *Selected Works*, p.380.
150. *Beijing Daily*, May 28, 1991.
151. SCMP, March 13, 1991.
152. ibid.
153. *People's Daily*, September 1, 1991; SCMP, September 4, 1991.
154. Author's Chinese sources quoting internal documents.
155. *Wen Zai Bao* (*Paper of Article Excerpts*) (Beijing), June 30, 1991.
156. CNS, March 14, 1994.
157. SCMP, June 25, 1991.
158. ibid.
159. *The Nineties* monthly (Hong Kong), September 1990.

160. *People's Daily*, July 18, 1989.
161. Up to mid-1994, Guangdong and Shanghai continued to enjoy special status so far as the reshuffle of regional cadres is concerned. Beijing showed a particular concern for not upsetting stability by appointing unpopular politicians from out of the two areas.
162. CNS, March 19, 1993.
163. NCNA, January 27, 1994.
164. NCNA, March 4, 1994.
165. *The Mirror*, January 1994.
166. *Nanfang Daily* (Guangzhou), February 1, 1994.
167. Another major reason behind the reshuffles in late 1993 and early 1994 was the power struggle: leading players like Jiang Zemin and Zhu Rongji were eager to promote their protégés.
168. SCMP, January 31, 1991; HKCNA, April 24, 1991.
169. NCNA, January 20, 1992.
170. Quoted by sources close to the Propaganda Department.
171. CNS, May 3, 1991.
172. NCNA, May 29, 1991.
173. NCNA, January 20, 1992.
174. SCMP, January 22, 1992.
175. NCNA, January 30, 1991.
176. *Ming Pao*, August 17, 1991.
177. NCNA, March 24, 1993.
178. *Wen Wei Po*, June 21, 1993.
179. AFP, March 16, 1993; *Wen Wei Po*, March 15, 1993.
180. CNS, June 8, 1993; *Wen Wei Po*, April 17, 1993.
181. ibid.
182. CNS, May 3, 1993; CNS, June 22, 1993.
183. CNS, April 6, 1993.
184. CNS, June 22, 1993.
185. *Wen Wei Po*, May 5, 1993; *Economic Daily*, February 11, 1993; *United Daily News*, March 1, 1993.
186. AP, August 20, 1993.
187. *Ming Pao*, March 22, 1993.
188. CNS, September 10, 1993.
189. NCNA, August 18, 1993.
190. *Wen Wei Po*, October 9, 1993.
191. *Guangming Daily*, June 7, 1986.
192. For a discussion of the democratisation ideals raised in the mid-1980s, see, for example, Willy Wo-Lap Lam, *The Era of Zhao Ziyang*, (Hong Kong: A.B. Books and Stationery, 1989), pp.19-44.

193. *Political Report of the 13th Party Congress*, Beijing Review Press, 1987, pp. xv-xvi.

194. NCNA, March 12, 1990.

195. *People's Daily*, March 13, 1990.

196. *Wen Wei Po*, March 22, 1994.

197. SCMP, February 7, 1991; *People's Daily*, December 1, 1993.

198. *People's Daily*, August 16, 1990.

199. Li Ruihuan, *On Doing Concrete Things for the People*, (Tianjin: Hundred Flowers Literature & Arts Press, 1991), pp. 4-5.

200. NCNA, January 27, 1994.

201. NCNA February 3, 1994.

202. CNS, January 26, 1994.

203. NCNA, February 7, 1990.

204. *People's Daily*, February 8, 1990.

205. CNS, June 14, 1990.

206. SCMP, January 5, 1990.

207. CNS, June 15, 1991.

208. CNS, February 11, 1990; *People's Daily*, 2 November 2, 1991.

209. SCMP, February 12, 1990; SCMP, January 2, 1990.

210. *Ming Pao*, March 28, 1990.

211. NCNA, November 25, 1993.

212. *United Daily News*, November 4, 1993.

213. *Wen Wei Po*, March 28, 1993.

214. NCNA, October 9, 1993.

215. *Wen Wei Po*, March 9, 1994.

216. *Wen Wei Po*, February 14, 1994.

217. *Wen Wei Po*, June 19, 1993.

218. *Wen Wei Po*, June 23, 1993; CNS, February 2, 1993.

219. CNS, 6 February, 1993.

220. Author's interview with Xu Simin.

221. *Shenzhen Special Zone Daily*, January 31, 1993.

222. NCNA, May 17, 1993.

223. Quoted by Chinese sources.

224. SCMP, February 28, 1990.

225. SCMP, March 29, 1990.

226. CNS, February 25, 1991.

227. *Ta Kung Pao*, January 24, 1992.

228. Author's interview with Yan Jiaqi.

229. It is an indication of their cautiousness that Qiao Shi and Tian Jiyun did not make any proposals towards revamping the NPC structure.

230. CNS, July 5, 1989.

231. SCMP, April 7, 1991.

232. *China Daily*, October 30, 1993; SCMP, February 2, 1994; SCMP, January 6, 1994.

233. HKCNA, March 24, 1989.

234. Cited by the author's Chinese sources.

235. ibid.

236. SCMP, December 27, 1991; *Wen Wei Po*, January 27, 1992.

237. *Ming Pao*, April 4, 1992.

238. Author's interview with Dai Qing; SCMP, November 24, 1993.

239. CNS, January 21, 1994.

240. SCMP, April 7, 1993.

241. *Ming Pao*, April 15, 1993.

242. NCNA, April 6, 1993.

243. CNS, September 2, 1993.

244. CNS, September 2, 1993.

245. SCMP, April 7, 1993.

246. *China Times Weekly*, January 9, 1994.

247. *Ming Pao*, April 16, 1993; April 20, 1993.

248. *Wen Wei Po*, May 15, 1993; *Nanfang Daily* (Guangzhou), February 2, 1994; CNS, February 3, 1994.

249. *Ming Pao*, March 16, 1994.

250. For a discussion of the political rivalry between the Qiao-Tian group and the "mainstream faction" led by Jiang Zemin, see, for example, SCMP, April 7, 1993.

251. SCMP, June 12, 1990.

252. *Economic Reporter*, October 16, 1989.

253. NCNA, December 3, 1991.

254. CNS, December 8, 1991.

255. CNS, July 16, 1989.

256. Author's interview with Yu Haocheng.

257. Investigations of "economic crimes" by Zhao's sons never became official or publicised in the media. In 1993 and 1994, Zhao privately denied the complicity of his sons.

258. NCNA, August 19, 1991.

259. CNS, March 27, 1990.

260. CNS, November 12, 1993.

261. *Ming Pao*, March 14, 1994; *Wen Wei Po*, March 16, 1994.

262. NCNA, October 22, 1993.

263. NCNA, November 8, 1993; *Wen Wei Po*, August 14, 1993.

264. *Ming Pao*, August 12, 1993; HKCNA, October 20, 1993; CNS, October 18, 1993.

265. *People's Daily*, October 8, 1993.

266. *People's Daily*, October 23, 1993.

267. *United Daily News*, November 1, 1993.

268. *Ming Pao*, December 25, 1993; *Ming Pao*, September 13, 1993; *United Daily News*, November 10, 1993.

269. *Ming Pao*, April 12, 1994.

270. *Wen Wei Po*, February 26, 1994.

271. NCNA, October 13, 1993; *People's Daily*, November 30, 1993.

272. NCNA, October 4, 1993; NCNA, September 17, 1993.

273. In the elections of county-level cadres, party control had by the early 1990s been weakened. Local barons, for example, millionaire private entrepreneurs and heads of "feudalistic" clans, were often elected with the connivance of party functionaries.

274. *United Daily News*, February 1, 1993.

275. ibid.

276. *Wen Wei Po*, February 7, 1993.

277. SCMP, February 6, 1993.

278. *Ming Pao*, March 30, 1993.

279. CNS, November 24, 1993.

280. *Ming Pao*, March 28, 1993.

281. NCNA, April 16, 1993.

282. AFP, March 1, 1993.

283. AFP, May 10, 1993.

284. SCMP, April 2, 1993.

Chapter 6

1. This particular outburst against conservative cadres was not contained in the official version of the *nanxun* talks in Volume III of Deng's *Selected Works*. However, it was reported in Zhuhai and Hong Kong papers. See, for example, *Wen Wei Po* (Hong Kong), April 17, 1992.

2. *Volume III of the Selected Works of Deng Xiaoping*, (Beijing: The People's Press, 1993), p.380.

3. *Wen Wei Po*, October 14, 1992.

4. *South China Morning Post* (SCMP) (Hong Kong), October 20, 1992; *Far Eastern Economic Review* (Hong Kong), December 10, 1992.

5. For a discussion of the purge of the Yang clan, see, for example, *The Mirror* monthly (Hong Kong), January 1993; *Contemporary* monthly, (Hong Kong), November 1992.

6. For a complete line-up of the new leadership, see *The Mirror*, November 1992; *Contemporary*, November 1992.

7. *People's Daily*, October 13, 1992; *The Express* (Hong Kong), October 5, 1992.

8. For the role played by Liu Huaqing and Zhang Zhen, see, for example, *Wide Angle* monthly (Hong Kong), December 1992.

9. Author's interview with sources in Beijing.

10. *The Mirror*, November 1992.

11. *Ming Pao*, March 28, 1993.

12. *Hong Kong Economic Journal* (HKEJ), May 5, 1994.

13. *Wen Wei Po*, November 14, 1993.

14. China News Service (CNS), May 12, 1994.

15. Hu Qili largely abstained from commenting on political and economic affairs, probably to save his neck.

16. SCMP, March 26, 1993.

17. From early 1994 onwards, Li Tieying surprised observers by espousing market reforms, see, for example, CNS, May 17, 1994.

18. HKEJ, May 18, 1994.

19. Wang Qishan reportedly said soon after the June 4 massacre that it was necessary for the party to take "resolute action" to ensure stability for the next generation.

20. SCMP, January 28, 1994.

21. Shanghai here refers to the Greater Shanghai area and environs, including Jiangsu and Zhejiang. The Shanghai Faction was equally dominant during the reign of Chiang Kai-shek and the Gang of Four.

22. CNS, February 12, 1993.

23. *United Daily News* (Taipei), October 15, 1992.

24. For an analysis of the Gansu Faction, see, for example, SCMP, September 7, 1990.

25. Since the Cultural Revolution, none of the top leaders of Shanghai can be called mavericks or independently-minded cadres. They include Wang Daohan, Rui Xingwen, Jiang Zemin, Zhu Rongji and Wu Bangguo.

26. Quoted by author's Chinese sources in Beijing.

27. SCMP, July 23, 1991.

28. For a discussion of Deng's support of Shanghai, see *The Mirror*, January 1994.

29. SCMP, April 15, 1991.

30. For a discussion of the ideas of Hu Jintao, see, for example, HKEJ, January 28, 1994; *Wen Wei Po*, January 24, 1994.

31. *Oriental Daily News* (Hong Kong), June 14, 1989.

32. *United Daily News*, October 8, 1992.

33. SCMP, March 26, 1993.

34. SCMP, June 5, 1993.

35. SCMP, April 10, 1991.

36. SCMP, August 10, 1990.

37. *Wide Angle*, June 1991.

38. Given Jiang's relationship with Li Xiannian and Chen Yun, it is not surprising that he should have co-opted ideologues under their wing.

39. In late 1993, Jiang also signed on He Xin, a former adviser to Li Peng, as his consultant on international strategic affairs. He is a leading neo-conservative.

40. For a discussion of the rise of Jiang Zemin, see SCMP, May 25, 1994.

41. NCNA, September 14, 1989.

42. Deng Xiaoping told North Korean leader Kim Il Sung that his heart was at ease with Jiang at the helm, see SCMP, October 10, 1992.

43. SCMP, November 11, 1992.

44. According to Chinese sources, Deng complained during his inspection trip to Capital Iron and Steel Works in May 1992 about "cadres in Zhongnanhai who do nothing but engage in empty talk". This is taken as a reference to Jiang Zemin and Li Peng. See also *The Mirror*, July and August, 1992.

45. *Ta Kung Pao*, October 26, 1992.

46. CNS, December 16, 1992.

47. *Ta Kung Pao*, June 15, 1992.

48. NCNA, November 22, 1992.

49. SCMP, October 15, 1992; *Hong Kong Standard*, September 11, 1992.

50. CNS, March 12, 1994.

51. After Jiang became party General Secretary, the official media heaped praise on his record in Shanghai. Yet residents and foreigners in the city said his performance as mayor and party boss was most mediocre.

52. *Wen Wei Po*, November 11, 1993.

53. *Ming Pao*, June 2, 1993.

54. For a discussion of the Qinghua Faction, see CNS, February 12, 1993.

55. SCMP, August 3, 1993.

56. SCMP, October 12, 1993.

57. SCMP, January 22, 1994.

58. NCNA, November 27, 1992.

59. Quoted by American sources travelling with Zhu in 1990.

60. *Wen Wei Po*, October 16, 1992.

61. *The Mirror*, February 1994.

62. *People's Daily*, July 23, 1992; HKCNA, July 28, 1992.

63. HKEJ, October 22, 1993.

64. CNS, April 23, 1994.

65. *Ta Kung Pao*, December 21, 1992; *China Daily*, February 1, 1993.

66. HKEJ, September 15, 1993.

67. HKEJ, March 28, 1993.

68. SCMP, December 8, 1993.

69. CNS, April 22, 1994.

70. Zhu said in October 1993 that he did not fire too many PBoC officials because if he had done so, the banking system would have been paralysed. Quoted by Chinese sources in Hong Kong.

71. Quoted by author's Chinese sources.

72. See Gao Xin and Ho Pin, *Archives of Senior Cadres*, (Taipei: The Journalist Press, 1993), p. 94.

73. NCNA, November 24, 1992; *Ming Pao*, August 26, 1993.

74. For one version of Zhu's TV message to the people of Shanghai, see Jonathan Unger, ed. *The Pro-Democracy Protests in China*, (Armonk, New York: M.E. Sharpe, 1991), p. 227.

75. SCMP, December 2, 1992.

76. SCMP, April 23, 1991.

77. SCMP, December 2, 1992.

78. HKEJ, October 22, 1993.

79. *Ming Pao*, April 4, 1994.

80. In 1993 and 1994, Zhu Rongji ensured that as much funding as was possible under the tight-money regime be made available to Shanghai and Pudong. Pudong would be to Zhu what the Great Wall was to the First Emperor Qin.

81. *Ming Pao*, June 28, 1993.

82. In spite of his skills in massaging the egos of elders who used to stay in Shanghai, Zhu ran afoul of the late president Li Xiannian, see *Ming Pao*, June 26, 1992.

83. For an assessment of Zhu's place in history, see SCMP, December 2, 1992; HKEJ, September 10, 1993.

84. *Ta Kung Pao*, October 26, 1992.

85. ibid.

86. *Ming Pao*, November 21, 1992; *United Daily News*, December 1, 1992.

87. SCMP, November 28, 1992.

88. *China Daily*, November 29, 1992.

89. HKEJ, January 1, 1993.

90. *Wen Wei Po*, December 31, 1992; SCMP, January 1, 1993.

91. SCMP, May 18, 1994.

92. In the five years after Tiananmen Square, there was an uneasy co-existence between Li and Zhu. Upon his severe heart attack and subsequent incapacitation in mid-1993, Li refused to name Zhu acting premier.

93. In the first few years after the massacre, Deng repeatedly praised Li Peng for the success of China's foreign policy. However, Li continued to receive criticism from the patriarch for foot-dragging in economic reform.

94. NCNA, December 27, 1992.

95. NCNA, November 1, 1993.

96. *Contemporary*, April 1994.

97. Largely because of support from Li Peng, Li Guixian retained his position of State Councillor despite having been widely criticised for his failure as People's Bank of China Governor.

98. *Wide Angle*, November 1993.

99. CNS, April 2, 1993.

100. For a graphic description of the pro-democracy movement in Beijing, see Unger, op. cit., pp.8-58.

101. *Wah Kiu Yat Po*, March 15, 1992; HKET, March 12, 1992.

102. *People's Daily*, October 10, 1992.

103. Author's interview with Bao Pu, son of Bao Tong.

104. SCMP, July 6, 1993.

105. *Ming Pao*, August 15, 1992.

106. HKEJ, June 29, 1993.

107. For a discussion of Zhao's "crimes", see, for example, *China Daily*, July 12, 1989; NCNA, August 18, 1991.

108. SCMP, October 30, 1989.

109. *Economic Reporter*, October 30, 1989; *The Mirror*, November 1993.

110. SCMP, October 14, 1992.

111. Quoted by Chinese sources in Beijing.

112. *Wah Kiu Yat Po*, April 19, 1993.

113. *The Mirror*, May 1994.

114. When Zhao became party chief in early 1987, he did not have control over such departments as organisation or propaganda, a factor behind his downfall in 1989.

115. SCMP, October 14, 1992.

116. *Wen Wei Po*, April 30, 1993.

117. CNS, December 8, 1992.

118. *Ming Pao*, March 31, 1993.

119. *China Review*, 1992 ed. Kuan Hsin-chi and Maurice Brosseau, (Hong Kong: Chinese University Press, 1992) p.xxii.

120. *China Youth Daily*, October 27, 1992.

121. For a discussion of the career of Yan Mingfu, see, for example, SCMP, September 22, 1993.

122. SCMP, October 19, 1992; SCMP, September 7, 1991.

123. For a description of the younger followers of Zhao, see, for example, *Pai Shing* weekly (Hong Kong), December 1, 1989.

124. *China Times* (Taipei), July 30, 1993.

125. *Ming Pao*, May 8, 1993; August 5, 1994.

126. Hu Yaobang's followers had a larger regional representation than Zhao Ziyang's partly because Hu, a former head of the Organisation Department as well as the Communist Youth League, was more adept at building his own network.

127. CNS, October 20, 1993.

128. Quoted by author's Chinese sources in Beijing.

129. For a discussion of the influence of Zhu Houze, see SCMP, May 11, 1994.

130. For a discussion of the "liberalising" influence of Li Ruihuan on ideology, see, for example, *China Review*, ed. Hsin-chi Kuan and Maurice Brosseau, (Hong Kong: Chinese University Press, 1991), pp. 20.3-20.9.

131. SCMP, June 20, 1990.

132. NCNA, June 19, 1990.

133. HKCNA, June 28, 1990; *People's Daily*, May 1, 1990.

134. *Ming Pao*, August 15, 1992.

135. *People's Daily*, June 13, 1990.

136. Li's transfer to the CPPCC, just like Qiao's move to the NPC, was a reflection of Deng's desire to accommodate the wishes of the Mainstream Faction headed by Jiang Zemin and Zhu Rongji. Li's liberalism was perceived as a threat to the Mainstream Faction.

137. *People's Daily*, March 28, 1993.

138. SCMP, April 4, 1992.

139. SCMP, October 13, 1992.

140. For an analysis of the regional affiliation of the new Central Committee members, see *The Fourteenth Party Congress and China's Future*, (Hong Kong: Contemporary Magazine Press, 1992) pp.36-41.

141. *United Daily News*, July 23, 1992.

142. For a discussion of how different provinces revised their development plans after the *nanxun*, see, for example, *Wen Wei Po*, August 17, 1992.

143. NCNA, December 7, 1992.

144. HKCNA, December 21, 1992.

145. NCNA, August 22, 1992.

146. *Ming Pao*, August 21, 1992; *Wen Wei Po*, December 21, 1992.

147. *Wide Angle*, November 1993.

148. The clout of the regional "warlords" was boosted by the fact that many heavyweight cadres had stakes in businesses in the provinces, particularly along the coast.

149. SCMP, March 18, 1993.

150. Cited by sources in Guangdong.

151. According to Chinese sources, Deng Xiaoping told Ye Jianying that his son, Ye Xuanping, would be allowed to stay in Guangdong for as long as he liked.

152. *Wen Wei Po*, June 21, 1993; *Wen Wei Po*, February 20, 1994.

153. *Ming Pao*, December 7, 1992.

154. SCMP, January 1, 1993.

155. NCNA, January 17, 1993; *United Daily News*, March 18, 1994.

156. CNS, July 15, 1993.

157. CNS, July 10, 1992; *Sing Tao Jih Pao* (Hong Kong), July 11, 1992.

158. HKET, December 31, 1992; CNS, June 20, 1993.

159. There were many instances of a conservative central cadre becoming market-oriented after having served in a coastal city for a few years.

160. The following published sources are used for Bo Xilai, *Wen Wei Po*, January 19, 1993; Chi Fulin, SCMP, August 1, 1994; Liu Chengye, HKET, July 1, 1993 and HKET, May 31, 1993; Tang Ruoxin, *Wen Wei Po*, July 16, 1993; Wu Guanzheng, CNS, December 2, 1992; Xi Jinping, HKEJ, January 11, 1994; Yu Zhengsheng, *Ming Pao*, January 16, 1993; Zhao Baojiang, *Wen Wei Po*, December 16, 1993.

161. For a discussion of the growth of regional power, see, Ho Pin, "Regional Warlords Showing Their Power," in *Hong Kong Economic Journal Monthly*, August 1992, pp.78-81.

162. *Wide Angle*, February 1992.

163. NCNA, December 6, 1992.

164. NCNA, November 19, 1992.

165. *Wen Wei Po*, January 13, 1993.

166. *Ta Kung Pao*, July 24, 1992.

167. For a discussion of the business interests of *gaoganzidi*, see *The Gang of Princelings of the Chinese Communist Party*, by Ho Pin and Gao Xin, (Taipei: China Times Press, 1992).

168. SCMP, December 2, 1992.

169. NCNA February 23, 1994.

170. Author's interviews with private entrepreneurs in Beijing and Guangdong.

171. *Wide Angle*, February 1993.

172. NCNA, December 1, 1992.

173. *Ta Kung Pao*, December 14, 1992.

174. HKCNA, October 29, 1992.

175. CNS, March 20, 1994.

176. *United Daily News*, November 5, 1993.

177. *United Daily News*, June 23, 1993.

178. *Hong Kong Commercial Daily*, January 25, 1994.

179. *Ming Pao*, March 30, 1994.

180. *Ming Pao*, December 29, 1992.

181. *Wen Wei Po*, February 23, 1993.

182. *Ming Pao*, January 28, 1994.

183. *Wen Wei Po*, March 27, 1993.

184. CNS, October 13, 1993; CNS, October 17, 1993.

185. HKCNA, March 20, 1993.

186. NCNA, March 15, 1993.

187. Author's interview with Liu Binyan.

188. The head of the Stone Corp, Wan Runnan, who fled China soon after the massacre, remained active in the overseas dissident movement. Based on author's interview with Wan.

189. HKEJ, May 28, 1993; HKCNA, March 15, 1994.

190. CNS, September 17, 1993.

191. *China Review* 1993, ed. Joseph Cheng Yu-shek & Maurice Brosseau, (Hong Kong: Chinese University Press, 1993), p. 2.41.

192. Author's interview with Wang Ruowang.

193. Dissidents who were frustrated in their business attempts partly because of official interference included Wang Dan, Zhou Duo, Zhang Xianliang, and Wang Xizhe.

194. HKET, April 29, 1993.

195. *United Daily News*, August 4, 1993.

196. HKCNA, January 28, 1994.

197. NCNA, April 15, 1994.

198. SCMP, July 2, 1993.

199. SCMP, January 29, 1994.

200. SCMP, March 2, 1994.

201. *Wen Wei Po*, February 15, 1994; CNS, February 21, 1994.

Chapter 7

1. New China News Agency (NCNA), March 1, 1994.

2. NCNA, September 2, 1994.

3. In early 1994, Taiwan President Lee Teng-hui used a native-Taiwanese expression, "stubborn as concrete", to describe the Beijing administration.

4. NCNA, July 4, 1994.

5. *South China Morning Post* (SCMP), Hong Kong, July 6, 1994.

6. *Ming Pao*, April 3, 1994.

7. *Hong Kong Economic Journal* (HKEJ), July 29, 1994.

8. *Wen Wei Po*, June 23, 1994.

9. HKEJ, August 19, 1994.

10. *Wen Wei Po*, February 21, 1994; SCMP, February 23, 1994.

11. SCMP, July 15, 1994; *Wen Wei Po*, August 31, 1994.

12. China News Service (CNS), 4 July 1994.

13. Legal Daily (Beijing), May 3, 1994.

14. NCNA, August 30, 1994; CNS, August 12, 1994; SCMP, August 13, 1994.

15. AFP, June 19, 1994.

16. SCMP, January 19, 1994.

17. NCNA, January 23, 1994.

18. *Next* magazine (Hong Kong), July 21, 1994.

19. AP, July 6, 1994.

20. NCNA, January 2, 1994.

21. SCMP, July 18, 1994.

22. Quoted by Chinese sources in Beijing.

23. CNS, April 20, 1994.

24. NCNA, September 1, 1994.

25. SCMP, November 28, 1992; *China Trade Report* monthly, (Hong Kong), June 1994.

26. *Jianghan Academy Journal* (Nanjing), Vol. III, 1994.

27. There was no official record of Jiang Zemin being transferred to Beijing in late May 1994. But it was widely reported by Chinese sources and diplomats in Shanghai and Beijing.

28. SCMP, March 29, 1994.

29. HKEJ, November 3, 1993.

30. The "duplicitous" nature of Chinese cadres was also illustrated by the large number of cadres who expressed sympathies for the students in May 1989. Chinese officials might again show support for a liberal leader after Deng's death.

31. Thanks to the so-called "psychological engineering" of Jiang Zemin, taboo subjects such as the proper relationship of the army and the state were banished from open forums. However, such topics were discussed in underground "salons".

32. *Wide Angle* monthly (Hong Kong), June 1994.

33. *Contemporary* monthly (Hong Kong), July 1994; *Wen Wei Po*, June 12, 1994.

34. Wang Dongxin's role in the coup that toppled the Gang of Four was well-known. It was discussed in such Beijing best-sellers as *Ye Jianying in 1976* and *Deng Xiaoping in 1976*.

35. *Yearbook of Who's Who in China*, 1993, (Beijing: Huaye Press, 1994), p.42.

36. SCMP, August 3, 1994.

37. *The Mirror*, September 1994.

38. *People's Liberation Army Daily*, July 29, 1994.

39. Quoted by Chinese sources.

40. *People's Daily*, July 23, 1994.

41. *People's Daily*, July 31, 1994.

42. *The Mirror*, August 1994; NCNA, August 1, 1994.

43. *People's Daily*, July 31, 1994; NCNA, July 31, 1994; HKCNA, August 1, 1994.

44. *Ming Pao*, February 2, 1994.

45. NCNA, March 1, 1994; *Ming Pao*, March 2, 1994.

46. *China Times Business Weekly* (CTBW), (Taipei), July 10, 1994; NCNA, August 31, 1994.

47. *Washington Post*, May 8, 1994.

48. SCMP, June 25, 1994.

49. For a discussion of the diplomatic role of the generals, see SCMP, July 29, 1994.

50. SCMP, August 2, 1994.

51. SCMP, July 8, 1994.

52. *People's Daily*, August 1, 1994; *PLA Daily*, August 1, 1994.

53. *Contemporary*, August 1994.

54. CTBW, July 10, 1994.

55. HKET, July 25, 1994; CTBW, July 10, 1994.

56. SCMP, July 9, 1994.

57. NCNA, September 1, 1994.

58. SCMP, August 14, 1992.

59. Army sources said that to prevent coups and internal disorder, the CMC had ordered army intelligence to boost surveillance over potentially disloyal officers.

60. SCMP, December 15, 1993.

61. NCNA, July 1, 1994.

62. NCNA, March 22, 1994.

63. *Hong Kong Economic Times* (HKET), May 10, 1994.

64. NCNA, June 1, 1994.

65. NCNA, August 16, 1994.

66. CNS, May 11, 1994.

67. HKEJ, June 23, 1994.

68. *Ming Pao*, August 21, 1994; *Newsweek*, August 22, 1994.

69. CNS, June 1, 1994.

70. SCMP, June 2, 1994.

71. Hong Kong China News Agency (HKCNA), April 22, 1994.

72. *Wen Wei Po*, July 14, 1994.

73. *Wen Wei Po*, July 5, 1994.

74. *Wen Wei Po*, July 14, 1994.

75. UPI, June 19, 1994.

76. *Ming Pao*, June 16, 1994; *Ming Pao,* June 24, 1994.

77. *Ming Pao*, July 26, 1994; *Economic Reporter* weekly (Hong Kong) July 30, 1994.

78. *Ming Pao*, July 7, 1993.

79. SCMP, June 26, 1994.

80. Cited in internal economic reports.

81. SCMP, July 28, 1994.

82. NCNA October 9, 1994; NCNA, August 1, 1994.

83. HKEJ, May 26, 1994.

84. *Ming Pao*, July 20, 1994.

85. CNS, July 14, 1994.

86. *Ming Pao*, May 28, 1994; CNS, August 15, 1994.

87. NCNA, June 28, 1994.

88. *Wen Wei Po*, July 21, 1994.

89. HKCNA, May 19, 1994; SCMP, May 18, 1994.

90. *Ming Pao*, June 24, 1993.

91. NCNA, May 31, 1994.

92. HKCNA, June 21, 1994.

93. CNS, August 21, 1994.

94. SCMP, March 31, 1994.

95. *Ming Pao*, July 30, 1994; SCMP, August 2, 1994.

96. CNS, April 22, 1994; Reuters, June 16, 1994; *Wen Wei Po*, June 14, 1994.

97. *Ming Pao*, August 19, 1994.

98. An influential American bank played a sizeable role in helping the PBoC put together China's new fiscal and exchange-rate policies of late 1993 and early 1994.

99. The year 1994 saw a further expansion of the business empires of several Deng children and relatives.

100. HKEJ, June 3, 1994.

101. NCNA, July 26, 1994.

102. HKEJ, June 3, 1994.

103. CNS, August 15, 1994; HKET, June 7, 1994.

104. *People's Daily*, August 15, 1994.

105. NCNA, July 27, 1994.

106. *People's Daily*, August 15, 1994; *United Daily News*, August 16, 1994.

107. NCNA, June 22, 1994.

108. CNS, August 15, 1994.

109. *Contemporary*, August 1994.

110. NCNA, June 22, 1994; *Wen Wei Po*, April 8, 1994.

111. NCNA, August 2, 1994.

112. SCMP, August 3, 1994.

113. *Ming Pao*, August 26, 1994.

114. *Wen Wei Po*, October 31, 1993; NCNA, August 15, 1994; *Wen Wei Po*, August 4, 1994.

115. *Wen Wei Po*, July 27, 1994.

116. CNS, August 17, 1994.

117. The amount of "special contributions" from the regions, which began in the mid-1980s, is difficult to estimate because they were not recorded in the official budget.

118. SCMP, July 21, 1994.

119. ibid.

120. *Wen Wei Po*, July 21, 1994.

121. In early 1994, Zhu Rongji and his senior PBoC staff made enquiries of bank officials in Guangdong concerning the exact fiscal conditions of the province.

122. *Wen Wei Po*, June 25, 1994.

123. Quoted by Chinese sources in Beijing.

124. "The State, Civil Society, and Uncivil Society", a paper written by Dali L. Yang and presented at the Association for Asian Studies Annual Convention, Boston, March 24-27, 1994.

125. Gordon White, "Democratisation and Economic Reform in China", *Australian Journal of Chinese Affairs*, January 1994.

126. *People's Daily*, June 20, 1994.

127. SCMP, August 8, 1994.

128. NCNA, July 11, 1994; HKCNA, July 24, 1994.

129. HKCNA, May 31, 1994.

130. SCMP, June 22, 1994.

131. By mid-1994, even Wang Dan had indicated a wish to start his own business.

132. *Wide Angle*, June 1994.

133. SCMP, June 7, 1994.

134. *Ming Pao*, July 12, 1994.

135. *Ming Pao*, July 18, 1994.

136. *Ming Pao*, April 28, 1994.

137. For a discussion of the influence of Hong Kong culture on the mainland, see *Contemporary*, June 1994.

138. *Wen Wei Po*, July 7, 1994.

139. NCNA, July 4, 1994.

140. *Ming Pao*, August 6, 1994.

141. *Legal Daily*, July 21, 1994; *China Daily*, August 3, 1994; AFP, July 21, 1994.

142. For example, in September 1994, about 100 investors in the ill-fated Qingyuan Tongyu International Futures Commodities Brokers Co, which was located in a city a few hours from Guangzhou, protested outside the premises of the Guangdong Government. They claimed to have lost 300 million yuan. See *Ming Pao*, September 3, 1994. The phenomenon of *gumin* in action was also illustrated in Russia at about the same time: the incident of the defaulting MMM Co, over which investors staged massive protests.

143. SCMP, August 14, 1992.

144. *Wen Wei Po*, June 23, 1994.

145. For an analysis of General Ba and his successors in the Shanghai garrison, see *Wide Angle*, August 1994.

146. NCNA, August 16, 1994; *Wen Wei Po*, August 30, 1994.

147. *Looking at China with a Third Eye*, (Taiyuan: Shansi People's Press, 1994). This book became a bestseller after the publicity generated about its "political message".

148. SCMP, August 17, 1994.
149. CNS, March 24, 1989.
150. *Ming Pao*, December 16, 1992.
151. Quoted by Chinese sources in Hong Kong.
152. Under Zhao Ziyang's administration, other places which had contemplated a limited degree of "participatory politics" and "direct elections" included the Tianjin economic development zone.

Index

Ai Zhisheng 171,173

agriculture 55, 60-61, 66, 68-70, 79-80, 99, 129-130, 157, 167, 179, 183, 202, 350, 358, 408, 410, 412

Agriculture, Ministry of 98, 102, 130, 331, 389

All China Federation for Industry and Commerce (ACFIC) 301, 376, 420

All China Federation of Trade Unions (ACFTU) 273-276

Amnesty International 156, 265, 267

Anhui Province 313, 360

Anti-Rightist Movement 36, 45, 135-137, 146, 151, 168

arms sales 200

Asia 51, 53, 76, 109, 110, 114, 127, 178, 189, 197, 301, 377, 398

Asia Watch (Human Rights Watch/Asia) 156, 265, 266, 267

Asia-Pacific Region 127, 128, 141, 324

Association of South-East Asian Nations (ASEAN) 368, 398

austerity programme 24, 28, 47, 64, 76, 107, 119-120, 123-126, 129, 132-133; 285, 331, 334-335, 346, 351, 361, 366, 369, 406, 417, 418, 422

16-point programme 345

Australia 87, 140

Ba Zhongtan 238, 261, 340, 426

Bai Lanfeng 380

Bai Nansheng 422

Bangladesh 220

bankruptcy, 345, 405, 425; bankruptcy law 405

banks (also banking) 20, 26-27, 71-72, 77-78, 84, 87, 89, 91-92, 97-

98, 100, 111-112, 118-120, 123-124, 128, 130-131, 133, 290, 302, 309, 331, 342, 344
Agriculture Bank 91, 123
Import and Export Credit Bank 91
People's Bank of China 27, 56, 91, 111, 120, 123-2, 124, 161, 186, 191, 245, 254, 314, 319, 331, 341-342, 346, 348, 352, 406-407
State Long-term Development Trust Bank 91
Bao Tong 34-35, 140, 155, 245, 269, 293, 354, 358
baojia huhang 198-199
Bauhinia 39, 117, 167
Beijing Military Region 207, 209-210, 213-215, 220, 260
Beijing University (Beida) 36, 99-100, 169, 177, 185, 196, 260, 267-268, 278, 360, 374, 380-381, 390
bingshang (also *junshang*) 227-229, 231-232, 236-237, 397
Bo Xicheng 247, 254-256, 328, 372
Bo Xilai 369
Bo Yibo 6, 10, 98, 183, 249-252, 254, 328, 369, 372, 382
Bohai 414
bonds 101-103, 112, 115, 412, 422
bourgeois liberalisation 3-4, 8-9, 11, 30-31, 33-34, 40, 42-43, 55, 113, 135-140, 143, 145-148, 150, 152, 161, 165-166, 171-172, 176, 203, 207-208, 239, 244, 251, 256, 278, 294, 303, 323, 332, 338, 348, 354, 363
Britain 71
budget 53, 57, 90, 188, 197, 199, 205, 230, 234, 287, 289, 400, 415

army budget 200-201
budget deficits 404, 416
Burma 108-109, 398

Canada 89, 347
Cao Pengsheng 210, 213
Cao Shuangming 214
Capital Iron and Steel Works (Shougang) 20, 46, 58, 77, 90, 339, 344
capitalism 8, 10-12, 19-21, 75, 82, 105, 111, 113, 136-137, 139, 147-148, 153, 158-159, 162, 174, 180-181, 232-234, 248, 250, 275, 343, 349, 353, 370, 401
quasi-capitalist road 77, 136, 186, 188, 324, 353
Catholics 153-154
Ceausescu, Nicolae 428
censorship 203, 273, 304, 389, 422
Central Advisory Commission (CAC) 10, 98, 167, 162, 165, 213, 190, 213, 249, 250-252, 328
Central Committee Document No. 2, 18-19, 21-22, 75-77, 132, 178
Document No. 4 78, 82, 110, 364, 366, 372
Document No. 5 19, 79
Central Commission for the Comprehensive Management of Social Order (CCCMSO) 258
Central Commission for Disciplinary Inspection (CCDI) 189-190, 209, 312, 327, 355, 385, 387
Central Intelligence Agency (CIA) 140
Central Military Commission (CMC) 33, 38, 40, 150, 194, 197, 199-200, 202-209, 212-224, 226-228, 230-238, 257, 304, 326-329, 335,

337, 340, 392, 393, 394-395,
396-397, 400

Central Party School   21, 37, 40, 80,
126, 138, 167, 188, 197, 199,
279, 284, 286, 336, 340-341, 391,
420

central planning   10, 51, 161, 164,
343, 349, 351-353, 378

China Times   178

Chai Ling   208

Changcheng Electronics, Machinery
and High-Technology Corp   120,
270, 314, 353

Chen Jinhua   15, 23, 129, 330, 351,
409

Chen Junsheng   412

Chen Muhua   306

Chen Shineng   318

Chen Weili   256

Chen Xiaolu   380

Chen Xilian   199

Chen Xitong   13, 139, 140, 176, 327,
334, 392

Chen Yuan   56, 91, 124, 191, 247,
254-255, 328, 370

Chen Yun   16, 32, 49, 53, 56, 60-61,
76, 110, 136, 161-164, 171, 197-
180, 186-188, 192, 195, 228, 249,
250-251, 255-256, 280-281, 306,
310, 326, 328, 331-332, 338, 349,
352, 372, 380, 388, 400, 408

Chen Zhihan   315

Chen Ziming   35, 266, 269

Chengdu   105, 110, 358, 368

Chengdu Military Region   210, 213-
214, 398

Chi Fulin   369

Chi Haotian   34, 195, 197, 201, 203,
206, 213, 217, 219, 221, 230,
238, 252, 328, 395, 399

Chiang Ching-kuo   128, 428

China Daily   101, 185, 321, 350

China International Trust and
Investment Corp (CITIC)   98,
140, 253, 256

China News Service (CNS)   11, 24,
41, 58, 61, 63, 96, 102-103, 105,
203, 232, 259, 260, 275, 278,
287, 290, 296, 300, 303, 319,
331, 346, 378

China Sociological Society   423

China Youth Daily   247, 359

Chinese Academy of Sciences (CAS)
40, 131, 140-141, 147, 158, 172,
183, 187, 189, 190, 279

Chinese Academy of Social Sciences
(CASS)   41, 57, 63, 67, 140-141,
147, 158, 172, 183, 187, 189-190,
223-224, 246, 278-279, 293, 304,
332

Chinese People's Political Consultative
Conference (CPPCC)   87, 99,
114, 117-118, 127, 174, 186, 190,
242, 247, 239, 284, 295-296,
299-302, 305-306, 310, 320, 332,
346, 363, 374-376, 385-386, 389,
410, 429

Chinese Non-Governmental Chamber
of Commerce (CNGCC)   376,
420

Chinese Social Sciences Quarterly
422

Chinese Business Times   417

civil service   252, 285-286, 291-292,
396

civil society   384, 410, 418-419, 421-
422, 424

clans   153-155, 262, 338, 343, 429,
430

class struggle   161, 188, 256, 262,
264-265, 294

Clinton, Bill   2, 238, 338

Cohen, Jerome 368
command economy
  (also diktat economy) 117, 126,
    331-332, 346, 361, 409
Commission for Political and Legal
    Affairs (CPLA) 312, 269, 270,
    312
Commission of Science, Technology
    and Industry for National
    Defence (COSTIND) 254
commune 427
communism 5-6, 8, 49, 188, 242,
    248, 250, 284, 298, 324
Communist Youth League (CYL)
    274, 291, 359-361, 428
Confucianism 391
Contemporary 257-258
corruption 241-242, 245, 249, 291,
    295, 301, 307-316, 352, 368, 370,
    385-388, 397, 401, 405, 411, 429
coup d'etat 128, 281, 320, 394, 399,
    400-401
courts 256, 263-300, 304, 308-309,
    312, 387, 424
crime 256, 258-261, 264-266, 268-
    269, 295, 310, 313, 356-357, 387
cross leadership 247, 329, 385
cult of personality 36-38, 40-42, 238
Cultural Revolution
  (also Ten Years of Chaos) 5, 35,
    41, 80, 253, 285, 299, 312, 334,
    385, 400

Dai Qing 306
Dai Xianglong 331
Dalian 115, 366, 369, 414
Daqing Oilfield 149
Daqiuzhuang 270
democracy 240, 242-244, 252, 259,
    26-261, 265, 267, 271, 274, 279,

    285, 297, 299-303, 309-310, 317-
    33, 347, 354, 360, 377, 379, 380-
    381, 424, 428-429
  pro-democracy movements 46,
    189, 252, 261, 310, 360
Deng Liqun 136, 142, 145, 148, 161,
    165, 172, 183, 186, 190-191
Deng Nan 254, 316, 328, 395
Deng Pufang 46, 311, 395
Deng Rong 254, 395
Deng Xiaoping
  1-59 *passim,* 88-89, 117, 119, 121,
    191, 249-251, 263, 284, 306, 320,
    372, 379, 372, 379, 382, 391-392,
    404, 408, 410, 428-429
  views on and relations with the
    army 32-33, 190-191, 197, 199,
    201-204, 209-222, 225, 228, 231,
    235, 258, 396, 397, 398, 401
  views on bourgeois liberalisation
    42, 135-139, 142-151
  relations with the Communist
    Youth League 360-361, 363
  on corruption 45, 310-311, 314-
    315, 388, 411
  on dissidents and rightists 34-36
  on the Eastern bloc and Russia 6,
    29, 51, 245
  controversy over the economic
    growth rate 14-15, 23-25, 27,
    61-62, 64, 124, 126, 364
  "economics first" theory 4, 5, 157
  relations with Jiang Zemin 236-
    238, 330
  relations with Li Peng 348-353
  relations with Mao Zedong 48
  on the market economy and market
    reforms 4, 6, 10-11, 18-19, 54,
    56-57
  the *nanxun* 75-80, 82-82
  on neo-authoritarianism 128, 131-

137, 426

personality cult of Deng   36-41

on political reform   40, 239-242, 286, 317, 384-386

on regionalism   5, 12, 22, 59, 367-370, 412, 416-418

on science and technology   7, 279, 280

on Shanghai   16, 26, 28, 110-113

relations with the Shanghai Faction 333-340

on the succession problem   323-329, 425

on party supremacy   235-248

on the special economic zones   17, 24

on thought liberation   11-13, 43, 44

relations with Zhao Ziyang   354, 357, 359, 377

relations with Zhu Rongji   343-344, 346, 348

Deng Zhenglai   422

Deng Zhifang   41, 45, 46, 128, 229, 253, 256

development zones   345, 408

dictatorship of the proletariat   242, 256, 258, 263-264, 270-271, 286, 292, 317, 419

Ding Guan'gen   171-172, 174, 270, 327, 335, 356, 391

Ding Henggao   228, 254

Ding Shisun   301

dissidents   251, 258, 260, 263, 265, 266-267, 269, 671, 277, 301, 310, 323, 336, 379, 380, 400-421, 423, 428-429

Dong Fureng   378, 407

Du Runsheng   76

Du Tiehuan   215

Du Ying   191

Duan Lunyi   413

East-Asiatic model   127, 129

Eastern bloc   148, 159, 167, 207, 218, 234, 248, 253, 317, 329, 353, 377, 429

economic development zones (EDZs) 113-116, 118, 120-121, 408

education   32, 67, 130, 147, 152, 156-157, 159-160, 171-172, 176, 179, 196, 200, 205, 208, 217, 232, 243, 245, 256, 266, 277, 279, 285, 287, 292, 304, 328, 330-331, 377-378, 393, 400, 409, 429

Eight Immortals   39, 249, 255

elections   119, 158, 185-186, 281, 303, 309, 317-319, 368, 370, 390, 420, 428-429

cha'er elections   317

electronics   62, 113, 120, 130, 200, 202, 224, 232, 237, 270, 290, 316, 330, 336-337, 340, 353, 358, 402

Elegy of the Barracks   238, 340

Elite   177

enterprises   17, 20, 24, 54-59, 62, 71-77, 80, 82, 84-90, 92, 94-97, 99, 101-102, 104, 112, 114-115, 120-123, 127-128, 131, 138, 147, 154, 180-181, 184, 188, 230, 240, 246-248, 261, 272, 275-276, 280, 288, 295-296, 315-316, 331, 341, 344, 346, 350, 358, 364, 366-368, 370, 372-377, 387-389, 402-407, 410, 412-415, 419-422, 424

enterprise reform   20, 387, 389, 404

private enterprises   77, 90, 93, 95, 97, 99, 127, 280, 372, 374, 376-

377, 407, 419, 420
private entrepreneurs   85, 87, 95,
    98, 100, 138, 154, 327, 355, 366,
    371, 372, 374, 376-381, 411,
    418-420, 423, 429
rural enterprises   78, 97, 102, 154
village and township enterprises
    24, 76, 80, 94, 96, 114, 122, 368,
    375, 413, 415, 419

Fan Gang   422
Fang Lizhi   35, 77, 138, 239, 269,
    271, 379
Fang Zuqi   215
federal system   418
Fei Xiaotong   109, 298-299, 316
Finance, Ministry of   89, 161, 314
financial contract responsibility
    system (FCRS)   90
financial reform   16, 91, 103, 118,
    121-122
Five-Year Plans   14, 55, 157
    Eighth Five-Year Plan   7, 13-14,
    23, 56-57, 59, 61, 63, 95, 98,
    101, 116
Fok, Henry   115, 369
Foreign Affairs, Ministry of   257, 330
foreign exchange   67, 92, 99, 114,
    230, 389, 396, 410
foreign investment   21, 87, 100, 107,
    113, 116, 167, 227, 246, 367, 386
foreign policy   182, 196, 238, 330,
    352, 397, 398
Fortnightly Chat   408
Foshan   262, 367
Four Cardinal Principles   4, 37, 55,
    78, 84, 137, 145-146, 152, 181,
    241, 256, 270, 282, 287, 303, 340
Fourth Field Army   400
France   197

Friedman, Milton   96, 125
Fu Quanyou   197, 210, 213, 215, 221,
    238, 328, 397
Fu Rui   254, 328, 355, 370
Fujian Province   17, 86, 95, 338, 370,
    376
fupin   42, 414
futures   409-410, 412-413, 424

Gang of Four   21, 47, 128, 161, 164-
    166, 171, 173, 332, 354, 362,
    394, 399
Gansu Province   358
Gao Di   21, 171, 179, 186, 189, 332,
    340
Gao Qiang   89
Gao Shan   379
Gao Shangquan   87, 126
gaoganzidi   46, 253, 254-256, 311,
    317, 369-370, 411
Ge Hongsheng   318
General Agreement on Tariffs and
    Trade (GATT)   92, 410
General Logistics Department (GLD)
    230, 238
General Office of the Central
    Committee   7, 336, 358
General Political Department (GPD)
    199, 203-209, 213-216, 269, 231-
    232, 236, 238, 395
General Staff Department (GSD)
    217, 222, 224, 226-227, 331
Germany   41, 109, 127, 131, 228,
    307, 385, 389
getihu   80, 90, 94, 97-98, 100, 105,
    114, 131, 138, 154, 371-372, 375,
    377, 380, 422
Gold Coast   16, 22, 88-89, 106-107,
    324, 364, 378
Gorbachev, Mikhail   29, 43, 62, 136,

184-185, 194

grain   54-55, 60, 65-68, 80, 93-94,
    130, 154, 167, 195, 233, 295,
    388, 396, 408-409
    grain as the key link   67, 80, 408
Great Leap Forward   22-23, 25, 46-
    48, 76, 150, 164, 350
Gu Hui   209, 211, 213
Gu Mu   114
Gu Shanqing   210, 213
guandao   182
Guangdong Province   10, 15-16, 22,
    58, 60-61, 74, 76, 88, 90, 94,
    101, 107, 110, 115-119, 121, 123,
    130, 160, 175, 180, 208, 227,
    237, 247, 252, 254, 258, 260,
    262, 276, 283-285, 289, 309, 311,
    334, 354-357, 364, 366-367, 370,
    373-374, 376, 382, 385-386, 407-
    408, 412-418, 423, 428
Guangming Daily   145, 170, 176,
    180, 272, 292
Guangxi Province   67, 107, 109, 316,
    357, 369, 417
Guangzhou   15, 22, 74, 94, 102, 104-
    105, 115-119, 124-125, 207, 210-
    211, 213, 215-216, 229, 248, 251,
    260-261, 272, 284, 289, 301, 334,
    343, 366-367, 369, 376, 392, 408,
    414-417, 420-422, 424
Guizhou Province   54, 60, 81, 107,
    109, 110, 120, 204, 315, 317-318,
    361, 365, 408, 424
Gulf War   7, 61, 140-141, 190, 198-
    199, 201-202, 223-224, 226, 237,
    279, 306, 337
gumin   104-106, 410, 424-425
Guo Luoji   36, 269
Guo Shuqing   342, 390
Guo Zhengmin   315

Hainan Academy of Economic
    Research   380
Hainan Province   2, 6, 16, 52, 66, 78,
    102, 104, 107, 109, 113, 115,
    122-123, 125, 247, 311, 314-315,
    334, 355, 361, 366, 368-369, 380,
    396
Han Fucai   311
He Guanghui   63, 86, 409
He Jingzhi   21, 165-166, 171, 172,
    186
He Long   228, 254
He Pengfei   254
He Qizhong   214
He Xin   140-141, 158, 190, 223, 338,
    375
Hebei Province   120, 125, 153-154,
    160, 171, 210, 278, 283, 314, 370
Heilongjiang Province   109, 247, 251,
    365-366, 406
Henan Province   68, 70, 153, 165,
    254, 283, 365
Heng Tong Group   380-381
Hong Kong   3, 11, 15-18, 20, 22-24,
    26, 28-29, 32, 36, 39, 40, 46, 70,
    75, 77-79, 90, 97-100, 102, 104,
    106-107, 109-110, 112-115, 117,
    119, 124, 139, 140, 147, 167,
    173, 176, 178, 190-191, 200, 203,
    205, 214, 216, 218, 225, 228-232,
    241, 245, 249, 254-255, 257, 263,
    270, 276, 287, 290, 299, 300-301,
    304-305, 307, 309, 310-311, 314-
    316, 318, 329, 341, 346, 348,
    352, 353, 357, 365-366, 367-370,
    382, 386, 396-398, 400, 414-416,
    418, 421-413, 428-429
Hong Kong China News Agency
    (HKCNA)   55, 62, 65, 67-68, 75,
    81, 92-93, 99, 123, 149, 262, 316,
    374, 388, 404

Hong Kong Economic Journal 147,
    220
Hong Xuezhi   220, 400
Hong Yonglin   315
household contract responsibility sys-
    tem   57-58, 66, 68-70, 79-80, 88,
    90, 101, 120, 167, 184, 225, 246,
    279, 427
Hubei Province   5, 81, 101, 183, 247,
    305-306, 365, 416
Hu Angang   131, 397
Hu Deping   361, 420
Hu Jintao   171, 172, 276, 284-285,
    327-328, 335, 341-342, 391
Hu Jiwei   169-170, 177, 304, 378
Hu Ping   41, 120
Hu Qiaomu   187, 191
Hu Qili   3, 11-12, 34, 49, 152, 156,
    165, 380, 336, 358, 360, 382,
    427-428
Hu Sheng   140, 172, 183
Hu Yaobang   1-2, 11-13, 23, 32, 34,
    40, 43, 45, 47, 49, 59, 83, 126,
    27, 136, 138, 145-146, 152, 156,
    165-166, 172, 185, 202, 219, 237,
    240, 250-251, 253, 274, 280, 310,
    320, 324, 331, 333, 338, 346,
    347, 352, 354-355, 357-361, 368,
    379, 420
Hua Guofeng   38-39, 41, 146, 164,
    171, 238, 339, 341
Huang Ju   13, 16, 111-112, 284
Huang Puping   19, 52, 173
Huizhou   315-316
human rights   247, 263, 265, 268,
    287, 298, 321, 347
Hunan Province   81, 149, 154, 183,
    202, 357, 365, 417
Hungary   53, 428

ideology   5, 8, 29, 31, 86, 136, 144,
    146-147, 149, 157, 161, 165,
    172-174, 177, 191-192, 205, 222-
    223, 226, 234, 236, 254, 278,
    289, 295, 331, 340, 344-345,
    361-362, 422, 424
ideologues   7, 32, 34, 48, 52, 113,
    137-140, 143-144, 148-149, 151,
    157, 161, 163, 168-170, 174-175,
    180-191, 199, 206, 314, 223, 238,
    250, 278-279, 323-324, 326, 334,
    337, 343, 359, 362, 363
ideological and political work   5, 32,
    74, 113, 145-147, 151, 160, 175,
    182, 206, 210, 223, 244, 295,
Iliescu, Ion   428
imperialism   139-142, 159, 223, 234
Independent Commission Against
    Corruption (Hong Kong)   311
India   109, 299
inflation   25-28, 40, 43, 47, 53, 63,
    64-66, 94, 107, 130, 133, 182,
    188, 200, 232, 258, 272, 274,
    295, 345, 376, 388-390, 408, 412,
    421-422
infrastructure   16-17, 54, 61, 68, 77,
    87, 112, 116, 345, 396, 413
Inner Mongolia   70, 108-210, 287-
    288, 417
intellectuals   11, 20-21, 35-36, 39,
    45, 48, 55, 136-138, 140, 151-
    152, 155-156, 158-159, 168-170,
    172-173, 176-179, 181, 186-187,
    209, 231, 239, 241-242, 251, 255,
    266-267, 271, 277, 279-280, 293,
    302-306, 310, 326, 337, 339, 340,
    347, 353-355, 357-361, 363, 368-
    369, 378-380, 389, 417, 419, 421,
    428
Israel   2

Japan 41, 49, 701, 109, 115, 128, 130, 141, 189, 250, 253, 320, 330, 343, 356, 359, 371, 400, 410, 412
Jia Zhijie 13
Jiang Chunyun 327, 364
Jiang Jiafu 108
Jiang Liu 130, 279, 332
Jiang Qing 42, 161, 164, 166, 349
Jiang Zemin 7, 15, 31, 37, 39, 108, 136, 143, 153, 155, 159, 168, 182, 185, 246-247, 249-250, 256, 270, 273, 277, 290, 294, 300, 307, 310, 313, 319, 323, 327-329, 349, 359, 361, 382, 384, 390, 404, 414, 418, 427, 429
   views on agriculture 55, 61, 69-70
   views on and relations with the army 194-195, 197-198, 201-202, 206-207, 209, 211-213, 217-219, 223, 227, 235-236, 335, 393-394, 399-401
   relations with Deng Xiaoping 41-42, 425-426
   on enterprises 71, 82
   on leftism 9, 173-177, 338
   relations with Li Xiannian 252
   on macro-level economic control 63, 121
   on the political system 243-264, 284-285, 296-298
   on reform 11, 124, 391
   relations with the Shanghai Faction 111, 320, 332-333, 336
Jiang Wei 315
Jiangsu Province 22, 26, 73, 76, 123, 167, 183, 369, 391, 416
Jiangxi Province 171, 342, 370
Jianlibao Group 116
Jilin Province 63, 72, 109, 189, 213, 330, 406
Jin Xin 389
Jinan Military Region 210, 215
joint ventures 16, 21, 24, 74-75, 77, 85, 93, 96, 112, 115, 178, 184, 228, 231, 246, 372, 405, 423
judiciary 229, 241, 263-264, 266, 268, 316, 384, 386
   judicial independence 44
June 4 massacre 1-4, 111, 107, 147, 149, 162, 164, 187, 189, 194, 206, 220, 211, 213, 239, 241, 249, 253, 255, 260, 263, 272, 277, 299, 305, 332, 340, 358, 362, 369, 371, 380-381, 390, 392, 418

Kazakhstan 109
Kui Fulin 222
Kumagai Gumi 115
Kuomintang 24, 248, 334

labour 70, 80-81, 98, 116, 119, 146, 152, 170, 266-267, 271-277, 283, 309, 330, 360, 373, 389, 416, 426
   labour union 277, 429
laosanjie 226
Leading Group on Finance and Economics 330
Leading Group on Foreign Affairs 330, 352
Leading Group on Overseas Propaganda 172
Lee Kuan Yew 428
leftism 11, 20-21, 31, 39, 47-48, 145, 166-170, 172-173, 179, 309, 340, 363, 369, 378
Lei Feng 159, 175, 189, 203, 261, 281, 294, 362

Lei Yu 22, 104, 118, 366, 368
legislature 30, 234, 247, 262, 276,
    303, 307, 309, 313, 319, 321,
    329, 375, 385-386, 429
Li Boyong 276
Li Chang 378
Li Gang 127
Li Guixian 27, 111, 186, 319, 353
Li Hao 366
Li Jiange 342
Li Jinai 214
Li Jing 214
Li Jiulong 210, 213, 398
Li Ka-shing 17-18, 46
Li Keqiang 360
Li Lanqing 316, 327
Li Lianjin 423
Li Luoli 368
Li Peng 3, 6, 15, 41, 45, 52, 54, 56,
    59, 61, 130, 140, 124, 145, 178,
    158, 161, 167, 172, 174, 186,
    190, 197, 223, 256, 267, 280,
    291, 310, 316, 319-320, 327, 330,
    335, 337-339, 341, 359, 389-390,
    404, 409, 412, 425, 428
    views on agriculture 68
    on the austerity programme 63-
    64, 129, 350, 401
    on defence 201-202
    relations with Deng Xiaoping 13,
    23, 27, 344, 382, 384
    on enterprises 72-72, 95-97, 101
    on Guangdong and the special eco-
    nomic zones 114, 118
    relations with the June 4 crack-
    down and dissidents 170, 196,
    263-265, 304, 392
    on political reform 242, 285-286
    on price reform 66, 352
    relations with the "pro-Soviet fac-
    tion" 253, 331, 333

    on regionalism 365
    relations with Shanghai 111, 348
    on the Three Gorges project 305-
    307
    relations with Zhao Ziyang 356
    relations with Zhu Rongji 345-
    346
Li Qiyan 172, 318
Li Rui 169-170, 177, 307
Li Ruihuan 5, 7, 35, 99, 166, 172-
    175, 180, 187, 244, 247, 282,
    293, 294, 299-302, 320, 327, 329,
    340, 347, 361, 382, 393
Li Shenzhi 279
Li Tieying 186, 253, 277, 318, 327,
    331, 353
Li Tsung-dao 4
Li Xiannian 14, 31-32, 187, 249, 252,
    331, 337-338, 349, 359, 401
Li Xiaoshi 316, 353, 388
Li Xilin 213
Li Ximing 21, 68, 171-172, 281,
    318, 327, 334, 392
Li Yining 100-101, 106, 343, 360,
    390
Li Youwei 366, 368
Li Ziliu 301, 367
Liang Ningguang 417
Liang Xiang 310, 312, 368
Liaoning Province 38, 73, 109, 122,
    189, 219, 230, 267, 283, 365,
    404, 407
Liberation Daily 12, 27, 52, 166, 173
Light Industry, Ministry of 290, 350
Lin Biao 38, 213, 339, 400
Lin Hanxiong 311-312
Lin Ruo, 61, 116, 386
Lin Yifu, Justin 422
Liu Anyuan 213, 215
Liu Binyan 138, 377, 379
Liu Chengye 370

Liu Ji 336
Liu Jiang 331, 389
Liu Jingsong 209, 225
Liu Mingkang 370
Liu Shaoqi 165, 254, 355
Liu Xirong 102
Liu Yonghao 421
Liu Zhengwei 110
Liu Zhongde 172
Liu Zhongli 122, 20, 331, 415
Looking at China with a Third Eye
    426
Lou Jiwei 342, 390
Lu Feng 171, 325
Lu Ping 348
Luo Gan 186, 259, 286, 290, 331
Luo Yun'guang 311

Ma Dayou 305
Ma Lin 110
Mainstream Faction 33, 320, 323,
    329, 332, 382, 384, 418
Mammonism 81, 176, 179-180, 229,
    232
Mao Zedong 2, 23, 38, 48, 53, 59,
    68, 80, 137, 148-150, 160, 166,
    188, 219, 223, 250, 338, 385, 393
    Mao Zedong Thought 38, 137,
    250
    Maoism 4, 8, 148, 157, 165, 168,
    173, 180, 182-183, 188, 225
market (also market place) 2, 8, 10-
    13, 16, 18-19, 24, 26, 30-31, 52-
    57, 64-67, 70, 72-77, 79-82, 84-
    85, 87-88, 90, 92-93, 95-96, 97,
    99, 101, 103-110, 114-115, 118-
    119, 123, 125-132, 136-137, 141,
    148, 158, 160, 164-165, 169-170,
    174-175, 178-181, 183-189, 191,
    200, 229, 231-233, 244, 251, 258,
262, 264-265, 284, 289, 291,
    307-308, 314-315, 321-326, 331-
    332, 337-339, 343-344, 346, 349-
    354, 358, 366-373, 375-376, 378-
    381, 386-389, 391, 396, 399,
    401-404, 407-413, 416, 419, 423-
    425, 429
market reforms 42, 45, 49, 76-77,
    165, 169, 183-184, 191, 259, 315,
    322-325, 332, 343-344, 358, 378,
    382, 389, 391, 399, 401, 409,
    410, 429
martial law 32, 36, 139, 194, 196,
    203-204, 210, 214, 249, 257, 304,
    358, 425
Marx 4, 18, 39, 43, 126, 138, 162,
    181, 183, 253, 324, 383-384, 419,
    Marxism 4, 8, 11-12, 16, 37-38,
    41, 43-44, 46, 54, 81-82, 137,
    143, 146, 148, 156, 162, 179-180,
    209, 246, 250, 270, 278, 281,
    290, 302, 340
Marxism-Leninism 4, 8, 41, 137,
    209, 246, 270, 278, 281, 297
mass movements 4, 142, 147, 157,
    159, 160, 169-170, 175, 268, 311,
    314
Miao Fuchun 412
middle class 138, 377, 419
Ming Dynasty 185
Ming Pao 178, 270
millionaires 90, 379, 380, 421, 425
Ministry of International Trade and
    Industry (Japan) 330, 343
money supply 23, 64, 91, 133
Mongolia 70, 108-109, 210, 287-
    288, 417
Most Favoured Nation status (MFN)
    35
Muslim 59, 109, 223

Nande Economic Group 374
Nanjing 36, 123, 197, 209, 210-211,
213-215, 222
Nanjing Military Region 209
nanxun 2-3, 15, 17-25, 30-33, 36,
39, 42-45, 49-50, 52, 54, 64, 75-
76, 79-83, 106, 110, 113, 119,
124, 126, 128, 132, 136, 148,
164, 166-168, 170-171, 178-179,
181, 183, 190, 198-199, 213, 227,
245, 247-248, 258, 280, 313-314,
321, 324-326, 339-340, 351-352,
354, 360, 363-364, 367, 369, 418
National People's Congress (NPC)
15, 22, 27, 30, 35, 66, 68, 89, 98,
106, 152, 159, 167, 173, 179,
186, 198-199, 201-202, 229, 231,
235-236, 240-242, 247, 249, 263,
276-277, 279, 289, 293, 297,
301-310, 313, 315, 317-320, 327,
329-331, 335, 337-338, 351, 353,
358, 360, 363, 366, 375-377, 382,
385-387, 389, 392-393, 414, 428,
429
navy 200, 221
neo-authoritarianism 390
Nepal 109, 299
New Party 49, 365
Ni Zhifu 171, 275
Nie Li 228, 254
Ningxia Province 122
North Korea 109, 398
Northern Expedition 11-12, 334

Olympics 167, 176, 268, 294
Organisation Department 117, 151,
155, 246, 249, 254, 274, 278,
281, 284-285, 288, 292, 317-318,
355, 359, 365, 370, 372, 391
Ou Guangyuan 367

ownership 54-55, 82-87, 95-96, 98,
100-101, 103, 137, 181, 247, 343,
368, 403-404, 421

Pakistan 109, 218, 299
Pan Weiming 172, 347
Pao, Y.K. Sir, 316, 373-374
Party Congress, 13th 3, 34, 55, 57,
59, 83, 95-96, 165, 196, 240-242,
244-245, 251, 293
14th Party Congress 18, 23, 30,
33, 34, 37, 82, 168, 170-172, 178,
186, 196, 211, 213-214, 217, 221,
223, 225, 238, 247, 251, 253,
281, 323, 325, 327, 329, 334-335,
339, 340, 343-344, 349, 354,
357-358, 361, 363, 364, 371
Party School Forum 420
patriotism 17, 41, 149, 152, 157,
175-178, 340
Patten, Chris 29, 423
peaceful evolution 2, 6, 8-9, 20, 40,
42-43, 49, 53, 96, 135, 137-140,
142, 148, 151-152, 169, 175-176,
186, 188, 191, 239, 244, 256,
258, 287, 296-297, 349, 379
Pearl River Delta 367, 379
Peng Zhen 159, 191, 249, 254, 328,
349, 355, 370, 332, 382, 400
People's Armed Police (PAP) 105,
208, 212, 233, 238, 254, 256-257,
259-262, 277, 316, 340, 389, 393,
400, 426
People's Bank of China (PBoC) 27,
56, 91, 111, 120, 123-2, 124, 161,
186, 191, 245, 254, 314, 319,
331, 341-342, 346, 348, 352,
406-407
People's Daily 7, 21, 36, 41, 67, 85,
97, 137-138, 145, 150, 152, 155,

157-158, 169-170, 173-174, 176-
177, 179, 189-190, 196, 206, 217,
273, 281, 294-295, 297, 302, 315,
332, 340, 390, 413, 419
People's Liberation Army (PLA) 32-
33, 150, 193-202, 204-212, 214-
218, 220-239, 245, 252, 254,
257-258, 260-261, 324, 332, 340,
345, 349, 368, 393-400, 426, 429,
People's Liberation Army Daily 32,
194-195, 206, 214, 217, 219, 221,
225-226, 229, 237-238, 341
police 30, 36, 78, 104, 156, 178,
182, 256-262, 266, 269, 274, 277,
287-288, 315-316, 322, 329, 379,
380, 424
  police state 2, 4, 30, 128, 241,
256, 258, 261, 383-384, 417
political reform 2-3, 31, 40, 45, 49, 133,
169, 170, 186, 196, 329, 240, 242-
244, 248, 252, 256, 258, 269, 273,
277, 285, 297, 303, 317, 321, 340,
354, 363, 384
price reform 47, 61, 64-66, 79, 82,
92-93, 101, 352, 408
princelings 254-256, 310, 328, 372
productivity 5, 10, 16, 20, 53-54, 75-
76, 83-84, 101, 168, 178, 181,
184, 353, 376, 383, 401, 404
Propaganda Department 9, 22, 33,
37-38, 128, 138, 144, 161, 166,
170, 172-173, 175-176, 189-190,
274, 288, 232, 335, 340, 390, 423
property 46, 85, 90-91, 100, 114,
229, 235, 367, 374, 379, 405,
412, 415, 423
Public Relations Journal 321
Public Security, Ministry of 256-
259, 261, 264, 268-269, 277,
314-316, 341, 370, 391
Pudong 15-17, 107, 110-115, 118,

125, 334, 348
purges 135, 143, 151, 155-156, 166,
171-173, 195, 208-209, 215, 251,
260, 312, 327, 334, 340, 426

Qian Qichen 142, 182, 327, 335
Qian Xuesen 279
Qian Yongchang 311
Qian Zhengying 170, 305
Qiao Shi 6, 21, 35, 37, 45, 167, 173,
21, 212, 247, 253, 269, 302, 307,
312, 320, 327, 329, 335-336, 341,
347, 361, 363, 392, 393, 418
Qin Chuan 167, 177, 179
Qin Jiwei 204, 210, 212, 225, 234,
252, 327
Qin Wenjun 113
Qinghai Province 109, 154, 259,
311, 342
Qinghua University 278, 342
Qinghua Faction 332, 342
quanmin jieshang 18, 43, 81, 315,
381
Qunyan 306
qunzhong yundong (see mass move-
ments) 175, 314

Radio, Film and Television, Ministry
of 171, 173, 176, 350
real estate 19, 77, 79, 90, 104, 113,
119, 121-123, 181, 227, 228, 263,
345-346, 359, 365, 380, 412-413,
421
recentralisation 57, 88, 91, 06, 113,
116, 119, 286
red capitalists 46, 53, 95-99, 138,
154, 184, 191, 253, 299, 371,
372, 373-374, 377, 421
Red Flag 138, 143

regionalism 29, 59, 106, 109, 111, 202, 283, 324, 363, 365, 412, 418, 425,

religion 153

Ren Jianxin 263, 265, 268, 269, 312, 327

Ren Kelei 368

Ren Zhongyi 364

renminbi 112

Research Institute for the Reform of the Economic Structure (RIRES) 75, 140, 165, 293, 380, 165, 380

Research Office for the Reform of the Political Structure 379

responsibility system (see household contract responsibility system) 57-58, 66, 68-70, 88, 90, 101, 120, 167, 184, 245-246, 279, 427

Romania 167, 207, 260, 297, 401, 428

Rong Yiren 98, 299, 300, 301

Rui Xingwen 358-359, 375

Russia 53, 109, 142, 218, 228, 232, 339, 359, 396, 429

Second Field Army 395

Secretariat of the Central Committee 327

Selected Works of Deng Xiaoping 36, 40-41, 137, 219, 239

Selected Works of Deng Xiaoping Vol III 39-41, 75, 125, 132, 143, 182, 216

securities (see stocks) 101, 103-106, 309, 343

Seeking Truth 81, 117, 159, 170, 181, 403

Sha Jianxun 190

Shaanxi Province 122

Shandong Province 61, 68, 210, 230,

274, 288-289, 371, 374-375, 394

Shanghai 12-17, 19, 21-22, 25-29, 38, 40, 52, 74, 76, 88, 93, 101-104, 107, 110-113, 117-118, 121, 123-125, 132, 152, 154, 161-162, 164-166, 171-173, 180, 190, 197, 210, 229, 237, 238, 252, 257-258, 260, 267, 272, 275, 284, 294, 298, 301, 303, 313, 315, 318, 320, 323-324, 329, 330-338, 340-344, 346-349, 359, 364, 366-367, 372, 375-376, 380, 392, 394, 406, 410, 413-41, 416-417, 420, 425-426

Shanghai Faction 14, 161, 173, 320-322, 329-330, 332-334, 342, 426

Shanghai Stock Exchange 102

Shanxi Province 13, 210, 294, 296, 365, 397

Shao Qihui 406

Shao Yanxiang 170 177

shareholding economy (see stock economy) 100, 103, 105-106, 409

Shen Daren 122

Shen Taifu 270, 316

Shenyang 74, 104, 209, 214, 221, 225, 398

Shenyang Military Region 209, 214, 221, 225, 398

Shenzhen 16, 18-19, 22-24, 58, 95, 102-105, 111-113, 115-116, 119-120, 178, 186, 199, 248, 260, 262, 275-276, 301-302, 309, 324, 353, 366-368, 370, 396, 406, 410, 413-414, 416, 424, 429

Shenzhen Stock Exchange 410

Shi Yuxiao 209, 211, 213

Shishi 95, 319, 370

shock therapy 401, 404, 429

Sichuan Province 7, 38, 41, 73, 81,

105, 107, 109-110, 150, 237,
304-306, 315, 347, 356, 358, 364,
368, 376, 413, 416
Sing Tao Group   178
Singapore   2, 16, 26, 3, 112, 127-128,
132, 343, 411, 428-429
Singapore model   51, 53, 127-128
smuggling   229-231, 316, 370
socialism   5-6, 8, 10, 19, 32, 34, 37,
41, 43-44, 49, 52, 70, 75, 82-83,
95-96-, 98, 135, 139, 142-143,
146-148, 152, 156, 158-160, 162,
164-165, 167, 177, 178, 180-181,
187, 194, 216, 222, 243, 271,
275, 277, 284-285, 315, 340, 349,
401, 405, 427
socialism with Chinese characteristics   10, 32, 37, 222
socialist education campaign   67,
156, 159, 287
Song Defu   291, 330, 360
Song Keda   210, 214, 225
Song Ping   21, 70, 151, 159-160,
168, 171-172, 180, 186, 189, 249,
278, 281-283, 325, 327-328, 334-
335, 358, 382
Song Qingwai   210
Song Renqiong   249, 349
Soros Foundation   140
South Africa   2, 87
South Korea   41, 128, 200, 226, 230-
231, 369, 371
Special Economic Zone Daily   15,
113, 161, 187, 199, 413
special economic zones (SEZs)   15-
16, 19, 24, 38, 40, 76-77, 80,
111, 113-115, 118-119, 120-121,
188, 275, 364, 413
special political zones (SPZs)   113,
428-429
spiritual pollution   137

Spratly Islands   398
Stalinism   44, 52, 71, 129, 135, 156,
166, 201, 332, 349-350, 388, 392,
410
State Commission for the Reform of
the Economic Structure (SCRES)
15, 63, 86-87, 103, 351, 391,
State Economic and Trade
Commission (SETC)   290, 330,
342-343, 351, 402-403
State Education Commission   171-
172, 176, 179, 245, 277
State Gold Administration Bureau   89
State Nationalities Affairs
Commission   108
State Planning Commission (SPC)
14, 56, 63, 78, 94, 126, 129-130,
161, 198, 202, 330, 342, 350-351,
359, 402, 409
State Security, Ministry of (MSS)   79,
257-259, 261, 269, 273-274, 277,
421
stocks   16-17, 24, 26, 52, 74, 77, 79,
85-86, 89-91, 95, 100-106, 118,
123, 181, 187, 228, 231, 294,
309, 313, 315, 343-346, 353, 360,
365-368, 374, 379, 396, 403, 405,
408-410, 412-413, 423-425, 428
stock companies   16, 24, 77, 85-
86, 100-102, 104, 365
"stock economy"   101, 103, 105,
123, 231, 346, 368, 391, 410, 425
streamlining, administrative   64, 78,
84, 93, 186, 218, 222, 241, 243,
247, 265, 268, 285-287, 288-291,
308-309, 312, 337, 350-351, 374,
387, 397, 429
strikes   2, 224, 267, 273, 275-277,
292, 344, 399, 402, 407
Study, Research, Reference   82
succession   3, 31, 33, 177, 193, 195,

235-236, 238, 241, 254, 317,
    322-323, 394, 398, 425
Sun Changjiang   146, 169, 360
Sun Weiben   406
Supervision Ministry   387
Supreme People's Court (also courts)
    263, 268-269, 300
Supreme People's Procuratorate   264,
    269, 300, 311, 313

Ta Kung Pao   11, 315-316, 373-374
Taiwan   17, 24, 41, 49, 79, 124, 139-
    140, 173, 176, 178, 189, 197,
    201, 203, 226, 232, 241, 246-247,
    305, 307, 316, 330, 336, 346,
    357, 359, 366, 398, 418, 423,
    428, 429
Taipei   398
Tang Dynasty   185, 222
Tang Ruoxin   191, 370
Tao Bojun   215
Tao Siju   256
tax (also taxation)   42, 57-60, 66, 71,
    88-91, 97, 106, 111-112, 114,
    120-122, 164, 229, 231, 288, 290,
    314, 365-367, 373-374, 388-389,
    397, 402, 415-416, 421, 427
    dual tax system   58-59, 88, 106,
    120-122, 415
    value-added tax   89, 388, 415
technocrats   322, 326-327, 329-333,
    338, 341-344, 346, 348, 351, 390,
    406
telecommunications   113, 224, 415,
    421-422
telephones   289, 314, 422
Ten-Year Economic Blueprint   7, 14,
    55-57, 98, 101, 157, 336, 351,
    364
Textile Industry, Ministry of (MTI)

290, 350
Thailand   109, 128, 215, 401
The East is Red   182
The Tides of History   170
Third Field Army   221, 238, 399
thought liberation   3, 11-13, 18-19,
    28, 30, 44, 146, 169, 219, 361
Three Gorges project   305-306
Tian Chengping   342
Tian Jiyun   21, 35, 45, 69, 40, 79-80,
    99, 115, 118, 167, 170, 173, 247,
    256, 307, 320, 327, 341, 363,
    382, 393
Tiananmen Square crackdown, (also
    June 4)   67, 144, 201, 269, 293,
    351
Tianjin   46, 62, 104, 115, 210, 215,
    230, 257, 258, 270, 295, 300,
    343, 361-362, 364, 376, 380, 414,
    417
Tibet   59, 107, 171, 230, 259, 266,
    287, 319, 396, 412, 415, 417-418
Tong Dalin   126, 361
trade   57, 61, 74, 77-78, 85, 87, 91-
    92, 97, 102-103, 105-106, 108-
    109, 112, 127, 168, 171, 227,
    266, 270, 271, 273-276, 290, 315,
    330-331, 341-344, 350-351, 369,
    372, 375-376, 387, 389, 402, 410,
    413, 420, 424-425
    border trade   108, 372
    foreign trade   74, 77-78, 92, 331,
    344, 369, 375, 387, 402, 413
trade unions   127, 171, 266, 270-271,
    273-274, 276, 429
triangular debts   70, 72, 75, 124, 330,
    346, 407
triads   259, 261-263
Turkey   109

Uighurs 108-109

unemployment 258, 272, 275, 389-390, 403, 405

United Daily News 178

united front 17, 254, 297-298, 329, 356, 358-359, 361, 420

United Front Department 356, 358, 361, 420

United States of America 2, 6, 9, 17-18, 41, 92, 131, 135, 137, 139-141, 176, 195, 197, 200, 223-224, 228, 238, 253, 267, 279, 336, 338, 343, 377, 380, 398, 410, 422

USSR (Soviet Union) 2, 5-6, 18, 52, 62, 65, 108-109, 135, 141-142, 184, 194, 201, 220, 242, 244, 246, 248, 253, 281, 296, 329, 386, 388, 417

wages 9, 12, 52, 58, 61-63, 65, 73, 77, 138, 146, 148, 160, 176, 200, 256, 288, 296, 406

Wan Li 15, 66, 80, 239, 242, 251-252, 293, 301, 310, 327, 329, 356-357, 380, 382, 393

Wan Runnan 138

Wan Xueyuan 318

Wang Bingqian 57, 201, 350

Wang Chaowen 318

Wang Chengbin 209-211, 213, 215

Wang Dan 266, 379, 380-381

Wang Daohan 111, 340

Wang Hui 423

Wang Juntao 35, 266, 269

Wang Jue 126

Wang Ke 214, 221, 398

Wang Maolin 13

Wang Meng 170, 172, 177, 338

Wang Qishan 332

Wang Shaoguang 131

Wang Renzhi 9, 21, 138, 143, 146, 157, 171-173, 189, 206

Wang Ruilin 33, 215-216, 236, 394-395, 400

Wang Ruoshui 146, 169, 177

Wang Ruowang 138, 379, 428

Wang Weicheng 171, 337

Wang Xizhe 380

Wang Yizhou 131

Wang Zhaoguo 336

Wang Zhen 153, 166, 191, 194, 228, 249, 250-251, 256, 328, 341, 372

Wang Zhongyu 330, 351, 403-404

Wang Zuo 60

Wei Jianxing 172, 312, 316, 327

Wei Jingsheng 35-36, 44, 145, 267, 269

Wen Jiabao 327, 336, 357

Wen Yuankai 138

Wenzhou 102, 407

White, Gordon 409

White Snow, Red Blood 238

Wind Faction 168, 172, 338

World Economic Herald 340

Wu Bangguo 38, 125, 252, 284, 327, 342

Wu Guanzheng 342, 370

Wu Jiaxiang 379

Wu Jianchang 46, 236

Wu Jinglian 127, 177, 342, 378

Wu Mingyu 126, 361, 378

Wu Quanxu 222

Wu Xiang 378

Wu Xiaoling 342, 391

Wu Zongguo 185

Wu Zuguang 169

Wuhan 104, 261, 264, 370-371, 376, 413

Xi Jinping 254, 370

Xi Yang 270, 348
Xia Yan 170, 177
xiahai 81, 256, 314, 380
Xiang Huizheng 415
Xiang Nan 108, 360, 361, 366
Xiamen 15, 17, 104, 115, 315, 319, 361
Xiang Huizheng 415
Xiao Ke 213, 252
Xiao Yang 74, 364, 368
Xiao Zhuoji 99, 346, 374
Xie Fei 121, 244, 327, 364, 367, 385
Xinjiang Autonomous Region 109
Xiong Guangkai 222
Xizong 185
Xu Caihou 215
Xu Dasen 139-140
Xu Qinxian 205
Xu Weicheng 128, 161, 165, 171, 173, 186, 332
Xu Xin 214, 232
Xuanzong 185
Yan Jiaqi 1, 48, 146, 292, 304, 418
Yan Mingfu 34, 156, 356, 358
Yan'an 44, 48-49, 138, 147, 166, 174, 188, 203, 232, 240, 247, 255, 338, 393
yanda 268
Yang Baibing 33, 158, 197-199, 205-207, 209-212, 214-215, 220-221, 223-225, 236-238, 251-252, 326-327, 340, 394, 399
Yang Chengwu 199
Yang Dali 419
Yang Dezhi 199, 213, 225
Yang Dezhong 394
Yang Clan, the 33, 35, 198, 211, 213-216, 221, 236, 237, 326, 327, 332, 399
Yang Peixin 375
Yang Shangkun 6, 9, 45, 59, 128, 185, 190, 197, 203, 209, 212, 220, 234, 237, 243, 249, 251, 252, 310, 326, 327, 329, 336, 354, 357, 359, 372, 382, 393
Yang Rudai 327
Yang Xingfu 274
Yangpu 115
Yangtze River Delta 19, 28, 77, 305, 334, 370, 371
Yao Yilin 3, 13-15, 23, 26, 53-54, 67, 147, 161-162, 171, 252, 327, 330-332, 335, 339, 348, 350, 352, 359, 382
Ye Jianying 228, 253, 367, 372, 394
Ye Xuanping 58, 117, 186, 284, 302, 364, 367, 393
Yeltsin, Boris 53, 142, 163, 281
You Lin 190
Yu Guangyuan 126, 170, 378
Yu Yongbo 197, 213, 215, 217, 328
Yu Zhengsheng 370
Yuan Hongbin 169, 170, 277
Yuan Mu 63, 145, 158, 183, 186, 190, 337, 356
Yugoslavia 53, 131, 418
Yunnan Province 107-109, 168, 203, 314

Zeng Jianhui 172
Zeng Qinghong 330, 336, 394
Zhang Aiping 213, 221, 225, 252
Zhang Gong 209-210, 213-215
Zhang Kangkang 177
Zhang Siqing 311, 313
Zhang Shaojie 380
Zhang Shutian 261
Zhang Taiheng 210, 213
Zhang Wannian 197, 210, 213, 218, 221, 328
Zhang Xianliang 379-380
Zhang Zhen 33, 197, 213, 215-217,

221-222, 232, 236, 239, 328, 395, 398-400
Zhang Zhenglong 238
Zhang Zhongxian 210
Zhao Baojiang 371
Zhao Zhihao 58
Zhao Ziyang 1, 2, 9, 11, 13, 15, 19-
   21, 23-24, 32, 34-35, 40, 45-47,
   52-55, 59-61, 74, 78, 83, 87-88,
   100, 106, 114, 116, 126-128, 136,
   138, 140, 144, 152, 155-156,
   164-166, 174, 185, 188, 202,
   203-204, 206, 219, 225, 234, 237,
   239-240, 244-245, 250, 259, 280-
   281, 293, 309-312, 320, 324,
   331-334, 328, 342-344, 346-348,
   352-354, 356, 361, 363, 368-369,
   371, 377, 379, 393, 418
Zheng Bijian 41, 171-173, 340
Zheng Kaizhao 354
Zheng Liangyu 116, 368
zhengji 280, 282, 284
Zhejiang Province 95, 102, 160, 163,
   188, 238, 314, 317-318, 365, 408,
   419
zhongyang 89, 106, 110, 121-122,
   127, 132, 241, 325, 332, 411-412
Zhou Duo 379
Zhou Enlai 39, 253, 255, 352, 363
Zhou Nan 348
Zhou Youliang 215
Zhu Dunfa 210-211
Zhu Houze 49, 126-127, 152, 165,
   172, 274, 346, 360-361, 378
Zhu Rongji 23, 26, 29, 32, 46-47,
   71, 78, 91, 94, 111, 120-121, 132,
   163, 179, 185, 188, 231, 237,
   252, 253, 256, 270, 284, 285,
   291, 296, 316, 320, 322, 327,
   329-333, 336, 338, 341-342, 344,
   351-352, 355, 361, 365, 369, 372,

383, 384, 390, 393, 403-405,
   408-409, 412, 419, 421-422, 425
Zhu Senlin 103, 117, 121, 284, 367,
   376, 423
Zhu Xiaohua 331
Zhu Yongming 110
Zhuhai 16, 18, 22-23, 102, 113, 115,
   178, 185, 199, 251, 260, 275,
   280, 324, 380, 382, 414
Zhuhai Special Zone Daily 178
Zou Jiahua 56, 59, 61, 124, 128,
   161, 199, 201, 202, 253, 327,
   325, 364
Zou Jun 95
Zuo Dapei 422